Blackstone's

Magistrates'
Handbook

CU00904370

Preface to the 2017 Edition

This book aims to provide a portable resource to busy criminal lawyers seeking answers to the common issues that arise at court. I use it to replace the file of papers I used to carry, to which I might need to refer. I have added subjects this year that have been raised in my presence in court but were not covered by the text. I have excluded subjects that do seem to arise in practice. It is difficult to balance the availability of space with the number of subjects to be covered. I have worked on the principle that it is more important to concentrate on matters that arise without warning and to omit matters that more commonly arise on notice, or where there is time for preparation. I have this year maintained the principle that the book does not deal with indictable-only offences or with either-way matters that only in the most exceptional circumstances would be concluded in the magistrates' court, although this is being reviewed because of the demands of Better Case Management to identify early the issues that might arise in the Crown Court. I have again reorganized some headings to make them easier to consider and to save space.

The criminal law is constantly changing and I have included *in italics* subjects that are likely to change during the life of this edition.

Where there is a reference merely to a fine, it is reference to an unlimited fine.

I welcome feedback on this book. The text must meet the needs of the practising lawyer and be completely accurate. The intention is that it will continue to be the most easily accessed source of answers to questions that arise pre-trial at the magistrates' court level. The law is cited as at 31 July 2016. I wish to acknowledge the help given by District Judge Naomi Redhouse and my colleague Mark Ashford in relation to youths; by my colleagues Carolyn Taylor in relation to mental health issues and William Bergstrom in writing the section on extradition; by Philip Houlden, Clerk to the Justices, for the inspiration behind the diagram at the start of the section on bail; and to Fiona Sinclair and all at Oxford University Press for their skills and patience in the preparation of this edition of the *Handbook*. The remaining mistakes are my responsibility alone.

Anthony Edwards
London

Contents

Part A Procedure and Evidence

Contents

Part B Youths in the Adult Court

Part C Offences

Part D Sentencing

Contents

Icons List

The following icons are used throughout this book:

DO Dangerous Offender

EW Either Way

Sentence

SO Summary Only

Cross-reference to *Blackstone's Criminal Practice 2017*

Table of Cases

Table of Cases

Table of Cases

Table of Cases

Table of Cases

Table of Cases

Table of Cases

Table of Cases

Table of Cases

Table of Cases

Table of Primary Legislation

Table of Primary Legislation

Table of Primary Legislation

Table of Primary Legislation

Table of Primary Legislation

Table of Primary Legislation

Table of Primary Legislation

Table of Primary Legislation

Table of Primary Legislation

Table of Secondary Legislation

Table of Secondary Legislation

Table of Conventions

Table of Practice Directions

Table of European Legislation

Directives

Part A
Procedure and Evidence

A1 Abuse of Process

A1.1 Introduction

Abuse of process is something so unfair and wrong with the prosecution that the court should not allow a prosecutor to proceed with what is, in all other respects, a regular proceeding: *Hui-chi Ming v R* [1992] 1 AC 34.

A stay on these grounds falls into two main categories:

- where a fair trial of the particular defendant is impossible (eg due to loss of evidence);
- where there is a misuse of court process (where it offends the court's sense of justice and propriety to be asked to try the accused in the circumstances of the particular case). In relation to this category of case, the magistrates' court does not have jurisdiction to determine the issue and proceedings might be adjourned in order that the defence may seek a judicial review. It was confirmed in *Woolls v N Somerset Council* EWHC 1410 (Admin), applying *Nembhard v DPP* [2009] EWHC 194, that it is also proper for the magistrates to proceed to a conclusion and make findings of fact so that the original issue can be resolved by the court stating a case for the High Court. Cases involving human trafficking will be considered under this head (*L; HVN; THN; T v R* [2013] EWCA Crim 991).

A stay of proceedings based on an abuse of process will be rare and should be allowed only in exceptional circumstances (see *Attorney General's Reference No 1 of 1990* (1992) 95 Cr App R 296); and if the court process can compensate for any unfairness or wrongs, so as to allow for a fair trial, that is the way in which it should proceed.

On an application to stay for abuse of process, it is for the defendant to satisfy the court on a balance of probabilities that no fair trial is possible. The application should be decided on material adduced by the prosecution and defence, with both parties having the right (subject to usual judicial discretion) to call evidence (*R v Clerkenwell Magistrates' Court, ex p Bell* [1991] Crim LR 468).

A1.2 Relevant grounds

A1.2.1 *Missing evidence or disclosure*

The issues identified in *R v Dobson* [2001] EWCA Crim 1606 are as follows:

- What was the duty of the police?
- Did the police fail in their duty by not obtaining or retaining the appropriate (material)?
- If so, was there serious prejudice which rendered a fair trial impossible in the light of such failure?
- Alternatively, did the police failure result from such bad behaviour, in the sense of bad faith or serious fault, as to render it unfair that the accused should be tried at all? The requirement for bad faith was doubted in *Clay v South Cambridgeshire JJ* [2104] EWHC 321 (Admin) which held that the issue was whether or not there could be a fair trial.

There is a duty on the police to contact identified witnesses (*Morris v DPP* [2014] EWHC 105 (Admin)). There is no *general* duty on the prosecution to retain CCTV evidence that might have given insight into whether a warning was given to a detainee during a breath test procedure (*Morris v Director of Public Prosecutions* [2008] EWHC 2788 (Admin)). This decision follows the leading case of *R v Feltham Magistrates' Court and another, ex p Ebrahim* [2001] EWHC Admin 130.

That case emphasizes that the early identification of the significance of the relevant material is a key factor to ensure that the prosecution are under a duty, not least under the code of practice made under the Criminal Procedure and Investigations Act 1996. The case confirms the possibility of using section 78 of the Police and Criminal Evidence Act 1984 to exclude some or all of the prosecution evidence if the failure to produce the material sought or to comply with disclosure obligations may render the trial unfair.

The duties of the prosecution are set out in the Attorney General's guidelines on the disclosure of unused material.

A1.2.2 *Alternative remedy*

The exclusion of evidence under section 78 Police and Criminal Evidence Act 1984 (PACE) to secure a fair trial is to be preferred to using the abuse jurisdiction (see **A2.2.4**). In *R v DS and TS* [2015] EWCA Crim 662 the court held that whether the breach by the Crown is of a general or specific nature the consequences should be the same; and whether the failure related to evidence (*Boardman*, see **A2.2.4**) or disclosure (in this case), all such breaches affect the fairness of the trial and undermine public confidence in the criminal justice system. Whether a breach is dealt with by a stay or by exclusion of evidence under section 78 PACE the same considerations apply. They include:

- the gravity of the charges;
- the denial of justice to the complainants;
- the importance of disclosure in sexual offences;
- the necessity for proper attention to be paid to disclosure;
- the nature and materiality of the failures;
- any failures by the defence;
- the waste of court resources and the effect on the court;
- the availability of other sanctions.

A1.2.3 *Failure to supply initial details of the prosecution case*

There is no jurisdiction to stay proceedings for failures in service of initial details of the prosecution case under Part 8 of the Criminal Procedure Rules; the appropriate remedy is to adjourn (*R v Leeds Youth Court, ex p P(A)* [2001] EWHC 215 (Admin)), although repeated failure to comply with the rules may provide for a stay in truly exceptional circumstances (*R v Willesden Magistrates' Court, ex p Clemmings* (1988) 152 JPN 46). A threat to stay a prosecution if there were further disclosure breaches did not give rise to any legitimate expectation on the part of the defendant so as to require the court to carry through its threat on the next occasion (*R v Leeds Youth Court, ex p AP and others* [2001] EWHC 215 (Admin)).

A1.2.4 *Improper motive*

The fact that there was a mixed motive for launching a private prosecution will justify a stay only if the conduct of the prosecutor is truly oppressive, as it was obvious that many private prosecutions would be brought with mixed motives (*Dacre v City of Westminster Magistrates' Court* [2009] 1 Cr App R 6).

In *Nembhard v Director of Public Prosecutions* [2009] EWHC 194 (Admin), the court ruled that a magistrates' court was correct to refuse to stay proceedings on the ground that a request to produce traffic documents was motivated by improper considerations—namely a desire to harass the defendant. In such cases the proper course of action would be either to stay the prosecution pending determination of the issue by the High Court, or to apply for judicial review of the decision to prosecute. This case is an important reminder that in instances where an abuse of state power is being alleged, a magistrates' court has no jurisdiction to stay proceedings (*R v Horseferry Road Magistrates' Court, ex p Paul James Bennett* [1994] 1 AC 42).

A1.2.5 *Delay*

In the absence of other compelling reasons, a lengthy delay, in itself, does not justify a stay of criminal proceedings (*Spiers v Ruddy* [2008] 1 AC 873, PC).

In *Ali v Crown Prosecution Service* [2007] EWCA Crim 691, proceedings brought seven years after the incident should have been stayed, as important documentary evidence, relevant to assessing the victim's credibility, had been lost. The court emphasized that:

> this is a rare case where prejudice following from the delay was not alleviated and probably could never have been cured during the course of the trial.

In *Halahan* [2014] EWCA Crim 2079, the court held that in a case where prejudice by delay, resulting in the loss of documents, was alleged, it is necessary to show more than speculation that the document would assist the defence. It was necessary that the missing evidence represented a significant and demonstrable chance of the disclosure of strongly supportive evidence emerging on a specific issue in the case.

In *R (Flaherty) v City of Westminster Magistrates' Court* [2008] EWHC 2589 (Admin), the last two years of a ten-year delay in enforcing a confiscation order were attributable to the prosecution. The proceedings ought to have been stayed, as confiscation proceedings must be determined within a reasonable time.

Earlier cases, such as *R v Clerk to the Medway Justices, ex p DHSS* [1986] Crim LR 686, DC, in which a prosecution was stayed where the prosecution laid the information on the last day before it was time-barred, should be treated with extreme caution in the light of considerable and more recent appellate-level scrutiny of the principles that apply. It is almost inconceivable that the *Medway* case would be decided similarly today.

A1.2.6 *Legitimate expectation*

The prosecution of a person who has received a promise, an undertaking, or a representation from the police that he will not be prosecuted is capable of being an abuse of process (*Croydon Justices, ex p Dean* [1993] QB 769). So too will be the prosecution of a person denied a caution by the failure of the police to make appropriate disclosure to enable legal advice to be given (*DPP v Ara* [2001] EWHC 493 (Admin)). The administration of a caution may make it an abuse for there to be a later prosecution (*Jones v Whalley* [2007] 1 AC 63) but the Crown may in appropriate cases, where there is a proper basis, change its mind as to how to proceed. The Crown is required, absent a change of circumstances, to proceed in a single prosecution with all the charges it proposes to bring arising out of the same incident (*Connelly v DPP* [1964] AC 1254; *R v Beedie* [1997] EWCA Crim 714).

A1.2.7 *Autrefois acquit*

This bar is confined to cases that are the same in fact and law. The rule will be construed narrowly and if this causes injustice amounting to oppression the remedy is to stay the proceedings. Although on an allegation of common assault the Crown offered no evidence, it could proceed with an allegation of occasioning ABH if the defendant had never been in peril of trial on the lesser offence (*R v JFJ* [2013] EWCA Crim 569). Where a case is dismissed for the failure of the prosecution to appear (s 15 Magistrates' Court Act (MCA) 2000) it is not an abuse to commence again as the defendant was not in jeopardy (*DPP v Jarman* [2013] EWHC 4391 (Admin)). Magistrates cannot dismiss a case without hearing evidence. *DPP v Bird* [2016] EWHC 4077 (Admin) confirms that the doctrine of *autrefois acquit* only applies if the defendant was put at risk of conviction and the case was heard on the merits; that is, the court could have convicted but did not do so.

A1.2.8 *Decisions to prosecute*

Whilst *R (Barons Pub Company Limited v Staines Magistrates' Court* [2013] EWHC 898 (Admin)) confirmed that a decision to prosecute is susceptible to review, as an abuse of process, if it is one that no reasonable prosecutor would make, or which misapplies a policy, or is based on a policy which is unlawful, in individual cases it is for the Crown and not the court to show the proportionality for the purposes of Articles 10 and 11 of the European Convention on Human Rights (ECHR) of a decision to prosecute. The court merely considers admissible evidence and this may require human rights issues to be considered at that stage (*James v DPP* [2015] EWHC 3296 (Admin)).

These decisions confirm that this issue goes to the fairness of the individual proceedings and should therefore be resolved in the proceedings themselves and not by judicial review.

 See *Blackstone's Criminal Practice 2017* **D3**

A2 **Adjournments**

A2.1 **Time limits applicable to adjournments**

It should be noted that time limits apply to remands under the Magistrates' Courts Act 1980 (eg ss 5, 10, 11, 17, 130, etc). When a person is sent for trial to the Crown Court, the eight-clear-day limit on initial remand (if in custody) does not apply as the court has not remanded the case. The details appear at **A25.**

A2.2 **Principles to be applied**

Part 3 of the Criminal Procedure Rules requires active case management. This includes discouraging delay, and dealing with as many aspects of the case as possible on the same occasion and avoiding unnecessary hearings (r 3.2(2)(f)). At every hearing, if the case cannot be concluded there and then, the court must give directions so that it can be concluded at the next hearing or as soon as possible after that (r 3.9(1)). Unless this has been done already, the court must take the defendant's plea (r 3.9(2)(b)). This obligation does not depend on the extent of initial disclosure, service of evidence, disclosure of unused material, or the grant of legal aid. There are still many instances where an adjournment is required. In such instances advocates can expect those applications to be closely scrutinized (*R v Hereford Magistrates' Court, ex p Rowland* [1998] QB 110).

In *Crown Prosecution Service v Picton* [2006] EWHC 1108 (Admin), the court laid down the following general approach:

- A decision whether to adjourn is a decision within the discretion of the trial court. An appellate court will interfere only if very clear grounds for doing so are shown.
- Magistrates should pay great attention to the need for expedition in the prosecution of criminal proceedings; delays are scandalous; they bring the law into disrepute; summary justice should be speedy justice; an application for an adjournment should be rigorously scrutinized.
- Where an adjournment is sought by the prosecution, magistrates must consider both the interest of the defendant in getting the matter dealt with, and the interest of the public that criminal charges should be adjudicated upon: the guilty convicted as well as the innocent acquitted. With a more serious charge, the public interest that there be a trial will carry greater weight.

- Where an adjournment is sought by the accused, the magistrates must consider whether, if it is not granted, the accused will be able fully to present his defence and, if he will not be able to do so, the degree to which his ability to do so is compromised.
- In considering the competing interests of the parties, the magistrates should examine the likely consequences of the proposed adjournment, in particular, its likely length, and the need to decide the facts while recollections are fresh.
- The reason that the adjournment is required should be examined and, if it arises through the fault of the party asking for the adjournment, that is a factor against granting the adjournment, carrying weight in accordance with the gravity of the fault. If that party was not at fault then that may favour an adjournment. Likewise, if the party opposing the adjournment has been at fault then that will favour an adjournment.
- The magistrates should take appropriate account of the history of the case, and whether there have been earlier adjournments and at whose request, and why.
- Lastly, of course, the factors to be considered cannot be comprehensively stated but depend upon the particular circumstances of each case, and they will often overlap. The court's duty is to do justice between the parties in the circumstances as they have arisen.

In *Aravinthan Visvaratnam v Brent Magistrates' Court* [2009] EWHC 3017 (Admin), the court made these observations:

> The prosecution must not think that they are always allowed at least one application to adjourn the case. If that idea were to gain currency, no trial would ever start on the first date set for trial.

> So these are the competing considerations. I have no doubt that there is a high public interest in trials taking place on the date set for trial, and that trials should not be adjourned unless there is a good and compelling reason to do so. The sooner the prosecution understand this—that they cannot rely on their own serious failures properly to warn witnesses— the sooner the efficiency in the Magistrates' Court system improves. An improvement in timeliness and the achievement of a more effective and efficient system of criminal justice in the Magistrates' Court will bring about great benefits to victims and to witnesses and huge savings in time and money.

On an application for an adjournment by the defence, the court in *R (Anderson) v Guildford MC* [2015] EWHC 2454 (Admin) held that the issue was whether a fair trial could take place. Whilst speed was important an adjournment was granted where:

(1) The defence had voluntarily submitted a full and very detailed defence case statement even though initial disclosure had not yet been made.

(2) The defence had identified the need for two expert reports on the 'victim's' pathology (nature of the injury) and toxicology (drugs taken), and it was not for a court to prejudge whether these would be relevant or not.

(3) Other outstanding material identified a potential witness who might testify to the 'victim's' condition, and related to bad character.

Notwithstanding that the not guilty plea had been entered on 16 April (by a duty solicitor), and the trial was on 29 June, the application to adjourn was made (by the defendant's own solicitor) on 1 June.

A2.2.1 *Diversion from prosecution*

Although courts are discouraged from allowing adjournments for this reason and there is no right to such an adjournment (*R (F) v CPS and the Chief Constable of Merseyside* (2004) 168 JP 93), such adjournments are regularly granted whenever the CPS on review agree that such an outcome is appropriate. This happens particularly where the charging decision has been made by the police or when defendants are receiving informed legal advice for the first time. It also applies when there are issues of mental disorder. Whilst a plea of not guilty can be entered, the Crown will often be willing to consider informed representations to comply with their duties under the Code for Crown Prosecutors.

Paragraph 3.6 of the Code for Crown Prosecutors states that:

> #### Code for Crown Prosecutors, para 3.6
>
> Prosecutors review every case they receive from the police or other investigators. Review is a continuing process and prosecutors must take account of any change in circumstances that occurs as the case develops, including what becomes known of the defence case. Wherever possible, they should talk to the investigator when thinking about changing the charges or stopping the case. Prosecutors and investigators work closely together, but the final responsibility for the decision whether or not a case should go ahead rests with the CPS.

A2.2.2 *Legal aid*

A common issue that arises is in relation to adjournments for the purposes of legal aid being granted. Much will depend on the circumstances, and in particular, how much time the defendant has had, if any, to arrange appropriate representation. The court will also be mindful of payments that can be made to firms if legal aid is refused—thereby diluting the force of any argument that work would otherwise be unfunded. However, in *Stopya v District Court of Lublin Poland* [2012] EWHC 1787 (Admin) it was held that 'delays occasioned by means testing which are not occasioned by the fault of the requested person or his legal advisers cannot be held against the requested person'.

A2.2.3 *Absence of the defendant*

R (Drinkwater) v Solihull Magistrates' Court [2012] EWHC 765 (Admin) (applying *R v Jones* [2002] UKHL 5) suggested that a trial may take place in the absence of the defendant only in exceptional circumstances. However, the case did not take account of the amendments made to section 11 of the Magistrates' Court Act 1980. The section requires that the trial proceed unless it is contrary to the interests of justice to do so. The defence should show acceptable reason for the failure to appear (s 11(2A)). A failure to make proper inquiry into a defendant's absence which, had it been carried out, would have led to the adjournment of the matter, will result in 'any resulting conviction following trial in absence being quashed' (*R (James) v Tower Bridge Magistrates' Court*, unreported, 9 June 2009, DC). (See also **A23.3**)

Where a defendant provides a medical note in relation to non-attendance, a court should give reasons for finding such medical excuses spurious, it being rarely, if ever, appropriate to reject a medical certificate (even if not meeting the normal requirements as to information required) without first giving the defendant an opportunity to respond (*Evans v East Lancashire Magistrates' Court* [2010] EWHC 2108 (Admin)).

In *R v Bolton Magistrates' Court, ex p Merna* [1991] Crim LR 848, the court said:

if the court suspects the [medical] grounds to be spurious or believes them to be inadequate, the court should ordinarily express its doubts and thereby give the defendant an opportunity to seek to resolve the doubts. It may call for better evidence, require further inquiries to be made or adopt any other expedient fair to both parties. The ultimate test must always be one of fairness and if a defendant claims to be ill with apparently responsible professional support for his claim, the court should not reject that claim and proceed to hear the case in a defendant's absence without satisfying itself that the claim may properly be rejected and that no unfairness will thereby be done.

The issues were re-examined and confirmed in *Killick v West London Magistrates' Court* [2012] EWHC 3864 (Admin):

Section 11(1)(b) and (2A) of the Magistrates' Courts Act 1980 allow the court to proceed in the absence of a defendant unless it appears contrary to the interests of justice, but it should not do so if it considers that there is an acceptable reason for his failure to attend. The jurisdiction must be exercised with the utmost care and caution. The case should not proceed without the court satisfying itself that the claim for an adjournment may properly be rejected and that no unfairness will thereby be done.

Where a defendant wished to resist a criminal charge and is shown by medical evidence to be unfit to attend court either as a result of involuntary illness or incapacity, it would be very rarely, if ever, right for the court to exercise its discretion in favour of proceeding. If the court suspects the grounds to be spurious or inadequate, it should express its doubts to give the defence a chance to resolve them. The court must distinguish genuine grounds from those that are spurious and designed to frustrate the process. If the court concludes the latter is the case, it may proceed as if there is a truly compelling reason for doing so, notwithstanding the justified non-attendance.

If a court proceeds, it should set aside the order under section 142 of the Magistrates' Court Act 1980 if compelling medical evidence is then produced.

Criminal Practice Direction 5C contains specific provisions on the production of medical certificates:

Criminal Practice Direction (CPD) 5C

5C.1 Doctors will be aware that medical notes are normally submitted by defendants in criminal proceedings as justification for not answering bail. Medical notes may also be submitted by witnesses who are due to give evidence and jurors.

5C.2 If a medical certificate is accepted by the court, this will result in cases (including contested hearings and trials) being adjourned rather than the court issuing a warrant for the defendant's arrest without bail. Medical certificates will also provide the defendant with sufficient evidence to defend a charge of failure to surrender to bail.

5C.3 However, a court is not absolutely bound by a medical certificate. The medical practitioner providing the certificate may be required by the court to give evidence. Alternatively the court may exercise its discretion to disregard a certificate which it finds unsatisfactory: *R v Ealing Magistrates' Court ex P. Burgess [2001] 165 J.P. 82*

5C.4 Circumstances where the court may find a medical certificate unsatisfactory include

  (a) where the certificate indicates that the defendant is unfit to attend work (rather than to attend court);
  (b) where the nature of the defendant's ailment (e.g. broken arm) does not appear to be capable of preventing his attendance at court;
  (c) where the defendant is certified as suffering from stress/anxiety/depression and there is no indication of the defendant recovering within a realistic timescale.

5C.5 It therefore follows that the minimum standards a medical certificate should set out are:

  (a) the date on which the medical practitioner examined the defendant;
  (b) the exact nature of the defendant's ailments;

(c) if it is not self-evident, why the ailment prevents the defendant attending court;

(d) an indication as to when the defendant is likely to be able to attend court, or a date when the current certificate expires.

5C.6 Medical practitioners should be aware that when issuing a certificate to a defendant in criminal proceedings they make themselves liable to being summonsed to court to give evidence about the content of the certificate, and they may be asked to justify their statements.

A2.2.4 *Witnesses*

Where a party was unable, through no fault of his own, to call an important witness, an adjournment should be granted to give an opportunity for that witness to be traced and steps taken to secure attendance (*Khurshied v Peterborough Magistrates' Court* [2009] EWHC 1136 (Admin) and *Nadour v Chester Magistrates' Court* [2009] EWHC 1505 (Admin)). In *Essen v Director of Public Prosecutions* [2005] EWHC 1077 (Admin), the court was concerned with a failure of the Crown Prosecution Service (CPS), due to administrative error, to warn its witnesses for trial. The court held that in the absence of some other counter-prevailing factor an adjournment ought not to be granted. The fact that a crime may go unpunished is not sufficient as:

in that case no prosecutor, however dilatory, need attend to the requirement to be ready for trial on the set date … The prejudice to the defendant [of an adjournment in those circumstances] was manifest. The CPS had no ground for seeking clemency. It was the sole author of its own misfortune.

A prosecutor should always be given some time to make inquiries as to why a witness is not present (*R v Swansea Justices, ex p Director of Public Prosecutions*, The Times, 30 March 1990).

A2.2.5 *Disclosure*

Section 7A(3) Criminal Procedure and Investigations Act 1996 requires that the Crown serve material as soon as reasonably practicable. The court must have regard to the overriding objective of the Criminal Procedure Rules. The defence must identify the possible significance of missing disclosure. If the prosecution have failed to carry out their statutory duties in relation to disclosure under the Act, an adjournment may be granted, on the Crown's application (*Swash v Director of Public Prosecutions* [2009] EWHC 803 (Admin)). If the application is refused, it is professionally improper for a lawyer to prosecute a case where there has been a breach of the duty to disclose. The CPS Disclosure Manual paragraph 11(1) indicates that prosecutors must facilitate proper disclosure as part of the general and personal professional responsibility to act fairly and impartially in the interests of justice (as confirmed in *DPP v Graham Petrie* [2015] EWHC 48 (Admin)). The courts may exclude all prosecution evidence under section 78 of the Police and Criminal Evidence Act 1984 as it may then be unfair in the proceedings to admit that evidence alone at trial (*R (Ibrahim) v Feltham Magistrates' Court* 2001 EWHC 130 (Admin)). In *R v Boardman* [2015] EWCA Crim 175, all the key prosecution evidence was excluded under this provision. Where the material sought would amount to further disclosure, a defence case statement must be lodged and an application made under section 8 of the Criminal Procedure and Investigations Act 1996 (*R v Austin* [2013] EWCA Crim 1028). Adjournments in relation to unused material will not be granted if the defence do not follow the correct formal procedures (*DPP v Graham Petrie*).

The Magistrates' Court disclosure review in May 2014 considered the issues involved:

Magistrates' Court disclosure review

146. The question has been raised as to what should happen on the day of trial if the prosecution has not complied with its disclosure obligations.

147. The first point for consideration is whether the Crown has indeed failed to comply. In some cases it is reported that there are late section 8 CPIA applications and that the fault, if any, therefore lies with the defence. However, if the failure is clearly at the door of the prosecution, then it is the prosecution who must make the application for an adjournment to comply with its obligations.

148. If the application for an adjournment is refused, the consequence must be that the prosecution should offer no evidence, in line with the guidance set out in Chapter 1 of the CPS/ACPO Disclosure Manual. It would be against the professional code of conduct for prosecutors to proceed to trial having not complied with their statutory disclosure obligations. Generally an abuse of process argument is neither necessary nor appropriate.

149. A common and very unfortunate situation is that the prosecution serve, on the day of trial, disclosure or a notice stating that there is nothing to disclose. Here the Bench should proceed in the interests of justice, applying common sense. Although the defence would be entitled to make a section 8 application within 14 days, it will often be appropriate for the court to expect the defence to set out its full defence case in order to trigger the section 8 application.

150. In some situations, the section 8 application can be dealt with there and then. If, having heard such an application, the court decides that there is no obligation for further disclosure, then, unsatisfactory as late service may be, the interests of justice may require the case to proceed. Similarly, where disclosure is made on the day of the hearing, it will often

be possible, without injustice, for there to be a short adjournment on the day of trial for the defence to assimilate the new information, but for the trial itself nevertheless to proceed.

151. There will be occasions when it is unreasonable to expect the defence to assimilate new information on the day of trial, or where the court orders section 8 disclosure on the day of trial, and the prosecution cannot comply. In those circumstances an adjournment may be appropriate.

152. The key point is that this position should never have been reached. It is not simply a failing of the prosecution. The defence has an obligation to draw this to the attention of the court in advance, and it is the responsibility of the court to ensure that proper disclosure has been made sufficiently in advance of the trial.

See also **A16**.

A2.2.6 *Ambush defence*

If a defendant raises matters for the first time in the proceedings (so-called ambush defences), the court is fully justified in adjourning the matter in order to allow the prosecution to deal with them properly (eg *R (Lawson) v Stratford Magistrates' Court* [2007] EWHC 2490 (Admin), where compliance with signage regulations in relation to a prosecution for speeding was raised for the first time in cross-examination). The general principles are established by the series of decisions in *R v Gleeson* [2003] EWCA Crim 3357, *R v Chorley Justices* [2006] EWHC 1795 (Admin), and *Malcolm v Director of Public Prosecutions* [2007] EWHC 363 (Admin).

In *R (Taylor) v Southampton Magistrates' Court* [2008] EWHC 3006 (Admin), it was held that, during a trial for failing to comply with a notice under section 172 of the Road Traffic Act 1988, a District Judge was right to adjourn the case in order for the prosecution to be able to gather evidence (if such evidence existed) to prove service of the notice. There was no question of bias, even though the court acted of its own motion. In this case there was no issue of 'ambush', the prosecution having not only been put to proof of all issues but the specific issue having been raised. That was not enough for the court in this instance, in the absence of a positive defence case that the notice had not in fact been served.

 See *Blackstone's Criminal Practice 2017* **D4**

A3 Admissibility and Exclusion of Evidence

A3.1 Admissibility and exclusion

Given that magistrates deal with questions of both fact and law, the *voir dire* procedure adopted in the Crown Court is not always appropriate in summary proceedings when issues of admissibility arise. The timing of any challenge is a matter for the court, and whilst there is no right to have issues of admissibility determined as a preliminary issue (*R v Epping and Ongar Justices, ex p Manby* [1986] Crim LR 555s), Section 8A of the Magistrates' Courts Act 1980 provides for pre-trial rulings on issues of admissibility. Previous rulings on admissibility can be reversed, but this should happen only exceptionally (see **A9** for relevant provisions and cases).

When a party is seeking to exclude evidence under section 76 of the Police and Criminal Evidence Act 1984, a *voir dire* will be required as there is no discretion under section 76 (as opposed to s 78) and the prosecution carry the burden of disproving unfairness (*Vel v Owen* [1987] Crim LR 496).

When a party is inviting a court to exercise its discretion to exclude evidence under section 78 of the Police and Criminal Evidence Act 1984, the court has a choice as to whether to deal with the issue when it arises or once all evidence has been heard. The *voir dire* procedure is appropriate to such applications, as an accused may otherwise be denied the opportunity to remain silent in relation to the substantive matter. In *Halawa v Federation Against Copyright Theft* [1995] 1 Cr App R 496, the court laid down the following principles:

- absent a good reason, the defendant is entitled to a *voir dire* on the issue of exclusion under section 78;
- if section 78 is being argued as an alternative to section 76, a *voir dire* should be held;
- it will generally be appropriate to hear all of the prosecution evidence before embarking on a *voir dire* in relation to the disputed parts;
- if the argument is only to the circumstances in which evidence was gathered, a *voir dire* may not be necessary; if, however, the defendant contradicts the evidence, it is more likely that a *voir dire* is appropriate;
- the defence must be in a position to assist the court in determining the extent of any challenge.

Police and Criminal Evidence Act 1984, s 78

78 (1) In any proceedings the court may refuse to allow evidence on which the prosecution proposes to rely to be given if it appears to the court that, having regard to all the circumstances, including the circumstances in which the evidence was obtained, the admission of the evidence would have such an adverse effect on the fairness of the proceedings that the court ought not to admit it.

(2) Nothing in this section shall prejudice any rule of law requiring a court to exclude evidence.

(3) This section shall not apply in the case of proceedings before a magistrates' court inquiring into an offences as examining justices.

It should be noted that section 78 may only be used to exclude prosecution evidence, not that led by a co-defendant.

A4 **Allocation and Plea Before Venue**

A4.1 Cases that must be sent to the Crown Court

The court must send the case to the Crown Court if:

- there is an indictable-only offence (see **Appendix 3**);
- a notice has been served under section 51B (serious fraud) or section 51C (children) of the Crime and Disorder Act 1998; or
- the offence is related to an indictable/notice offence for which the defendant or another defendant is sent for trial (unless the defendant appears on a subsequent occasion when there is a discretion);
- the defendant is charged with an either-way offence or relevant (imprisonable or disqualifiable) summary offence, and is or has been sent to the Crown Court for a related offence;
- the defendant is jointly charged with another defendant who is or has been sent to the Crown Court for a related offence;
- the defendant is jointly charged or is charged with a related offence with a youth defendant who is or has been sent to the Crown Court for trial.

In each case where there is a co-defendant, the duty exists when the defendants appear on the same occasion, but becomes a discretion if this defendant appears on a subsequent occasion.

For the procedure on sending see **A27**.

A4.2 Cases that may be sent to the Crown Court

A plea before venue is conducted for all other either-way offences. The defendant is asked to indicate a plea.

Magistrates' Courts Act 1980, s 17A

17A Initial procedure: accused to indicate intention as to plea

(1) This section shall have effect where a person who has attained the age of 18 years appears or is brought before a magistrates' court on an information charging him with an offence triable either way.

(2) Everything that the court is required to do under the following provisions of this section must be done with the accused present in court.

(3) The court shall cause the charge to be written down, if this has not already been done, and to be read to the accused.

Allocation Procedure for Adults

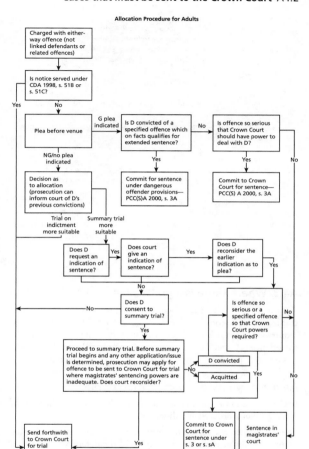

Figure 1 Allocation procedure for adults

(4) The court shall then explain to the accused in ordinary language that he may indicate whether (if the offence were to proceed to trial) he would plead guilty or not guilty, and that if he indicates that he would plead guilty—
    (a) the court must proceed as mentioned in subsection (6) below; and
    (b) he may (unless section 17D(2) below were to apply) be committed for sentence to the Crown Court under section 3 or (if applicable) 3A

> of the Powers of Criminal Courts (Sentencing) Act 2000 if the court is of such opinion as is mentioned in subsection (2) of the applicable section.
>
> (5) The court shall then ask the accused whether (if the offence were to proceed to trial) he would plead guilty or not guilty.
>
> (6) If the accused indicates that he would plead guilty the court shall proceed as if—
>
>   (a) the proceedings constituted from the beginning the summary trial of the information; and
>
>   (b) section 9(1) above was complied with and he pleaded guilty under it.
>
> (7) If the accused indicates that he would plead not guilty section 18(1) below shall apply.
>
> (8) If the accused in fact fails to indicate how he would plead, for the purposes of this section and section 18(1) below he shall be taken to indicate that he would plead not guilty.
>
> (9) Subject to subsection (6) above, the following shall not for any purpose be taken to constitute the taking of a plea—
>
>   (a) asking the accused under this section whether (if the offence were to proceed to trial) he would plead guilty or not guilty;
>
>   (b) an indication by the accused under this section of how he would plead.

A4.3 Where there is a guilty plea

If the indication of plea is guilty, the court proceeds to sentence, and this may include committal for sentence if Crown Court powers are required to deal with the defendant. It shall commit for sentence if the offence is a specified offence (see **Appendix 4**) and the dangerous offender provisions apply on the facts of the particular case.

A4.4 Not guilty or no indication of plea

If the indication of plea is not guilty, or there is no indication of plea, the court proceeds to allocation.

The court receives representations from the Crown, which may include details of previous convictions of the defendant, and from the defence.

The court determines, in accordance with section 19 of the Magistrates' Courts Act 1980 and the Allocation Guidelines, whether the case is more suitable for summary trial or trial on indictment.

A4.4.1 *Allocation procedure*

The court must hear representations from all parties before considering whether jurisdiction ought to be accepted or declined. The

procedure where there is more than one charge or more than one
defendant is set out in Rule 9 of the Criminal Procedure Rules:

Criminal Procedure Rules, r 9.2

9.2

(5) Where the court on the same occasion deals with two or more offences
    alleged against the same defendant, the court must deal with those
    offences in the following sequence—
    (a) any to which rule 9.6 applies (prosecutor's notice requiring Crown
        Court trial);
    (b) any to which rule 9.7 applies (sending for Crown Court trial, without
        allocation there), in this sequence—
        (i) any the court must send for trial; then
        (ii) any the court can send for trial; and
    (c) any to which rule 9.14 applies (allocation for Crown Court trial).

(6) Where the court on the same occasion deals with two or more defend-
    ants charged jointly with an offence that can be tried in the Crown
    Court then in the following sequence—
    (a) the court must explain, in terms each defendant can understand
        (with help, if necessary), that if the court sends one of them to the
        Crown Court for trial then the court must send for trial in the Crown
        Court, too, any other of them—
        (i) who is charged with the same offence as the defendant sent
            for trial, or with an offence which the court decides is related
            to that offence;
        (ii) who does not wish to plead guilty to each offence with which
            he or she is charged; and
        (iii) (if that other defendant is under 18, and the court would not
            otherwise have sent him or her for Crown Court trial) where
            the court decides that sending is necessary in the interests of
            justice,
        even if the court by then has decided to allocate that other defend-
        ant for magistrates' court trial; and
    (b) the court may ask the defendants questions to help it decide in
        what order to deal with them …

Section 19 of the Magistrates' Courts Act 1980 provides:

Magistrates' Courts Act 1980, s 19(1)–(4)

**19 Court to begin by considering which mode
of trial appears more suitable**

(1) The court shall decide whether the offence appears to it more suitable
    for summary trial or for trial on indictment.

(2) Before making a decision under this section, the court—
    (a) shall give the prosecution an opportunity to inform the court of the
        accused's previous convictions (if any); and

    (b) shall give the prosecution and the accused an opportunity to make representations as to whether summary trial or trial on indictment would be more suitable.

(3) In making a decision under this section, the court shall consider—

    (a) whether the sentence which a magistrates' court would have power to impose for the offence would be adequate; and

    (b) any representations made by the prosecution or the accused under subsection (2)(b) above,

and shall have regard to any allocation guidelines (or revised allocation guidelines) issued as definitive guidelines under section 170 of the Criminal Justice Act 2003.

(4) Where—

    (a) the accused is charged with two or more offences; and

    (b) it appears to the court that the charges for the offences could be joined in the same indictment or that the offences arise out of the same or connected circumstances,

subsection (3)(a) above shall have effect as if references to the sentence which a magistrates' court would have power to impose for the offence were a reference to the maximum aggregate sentence which a magistrates' court would have power to impose for all of the offences taken together.

A4.4.2 *Allocation guideline*

The Sentencing Council has issued a definitive guideline in relation to the allocation of cases between the magistrates' court and Crown Court.

It is important to ensure that all cases are tried at the appropriate level.

1. In general, either way offences should be tried summarily unless:
   - the outcome would clearly be a sentence in excess of the court's powers for the offence(s) concerned after taking into account personal mitigation and any potential reduction for a guilty plea; or
   - for reasons of unusual legal, procedural or factual complexity, the case should be tried in the Crown Court. This exception may apply in cases where a very substantial fine is the likely sentence. Other circumstances where this exception will apply are likely to be rare and case specific; the court will rely on the submissions of the parties to identify relevant cases.
2. In cases with no factual or legal complications the court should bear in mind its power to commit for sentence after a trial and may retain jurisdiction notwithstanding that the likely sentence might exceed its powers.
3. Cases may be tried summarily even where the defendant is subject to a Crown Court Suspended Sentence Order or Community Order.
4. All parties should be asked by the court to make representations as to whether the case is suitable for summary trial. The court should refer to definitive guidelines (if any) to assess the likely sentence for the offence in

the light of the facts alleged by the prosecution case, taking into account all aspects of the case including those advanced by the defence, including any personal mitigation to which the defence wish to refer.

Where the court decides that the case is suitable to be dealt with in the magistrates' court, it must warn the defendant that all sentencing options remain open and, if the defendant consents to summary trial and is convicted by the court or pleads guilty, the defendant may be committed to the Crown Court for sentence.

Committal for sentence

There is ordinarily no statutory restriction on committing an either-way case for sentence following conviction. The general power of the magistrates' court to commit to the Crown Court for sentence after a finding that a case is suitable for summary trial and/or conviction continues to be available where the court is of the opinion 'that the offence or the combination of the offence and one or more offences associated with it was so serious that the Crown Court should, in the court's opinion, have the power to deal with the offender in any way it could deal with him if he had been convicted on indictment'.

However, where the court proceeds to the summary trial of certain offences relating to criminal damage, upon conviction there is no power to commit to the Crown Court for sentence.

The court should refer to any definitive guideline to arrive at the appropriate sentence, taking into account all of the circumstances of the case including personal mitigation and the appropriate guilty plea reduction.

In borderline cases the court should consider obtaining a pre-sentence report before deciding whether to commit to the Crown Court for sentence.

Where the offending is so serious that the court is of the opinion that the Crown Court should have the power to deal with the offender, the case should be committed to the Crown Court for sentence even if a community order may be the appropriate sentence (this will allow the Crown Court to deal with any breach of a community order, if that is the sentence passed).

A4.5 Magistrates' court declines jurisdiction

If the court declines jurisdiction, it must send the case to the Crown Court. For the procedure on sending see **A27**.

A4.6 Magistrates' court accepts jurisdiction

If the court accepts jurisdiction, the defendant may request an indication whether the court is considering a custodial sentence. If the court is willing to give an indication, the defendant must be invited to reconsider his plea. If the indication was non-custodial and a plea of guilty is indicated, the court may neither impose a custodial sentence nor commit for sentence.

The defence must otherwise be asked if they consent to summary trial. If the defence elect trial on indictment, the case must be sent to the Crown Court. (See **A27**.)

If the defence consent to summary trial, the Crown may make further representations that the trial should be on indictment jurisdiction if new factors become relevant. However, there can be no change of venue once the trial has begun or an application in relation to the trial has been made.

If the case remains summary there is a trial, and in the event of a conviction the court may sentence within its own powers, unless:

- there is a specified offence and the requirements for an extended sentence are met by the facts of the particular case; or
- new factors have arisen during the trial, making the initial decision to accept jurisdiction inappropriate.

This follows the case law on 'expectation' preventing a court from changing its mind (*R v Nottingham Magistrates' Court, ex p Davidson* [2000] 1 Cr App R (S) 167). Under these procedures the court will have been fully advised about the defendant's previous convictions, and as the Crown will have had opportunities to emphasize particular seriousness, it will therefore be difficult for the court to say that the decision to accept summary jurisdiction did not give rise to a legitimate expectation of disposal within magistrates' court powers (*Sheffield Magistrates' Court, ex p Ojo* (2000) 164 JP 659). The power to commit for sentence arises when there is an acceptance an acceptance of jurisdiction that was so perverse as to be unlawful (*R (Nicholas) v Chester Magistrates' Court* [2009] EWHC 1504 (Admin)) or in total disregard of the relevant sentencing guideline (*Thornton v CPS* [2012] EWHC 346 (Admin)); or there have been new convictions since the allocation hearing; or the facts at trial were clearly more serious than originally described so that Crown Court sentencing powers are required.

The allocation guideline emphasizes these powers to commit for sentence (see **A4.4.2**) and there may as a result now be no general expectation of a summary disposal.

A4.7 Either-way offences that must be tried summarily

The court must determine venue for either-way offences. Some either-way offences have venue dictated by value (criminal damage, save arson and aggravated vehicle-taking). If the value of damage is less than £5,000, only summary trial will be offered. For multiple offences, the aggregate value must be considered (MCA 1980, s 22(11)). A court has a discretion but not a duty to hear evidence in relation to value (*R v Canterbury Justices, ex p Klisiak* [1981] 2 All ER 129). Value does not include consequential loss flowing from destruction (*R v Colchester Magistrates' Court, ex p Abbott* [2001] Crim LR 564). Where it is not clear whether or not the value exceeds £5,000, the defendant will be permitted, if he so wishes, to elect Crown Court trial but the maximum ten-year sentence is then available (*R v Alden* [2002] EWCA Crim 412).

Theft from a shop that does not exceed an aggregate value of £200 is a hybrid offence in that it can only be tried summarily (without a power to commit for sentence) unless the defendant elects to be tried on indictment: section 22A of the Magistrates' Courts Act 1980. If the defendant elects for trial on indictment full sentencing powers are available.

Section 22 of the Magistrates' Courts Act 1980 provides:

Magistrates' Courts Act 1980, ss 22 and 22A

22 Certain offences triable either way to be tried summarily if value involved is small

(1) If the offence charged by the information is one of those mentioned in the first column of Schedule 2 to this Act (in this section referred to as 'scheduled offences') then, subject to subsection 7 below, the court shall, before proceeding in accordance with section 19 above, consider whether, having regard to any representations made by the prosecutor or the accused, the value involved (as defined in subsection (10) below) appears to the court to exceed the relevant sum. For the purposes of this section the relevant sum is £5,000.

(2) If, where subsection (1) above applies, it appears to the court clear that, for the offence charged, the value involved does not exceed the relevant sum, the court shall proceed as if the offence were triable only summarily, and sections 19 to 21 above shall not apply.

(3) If, where subsection (1) above applies, it appears to the court clear that, for the offence charged, the value involved exceeds the relevant sum, the court shall thereupon proceed in accordance with section 19 above in the ordinary way without further regard to the provisions of this section.

(4) If, where subsection (1) above applies, it appears to the court for any reason not clear whether, for the offence charged, the value involved does or does not exceed the relevant sum, the provisions of subsections (5) and (6) below shall apply.

(5) The court shall cause the charge to be written down, if this has not already been done, and read to the accused, and shall explain to him in ordinary language—
   (a) that he can, if he wishes, consent to be tried summarily for the offence and that if he consents to be so tried, he will definitely be tried in that way; and

      (b) that if he is tried summarily and is convicted by the court, his liability to imprisonment or a fine will be limited as provided in section 33 below.

(6) After explaining to the accused as provided by subsection (5) above the court shall ask him whether he consents to be tried summarily and—

      (a) if he so consents, shall proceed in accordance with subsection (2) above as if that subsection applied;

      (b) if he does not so consent, shall proceed in accordance with subsection (3) above as if that subsection applied.

(7) [repealed]

(8) Where a person is convicted by a magistrates' court of a scheduled offence, it shall not be open to him to appeal to the Crown Court against the conviction on the ground that the convicting court's decision as to the value involved was mistaken.

(9) If, where subsection (1) above applies, the offence charged is one with which the accused is charged jointly with a person who has not attained the age of 17, the reference in that subsection to any representations made by the accused shall be read as including any representations made by the person under 18.

(10) In this section 'the value involved', in relation to any scheduled offence, means the value indicated in the second column of Schedule 2 to this Act, measured as indicated in the third column of that Schedule; and in that Schedule 'the material time' means the time of the alleged offence.

(11) Where—

      (a) the accused is charged on the same occasion with two or more scheduled offences and it appears to the court that they constitute or form part of a series of two or more offences of the same or a similar character; or

      (b) the offence charged consists in incitement to commit two or more scheduled offences, this section shall have effect as if any reference in it to the value involved were a reference to the aggregate of the values involved.

22A Low-value shoplifting to be a summary offence

(1) Low-value shoplifting is triable only summarily.

(2) But where a person accused of low-value shoplifting is aged 18 or over, and appears or is brought before the court before the summary trial of the offence begins, the court must give the person the opportunity of electing to be tried by the Crown Court for the offence and, if the person elects to be so tried—

      (a) subsection (1) does not apply, and

      (b) the court must proceed in relation to the offence in accordance with section 51(1) of the Crime and Disorder Act 1998.

(3) 'Low-value shoplifting' means an offence under section 1 of the Theft Act 1968 in circumstances where—

      (a) the value of the stolen goods does not exceed £200,

      (b) the goods were being offered for sale in a shop or any other premises, stall, vehicle or place from which there is carried on a trade or business, and

(c) at the time of the offence, the person accused of low-value shoplifting was, or was purporting to be, a customer or potential customer
of the person offering the goods for sale.

(4) For the purposes of subsection (3)(a)—

    (a) the value of the stolen goods is the price at which they were being
offered for sale at the time of the offence, and

    (b) where the accused is charged on the same occasion with two or
more offences of low-value shoplifting, the reference to the value
involved has effect as if it were a reference to the aggregate of the
values involved.

(5) A person guilty of low-value shoplifting is liable on summary conviction
to—

    (a) imprisonment for a period not exceeding 51 weeks (or 6 months, if
the offence was committed before the commencement of section
281(4) and (5) of the Criminal Justice Act 2003),

    (b) a fine, or

    (c) both.

(6) A person convicted of low-value shoplifting by a magistrates' court may
not appeal to the Crown Court against the conviction on the ground
that the convicting court was mistaken as to whether the offence was
one of low-value shoplifting.

(7) For the purposes of this section, any reference to low-value shoplifting
includes aiding, abetting, counselling or procuring the commission of
low-value shoplifting.

A4.8 Allocation in the absence of the defendant

Under section 17B Magistrates' Courts Act 1980, an advocate can
indicate a plea on a defendant's behalf if that defendant has been
removed for unruly behaviour, or the defendant is a company.

A4.9 Sentence discount for early indication
of plea

In *R v Caley* [2012] EWCA Crim 2821, the court appeared to indicate that the same discount will be given for a plea of guilty in the
magistrates' court, followed by a committal for sentence, as for an
indication given immediately, or immediately after, the case is sent
to the Crown Court.

See *Blackstone's Criminal Practice 2017* **D6**

A5 **Amending Charge**

A5.1 **Amendment within the time limit**

It should not be thought that prosecutors have an unfettered right to seek to amend charges that are not subject to any limitation of time (ie indictable and indictable-only charges). Amendments should be granted only where the application is judged to be proper and appropriate (*R v Redbridge Justices, ex p Whitehouse* (1992) 94 Cr App R 332).

A5.2 **Amendment outside the time limit**

An amendment outside the time limit, in order to allow the prosecution to proceed with a summary-only offence which would otherwise be time barred, may be permitted, provided that the new offence is based on the 'same misdoing' and that it is in the interests of justice to allow the amendment (*R v Scunthorpe Justices, ex p McPhee and Gallagher* (1998) 162 JP 635, DC).

The following principles emerge from *Scunthorpe Justices*:

- the purpose of the six-month time limit imposed by section 127 MCA 1980 is to ensure that summary offences are charged and tried as soon as reasonably practicable after their alleged commission;
- where an information has been laid within the six-month period it can be amended after the expiry of that period;
- an information can be amended after the expiry of the six-month period, even to allege a different offence or different offences, provided that:
  - the different offence or offences allege the 'same misdoing' as the original offence; and
  - the amendment can be made in the interests of justice.

The phrase 'same misdoing' should not be construed too narrowly. It means that the new offence should arise out of the same (or substantially the same) facts as gave rise to the original offence.

In *Shaw v Director of Public Prosecutions* [2007] EWHC 207 (Admin), the court ruled that an amendment to charge an offence which was based on similar misdoing ought not to have been permitted, as the original offence carried only a financial penalty whereas the new offence carried imprisonment. The court ruled similarly in *R (Crown Prosecution Service) v Everest* [2005] EWHC 1124 (Admin), observing that the new offence carried a higher penalty, had a statutory defence that the defence had to establish, and that the defendant was not legally represented.

The amendment of a charge to substitute failing to provide a specimen of breath with failing to provide a specimen of urine was held to be proper in *Williams v Director of Public Prosecutions* [2009] EWHC 2354 (Admin), although the court did allow the appeal as the alteration had not been made in a timely fashion (applying *DPP v Hammerton* [2009] EWHC 921 (Admin)). In *Crann v CPS* [2013] EWHC 552 (Admin), a very late amendment was allowed as the offence was no more serious and had been anticipated (contra *Williams v DPP* [2009] EWHC 2354 (Admin)).

An out-of-time amendment to allege a different defendant is not permissible (*Sainsbury's Supermarkets Ltd v HM Courts Service* [2006] EWHC 1749 (Admin)).

A6 **Appeals and Reopening**

A6.1 **Appeals**

An appeal against conviction and/or sentence lies as of right to the Crown Court. A notice of appeal must be served within 21 days of final disposal of the case. Section 113 MCA 1980 creates an obligation on the magistrates' court to consider an application for bail pending appeal in every case where a properly constituted application for bail is made (*Thomas v CPS* [2015] EWHC 4079 (Admin)).

If a custodial sentence is imposed it is not the normal practice to grant bail pending an appeal, and there is no statutory right to bail. Where the appeal is against conviction and the defendant was convicted after trial, many courts will look more favourably on bail pending appeal, particularly when the custodial sentence is short. In *R v Imdad Shah* (1980) 144 JP 460, the court rejected an argument that bail should be granted where the sentence was a short one and there was a risk that the sentence would be served prior to the appeal being heard. The court ruled that in such cases an early listing should be sought. By way of contrast, in *R (G) v Inner London Crown Court* [2003] EWHC 2715 (Admin) the applicant successfully judicially reviewed a decision by a Crown Court to refuse bail in a 'short sentence' case.

Section 108 of the Magistrates' Courts Act 1980 provides:

Magistrates' Courts Act 1980, s 108

108 Right of appeal to the Crown Court

(1) A person convicted by a magistrates' court may appeal to the Crown Court—
  (a) if he pleaded guilty, against his sentence;
  (b) if he did not, against the conviction or sentence.

(1A) Section 14 of the Powers of Criminal Courts (Sentencing) Act 2000 (under which a conviction of an offence for which an order for conditional or absolute discharge is made is deemed not to be a conviction except for certain purposes) shall not prevent an appeal under this Act, whether against conviction or otherwise.

(2) A person sentenced by a magistrates' court for an offence in respect of which an order for conditional discharge has been previously made may appeal to the Crown Court against the sentence.

(3) In this section 'sentence' includes any order made on conviction by a magistrates' court, not being—
  (b) an order for the payment of costs;
  (c) an order under section 37(1) of the Animal Welfare Act 2006 (which enables a court to order the destruction of an animal); or

---

> (d) an order made in pursuance of any enactment under which the court has no discretion as to the making of the order or its terms and also includes a declaration of relevance, within the meaning of section 23 of the Football Spectators Act 1989.
>
> (4) Subsection (3)(d) above does not prevent an appeal against a surcharge imposed under section 161A of the Criminal Justice Act 2003.

A6.2 Reopening cases

A6.2.1 *Jurisdiction*

Magistrates' Courts Act 1980, s 142

142 Power of magistrates' court to re-open cases to rectify mistakes etc

(1) A magistrates' court may vary or rescind a sentence or other order imposed or made by it when dealing with an offender if it appears to the court to be in the interests of justice to do so, and it is hereby declared that this power extends to replacing a sentence or order which for any reason appears to be invalid by another which the court has power to impose or make.

(1A) The power conferred on a magistrates' court by subsection (1) above shall not be exercisable in relation to any sentence or order imposed or made by it when dealing with an offender if—
　　(a) the Crown Court has determined an appeal against—
　　　　(i) that sentence or order;
　　　　(ii) the conviction in respect of which that sentence or order was imposed or made; or
　　　　(iii) any other sentence or order imposed or made by the magistrates' court when dealing with the offender in respect of that conviction (including a sentence or order replaced by that sentence or order); or
　　(b) the High Court has determined a case stated for the opinion of that court on any question arising in any proceeding leading to or resulting from the imposition or making of the sentence or order.

(2) Where a person is convicted by a magistrates' court and it subsequently appears to the court that it would be in the interests of justice that the case should be heard again by different justices, the court may so direct.

(2A) The power conferred on a magistrates' court by subsection (2) above shall not be exercisable in relation to a conviction if—
　　(a) the Crown Court has determined an appeal against—
　　　　(i) the conviction; or
　　　　(ii) any sentence or order imposed or made by the magistrates' court when dealing with the offender in respect of the conviction; or
　　(b) the High Court has determined a case stated for the opinion of that court on any question arising in any proceeding leading to or resulting from the conviction.

> (3) Where a court gives a direction under subsection (2) above—
>   (a) the conviction and any sentence or other order imposed or made in consequence thereof shall be of no effect; and
>   (b) section 10(4) above shall apply as if the trial of the person in question had been adjourned.
> (4) [repealed]
> (5) Where a sentence or order is varied under subsection (1) above, the sentence or other order, as so varied, shall take effect from the beginning of the day on which it was originally imposed or made, unless the court otherwise directs.

A6.2.2 *Principles*

Section 142 of the Magistrates' Courts Act 1980 relates to criminal proceedings and has no application to other areas of magistrates' court jurisdiction such as liability orders (*Liverpool City Council v Plemora Distribution Ltd* [2002] EWHC 2467 (Admin)), and detention and forfeiture in relation to proceeds of crime. Further, the court enjoys no common law jurisdiction to reopen civil matters such as a civil injunction (*Samuda v Birmingham Justices* [2008] EWHC 205 (Admin)). A defendant who has been convicted in absence can properly attempt to reopen under this section. Culpability on the part of the offender is relevant to whether it is in the interests of justice to reopen, but it is not determinative. It will normally be in the interests of justice for a defendant to be able to defend himself, and unless the evidence indicates that his absence from trial is deliberate and voluntary, a rehearing would normally be the appropriate course (*R (Morsby) v Tower Bridge Magistrates' Court* [2007] EWHC 2766 (Admin)). See also *R (Manorgate Ltd) v Thames Magistrates' Court* [2013] EWHC 535 (Admin). Any inconvenience to the court in allowing a reopening can never outweigh the interests of justice (*R (Blick) v Doncaster Magistrates' Court* (2008) 172 JP 651). Section 142(2) MCA 1980 does not require a mistake in every case but merely that rectification be in the interests of justice. However, there must be new material before the court (*R (Nkromah) v Willesden MC* [2014] EWHC 4455(Admin)).

Persons made subject to a hospital order under section 37(3) of the Mental Health Act 1983 fall within the definition of 'offender', and a person can use section 142 MCA 1980 to reopen a hearing determining the issue under the Mental Health Act (*R (Bartram) v Southend Magistrates' Court* [2004] EWHC 2691 (Admin)). An order to commit an offender to prison for non-satisfaction of a confiscation order made under the Proceeds of Crime Act 2002 in the Crown Court is capable of being reopened.

The court has power to revisit the issue of a warrant following non-payment of fines. A court does not have the power to rescind a costs order made in favour of a defendant who was not convicted as the section related only to orders post-conviction (*Coles v East Penwith Justices*, The Times, 27 July 1998).

The nature of the remedy afforded under MCA 1980 is akin to a 'slip rule', allowing a court to rectify a clear mistake or injustice. An applicant who entered an unequivocal plea of guilty cannot apply to reopen a plea under this section (*R v Croydon Youth Court, ex p Director of Public Prosecutions* [1997] 2 Cr App R 411), unless the plea was inappropriate and so now equivocal; however, this exception did not apply where the allegation was of professional impropriety by the defendant's legal representative as this did not fall within the word 'mistake' (*Williamson v City of Westminster Magistrates' Court* [2012] EWHC 1444 (Admin)).

Section 142 should not be used to advance new arguments, neither should it be used as an 'appeal' mechanism against an earlier decision (*Zykin v Crown Prosecution Service* [2009] EWHC 1469 (Admin); *R v Chajed* [2013] EWHC 188 (Admin)). Applications based on a change of law between conviction and application should not be entertained, under normal principles of finality of judgment.

A prosecutor cannot apply to reopen proceedings that have previously been withdrawn (*R (Green and Green Scaffolding Ltd) v Staines Magistrates' Court* (2008) 172 JP 353).

A6.2.3 *Applications*

An application may be made orally or in writing; the applicant does not have to attend the hearing. All parties must be given notice of the application and be heard if they so wish. Section 142(1A) and (2A) of the 1980 Act set out the instances in which a remedy under this provision is denied on account of an alternative avenue of appeal having been taken.

A procedure for an application under section 142 is provided by the Criminal Procedure Rules:

Criminal Procedure Rules, r 24.18

(4) A party who wants the court to exercise its power must—
  (a) apply in writing as soon as reasonably practicable after the conviction or order that that party wants the court to set aside, vary or rescind;
  (b) serve the application on—
    (i) the court officer, and
    (ii) each other party; and

> (c) in the application—
>   (i) explain why, as appropriate, the conviction should be set aside, or the order varied or rescinded,
>   (ii) specify any variation of the order that the applicant proposes,
>   (iii) identify any witness that the defendant wants to call, and any other proposed evidence,
>   (iv) say whether the defendant waives legal professional privilege, giving any relevant name and date, and
>   (v) if the application is late, explain why.
> (5) The court may—
>   (a) extend (even after it has expired) the time limit under paragraph (4), unless the court's power to set aside the conviction, or vary the order, can no longer be exercised;
>   (b) allow an application to be made orally.

There is no statutory time limit on reopening, but the former 28-day rule should act as a salutary guideline. Applications made much beyond this date might properly be refused on interests of justice grounds, as '[d]elay in matters of this sort is always harmful, memories fade, records may be lost and the essence of doing justice is that it should be done expeditiously' (*R v Ealing Magistrates' Court, ex p Sahota*, The Times, 9 December 1997). It is not, however, a decisive factor. It is not enough for the magistrates simply to say that the length of time is such that it is no longer proper to open the case under section 142. More substantial reasoning than that has to be given, so that the applicant (and any court on appeal) can understand why it is no longer proper to deal with the matter.

Applications may be made by both defence and prosecution, but the exercise of such discretion in favour of a prosecutor will be rare, and can never extend to the overturning of an acquittal. A prosecutor could properly make an application to reopen where the court had erroneously failed to impose penalty points or some other appropriate order. Similarly, if the court had been unaware of factors relevant to sentence, it could be invited to reopen sentence, even if that meant a risk that it would be increased. However, if it is appropriate for the powers under section 142 to be used to increase sentence then the power must be exercised very speedily (*R (Holme) v Liverpool Magistrates' Court* [2004] EWHC 3131 (Admin), where the court declined to allow the prosecution to exercise the power).

A6.2.4 *Interests of justice*

Justices are given wide discretion in determining what are relevant factors in relation to interests of justice, but decisions must be based on sound judicial reasoning. A defendant's late arrival at court was held not to be a proper ground, in itself, to refuse a rehearing (*R v Camberwell Green Magistrates' Court, ex p Ibrahim* (1984) 148 JP 400). Factors a court ought to consider include:

- why the convicted person did not appear at the original trial (if that was the case);
- timeliness of the application;
- reason for any delay;
- importance of the decision being questioned—note that the importance to all parties, including defendant, prosecution, and other interested parties (such as victim), should be assessed;
- inconvenience and prejudice caused to opposing parties;
- whether a more appropriate appeal remedy is available. It will not be appropriate to allow a reopening where a defendant is denied a right of appeal due to an unequivocal guilty plea (*R v Croydon Youth Court, ex p Director of Public Prosecutions* [1997] 2 Cr App R 411).

In addition, the court must always consider rule 1 of the Criminal Procedure Rules and the overriding objective.

 See *Blackstone's Criminal Practice 2017* **D29**

A6.2.5 *Effect of reopening*

A conviction will be set aside, as will any sentence or ancillary orders flowing from it. The matter is treated as adjourned for trial. Justices who sat on the original hearing, or the hearing to reopen, cannot sit on the adjourned trial. The prosecution retain the right to offer no evidence and the court lacks power to insist that a prosecutor proceeds with the case (*R (Rhodes-Presley) v South Worcestershire Magistrates' Court* [2008] EWHC 2700 (Admin)).

If a sentence or order is reopened, the court may vary or rescind the original finding and substitute any other lawful sentence or order that would have been available to the court at the original hearing. The new orders take effect from the date of the old order unless the court directs otherwise. A court must be careful not to offend against any legitimate expectation given to the offender (*Jane v Broome*, The Times, 2 November 1988).

A6.3 Reopening of guilty plea

Criminal Procedure Rules, r 24.10

Application to withdraw a guilty plea

(1) This rule applies where the defendant wants to withdraw a guilty plea.
(2) The defendant must apply to do so—
    (a) as soon as practicable after becoming aware of the reasons for doing so; and
    (b) before sentence.
(3) Unless the court otherwise directs, the application must be in writing and the defendant must serve it on—
    (a) the court officer; and
    (b) the prosecutor.
(4) The application must—
    (a) explain why it would be unjust not to allow the defendant to withdraw the guilty plea;
    (b) identify—
        (i) any witness that the defendant wants to call, and
        (ii) any other proposed evidence; and
    (c) say whether the defendant waives legal professional privilege, giving any relevant name and date.

The following principles emerge from the authorities:

- the fact that the defendant was not legally represented when he entered his guilty plea is not on its own grounds for allowing a change of plea (*R v South Tameside Magistrates' Court, ex p Rowland* [1983] 3 All ER 689);
- a misunderstanding as to the nature of the charge being pleaded to may justify a change of plea (and may well be an equivocal plea in any event) (*P Foster Haulage Ltd v Roberts* [1978] 2 All ER 751);
- evidence of the previous guilty plea may be adduced at any later trial, although its probative value will generally be so low that a court ought to decline to admit it (*R v Rimmer* [1972] 1 WLR 268).

In *S (An Infant) v Recorder of Manchester* [1971] AC 481, the court held that:

- the power to reopen plea was a discretionary one;
- the power ought to be used sparingly;
- the power is available up until sentence has been passed;
- the question for the court is whether justice requires the change of plea to be permitted.

A7 **Bad Character**

A7.1 **Introduction**

The admissibility of bad character is regulated by sections 98–113 of the Criminal Justice Act 2003, but section 27(3) Theft Act 1968 remains available to the Crown in cases of handling. The common law rules are now subsidiary to the statutory regime. The Act is concerned with the admission of bad character in relation to:

- the defendant;
- any co-defendant;
- a person other than a defendant in the case.

The Criminal Procedure Rules provide a strict regime for the admission of evidence of bad character. The court has the power to exclude otherwise admissible evidence of bad character on the grounds of non-compliance, if the effect would be to prejudice a party, for example by way of ambush defence (*R v Musone* [2007] EWCA Crim 1237). Provided that there is no prejudice, a court is free to admit evidence of bad character if to do so would satisfy the overriding objective of rule 1 of the Criminal Procedure Rules. Attempts to argue that evidence ought to be admitted following procedural non-compliance only in exceptional cases have been rejected (*R (Robinson) v Sutton Coldfield Magistrates' Court* [2006] EWHC 307 (Admin)). In *Robinson*, the court did say, however, that:

> a court would ordinarily wish to know when the relevant enquiries had been initiated, and in broad terms why they have not been completed within the time allowed. Any application for an extension will be closely scrutinised by the court. A party seeking an extension cannot expect the indulgence of the court unless it clearly sets out the reasons why it is seeking that indulgence.

Rule 21 of the Criminal Procedure Rules regulates the admission of bad character evidence:

Criminal Procedure Rules, r 21

21.2.—(1) A party who wants to introduce evidence of bad character must—
   (a) make an application under rule 21.3, where it is evidence of a non-defendant's bad character;
   (b) give notice under rule 21.4, where it is evidence of a defendant's bad character.

(2) An application or notice must—
   (a) set out the facts of the misconduct on which that party relies,

---

   (b) explain how that party will prove those facts (whether by
       certificate of conviction, other official record, or other evi-
       dence), if another party disputes them, and
   (c) explain why the evidence is admissible.

Notice to introduce evidence of a defendant's bad character

21.4.—(1) This rule applies where a party wants to introduce evidence of a
       defendant's bad character.

   (2) A prosecutor or co-defendant who wants to introduce such evi-
       dence must serve notice on—
       (a) the court officer; and
       (b) each other party.

   (3) A prosecutor must serve any such notice not more than—
       (a) 28 days after the defendant pleads not guilty, in a magis-
           trates' court; ...

   (4) A co-defendant must serve any such notice—
       (a) as soon as reasonably practicable; and in any event
       (b) not more than 14 days after the prosecutor discloses mate-
           rial on which the notice is based.

   (5) A party who objects to the introduction of the evidence identi-
       fied by such a notice must—
       (a) apply to the court to determine the objection;
       (b) serve the application on—
           (i) the court officer, and
           (ii) each other party
       not more than 14 days after service of the notice; and
       (c) in the application explain, as applicable—
           (i) which, if any, facts of the misconduct set out in the
               notice that party disputes,
           (ii) what, if any, facts of the misconduct that party admits
                instead,
           (iii) why the evidence is not admissible,
           (iv) why it would be unfair to admit the evidence, and
           (v) any other objection to the notice.

   (8) A defendant who wants to introduce evidence of his or her own
       bad character must—
       (a) give notice, in writing or orally—
           (i) as soon as reasonably practicable, and in any event
           (ii) before the evidence is introduced, either by the defend-
                ant or in reply to a question asked by the defendant of
                another party's witness in order to obtain that evidence...;

Court's power to vary requirements under this Part

21.6.—(1) The court may—
       (a) shorten or extend (even after it has expired) a time limit
           under this Part;
       (b) allow an application or notice to be in a different form to one
           set out in the Practice Direction, or to be made or given orally;
       (c) dispense with a requirement for notice to introduce evi-
           dence of a defendant's bad character.

> (2) A party who wants an extension of time must—
>   (a) apply when serving the application or notice for which it is needed; and
>   (b) explain the delay.

A7.2 What is bad character?

The Criminal Justice Act defines 'bad character' as the commission of an offence or other 'reprehensible behaviour'. It is important to note the effect of section 98 (see **A7.3**), which has the effect of excluding much bad character evidence from the statutory scheme, allowing for its admissibility subject only to the normal rules of probity and relevance.

In considering whether or not a party has committed an offence, regard can be had to:

* previous convictions;
* previous police cautions or youth cautions;
* offences for which the person has not been tried;
* offences for which the person has been acquitted (*R v Z* [2000] 2 AC 483) or found unfit to be tried (*R v Renda* [2005] EWCA Crim 2826).

Other examples include telling lies, taking illegal drugs (*R v AJC* [2006] EWCA Crim 284), being sexually promiscuous (*R v Ball* [2005] EWCA Crim 2826), and collecting photographs of people being violently attacked (*R v Saleem* [2007] EWCA Crim 1923). In *R v M* [2014] EWCA Crim 1407, it was held that attempted suicide and probably, self-harming do not amount to reprehensible behaviour but excessive drinking and illegal drug taking do fall within the meaning of the term. The Act also covers those with a disposition towards reprehensible conduct, for example an admission that a person is sexually attracted to children (*R v S* [2007] EWCA Crim 1387; but see also *R v Fox* [2009] EWCA Crim 653, where such evidence ought not to be admitted).

It is important to note that a defendant is entitled to dispute that he is guilty of a matter that has resulted in conviction (or caution); the procedure for doing so is discussed in *R v C* [2010] EWCA Crim 2971.

There are some particular considerations at play when admitting police cautions as evidence of bad character. In *R v Olu and others* [2010] EWCA Crim 2975, the court held:

> We accept the submission that there is a very considerable difference not only between a caution and a conviction for the reasons given in the authorities to which we have referred, but there is also a very

considerable difference between an admission contained in a caution without legal advice having been given and an admission made in a caution after legal advice or before a court by a plea. In such circumstances, the giving of legal advice or the formality of a court appearance will have made clear to the person the consequences of his admission. The processes that lead to a caution can differ widely between police area and police area; a court would be shutting its eyes to reality if it assumed that, where a person was not legally represented, the consequences of admitting an offence and accepting a caution were fully explained to a person in a manner that he understood the serious adverse consequences that would follow and what he was giving up by not exercising his right to legal advice—namely that what he was admitting would give him a criminal record, that the caution would be maintained on his PNC record for very many years and that it would be used against his interests in certain circumstances.

Penalty notices for disorder cannot, in themselves, be adduced as evidence of bad character (*R v Hamer* [2010] EWCA Crim 2053); neither can unsubstantiated allegations contained in crime reports (*R v Braithwaite* [2010] EWCA Crim 1082).

A7.3 Bad character excluded from application

Section 98 provides:

> **Criminal Justice Act 2003, s 98**
>
> **98 'Bad character'**
> References in this Chapter to evidence of a person's 'bad character' are to evidence of, or of a disposition towards, misconduct on his part, other than evidence which—
>
> (a) has to do with the alleged facts of the offence with which the defendant is charged, or
> (b) is evidence of misconduct in connection with the investigation or prosecution of that offence.

At a more obvious level this means that the allegation itself (obviously of misconduct) does not need to be subject to an application to admit bad character. It also covers the following:

- evidence of a previous conviction that might be a component of the offence alleged (eg a conviction for assault against a child in relation to a cruelty charge concerning that same child: *R v R* [2006] EWCA Crim 3196);
- preparatory acts (eg purchase of a murder weapon);
- background evidence (eg an act that provided motive for the offence: *R v Saleem* [2007] EWCA Crim 1923 and *R v McNeill* [2007] EWCA Crim 2927);

- a temporal connection is not essential for the evidence to be 'to do' with the offence if it goes to provide the motive, but it is otherwise if it is being used as evidence of propensity (*R v Sule* [2012] EWCA Crim 1130).

A7.4 Non-defendant's bad character

Section 100 provides:

Criminal Justice Act 2003, s 100

100 Non-defendant's bad character

(1) In criminal proceedings evidence of the bad character of a person other than the defendant is admissible if and only if—
  (a) it is important explanatory evidence,
  (b) it has substantial probative value in relation to a matter which—
    (i) is a matter in issue in the proceedings, and
    (ii) is of substantial importance in the context of the case as a whole, or
  (c) all parties to the proceedings agree to the evidence being admissible.
(2) For the purposes of subsection (1)(a) evidence is important explanatory evidence if—
  (a) without it, the court or jury would find it impossible or difficult properly to understand other evidence in the case, and
  (b) its value for understanding the case as a whole is substantial.
(3) In assessing the probative value of evidence for the purposes of subsection (1)(b) the court must have regard to the following factors (and to any others it considers relevant)—
  (a) the nature and number of the events, or other things, to which the evidence relates;
  (b) when those events or things are alleged to have happened or existed;
  (c) where—
    (i) the evidence is evidence of a person's misconduct, and
    (ii) it is suggested that the evidence has probative value by reason of similarity between that misconduct and other alleged misconduct,
    the nature and extent of the similarities and the dissimilarities between each of the alleged instances of misconduct;
  (d) where—
    (i) the evidence is evidence of a person's misconduct,
    (ii) it is suggested that that person is also responsible for the misconduct charged, and
    (iii) the identity of the person responsible for the misconduct charged is disputed,
    the extent to which the evidence shows or tends to show that the same person was responsible each time.
(4) Except where subsection (1)(c) applies, evidence of the bad character of a person other than the defendant must not be given without leave of the court.

A7.5 **Defendant's bad character**

Section 101 provides:

> ### Criminal Justice Act 2003, s 101
>
> #### 101 Defendant's bad character
> (1) In criminal proceedings evidence of the defendant's bad character is admissible if, but only if—
>   - (a) all parties to the proceedings agree to the evidence being admissible,
>   - (b) the evidence is adduced by the defendant himself or is given in answer to a question asked by him in cross-examination and intended to elicit it,
>   - (c) it is important explanatory evidence,
>   - (d) it is relevant to an important matter in issue between the defendant and the prosecution,
>   - (e) it has substantial probative value in relation to an important matter in issue between the defendant and a co-defendant,
>   - (f) it is evidence to correct a false impression given by the defendant, or
>   - (g) the defendant has made an attack on another person's character.
> (2) Sections 102 to 106 contain provision supplementing subsection (1).
> (3) The court must not admit evidence under subsection (1)(d) or (g) if, on an application by the defendant to exclude it, it appears to the court that the admission of the evidence would have such an adverse effect on the fairness of the proceedings that the court ought not to admit it.
> (4) On an application to exclude evidence under subsection (3) the court must have regard, in particular, to the length of time between the matters to which that evidence relates and the matters which form the subject of the offence charged.

A7.6 **Important explanatory evidence**

Section 102 provides:

> ### Criminal Justice Act 2003, s 102
>
> #### 102 'Important explanatory evidence'
> For the purposes of section 101(1)(c) evidence is important explanatory evidence if—
>   - (a) without it, the court or jury would find it impossible or difficult properly to understand other evidence in the case, and
>   - (b) its value for understanding the case as a whole is substantial.

A case which is truly one of propensity cannot and must not be dressed up as a case of important explanatory evidence. To say the evidence fills out the picture is not the same as saying that the rest of the picture is either impossible or difficult to see without it (*R v Lee* [2012] EWCA Crim 316).

A7.7 Matter in issue between defendant and prosecution

Section 103 provides:

Criminal Justice Act 2003, s 103

103 Matter in issue between the defendant and the prosecution

(1) For the purposes of section 101(1)(d) the matters in issue between the defendant and the prosecution include—
  (a) the question whether the defendant has a propensity to commit offences of the kind with which he is charged, except where his having such a propensity makes it no more likely that he is guilty of the offence;
  (b) the question whether the defendant has a propensity to be untruthful, except where it is not suggested that the defendant's case is untruthful in any respect.

(2) Where subsection (1)(a) applies, a defendant's propensity to commit offences of the kind with which he is charged may (without prejudice to any other way of doing so) be established by evidence that he has been convicted of—
  (a) an offence of the same description as the one with which he is charged, or
  (b) an offence of the same category as the one with which he is charged.

(3) Subsection (2) does not apply in the case of a particular defendant if the court is satisfied, by reason of the length of time since the conviction or for any other reason, that it would be unjust for it to apply in his case.

(4) For the purposes of subsection (2)—
  (a) two offences are of the same description as each other if the statement of the offence in a written charge or indictment would, in each case, be in the same terms;
  (b) two offences are of the same category as each other if they belong to the same category of offences prescribed for the purposes of this section by an order made by the Secretary of State.

(5) A category prescribed by an order under subsection (4)(b) must consist of offences of the same type.

(6) Only prosecution evidence is admissible under section 101(1)(d).

Whilst the matter in issue includes propensity, the provision is more likely to be relevant to ruling out a defence such as innocent association (*R v Vo* [2013] EWCA Crim 2292); self-defence (*R v Cox* [2014] EWCA Crim 804); or identity (*R Richardson* [2014] EWCA Crim 1785). It may assist to establish the credibility of the complainant (*R v Blake* [2014] EWCA Crim 2341). It must not be used to bolster a weak case (see *R v H* [2014] EWCA Crim 420).

A7.8 Matter in issue between the defendant and a co-defendant

Section 104 provides:

Criminal Justice Act 2003, s 104

104 'Matter in issue between the defendant and a co-defendant'

(1) Evidence which is relevant to the question whether the defendant has a propensity to be untruthful is admissible on that basis under section 101(1) only if the nature or conduct of his defence is such as to undermine the co-defendant's defence.

(2) Only evidence—
   (a) which is to be (or has been) adduced by the co-defendant, or
   (b) which a witness is to be invited to give (or has given) in cross-examination by the co-defendant, is admissible under section 101(1)(e).

A7.9 Evidence to correct a false impression

Section 105 provides:

Criminal Justice Act 2003, s 105

105 'Evidence to correct a false impression'

(1) For the purposes of section 101(1)(f)—
   (a) the defendant gives a false impression if he is responsible for the making of an express or implied assertion which is apt to give the court or jury a false or misleading impression about the defendant;
   (b) evidence to correct such an impression is evidence which has probative value in correcting it.

(2) A defendant is treated as being responsible for the making of an assertion if—
   (a) the assertion is made by the defendant in the proceedings (whether or not in evidence given by him),
   (b) the assertion was made by the defendant—
      (i) on being questioned under caution, before charge, about the offence with which he is charged, or
      (ii) on being charged with the offence or officially informed that he might be prosecuted for it,
      and evidence of the assertion is given in the proceedings,
   (c) the assertion is made by a witness called by the defendant,
   (d) the assertion is made by any witness in cross-examination in response to a question asked by the defendant that is intended to elicit it, or is likely to do so, or

    (e) the assertion was made by any person out of court, and the defendant adduces evidence of it in the proceedings.

(3) A defendant who would otherwise be treated as responsible for the making of an assertion shall not be so treated if, or to the extent that, he withdraws it or disassociates himself from it.

(4) Where it appears to the court that a defendant, by means of his conduct (other than the giving of evidence) in the proceedings, is seeking to give the court or jury an impression about himself that is false or misleading, the court may if it appears just to do so treat the defendant as being responsible for the making of an assertion which is apt to give that impression.

(5) In subsection (4) 'conduct' includes appearance or dress.

(6) Evidence is admissible under section 101(1)(f) only if it goes no further than is necessary to correct the false impression.

(7) Only prosecution evidence is admissible under section 101(1)(f).

A7.10 Attack on another person's character

Section 106 provides:

Criminal Justice Act 2003, s 106

106 'Attack on another person's character'

(1) For the purposes of section 101(1)(g) a defendant makes an attack on another person's character if—
    (a) he adduces evidence attacking the other person's character,
    (b) he (or any legal representative appointed under section 38(4) of the Youth Justice and Criminal Evidence Act 1999 (c. 23) to cross-examine a witness in his interests) asks questions in cross-examination that are intended to elicit such evidence, or are likely to do so, or
    (c) evidence is given of an imputation about the other person made by the defendant—
        (i) on being questioned under caution, before charge, about the offence with which he is charged, or
        (ii) on being charged with the offence or officially informed that he might be prosecuted for it.

(2) In subsection (1) 'evidence attacking the other person's character' means evidence to the effect that the other person—
    (a) has committed an offence (whether a different offence from the one with which the defendant is charged or the same one), or
    (b) has behaved, or is disposed to behave, in a reprehensible way;
    and 'imputation about the other person' means an assertion to that effect.

(3) Only prosecution evidence is admissible under section 101(1)(g).

 See *Blackstone's Criminal Practice 2017* **F12**

A7.11 Handling: special rules

Theft Act 1968, s 27

(3) Where a person is being proceeded against for handling stolen goods (but not for any offence other than handling stolen goods), then at any stage of the proceedings, if evidence has been given of his having or arranging to have in his possession the goods the subject of the charge, or of his undertaking or assisting in, or arranging to undertake or assist in, their retention, removal, disposal or realisation, the following evidence shall be admissible for the purpose of proving that he knew or believed the goods to be stolen goods:—

(a) evidence that he has had in his possession, or has undertaken or assisted in the retention, removal, disposal or realisation of, stolen goods from any theft taking place not earlier than twelve months before the offence charged; and

(b) (provided that seven days' notice in writing has been given to him of the intention to prove the conviction) evidence that he has within the five years preceding the date of the offence charged been convicted of theft or of handling stolen goods.

A7.11.1 Key points

Handling must be the only offence in issue. The provision goes only to proof of guilty knowledge, not dishonesty or possession (*Duffas* 1994 158 JP 245). Only the details admissible by reason of section 73(2) Police and Criminal Evidence Act 1984 should be admitted (*Hacker* 1994 1 All ER 45). *Hacker* also confirms that section 78 Police and Criminal Evidence Act 1984 can be used to exclude the evidence if it is unfair in the proceedings to admit it.

A8 **Bail**

A8.1 Introduction

The starting point is that there is a presumption in favour of bail being granted in criminal proceedings (see **A8.2** for the position in relation to defendants charged with murder appearing before a magistrates' court). The exceptions to that right under Schedule 1 to the Bail Act 1976 are summarized below:

Exception	Imprisonable— Pt I	Imprisonable— Pt IA triable only summarily	Non-imprisonable— Pt II
Fail to answer bail	Yes, but where there is a real likelihood of custody (para 2(1)(a))	Previously failed to answer bail in criminal proceedings and consequently court believes will fail to answer bail if bailed now, but only where real likelihood of custody (para 2)	Previously failed to answer bail in criminal proceedings and consequently court believes will fail to answer bail now (para 2)
Offend whilst on bail	Yes, but where real likelihood of custody (para 2(1)(b))	On bail at the date of the offence and consequently court believes would commit an offence on bail, but only if a real likelihood of custody (para 3)	NA
Interfere with witnesses or obstruct course of justice	Yes, but where real likelihood of custody (para 2(1)(c))	NA	NA
Substantial grounds for believing that if released on bail would commit an offence likely to cause physical or mental injury to an associated person, or cause an associated person to fear physical or mental injury	Yes (para 2ZA)	Yes (para 4)	NA

A8 Bail

Exception	Imprisonable—Pt I	Imprisonable—Pt IA triable only summarily	Non-imprisonable—Pt II
Arrested for breach of bail in same proceedings and substantial grounds to believe would fail to appear, commit offences, or interfere with witnesses or obstruct the course of justice	Yes, but must be a real likelihood of custody; if offence carries a life term the court may not grant bail unless satisfied there is no significant risk of failure to appear (para 6)	Yes, but must be real likelihood of custody (para 7)	Yes, including committing the offence by engaging in conduct likely to cause physical or mental injury to an associated person (paras 5 and 6)
Indictable or either-way offence and defendant on bail at the time of the offence	Yes, but note that if the offence carries a life term the court may not grant bail unless it is satisfied that there is no significant risk of an offence on bail. Must be a real likelihood of custody (para 2A)	NA	NA
Own protection or welfare	Yes (para 3)	Yes (para 5)	Yes (para 3)
Serving sentence	Yes (para. 4)	Yes (para 6)	Yes (para 4)
Insufficient information	Yes (para 5)	Yes (para 8)	NA
Reports	Yes (para 7)	NA	NA
Drugs scheme	Yes (para 6A)	Yes (para 9)	NA
Homicide or rape	No bail unless exceptional circumstances justified if charged or convicted of a CJPOA 1994, s 25 offence and previous convictions for a s 25 offence	NA	NA
Murder	Not in the magistrates' court	NA	NA

A8.1.1 *General exceptions*

That presumption does not apply in the following cases:

- in extradition proceedings where the person is alleged to have been convicted of the offence;
- following committal to the Crown Court for sentence or for breach of a Crown Court order;
- after conviction, unless the proceedings are adjourned for inquiries to be made or a report to be prepared for sentence;
- on appeal against conviction or sentence.

Where a defendant aged 18 or over has tested positive for heroin, cocaine, or crack cocaine, and is unwilling to undergo an assessment of his drug misuse and/or any proposed follow-up treatment, different rules apply. The defendant cannot be granted bail unless the court is satisfied that there is no significant risk of an offence being committed while on bail.

Bail may be granted only in exceptional circumstances where a defendant is charged with or convicted of an offence of:

- murder, or
- attempted murder, or
- manslaughter, or
- rape, or
- attempted rape,

and the defendant has been previously convicted in the United Kingdom of any such offence or of culpable homicide. (If the previous conviction was manslaughter or culpable homicide, the provision applies only if the defendant received a sentence of imprisonment/long-term detention.) Convictions in EU member states can be taken into account.

Bail need not be granted to a person on bail at the time of committing an indictable offence (Bail Act 1976, Sch 1, para 2A). Sections 14 and 15 of the Criminal Justice Act 2003 are partially in force and currently apply *only* to those charged with offences carrying life imprisonment. Offences carrying life imprisonment appear in **Appendix 3** to this book.

Criminal Justice Act 2003, s 14

14 Offences committed on bail

(1) For paragraph 2A of Part 1 of Schedule 1 to the 1976 Act (defendant need not be granted bail where he was on bail on date of offence) there is substituted—

'2A(1) If the defendant falls within this paragraph he may not be granted bail unless the court is satisfied that there is no significant risk of his committing an offence while on bail (whether subject to conditions or not).

- The defendant falls within this paragraph if—
    (a) he is aged 18 or over, and
    (b) it appears to the court that he was on bail in criminal proceedings on the date of the offence.'

(2) After paragraph 9 of that Part there is inserted—

'9AA(1) This paragraph applies if—
    (a) the defendant is a child or young person, and
    (b) it appears to the court that he was on bail in criminal proceedings on the date of the offence.

(2) In deciding for the purposes of paragraph 2(1) of this Part of this Schedule whether it is satisfied that there are substantial grounds for believing that the defendant, if released on bail (whether subject to conditions or not), would commit an offence while on bail, the court shall give particular weight to the fact that the defendant was on bail in criminal proceedings on the date of the offence.'

Criminal Justice Act 2003, s 15(1) and (2)

15 Absconding by persons released on bail

(1) For paragraph 6 of Part 1 of Schedule 1 to the 1976 Act (defendant need not be granted bail if having been released on bail he has been arrested in pursuance of section 7) there is substituted—

'6 (1) If the defendant falls within this paragraph, he may not be granted bail unless the court is satisfied that there is no significant risk that, if released on bail (whether subject to conditions or not), he would fail to surrender to custody.

(2) Subject to sub-paragraph (3) below, the defendant falls within this paragraph if—
    (a) he is aged 18 or over, and
    (b) it appears to the court that, having been released on bail in or in connection with the proceedings for the offence, he failed to surrender to custody.

(3) Where it appears to the court that the defendant had reasonable cause for his failure to surrender to custody, he does not fall within this paragraph unless it also appears to the court that he failed to surrender to custody at the appointed place as soon as reasonably practicable after the appointed time.

(4) For the purposes of sub-paragraph (3) above, a failure to give to the defendant a copy of the record of the decision to grant him bail shall not constitute a reasonable cause for his failure to surrender to custody.'

(2) After paragraph 9AA of that Part (inserted by section 14(2)) there is inserted—

'9AB (1) Subject to sub-paragraph (2) below, this paragraph applies if—
    (a) the defendant is a child or young person, and

> (b) it appears to the court that, having been released on bail in or
>   in connection with the proceedings for the offence, he failed to
>   surrender to custody
> (2) Where it appears to the court that the defendant had reasonable
>   cause for his failure to surrender to custody, this paragraph does not
>   apply unless it also appears to the court that he failed to surrender
>   to custody at the appointed place as soon as reasonably practicable
>   after the appointed time.
> (3) In deciding for the purposes of paragraph 2(1) of this Part of this
>   Schedule whether it is satisfied that there are substantial grounds
>   for believing that the defendant, if released on bail (whether subject
>   to conditions or not), would fail to surrender to custody, the court
>   shall give particular weight to—
>   (a) where the defendant did not have reasonable cause for his failure
>   to surrender to custody, the fact that he failed to surrender to
>   custody, or
>   (b) where he did have reasonable cause for his failure to surrender
>   to custody, the fact that he failed to surrender to custody at
>   the appointed place as soon as reasonably practicable after the
>   appointed time.
> (4) For the purposes of this paragraph, a failure to give to the defend-
>   ant a copy of the record of the decision to grant him bail shall not
>   constitute a reasonable cause for his failure to surrender to custody.'

A8.2 Right to apply for bail

An application for bail may be made at the first hearing of the case
before a magistrates' court, save in respect of a defendant facing a
charge of murder (or murder and any other charge(s)), in which
case the issue of bail must be resolved before a Crown Court judge
within 48 hours (excluding public holidays) beginning the day after
the defendant's appearance in the magistrates' court (Coroners and
Justice Act 2009, s 115). If bail is refused, an application may be
made at the subsequent hearing, and may be based on the same
grounds as the first. A refusal of bail on the grounds of insufficient
information should not be counted as a decision to refuse bail,
thereby exhausting one of the two attempts (*R v Calderdale Justices,
ex p Kennedy*, The Times, 18 February 1992). Similarly, a remand
in absence should be discounted (*R v Dover and East Kent Justices,
ex p Dean*, The Times, 22 August 1991).

Note, however, that if a fully argued application is not made by the
defendant at the first hearing, the effect is that one opportunity
to argue for bail is lost, meaning that if bail is refused at the subsequent hearing, the two opportunities for bail have been spent.
Similarly, if an argument is made at the first hearing but not at the
second hearing, there is no right to a second application for bail at
the third hearing. Advocates should always obtain certificates of

full argument in order to support any further Crown Court bail application (Bail Act 1976, s 5(6A)). This should appear on the bail form issued by the court.

Following two refusals to grant bail, further applications may be made if there are new arguments as to fact or law (Bail Act 1976, Sch 1, Pt IIA). This includes but is not limited to a change in circumstances, for example:

- change in the case alleged against the defendant (*R v Reading Crown Court, ex p Malik* [1981] QB 451 and *R v Slough Justices, ex p Duncan* [1981] QB 451);
- increased surety (*R v Isleworth Crown Court, ex p Commissioners of Customs and Excise*, The Times, 27 July 1990);
- passage of time (*Neumeister v Austria (No 1)* (1979–80) 1 EHRR 91).

In *R (B) v Brent Youth Court* [2010] EWHC 1893 (Admin), the court held that a change of address presented for residence purposes amounted to a change of circumstances. It was not necessary that any new factor be exceptional in nature. The correct test is whether there are any new considerations which were not before the court when the accused was last remanded in custody. Similarly, an argument that the prosecution case against the defendant was significantly weaker than at first presented would qualify as a new argument. The court ended by saying that:

> even if the Bench had been entitled to form the view that each and every argument as to fact or law was an argument which it had heard previously, it manifestly failed to go on to consider whether, notwithstanding that, it should nonetheless consider substantively a bail application, given the provisions of Section 44 [Children and Young Persons Act 1933], having regard to the welfare of a child or young person.

A8.3 Grounds for refusing bail

The seriousness of the offence (and the likely penalty) cannot of itself justify a refusal of bail on the inference that the person is likely to abscond (*Lettelier v France* (1992) 14 EHRR 83), although a judge is perfectly entitled to regard that as a significant factor (*R (Thompson) v Central Criminal Court* [2005] EWHC 2345 (Admin)). Before bail can be refused on the grounds of interfering with witnesses or obstructing justice, the prosecution must point to an identifiable risk and provide supporting evidence (*Clooth v Belgium* (1991) 14 EHRR 717). The court should not take the prosecution case at its highest, but rather follow the statute and consider the strength overall of the prosecution evidence (*R (E) v Wood Green Crown Court* [2013] EWHC 1869 (Admin)).

In deciding whether to refuse bail the relevant considerations include (Bail Act 1976, Sch 1, para 9):

- the nature and seriousness of the offence or default (and the probable method of dealing with the defendant for it);
- the character, antecedents, associations, and community ties of the defendant;
- the defendant's record as respects the fulfilment of his obligations under previous grants of bail in criminal proceedings:
  - except in the case of a defendant whose case is adjourned for inquiries or a report, the strength of the evidence of his having committed the offence or having defaulted;
- the court is satisfied that there are substantial grounds for believing that the defendant, if released on bail (whether subject to conditions or not), would commit an offence while on bail, it is a relevant consideration that there is a risk that the defendant may do so by engaging in conduct that would, or would be likely to, cause physical or mental injury to any person other than the defendant;
- any other considerations that appear to be relevant.

Section 6ZA Bail Act 1976 provides that:

> if the defendant is charged with murder, the defendant may not be granted bail unless the court is of the opinion that there is no significant risk of the defendant committing, while on bail, an offence that would, or would be likely to, cause physical or mental injury to any person other than the defendant.

A8.3.1 *Classifying the offence*

There are three categories of offences to consider:

- indictable imprisonable offences (Sch 1, Pt 1);
- summary-only imprisonable offences (which includes offences triable summarily only due to the value of the offence, eg criminal damage) (Sch 1, Pt 1A), although it is unclear whether the hybrid offence of low-value theft from a shop falls into this group because of the defendant's right to elect; and
- summary-only non-imprisonable offences (Sch 1, Pt II).

A8.4 Indictable imprisonable offences

Bail cannot be refused if there is no real prospect that the defendant will be sentenced to a custodial sentence in the proceedings.

A court may refuse bail on the grounds:

- that the defendant is already a serving prisoner (para 4 remand); or
- that there is insufficient information on which to base a decision (para 5 remand).

Refusal of bail can be for the defendant's own protection or, for a defendant under 18 years of age, his own welfare (para 3 remand).

Bail may be refused if there are substantial grounds for believing that, if released on bail, the defendant would:

- fail to surrender;
- commit further offences;
- commit an offence on bail by engaging in conduct that would or would be likely to cause physical or mental injury to an associated person, or that an associated person would fear physical or mental injury—under section 62 of the Family Law Act 1996, 'associated person' includes:
  - those who are or have been married to each other or in a civil partnership,
  - present or former cohabitants,
  - those who live or have lived in the same household other than as employees, tenants, or lodgers,
  - relatives,
  - those who are or have been engaged to marry or enter into a civil partnership,
  - those who have or have had intimate personal relationships of significant duration,
  - the parents of children and those with parental responsibility,
  - parties to the same family proceedings; or
- interfere with witnesses or otherwise obstruct the course of justice.

Bail may also be refused if the offender was:

- on bail at the time of the offence;
- arrested for breach of bail in the same proceedings and there are substantial grounds to believe he would fail to appear, commit offences, or interfere with witnesses or obstruct the course of justice.

A8.5 Summary-only imprisonable offences

Bail cannot be refused if there is no real prospect that the defendant will be sentenced to a custodial sentence in the proceedings.

Bail can be refused on one or more of the following grounds only:

- failure to surrender (if the defendant has previously failed to surrender);
- commission of further offences (if the instant offence was committed on bail);

- fear of commission of offences likely to cause an associated person to suffer or fear physical or mental injury;
- the defendant's own protection (for his own welfare if aged under 18);
- the defendant is serving custody;
- fear of failure to surrender, commission of offences, interference with witnesses, or obstruction of justice (if the defendant has been arrested for breach of bail in respect of the instant offence); and
- lack of sufficient information.

A8.6 Summary-only non-imprisonable offences (Sch 1, Pt II)

Bail can be denied only if there has been a previous failure to surrender in the proceedings and the court believes that if granted bail the defendant would fail to surrender again, or:

- for the defendant's own protection (for his own welfare if aged under 18);
- where the defendant is already in custody;
- where, following a breach of bail, or the defendant absconding, there are substantial grounds for believing that if released on bail the defendant would:
  - fail to surrender,
  - commit further offences, or
  - interfere with witnesses or otherwise obstruct the course of justice.

A8.7 Conditional bail

Conditional bail may be imposed if the court believes there to be a risk that:

- the defendant will fail to surrender; a surety should only be used for this reason (*R (Shea) v Winchester Crown Court* [2013] EWHC 1050 (Admin));
- the defendant will commit an offence while on bail;
- the defendant would interfere with witnesses or obstruct justice;
- the defendant would not cooperate with the making of pre-sentence or other reports; or
- the defendant would not attend appointments with his legal adviser.

A person granted bail on a charge of murder must be required to undergo a psychiatric examination (Bail Act 1976, s 3(6A)).

A8.8 Insufficient information

The accused need not be granted bail if the court is satisfied that, owing to lack of time since the commencement of the proceedings, it has not been practicable to obtain sufficient information for taking the bail decision. This may apply if the defence need to confirm an address, or immigration status, or the mental health of the defendant; or the police have enquiries outstanding which might make the allegation more serious. There is no restriction in the Bail Act which has the effect of limiting the number of times on which the provision can be used. Whilst it should not allow the police to delay their enquiries, it has the benefit of not counting as a bail application.

A8.9 Pre-release conditions

Bail Act 1976, ss 3 and 8

3 General provisions

(1) A person granted bail in criminal proceedings shall be under a duty to surrender to custody, and that duty is enforceable in accordance with section 6 of this Act.

...

(4) He may be required, before release on bail, to provide a surety or sureties to secure his surrender to custody.

...

8 Bail with sureties

(1) This section applies where a person is granted bail in criminal proceedings on condition that he provides one or more surety or sureties for the purpose of securing that he surrenders to custody.

(2) In considering the suitability for that purpose of a proposed surety, regard may be had (amongst other things) to—
   (a) the surety's financial resources;
   (b) his character and any previous convictions of his; and
   (c) his proximity (whether in point of kinship, place of residence or otherwise) to the person for whom he is to be surety.

(3) Where a court grants a person bail in criminal proceedings on such a condition but is unable to release him because no surety or no suitable surety is available, the court shall fix the amount in which the surety is to be bound and subsections (4) and (5) below, or in a case where the proposed surety resides in Scotland subsection (6) below, shall apply for the purpose of enabling the recognizance of the surety to be entered into subsequently.

(4) Where this subsection applies the recognizance of the surety may be entered into before such of the following persons or descriptions of persons as the court may by order specify or, if it makes no such order, before any of the following persons, that is to say—
   (a) where the decision is taken by a magistrates' court, before a justice of the peace, a justices' clerk or a police officer who either is of

the rank of inspector or above or is in charge of a police station or, if magistrates' courts rules so provide, by a person of such other description as is specified in the rules ...

(5) Where a surety seeks to enter into his recognizance before any person in accordance with subsection (4) above but that person declines to take his recognizance because he is not satisfied of the surety's suitability, the surety may apply to—

  (a) the court which fixed the amount of the recognizance in which the surety was to be bound, or

  (b) a magistrates' court

for that court to take his recognizance and that court shall, if satisfied of his suitability, take his recognizance.

(6) Where this subsection applies, the court, if satisfied of the suitability of the proposed surety, may direct that arrangements be made for the recognizance of the surety to be entered into in Scotland before any constable, within the meaning of the M1Police (Scotland) Act 1967, having charge at any police office or station in like manner as the recognizance would be entered into in England or Wales.

(7) Where, in pursuance of subsection (4) or (6) above, a recognizance is entered into otherwise than before the court that fixed the amount of the recognizance, the same consequences shall follow as if it had been entered into before that court. A surety may be taken by a police officer under these provisions unless the court otherwise orders.

Courts wish to see some evidence of a surety's means. A surety must understand the risks to them, including of imprisonment, if the defendant fails to appear and the recognizance cannot be found.

For the convenience of all parties sureties should normally be made continuous for each hearing at which the defendant is required to attend.

A surety may only be used to secure attendance and is not appropriate to prevent further offences (*R (Shea) v Winchester Crown Court* [2013] EWHC 1050(Admin)).

A8.9.1 *Security*

This may be money or items of value. The Money Laundering Regulations require that those handling the money (including a court) are satisfied as to its source. There is no limitation on what may be provided as the security, though jointly owned property may not be accepted. The courts are ill equipped to hold substantial securities and solicitors will often give undertakings, backed by irrevocable authorities from the owner of the security, to account to the court should the defendant fail to appear.

A8.10 Electronic monitoring

Section 3AB of the Bail Act 1976 deals with electronic monitoring for adults; and section 3AC is applicable to all defendants. The court must be satisfied that without electronic monitoring bail would not be granted.

A8.11 Prosecution appeals against the grant of bail

The Bail (Amendment) Act 1993 allows a prosecutor to appeal the grant of bail in any case where the offence is imprisonable. The prosecution must have objected to bail, and following the grant of bail, must orally in court state their intention to appeal the decision. A written notice must be served on both the court and the defendant within two hours of the oral notice having been given. A delay of five minutes in giving an oral indication to the court (and after the defendant had been taken from the courtroom) was deemed to comply with the Act in *R v Isleworth Crown Court, ex p Clarke* [1998] 1 Cr App R 257. In *R (Jeffrey) v Crown Court at Warwick* [2003] Crim LR 190, a written notice was served three minutes late due to no fault on the part of the prosecutor. A challenge to the validity of that service failed and the court suggested that section 1(7) of the Act should have read into it the following words:

> unless such failure was caused by circumstances outside the control of the prosecution and not due to any fault on its part.

Service of the written notice on a jailer who hands the notice to a defendant suffices, and solicitors who accept such notices do so on the implicit understanding that they will be immediately communicated to the defendant.

A8.12 Breach of bail conditions

Offences of failing to appear are dealt with at **C3**.

Bail Act 1976, s 7

(4) a person arrested in pursuance of subsection (3) above—

    (a) shall, except where he was arrested within 24 hours of the time appointed for him to surrender to custody, be brought as soon as practicable and in any event within 24 hours after his arrest before a justice of the peace; and

    (b) in the said excepted case shall be brought before the court at which he was to have surrendered to custody.

(5) A justice of the peace before whom a person is brought under subsection (4) above may, subject to subsection (6) below, if of the opinion that that person—

(a) is not likely to surrender to custody, or

(b) has broken or is likely to break any condition of his bail,

remand him in custody or commit him to custody, as the case may require, or alternatively, grant him bail subject to the same or to different conditions, but if not of that opinion shall grant him bail subject to the same conditions (if any) as were originally imposed.

Following an alleged breach of bail conditions, the defendant must be brought before a magistrates' court within 24 hours of arrest. This means that the hearing must commence at court within those 24 hours, and any delay must result in the defendant's automatic release from custody (*R v Governor of Glen Parva Young Offender Institution, ex p G (A Minor)* [1998] 2 Cr App R 349). A court can, however, bring a defendant into the dock and then adjourn the hearing until later in the court list (*R (Hussein) v Derby Magistrates' Court* [2001] 1 WLR 254). A magistrates' court has no power simply to commit an offender to the Crown Court in order for the breach to be decided (*R v Teeside Magistrates' Court, ex p Ellison* (2001) 165 JP 355).

Only one magistrate need deal with an alleged bail breach, and there is no requirement for formal evidence to be called by prosecution or defence. There is no defence of 'reasonable excuse' in relation to the breaking of bail conditions (*R (Vickers) v West London Magistrates' Court* [2004] Crim LR 63), although the reasons for breach would be relevant to the determination of whether or not to grant bail again.

In *R v Liverpool Justices, ex p Director of Public Prosecutions* (1992) 95 Cr App R 222, the court laid down the following guidance for a court to follow when considering bail breaches:

- strict rules of evidence did not apply and hearsay was admissible;
- the court must consider the type of evidence called and take account of the fact that there had been no cross-examination;
- the prosecution and defence can call witnesses if they so wish, and the other party has the right to cross-examine;
- the defendant has a right to give oral evidence.

In practice a statement will be read to the court. It follows as a result of the above that no issue in relation to hearsay arises (*R (Thomas) v Greenwich Magistrates' Court* [2009] EWHC 1180 (Admin)).

If the breach is not proved, the defendant must be released on the same conditions as existed previously. If the breach is proved, that does not mean an automatic remand into custody; *R (DPP) v*

Havering Magistrates' Court [2001] 1 WLR 805 confirms that it is simply a factor to be considered when the court decides whether or not it should re-bail the defendant.

A8.13 Criminal Procedure Rules applicable to the grant of bail

Part 14 of the Criminal Procedure Rules applies to bail.

A8.14 Provision of bail for youths

The rules relating to the provision of bail for youths are discussed in **B2**.

A8.15 Appeals in relation to bail

A8.15.1 *Appeal against conditional bail*

If a defendant is dissatisfied with the conditions of bail he may appeal to the Crown Court, provided that he has first applied to a magistrates' court to vary those conditions and has been unsuccessful. An appeal lies only in relation to the following conditions:

- residence (but not in relation to any bail hostel);
- surety or security;
- curfew;
- non-contact.

In other circumstances it may be necessary to apply for a judicial review.

A8.15.2 *Appeal against refusal of bail*

Following full argument in the magistrates' court (and a certificate of full argument having been issued; Rule 19 CPR requires that the document confirming the refusal of bail contain such a certificate), an appeal lies as of right to the Crown Court.

There is no longer any appeal route to the High Court, save in an exceptional case by way of judicial review.

 See *Blackstone's Criminal Practice 2017* **D7**

A9 **Binding Rulings**

Section 8A of the Magistrates' Courts Act 1980 deals with pre-trial rulings and section 8B allows a magistrates' court to make binding rulings.

Sections 8A and 8B of the Magistrates' Courts Act 1980 provide:

Magistrates' Courts Act 1980, ss 8A and 8B

8A Power to make rulings at pre-trial hearing

(1) For the purposes of this section a hearing is a pre-trial hearing if—
    (a) it relates to an information—
        (i) which is to be tried summarily, and
        (ii) to which the accused has pleaded not guilty, and
    (b) it takes place before the start of the trial.
(2) …
(3) At a pre-trial hearing, a magistrates' court may make a ruling as to any matter mentioned in subsection (4) if—
    (a) the condition in subsection (5) is met,
    (b) the court has given the parties an opportunity to be heard, and
    (c) it appears to the court that it is in the interests of justice to make the ruling.
(4) The matters are—
    (a) any question as to the admissibility of evidence;
    (b) any other question of law relating to the case.
(5) …
(6) A ruling may be made under this section—
    (a) on an application by a party to the case, or
    (b) of the court's own motion.
(7) For the purposes of this section and section 8B, references to the prosecutor are to any person acting as prosecutor, whether an individual or body.

8B Effect of rulings at pre-trial hearing

(1) Subject to subsections (3) and (6), a ruling under section 8A has binding effect from the time it is made until the case against the accused or, if there is more than one, against each of them, is disposed of.
(2) The case against an accused is disposed of if—
    (a) he is acquitted or convicted,
    (b) the prosecutor decides not to proceed with the case against him, or
    (c) the information is dismissed.
(3) A magistrates' court may discharge or vary (or further vary) a ruling under section 8A if—
    (a) the condition in section 8A(5) is met,
    (b) the court has given the parties an opportunity to be heard, and
    (c) it appears to the court that it is in the interests of justice to do so.

> (4) The court may act under subsection (3)—
>   (a) on an application by a party to the case, or
>   (b) of its own motion.
> (5) No application may be made under subsection (4)(a) unless there has been a material change of circumstances since the ruling was made or, if a previous application has been made, since the application (or last application) was made.
> (6) A ruling under section 8A is discharged in relation to an accused if—
>   (a) the magistrates' court commits or sends him to the Crown Court for trial for the offence charged in the information, or
>   (b) a count charging him with the offence is included in an indictment by virtue of section 40 of the Criminal Justice Act 1988.

Because of the binding nature of these rulings, it is not open to a later bench simply to reverse the ruling because it would have reached a different conclusion.

In *Brett v Director of Public Prosecutions* [2009] EWHC 440 (Admin), the court took a far less restrictive approach than that taken in previous cases in holding a judge to have erred in feeling that he was bound by a previous ruling under section 8A of the Magistrates' Courts Act 1980. However, a later court cannot simply annul a previous decision on the sole ground that it simply disagrees with it (*Crown Prosecution Service v Gloucester Justices and Loveridge* [2008] EWHC 1488 (Admin)). In *R (Jones) v South East Surrey Local Justice Area* [2010] EWHC 916 (Admin), the court, having previously disallowed a prosecution application to adjourn, later granted it due to the fact that the information presented on the renewed application was different and that it was in the interests of justice that the previous ruling be reversed.

Where the court acts of its own motion to vary a previous ruling, the grounds for discharge or variation are simply the interests of justice; and where an application is made by a party, there is an additional requirement for proof of material change of circumstances (*Crown Prosecution Service v Gloucester Justices and Alan Loveridge* [2008] EWHC 1488 (Admin)).

 See *Blackstone's Criminal Practice 2017* **D21**

A10 **Case Management**

A10.1 Overview

All parties are expected to manage cases proactively through the system. The most notable impact has been to limit the use of so-called ambush defences. However, a strong defendant, aware of the risks, is still able to put the Crown to proof.

For information on the completion of the case management form, see **Appendix 1**.

A10.2 Application of the rules to civil proceedings

The Criminal Procedure Rules have no application in relation to civil procedure in the magistrates' court, and the Civil Procedure Rules do not apply either.

Rule 3A of the Magistrates' Courts Rules 1981 provides the court with case management powers identical to those enjoyed in relation to criminal cases.

A10.3 Alternative charges

When the Crown prefers an aggravated offence and in the alternative the underlying offence, the latter should be adjourned *sine die* if the court convicts on the more serious matter. If the defendant offers a plea to the lesser offence it should be noted but not taken (*Henderson v CPS* [2016] EWHC 464 (Admin)).

A10.4 The overriding objective and case management

Criminal Procedure Rules 1 and 3 deal with the overriding objective and case management powers. Extracts from these rules are reproduced in **Appendix 2**.

A10.5 Prosecution witnesses

Once the Crown has served witness statements as initial details of the prosecution case, it must, if the defence so request, call or at least tender as witnesses all those whose statements have been served, unless the statement is to be read or the witness is not capable of belief (*R v Russell Jones* [1995] 3 All ER 239). If the prosecution choose not to call a particular witness, and the court is satisfied that the interests of justice require that the witness be called, and that it would be unfair to the defence not to do so, the court may in appropriate cases call the witness itself (*R v Haringey Justices ex p DPP* [1996] 1 All ER 828). These cases were not referred to in *Azzaz v DPP* 2015 EWHC 3016 when the case proceeded without the unwilling complainant, there being another witness to the events. Neither party made a hearsay application in relation to the statement of the missing witnesses nor sought to follow the procedure in *Haringey Justices*. The result of any cross-examination was speculative.

A10.6 **Alibi notices**

An alibi notice is required (in summary proceedings within 14 days of initial disclosure by the Crown) if the defendant believes that a witness may be able to assist his defence. Because it is based on belief, not actuality, it is not proper to wait until there is a signed proof from the witness in question. (In the matter of a wasted costs order against see *Joseph Hill & Company* [2013] EWCA Crim775.)

A10.7 **Defence case statements**

These are not obligatory in summary proceedings but if given should be served within 14 days of initial disclosure by the Crown. An application for further disclosure under section 8 of the Criminal Procedure and Investigations Act 1996 cannot be made unless a defence case statement has been served (see **A16**).

A10.8 **Defence witnesses—notification of intention to call**

Section 6C of the Criminal Procedure and Investigations Act 1996 imposes duties on a defendant intending to call defence witnesses at trial. Failure to comply is most likely to result in an adjournment and wasted costs, so solicitors should ensure that they have taken all reasonable steps to ensure that a defendant is made aware of his obligations to provide such information. Notice of the name, address, and date of birth, if available, should be given in summary proceedings within 14 days of initial disclosure. A form is prescribed at Criminal Procedure Rules forms 15.4. It is likely that the prosecution will supply such information to the police. There is a code of practice for arranging and conducting interviews of witnesses notified by the accused, and this governs police conduct.

A10.8.1 *Time limits*

The time for service begins with the day on which the prosecutor complies or purports to comply with Criminal Procedure and Investigations Act 1996, section 3 (initial duty of the prosecutor to disclose) and expires at the end of 14 days.

The rules for service are contained in the Criminal Procedure and Investigations Act 1996.

Criminal Procedure and Investigations Act 1996 (Defence Disclosure Time Limits) Regulations 2011, reg 3

3(2) The court may by order extend (or further extend) the relevant period by so many days as it specifies but may only make such an order

   (a) on an application by the accused; and

   (b) if it is satisfied that it would be unreasonable to require the accused to give a defence statement under section 5 or section 6, or give notice under section 6C, as the case may be, within the relevant period.

The application must—

   (a) be made within the relevant period;

   (b) specify the grounds on which it is made; and

   (c) state the number of days by which the accused wishes the relevant period to be extended.

There is no limit on the number of applications that may be made under paragraph (2)(a).

A10.9 Preparation for trial

Part 24.3 Criminal Procedure Rules requires that both prosecution and defence prepare their cases because, at the start of a trial,

(1) the prosecutor may summarize the prosecution case, concisely identifying the relevant law, outlining the facts, and indicating the matters likely to be in dispute;

(2) to help the members of the court to understand the case and resolve any issue in it, the court may invite the defendant concisely to identify what is in issue.

A10.10 Case law

The courts deprecate any attempts to take a tactical advantage.

In *Writtle v Director of Public Prosecutions* [2009] EWHC 236 (Admin), the court held:

the present regime of case management should in general ensure that the issues in the case are identified well before a hearing. There will, of course, be cases where something occurs in the course of a trial which may properly give rise to a new issue, but this was not such a case. The days when the defence can assume that they will be able successfully to ambush the prosecution are over.

The court adopted the earlier ruling in *Malcolm v Director of Public Prosecutions* [2007] EWHC 363 (Admin), in which Burnton J stated that it is the duty of the defence to make clear to the prosecution and the court at an early stage both the defence and the issues it raises:

In my judgment, [counsel's] submissions, which emphasised the obligation of the prosecution to prove its case in its entirety before closing its case, and certainly before the end of the final speech for the defence, had an anachronistic, and obsolete, ring. Criminal trials are no longer to be treated as a game, in which each move is final and any omission by the prosecution leads to its failure. It is the duty of the defence to make its defence and the issues it raises clear to the prosecution and to the court at an early stage. That duty is implicit in rule 3.3 of the Criminal Procedure Rules, which requires the parties actively to assist the exercise by the court of its case management powers, the exercise of which requires early identification of the real issues. Even in a relatively straightforward trial such as the present, in the magistrates' court (where there is not yet any requirement of a defence statement or a pre-trial review), it is the duty of the defence to make the real issues clear at the latest before the prosecution closes its case.

In *Director of Public Prosecutions v Bury Magistrates' Court* [2007] EWHC 3256 (Admin), the court deprecated the practice of the defence of failing to notify the court of prosecution failures when certifying a case ready for trial, in order to take a tactical advantage. Further, that defence breach of the rules may have an impact on the amount of any costs to be recovered (in this case wasted costs).

In *R (Lawson) v Stratford Magistrates' Court* [2007] EWHC 2490 (Admin), it was held that a court was correct to allow a prosecution adjournment in order to address issues raised for the first time by the defence during a closing speech. The issues related to signage and device calibration.

A10.11 Sanctions

Failure to abide by the Criminal Procedure Rules brings sanctions specified by statute (eg adverse inferences).

However, for a defendant prepared to take the consequences, there is no power under the Rules to make hearsay statements admissible other than by a proper application of the hearsay provisions of the Criminal Justice Act 2003. *T v R* [2012] EWCA Crim 2358 confirms that a failure to comply with procedural rules could not affect the law on the admissibility of evidence.

A failure by a defendant to serve a defence statement did not amount to a contempt of court on either the part of the advocate or defendant. (*R v Rochford* [2010] EWCA Crim 1928 and *Joseph Hill & Co* [2013] EWCA Crim 775.) In *SVS Solicitors* [2012] EWCA Crim 319, a wasted costs order was upheld in a case where the solicitors were said to be complicit in their client's disobedience of the Rules, failing to file a counter-notice to an application to admit hearsay evidence. The court stated (albeit *obiter*) that a solicitor instructed by a client to ignore the requirements of the Criminal Procedure Rules should withdraw from the case. It is wise to seek directions from the court in that eventuality.

 See *Blackstone's Criminal Practice 2017* **D4**

A11 **Civil Orders**

A full list of possible civil proceedings, and the relevant statutes, appears at **A20.1** (Criminal Legal Aid (General) Regulations 2013, reg 9).

A11.1 **Closure orders**

It should be noted that applications for closure orders will only be prescribed proceedings for the purposes of Regulation 9 of the Criminal Legal Aid (General) Regulations 2013 where a person has engaged in, or is likely to engage in, behaviour that constitutes a criminal offence on the premises. This will include where the closure order relates to criminal behaviour and a combination of other grounds; but not closure orders that relate to nuisance or disorderly behaviour only, unless they amount to a common law public nuisance.

Anti-social Behaviour Crime and Policing Act 2014, ss 76, 80, and 81

76 Power to issue closure notices

(1) A police officer of at least the rank of inspector, or the local authority, may issue a closure notice if satisfied on reasonable grounds—
  (a) that the use of particular premises has resulted, or (if the notice is not issued) is likely soon to result, in nuisance to members of the public, or
  (b) that there has been, or (if the notice is not issued) is likely soon to be, disorder near those premises associated with the use of those premises,
  and that the notice is necessary to prevent the nuisance or disorder from continuing, recurring or occurring.
  …

80 Power of court to make closure orders.

(1) Whenever a closure notice is issued an application must be made to a magistrates' court for a closure order (unless the notice has been cancelled under section 78).
(2) An application for a closure order must be made—
  (a) by a constable, if the closure notice was issued by a police officer;
  (b) by the authority that issued the closure notice, if the notice was issued by a local authority.
(3) The application must be heard by the magistrates' court not later than 48 hours after service of the closure notice.
(4) In calculating when the period of 48 hours ends, Christmas Day is to be disregarded.

---

(5) The court may make a closure order if it is satisfied—
  (a) that a person has engaged, or (if the order is not made) is likely to engage, in disorderly, offensive or criminal behaviour on the premises, or
  (b) that the use of the premises has resulted, or (if the order is not made) is likely to result, in serious nuisance to members of the public, or
  (c) that there has been, or (if the order is not made) is likely to be, disorder near those premises associated with the use of those premises,
  and that the order is necessary to prevent the behaviour, nuisance or disorder from continuing, recurring or occurring.
(6) A closure order is an order prohibiting access to the premises for a period specified in the order.
  The period may not exceed 3 months.
(7) A closure order may prohibit access—
  (a) by all persons, or by all persons except those specified, or by all persons except those of a specified description;
  (b) at all times, or at all times except those specified;
  (c) in all circumstances, or in all circumstances except those specified.
(8) A closure order—
  (a) may be made in respect of the whole or any part of the premises;
  (b) may include provision about access to a part of the building or structure of which the premises form part.
(9) The court must notify the relevant licensing authority if it makes a closure order in relation to premises in respect of which a premises licence is in force.

81 Temporary orders.

(1) This section applies where an application has been made to a magistrates' court under section 80 for a closure order.
(2) If the court does not make a closure order it may nevertheless order that the closure notice continues in force for a specified further period of not more than 48 hours, if satisfied—
  (a) that the use of particular premises has resulted, or (if the notice is not continued) is likely soon to result, in nuisance to members of the public, or
  (b) that there has been, or (if the notice is not continued) is likely soon to be, disorder near those premises associated with the use of those premises,
  and that the continuation of the notice is necessary to prevent the nuisance or disorder from continuing, recurring or occurring.
(3) The court may adjourn the hearing of the application for a period of not more than 14 days to enable—
  (a) the occupier of the premises,
  (b) the person with control of or responsibility for the premises, or
  (c) any other person with an interest in the premises,
  to show why a closure order should not be made.
(4) If the court adjourns the hearing under subsection (3) it may order that the closure notice continues …

A11.2 Domestic violence protection orders

Crime and Security Act 2010, ss 27 and 28

27 Application for a domestic violence protection order

(1) If a DVPN (Domestic Violence protection notice) has been issued, a constable must apply for a domestic violence protection order ('a DVPO').

(2) The application must be made by complaint to a magistrates' court.

(3) The application must be heard by the magistrates' court not later than 48 hours after the DVPN was served pursuant to section 25(2).

(4) In calculating when the period of 48 hours mentioned in subsection (3) ends, Christmas Day, Good Friday, any Sunday and any day which is a bank holiday in England and Wales under the Banking and Financial Dealings Act 1971 are to be disregarded.

(5) A notice of the hearing of the application must be given to (the respondent) P.

(6) The notice is deemed given if it has been left at the address given by P (when asked at the time of service of the DVPN).

(7) But if the notice has not been given because no address was given by P under section 25(3), the court may hear the application for the DVPO if the court is satisfied that the constable applying for the DVPO has made reasonable efforts to give P the notice.

(8) The magistrates' court may adjourn the hearing of the application.

(9) If the court adjourns the hearing, the DVPN continues in effect until the application has been determined.

(10) On the hearing of an application for a DVPO, section 97 of the Magistrates' Courts Act 1980 (summons to witness and warrant for his arrest) does not apply in relation to a person for whose protection the DVPO would be made, except where the person has given oral or written evidence at the hearing.

28 Conditions for and contents of a domestic violence protection order

(1) The court may make a DVPO if two conditions are met.

(2) The first condition is that the court is satisfied on the balance of probabilities that P has been violent towards, or has threatened violence towards, an associated person.

(3) The second condition is that the court thinks that making the DVPO is necessary to protect that person from violence or a threat of violence by P.

(4) Before making a DVPO, the court must, in particular, consider—

  (a) the welfare of any person under the age of 18 whose interests the court considers relevant to the making of the DVPO (whether or not that person is an associated person), and

  (b) any opinion of which the court is made aware—

    (i) of the person for whose protection the DVPO would be made, and

    (ii) in the case of provision included by virtue of subsection (8), of any other associated person who lives in the premises to which the provision would relate.

(5) But the court may make a DVPO in circumstances where the person for whose protection it is made does not consent to the making of the DVPO.

(6) A DVPO must contain provision to prohibit P from molesting the person for whose protection it is made.

(7) Provision required to be included by virtue of subsection (6) may be expressed so as to refer to molestation in general, to particular acts of molestation, or to both.

(8) If P lives in premises which are also lived in by a person for whose protection the DVPO is made, the DVPO may also contain provision—
   (a) to prohibit P from evicting or excluding from the premises the person for whose protection the DVPO is made,
   (b) to prohibit P from entering the premises,
   (c) to require P to leave the premises, or
   (d) to prohibit P from coming within such distance of the premises as may be specified in the DVPO.

(9) A DVPO must state that a constable may arrest P without warrant if the constable has reasonable grounds for believing that P is in breach of the DVPO.

(10) A DVPO may be in force for—
   (a) no fewer than 14 days beginning with the day on which it is made, and
   (b) no more than 28 days beginning with that day.

(11) A DVPO must state the period for which it is to be in force.

A11.2.1 Key points

1. These proceedings are civil in nature.

2. Whilst section 54 of the Magistrates' Courts Act 1980 allowed for adjournment of this power to exceed the time limits in the legislation, this should only be used when there would otherwise be a breach of a person's rights under the European Convention on Human Rights (*MPC v Hooper* [2005] EWHC 199 (Admin); *R (Turner) v Highbury Corner Magistrates' Court* [2005] EWHC 2568 (Admin)).

3. Procedural safeguards were recommended in *R (Cleary) v Highbury Corner Magistrates' Court* [2006] EWHC 1869 (Admin) on the service of evidence, the use of hearsay evidence, and disclosure:

   As to the service of evidence fairness requires that the police must normally serve written versions of the evidence they propose to adduce in sufficient time before the hearing to enable the defendant fairly to deal with it.

   As to hearsay evidence, this is in principle admissible under section 1 of the Civil Evidence Act 1995. But, by section 2(1), a party proposing to adduce hearsay evidence in civil proceedings has to give the other party notice of that fact and, on request, such particulars of or relating to the evidence as is reasonable and practicable in the circumstances for the purpose of enabling him to deal with any matters arising from it being hearsay. Syntactically, the 'reasonable and practicable' requirement applies to the notice as well as the particulars.

Section 3 provides that the rules may provide that another party to the proceedings may with the leave of the court call as a witness and cross-examine the maker of the hearsay statement. Thus to expect to adduce, as hearsay, evidence of a person who is not identified offends the spirit if not the letter of section 3, since a defendant cannot seek leave to call and cross-examine a witness whose identity is not revealed … an easy assumption that hearsay evidence is routine in these cases risks real injustice. The willingness of a civil court to admit hearsay evidence carries with it inherent dangers. It is much more difficult for a court to assess the truth of what they are being told if the original maker of the statement does not attend to be cross-examined. More attention should be paid by claimants to the need to state by convincing direct evidence why it is not reasonable and practicable to produce the original maker of the state-ment as a witness. Magistrates should have these matters well in mind. The use of the words 'if any' in section 4 of the 1995 Act shows that some hearsay evidence may be given no weight at all. Credible direct evidence of a defendant in an application for a closure order may well carry greater weight than uncross-examined hearsay from an anony-mous witness or several anonymous witnesses [as to hearsay generally in civil proceedings see **A11.4**].

The police should disclose documents which clearly and materially affect their case adversely or support the defendant's case.

4. These proceedings are 'prescribed' for the purposes of Regulation 9 of the Criminal Legal Aid (General) Regulations 2013 and so legal aid is available on forms CRM14 and 15.

5. Any breach of a domestic violence protection order is dealt with under section 63 of the Magistrates' Courts Act 1980 which provides for a penalty of up to £50 per day that the breach con-tinues to a maximum of £5,000, or for committal to custody for a maximum of two months.

A11.3 **Evidence**

A11.3.1 *Hearsay*

Civil behaviour orders such as closure orders and domestic vio-lence protection orders are now commonplace in criminal courts, and very often involve issues of hearsay. Hearsay evidence in these cases is not regulated by the Criminal Justice Act 2003 but, in so far as it relates to ancillary orders in criminal proceedings, by Part 31 of the Criminal Procedure Rules; and by the Civil Evidence Act 1995.

A11.3.2 *Procedure*

The procedure for a contested hearing is governed by section 55 Magistrates Courts Act 1980 and rule 14 Magistrates' Court Rules 1981.

By section 2(1) Civil Evidence Act 1995 a party which proposes to adduce hearsay evidence must give notice of that intention to the other party or parties. A failure does not affect the admissibility of the evidence but may be taken into account in considering the exercise of its powers with respect to the course of proceedings and costs and as a matter adversely affecting the weight to be given to the evidence.

The Magistrates' Court (Hearsay Evidence in Civil Proceedings) Rules 1999 provide time limits:

- 21 days before the hearing date: notice of the intention to give hearsay evidence;
- within seven days: counter-notice with reasons why there should be cross-examination and a party must also give notice of any intention to attack the credibility of a hearsay witness.

A11.3.3 *Challenging the weight to be attached to hearsay evidence*

Regard should be had to section 4 of the Civil Evidence Act 1995, which provides:

Civil Evidence Act 1995, s 4

4 Considerations relevant to weighing of hearsay evidence

(1) In estimating the weight (if any) to be given to hearsay evidence in civil proceedings the court shall have regard to any circumstances from which any inference can reasonably be drawn as to the reliability or otherwise of the evidence.

(2) Regard may be had, in particular, to the following—

    (a) whether it would have been reasonable and practicable for the party by whom the evidence was adduced to have produced the maker of the original statement as a witness;

    (b) whether the original statement was made contemporaneously with the occurrence or existence of the matters stated;

    (c) whether the evidence involves multiple hearsay;

    (d) whether any person involved had any motive to conceal or misrepresent matters;

    (e) whether the original statement was an edited account, or was made in collaboration with another or for a particular purpose;

    (f) whether the circumstances in which the evidence is adduced as hearsay are such as to suggest an attempt to prevent proper evaluation of its weight.

A11.3.4 *Credibility and previous inconsistent statements*

Sections 5(2) and 6 of the Civil Evidence Act 1995 provide:

Civil Evidence Act 1995, ss 5(2) and 6

5 Competence and credibility

(2) Where in civil proceedings hearsay evidence is adduced and the maker of the original statement, or of any statement relied upon to prove another statement, is not called as a witness—

    (a) evidence which if he had been so called would be admissible for the purpose of attacking or supporting his credibility as a witness is admissible for that purpose in the proceedings; and

    (b) evidence tending to prove that, whether before or after he made the statement, he made any other statement inconsistent with it is admissible for the purpose of showing that he had contradicted himself. Provided that evidence may not be given of any matter of which, if he had been called as a witness and had denied that matter in cross-examination, evidence could not have been adduced by the cross-examining party.

6 Previous statements of witness

(1) Subject as follows, the provisions of this Act as to hearsay evidence in civil proceedings apply equally (but with any necessary modifications) in relation to a previous statement made by a person called as a witness in the proceedings.

(2) A party who has called or intends to call a person as a witness in civil proceedings may not in those proceedings adduce evidence of a previous statement made by that person, except—

    (a) with the leave of the court, or

    (b) for the purpose of rebutting a suggestion that his evidence has been fabricated.

This shall not be construed as preventing a witness statement (that is, a written statement of oral evidence which a party to the proceedings intends to lead) from being adopted by a witness in giving evidence or treated as his evidence.

(3) Where in the case of civil proceedings section 3, 4 or 5 of the Criminal Procedure Act 1865 applies, which make provision as to—

    (a) how far a witness may be discredited by the party producing him,

    (b) the proof of contradictory statements made by a witness, and

    (c) cross-examination as to previous statements in writing,

this Act does not authorise the adducing of evidence of a previous inconsistent or contradictory statement otherwise than in accordance with those sections.

    This is without prejudice to any provision made by rules of court under section 3 above (power to call witness for cross-examination on hearsay statement).

---

(4) Nothing in this Act affects any of the rules of law as to the circumstances in which, where a person called as a witness in civil proceedings is cross-examined on a document used by him to refresh his memory, that document may be made evidence in the proceedings.

(5) Nothing in this section shall be construed as preventing a statement of any description referred to above from being admissible by virtue of section 1 as evidence of the matters stated.

A12.1 Time limits

A12.1.1 *Overview*

Generally speaking, summary proceedings must be started within six months of the criminality complained of.

Section 127 of the Magistrates' Courts Act 1980 provides:

Magistrates' Courts Act 1980, s 127

127 Limitation of time

(1) Except as otherwise expressly provided by any enactment and subject to subsection (2) below, a magistrates' court shall not try an information or hear a complaint unless the information was laid, or the complaint made, within 6 months from the time when the offence was committed, or the matter of complaint arose.

(2) Nothing in—
   (a) subsection (1) above; or
   (b) subject to subsection (4) below, any other enactment (however framed or worded) which, as regards any offence to which it applies, would but for this section impose a time-limit on the power of a magistrates' court to try an information summarily or impose a limitation on the time for taking summary proceedings,
   shall apply in relation to any indictable offence.

...

The following principles emerge from the case law:

- the date of the offence is excluded from the time calculation (*Radcliffe v Bartholomew* [1892] 1 QB 161);
- in relation to a continuing offence, it is the date of the last act that is relevant (*Director of Public Prosecutions v Baker* [2004] EWHC 2782 (Admin));
- month means calendar month;
- limitation ends at midnight on the last day;
- if there is doubt as to whether an information has been laid in time, it must be resolved in favour of the defendant (*Lloyd v Young* [1963] Crim LR 703).

The six-month time limit does not apply to allegations of criminal damage of whatever value as they are either-way offences that, under £5000 in value, may only be tried summarily (*DPP v Bird* 2015 EWHC 4077 (Admin)).

See **A5** for the rules relating to amendment of a charge to substitute an offence that would otherwise be time-barred.

A12.1.2 *Exceptions*

A large number of offences that can be tried only summarily are, in certain circumstances, exempt from the six-month time bar.

In relation to some offences, time runs only from when an offence is 'discovered' by the prosecutor, which means when there was a reasonable belief that an offence had been committed (*Tesco Stores Ltd v London Borough of Harrow* (2003) 167 JP 657, DC). Where the relevant statute provides for a certificate to be signed by a prosecutor as to when he first had knowledge of the relevant facts, and there is a defence challenge to such a certificate, the matter should be dealt with by an application to stay the case for abuse (*Lamont-Perkins v RSPCA* [2012] EWHC 1002 (Admin)). The matter was further considered in *Letherbarrow v Warwickshire County Council* [2015] EWHC 4820 (Admin). This held that, where the time ran from the date on which evidence that a prosecutor considers sufficient to justify proceeding comes to his knowledge, the date referred to is that on which a decision-maker considered the evidence and not the date on which any employee became aware of the case. That decision is not merely whether there is a *prima facie* case but effectively the application of both parts of a prosecutor's duty (both evidential and public interest tests) to review a case before authorizing a prosecution.

 See *Blackstone's Criminal Practice 2017* **D2**

...provisions in relation to costs are contained in the
Practice Direction (Costs in Criminal Proceedings) 2015 EWCA
Crim 1568 (as amended by 2016 EWCA Crim 98).

A13.1 Statutory basis for awarding defence costs (defence costs orders)

Section 16(1) of the Prosecution of Offences Act 1985 provides:

> **Prosecution of Offences Act 1985, s 16(1)**
>
> **16 Defence costs**
> (1) Where—
>   (a) an information laid before a justice of the peace for any area, charg-
>   ing any person with an offence, is not proceeded with;
>   (b) a magistrates' court dealing summarily with an offence dismisses
>   the information;
>   that court or, in a case falling within paragraph (a) above, a magistrates'
>   court for that area, may make an order in favour of the accused for
>   a payment to be made out of central funds in respect of his costs (a
>   'defendant's costs order').

Section 16(1) does not apply to proceedings in respect to breach
of community penalty as the information does not charge a person with an offence. Similarly, the provision has no application in
relation to civil proceedings (eg in relation to domestic violence
protection orders).

Costs should generally be awarded to a defendant who can satisfy
section 16(1). This includes:

- where the case is withdrawn so that a caution can be administered (*R (Stoddard) v Oxford Magistrates' Court* (2005) 169
  JP 683);
- where there is a stay for abuse of process (*R (RE Williams & Sons
  (Wholesale) Ltd) v Hereford Magistrates' Court* [2008] EWHC
  2585 (Admin));
- where a case is resolved by way of bind over (*Emohare v Thames
  Magistrates' Court* [2009] EWHC 689 (Admin)).

In *R (Spiteri) v Basildon Crown Court* [2009] EWHC 665 (Admin),
the applicant successfully appealed a refusal to make a defendant's
costs order on the grounds that he was acquitted on a 'technicality'.
It was held that a costs order could not be refused on the sole
ground that the applicant had brought the proceedings upon

himself, as more was required, such as the defendant's having misled the prosecution as to the strength of the case against him. A similar point arose in *Dowler v MerseyRail* [2009] EWHC 558 (Admin), where the court ruled that, when refusing costs, courts should give reasons for the refusal contemporaneously with the ruling. In *R (Rees) v Snaresbrook Crown Court* [2012] EWHC 3879 (Admin), the court left open the possibility of refusing a defence costs order where the defendant had committed perjury or succeeded by ambushing the Crown.

A court should not limit the amount of costs recoverable from central funds to those of the final hearing, at which a bind over was accepted, where the Crown would not have discontinued the proceedings (*Newcombe v CPS* [2013] EWHC 2160 (Admin)).

A13.1.1 *Orders against a party to pay costs thrown away*

Such orders may benefit defendants who suffer financial prejudice as a result of CPS actions or failures to act.

Section 19 of the Prosecution of Offences Act 1985 provides:

> **Prosecution of Offences Act 1985, s 19**
>
> **19 Provision for orders as to costs in other circumstances**
>
> (1) The Lord Chancellor may by regulations make provision empowering magistrates' courts ... in any case where the court is satisfied that one party to criminal proceedings has incurred costs as a result of an unnecessary or improper act or omission by, or on behalf of, another party to the proceedings, to make an order as to the payment of those costs.

The Regulations are the Costs in Criminal Cases (General) Regulations 1986:

> **Costs Practice Direction 4.1.1**
>
> **Costs against a party to the proceedings**
>
> A Magistrates' Court ... may order the payment of any costs incurred as a result of any unnecessary or improper act or omission by or on behalf of any party to the proceedings as distinct from his legal representative: section 19 of the Act and regulation 3 of the General Regulations. The court may find it helpful to adopt a three-stage approach (a) Has there been an unnecessary or improper, act or omission? (b) As a result have any costs been incurred by another party? (c) If the answers to (a) and (b) are 'yes', should the court exercise its discretion to order the party responsible to meet the whole or any part of the relevant costs, and if so what specific sum is involved?

In *DPP v Denning* (1991) 2QB 532 an act was defined as unnecessary or improper if events would have occurred if the party had conducted itself properly. In *R (Singh) v Ealing Magistrates' Court* [2014] EWHC 1443 (Admin) it was held that a mere mistake without repetition can be grounds for a costs order under section 19 if additional costs arise from someone on the prosecution side not conducting the case properly. It is not an answer to be unsure whether the CPS or police are responsible. The prosecution is indivisible. The section does, however, contain a discretion not a duty to make an order if there is a satisfactory explanation. In *R (DPP) v Sheffield Crown Court* [2014] EWHC 2014 (Admin), the court held that the word 'improper' should be interpreted as set out in *Ridehalgh v Horsefield* (see **A13.1.2** below), but that case was considering the differently worded section 19A, and the decision was doubted in *Evans and others v SFO* [2015] EWHC 263(QB). The judge held that cases on section 19A and the wasted cost jurisdiction could not be carried over to section 19.

In considering an application under section 19 Prosecution of Offences Act 1985 the principles to be applied in respect of an application under that section and Regulation 3 were set out in *Evans* and in *R v Cornish and Maidstone and Tunbridge Wells NHS Trust* [2016] EWHC 779 (QB). It should be noted that these cases were concerned with an application for the total costs of a failed prosecution. More common will be applications in relation to unnecessary hearings or extra work caused by the failure of a party to comply in a timely fashion with an order of the court. These orders should be more common in such situations. It is suggested that failure to comply with a court order amounts to impropriety, as a party, however busy, can always apply for further time. *Evans* set out the following principles:

i) When any court is considering a potential costs order against any party to criminal proceedings, it must clearly identify the statutory power(s) upon which it is proposing to act; and thus the relevant threshold and discretionary criteria that will be applicable.

ii) In respect of an application under section 19 of the 1985 Act, a threshold criterion is that there must be 'an unnecessary or improper act or omission' on the part of the paying party, i.e. an act or omission which would not have occurred if the party concerned had conducted his case properly or which could otherwise have been properly avoided.

iii) In assessing whether this test is met, the court must take a broad view as to whether, in all the circumstances, the acts of the relevant party were unnecessary or improper.

iv) Recourse to cases concerning wasted costs applications under section 19A or its civil equivalent, such as *Ridehalgh*, will not be helpful.

Similarly, in wasted costs applications under section 19A, recourse to cases under section 19 will not be helpful.

v) The section 19 procedure is essentially summary; and so a detailed investigation into (e.g.) the decision-making process of the prosecution will generally be inappropriate.

vi) Each case will be fact-dependent; but cases in which a section 19 application against a public prosecutor will be appropriate will be very rare, and generally restricted to those exceptional cases where the prosecution has acted in bad faith or made a clear and stark error as a result of which a defendant has incurred costs for which it is appropriate to compensate him. The court will be slow to find that such an error has occurred. Generally, a decision to prosecute or similar prosecutorial decision will only be an improper act by the prosecution for these purposes if, in all the circumstances, no reasonable prosecutor could have come to that decision (paragraph 148).

Cornish added that:

(a) Simply because a prosecution fails, even if the defendant is found to have no case to answer, [this] does not of itself overcome the threshold criteria of s. 19

(b) Improper conduct means an act or omission that would not have occurred if the party concerned had conducted his case properly

(c) The test is one of impropriety, not merely unreasonableness. The conduct of the prosecution must be starkly improper such that no great investigation into the facts or decision-making process is necessary to establish it …

A13.1.2 *Wasted costs*

Defence solicitors may not benefit from a wasted costs order if there is a representation order in place as they are not a party to the proceedings (*R (CPS) v Bolton Crown Court* (2013) Costs LR 220), though a privately paying defendant may do so if there is a liability to indemnify.

Such orders may, however, be made against defence solicitors in the prescribed circumstances.

Prosecution of Offences Act 1985, s 19A

Costs against legal representatives etc

(1) In any criminal proceedings—

...

(c) a magistrates' court,

may disallow, or (as the case may be) order the legal or other representative concerned to meet, the whole of any wasted costs or such part of them as may be determined in accordance with regulations.

...

---

(3) In this section—

'wasted costs' means any costs incurred by a party—

(a) as a result of any improper, unreasonable, or negligent act or omission on the part of any representative or any employee of a representative; or

(b) which, in the light of any such act or omission occurring after they were incurred, the court considers it is unreasonable to expect that party to pay.

The Practice Direction (Costs in Criminal Proceedings) 2013 EWCA Crim 1632 deals with wasted costs in paragraph 4.2:

Practice Direction (Costs in Criminal Proceedings) 2013 EWCA Crim 1632

Part 4.2.4

(iv) A three-stage test or approach is recommended when a wasted costs order is contemplated:

(a) Has there been an improper, unreasonable or negligent act or omission?

(b) As a result have any costs been incurred by a party?

(c) If the answers to (a) & (b) are 'yes', should the court exercise its discretion to disallow or order the representative to meet the whole or any part of the relevant costs, and if so what specific sum is involved?

...

(vi) The judge must specify the sum to be allowed or ordered. Alternatively the relevant available procedure should be substituted should it be impossible to fix the sum.

Part 4.2.5

(i) The primary object is not to punish but to compensate, albeit as the order is sought against a non party, it can from that perspective be regarded as penal.

...

(iv) Because of the penal element a mere mistake is not sufficient to justify an order, there must be a more serious error.

...

(vi) The normal civil standard of proof applies but if the allegation is one of serious misconduct or crime clear evidence will be required to meet that standard.

In *Ridehalgh v Horsefield* [1994] Ch 205 the court stated:

Improper, unreasonable or negligent: ... In our view the meaning of these expressions is not open to serious doubt.

'Improper' means what it has been understood to mean in this context for at least half a century. The adjective covers, but is not confined to, conduct which would ordinarily be held to justify disbarment, striking off, suspension from practice or other serious professional penalty. It covers any significant breach of a substantial duty imposed by a relevant code of professional conduct. But it is not in our judgment limited to that. Conduct which would be regarded as improper according to the consensus of professional (including judicial) opinion can be fairly stigmatised as such whether or not it violates the letter of a professional code.

'Unreasonable' also means what it has been understood to mean in this context for at least half a century … But conduct cannot be described as unreasonable simply because it leads in the event to an unsuccessful result or because other more cautious legal representatives would have acted differently. The acid test is whether the conduct permits of a reasonable explanation. If so, the course adopted may be regarded as optimistic and as reflecting on a practitioner's judgment, but it is not unreasonable.

…[W]e are clear that 'negligent' should be understood in an untechnical way to denote failure to act with the competence reasonably to be expected of ordinary members of the profession. In adopting an untechnical approach to the meaning of negligence in this context, we would however wish firmly to discountenance any suggestion that an applicant for a wasted costs order under this head need prove anything less than he would have to prove in an action for negligence: 'advice, acts or omissions in the course of their professional work which no member of the profession who was reasonably well-informed and competent would have given or done or omitted to do'; an error 'such as no reasonably well-informed and competent member of that profession could have made' … We were invited to give the three adjectives (improper, unreasonable and negligent) specific, self-contained meanings, so as to avoid overlap between the three. We do not read these very familiar expressions in that way. Conduct which is unreasonable may also be improper, and conduct which is negligent will very frequently be (if it is not by definition) unreasonable. We do not think any sharp differentiation between these expressions is useful or necessary or intended.

Under the provisions of section 19B of the Prosecution of Offences Act 1985, to make a wasted costs order against a third party the court must find serious misconduct as required by section 19B of the Prosecution of Offenders Act 1986. There must therefore be a history of failure to address an underlying issue (*R v Allied Language Solutions* (2013) (QB)).

A13.2 Costs in relation to civil complaints

Section 64 of the Magistrates' Courts Act 1980 provides:

Magistrates' Courts Act 1980, s 64

64 Power to award costs and enforcement of costs

(1) On the hearing of a complaint, a magistrates' court shall have power in its discretion to make such order as to costs—

   (a) on making the order for which the complaint is made, to be paid by the defendant to the complainant;

> (b) on dismissing the complaint, to be paid by the complainant to the defendant,
>
> as it thinks just and reasonable; but if the complaint is for an order for the periodical payment of money, or for the revocation, revival or variation of such an order, or for the enforcement of such an order, the court may, whatever adjudication it makes, order either party to pay the whole or any part of the other's costs.
>
> (2) The amount of any sum ordered to be paid under subsection (1) above shall be specified in the order, or order of dismissal, as the case may be.

The discretion here is narrower than under section 16 of the Prosecution of Offences Act 1985 (see **A13.1**), and can be invoked if the court makes an order or dismisses the complaint, or the proceedings are withdrawn (s 52 Courts Act 1971). Applicants may also rely upon *Baxendale-Walker v Law Society* [2007] 3 All ER 330 (and other similar cases) to avoid costs on the basis that they are public bodies acting in the wider public interest and should not be exposed to the risk of adverse costs orders:

- in relation to civil proceedings commenced under Part 2 of the Proceeds of Crime Act 2002 (*Perinpanathan v City of Westminster Magistrates' Court* [2010] EWCA Civ 40) in relation to cash seizure cases that have been successfully defended;
- in relation to proceedings under section 1 of the Crime and Disorder Act 1998 (ASBO application) (*Manchester City Council v Manchester Magistrates' Court* [2009] EWHC 1866 (Admin));
- in withdrawal cases—see *Chief Constable of Warwickshire v MT* 2015 EWHC 2303 (Admin).

A13.3 Costs in relation to witnesses

Costs in relation to character witnesses' attendance at court can be recovered only when the court has certified that the interests of justice required the witnesses' attendance (Costs in Criminal Cases (General) Regulations 1986 (SI 1986/1335), reg 15). Advocates should ensure that an application is made to the court either prior to or immediately after the witnesses' attendance.

 See *Blackstone's Criminal Practice 2017* **D33**

A14 **Court-Appointed Legal Representatives**

A14.1 Overview

In circumstances defined by section 34 of the Youth Justice and Criminal Evidence Act 1999 (complainants in proceedings for sexual offences); section 35 (child complainants and other child witnesses); and section 36 (more generally), a defendant is prohibited from cross-examining witnesses. In the event that the defendant has declined or is not eligible for legal funding, the court has power under section 38 to appoint a legal representative to carry out this function on behalf of the court.

A14.2 Key points

Fees for this work are authorised under section 19 of the Prosecution of Offences Act 1985 and are as agreed by the court or allowed following taxation at private client rates. Solicitors should not agree to fees that are less than those that would be allowed for in line with civil guideline costs rates.

In *Abbas v CPS* [2015] EWHC 579 (Admin), the court held that to allow for effective cross-examination there was a need for a pre-trial conference and also for presence at pre-trial applications such as over bad character or disclosure.

Criminal Procedure Rule 23 applies.

A14.3 Statutory provisions

> **Youth Justice and Criminal Evidence Act 1999, ss 34, 35, 36, and 38**
>
> **34 Complainants in proceedings for sexual offences**
> No person charged with a sexual offence may in any criminal proceedings cross-examine in person a witness who is the complainant, either—
>
> (a) in connection with that offence, or
> (b) in connection with any other offence (of whatever nature) with which that person is charged in the proceedings.
>
> **35 Child complainants and other child witnesses**
> (1) No person charged with an offence to which this section applies may in any criminal proceedings cross-examine in person a protected witness, either—
>   (a) in connection with that offence, or

    (b) in connection with any other offence (of whatever nature) with which that person is charged in the proceedings.
(2) For the purposes of subsection (1) a 'protected witness' is a witness who—
    (a) either is the complainant or is alleged to have been a witness to the commission of the offence to which this section applies, and
    (b) either is a child or falls to be cross-examined after giving evidence in chief (whether wholly or in part)—
        (i) by means of a video recording made (for the purposes of section 27) at a time when the witness was a child, or
        (ii) in any other way at any such time.
(3) The offences to which this section applies are—
    (a) any offence under—
        (iva) any of sections 33 to 36 Sexual Offences Act 1956,
        (v) the Protection of Children Act 1978;
        (vi) part 1 of the Sexual Offences Act 2003 or any relevant superseded enactment; or
        (vii) sections 1 and 2 of the Modern Slavery Act 2015;
    (b) kidnapping, false imprisonment or an offence under section 1 or 2 of the Child Abduction Act 1984;
    (c) any offence under section 1 of the Children and Young Persons Act 1933;
    (d) any offence (not within any of the preceding paragraphs) which involves an assault on, or injury or a threat of injury to, any person.
(4) In this section 'child' means—
    (a) where the offence falls within subsection (3)(a), a person under the age of 17; or
    (b) where the offence falls within subsection (3)(b), (c) or (d), a person under the age of 14.
(5) For the purposes of this section 'witness' includes a witness who is charged with an offence in the proceedings.

36 Direction prohibiting accused from cross-examining particular witness

(1) This section applies where, in a case where neither of sections 34 and 35 operates to prevent an accused in any criminal proceedings from cross-examining a witness in person—
    (a) the prosecutor makes an application for the court to give a direction under this section in relation to the witness, or
    (b) the court of its own motion raises the issue whether such a direction should be given.
(2) If it appears to the court—
    (a) that the quality of evidence given by the witness on cross-examination—
        (i) is likely to be diminished if the cross-examination (or further cross-examination) is conducted by the accused in person, and
        (ii) would be likely to be improved if a direction were given under this section, and
    (b) that it would not be contrary to the interests of justice to give such a direction,
the court may give a direction prohibiting the accused from cross-examining (or further cross-examining) the witness in person.

(3) In determining whether subsection (2)(a) applies in the case of a witness the court must have regard, in particular, to—

    (a) any views expressed by the witness as to whether or not the witness is content to be cross-examined by the accused in person;

    (b) the nature of the questions likely to be asked, having regard to the issues in the proceedings and the defence case advanced so far (if any);

    (c) any behaviour on the part of the accused at any stage of the proceedings, both generally and in relation to the witness;

    (d) any relationship (of whatever nature) between the witness and the accused;

    (e) whether any person (other than the accused) is or has at any time been charged in the proceedings with a sexual offence or an offence to which section 35 applies, and (if so) whether section 34 or 35 operates or would have operated to prevent that person from cross-examining the witness in person;

    (f) any direction under section 19 which the court has given, or proposes to give, in relation to the witness.

(4) For the purposes of this section—

    (a) 'witness', in relation to an accused, does not include any other person who is charged with an offence in the proceedings; and

    (b) any reference to the quality of a witness's evidence shall be construed in accordance with section 16(5) ....

38 Defence representation for purposes of cross-examination

(1) This section applies where an accused is prevented from cross-examining a witness in person by virtue of section 34, 35 or 36.

(2) Where it appears to the court that this section applies, it must—

    (a) invite the accused to arrange for a legal representative to act for him for the purpose of cross-examining the witness; and

    (b) require the accused to notify the court, by the end of such period as it may specify, whether a legal representative is to act for him for that purpose.

(3) If by the end of the period mentioned in subsection (2)(b) either—

    (a) the accused has notified the court that no legal representative is to act for him for the purpose of cross-examining the witness, or

    (b) no notification has been received by the court and it appears to the court that no legal representative is to so act,

the court must consider whether it is necessary in the interests of justice for the witness to be cross-examined by a legal representative appointed to represent the interests of the accused.

(4) If the court decides that it is necessary in the interests of justice for the witness to be so cross-examined, the court must appoint a qualified legal representative (chosen by the court) to cross-examine the witness in the interests of the accused.

(5) A person so appointed shall not be responsible to the accused.

 See *Blackstone's Criminal Practice 2017* **F7.2** and **F7.3**

A15 **Custody Time Limits**

A15.1 **Overview**

Category	Time limit
Cases sent to the Crown Court	An overall time limit of 182 days applies, which includes any time spent in custody at the magistrates' court.
Either-way offences	Maximum 56 days from first appearance to hearing evidence in a summary trial (unless case was originally destined for sending and court reverts to summary trial after 56 days have elapsed, in which case the limit is 70 days).
Summary-only offences	56 days to start of summary trial.
Youths	As above, save that indictable-only cases that are tried summarily in the youth court are subject to the same time limits as either-way cases (*R v Stratford Youth Court, ex p S (A Minor)* [1998] 1 WLR 1758).

A15.2 **Exceptions**

Defendants who abscond from prison, or who have been released on bail following expiry of a custody time limit, but are then remanded following a breach of bail, do not enjoy the protections offered by custody time limits.

If a person is granted bail and is later remanded into custody, the earlier period on remand will count towards the custody time limit.

Custody time limits start at the end of the first day of remand and expire at midnight on the last day. A time limit expiring on one of the following days will be treated as having expired on the next preceding day which is not one of those days: a Saturday, a Sunday, Christmas Day, Good Friday, or a bank holiday.

A15.3 **Extending custody time limits**

In general, the following considerations are relevant:

- the prosecution should give two days' notice of an intention to apply, but lack of notice is not fatal to the application and the court retains a discretion to extend the time limits (*R v Governor of Canterbury Prison, ex p Craig* [1991] 2 QB 195);
- there is no power to extend once a time limit has lapsed (*R v Sheffield Justices, ex p Turner* [1991] 2 WLR 987);

- the court must be satisfied, on a balance of probabilities, that the need for the extension is due to the illness or absence of the accused, a necessary witness, a judge or magistrate; or a postponement which is occasioned by the ordering of separate trials, or some other good and sufficient cause; and that the prosecution have acted with all due diligence and expedition;
- the following have been held not to amount to good and sufficient cause, certainly in cases that are routine (*R (McAuley) v Coventry Crown Court* [2012] EWHC 680 (Admin) and *R (Raeside) v Luton Crown Court* [2012] EWHC 1064 (Admin)): lack of court time, listing difficulties attributable to the nature of the case, lack of a suitably experienced judge (or lack of any judge at all). Absent exceptional circumstances, resource difficulties do not amount to a good and sufficient cause.

 See *Blackstone's Criminal Practice 2017* **D15.7–D15.38**

A16 **Disclosure**

A16.1 Overview

Disclosure comes in stages:

(1) Initial disclosure of the prosecution case.
(2) Common law disclosure.
(3) Disclosure in relation to unused material.
(4) Consideration also has to be given to third party disclosure.

A16.2 Initial details of the prosecution case

The term 'advance information' is no longer accurate as the Criminal Procedure Rules refer only to initial details of the prosecution case. Part 8 of the Criminal Procedure Rules requires that initial disclosure should be available no later than the start of the day of the first hearing.

Part 8 provides for disclosure of such information in relation to all cases in a magistrates' court. It can be seen from Rule 8 (see **A16.3**) that prosecutors enjoy a wide discretion as to what is served prior to plea. Criminal Practice Direction 2015 EWCA Crim 1253 directions 3A4 and 3A12 require that there is sufficient information to enable the defendant to make an informed decision on plea and for the court to decide whether the case is suitable for summary trial.

Frequent problems arise in relation to the service of video and other recorded evidence. If the Crown is not relying on the undisclosed video evidence then no issue in relation to initial disclosure arises. In any event, the prosecution are under a duty to serve only a summary of their case, not the case in its entirety. The defendant's remedy is to enter a not guilty plea and put the Crown to proof.

A16.3 Extent of disclosure

Part 8 of the Criminal Procedure Rules provides:

> ### Criminal Procedure Rules, Pt 8
>
> #### 8.1 When this Part applies
> This Part applies in a magistrates' court.
>
> #### 8.2
> (1) The prosecutor must serve initial details of the prosecution case on the court officer—
>   (a) as soon as practicable; and
>   (b) in any event, no later than the beginning of the day of the first hearing.

(2) Where a defendant requests those details, the prosecutor must serve them on the defendant—
  (a) as soon as practicable; and
  (b) in any event, no later than the beginning of the day of the first hearing.
(3) Where a defendant does not request those details, the prosecutor must make them available to the defendant at, or before, the beginning of the day of the first hearing.

8.3 Content of initial details
Initial details of the prosecution case must include—

(a) where, immediately before the first hearing in the magistrates' court, the defendant was in police custody for the offence charged—
  (i) a summary of the circumstances of the offence, and
  (ii) the defendant's criminal record, if any;
(b) where paragraph (a) does not apply—
  (i) a summary of the circumstances of the offence,
  (ii) any account given by the defendant in interview, whether contained in that summary or in another document,
  (iii) any written witness statement or exhibit that the prosecutor then has available and considers material to plea, or to the allocation of the case for trial, or to sentence,
  (iv) the defendant's criminal record, if any, and
  (v) any available statement of the effect of the offence on a victim, a victim's family or others.

 See *Blackstone's Criminal Practice 2017* **D5**

A16.4 Common law disclosure

There is a common law duty to disclose material which may assist the defence at bail hearings or in the early preparation of their case or in mitigation. Following the decision in *R v DPP, ex p Lee* [1999] 2 All ER 737, the prosecutor must always be alive to the need to make advance disclosure of material of which he is aware (either from his own consideration of the papers or because his attention has been drawn to it by the defence), and which he, as a responsible prosecutor, recognizes should be disclosed at an earlier stage. Examples include:

• previous convictions of a complainant or deceased if that information could reasonably be expected to assist the defence when applying for bail;
• material which will enable the defence to make preparations for trial which may be significantly less effective if disclosure is

delayed (eg names of eyewitnesses who the prosecution do not intend to use);
• the withdrawal of support for the prosecution by a witness.

This material must be revealed to the prosecutor for service on the defence with the initial details of the prosecution case.

A16.5 Disclosure of unused material

Prosecution disclosure of unused material following a not guilty plea is regulated under section 3(1)(a) of the Criminal Procedure and Investigations Act 1996 and by the Judicial Protocol on disclosure of unused material:

> ### Criminal Procedure and Investigations Act 1996, s 3(1)(a)
>
> **3 Initial duty of prosecutor to disclose**
> (1) The prosecutor must—
>   (a) disclose to the accused any prosecution material which has not previously been disclosed to the accused and which might reasonably be considered capable of undermining the case for the prosecution against the accused or of assisting the case for the accused ....

In the magistrates' court there is no duty to serve a defence case statement but in the absence of one, a prosecutor may not be able adequately or at all to discover which information might be disclosable. Particular problems arise with CCTV. Courts are unlikely to adjourn for CCTV where its content is purely speculative. If an early request was made, forensic advantage could be taken of its absence (*DPP v Petrie* [2015] EWHC 48 (Admin)). However it is otherwise when the CCTV has been referred to in interview by the police, or has been viewed by the police who decided not to retain it because it did not assist their case, without performing their duty to consider whether it might assist the defendant's case. The court considered that the trial in the latter situation would not be fair (*Birmingham* [1992] Crim LR 117)).

A failure to disclose in accordance with the statutory scheme may lead to an adjournment (see **A2.2**). In the alternative, courts may exclude all or any prosecution evidence under section 78 of the Police and Criminal Evidence Act 1984 where there has been a failure in accordance with statutory time limits to provide initial or further disclosure, and this makes the trial unfair (*R (Ibrahim) v Feltham MC* [2001] EWHC 130 (Admin) and *R v Boardman* [2015] EWCA Crim 175). The need for a defence case statement cannot arise until initial disclosure had been served by the Crown.

A16.6 Section 8 disclosure applications

A party aggrieved in relation to prosecution disclosure can apply to
the court under section 8 of the 1996 Act, but *must* serve a defence
case statement in order to do so.

Criminal Procedure and Investigations Act 1996, s 8

8 Application by accused for disclosure

(1) This section applies where the accused has given a defence statement
under section 5, 6 or 6B and the prosecutor has complied with section
7A(5) or purported to comply with it or has failed to comply with it.

(2) If the accused has at any time reasonable cause to believe that there is
prosecution material which is required by section 7A to be disclosed to
him and has not been, he may apply to the court for an order requiring
the prosecutor to disclose it to him.

(3) For the purposes of this section prosecution material is material—

    (a) which is in the prosecutor's possession and came into his possession
in connection with the case for the prosecution against the accused,

    (b) which, in pursuance of a code operative under Part II, he has inspected
in connection with the case for the prosecution against the accused, or

    (c) which falls within subsection (4).

(4) Material falls within this subsection if in pursuance of a code operative
under Part II the prosecutor must, if he asks for the material, be given a
copy of it or be allowed to inspect it in connection with the case for the
prosecution against the accused.

(5) Material must not be disclosed under this section to the extent that the
court, on an application by the prosecutor, concludes it is not in the
public interest to disclose it and orders accordingly.

(6) Material must not be disclosed under this section to the extent that
it is material the disclosure of which is prohibited by section 17 of the
Regulation of Investigatory Powers Act 2000.

A16.7 Third party disclosure

A16.7.1 *CPIA Code of Practice*

3.5 In conducting an investigation, the investigator should pursue all reasonable lines of inquiry, whether these point towards or away from the
suspect. What is reasonable in each case will depend on the particular
circumstances …

3.6 If the officer in charge of an investigation believes that other persons may
be in possession of material that may be relevant to the investigation, and
if this has not been obtained under paragraph 3.5 above, he should ask
the disclosure officer to inform them of the existence of the investigation
and to invite them to retain the material in case they receive a request
for its disclosure. The disclosure officer should inform the prosecutor
that they may have such material. However, the officer in charge of an

investigation is not required to make speculative enquiries of other persons; there must be some reason to believe that they may have relevant material. That reason may come from information provided to the police by the accused or from other inquiries made or from some other source.

...

4.3 Negative information is often relevant to an investigation. If it may be relevant it must be recorded. An example might be a number of people present in a particular place at a particular time who state that they saw nothing unusual.

A16.7.2 *Case law*

In *R v Alibhai* [2004] EWCA Crim 681, the Court of Appeal held that under the CPIA 1996 the prosecutor is only under a duty to disclose a third party's material if that material had come into the prosecutor's possession and the prosecutor was of the opinion that such material satisfied the disclosure test. Before taking steps to obtain third party material, the Court emphasized that it must be shown that there was a suspicion that the third party not only had relevant material and that the material was not merely neutral or damaging to the accused, but it also satisfied the disclosure test.

Furthermore, *R v Alibhai* states that even if there is the necessary suspicion, the prosecutor has a 'margin of consideration' as to what steps to take in any particular case and was not thus under an absolute obligation to obtain material that was suspected to satisfy the disclosure test.

There may be cases where the investigator, disclosure officer, or prosecutor believes that a third party (eg a local authority, a social services department, a hospital, a doctor, a school, a provider of forensic services) has material or information which might be relevant to the prosecution case. In such cases, investigators, disclosure officers, and prosecutors should take reasonable steps to identify, secure, and consider material held by any third party where it appears to the investigator, disclosure officer, or prosecutor that (a) such material exists, and (b) it may be relevant to an issue in the case.

A16.7.3 *Judicial protocol*

The judicial protocol places responsibilities on the Crown:

44. Where material is held by a third party such as a local authority, a social services department, hospital or business, the investigators and the prosecution may need to make enquiries of the third party, with a view to inspecting the material and assessing whether the relevant test for disclosure is met and determining whether any or all of the material should be retained, recorded and, in due course, disclosed to the accused. If access by the prosecution is granted, the investigators and the prosecution will need to establish whether the custodian of the material intends to raise PII issues, as a result of which the material may have to be placed before the court for a decision. This does not obviate the need for the defence to conduct its own enquiries as appropriate. Speculative enquiries without any proper basis in relation to third party material—whether by the prosecution or the defence—are to be discouraged, and, in appropriate cases, the court will consider making an order for costs where an application is clearly unmeritorious and misconceived.

A16.7.4 *Statutory procedure to obtain third party material*

If material evidence is in the hands of a third party a summons may be issued under section 97 Magistrates Courts Act 1980 (see **A32**). The statutory requirements in section 97 are more stringent than the disclosure test. Items sought under the summons procedure must be 'likely to be material evidence' (which the House of Lords in *R v Derby Magistrates' Court ex parte B* [1995] 4 All ER 526 has construed to mean 'immediately admissible per se').

A16.8 The judicial protocol on disclosure 2013

The section on magistrates' courts confirms:

Judicial Protocol on the Disclosure of Unused Material in Criminal Cases, paras 30–37

30. The principles relating to disclosure apply equally in the magistrates' courts. It follows that whilst disclosure of unused material in compliance with the statutory test is undoubtedly essential in order to achieve justice, it is critical that summary trials are not delayed or made overcomplicated by misconceived applications for, or inappropriate disclosure of, prosecution material.

31. Magistrates will rely on their legal advisers for guidance, and the latter should draw the attention of the parties and the court to the statutory provisions and the applicable case law. Cases raising disclosure issues of particular complexity should be referred to a District Judge (Magistrates' Courts), if available.

32. Although service of a defence statement is voluntary for summary trials (section 6 CPIA), the defendant cannot make an application for specific disclosure under section 8 CPIA, and the court cannot make any orders in this regard, unless a proper defence statement has been provided. It follows that although providing a defence statement is not mandatory, it remains a critical stage in the disclosure process. If disclosure issues are to be raised by the defence, a defence statement must be served well in advance of the trial date. Any section 8 application must be made in strict compliance with the Rules.

33. The case-management forms used in the magistrates' courts fulfil some of the functions of a defence statement, and the prosecution must take into account the information provided as to the defence case when conducting its ongoing review of unused material. As the Court of Appeal noted in *R v Newell* (*supra*), admissions can be made in the Trial Preparation Form and the defence is able to identify the matters that are not in issue. Admissions made in these circumstances may be admissible during the trial. However, other information on the form that does not come within the section relating to admissions should be treated in the same way as the contents of a PCMH form in the Crown Court and it should not generally be introduced as part of the evidence at trial. However, the contents of the Trial Preparation Form do not replace the need to serve a defence statement if the defendant seeks to apply for disclosure under section 8 CPIA.

34. The standard directions require that any defence statement is to be served within 14 days of the date upon which the prosecution has complied with, or purported to comply with, the duty to provide initial disclosure. There may be some instances when there will be a well-founded defence application to extend the 14-day time limit for serving the defence statement. These applications must be made in accordance with the Criminal Procedure Rules, in writing and before the time limit expires.

35. Although CCTV footage frequently causes difficulties, it is to be treated as any other category of unused material and it should only be disclosed if the material meets the appropriate test for disclosure under the CPIA. The defence should either be provided with copies of the sections of the CCTV or afforded an opportunity to view them. If the prosecution refuses to disclose CCTV material that the defence considers to be discloseable, the courts should not make standard or general directions requiring the prosecutor to disclose material of this kind in the absence of an application under section 8. When potentially relevant CCTV footage is not in the possession of the police, the guidance in relation to third party material will apply, although the police remain under a duty to pursue all reasonable lines of inquiry, including those leading away from a suspect, whether or not defence requests are made.

36. The previous convictions of witnesses and any disciplinary findings against officers in the case are frequently discloseable and care should be taken to disclose them as appropriate. Documents such as crime reports or records of emergency calls should not be provided on a routine basis, for instance as part of a bundle of disclosed documents, irrespective of whether the material satisfies the appropriate test for disclosure. Defence advocates should not request this material in standard or routine correspondence, and instead focussed consideration should be given to the circumstances of the particular case. Unjustified requests for disclosure of material of this kind are routinely made, frequently leading to unnecessary delays and adjournments. The prosecution should always consider whether the request is properly made out.

37. The supervisory role of the courts is critical in this context, and magistrates must guard against granting unnecessary adjournments and issuing unjustified directions.

 See *Blackstone's Criminal Practice 2017* **D9**

A17 **Extradition**

A17.1 **Jurisdiction**

The Extradition Act 2003 sets out the procedures to be adopted during the extradition process. The power to extradite rests with the Senior Magistrate and authorised District Judges, and cases are generally heard only at City of Westminster Magistrates' Court. This section details the most important initial checks that a solicitor or barrister should make when seized of the case for the first time. Unless absolutely satisfied that extradition can proceed properly unopposed under Part 1 of the Act, recourse should be had to the detailed practitioner works and to specialist practitioners, as well as fast-developing case law.

Countries issuing extradition requests are divided into category 1 (Part 1 Extraditions) and category 2 countries (Part 2 Extraditions). Category 1 states utilize the European Arrest Warrant (EAW) procedure, and extradition will generally be ordered save in the most exceptional defined circumstances. More robust evidential protections are in place in relation to most category 2 states. The United Kingdom also has special arrangements in place with certain states, for example the United States of America.

A17.2 **The arrest warrant**

A17.2.1 *Part 1 Extradition*

The following states have been designated under Part 1 of the Extradition Act 2003: Austria, Belgium, Bulgaria, Croatia, Cyprus, Czech Republic, Denmark, Estonia, Finland, France, Germany, Gibraltar, Greece, Hungary, Ireland, Italy, Latvia, Lithuania, Luxembourg, Malta, the Netherlands, Poland, Portugal, Romania, Slovakia, Slovenia, Spain, and Sweden.

Following the issuing of an arrest warrant, the police will execute that warrant and bring the individual before the court.

The arrest warrant should be in the standard format and detail the statutory particulars as required under section 2 of the Act.

A17.2.2 *Part 2 Extradition*

A request for an arrest warrant is made to the Secretary of State, who must issue to the court a certificate, unless certain exceptions apply, if a valid extradition request is received (s 70). This will result in the wanted person being brought before the court pursuant to an arrest warrant being issued by the court (s 71).

A17.3 **Funding**

Extradition work is funded under the Standard Crime Contract, as provided by section 14(c) Legal Aid Sentencing and Punishment of Offenders Act 2012. An application for representation should be made in the usual way. Extradition proceedings are the only proceedings in the magistrates' court that allow for representation by Queen's Counsel. It is rare for legal aid to be refused on merits, but means inquiries can cause considerable difficulty and delay. Extradition should not proceed in the absence of a representation order if the requested person and his representatives have been guilty of no fault (*Stopya v District Court of Lublin Poland* [2012] EWHC 1787 (Admin)).

A17.4 **Timing of appearance and time limits**

In the case of a provisional arrest under Part 1 of the Act, where a constable has reasonable grounds to believe that a warrant is being or will be issued, the first appearance must be within 48 hours of arrest (weekends and holidays excepted). In all other cases the appearance must be as soon as is practicable. A failure to comply should lead to the person's discharge.

In Part 1 cases where there has been a provisional arrest, section 4(2) requires service of the warrant, failure of which may result in a discharge at the discretion of the District Judge.

The initial hearing may be adjourned to a later date.

If consent to extradition is not given, the judge will set the appropriate timetable, the limits of which may be extended by the District Judge:

- under Part 1—21 days from arrest, or a later date if it is in the interests of justice or there are domestic proceedings (Extradition Act 2003, s 8);
- under Part 2—not later than two months from first appearance, or a later date if it is in the interests of justice (Extradition Act 2003, s 75).

A17.5 **Statutory bars to extradition**

The statutory bars to extradition are:

- age (s 15)—the fugitive must not be less than 10 years old at the date of the crime;
- double jeopardy (ss 12 and 80) (so that a defendant is not prosecuted twice for the same offence in different jurisdictions, etc);
- no decision has been made in Part 1 countries whether to charge or to try the requested person (s 12A) where the person's absence

from the country is not the sole reason for that failure: see *Kandola v Germany* [2015] EWHC 619 (Admin);

- earlier extradition (Pt 1, ss 18 and 19) (prohibition of defendant's extradition where he has already been extradited to the United Kingdom from a category 1 or non-category 1 territory, and certain other circumstances apply);

- extraneous considerations (ss 13 and 81) (eg disguised extradition request and the defendant is in reality wanted on account of his political opinions, race, religion, nationality, gender, or sexual orientation, etc; or if the defendant would be prejudiced at his trial, or punished or detained because of such extraneous considerations);

- passage of time (ss 14 and 82) (if it appears that it would be 'unjust or oppressive' to extradite by reason of passage of time since the defendant allegedly committed the extradition offence or became unlawfully at large, in accordance with the meaning of that phrase in *Kakis v Cyprus* [1978] 1 WLR 779, 782, and subsequent case law). 'Unjust' may include risk of prejudice to the accused in the conduct of the trial itself, for example if defence witnesses or other evidence would have disappeared due to lapse of time. 'Oppressive' includes hardship to the accused resulting from change in circumstances that has occurred during the period to be taken into consideration (eg if the client has set up a family in the United Kingdom and would suffer serious hardship). It should be noted that this ground cannot be used if it can be shown the defendant is a fugitive (ie he knew about the case and fled the country);

- speciality (ss 17 and 95) (the burden is on the defendant to show that there are not adequate speciality arrangements in place, etc—a speciality arrangement is a legal protection that guarantees that the requested person may be prosecuted only for conduct that appears in the extradition warrant);

- asylum claim pending (ss 39, 40, and 121);

- competing claims for extradition (ss 24 and 90);

- convictions in absence (ss 20 and 86) (if the defendant was convicted *in absentia*, did not deliberately absent himself from trial, and if he would not be entitled to a retrial, etc);

- domestic UK criminal proceedings taking precedence even if this is discovered after an order is made (ss 22 and 88);

- person serving prison sentence(s) in the United Kingdom (ss 23 and 89);

- physical or mental health (ss 25 and 91) (if such that it would be unjust or oppressive to extradite the defendant, in accordance with the meaning in the case law). If physical illness is raised as an objection, that is, it would be unjust or oppressive to extradite, it would have to be very serious. If so, and if a treatment plan is in place in the United Kingdom, this may justify an adjournment to explore it by further inquiry. With mental health issues and a potential risk of suicide, a real and substantial risk of suicide must be shown, but the court looks at the measures in place to prevent suicide while the requested person is in the United Kingdom, while being transferred to the requesting state, and when received by the requesting state. It is only in a very rare case that a requested person would be likely to establish that measures to prevent a substantial risk of suicide would not be effective (see *Wolkowicz v Poland* [2013] EWHC 102 (Admin));

- human rights considerations (ss 21 and 87) (if ordering extradition would be incompatible with the defendant's Convention rights within the meaning of the Human Rights Act 1998—most commonly raised are Arts 2, 3, 5, 6, and 8);
- forum issues (accusation cases only: ss 19B and 83A) (the extradition is barred if it is not in the interests of justice because a substantial measure of the defendant's relevant activity was performed in the United Kingdom and the court decides, having regard to the specified matters (and only those), that the extradition should not take place). The specified matters are set out and include the belief of a prosecutor that the United Kingdom is not the most appropriate jurisdiction. If a prosecutor has considered the offences, the judge must make the prosecutor a party to the proceedings. The bar ceases to apply if the judge receives a prosecutor's certificate as prescribed by the Act;
- proportionality in Part 1 accusation cases (s 21A): in addition to considering the bars and human rights issues, the court must consider whether extradition is disproportionate. However, this is tightly defined by reference to the seriousness of the conduct; the likely penalty; and the possibility of less coercive measures being used. The issue was considered in *Mirasjewski v Poland* 2014 EWHC 4261 (Admin) and guidance is given in Criminal Practice Direction 50.

Criminal Practice Directions 2015, Pt 50 Extradition

50A.3 In any case where the conduct alleged to constitute the offence falls into one of the categories in the table at paragraph 50A.5 below, unless there are exceptional circumstances, the judge should generally determine that extradition would be disproportionate. It would follow under the terms of s. 21A (4) (b) of the Act that the judge must order the person's discharge.

50A.4 The exceptional circumstances referred to above in paragraph 50A.3 will include:
   i.   Vulnerable victim

    ii. Crime committed against someone because of their disability, gender identity, race, religion or belief, or sexual orientation
    iii. Significant premeditation
    iv. Multiple counts
    v. Extradition also sought for another offence
    vi. Previous offending history.

50A.5 The table is as follows:

Category of offence	Examples
Minor **theft**—(not robbery/burglary or theft from the person)	Where the theft is of a low monetary value and there is a low impact on the victim or indirect harm to others, for example: (a) Theft of an item of food from a supermarket (b) Theft of a small amount of scrap metal from company premises (c) Theft of a very small sum of money
Minor financial offences (**forgery, fraud** and **tax** offences)	Where the sums involved are small and there is a low impact on the victim and/or low indirect harm to others, for example: (a) Failure to file a tax return or invoices on time (b) Making a false statement in a tax 117 return (c) Dishonestly applying for a tax refund (d) Obtaining a bank loan using a forged or falsified document (e) Non-payment of child maintenance
Minor **road traffic, driving** and related offences	Where no injury, loss or damage was incurred to any person or property, for example: (a) Driving whilst using a mobile phone (b) Use of a bicycle whilst intoxicated
Minor **public order** offences	Where there is no suggestion the person started the trouble, and the offending behaviour was for example: (a) Non-threatening verbal abuse of a law enforcement officer or government official (b) Shouting or causing a disturbance, without threats (c) Quarrelling in the street, without threats
Minor **criminal damage,** (other than by fire)	For example, breaking a window
Possession of controlled substance (other than one with a high capacity for harm such as heroin, cocaine, LSD or crystal meth)	Where it was possession of a very small quantity and intended for personal use

A17.5.1 *Temporary transfer (s 21B)*

Temporary transfer requires the consent of both parties, will lead to the withdrawal of the relevant EAW, and will allow discussions to take place between the parties before the transfer takes place. The court is entitled to receive clear and particularized details of the person to whom the fugitive will speak in the requesting state and the purpose of that conversation. The timing of the request is a relevant consideration in deciding whether an adjournment should be allowed (*Duncan v Presiding Magistrate Malaga* [2015] EWHC 3446 (Admin)).

A17.6 **Human rights**

A17.6.1 *Articles 2 and 3 ECHR*

Right to life (Art 2) and prohibition of inhuman or degrading treatment or punishment (Art 3):

- may be argued if it can be shown that there are 'substantial grounds for believing there is a real risk of breach'—this is a high test, but can be explored if the client instructs that his life is in danger in the requesting state;
- if it is alleged that there is a risk of breach due to the actions of non-state agents, such as a gang of organized criminals, it must be shown that there is inadequate protection available from the requesting state. The court presumes that an EU member state will be able to comply with its obligations as a member state.

A17.6.2 *Articles 5 and 6 ECHR*

These relate to 'flagrant denial of justice in requesting state' (Art 5) and 'real risk that defendant will suffer a flagrant denial of a fair trial' (Art 6).

There is a presumption that an EU member state will honour its treaty obligations, and these rights are guaranteed.

A17.6.3 *Article 8 ECHR*

This sets out the right to respect for private and family life. See *R (on the application of HH) v Westminster City Magistrates' Court* [2012] UKSC 25. In deciding whether Article 8 rights are outweighed by the public interest in extradition, *Polish Judicial Authorities v Celinski and others* [2015] EWHC 1274 (Admin) held that the judicial authorities of member states must be accorded a proper degree of mutual confidence and respect; and factors mitigating the gravity of an offence will ordinarily be matters for the courts of the requesting state.

A17.7 **Procedure in category 2 cases**

Applicable where the defendant is wanted by a non-EU country:

- The prosecution will serve either a provisional request (warrant) with limited information about the crime for which the defendant is wanted, or full extradition papers. Section 74 of the Extradition Act 2003 applies if the defendant has been arrested under a provisional warrant. The warrant must be shown to the defendant upon arrest, or as soon as practicable after his arrest (s 74(2)). The defendant must also be brought before the appropriate judge as soon as practicable (s 74(3)), unless the defendant is granted bail by police, or the Secretary of State decides under section 126 that the request is not to be proceeded with. If these requirements are not complied with and the defendant applies to be discharged, the judge must order his discharge (s 74(5)).

- The judge must give the defendant information in accordance with section 74(7), which is that he is accused of the commission of an offence in a category 2 territory or that he is alleged to be unlawfully at large after conviction of an offence by a court in a category 2 territory, and the required information about consent (ie that the requested person may consent to his extradition, the effect of consent, the procedure that will apply if he gives consent, and that the consent must be given in writing and is irrevocable).

- If section 70(9) has been complied with (ie the judge has received the request and certificate), the judge must fix a hearing date, which must not be later than two months starting with the date on which the judge receives the documents. This period may be extended under section 76(4).

- The court should seek to identify the potential issues that will be raised against extradition (*Antonov v Lithuania* [2015] EWHC 1243 (Admin)).

- The judge must remand the requested person in custody or on bail. See further **A17.9**.

A17.8 **Procedure in category 1 cases**

Applicable where the defendant is wanted by a country within the EAW system.

The court may wish to proceed with the extradition hearing forthwith but will adjourn, for example, upon request of the defence to obtain and present evidence in relation to a bar that has been raised. Well-reasoned arguments on sound grounds are required. The following matters must be considered.

A17.8.1 *The contents of the EAW*

A technically valid warrant must contain certain specific information, the absence of which will make it invalid and the requested person must be discharged.

A17.8.1.1 *Accusation case*

The EAW must contain:

- a statement that the defendant is wanted for the purpose of prosecution (rather than mere investigation);
- the defendant's identity (ie personal details);
- details of any other warrants issued for the same offence;
- details of the alleged offence, date, place.

The offence must constitute an extradition offence; that is, an offence over which the United Kingdom takes jurisdiction (framework, dual criminality, or recognized by international law), and be punishable with at least 12 months' imprisonment or as provided in sections 64 and 65 of the Extradition Act 2003 for extraterritorial offences.

A17.8.1.2 *Conviction case*

The EAW must contain:

- a statement that the defendant is wanted for the purpose of sentencing or serving a sentence of imprisonment;
- the defendant's identity (ie personal details);
- particulars of conviction, date, court;
- any other warrants issued for the same offence;
- the sentence that has been imposed—which must be four months' custody or over to extradite if the requested person is alleged to be unlawfully at large after conviction, and has been sentenced for an offence over which the United Kingdom takes jurisdiction.

A17.8.2 *Extradition offences*

The offence outlined in the warrant must be an extradition offence. This means that it must have dual criminality with an offence in the United Kingdom, must be one that carries a sentence of imprisonment of over 12 months or as provided in sections 64 and 65 of the Extradition Act 2003 for extraterritorial offences, or one for which a sentence of four months or more has been imposed in a conviction case. The offence will also qualify if it is a specified offence included in the schedule to the EAW or recognized by international law, etc.

A17.8.3 *Identity*

If identity is not admitted, the requesting state must be in a position to prove it (Extradition Act 2003, s 7). Some examples of identification methods include:

- photographic or video evidence;
- possession of (or proximity to) papers bearing the same or essentially the same details;
- unusual name;
- fingerprints;
- admissions.

The defendant at court must be the person named in the EAW.

The court will decide this issue on the balance of probabilities, taking into account the information available to the court at the initial hearing.

A17.8.4 *Requirement regarding production at court*

If the defendant is not produced as soon as practicable at court, the judge must discharge (Extradition Act 2003, s 4(3) and (5)).

A17.8.5 *Requirement of service of the warrant*

The requested person must be given a copy of the warrant as soon as practicable after his arrest, if not the judge has a discretion to discharge, though this is seldom exercised (Extradition Act 2003, s 4(2) and (4)).

A17.8.6 *Consent*

A person who is legally represented (or is ineligible for legal aid, has declined it, or has had it withdrawn) may consent to extradition; such consent cannot be revoked.

Consenting to extradition might be advisable only if the requested person expressly wishes to give consent, and should be given only when the legal adviser is satisfied that none of the statutory or other bars to extradition is at issue.

The court will ask if the defendant will be consenting to his or her extradition. By indicating consent, the requested person no longer waives speciality protection; that is, a legal protection that guarantees that the requested person may be prosecuted only for conduct that appears in the EAW.

The court will seek to identify any bars or arguments against the extradition request. If any realistically arguable bars or arguments are raised, the usual procedure is for the court to open the extradition hearing and to adjourn to allow for preparation or gathering of evidence. The court may also fix a timetable in relation to filing and service of evidence, skeleton arguments, etc and should seek to identify the issues in the case (*Antonov v Lithuania* [2015] EWHC 1243 (Admin)).

If the extradition is not challenged (even though the defendant has not consented), the court will proceed with an uncontested extradition hearing, which is usually resolved within a short time. The result of such an uncontested hearing will be an order for the defendant's extradition.

A17.8.7 *Appeals*

The order for extradition is subject to a right of appeal, with leave from the Administrative Court, to that court. The appeal procedure is subject to a statutory time limit of seven days (including the date of the order for extradition), which is strict but can be extended if the requested person did everything possible to ensure the notice was given as soon as possible, under section 160 Anti-social Behaviour Crime and Policing Act 2014, in relation to the filing and service requirements. Only specialist practitioners should undertake such appeals.

A17.9 **Bail**

The court will invariably consider bail, whether or not the extradition hearing is adjourned or the defendant's extradition is ordered.

Usual Bail Act considerations apply, although there is no presumption in favour of bail in conviction cases. A security is often required.

 See *Blackstone's Criminal Practice 2017* **D31**

A18 **Hearsay**

A18.1 Overview

Hearsay evidence in criminal proceedings is regulated by sections 114–126 of the Criminal Justice Act 2003. The main legislative provisions are set out in **A18.3**.

A18.2 Criminal Procedure Rules

Part 20 of the Criminal Procedure Rules regulates the admission of hearsay evidence:

Criminal Procedure Rules, Pt 20

20.2 (1) This rule applies where a party wants to introduce hearsay evidence for admission under any of the following sections of the Criminal Justice Act 2003—
   (a) section 114(1)(d) (evidence admissible in the interests of justice);
   (b) section 116 (evidence where a witness is unavailable);
   (c) section 117(1)(c) (evidence in a statement prepared for the purposes of criminal proceedings);
   (d) section 121 (multiple hearsay).
(2) That party must—
   (a) serve notice on—
      (i) the court officer, and
      (ii) each other party;
   (b) in the notice—
      (i) identify the evidence that is hearsay,
      (ii) set out any facts on which that party relies to make the evidence admissible,
      (iii) explain how that party will prove those facts if another party disputes them, and
      (iv) explain why the evidence is admissible; and
   (c) attach to the notice any statement or other document containing the evidence that has not already been served.
(3) A prosecutor who wants to introduce such evidence must serve the notice not more than—
   (a) 28 days after the defendant pleads not guilty, in a magistrates' court; ...
(4) A defendant who wants to introduce such evidence must serve the notice as soon as reasonably practicable.
(5) A party entitled to receive a notice under this rule may waive that entitlement by so informing—
   (a) the party who would have served it; and
   (b) the court.

20.5 (1) The court may—
   (a) shorten or extend (even after it has expired) a time limit under this Part;
   (b) allow an application or notice to be in a different form to one set out in the Practice Direction, or to be made or given orally;
   (c) dispense with the requirement for notice to introduce hearsay evidence.
   (2) A party who wants an extension of time must—
   (a) apply when serving the application or notice for which it is needed; and
   (b) explain the delay.

A18.3 Legislative scheme

Sections 114–120 of the Criminal Justice Act 2003 are the main statutory provisions.

Criminal Justice Act 2003, s 114

114 Admissibility of hearsay evidence

(1) In criminal proceedings a statement not made in oral evidence in the proceedings is admissible as evidence of any matter stated if, but only if—
   (a) any provision of this Chapter or any other statutory provision makes it admissible,
   (b) any rule of law preserved by section 118 makes it admissible,
   (c) all parties to the proceedings agree to it being admissible, or
   (d) the court is satisfied that it is in the interests of justice for it to be admissible.

(2) In deciding whether a statement not made in oral evidence should be admitted under subsection (1)(d), the court must have regard to the following factors (and to any others it considers relevant)—
   (a) how much probative value the statement has (assuming it to be true) in relation to a matter in issue in the proceedings, or how valuable it is for the understanding of other evidence in the case;
   (b) what other evidence has been, or can be, given on the matter or evidence mentioned in paragraph (a);
   (c) how important the matter or evidence mentioned in paragraph (a) is in the context of the case as a whole;
   (d) the circumstances in which the statement was made;
   (e) how reliable the maker of the statement appears to be;
   (f) how reliable the evidence of the making of the statement appears to be;
   (g) whether oral evidence of the matter stated can be given and, if not, why it cannot;
   (h) the amount of difficulty involved in challenging the statement;
   (i) the extent to which that difficulty would be likely to prejudice the party facing it.

(3) Nothing in this Chapter affects the exclusion of evidence of a statement on grounds other than the fact that it is a statement not made in oral evidence in the proceedings.

It will rarely be appropriate to use section 114 in order to circumvent section 116 (cases where a witness is unavailable) (*R v Ibrahim* [2010] EWCA Crim 1176). This principle takes on a particular importance in the magistrates' court in relation to 'missing' or reluctant witnesses (eg in domestic violence cases). Whilst there would be occasions when, in domestic violence proceedings, it would be necessary to admit hearsay evidence from the complainant the correct procedures must be followed. Section 114(1)(d) CJA 2003 (the interest of justice) could not be considered until all due enquiries and applications had been made and evidence heard under section 116 (*R v Jones (Kane)* [2015] EWCA Crim 1317). Section 114 should not be used simply to bypass other procedures available to the prosecution, for example the witness summons. In *R v Freeman* [2010] EWCA Crim 1997, the court quashed a conviction where section 114 was used in relation to a witness who had retracted his previous statement.

Regard must be had to all of the criteria in section 114(2), although not all factors need be decided in favour of admissibility.

Section 114(2)(e) requires the court to consider the reliability of the maker of the statement. The principles were considered further in *R v Riat and others* [2012] EWCA Crim 1509. The court must:

- be satisfied that there is proper statutory basis for admitting hearsay;
- identify if there is any material assisting in the test of credibility (s 124);
- consider as appropriate any interests of justice test;
- if there is no specific gateway, consider section 114(1)(d);
- consider any application to exclude under section 78 of the Police and Criminal Evidence Act 1984 or section 126 of the Criminal Justice Act 2003.

The criteria in section 114(2) are a useful aide-mémoire in identifying the relevant issues.

A focused decision must be made considering:

- the importance of the evidence in the case;
- the risks of unreliability;
- issues as to whether the reliability of the maker of the statement can be tested and assessed.

Of particular relevance are:

- the circumstances of the making of the hearsay statement,
- interest or disinterest of the maker,
- the existence of supporting evidence,
- information on the reliability of the maker,
- any means of testing reliability.

Criminal Justice Act 2003, ss 115 and 116

115 Statements and matters stated

(1) In this Chapter references to a statement or to a matter stated are to be read as follows.

(2) A statement is any representation of fact or opinion made by a person by whatever means; and it includes a representation made in a sketch, photofit or other pictorial form.

(3) A matter stated is one to which this Chapter applies if (and only if) the purpose, or one of the purposes, of the person making the statement appears to the court to have been—
   (a) to cause another person to believe the matter, or
   (b) to cause another person to act or a machine to operate on the basis that the matter is as stated.

Principal categories of admissibility

116 Cases where a witness is unavailable

(1) In criminal proceedings a statement not made in oral evidence in the proceedings is admissible as evidence of any matter stated if—
   (a) oral evidence given in the proceedings by the person who made the statement would be admissible as evidence of that matter,
   (b) the person who made the statement (the relevant person) is identified to the court's satisfaction, and
   (c) any of the five conditions mentioned in subsection (2) is satisfied.

(2) The conditions are—
   (a) that the relevant person is dead;
   (b) that the relevant person is unfit to be a witness because of his bodily or mental condition;
   (c) that the relevant person is outside the United Kingdom and it is not reasonably practicable to secure his attendance;
   (d) that the relevant person cannot be found although such steps as it is reasonably practicable to take to find him have been taken;
   (e) that through fear the relevant person does not give (or does not continue to give) oral evidence in the proceedings, either at all or in connection with the subject matter of the statement, and the court gives leave for the statement to be given in evidence.

(3) For the purposes of subsection (2)(e) 'fear' is to be widely construed and (for example) includes fear of the death or injury of another person or of financial loss.

(4) Leave may be given under subsection (2)(e) only if the court considers that the statement ought to be admitted in the interests of justice, having regard—
   (a) to the statement's contents,
   (b) to any risk that its admission or exclusion will result in unfairness to any party to the proceedings (and in particular to how difficult it will be to challenge the statement if the relevant person does not give oral evidence),
   (c) in appropriate cases, to the fact that a direction under section 19 of the Youth Justice and Criminal Evidence Act 1999 (c. 23) (special

measures for the giving of evidence by fearful witnesses etc) could
be made in relation to the relevant person, and

(d) to any other relevant circumstances.

(5) A condition set out in any paragraph of subsection (2) which is in fact
satisfied is to be treated as not satisfied if it is shown that the circumstances described in that paragraph are caused—

(a) by the person in support of whose case it is sought to give the state
in evidence, or

(b) by a person acting on his behalf,

in order to prevent the relevant person giving oral evidence in the proceedings (whether at all or in connection with the subject matter of the
statement).

In considering whether it is reasonably practicable to secure the
attendance of a witness, the court must consider what steps have,
and have not, been taken. The reasonableness will be judged in
relation to many factors, including the resources available to the
party (*R v Maloney* [1994] Crim LR 525).

Even where the attendance of a witness is not practicable (or some
other factor in s 116 is present), the court should then go on to
consider section 126 of the Act and section 78 of the Police and
Criminal Evidence Act 1984 in order to decide whether the evidence ought, in fairness, to be admitted.

Criminal Justice Act 2003, ss 117 and 118

117 Business and other documents

(1) In criminal proceedings a statement contained in a document is admissible as evidence of any matter stated if—

(a) oral evidence given in the proceedings would be admissible as evidence of that matter,

(b) the requirements of subsection (2) are satisfied, and

(c) the requirements of subsection (5) are satisfied, in a case where
subsection (4) requires them to be.

(2) The requirements of this subsection are satisfied if—

(a) the document or the part containing the statement was created or
received by a person in the course of a trade, business, profession
or other occupation, or as the holder of a paid or unpaid office,

(b) the person who supplied the information contained in the statement (the relevant person) had or may reasonably be supposed to
have had personal knowledge of the matters dealt with, and

(c) each person (if any) through whom the information was supplied
from the relevant person to the person mentioned in paragraph
(a) received the information in the course of a trade, business, profession or other occupation, or as the holder of a paid or unpaid office.

(3) The persons mentioned in paragraphs (a) and (b) of subsection (2) may
be the same person.

(4) The additional requirements of subsection (5) must be satisfied if the statement—

    (a) was prepared for the purposes of pending or contemplated criminal proceedings, or for a criminal investigation, but

    (b) was not obtained pursuant to a request under section 7 of the Crime (International Co-operation) Act 2003 (c. 32) or an order under paragraph 6 of Schedule 13 to the Criminal Justice Act 1988 (c. 33) (which relate to overseas evidence).

(5) The requirements of this subsection are satisfied if—

    (a) any of the five conditions mentioned in section 116(2) is satisfied (absence of relevant person etc), or

    (b) the relevant person cannot reasonably be expected to have any recollection of the matters dealt with in the statement (having regard to the length of time since he supplied the information and all other circumstances).

(6) A statement is not admissible under this section if the court makes a direction to that effect under subsection (7).

(7) The court may make a direction under this subsection if satisfied that the statement's reliability as evidence for the purpose for which it is tendered is doubtful in view of—

    (a) its contents,

    (b) the source of the information contained in it,

    (c) the way in which or the circumstances in which the information was supplied or received, or

    (d) the way in which or the circumstances in which the document concerned was created or received.

118 Preservation of certain common law categories of admissibility

(1) The following rules of law are preserved.

Public information etc

(1) Any rule of law under which in criminal proceedings—

    (a) published works dealing with matters of a public nature (such as histories, scientific works, dictionaries and maps) are admissible as evidence of facts of a public nature stated in them,

    (b) public documents (such as public registers, and returns made under public authority with respect to matters of public interest) are admissible as evidence of facts stated in them,

    (c) records (such as the records of certain courts, treaties, Crown grants, pardons and commissions) are admissible as evidence of facts stated in them, or

    (d) evidence relating to a person's age or date or place of birth may be given by a person without personal knowledge of the matter.

Reputation as to character

(2) Any rule of law under which in criminal proceedings evidence of a person's reputation is admissible for the purpose of proving his good or bad character.

[*Note*. The rule is preserved only so far as it allows the court to treat such evidence as proving the matter concerned.]

Reputation or family tradition

(3) Any rule of law under which in criminal proceedings evidence of reputation or family tradition is admissible for the purpose of proving or
disproving—
   (a) pedigree or the existence of a marriage,
   (b) the existence of any public or general right, or
   (c) the identity of any person or thing.

[Note: The rule is preserved only so far as it allows the court to treat such
evidence as proving or disproving the matter concerned.]

Res gestae

(4) Any rule of law under which in criminal proceedings a statement is
admissible as evidence of any matter stated if—
   (a) the statement was made by a person so emotionally overpowered
   by an event that the possibility of concoction or distortion can be
   disregarded,
   (b) the statement accompanied an act which can be properly evaluated
   as evidence only if considered in conjunction with the statement, or
   (c) the statement relates to a physical sensation or a mental state (such
   as intention or emotion).

Confessions etc

(5) Any rule of law relating to the admissibility of confessions or mixed statements in criminal proceedings.

Admissions by agents etc

(6) Any rule of law under which in criminal proceedings—
   (a) an admission made by an agent of a defendant is admissible against
   the defendant as evidence of any matter stated, or
   (b) a statement made by a person to whom a defendant refers a person
   for information is admissible against the defendant as evidence of
   any matter stated.

Common enterprise

(7) Any rule of law under which in criminal proceedings a statement made
by a party to a common enterprise is admissible against another party
to the enterprise as evidence of any matter stated.

Expert evidence

(8) Any rule of law under which in criminal proceedings an expert witness
may draw on the body of expertise relevant to his field.

(9) With the exception of the rules preserved by this section, the common
law rules governing the admissibility of hearsay evidence in criminal
proceedings are abolished.

No notice was required to admit *res gestae* evidence under section
118(1)(4) Criminal Justice Act 2003. The law was described in *R
v Andrews* [1987] AC 281 and the court had considered whether
the complainant was a person so emotionally overpowered that the
court could rule out concoction or distortion. In *Barnaby v DPP*

[2015] EWHC 232 (Admin) the magistrates had been correct to admit the content of three 999 calls and of the first statements by the victim to police when they arrived six minutes after the calls.

Criminal Justice Act 2003, ss 119 and 120

119 Inconsistent statements

(1) If in criminal proceedings a person gives oral evidence and—
   (a) he admits making a previous inconsistent statement, or
   (b) a previous inconsistent statement made by him is proved by virtue of section 3, 4 or 5 of the Criminal Procedure Act 1865 (c. 18),
   the statement is admissible as evidence of any matter stated of which oral evidence by him would be admissible.

(2) If in criminal proceedings evidence of an inconsistent statement by any person is given under section 124(2)(c), the statement is admissible as evidence of any matter stated in it of which oral evidence by that person would be admissible.

120 Other previous statements of witnesses

(1) This section applies where a person (the witness) is called to give evidence in criminal proceedings.

(2) If a previous statement by the witness is admitted as evidence to rebut a suggestion that his oral evidence has been fabricated, that statement is admissible as evidence of any matter stated of which oral evidence by the witness would be admissible.

(3) A statement made by the witness in a document—
   (a) which is used by him to refresh his memory while giving evidence,
   (b) on which he is cross-examined, and
   (c) which as a consequence is received in evidence in the proceedings,
   is admissible as evidence of any matter stated of which oral evidence by him would be admissible.

(4) A previous statement by the witness is admissible as evidence of any matter stated of which oral evidence by him would be admissible, if—
   (a) any of the following three conditions is satisfied, and
   (b) while giving evidence the witness indicates that to the best of his belief he made the statement, and that to the best of his belief it states the truth.

(5) The first condition is that the statement identifies or describes a person, object or place.

(6) The second condition is that the statement was made by the witness when the matters stated were fresh in his memory but he does not remember them, and cannot reasonably be expected to remember them, well enough to give oral evidence of them in the proceedings.

(7) The third condition is that—
   (a) the witness claims to be a person against whom an offence has been committed,
   (b) the offence is one to which the proceedings relate,

    (c) the statement consists of a complaint made by the witness (whether to a person in authority or not) about conduct which would, if proved, constitute the offence or part of the offence,

    (d) [repealed]

    (e) the complaint was not made as a result of a threat or a promise, and

    (f) before the statement is adduced the witness gives oral evidence in connection with its subject matter.

(8) For the purposes of subsection (7) the fact that the complaint was elicited (for example, by a leading question) is irrelevant unless a threat or a promise was involved.

 See *Blackstone's Criminal Practice 2017* **A7.83–A7.89** and **F16**

A19 **Identification Evidence**

A19.1 *Turnbull* direction: visual identification

In *R v Turnbull* (1976) 63 Cr App R 132, the court laid down the following guidance:

> First, whenever the case against an accused depends wholly or substantially on the correctness of one or more identifications of the accused which the defence alleges to be mistaken, the judge should warn the jury of the special need for caution before convicting the accused in reliance on the correctness of the identification or identifications. In addition he should instruct them as to the reason for the need for such a warning and should make some reference to the possibility that a mistaken witness can be a convincing one and that a number of such witnesses can all be mistaken. Provided this is done in clear terms the judge need not use any particular form of words.

> Secondly, the judge should direct the jury to examine closely the circumstances in which the identification by each witness came to be made. How long did the witness have the accused under observation? At what distance? In what light? Was the observation impeded in any way, as for example, by passing traffic or a press of people? Had the witness ever seen the accused before? How often? If only occasionally, had he any special reason for remembering the accused? How long elapsed between the original observation and the subsequent identification to the police? Was there any material discrepancy between the description of the accused given to the police by the witness when first seen by them and his actual appearance? If in any case, whether it is being dealt with summarily or on indictment, the prosecution has reason to believe that there is such a material discrepancy it should supply the accused or his legal advisers with particulars of the description the police were first given. In all cases if the accused asks to be given particulars of such descriptions, the prosecution should supply them. Finally, he should remind the jury of any specific weaknesses which had appeared in the identification evidence.

> Recognition may be more reliable than identification of a stranger; but even when the witness is purporting to recognise someone whom he knows, the jury should be reminded that mistakes in recognition of close relatives and friends are sometimes made.

> All these matters go to the quality of the identification evidence. If the quality is good and remains good at the close of the accused's case, the danger of a mistaken identification is lessened; but the poorer the quality, the greater the danger.

> In our judgment when the quality is good as for example when the identification is made after a long period of observation, or in satisfactory conditions by a relative, a neighbour, a close friend, a workmate and the like, the jury can safely be left to assess the value of the identifying evidence even though there is no other evidence to support it: provided always,

however, that an adequate warning has been given about the special need for caution.

Were the Courts to adjudge otherwise, affronts to justice would frequently occur. A few examples, taken over the whole spectrum of criminal activity, will illustrate what the effects upon the maintenance of law and order would be if any law were enacted that no person could be convicted on evidence of visual identification alone.

A19.2 Audio identification

For the protections necessary when there is evidence of voice recognition, reference should be made to *Flynn and St John* [2008] EWCA Crim 970. But such evidence may be admitted, with appropriate warnings, when the quality of the recording is good and the length sufficient (*R v Kapikanya (Alick)* [2015] EWCA Crim 1507). In Facebook identification cases, reference should be made to *R v Alexander and McGill* [2012] EWCA Crim 2768.

 See *Blackstone's Criminal Practice 2017* **F18**

A20 **Legal Aid**

A20.1 **Overview**

Legal aid is available for criminal proceedings. These are defined by the Legal Aid, Sentencing and Punishment of Offenders Act 2012 as including the following:

Legal Aid, Sentencing and Punishment of Offenders Act 2012, s 14

14 Criminal proceedings

In this Part 'criminal proceedings' means—

(a) proceedings before a court for dealing with an individual accused of an offence,

(b) proceedings before a court for dealing with an individual convicted of an offence, including proceedings in respect of a sentence or order,

(c) proceedings for dealing with an individual under the Extradition Act 2003,

(d) proceedings for binding an individual over to keep the peace or to be of good behaviour under section 115 of the Magistrates' Courts Act 1980 and for dealing with an individual who fails to comply with an order under that section,

(e) proceedings on an appeal brought by an individual under section 44A of the Criminal Appeal Act 1968 (appeal in case of death of appellant),

(f) proceedings on a reference under section 36 of the Criminal Justice Act 1972 on a point of law following the acquittal of an individual on indictment,

(g) proceedings for contempt committed, or alleged to have been committed, by an individual in the face of a court, and

(h) such other proceedings, before any court, tribunal or other person, as may be prescribed.

The proceedings referred to in section 14(h) are set out at regulation 9 of the Criminal Legal Aid (General) Regulations 2013 (SI 2013/9):

Criminal Legal Aid (General) Regulations 2013, reg 9

Criminal proceedings

9. The following proceedings are criminal proceedings for the purposes of section 14(h) of the Act (criminal proceedings)—

    (a) civil proceedings in a magistrates' court arising from a failure to pay a sum due or to obey an order of that court where such failure carries the risk of imprisonment;

(b)   proceedings under sections 14B, 14D, 14G, 14H, 21B and 21D of the Football Spectators Act 1989 in relation to banning orders and references to a court;

(c)   proceedings under section 5A of the Protection from Harassment Act 1997 in relation to restraining orders on acquittal;

…

(f)   proceedings in relation to parenting orders made under section 8(1)(b) of the Crime and Disorder Act 1998(1) where an order under section 22 of the Anti-social Behaviour, Crime and Policing Act 2014 or a sexual harm prevention order under section 103A of the Sexual Offences Act 2003 is made;

(g)   proceedings under section 8(1)(c) of the Crime and Disorder Act 1998 in relation to parenting orders made on the conviction of a child;

(h)   proceedings under section 9(5) of the Crime and Disorder Act 1998 to discharge or vary a parenting order made as set out in sub-paragraph (f) or (g);

(i)   proceedings under section 10 of the Crime and Disorder Act 1998 in relation to an appeal against a parenting order made as set out in sub-paragraph (f) or (g);

(j)   proceedings under Part 1A of Schedule 1 to the Powers of Criminal Courts (Sentencing) Act 2000 in relation to parenting orders for failure to comply with orders under section 20 of that Act;

(ja)   proceedings in a youth court (or on appeal from such a court) in relation to the breach or potential breach of a provision of an injunction under Part 1 of the Anti-social Behaviour, Crime and Policing Act 2014 where the person who is subject to the injunction is aged under 14;

(k)   proceedings under sections 80, 82, 83 and 84 of the Anti-social Behaviour, Crime and Policing Act 2014 in relation to closure orders made under section 80(5)(a) of that Act where a person has engaged in, or is likely to engage in behaviour that constitutes a criminal offence on the premises;

(ka)   proceedings under paragraph 3 of Schedule 2 to the Female Genital Mutilation Act 2003 in relation to female genital mutilation protection orders made other than on conviction and related appeals;

(kb)   proceedings under paragraph 6 of Schedule 2 to the Female Genital Mutilation Act 2003 in relation to female genital mutilation protection orders made under paragraph 3 of that Schedule;

(l)   proceedings under sections 20, 22, 26 and 28 of the Anti-social Behaviour Act 2003 in relation to parenting orders—
   (i)   in cases of exclusion from school; or
   (ii)   in respect of criminal conduct and anti-social behaviour;

(m)   proceedings under sections 97, 100 and 101 of the Sexual Offences Act 2003 in relation to notification orders and interim notification orders;

(n)   proceedings under sections 103A, 103E, 103F and 103H of the Sexual Offences Act 2003 in relation to sexual harm prevention orders;

…

(p) proceedings under sections 122A, 122D, 122E and 122G of the Sexual Offences Act 2003 in relation to sexual risk orders;

...

(r) proceedings under section 13 of the Tribunals, Courts and Enforcement Act 2007 on appeal against a decision of the Upper Tribunal in proceedings in respect of—
   (i) a decision of the Financial Conduct Authority
   (ia) a decision of the Prudential Regulation Authority;
   (ii) a decision of the Bank of England; or
   (iii) a decision of a person in relation to the assessment of any compensation or consideration under the Banking (Special Provisions) Act 2008 or the Banking Act 2009;

(s) proceedings before the Crown Court or the Court of Appeal in relation to serious crime prevention orders under sections 19, 20, 21 and 24 of the Serious Crime Act 2007;

(t) proceedings under sections 100, 101, 103, 104 and 106 of the Criminal Justice and Immigration Act 2008 in relation to violent offender orders and interim violent offender orders;

(u) proceedings under sections 26, 27 and 29 of the Crime and Security Act 2010 in relation to—
   (i) domestic violence protection notices; or
   (ii) domestic violence protection orders;

(ua) proceedings under sections 14(1)(b) and (c), 15 and 20 to 22 of the Modern Slavery Act 2015 in relation to slavery and trafficking prevention orders;

(ub) proceedings under sections 23 and 27 to 29 of the Modern Slavery Act 2015 in relation to slavery and trafficking risk orders; and

(v) any other proceedings that involve the determination of a criminal charge for the purposes of Article 6(1) of the European Convention on Human Rights.

Legal aid is subject to a merits test, and means assessment in some cases. There is no means assessment:

- for those under 18 years;
- for those in receipt of income support;
- for those in receipt of income-based employment and support allowance (ESA);
- for those in receipt of income-based job-seeker's allowance (JSA);
- for those in receipt of guaranteed state pension credit; or
- for those in receipt of Universal Credit.

Legal aid extends automatically to the Crown Court if the case is committed for sentence (note that there is no additional contribution payable in respect of these Crown Court proceedings).

Legal aid automatically extends, without a merits test, to any case sent to the Crown Court, but proceedings in the Crown Court are subject to a means test before an order can be granted. A contribution may then be required or legal aid be refused.

Appeals to the Crown Court require a fresh legal aid application to be lodged, and are subject to interests of justice and means criteria. A contribution may be payable in the Crown Court, dependent on means, or legal aid be refused.

A20.2 The interests of justice test

When assessing whether the grant of representation is in the interests of justice, regard should be had to the provisions of section 17(2) of the Legal Aid, Sentencing and Punishment of Offenders Act 2012 (the *Widgery* criteria). The defendant must be able to demonstrate one or more of the following:

- It is likely that I will lose my liberty.
- I have been given a sentence that is suspended or non-custodial. If I break this, the court may be able to deal with me for the original offence.
- It is likely that I will lose my livelihood.
- It is likely that I will suffer serious damage to my reputation.
- A substantial question of law may be involved.
- I may not be able to understand the court proceedings or present my own case.
- I may need witnesses to be traced or interviewed on my behalf.
- The proceedings may involve expert cross-examination of a prosecution witness.
- It is in the interests of another person that I am represented.
- Any other reasons.

Refusal on the basis of the interests of justice test can be appealed to justices or an officer of the Crown Court (Criminal Legal Aid (General) Regulations 2013 (SI 2013/9), regs 29 and 30), and regard should be had to the following:

- the likely penalty, not the theoretical maximum: *R v Highgate Justices, ex p Lewis* [1977] Crim LR 611;
- in *R (Punatar) v Horseferry Road Magistrates' Court* [2002] EWHC 1196 (Admin), the solicitor attended court to defend an imprisonable matter and submitted an application for representation at the end of those proceedings. At that stage the imprisonable matter had been replaced by a non-imprisonable one and legal aid was refused. The court held that the refusal was wrong in law; the court should not apply hindsight but instead look at what had been in the mind of the solicitor when he made the decision to attend court;

- a 16-year-old would not have the skills to cross-examine a police officer effectively: *Scunthorpe Justices, ex p S*, The Times, 5 March 1998;

- in *R (GKR Law Solicitors) v Liverpool Magistrates' Court* [2008] EWHC 2974 (Admin), the court held that it was appropriate to grant representation to a defendant in relation to a special reasons hearing, where a witness in the case was the defendant's 12-year-old son. The child was a witness entitled to and requiring special measures, and consideration would need to be given to video-interviewing the young witness in order to ensure best evidence was given; such measures would be outside the competence and resources of the defendant;

- in *R v Chester Magistrates' Court, ex p Ball* (1999) 163 JP 757, it was said that any defendant of previous good character pleading not guilty to a charge equal to, or more significant than, section 5 of the Public Order Act 1986 in terms of nature and seriousness, should be granted legal aid regardless of his social or professional standing. This is very unlikely to include non-imprisonable road traffic or regulatory offences;

- in *R v Gravesend Magistrates' Court ex p Baker* [1977] 161 JP 765 the defendant was charged with driving with excess alcohol and put forward special reasons based on spiked drinks. The court held that the applicant should be granted legal aid because a scientific expert would be required and the assistance of a solicitor would be necessary to identify witnesses, to take proper proofs, and to extract the defence in the witness box.

A20.3 Transfer of representation

The law is contained in regulation 14 of the Criminal Legal Aid (Determinations by a Court and Choice of Representative) Regulations 2013 (SI 2013/614):

Criminal Legal Aid (Determinations by a Court and Choice of Representative) Regulations 2013, reg 14

Change of provider

14 (1) Subject to paragraph (2), where an individual has selected a provider in criminal proceedings, the right conferred by section 27(4) of the Act does not include a right to select a provider in place of the original provider.

(2) The relevant court may determine that the individual can select a provider in place of the original provider in the circumstances set out in paragraphs (3) or (4).

---

(3) The circumstances are that the relevant court determines that—
  (a) there has been a breakdown in the relationship between the individual and the original provider such that effective representation can no longer be provided by the original provider; or
  (b) there is some other compelling reason why effective representation can no longer be provided by the original provider.
(4) The circumstances are that the relevant court determines that—
  (a) the original provider—
    (i) considers there to be a duty to withdraw from the case in accordance with the provider's professional rules of conduct; or
    (ii) is no longer able to represent the individual through circumstances outside the provider's control; and
  (b) the original provider has supplied the relevant court with details as to—
    (i) the nature of any such duty to withdraw from the case; or
    (ii) the particular circumstances that render the provider unable to represent the individual.

Solicitors seeking a transfer must exercise a proper and independent judgment when considering whether the supplicant's grounds were justified: *R (Sanjari) v Birmingham CC* 2015 EWHC 2037 (Admin).

Part 46 of the Criminal Procedure Rules provides that:

Criminal Procedure Rules, Pt 46

46.3 (1) This rule applies—
  (a) in relation to a party who has legal aid for the purposes of a case;.
  (b) where such a party wants to select a legal representative in place of the representative named in the legal aid representation order.
(2) Such a party must—
  (a) apply in writing as soon as practicable after becoming aware of the grounds for doing so; and
  (b) serve the application on—
    (i) the court officer, and
    (ii) the legal representative named in the legal aid representation order ...
(3) The application must—
  (a) explain what the case is about, including what offences are alleged, what stage it has reached and what is likely to be in issue at trial;
  (b) explain how and why the applicant chose the legal representative named in the legal aid representation order;
  (c) if an advocate other than that representative has been instructed for the applicant, explain whether the applicant wishes to replace that advocate;

(d) explain, giving relevant facts and dates—
    (i) in what way, in the applicant's opinion, there has been a breakdown in the relationship between the applicant and the current representative such that neither the individual representing the applicant nor any colleague of his or hers any longer can provide effective representation, or
    (ii) what other compelling reason, in the applicant's opinion, means that neither the individual representing the applicant nor any colleague of his or hers any longer can provide effective representation;

(e) give details of any previous application by the applicant to replace the legal representative named in the legal aid representation order;

(f) state whether the applicant—
    (i) waives the legal professional privilege attaching to the applicant's communications with the current representative, to the extent required to allow that representative to respond to the matters set out in the application, or
    (ii) declines to waive that privilege and acknowledges that the court may draw such inferences as it thinks fit in consequence;

(g) explain how and why the applicant has chosen the proposed new representative;

(h) include or attach a statement by the proposed new representative which—
    (i) confirms that that representative is eligible and willing to conduct the case for the applicant,
    (ii) confirms that that representative can and will meet the current timetable for the case, including any hearing date or dates that have been set, if the application succeeds,
    (iii) explains what, if any, dealings that representative has had with the applicant before the present case; and.

(i) ask for a hearing, if the applicant wants one, and explain why it is needed.

 See *Blackstone's Criminal Practice 2017* **D32**

A21 **Mental Disorder**

A21.1 **Fitness to plead**

In a strict legal sense the issue of fitness to plead does not arise in the magistrates' court as the relevant legislation does not provide for any summary procedures.

If the offence is an either-way offence the court may decline jurisdiction, but the defendant will not be able to consent to summary trial. However, if the accused is being tried for an imprisonable offence, and it is shown that the accused did the act or made the omission charged, *Lincoln (Kesteven) Justices, ex p O'Connor* [1983] 1 WLR 335 confirms that he can be made subject to a hospital order under section 37(3) of the Mental Health Act 1983.

Subject to having obtained two satisfactory reports, and the court can remand under section 35 of the Mental Health Act 1983 for that purpose, the court can then go on to make a hospital order under section 37(3). The stages are:

- raise issue of mental disorder;
- prove that the accused did the act or made the omission charged;
- obtain requisite medical assessment;
- make hospital order.

The prosecution will be required to prove only the *actus reus* of the offence (*R v Antoine* [2000] 2 All ER 208, HL). If the prosecution cannot prove the act or omission, the defendant must be discharged.

In the alternative, if the Crown will not follow that route, the defendant can plead not guilty and put the Crown to proof of the mental element.

The procedure under section 37(3) of the Mental Health Act 1983 is not available for indictable-only offences.

A21.2 **Fitness to stand trial**

If the defendant does not require a hospital/guardianship order under section 37(3) and suffers from mental disorder or some other significant impairment of intelligence, he may be able to participate in criminal proceedings if necessary with adaptations to the trial process tailored to suit his particular needs; see Criminal Practice Direction 2013 EWCA Crim 1631(as amended by 2016 EWCA Crim 97), paragraphs 3D–3F, including the use of an intermediary. However, if the defendant's illness or disability is so severe that he will be unable to participate in any way in his trial, then the Crown Prosecution Service should be invited to consider discontinuing the proceedings, or the court could stay the proceedings on the grounds of an abuse of process, or of its own volition adjourn the case *sine die*.

A21.3 Insanity

Insanity is available as a defence in the magistrates' court, but the defendant does not have an absolute right to have the issue determined at trial if the court feels that a disposal under section 37(3) of the Mental Health Act 1983 might be more appropriate. There is no 'special verdict' of not guilty by reason of insanity; a finding of insanity prevents conviction (*R (Singh) v Stratford Magistrates' Court* [2007] EWHC 1582 (Admin)).

A21.4 Medical reports

In order to decide whether the person should be tried or made subject to the fitness to plead procedure, the court may need to consider the report of a medical practitioner, and a remand to hospital under section 11 of the Powers of Criminal Courts (Sentencing) Act 2000 may be ordered.

Powers of Criminal Courts (Sentencing) Act 2000, s 11

11 Remand by magistrates' court for medical examination

(1) If, on the trial by a magistrates' court of an offence punishable on summary conviction with imprisonment, the court—

    (a) is satisfied that the accused did the act or made the omission charged, but

    (b) is of the opinion that an inquiry ought to be made into his physical or mental condition before the method of dealing with him is determined,

the court shall adjourn the case to enable a medical examination and report to be made, and shall remand him.

(2) An adjournment under subsection (1) above shall not be for more than three weeks at a time where the court remands the accused in custody, nor for more than four weeks at a time where it remands him on bail.

(3) Where on an adjournment under subsection (1) above the accused is remanded on bail, the court shall impose conditions under paragraph (d) of section 3(6) of the Bail Act 1976 and the requirements imposed as conditions under that paragraph shall be or shall include requirements that the accused—

    (a) undergo medical examination by a registered medical practitioner or, where the inquiry is into his mental condition and the court so directs, two such practitioners; and

---

(b) for that purpose attend such an institution or place, or on such practitioner, as the court directs and, where the inquiry is into his mental
condition, comply with any other directions which may be given to
him for that purpose by any person specified by the court or by a
person of any class so specified.

A21.5 Legal aid

The Legal Aid Agency's (LAA) criminal legal aid manual confirms:

Criminal Legal Aid Manual, paras 3.5.6 and 3.5.7

3.5.6 Signing the form

For audit purposes and *with the exception of applicants with severe mental
health problems,* the applicant must sign the application form in all cases.

3.5.7 Applicants with mental health problems

There are some applicants who, because of mental health problems, are
unable to give instructions to their solicitor, to understand the declaration
on the CRM14 & CRM15 and/or are unable to sign the application form. It
is likely that these applicants will be detained under the Mental Health Act
or will be being kept under medical supervision.

Where the applicant lacks capacity, within the meaning of the Mental
Capacity Act 2005, to instruct a solicitor as their representative and to sign
the declaration on the CRM14 and CRM15, the LAA's contract does allow the
solicitor to get someone else to sign the application on the applicant's behalf.

The application form may be signed by

- The applicant's attorney or deputy appointed under the Mental Capacity
  Act 2005
- The applicant's nearest relative or guardian
- A person acting as a Litigation friend
- Any other person who is acting in the applicant's best interest and who
  has sufficient knowledge of the applicant's financial affairs to be able to
  sign the declaration on the applicant's behalf

The solicitor or any other member, employee or associate of the solicitor's
firm cannot sign the form.

In addition to the signature, the third party must also be in a position to
provide details of the applicant's finances or the application form will be
rejected ... Solicitors should record in the 'Further Information' section of
the application form where someone other than the applicant has signed
the form, explaining why this was necessary. The person signing on the
applicant's behalf must also print their name and state their relationship
to the applicant.

In cases where the applicant does not have sufficient capacity to instruct
a solicitor, is unwilling or physically unable to sign the declaration on
the CRM14 and CRM15 forms themselves and there is no one available
to sign on the applicant's behalf, then special circumstances may apply.

We recognise the difficulties faced by the solicitor in obtaining information in these circumstances. A solicitor who wishes to act for the client in this situation should refer the application (as far as it can be completed) to the National Crime Team (NCT) for consideration. The NCT will work with you to build a picture of the applicant's circumstances and assess the level of risk the client presents.

Please note: Legal Advisers and Judges do not have the authority to accept unsigned forms for applicants in these circumstances,

A21.6 **Diversion**

The Code for Crown Prosecutors indicates that, in applying the public interest test, prosecutors should also have regard when considering culpability as to whether the suspect is, or was at the time of the offence, suffering from any significant mental or physical ill-health as in some circumstances this may mean that it is less likely that a prosecution is required. However, prosecutors will also need to consider how serious the offence was, whether it is likely to be repeated, and the need to safeguard the public or those providing care to such persons.

In legal guidance on mentally disordered offenders the following principle is set out:

The CPS uses the term 'mentally disordered offender' to describe a person who has a disability or disorder of the mind and has committed or is suspected of committing a criminal offence. This term covers a range of offences, disabilities and disorders. A mental disorder may be relevant to:

• The decision to prosecute or divert;
• Fitness to plead; and
• Sentencing/disposal.

Each case must be considered on its merits, taking into account all available information about any mental health problem, and its relevance to the offence, in addition to the principles set out in the Code for Crown Prosecutors. The Code explains that there is a balance to be struck between the public interest in diverting a defendant with significant mental illness from the criminal justice system and other public interest factors in favour of prosecution including the need to safeguard the public.

If there is significant evidence to establish that a defendant or suspect has a significant mental illness, a prosecution may not be appropriate unless the offence is serious or there is a real possibility that it may be repeated.

If proceedings have been started or are being considered and the CPS is provided with a medical report which states that the strain of criminal proceedings may lead to a considerable worsening of the defendant's mental health, the implications of the report should be considered very carefully.

This is a difficult field because in some cases the defendant may have become disturbed and depressed by the mere fact that his or her conduct has been discovered, and any suggestions that continuing the criminal proceedings will significantly worsen the defendant's condition should be evaluated carefully. In serious cases where a prosecution is plainly needed unless there is clear evidence that continuing the case would be likely to result in a permanent deterioration in the defendant's condition, it may be appropriate to obtain an independent medical report. Where the prosecutor is satisfied that the probable effect on the defendant's health outweighs the public interest considerations in favour of a prosecution, the case should be discontinued and full reasons recorded on the file.

 See *Blackstone's Criminal Practice 2017* **D20.27** and **E22**

A22 **Misbehaviour at Court**

A22.1 **Misbehaviour during allocation and summary trial**

Section 18(3) of the Magistrates' Courts Act 1980 provides:

Magistrates' Courts Act 1980, s 18(3)

18 Initial procedure on information against adult for offence triable either way

...

(3) The court may proceed in the absence of the accused in accordance with such of the provisions of sections 19 to 22 below as are applicable in the circumstances if the court considers that by reason of his disorderly conduct before the court it is not practicable for the proceedings to be conducted in his presence; and subsections (3) to (5) of section 23 below, so far as applicable, shall have effect in relation to proceedings conducted in the absence of the accused by virtue of this subsection (references in those subsections to the person representing the accused being for this purpose read as references to the person, if any, representing him).

...

A22.2 **Contempt of Court Act 1981**

Section 12 of the Contempt of Court Act 1981 provides:

Contempt of Court Act 1981, s 12

12 Offences of contempt of magistrates' courts

(1) A magistrates' court has jurisdiction under this section to deal with any person who—
  (a) wilfully insults the justice or justices, any witness before or officer of the court or any solicitor or counsel having business in the court, during his or their sitting or attendance in court or in going to or returning from the court; or
  (b) wilfully interrupts the proceedings of the court or otherwise misbehaves in court.

(2) In any such case the court may order any officer of the court, or any constable, to take the offender into custody and detain him until the rising of the court; and the court may, if it thinks fit, commit the offender to custody for a specified period not exceeding one month or impose on him a fine not exceeding £2,500, or both.

(2A) A fine imposed under subsection (2) above shall be deemed, for the purposes of any enactment, to be a sum adjudged to be paid by a conviction.

(3) A magistrates' court may at any time revoke an order of committal made under subsection (2) and, if the offender is in custody, order his discharge.

(4) Section 135 of the Powers of Criminal Courts (Sentencing) Act 2000 (limit on fines in respect of young persons) and the following provisions of the Magistrates' Courts Act 1980 apply in relation to an order under this section as they apply in relation to a sentence on conviction or finding of guilty of an offence; and those provisions of the Magistrates' Courts Act 1980 are section 36 (restriction on fines in respect of young persons); sections 75 to 91 (enforcement); section 108 (appeal to Crown Court); section 136 (overnight detention in default of payment); and section 142(1) (power to rectify mistakes).

It should be noted that there is no power to adjourn, and the matter must be dealt with before the end of the court day. There will be few cases that cannot be handled adequately by a suitable apology. See also Part 48 of the Criminal Procedure Rules.

 See *Blackstone's Criminal Practice 2017* **B14.79–B14.128**

A23 **Presence of Defendant in Court**

A23.1 General principles

If a defendant has been bailed to attend court, his presence is mandatory unless and until it is excused by the court. Where a defendant on bail fails to appear, a warrant may be issued for his arrest.

Statutory provisions are contained in section 129 of the Magistrates' Court Act 1980:

Magistrates' Court Act 1980, s 129

129 Further remand

(1) If a magistrates' court is satisfied that any person who has been remanded is unable by reason of illness or accident to appear or be brought before the court at the expiration of the period for which he was remanded, the court may, in his absence, remand him for a further time; and section 128(6) above shall not apply.

(2) Notwithstanding anything in section 128(1) above, the power of a court under subsection (1) above to remand a person on bail for a further time—

   (a) where he was granted bail in criminal proceedings, includes power to enlarge the recognizance of any surety for him to a later time;

(3) Where a person remanded on bail is bound to appear before a magistrates' court at any time and the court has no power to remand him under subsection (1) above, the court may in his absence—

   (a) where he was granted bail in criminal proceedings, appoint a later time as the time at which he is to appear and enlarge the recognizances of any sureties for him to that time;

   and the appointment of the time or the enlargement of his recognizance shall be deemed to be a further remand.

(4) Where a magistrates' court sends a person to the Crown Court for trial on bail and the recognizance of any surety for him has been conditioned in accordance with paragraph (a) of subsection (4) of section 128 above, the court may, in the absence of the surety, enlarge his recognizance so that he is bound to secure that the person so sent for trial appears also before the Crown Court.

On summons and certain other matters, the defendant may be represented by a legal representative.

Section 122 of the Magistrates' Courts Act 1980 provides:

> ## Magistrates' Courts Act 1980, s 122
>
> ### 122 Appearance by counsel or solicitor
> (1) A party to any proceedings before a magistrates' court may be represented by a legal representative.
> (2) Subject to subsection (3) below, an absent party so represented shall be deemed not to be absent.
> (3) Appearance of a party by legal representative shall not satisfy any provision of any enactment or any condition of a recognizance expressly requiring his presence.

Section 122(2) does not apply to a hearing at which a defendant is sent to the Crown Court. A personal attendance, but no contribution from the defendant, is required (*R (Lord Janner) v Westminster Magistrates' Court* [2015] EWHC 2578).

A23.2 Defendants in custody

A further remand of a defendant in custody can only be ordered if there is illness or accident in accordance with section 129 of the Magistrates' Court Act 1980.

Whilst an error in the administrative process (eg inserting the wrong court date on the record) could amount to an accident within the meaning of section 129 of the Magistrates' Court Act 1980 and so justify a remand in custody in the absence of the defendant (*Hillman v Governor of Bronzefield Prison* 24 May 2013 (DC)), a failure otherwise to produce the defendant in person or by video link may not. There is no limit to the length of a remand under these provisions.

A23.3 Defendant's presence at trial

Section 11 of the Magistrates' Courts Act 1980 details the court's powers when a defendant does not appear for trial:

> ## Magistrates' Courts Act 1980, s 11
>
> ### 11 Non-appearance of accused: general provisions
> (1) Subject to the provisions of this Act, where at the time and place appointed for the trial or adjourned trial of an information the prosecutor appears but the accused does not—
>   (a) if the accused is under 18 years of age, the court may proceed in his absence; and

(b) if the accused has attained the age of 18 years, the court shall proceed in his absence unless it appears to the court to be contrary to the interests of justice to do so.

This is subject to subsections (2), (2A), (3) and (4).

(2) Where a summons has been issued, the court shall not begin to try the information in the absence of the accused unless either it is proved to the satisfaction of the court, on oath or in such other manner as may be prescribed, that the summons was served on the accused within what appears to the court to be a reasonable time before the trial or adjourned trial or the accused has appeared on a previous occasion to answer to the information.

(2A) The court shall not proceed in the absence of the accused if it considers that there is an acceptable reason for his failure to appear.

(3) In proceedings to which this subsection applies, the court shall not in a person's absence sentence him to imprisonment or detention in a detention centre or make a detention and training order or an order under paragraph 8(2)(a) or (b) of Schedule 12 to the Criminal Justice Act 2003 that a suspended sentence passed on him shall take effect.

(3A) But where a sentence or order of a kind mentioned in subsection (3) is imposed or given in the absence of the offender, the offender must be brought before the court before being taken to a prison or other institution to begin serving his sentence (and the sentence or order is not to be regarded as taking effect until he is brought before the court).

(4) In proceedings to which this subsection applies, the court shall not in a person's absence impose any disqualification on him, except on resumption of the hearing after an adjournment under section 10(3) above; and where a trial is adjourned in pursuance of this subsection the notice required by section 10(2) above shall include notice of the reason for the adjournment.

(5) Subsections (3) and (4) apply to—

(a) proceedings instituted by an information, where a summons has been issued; and

(b) proceedings instituted by a written charge.

(6) Nothing in this section requires the court to enquire into the reasons for the accused's failure to appear before deciding whether to proceed in his absence.

(7) The court shall state in open court its reasons for not proceeding under this section in the absence of an accused who has attained the age of 18 years; and the court shall cause those reasons to be entered in its register of proceedings.

In deciding whether or not to proceed in the defendant's absence, the court has to have regard to the following principles (*R v Jones and others* [2002] UKHL 5; *Shirzadeh v Maidstone Magistrates' Court* [2003] EWHC 2216 (Admin)):

• the nature and circumstances of the defendant's behaviour in absenting himself from the trial or disrupting it, as the case may be, and in particular, whether his behaviour was deliberate, voluntary, and such as plainly waived his right to appear;

- (in the case of a defendant aged under 18 years) whether an adjournment might result in the defendant being caught or attending voluntarily and/or not disrupting the proceedings;
- (in the case of a defendant aged under 18 years) the likely length of such an adjournment;
- whether the defendant, though absent, is, or wishes to be, legally represented at the trial or has, by his conduct, waived his right to representation;
- whether an absent defendant's legal representatives are able to receive instructions from him during the trial and the extent to which they are able to present his defence (*Note*: it is a matter for the professional judgment of the advocate whether they should continue to represent the absent defendant (*R v Ulcay* [2007] EWCA Crim 2379));
- the extent of the disadvantage to the defendant in not being able to give his account of events, having regard to the nature of the evidence against him;
- the risk of the jury reaching an improper conclusion about the absence of the defendant;
- the seriousness of the offence, which affects defendant, victim, and public;
- the general public interest and the particular interest of victims and witnesses that a trial should take place within a reasonable time of the events to which it relates;
- the effect of delay on the memories of witnesses;
- where there is more than one defendant and not all have absconded, the undesirability of separate trials, and the prospects of a fair trial for the defendant(s) who are present.

The court in *Shirzadeh* identified four additional factors relevant to trial in the magistrates' court:

> [first] that there ought to be less risk from either a trained lay justice or a district judge in drawing an impermissible inference from a defendant's absence; secondly, in a magistrates' court the finder of fact may ask its own questions and test the evidence of prosecution witnesses; thirdly, a defendant in summary proceedings can apply to set aside any resulting conviction under section 142 of the Magistrates' Courts Act 1980; and fourthly, a defendant in summary proceedings has an automatic right of appeal to the Crown Court.

The decision to try a person in his absence must be exercised with great care and only in cases such as where the absence was a deliberate absconding (*R (Drinkwater) v Solihull Magistrates' Court* [2012] EWHC 765 (Admin)). (See also case law in **A2**.)

A23.4 **Statutory declarations**

Where a defendant is convicted in absence, having not known of
the summons or proceedings, he may apply to the court for the
conviction to be set aside. Section 14 of the Magistrates' Courts
Act 1980 provides:

Magistrates' Courts Act 1980, s 14

14 Proceedings invalid where accused did not know of them

(1) Where a summons has been issued under section 1 above and a magistrates' court has begun to try the information to which the summons
relates, then, if—
   (a) the accused, at any time during or after the trial, makes a statutory
   declaration that he did not know of the summons or the proceedings until a date specified in the declaration, being a date after the
   court has begun to try the information; and
   (b) within 21 days of that date the declaration is served on the designated officer for the court, without prejudice to the validity of the
   information,
the summons and all subsequent proceedings shall be void.

(2) For the purposes of subsection (1) above a statutory declaration shall
be deemed to be duly served on the designated officer if it is delivered
to him, or left at his office, or is sent in a registered letter or by the
recorded delivery service addressed to him at his office.

(3) If on the application of the accused it appears to a magistrates' court
(which for this purpose may be composed of a single justice) that it was
not reasonable to expect the accused to serve such a statutory declaration as is mentioned in subsection (1) above within the period allowed
by that subsection, the court may accept service of such a declaration
by the accused after that period has expired; and a statutory declaration
accepted under this subsection shall be deemed to have been served as
required by that subsection.

(4) Where any proceedings have become void by virtue of subsection (1)
above, the information shall not be tried again by any of the same justices.

The procedure is provided for by Criminal Procedure Rule 24.17:

Criminal Procedure Rules, r 24.17

(1) This rule applies where—
   (a) the case started with—
      (i) an information and summons, or
      (ii) a written charge and requisition, or
      (iii) a written charge and single justice procedure notice; and
   (b) under section 14 of the Magistrates' Courts Act 1980, the defendant makes a statutory declaration of not having found out about the
   case until after the trial began.

---

(2) The defendant must
  (a) serve such a declaration on the court officer—
    (i) not more than 21 days after the date of finding out about the case; or
    (ii) with an explanation for the delay, if serving it more than 21 days after that date.
  (b) serve with the declaration one of the following, as appropriate, if the case began with a written charge and single justice procedure notice—
    (i) a notice under rule 24.9(4)(a) (notice of guilty plea), with any representations that the defendant wants the court to consider and a statement of the defendant's assets and other financial circumstances, as required by that rule,
    (ii) a notice under rule 24.9(4)(b) (notice of intention to plead guilty at a hearing before a court comprising more than one justice), or
    (iii) a notice under rule 24.9(4)(c) (notice of intention to plead not guilty.
(3) The court may extend that time limit, even after it has expired—
  (a) at a hearing, in public or in private; or
  (b) without a hearing.

In relation to the single justice procedure introduced by section 16A Magistrates' Courts Act 1980 a similar provision for the making of a statutory declaration is contained in section 16E.

 See *Blackstone's Criminal Practice 2017* **D22**

A24 **Pre-Charge Hearings**

A24.1 **Funding**

Advocacy assistance, without a means test, is available for all the hearings in this section.

A24.2 **Warrants of further detention and extended warrants of further detention**

Police and Criminal Evidence Act 1984, ss 43 and 44

43

(1) Where, on an application on oath made by a constable and supported by an information, a magistrates' court is satisfied that there are reasonable grounds for believing that the further detention of the person to whom the application relates is justified, it may issue a warrant of further detention authorising the keeping of that person in police detention.

(2) A court may not hear an application for a warrant of further detention unless the person to whom the application relates—
   (a) has been furnished with a copy of the information; and
   (b) has been brought before the court for the hearing ....
   ...

(4) A person's further detention is only justified for the purposes of this section or section 44 below if—
   (a) his detention without charge is necessary to secure or preserve evidence relating to an offence for which he is under arrest or to obtain such evidence by questioning him;
   (b) an offence for which he is under arrest is an indictable offence ; and
   (c) the investigation is being conducted diligently and expeditiously.

(5) Subject to subsection (7) below, an application for a warrant of further detention may be made—
   (a) at any time before the expiry of 36 hours after the relevant time; or
   (b) in a case where—
      (i) it is not practicable for the magistrates' court to which the application will be made to sit at the expiry of 36 hours after the relevant time; but
      (ii) the court will sit during the 6 hours following the end of that period,
   at any time before the expiry of the said 6 hours ....

(7) If—
   (a) an application for a warrant of further detention is made after the expiry of 36 hours after the relevant time; and
   (b) it appears to the magistrates' court that it would have been reasonable for the police to make it before the expiry of that period,
   the court shall dismiss the application.

---

(8) Where on an application such as is mentioned in subsection (1) above a magistrates' court is not satisfied that there are reasonable grounds for believing that the further detention of the person to whom the application relates is justified, it shall be its duty—
    (a) to refuse the application; or
    (b) to adjourn the hearing of it until a time not later than 36 hours after the relevant time.

(9) The person to whom the application relates may be kept in police detention during the adjournment.

(10) A warrant of further detention shall—
    (a) state the time at which it is issued;
    (b) authorise the keeping in police detention of the person to whom it relates for the period stated in it.

(11) Subject to subsection (12) below, the period stated in a warrant of further detention shall be such period as the magistrates' court thinks fit, having regard to the evidence before it.

(12) The period shall not be longer than 36 hours.

(13) If it is proposed to transfer a person in police detention to a police area other than that in which he is detained when the application for a warrant of further detention is made, the court hearing the application shall have regard to the distance and the time the journey would take.

(14) Any information submitted in support of an application under this section shall state—
    (a) the nature of the offence for which the person to whom the application relates has been arrested;
    (b) the general nature of the evidence on which that person was arrested;
    (c) what inquiries relating to the offence have been made by the police and what further inquiries are proposed by them;
    (d) the reasons for believing the continued detention of that person to be necessary for the purposes of such further inquiries.

(15) Where an application under this section is refused, the person to whom the application relates shall forthwith be charged or, subject to subsection (16) below, released, either on bail or without bail.

(16) A person need not be released under subsection (15) above—
    (a) before the expiry of 24 hours after the relevant time; or
    (b) before the expiry of any longer period for which his continued detention is or has been authorised under section 42 above.

(17) Where an application under this section is refused, no further application shall be made under this section in respect of the person to whom the refusal relates, unless supported by evidence which has come to light since the refusal.

44 Extension of warrants of further detention

(1) On an application on oath made by a constable and supported by an information a magistrates' court may extend a warrant of further detention issued under section 43 above if it is satisfied that there are reasonable grounds for believing that the further detention of the person to whom the application relates is justified.

(2) Subject to subsection (3) below, the period for which a warrant of further detention may be extended shall be such period as the court thinks fit, having regard to the evidence before it.

(3) The period shall not—
   (a) be longer than 36 hours; or
   (b) end later than 96 hours after the relevant time.

(4) Where a warrant of further detention has been extended under subsection (1) above, or further extended under this subsection, for a period ending before 96 hours after the relevant time, on an application such as is mentioned in that subsection a magistrates' court may further extend the warrant if it is satisfied as there mentioned; and subsections (2) and (3) above apply to such further extensions as they apply to extensions under subsection (1) above.

(5) A warrant of further detention shall, if extended or further extended under this section, be endorsed with a note of the period of the extension.

(6) Subsections (2), (3) and (14) of section 43 above shall apply to an application made under this section as they apply to an application made under that section.

(7) Where an application under this section is refused, the person to whom the application relates shall forthwith be charged or, subject to subsection (8) below, released, either on bail or without bail.

(8) A person need not be released under subsection (7) above before the expiry of any period for which a warrant of further detention issued in relation to him has been extended or further extended on an earlier application made under this section.

A24.3 Warrants of further detention and extensions in terrorist cases

Terrorism Act 2000, s 41

Arrest without warrant

(1) A constable may arrest without a warrant a person whom he reasonably suspects to be a terrorist.

(2) Where a person is arrested under this section the provisions of Schedule 8 (detention: treatment, review and extension) shall apply.

(3) Subject to subsections (4) to (7), a person detained under this section shall (unless detained under any other power) be released not later than the end of the period of 48 hours beginning—.
   (a) with the time of his arrest under this section, or.
   (b) if he was being detained under Schedule 7 when he was arrested under this section, with the time when his examination under that Schedule began.

(4) If on a review of a person's detention under Part II of Schedule 8 the review officer does not authorise continued detention, the person shall (unless detained in accordance with subsection (5) or (6) or under any other power) be released.

---

(5) Where a police officer intends to make an application for a warrant under paragraph 29 of Schedule 8 extending a person's detention, the person may be detained pending the making of the application.

(6) Where an application has been made under paragraph 29 or 36 of Schedule 8 in respect of a person's detention, he may be detained pending the conclusion of proceedings on the application.

(7) Where an application under paragraph 29 or 36 of Schedule 8 is granted in respect of a person's detention, he may be detained, subject to paragraph 37 of that Schedule, during the period specified in the warrant.

(8) The refusal of an application in respect of a person's detention under paragraph 29 or 36 of Schedule 8 shall not prevent his continued detention in accordance with this section.

Schedule 8 Terrorism Act 2000, paras 29–36

29 (1) Each of the following—

  (a) in England and Wales, a Crown Prosecutor, …

  (d) in any part of the United Kingdom, a police officer of at least the rank of superintendent,

  may apply to a judicial authority for the issue of a warrant of further detention under this Part.

(2) A warrant of further detention—

  (a) shall authorise the further detention under section 41 of a specified person for a specified period, and

  (b) shall state the time at which it is issued.

(3) Subject to sub-paragraph (3A) and paragraph 36, the specified period in relation to a person shall be the period of seven days beginning—

  (a) with the time of his arrest under section 41, or

  (b) if he was being detained under Schedule 7 when he was arrested under section 41, with the time when his examination under that Schedule began.

(3A) A judicial authority may issue a warrant of further detention in relation to a person which specifies a shorter period as the period for which that person's further detention is authorised if—

  (a) the application for the warrant is an application for a warrant specifying a shorter period; or

  (b) the judicial authority is satisfied that there are circumstances that would make it inappropriate for the specified period to be as long as the period of seven days mentioned in sub-paragraph (3)

(4) In this Part 'judicial authority' means—

  (a) in England and Wales, … a District Judge (Magistrates' Courts) who is designated for the purpose of this Part by the Lord Chief Justice of England and Wales

Time limit

30 (1) An application for a warrant shall be made—

  (a) during the period mentioned in section 41(3), or

  (b) within six hours of the end of that period.

    (2) The judicial authority hearing an application made by virtue of sub-paragraph (1)(b) shall dismiss the application if he considers that it would have been reasonably practicable to make it during the period mentioned in section 41(3).

    (3) For the purposes of this Schedule, an application for a warrant is made when written or oral notice of an intention to make the application is given to a judicial authority.

Notice

31 An application for a warrant may not be heard unless the person to whom it relates has been given a notice stating—

    (a) that the application has been made,

    (b) the time at which the application was made,

    (c) the time at which it is to be heard, and

    (d) the grounds upon which further detention is sought.

Grounds for extension

32 (1) A judicial authority may issue a warrant of further detention only if satisfied that—

    (a) there are reasonable grounds for believing that the further detention of the person to whom the application relates is necessary as mentioned in sub-paragraph (1A), and

    (b) the investigation in connection with which the person is detained is being conducted diligently and expeditiously.

    (1A) The further detention of a person is necessary as mentioned in this sub-paragraph if it is necessary—

    (a) to obtain relevant evidence whether by questioning him or otherwise;

    (b) to preserve relevant evidence; or

    (c) pending the result of an examination or analysis of any relevant evidence or of anything the examination or analysis of which is to be or is being carried out with a view to obtaining relevant evidence.

    (2) In this paragraph 'relevant evidence' means, in relation to the person to whom the application relates, evidence which—

    (a) relates to his commission of an offence under any of the provisions mentioned in section 40(1)(a), or

    (b) indicates that he is a person falling within section 40(1)(b) …

Representation

33 (3) A judicial authority may exclude any of the following persons from any part of the hearing—

    (a) the person to whom the application relates;

    (b) anyone representing him.

    (4) A judicial authority may, after giving an opportunity for representations to be made by or on behalf of the applicant and the person to whom the application relates, direct—

    (a) that the hearing of the application must be conducted, and

    (b) that all representations by or on behalf of a person for the purposes of the hearing must be made,

by such means (whether a live television link or other means) falling within sub-paragraph (5) as may be specified in the direction and not in the presence (apart from by those means) of the applicant, of the person to whom the application relates or of any legal representative of that person.

(5) A means of conducting the hearing and of making representations falls within this sub-paragraph if it allows the person to whom the application relates and any legal representative of his (without being present at the hearing and to the extent that they are not excluded from it under sub-paragraph (3))—

    (a) to see and hear the judicial authority and the making of representations to it by other persons; and

    (b) to be seen and heard by the judicial authority.

(6) If the person to whom the application relates wishes to make representations about whether a direction should be given under sub-paragraph (4), he must do so by using the facilities that will be used if the judicial authority decides to give a direction under that sub-paragraph.

(7) Sub-paragraph (2) applies to the hearing of representations about whether a direction should be given under sub-paragraph (4) in the case of any application as it applies to a hearing of the application ...

(9) If in a case where it has power to do so a judicial authority decides not to give a direction under sub-paragraph (4), it shall state its reasons for not giving it.

Information

34 (1) The person who has made an application for a warrant may apply to the judicial authority for an order that specified information upon which he intends to rely be withheld from—

    (a) the person to whom the application relates, and

    (b) anyone representing him.

(2) Subject to sub-paragraph (3), a judicial authority may make an order under sub-paragraph (1) in relation to specified information only if satisfied that there are reasonable grounds for believing that if the information were disclosed—

    (a) evidence of an offence under any of the provisions mentioned in section 40(1)(a) would be interfered with or harmed,

    (b) the recovery of property obtained as a result of an offence under any of those provisions would be hindered,

    (c) the recovery of property in respect of which a forfeiture order could be made under section 23 or 23A would be hindered,

    (d) the apprehension, prosecution or conviction of a person who is suspected of falling within section 40(1)(a) or (b) would be made more difficult as a result of his being alerted,

    (e) the prevention of an act of terrorism would be made more difficult as a result of a person being alerted,

    (f) the gathering of information about the commission, preparation or instigation of an act of terrorism would be interfered with, or

    (g) a person would be interfered with or physically injured.

(3) A judicial authority may also make an order under sub-paragraph (1) in relation to specified information if satisfied that there are reasonable grounds for believing that—

    (a) the detained person has benefited from his criminal conduct, and

      (b) the recovery of the value of the property constituting the benefit would be hindered if the information were disclosed.

(3A) For the purposes of sub-paragraph (3) the question whether a person has benefited from his criminal conduct is to be decided in accordance with Part 2 or 3 of the Proceeds of Crime Act 2002.

  (4) The judicial authority shall direct that the following be excluded from the hearing of the application under this paragraph—

      (a) the person to whom the application for a warrant relates, and

      (b) anyone representing him.

Adjournments

35 (1) A judicial authority may adjourn the hearing of an application for a warrant only if the hearing is adjourned to a date before the expiry of the period mentioned in section 41(3).

  (2) This paragraph shall not apply to an adjournment under paragraph 33(2).

Extensions of warrants

36 (1) Each of the following—

      (a) in England and Wales, a Crown Prosecutor, ...

      (d) in any part of the United Kingdom, a police officer of at least the rank of superintendent,

    may apply ... for the extension or further extension of the period specified in a warrant of further detention.

(1A) The person to whom an application under sub-paragraph (1) may be made is—

      (a) a judicial authority;

(1B) An application for the extension or further extension of a period falls within this sub-paragraph if—

      (a) the grant of the application otherwise than in accordance with sub-paragraph (3AA)(b) would extend that period to a time that is no more than 14 days after the relevant time;

  (2) Where the period specified is extended, the warrant shall be endorsed with a note stating the new specified period.

  (3) Subject to sub-paragraph (3AA), the period by which the specified period is extended or further extended shall be the period which—

      (a) begins with the time specified in sub-paragraph (3A); and

      (b) ends with whichever is the earlier of—

         (i) the end of the period of seven days beginning with that time; and

         (ii) the end of the period of 14 days beginning with the relevant time.

(3A) The time referred to in sub-paragraph (3)(a) is—

      (a) in the case of a warrant specifying a period which has not previously been extended under this paragraph, the end of the period specified in the warrant, and

      (b) in any other case, the end of the period for which the period specified in the warrant was last extended under this paragraph.

(3AA) A judicial authority … may extend or further extend the period specified in a warrant by a shorter period than is required by sub-paragraph (3) if—
  (a) the application for the extension is an application for an extension by a period that is shorter than is so required; or
  (b) the judicial authority … is satisfied that there are circumstances that would make it inappropriate for the period of the extension to be as long as the period so required.
(3B) In this paragraph 'the relevant time', in relation to a person, means—
  (a) the time of his arrest under section 41, or
  (b) if he was being detained under Schedule 7 when he was arrested under section 41, the time when his examination under that Schedule began.
(4) Paragraphs 30(3) and 31 to 34 shall apply to an application under this paragraph as they apply to an application for a warrant of further detention …
(5) A judicial authority … may adjourn the hearing of an application under sub-paragraph (1) only if the hearing is adjourned to a date before the expiry of the period specified in the warrant.
(6) Sub-paragraph (5) shall not apply to an adjournment under paragraph 33(2).

A24.4 Appeal against pre-charge bail conditions

An application to the court, by way of appeal, from the decision to impose conditions on the grant of police bail, is provided for by section 47 Police and Criminal Evidence Act 1984.

Police and Criminal Evidence Act 1984, s 47

(1C) Subsections (1D) to (1F) below apply where a person released on bail under section 37, 37C(2)(b) or 37CA(2)(b) above is on bail subject to conditions.......
(1E) A magistrates' court may, on an application by or on behalf of the person, vary the conditions of bail; and in this subsection 'vary' has the same meaning as in the Bail Act 1976.
(1F) Where a magistrates' court varies the conditions of bail under subsection (1E) above, that bail shall not lapse but shall continue subject to the conditions as so varied.

The procedure is provided for by rule 14 of the Criminal Procedure Rules:

Criminal Procedure Rules, r 14.6

14.6—(1) This rule applies where a party wants a magistrates' court to reconsider a bail decision by a police officer.

(2) An application under this rule must be made to—
- (a) the magistrates' court to whose custody the defendant is under a duty to surrender, if any; or
- (b) any magistrates' court acting for the police officer's local justice area, in any other case.

(3) The applicant party must—
- (a) apply in writing; and
- (b) serve the application on—
  - (i) the court officer,
  - (ii) the other party, and
  - (iii) any surety affected or proposed.

(4) The application must—
- (a) specify—
  - (i) the decision that the applicant wants the court to make,
  - (ii) each offence charged, or for which the defendant was arrested, and
  - (iii) the police bail decision to be reconsidered and the reasons given for it;
- (b) explain, as appropriate—
  - (i) why the court should grant bail itself, or withdraw it, or impose or vary a condition, and
  - (ii) if the applicant is the prosecutor, what material information has become available since the police bail decision was made;
- (c) propose the terms of any suggested condition of bail; and
- (d) if the applicant wants an earlier hearing than paragraph (7) requires, ask for that, and explain why it is needed …

(7) Unless the court otherwise directs, the court officer must arrange for the court to hear the application as soon as practicable and in any event—
- (a) if it is an application to withdraw bail, no later than the second business day after it was served;
- (b) in any other case, no later than the fifth business day after it was served.

(8) The court may—
- (a) vary or waive a time limit under this rule;
- (b) allow an application to be in a different form to one set out in the Practice Direction;
- (c) if rule 14.2 allows, determine without a hearing an application to vary a condition.

A25 **Remand Periods**

A25.1 **Continuing investigations**

The power under section 128(7) and (8) MCA 2000 to remand to police custody does not arise until the court has decided that bail cannot be granted and must relate to allegations that are not already before the court. The court should then consider whether the remand should be to custody or to a police station, depending on whether further evidence is likely to be obtained, and if to a police station how long is required, with three days being the maximum for an adult and 24 hours for a youth.

Under section 152 Criminal Justice Act 1988 the courts have power to commit a person facing certain drugs offences to police custody for up to 192 hours.

A25.2 **Prior to conviction**

A25.2.1 *In custody*

The courts may remand to custody for a maximum of eight clear days on first remand.

A defendant may subsequently be remanded to custody for up to 28 clear days, provided the next stage in the proceedings will be dealt with. If it is known that the next stage cannot be dealt with in that period then eight-day remands will have to follow, until such time as completion of the next stage within 28 days is achievable.

However, the defendant can agree not to be produced for these hearings.

A further subsequent remand to custody for 28 clear days is allowed if the defendant is already in custody serving a sentence and will not be released before that date.

A25.2.2 *On bail*

The courts may remand on bail for eight days, or longer if the defendant consents.

A25.3 **Upon sending**

After a case has been sent to the Crown Court, the magistrates have the power to adjourn for a period up to the date of trial. It is important to note that the expression 'remand' has a particular meaning within the 1980 Act, and the court is not remanding a person when it sends someone for trial—therefore, when a court sends a person

for trial during his first appearance, it can do so in custody for a
period in excess of eight days.

A25.4 Illness or accident

Section 129 of the Magistrates' Courts Act 1980 allows for the
remands of persons not produced before the court due to illness
or accident. The court must have 'solid grounds' to justify an
opinion that failure to be produced was due to illness or accident
(*R v Liverpool Justices, ex p Grogan*, The Times, 8 October 1990).
A remand under this provision may be of any length (see **A23.2**).

A25.5 During trial

No limit (MCA 1980, s 10).

A25.6 Post-conviction

Maximum three weeks if in custody; four weeks if on bail.

See *Blackstone's Criminal Practice 2017* **D5.21–D5.37**

A26 **Reporting Restrictions**

A26.1 **Youths**

Section 39 of the Children and Young Persons Act 1933 has been disapplied from criminal proceedings. The law in relation to youth defendants in the adult court is set out in section 45 Youth Justice and Criminal Evidence Act 1999 (see **B8**).

A26.1.1 *Lifetime reporting restrictions in criminal proceedings for witnesses and victims under 18*

Section 45A Youth Justice and Criminal Evidence Act 1999 provides:

Youth Justice and Criminal Evidence Act 1999, s 45A

Power to restrict reporting of criminal proceedings for lifetime of witnesses and victims under 18

(1) This section applies in relation to—
   (a) any criminal proceedings in any court (other than a service court) in England and Wales, and
   (b) any proceedings (whether in the United Kingdom or elsewhere) in any service court.

(2) The court may make a direction ('a reporting direction') that no matter relating to a person mentioned in subsection (3) shall during that person's lifetime be included in any publication if it is likely to lead members of the public to identify that person as being concerned in the proceedings.

(3) A reporting direction may be made only in respect of a person who is under the age of 18 when the proceedings commence and who is—
   (a) a witness, other than an accused, in the proceedings;
   (b) a person against whom the offence, which is the subject of the proceedings, is alleged to have been committed.

(4) For the purposes of subsection (2), matters relating to a person in respect of whom the reporting direction is made include—
   (a) the person's name,
   (b) the person's address,
   (c) the identity of any school or other educational establishment attended by the person,
   (d) the identity of any place of work of the person, and
   (e) any still or moving picture of the person.

(5) The court may make a reporting direction in respect of a person only if it is satisfied that—
   (a) the quality of any evidence given by the person, or
   (b) the level of co-operation given by the person to any party to the proceedings in connection with that party's preparation of its case, is likely to be diminished by reason of fear or distress on the part of the person in connection with being identified by members of the public as a person concerned in the proceedings.

---

(6) In determining whether subsection (5) is satisfied, the court must in particular take into account—
  (a) the nature and alleged circumstances of the offence to which the proceedings relate;
  (b) the age of the person;
  (c) such of the following as appear to the court to be relevant—
      (i) the social and cultural background and ethnic origins of the person,
      (ii) the domestic, educational and employment circumstances of the person, and
      (iii) any religious beliefs or political opinions of the person;
  (d) any behaviour towards the person on the part of—
      (i) an accused,
      (ii) members of the family or associates of an accused, or
      (iii) any other person who is likely to be an accused or a witness in the proceedings.

(7) In determining that question the court must in addition consider any views expressed—
  (a) by the person in respect of whom the reporting restriction may be made, and
  (b) where that person is under the age of 16, by an appropriate person other than an accused.

(8) In determining whether to make a reporting direction in respect of a person, the court must have regard to—
  (a) the welfare of that person,
  (b) whether it would be in the interests of justice to make the direction, and
  (c) the public interest in avoiding the imposition of a substantial and unreasonable restriction on the reporting of the proceedings.

(9) A reporting direction may be revoked by the court or an appellate court.

(10) The court or an appellate court may by direction ('an excepting direction') dispense, to any extent specified in the excepting direction, with the restrictions imposed by a reporting direction.

(11) The court or an appellate court may only make an excepting direction if—
  (a) it is satisfied that it is necessary in the interests of justice to do so, or
  (b) it is satisfied that—
      (i) the effect of the reporting direction is to impose a substantial and unreasonable restriction on the reporting of the proceedings, and
      (ii) it is in the public interest to remove or relax that restriction.

(12) No excepting direction shall be given under subsection (11)(b) by reason only of the fact that the proceedings have been determined in any way or have been abandoned.

(13) In determining whether to make an excepting direction in respect of a person, the court or the appellate court must have regard to the welfare of that person.

(14) An excepting direction—
  (a) may be given at the time the reporting direction is given or subsequently, and
  (b) may be varied or revoked by the court or an appellate court.

A26.2 **Adults**

A26.2.1 *Withholding names or other details*

Under section 11 of the Contempt of Court Act 1981, where a court exercises its powers to allow a name or any other matter to be withheld from the public in criminal proceedings, the court may make such directions as are necessary prohibiting the publication of that name or matter in connection with the proceedings.

The Judicial College has published the following guidance:

> 4.4 ... Section 11 can only be invoked where the court allows a name or matter to be withheld from being mentioned in open court. It follows that there is no power to prohibit publication of any name or other matter which has been given in open court in the proceedings. For this reason, applications for an order under s. 11 may be heard in private provided there is good reason for doing so.
>
> Section 11 does not itself give the court power to withhold a name or other matter from the public. The power to do this must exist either at common law or from some other statutory provision.

Consistent with the requirement to protect the open justice principle and freedom of expression, courts should only make an order under section 11 where the nature or circumstances of the proceedings are such that hearing all evidence in open court would frustrate or render impractical the administration of justice. It follows that a defendant in a criminal trial must be named save in rare circumstances. It is not appropriate therefore to invoke the section 11 power to withhold matters for the benefit of a defendant's feelings or comfort or to prevent financial damage, or damage to reputation resulting from proceedings concerning a person's business. Nor can the power be invoked to prevent identification and embarrassment of the defendant's children, because of the defendant's public profile.

Where the ground for seeking a section 11 order is that the identification of a witness or a defendant will expose that person to a real and immediate risk to his life, engaging the state's duty to protect life under Article 2 ECHR, the court will consider whether the fear is objectively well-founded. In practical terms, the applicant will have to provide clear and cogent evidence to show that publication of his name will create or materially increase a risk of death or serious injury.

In appropriate cases consideration should be given to section 46 of the Youth Justice and Criminal Evidence Act 1999 if the evidence of a witness may be affected by fear that the identity of her children may become known. *Re ITN News*, [2013] EWCA Crim

773 (Admin) confirms that this does not follow automatically from a special measures direction but requires a separate fact-finding exercise.

When considering an application under the old law it was held that the court must balance the Article 10 rights of free expression and the Article 8 rights of the child. Particular weight is attached to the interests of the child if their interests were likely on the facts to be harmed, but there was a presumption that there should be open justice. In *R (A) v Lowestoft Magistrates' Court* [2013] EWHC 659 an elected councillor with a caution already was drunk in charge of the child. The child was under three years of age and would know nothing of the publicity. By contrast, in *Z v News Group Newspapers* [2013] EWHC 1150 (Fam), when a mother of eight children was involved in a benefit fraud, claiming by reference to disabilities and incapacities of those children, all of whom were innocent of any involvement, the balance was in favour of preventing the children (and so the mother) being named. The heavy burden to prevent publicity had been met, not least because the medical conditions of the children would be extensively examined and some of them were vulnerable. However, once the mother had been convicted the balance was in favour of naming her.

In rare circumstances, the right to private and family life under Article 8 ECHR may mean that normal media reporting has to be curtailed, but injunctions to cover these cases are dealt with by the High Court rather than the criminal courts. In *A v BBC* [2014] UKSC 325 the Supreme Court held that section 11 of the Contempt of Court Act 1981 could be used to protect a person's ECHR rights and not only to protect the public interest. It was not necessary for a restriction to have been in place for those who attended court. In this case the identification of the defendant would, on her deportation, have endangered her Article 3 rights and given her new grounds to seek asylum.

The court may in appropriate circumstances limit information to protect a person's safety or commercial interests, or to prevent disclosure of intimate personal details of a complainant. Each case turned on its own facts and involved a balancing exercise.

A26.2.2 *Postponement of reports*

Section 4(2) of the Contempt of Court Act 1981 provides:

Contempt of Court Act 1981, s 4(2)

4 Contemporary reports of proceedings

(2) In any such proceedings the court may, where it appears to be necessary for avoiding a substantial risk of prejudice to the administration of justice in those proceedings, or in any other proceedings pending or imminent, order that the publication of any report of the proceedings, or any part of the proceedings, be postponed for such period as the court thinks necessary for that purpose.

...

A27 Sending and Transfer for Trial

A27.1 Overview

In the following instances the court may decline or be deprived of jurisdiction to try a matter:

- indictable-only matters—sent to the Crown Court;
- either-way matters where jurisdiction is declined or the defendant has elected Crown Court trial—sent to the Crown Court; transfer cases—transferred to the Crown Court;
- voluntary bill of indictment (not covered in this book).

Method	Notes
Sending. Section 51 of the Crime and Disorder Act 1998	The court will send any indictable-only matter, along with any related either-way matters. This may involve sending one or more co-defendants. *Note*: A sending is not a remand within the meaning of MCA 1980, ss 128, 128A, and therefore the initial eight-day limitation on a remand in custody does not apply.
	An either-way offence is related to an indictable offence if the charge for the either-way offence could be joined in the same indictment as the charge for the indictable offence.
	A summary offence is related to an indictable offence if it arises out of circumstances which are the same as or connected with those giving rise to the indictable offence. The court can send related summary offences if they are imprisonable or carry discretionary or obligatory disqualification from driving.
	It does not matter that all matters are not sent on the same occasion.
	In the case of a youth charged with an adult (not necessarily on the same occasion), the youth will be sent if it is in the interests of justice to try him with the adult. There is no power to send a case to the Crown Court in the absence of a defendant, even if that person is legally represented.
Transfer cases. *Note*: See ss 51B and 51C of the Crime and Disorder Act 1998	Applicable to fraud cases and child cases.

Where a person is arrested for an either-way offence and commits a summary-only assault whilst at the police station, there is no basis for dealing with the summary-only matter at the Crown Court; it did not arise out of the same facts, neither was it part of a series of offences, so section 40(1) of the Criminal Justice Act 1988 did not apply (*R v Walton* [2011] EWCA Crim 2832).

A27.2 Case management

When sending a case to the Crown Court the magistrates have certain management responsibilities.

Criminal Procedure Rules, r 9.7

(5) If the court sends the defendant to the Crown Court for trial, it must—
  (a) ask whether the defendant intends to plead guilty in the Crown Court and—
    (i) if the answer is 'yes', make arrangements for the Crown Court to take the defendant's plea as soon as possible, or
    (ii) if the defendant does not answer, or the answer is 'no', make arrangements for a case management hearing in the Crown Court; and
  (b) give any other ancillary directions.

A27.3 Better case management

The Senior Presiding Judge has issued guidance on the suggested Defence Time Table:

Defendant charged	
Custody	**Bail**
Defence representative should: • consider initial details of the prosecution case (IDPC) • take instructions on bail/plea(s))/venue for trial; • apply for legal aid; • notify court and CPS of contact details of representative responsible for the case.	**Defence representative should:** • consider IDPC; • take instructions on bail/plea)s)/venue for trial; • apply for legal aid; • notify court and CPS of contact details of representative responsible for the case; **AND** • **communicate with CPS** to proactively explore pleas and issues including any additional information necessary to address them.

↓

Magistrates' court hearing	
BEFORE hearing—help the CPS complete the Better Case Management (BCM) questionnaire [and advise on alternative pleas, discount for guilty plea, and about any linked offences]	
At hearing—defence actions	
• Plea before venue [for allocation see **A4.6**]. • Guilty plea—consider requirement for a pre-sentence report (PSR) [for grounds for PSR see D28.2]. • Bail application.	• Not guilty plea/no indication—identify issues and agree with the CPS any necessary court directions that will assist an effective plea and trial preparation hearing (PTPH) [including the need for further evidence and for an interpreter; magistrates are discouraged from making specific orders]. • Assist the court to finalise the BCM questionnaire.

Magistrates should:

send to the **PTPH** no sooner than 28 days after the magistrates' court hearing (but not more than 35 days) UNLESS there are witnesses under 10 years of age; or section 28 of the Youth Justice and Criminal Evidence Act 1999 applies; or the offence is murder or a terrorism case where BCM processes have been adapted).

A27.4 Relevant legislation

Crime and Disorder Act 1998, ss 50A–51D

50A Order of consideration for either-way offences

(1) Where an adult appears or is brought before a magistrates' court charged with an either-way offence (the 'relevant offence'), the court shall proceed in the manner described in this section.

(2) If notice is given in respect of the relevant offence under section 51B or 51C below, the court shall deal with the offence as provided in section 51 below.

(3) Otherwise—

    (a) if the adult (or another adult with whom the adult is charged jointly with the relevant offence) is or has been sent to the Crown Court for trial for an offence under section 51(2)(a) or 51(2)(c) below—

        (i) the court shall first consider the relevant offence under subsection (3), (4), (5) or, as the case may be, (6) of section 51 below and, where applicable, deal with it under that subsection;

        (ii) if the adult is not sent to the Crown Court for trial for the relevant offence by virtue of sub-paragraph (i) above, the court shall then proceed to deal with the relevant offence in accordance with sections 17A to 23 of the 1980 Act;

    (b) in all other cases—

        (i) the court shall first consider the relevant offence under sections 17A to 20 (excluding subsections (8) and (9) of section 20) of the 1980 Act;

        (ii) if, by virtue of sub-paragraph (i) above, the court would be required to proceed in relation to the offence as mentioned in section 17A(6), 17B(2)(c) or 20(7) of that Act (indication of guilty plea), it shall proceed as so required (and, accordingly, shall not consider the offence under section 51 or 51A below);

        (iii) if sub-paragraph (ii) above does not apply—

    (a) the court shall consider the relevant offence under sections 51 and 51A below and, where applicable, deal with it under the relevant section;

    (b) if the adult is not sent to the Crown Court for trial for the relevant offence by virtue of paragraph (a) of this sub-paragraph, the court shall then proceed to deal with the relevant offence as contemplated by section 20(9) or, as the case may be, section 21 of the 1980 Act.

(4) Subsection (3) above is subject to any requirement to proceed as mentioned in subsections (2) or (6)(a) of section 22 of the 1980 Act (certain offences where value involved is small).

(5) Nothing in this section shall prevent the court from committing the adult to the Crown Court for sentence pursuant to any enactment, if he is convicted of the relevant offence.

51 Sending cases to the Crown Court: adults

(1) Where an adult appears or is brought before a magistrates' court ('the court') charged with an offence and any of the conditions mentioned in subsection (2) below is satisfied, the court shall send him forthwith to the Crown Court for trial for the offence.

(2) Those conditions are—

    (a) that the offence is an offence triable only on indictment other than one in respect of which notice has been given under section 51B or 51C below;

    (b) that the offence is an either-way offence and the court is required under section 20(9)(b), 21, 22A(2)(b), 23(4)(b) or (5) or 25(2D) of the Magistrates' Courts Act 1980 to proceed in relation to the offence in accordance with subsection (1) above;

    (c) that notice is given to the court under section 51B or 51C below in respect of the offence.

(3) Where the court sends an adult for trial under subsection (1) above, it shall at the same time send him to the Crown Court for trial for any either-way or summary offence with which he is charged and which—

    (a) (if it is an either-way offence) appears to the court to be related to the offence mentioned in subsection (1) above; or

    (b) (if it is a summary offence) appears to the court to be related to the offence mentioned in subsection (1) above or to the either-way offence, and which fulfils the requisite condition (as defined in subsection (11) below).

(4) Where an adult who has been sent for trial under subsection (1) above subsequently appears or is brought before a magistrates' court charged with an either-way or summary offence which—

    (a) appears to the court to be related to the offence mentioned in subsection (1) above; and

    (b) (in the case of a summary offence) fulfils the requisite condition, the court may send him forthwith to the Crown Court for trial for the either-way or summary offence.

(5) Where—

    (a) the court sends an adult ('A') for trial under subsection (1) or (3) above;

    (b) another adult appears or is brought before the court on the same or a subsequent occasion charged jointly with A with an either-way offence; and

    (c) that offence appears to the court to be related to an offence for which A was sent for trial under subsection (1) or (3) above, the court shall where it is the same occasion, and may where it is a subsequent occasion, send the other adult forthwith to the Crown Court for trial for the either-way offence.

(6) Where the court sends an adult for trial under subsection (5) above, it shall at the same time send him to the Crown Court for trial for any either-way or summary offence with which he is charged and which—

  (a) (if it is an either-way offence) appears to the court to be related to the offence for which he is sent for trial; and

  (b) (if it is a summary offence) appears to the court to be related to the offence for which he is sent for trial or to the either-way offence, and which fulfils the requisite condition.

(7) Where—

  (a) the court sends an adult ('A') for trial under subsection (1), (3) or (5) above; and

  (b) a child or young person appears or is brought before the court on the same or a subsequent occasion charged jointly with A with an indictable offence for which A is sent for trial under subsection (1), (3) or (5) above, or an indictable offence which appears to the court to be related to that offence,

  the court shall, if it considers it necessary in the interests of justice to do so, send the child or young person forthwith to the Crown Court for trial for the indictable offence.

(8) Where the court sends a child or young person for trial under subsection (7) above, it may at the same time send him to the Crown Court for trial for any indictable or summary offence with which he is charged and which—

  (a) (if it is an indictable offence) appears to the court to be related to the offence for which he is sent for trial; and

  (b) (if it is a summary offence) appears to the court to be related to the offence for which he is sent for trial or to the indictable offence, and which fulfils the requisite condition.

(9) Subsections (7) and (8) above are subject to sections 24A and 24B of the Magistrates' Courts Act 1980 (which provide for certain cases involving children and young persons to be tried summarily).

(10) The trial of the information charging any summary offence for which a person is sent for trial under this section shall be treated as if the court had adjourned it under section 10 of the 1980 Act and had not fixed the time and place for its resumption.

(11) A summary offence fulfils the requisite condition if it is punishable with imprisonment or involves obligatory or discretionary disqualification from driving.

(12) In the case of an adult charged with an offence—

  (a) if the offence satisfies paragraph (c) of subsection (2) above, the offence shall be dealt with under subsection (1) above and not under any other provision of this section or section 51A below;

  (b) subject to paragraph (a) above, if the offence is one in respect of which the court is required to, or would decide to, send the adult to the Crown Court under—

    (i) subsection (5) above; or

    (ii) subsection (6) of section 51A below,

the offence shall be dealt with under that subsection and not under any other provision of this section or section 51A below.

(13) The functions of a magistrates' court under this section, and its related functions under section 51D below, may be discharged by a single justice.

51A Sending cases to the Crown Court: children and young persons

[See **B5.5**]

51B Notices in serious or complex fraud cases

(1) A notice may be given by a designated authority under this section in respect of an indictable offence if the authority is of the opinion that the evidence of the offence charged—

   (a) is sufficient for the person charged to be put on trial for the offence; and

   (b) reveals a case of fraud of such seriousness or complexity that it is appropriate that the management of the case should without delay be taken over by the Crown Court ...

51C Notices in certain cases involving children

(1) A notice may be given by the Director of Public Prosecutions under this section in respect of an offence falling within subsection (3) below if he is of the opinion—

   (a) that the evidence of the offence would be sufficient for the person charged to be put on trial for the offence;

   (b) that a child would be called as a witness at the trial; and

   (c) that, for the purpose of avoiding any prejudice to the welfare of the child, the case should be taken over and proceeded with without delay by the Crown Court.

(2) That opinion must be certified by the Director of Public Prosecutions in the notice.

(3) This subsection applies to an offence—

   (a) which involves an assault on, or injury or a threat of injury to, a person;

   (b) under section 1 of the Children and Young Persons Act 1933 (cruelty to persons under 16);

   (c) under the Sexual Offences Act 1956, the Protection of Children Act 1978 or the Sexual Offences Act 2003;

   (d) of kidnapping or false imprisonment, or an offence under section 1 or 2 of the Child Abduction Act 1984;

   (e) which consists of attempting or conspiring to commit, or of aiding, abetting, counselling, procuring or inciting the commission of, an offence falling within paragraph (a), (b), (c) or (d) above ...

(7) In this section 'child' means—

   (a) a person who is under the age of 17; or

   (b) any person of whom a video recording (as defined in section 63(1) of the Youth Justice and Criminal Evidence Act 1999) was made when he was under the age of 17 with a view to its admission as his evidence in chief in the trial referred to in subsection (1) above.

51D Notice of offence and place of trial

(1) The court shall specify in a notice—
   (a) the offence or offences for which a person is sent for trial under section 51 or 51A above; and
   (b) the place at which he is to be tried (which, if a notice has been given under section 51B above, must be the place specified in that notice) …

(4) Where the court selects the place of trial for the purposes of subsection (1) above, it shall have regard to—
   (a) the convenience of the defence, the prosecution and the witnesses;
   (b) the desirability of expediting the trial; and
   (c) any direction given by or on behalf of the Lord Chief Justice with the concurrence of the Lord Chancellor under section 75(1) of the Supreme Court Act 1981.

=

 See *Blackstone's Criminal Practice 2017* **D10**

A28 Special Measures and Vulnerable Witnesses

A28.1 Special measures

Sections 16 and 17 of the Youth Justice and Criminal Evidence Act 1999 provide for special measures. Those aged under 18 may always benefit, as well as those meeting the requirements for incapacity (s 16). Witnesses who seek assistance may always benefit if the allegation is of the serious offences listed in the Youth Justice and Criminal Evidence Act 1999, Schedule 1A, which will usually be tried in the Crown Court, as well as those who otherwise meet the criteria (s 17). Under Part 3 of the Criminal Procedure Rules, the courts are required to facilitate the participation of anyone taking part, both witnesses and defendant(s).

Youth Justice and Criminal Evidence Act 1999, ss 16 and 17

16 Witnesses eligible for assistance on grounds of age or incapacity

(1) For the purposes of this Chapter a witness in criminal proceedings (other than the accused) is eligible for assistance by virtue of this section—
   (a) if under the age of 18 at the time of the hearing; or
   (b) if the court considers that the quality of evidence given by the witness is likely to be diminished by reason of any circumstances falling within subsection (2).

(2) The circumstances falling within this subsection are—
   (a) that the witness—
      (i) suffers from mental disorder within the meaning of the Mental Health Act 1983, or
      (ii) otherwise has a significant impairment of intelligence and social functioning;
   (b) that the witness has a physical disability or is suffering from a physical disorder.

(3) In subsection (1)(a) 'the time of the hearing', in relation to a witness, means the time when it falls to the court to make a determination for the purposes of section 19(2) in relation to the witness.

(4) In determining whether a witness falls within subsection (1)(b) the court must consider any views expressed by the witness.

(5) In this Chapter references to the quality of a witness's evidence are to its quality in terms of completeness, coherence and accuracy; and for this purpose 'coherence' refers to a witness's ability in giving evidence to give answers which address the questions put to the witness and can be understood both individually and collectively.

---

17 Witnesses eligible for assistance on grounds of fear or distress about testifying

(1) For the purposes of this Chapter a witness in criminal proceedings (other than the accused) is eligible for assistance by virtue of this subsection if the court is satisfied that the quality of evidence given by the witness is likely to be diminished by reason of fear or distress on the part of the witness in connection with testifying in the proceedings.

(2) In determining whether a witness falls within subsection (1) the court must take into account, in particular—

  (a) the nature and alleged circumstances of the offence to which the proceedings relate;

  (b) the age of the witness;

  (c) such of the following matters as appear to the court to be relevant, namely—

    (i) the social and cultural background and ethnic origins of the witness,

    (ii) the domestic and employment circumstances of the witness, and

    (iii) any religious beliefs or political opinions of the witness;

  (d) any behaviour towards the witness on the part of—

    (i) the accused,

    (ii) members of the family or associates of the accused, or

    (iii) any other person who is likely to be an accused or a witness in the proceedings.

(3) In determining that question the court must in addition consider any views expressed by the witness.

(4) Where the complainant in respect of a sexual offence is a witness in proceedings relating to that offence (or to that offence and any other offences), the witness is eligible for assistance in relation to those proceedings by virtue of this subsection unless the witness has informed the court of the witness's wish not to be so eligible by virtue of this subsection.

(5) A witness in proceedings relating to a relevant offence (or to a relevant offence and any other offences) is eligible for assistance in relation to those proceedings by virtue of this subsection unless the witness has informed the court of the witness's wish not to be so eligible by virtue of this subsection.

(6) For the purposes of subsection (5) an offence is a relevant offence if it is an offence described in Schedule 1A.

The following special measures are available in the magistrates' court:

	Section 16 witnesses (children and vulnerable adults)	Section 17 witnesses (intimidated/fear or distress)
Section 23—screening witness from accused	Full availability	Full availability
Section 24—evidence via live link	Full availability	Full availability
Section 25—evidence given in private	Full availability	Full availability
Section 26—removal of wigs/ gowns	Not applicable	Not applicable
Section 27—video-recorded evidence-in-chief	Full availability	Full availability
Section 28—video-recorded cross-examination and re-examination	Available in pilot areas	Not available
Section 29—examination through an intermediary	Full availability	Not applicable
Section 30—aids to communication	Full availability	Not applicable

A28.2 Witness anonymity

Sections 86–95 of the Coroners and Justice Act 2009 provide for the making and discharge of witness anonymity orders. These are to be regarded as a special measure of last practicable resort (*R v Mayers* [2008] EWCA Crim 2989).

 See *Blackstone's Criminal Practice 2017* **D14**

A29 Submission of No Case

A29.1 Test for no case to answer

In *R v Galbraith* (1981) 73 Cr App R 124, the court laid down the following test:

(1) If there is no evidence that the crime alleged has been committed by the defendant, there is no difficulty. The judge will of course stop the case.

(2) The difficulty arises where there is some evidence but it is of a tenuous character, for example because of inherent weakness, or vagueness, or because it is inconsistent with other evidence.

   (a) Where the judge comes to the conclusion that the prosecution evidence, taken at its highest, is such that a jury properly directed could not properly convict upon it, it is his duty, upon a submission being made, to stop the case.

   (b) Where, however, the prosecution evidence is such that its strength or weakness depends on the view to be taken of a witness's reliability, or other matters which are generally speaking within the province of the jury and where on one possible view of the facts there is evidence upon which a jury could properly come to the conclusion that the defendant is guilty, then the judge should allow the matter to be tried by the jury.

It follows that we think the second of the two schools of thought is to be preferred.

 See *Blackstone's Criminal Practice 2017* **D16.54–D16.73**

A30 Transfer/Remittal of Criminal Cases

A30.1 Transfer between courts

Section 27A of the Magistrates' Courts Act 1980 provides for transfer between magistrates' courts:

> ### Magistrates' Courts Act 1980, s 27A
>
> #### 27A Power to transfer criminal proceedings
>
> (1) Where a person appears or is brought before a magistrates' court—
>   (a) to be tried by the court for an offence, or
>   (b) for the court to inquire into the offence as examining justices, the court may transfer the matter to another magistrates' court.
> (2) The court may transfer the matter before or after beginning the trial or inquiry.
> (3) But if the court transfers the matter after it has begun to hear the evidence and the parties, the court to which the matter is transferred must begin hearing the evidence and the parties again.
> (4) The power of the court under this section to transfer any matter must be exercised in accordance with any directions given under section 30(3) of the Courts Act 2003.

A30.2 Transfer of custodial remand hearings

> ### Magistrates Courts Act 2000, s 130
>
> #### 130 Transfer of remand hearings
>
> (1) A magistrates' court adjourning a case under section 5, 10(1) or 18(4) above, and remanding the accused in custody, may, if he has attained the age of 17, order that he be brought up for any subsequent remands before an alternate magistrates' court nearer to the prison where he is to be confined while on remand.
> (2) The order shall require the accused to be brought before the alternate court at the end of the period of remand or at such earlier time as the alternate court may require.
> (3) While the order is in force, the alternate court shall, to the exclusion of the court which made the order, have all the powers in relation to further remand (whether in custody or on bail) and which that court would have had but for the order.
> (4) The alternate court may, on remanding the accused in custody, require him to be brought before the court which made the order at the end of the period of remand or at such earlier time as that court may require;

and, if the alternate court does so, or the accused is released on bail, the order under subsection (1) above shall cease to be in force.

(4A) Where a magistrates' court is satisfied as mentioned in section 128(3A) above—

    (a) subsection (1) above shall have effect as if for the words 'he be brought up for any subsequent remands before' there were substituted the words 'applications for any subsequent remands be made to';

    (b) subsection (2) above shall have effect as if for the words 'the accused to be brought before' there were substituted the words 'an application for a further remand to be made to' and

    (c) subsection (4) above shall have effect as if for the words 'him to be brought before' there were substituted the words 'an application for a further remand to be made to'.

A30.3 Remittal of convicted defendants

Provision is made for the remittal of convicted defendants by section 10 of the Powers of Criminal Courts (Sentencing) Act 2000:

Powers of Criminal Courts (Sentencing) Act 2000, s 10

10 Power of magistrates' court to remit case to another magistrates' court for sentence

(1) Where a person aged 18 or over ('the offender') has been convicted by a magistrates' court ('the convicting court') of an offence to which this section applies ('the instant offence') and—

    (a) it appears to the convicting court that some other magistrates' court ('the other court') has convicted him of another such offence in respect of which the other court has neither passed sentence on him nor committed him to the Crown Court for sentence nor dealt with him in any other way, and

    (b) the other court consents to his being remitted under this section to the other court,

the convicting court may remit him to the other court to be dealt with in respect of the instant offence by the other court instead of by the convicting court.

(2) This section applies to—

    (a) any offence punishable with imprisonment; and

    (b) any offence in respect of which the convicting court has a power or duty to order the offender to be disqualified under section 34, 35 or 36 of the Road Traffic Offenders Act 1988 (disqualification for certain motoring offences).

 See *Blackstone's Criminal Practice 2017* **D21.5**

A31 **Video Links**

Sections 57A–57F of the Crime and Disorder Act 1998 provide for the use of live links in relation to preliminary hearings and sentence (see **A28** for special measure provisions).

A32 Witnesses, Issue of Summons, or Warrant

A32.1 Power to require attendance

Magistrates' Courts Act 1980, s 97

97 Summons to witness and warrant for his arrest

(1) Where a justice of the peace is satisfied that—

    (a) any person in England or Wales is likely to be able to give material evidence, or produce any document or thing likely to be material evidence, at the summary trial of an information or hearing of a complaint or of an application under the Adoption and Children Act 2002 (c. 38) by a magistrates' court, and

    (b) it is in the interests of justice to issue a summons under this sub-section to secure the attendance of that person to give evidence or produce the document or thing,

    the justice shall issue a summons directed to that person requiring him to attend before the court at the time and place appointed in the summons to give evidence or to produce the document or thing.

(2) If a justice of the peace is satisfied by evidence on oath of the matters mentioned in subsection (1) above, and also that it is probable that a summons under that subsection would not procure the attendance of the person in question, the justice may instead of issuing a summons issue a warrant to arrest that person and bring him before such a court as aforesaid at a time and place specified in the warrant; but a warrant shall not be issued under this subsection where the attendance is required for the hearing of a complaint or of an application under the Adoption and Children Act 2002 (c. 38).

(2A) A summons may also be issued under subsection (1) above if the justice is satisfied that the person in question is outside the British Islands but no warrant shall be issued under subsection (2) above unless the justice is satisfied by evidence on oath that the person in question is in England or Wales.

(2B) A justice may refuse to issue a summons under subsection (1) above in relation to the summary trial of an information if he is not satisfied that an application for the summons was made by a party to the case as soon as reasonably practicable after the accused pleaded not guilty.

(2C) In relation to the summary trial of an information, subsection (2) above shall have effect as if the reference to the matters mentioned in subsection (1) above included a reference to the matter mentioned in subsection (2B) above.

(3) On the failure of any person to attend before a magistrates' court in answer to a summons under this section, if—

    (a) the court is satisfied by evidence on oath that he is likely to be able to give material evidence or produce any document or thing likely to be material evidence in the proceedings; and

---

> (b) it is proved on oath, or in such other manner as may be pre-scribed, that he has been duly served with the summons, and that a reasonable sum has been paid or tendered to him for costs and expenses; and
>
> (c) it appears to the court that there is no just excuse for the failure,
>
> the court may issue a warrant to arrest him and bring him before the court at a time and place specified in the warrant.
>
> (4) If any person attending or brought before a magistrates' court refuses without just excuse to be sworn or give evidence, or to produce any document or thing, the court may commit him to custody until the expiration of such period not exceeding one month as may be speci-fied in the warrant or until he sooner gives evidence or produces the document or thing or impose on him a fine not exceeding £2,500 or both.

Conduct money should be served with any summons sufficient to enable the person to attend court.

The power to compel production of documents relates only to material evidence, and should not be used to compel the produc-tion of documents solely for the purpose of cross-examination (*R v Skegness Magistrates' Court, ex p Cardy* [1985] RTR 49). See also Part 17 of the Criminal Procedure Rules.

The alternative approach is to require the Crown to accept its responsibilities under paragraph 3.5 of the Code of Practice issued under the Criminal Procedure and Investigations Act 1996 to pur-sue all reasonable lines of enquiry, a duty recognized by paragraphs 46 to 48 of the Judicial Protocol on Disclosure of Unused Material.

 See *Blackstone's Criminal Practice 2017* **D21.27–D21.33**

Part B
Youths in the Adult Court

B1 Age of Offender and the Position of Those Attaining 18

It is the duty of a court to determine their age when a young person is brought before the court. In most cases there is no dispute and a simple confirmation of the youth's date of birth will suffice. The court is, however, able to hear evidence on the issue. If the age is later found to be incorrect, this has no bearing on any orders made by the court. Section 99 of the Children and Young Persons Act 1933 provides:

Children and Young Persons Act 1933, s 99

99 Presumption and determination of age

(1) Where a person, whether charged with an offence or not, is brought before any court otherwise than for the purpose of giving evidence, and it appears to the court that he is a child or young person, the court shall make due inquiry as to the age of that person, and for that purpose shall take such evidence as may be forthcoming at the hearing of the case, but an order or judgment of the court shall not be invalidated by any subsequent proof that the age of that person has not been correctly stated to the court, and the age presumed or declared by the court to be the age of the person so brought before it shall, for the purposes of this Act, be deemed to be the true age of that person, and, where it appears to the court that the person so brought before it has attained the age of eighteen years, that person shall for the purposes of this Act be deemed not to be a child or young person.

(2) Where in any charge or indictment for any offence under this Act or any of the offences mentioned in the First Schedule to this Act except as provided in that Schedule, it is alleged that the person by or in respect of whom the offence was committed was a child or young person or was under or had attained any specified age, and he appears to the court to have been at the date of the commission of the alleged offence a child or young person, or to have been under or to have attained the specified age, as the case may be, he shall for the purposes of this Act be presumed at that date to have been a child or young person or to have been under or to have attained that age, as the case may be, unless the contrary is proved.

(3) Where, in any charge or indictment for any offence under this Act or any of the offences mentioned in the First Schedule to this Act, it is alleged that the person in respect of whom the offence was committed was a child or was a young person, it shall not be a defence to prove that the person alleged to have been a child was a young person or the person alleged to have been a young person was a child in any case where the acts constituting the alleged offence would equally have been an offence if committed in respect of a young person or child respectively.

(4) Where a person is charged with an offence under this Act in respect of a person apparently under a specified age it shall be a defence to prove that the person was actually of or over that age.

B1.1 Youth becoming an adult during course of proceedings

B1.1.1 *Attaining 18 before first court appearance*

Notwithstanding the defendant's age at the date of allegation or charge, where a defendant is 18 years of age at the date of the first court appearance the hearing is in the adult magistrates' court. Section 24(1) of the Magistrates' Courts Act 1980 ('summary trial of information against child or young person for indictable offence') applies only to those who are under 18 years at the date of the first appearance in court. The youth court has no jurisdiction (*R v Amersham Juvenile Court, ex p Wilson* [1981] 2 All ER 315). This applies where the defendant does not appear and a warrant is issued prior to the defendant's 18th birthday. The charge must be laid again in the adult court (*R v Uxbridge Youth Court, ex p H* [1998] EWHC (Admin) 341).

B1.1.2 *Attaining 18 during court proceedings*

The relevant date is the date on which the plea is taken and/or the venue is determined. If the defendant attains 18 after the first appearance at court and the offence is indictable, and no plea has been taken/venue has not been determined, the adult sending and venue procedures apply. This includes the right to elect trial by jury (*Re Daley* [1983] 1 AC 327; *R v West London Justices, ex p Siley-Winditt* [2000] Crim LR 926).

Where the prosecution, during the course of the proceedings, seek to lay a new charge based on the same facts, the new charge must be laid in the adult court (*R v Chelsea Justices, ex p Director of Public Prosecutions* [1963] 3 All ER 657).

B1.1.3 *Sentence*

For the purposes of sentence, the relevant age is the age of the defendant at the date of conviction or guilty plea (*R v Danga* [1992] QB 476).

The starting point is the sentence the defendant would have been likely to receive if he had been sentenced at the date of the commission of the offence (*R v Ghafoor* [2002] EWCA Crim 1857):

> It will rarely be necessary for a court even to consider the passing of a sentence which is more severe than the maximum it would have had jurisdiction to pass at the time of the commission of the offence.

The defendant's age is a powerful, but not the sole, determining factor (*R v Bowker* [2007] EWCA Crim 1608):

> Whilst therefore it is clearly right that a person who has committed an offence whilst under the age of 18 should be sentenced on the basis

that his culpability is to be judged by reference to his age at the time of the offence, nonetheless, the necessary sentencing disposal has to take account of the matters set out in section 142(1) [of the Criminal Justice Act 2003] if he is convicted after he has reached the age of 18. When sentencing those under 18, the court will generally focus more on their requirements and their rehabilitation. Section 142 suggests that for those over the age of 18, however, more general public policy considerations, in particular deterrence, can play a greater part.

The age of the offender for the purposes of determining which of the statutory regimes under the Criminal Justice Act 2003 applies (dangerousness) is his age at date of conviction (*R v Robson* [2006] EWCA Crim 1414).

SGC Guideline: Overarching Principles—Sentencing Youths, para 5

5. Crossing a significant age threshold between commission of an offence and sentence

5.1 There will be occasions when an increase in the age of an offender will result in the maximum sentence on the date of conviction being greater than that available on the date on which the offence was committed.

5.2 In such circumstances, the approach should be:

- where an offender crosses a relevant age threshold between the date on which the offence was committed and the date of conviction or sentence, a court should take as its starting point the sentence likely to have been imposed on the date on which the offence was committed;

- where an offender attains the age of 18 after committing the offence but before conviction, section 142 of the Criminal Justice Act 2003 applies (whilst section 37 of the 1998 Act and section 44 of the 1933 Act ... apply to those aged under 18) and the sentencing disposal has to take account of the matters set out in that section;

- it will be rare for a court to have to consider passing a sentence more severe than the maximum it would have had jurisdiction to pass at the time the offence was committed even where an offender has subsequently attained the age of 18;

- however, a sentence at or close to that maximum may be appropriate, especially where a serious offence was committed by an offender close to the age threshold.

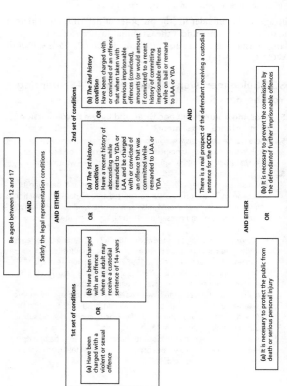

Figure 2 Remand to youth detention accommodation

With the following exceptions, the bases on which the Crown may oppose bail, and on which an application for bail, whether unconditional or conditional, may be made for a youth appearing in the adult court, are the same as for an adult (see **A8**).

If, under transitional arrangements, the offence carries a sentence of life imprisonment and at the time of the offence the defendant was on bail, Schedule 1, paragraphs 9AA and 9AB to the Bail Act 1976 (as amended) provide:

Bail Act 1976, Sch 1, paras 9AA and 9AB

9AA (1) This paragraph applies if—
   (a) the defendant is a child or young person, and
   (b) it appears to the court that he was on bail in criminal proceedings on the date of the offence.

(2) In deciding for the purposes of paragraph 2(1) of this Part of this Schedule whether it is satisfied that there are substantial grounds for believing that the defendant, if released on bail (whether subject to conditions or not), would commit an offence while on bail, the court shall give particular weight to the fact that the defendant was on bail in criminal proceedings on the date of the offence.

9AB (1) Subject to sub-paragraph (2) below, this paragraph applies if—
   (a) the defendant is a child or young person, and
   (b) it appears to the court that, having been released on bail in or in connection with the proceedings for the offence, he failed to surrender to custody.

(2) Where it appears to the court that the defendant had reasonable cause for his failure to surrender to custody, this paragraph does not apply unless it also appears to the court that he failed to surrender to custody at the appointed place as soon as reasonably practicable after the appointed time.

(3) In deciding for the purposes of paragraph 2(1) of this Part of this Schedule whether it is satisfied that there are substantial grounds for believing that the defendant, if released on bail (whether subject to conditions or not), would fail to surrender to custody, the court shall give particular weight to—
   (a) where the defendant did not have reasonable cause for his failure to surrender to custody, the fact that he failed to surrender to custody, or
   (b) where he did have reasonable cause for his failure to surrender to custody, the fact that he failed to surrender to custody at the appointed place as soon as reasonably practicable after the appointed time.

(4) …

If electronic monitoring is to be a condition of bail, the court must comply with section 3AA of the Bail Act 1976.

> **Bail Act 1976, ss 3AA(1)–(5)**
>
> **3AA Conditions for the imposition of electronic monitoring requirements: children and young persons**
>
> (1) A court may not impose electronic monitoring requirements on a child or young person unless each of the following conditions is met.
>
> (2) The first condition is that the child or young person has attained the age of twelve years.
>
> (3) The second condition is that—
>
>   (a) the child or young person is charged with or has been convicted of a violent or sexual offence, or an offence punishable in the case of an adult with imprisonment for a term of fourteen years or more; or
>
>   (b) he is charged with or has been convicted of one or more imprisonable offences which, together with any other imprisonable offences of which he has been convicted in any proceedings—
>
>   (i) amount, or
>
>   (ii) would, if he were convicted of the offences with which he is charged, amount, to a recent history of repeatedly committing imprisonable offences while remanded on bail or to local authority accommodation.
>
> (4) The third condition is that the court is satisfied that the necessary provision for dealing with the person concerned can be made under arrangements for the electronic monitoring of persons released on bail that are currently available in each local justice area which is a relevant area.
>
> (5) The fourth condition is that a youth offending team has informed the court that in its opinion the imposition of electronic monitoring requirements will be suitable in the case of the child or young person.

B2.1 Refusal of bail

If a youth is refused bail, the Legal Aid, Sentencing and Punishment of Offenders Act 2012, Part 3, Chapter 3 provides for the regime (see **B2.1.9** for ss 91–102).

It should be noted that remands both to local authority accommodation and to youth detention accommodation are custodial remands, and that time limits for such remands and custody time limits apply. In the case of a youth charged with murder, where the court has no power to grant bail, the court will still determine where the youth is to be remanded (*R (A) v Lewisham Youth Court* [2011] EWHC 1193 (Admin)) and there is no limit under the Bail Act 1976 to the number of occasions on which consideration can be given to this issue.

B2.1.1 *Youth remands*

Where a youth is not released on bail, section 91 of the Legal Aid, Sentencing and Punishment of Offenders Act 2012 requires the court to remand the child to local authority accommodation in accordance with section 92, unless one of the sets of conditions set out in sections 98 to 101 is fulfilled (see **B2.1.9**), in which case the court may instead remand the child to youth detention accommodation. Under section 92(2), a court that remands a child to local authority accommodation must designate the local authority that is to receive the child.

B2.1.2 *Remand to local authority accommodation*

The remand may be without conditions, but if appropriate, under section 93 of the Legal Aid, Sentencing and Punishment of Offenders Act 2012, after consultation with the designated local authority, the court may require:

- the child to comply with any conditions that could be imposed under section 3(6) of the Bail Act 1976;
- the child to comply with any conditions required for the purpose of securing compliance with electronic monitoring;
- the designated local authority to comply with any requirements to secure the child's compliance with a condition; and
- the designated local authority not to place the child with a named person.

An application may be made to the court in respect of a child who has been remanded to local authority accommodation to impose, vary, or revoke conditions.

B2.1.3 *Electronic monitoring as a condition of bail whilst remanded to local authority accommodation*

The court may not impose electronic monitoring of a child's compliance with a condition imposed under section 93 unless the conditions set out in section 94 (see **B2.1.9**) are satisfied.

B2.1.4 *Failure to surrender*

Where a child who is remanded on bail fails to surrender to court without reasonable cause, section 6 of the Bail Act 1976 will apply (see **C3**).

B2.1.5 *Breach of conditions of remand to local authority accommodation*

Under section 97 of the Legal Aid, Sentencing and Punishment of Offenders Act 2012, a constable may arrest a child without a warrant if the child has been remanded to local authority accommodation with conditions and the constable has reasonable grounds to suspect that the child has broken any of those conditions. The child must be brought before the court as soon as practicable and within 24 hours of the child's arrest. Where that 24-hour period includes the time appointed for the child's original court appearance then the child should appear before that same court.

If the court is of the opinion that a child has broken any of the conditions of a remand to local authority accommodation, the court may once again consider the conditions of bail and may attach new conditions to the remand to local authority accommodation or, if the conditions in sections 98–101 are met, remand the child to youth detention accommodation.

If the court is not of the opinion that the child has broken any of the conditions of his remand to local authority accommodation, it must remand the child subject to the original conditions imposed.

B2.1.6 *10- to 11-year-olds*

A child aged 10 to 11 years may only be remanded on bail or to local authority accommodation. If a child reaches the age of 12 during the course of a remand, it is possible that he may then be remanded to youth detention accommodation at the next court appearance should the relevant conditions (Legal Aid, Sentencing and Punishment of Offenders Act 2012, ss 98–101) be met.

B2.1.7 *Secure accommodation*

A child aged between 10 and 17 years who is remanded to local authority accommodation may be placed in secure local authority accommodation if the designated local authority obtains a court order permitting this under section 25 of the Children Act 1989 (as modified by the Children (Secure Accommodation) Regulations 1991 (SI 1991/1505)).

Section 25 of the Children Act 1989 provides:

> ### Children Act 1989, s 25
>
> #### 25 Use of accommodation for restricting liberty
> (1) Subject to the following provisions of this section, a child who is being looked after by a local authority may not be placed, and, if placed, may not be kept, in accommodation provided for the purpose of restricting liberty ('secure accommodation') unless it appears—
>   (a) that—
>   (i) he has a history of absconding and is likely to abscond from any other description of accommodation; and
>   (ii) if he absconds, he is likely to suffer significant harm; or

(b) that if he is kept in any other description of accommodation he is likely to injure himself or other persons.

(2) The appropriate national authority may by regulations—

    (a) specify a maximum period—

      (i) beyond which a child may not be kept in secure accommodation without the authority of the court; and

      (ii) for which the court may authorise a child to be kept in secure accommodation;

    (b) empower the court from time to time to authorise a child to be kept in secure accommodation for such further period as the regulations may specify; and

    (c) provide that applications to the court under this section shall be made only by local authorities.

(3) It shall be the duty of a court hearing an application under this section to determine whether any relevant criteria for keeping a child in secure accommodation are satisfied in his case.

(4) If a court determines that any such criteria are satisfied, it shall make an order authorising the child to be kept in secure accommodation and specifying the maximum period for which he may be so kept.

(5) On any adjournment of the hearing of an application under this section, a court may make an interim order permitting the child to be kept during the period of the adjournment in secure accommodation.

(6) No court shall exercise the powers conferred by this section in respect of a child who is not legally represented in that court unless, having been informed of his right to apply for representation funded by the Legal Aid Authority as part of the Civil Legal Aid or Criminal Legal Aid and having had the opportunity to do so, he refused or failed to apply.

(7) The appropriate national authority may by regulations provide that—

    (a) this section shall or shall not apply to any description of children specified in the regulations;

    (b) this section shall have effect in relation to children of a description specified in the regulations subject to such modifications as may be so specified;

    (c) such other provisions as may be so specified shall have effect for the purpose of determining whether a child of a description specified in the regulations may be placed or kept in secure accommodation.

(8) The giving of an authorisation under this section shall not prejudice any power of any court in England and Wales or Scotland to give directions relating to the child to whom the authorisation relates.

(9) This section is subject to section 20(8).

B2.1.8 *Children who turn 18 years of age during their remand*

Where a child turns 18 during the course of his remand, he will remain in youth detention accommodation until he is released or returned to court.

B2.1.9 *The statutory remand scheme*

Legal Aid, Sentencing and Punishment of Offenders Act 2012, ss 91–102

91 Remands of children otherwise than on bail

(1) This section applies where—
  (a) a court deals with a child charged with or convicted of one or more offences by remanding the child, and
  (b) the child is not released on bail.

(2) This section also applies where—
  (a) a court remands a child in connection with extradition proceedings, and
  (b) the child is not released on bail.

(3) Subject to subsection (4), the court must remand the child to local authority accommodation in accordance with section 92.

(4) The court may instead remand the child to youth detention accommodation in accordance with section 102 where—
  (a) in the case of a child remanded under subsection (1), the first or second set of conditions for such a remand (see sections 98 and 99) is met in relation to the child, or
  (b) in the case of a child remanded under subsection (2), the first or second set of conditions for such a remand in an extradition case (see sections 100 and 101) is met in relation to the child.

(5) This section is subject to section 128(7) of the Magistrates' Courts Act 1980 (remands to police detention for periods of not more than 3 days); but that provision has effect in relation to a child as if for the reference to 3 clear days there were substituted a reference to 24 hours.

(6) In this Chapter, 'child' means a person under the age of 18.

(7) References in this Chapter (other than in relation to extradition proceedings) to the remand of a child include a reference to—
  (a) the sending of a child for trial, and
  (b) the committal of a child for sentence,
  and related expressions are to be construed accordingly.

(8) Before the insertion of section 51A of the Crime and Disorder Act 1998 (sending cases to the Crown Court: children and young persons) by Schedule 3 to the Criminal Justice Act 2003 is fully in force, subsection (7) has effect as if it also referred to the committal of a child for trial.

(9) Subsection (7) also applies to any provision of an Act other than this Act that refers (directly or indirectly) to the remand of a child under this section.

92 Remands to local authority accommodation

(1) A remand to local authority accommodation is a remand to accommodation provided by or on behalf of a local authority.

(2) A court that remands a child to local authority accommodation must designate the local authority that is to receive the child.

(3) That authority must be—
  (a) in the case of a child who is being looked after by a local authority, that authority, and

---

    (b) in any other case, the local authority in whose area it appears to the court that the child habitually resides or the offence or one of the offences was committed.

(4) The designated authority must—

    (a) receive the child, and

    (b) provide or arrange for the provision of accommodation for the child whilst the child is remanded to local authority accommodation.

(5) Where a child is remanded to local authority accommodation, it is lawful for any person acting on behalf of the designated authority to detain the child.

93 Conditions etc on remands to local authority accommodation

(1) A court remanding a child to local authority accommodation may require the child to comply with any conditions that could be imposed under section 3(6) of the Bail Act 1976 if the child were then being granted bail.

(2) The court may also require the child to comply with any conditions imposed for the purpose of securing the electronic monitoring of the child's compliance with the conditions imposed under subsection (1) if—

    (a) in the case of a child remanded under section 91(1) (proceedings other than extradition proceedings), the requirements in section 94 are met, or

    (b) in the case of a child remanded under section 91(2) (extradition proceedings), the requirements in section 95 are met.

(3) A court remanding a child to local authority accommodation may impose on the designated authority—

    (a) requirements for securing compliance with any conditions imposed on the child under subsection (1) or (2), or

    (b) requirements stipulating that the child must not be placed with a named person.

(4) A court may only impose a condition under subsection (1) or (2), or a requirement under subsection (3), after consultation with the designated authority.

(5) Where a child has been remanded to local authority accommodation, a relevant court—

    (a) may, on the application of the designated authority, impose on that child any conditions that could be imposed under subsection (1) or (2) if the court were then remanding the child to local authority accommodation, and

    (b) where it does so, may impose on the authority requirements for securing compliance with the conditions imposed under paragraph (a).

(6) Where a child has been remanded to local authority accommodation, a relevant court may, on the application of the designated authority or that child, vary or revoke any conditions or requirements imposed under this section (including as previously varied under this subsection).

(7) A court that imposes conditions on a child under this section or varies conditions so imposed—

    (a) must explain to the child in open court and in ordinary language why it is imposing or varying those conditions, and

    (b) if the court is a magistrates' court, must cause a reason given under paragraph (a) to be specified in the warrant of commitment and entered in the register.

(8) In this section 'relevant court'—

    (a) in relation to a child remanded to local authority accommodation by virtue of section 91(1) (proceedings other than extradition proceedings), means—

      (i) the court by which the child was so remanded, or

      (ii) any magistrates' court that has jurisdiction in the place where the child is for the time being;

    (b) in relation to a child remanded to local authority accommodation by virtue of section 91(2) (extradition proceedings), means the court by which the child was so remanded.

(9) References in this section to consultation are to such consultation (if any) as is reasonably practicable in all the circumstances of the case.

94 Requirements for electronic monitoring

(1) The requirements referred to in section 93(2)(a) (requirements for imposing electronic monitoring condition: non-extradition cases) are those set out in subsections (2) to (6).

(2) The first requirement is that the child has reached the age of twelve.

(3) The second requirement is that the offence mentioned in section 91(1), or one or more of those offences, is an imprisonable offence.

(4) The third requirement is that—

    (a) the offence mentioned in section 91(1), or one or more of those offences, is a violent or sexual offence or an offence punishable in the case of an adult with imprisonment for a term of 14 years or more, or

    (b) the offence or offences mentioned in section 91(1), together with any other imprisonable offences of which the child has been convicted in any proceedings, amount or would, if the child were convicted of that offence or those offences, amount to a recent history of committing imprisonable offences while on bail or subject to a custodial remand.

(5) The fourth requirement is that the court is satisfied that the necessary provision for electronic monitoring can be made under arrangements currently available in each local justice area which is a relevant area.

(6) The fifth requirement is that a youth offending team has informed the court that, in its opinion, the imposition of an electronic monitoring condition will be suitable in the child's case.

(7) For the purposes of this section, a local justice area is a relevant area in relation to a proposed electronic monitoring condition if the court considers that it will not be practicable to secure the electronic monitoring in question unless electronic monitoring arrangements are available in that area.

(8) In this Chapter—

'electronic monitoring condition' means a condition imposed on a child remanded to local authority accommodation for the purpose of securing the electronic monitoring of the child's compliance with conditions imposed under section 93(1) or (5);

'imprisonable offence' means—

(a) an offence punishable in the case of an adult with imprisonment, or

(b) in relation to an offence of which a child has been accused or convicted outside England and Wales, an offence equivalent to an offence that, in England and Wales, is punishable in the case of an adult with imprisonment;

'sexual offence' means an offence specified in Part 2 of Schedule 15 to the Criminal Justice Act 2003;

'violent offence' means murder or an offence specified in Part 1 of Schedule 15 to the Criminal Justice Act 2003;

'youth offending team' means a team established under section 39 of the Crime and Disorder Act 1998.

(9) References in this Chapter to a child being subject to a custodial remand are to the child being—

(a) remanded to local authority accommodation or youth detention accommodation, or

(b) subject to a form of custodial detention in a country or territory outside England and Wales while awaiting trial or sentence in that country or territory or during a trial in that country or territory.

(10) The reference in subsection (9) to a child being remanded to local authority accommodation or youth detention accommodation includes—

(a) a child being remanded to local authority accommodation under section 23 of the Children and Young Persons Act 1969, and

(b) a child being remanded to prison under that section as modified by section 98 of the Crime and Disorder Act 1998 or under section 27 of the Criminal Justice Act 1948.

95 Requirements for electronic monitoring: extradition cases
[Mirrors s 94]

96 Further provisions about electronic monitoring

(1) Where a court imposes an electronic monitoring condition, the condition must include provision making a person responsible for the monitoring.

(2) A person who is made responsible by virtue of subsection (1) must be of a description specified in an order made by the Secretary of State.

(3) The Secretary of State may make rules for regulating—

(a) the electronic monitoring of compliance with conditions imposed under section 93(1) or (5), and

(b) in particular, the functions of persons made responsible by virtue of subsection (1) of this section.

(4) Rules under this section may make different provision for different cases.

(5) Any power of the Secretary of State to make an order or rules under this section is exercisable by statutory instrument.

(6) A statutory instrument containing rules under this section is subject to annulment in pursuance of a resolution of either House of Parliament.

97 Liability to arrest for breaking conditions of remand

(1) A child may be arrested without warrant by a constable if—
  (a) the child has been remanded to local authority accommodation,
  (b) conditions under section 93 have been imposed in respect of the child, and
  (c) the constable has reasonable grounds for suspecting that the child has broken any of those conditions.

(2) Subject to subsection (3), a child arrested under subsection (1) must be brought before a justice of the peace—
  (a) as soon as practicable, and
  (b) in any event within the period of 24 hours beginning with the child's arrest.

(3) If the child was arrested during the period of 24 hours ending with the time appointed for the child to appear before the court in pursuance of the remand, the child must be brought before the court before which the child was to have appeared.

(4) In reckoning a period of 24 hours for the purposes of subsection (2) or (3), no account is to be taken of Christmas Day, Good Friday or any Sunday.

(5) If a justice of the peace before whom a child is brought under subsection (2) is of the opinion that the child has broken any condition imposed in respect of the child under section 93, the justice of the peace must remand the child.

(6) Section 91 applies to a child in relation to whom subsection (5) applies as if—
  (a) except in a case within paragraph (b), the child was then charged with or convicted of the offence for which the child had been remanded, or
  (b) in the case of a child remanded in connection with extradition proceedings, the child was then appearing before the justice of the peace in connection with those proceedings.

(7) If a justice of the peace before whom a child is brought under subsection (2) is not of the opinion mentioned in subsection (5), the justice of the peace must remand the child to the place to which the child had been remanded at the time of the child's arrest subject to the same conditions as those which had been imposed on the child at that time.

98 First set of conditions for a remand to youth detention accommodation

(1) For the purposes of section 91(4)(a), the first set of conditions for a remand to youth detention accommodation is met in relation to a child if each of the following is met in relation to the child—
  (a) the age condition (see subsection (2)),
  (b) the offence condition (see subsection (3)),
  (c) the necessity condition (see subsection (4)), and
  (d) the first or second legal representation condition (see subsections (5) and (6)).

(2) The age condition is that the child has reached the age of twelve.

(3) The offence condition is that the offence mentioned in section 91(1), or one or more of those offences—

    (a) is a violent or sexual offence, or

    (b) is an offence punishable in the case of an adult with imprisonment for a term of 14 years or more.

(4) The necessity condition is that the court is of the opinion, after considering all the options for the remand of the child, that only remanding the child to youth detention accommodation would be adequate—

    (a) to protect the public from death or serious personal injury (whether physical or psychological) occasioned by further offences committed by the child, or

    (b) to prevent the commission by the child of imprisonable offences.

(5) The first legal representation condition is that the child is legally represented before the court.

(6) The second legal representation condition is that the child is not legally represented before the court and—

    (a) representation was provided to the child under Part 1 of this Act for the purposes of the proceedings, but was withdrawn—

        (i) because of the child's conduct, or

        (ii) because it appeared that the child's financial resources were such that the child was not eligible for such representation,

    (b) the child applied for such representation and the application was refused because it appeared that the child's financial resources were such that the child was not eligible for such representation, or

    (c) having been informed of the right to apply for such representation and having had the opportunity to do so, the child refused or failed to apply.

99 Second set of conditions for a remand to youth detention accommodation

(1) For the purposes of section 91(4)(a), the second set of conditions for a remand to youth detention accommodation is met in relation to a child if each of the following is met in relation to the child—

    (a) the age condition (see subsection (2)),

    (b) the sentencing condition (see subsection (3)),

    (c) the offence condition (see subsection (4)),

    (d) the first or second history condition or both (see subsections (5) and (6)),

    (e) the necessity condition (see subsection (7)), and

    (f) the first or second legal representation condition (see subsections (8) and (9)).

(2) The age condition is that the child has reached the age of twelve.

(3) The sentencing condition is that it appears to the court that there is a real prospect that the child will be sentenced to a custodial sentence for the offence mentioned in section 91(1) or one or more of those offences.

(4) The offence condition is that the offence mentioned in section 91(1), or one or more of those offences, is an imprisonable offence.

(5) The first history condition is that—

    (a) the child has a recent history of absconding while subject to a custodial remand, and

    (b) the offence mentioned in section 91(1), or one or more of those offences, is alleged to be or has been found to have been committed while the child was remanded to local authority accommodation or youth detention accommodation.

(6) The second history condition is that the offence or offences mentioned in section 91(1), together with any other imprisonable offences of which the child has been convicted in any proceedings, amount or would, if the child were convicted of that offence or those offences, amount to a recent history of committing imprisonable offences while on bail or subject to a custodial remand.

(7) The necessity condition is that the court is of the opinion, after considering all the options for the remand of the child, that only remanding the child to youth detention accommodation would be adequate—

    (a) to protect the public from death or serious personal injury (whether physical or psychological) occasioned by further offences committed by the child, or

    (b) to prevent the commission by the child of imprisonable offences.

(8) The first legal representation condition is that the child is legally represented before the court.

(9) The second legal representation condition is that the child is not legally represented before the court and—

    (a) representation was provided to the child under Part 1 of this Act for the purposes of the proceedings, but was withdrawn—

        (i) because of the child's conduct, or

        (ii) because it appeared that the child's financial resources were such that the child was not eligible for such representation,

    (b) the child applied for such representation and the application was refused because it appeared that the child's financial resources were such that the child was not eligible for such representation, or

    (c) having been informed of the right to apply for such representation and having had the opportunity to do so, the child refused or failed to apply.

(10) In this Chapter 'custodial sentence' means a sentence or order mentioned in section 76(1) of the Powers of Criminal Courts (Sentencing) Act 2000.

(11) The reference in subsection (5)(b) to a child being remanded to local authority accommodation or youth detention accommodation includes—

    (a) a child being remanded to local authority accommodation under section 23 of the Children and Young Persons Act 1969, and

    (b) a child being remanded to prison under that section as modified by section 98 of the Crime and Disorder Act 1998 or under section 27 of the Criminal Justice Act 1948.

100 First set of conditions for a remand to youth detention accommodation: extradition cases

[Mirrors s 98]

101 Second set of conditions for a remand to youth detention accommodation: extradition cases

[Mirrors s 99]

102 Remands to youth detention accommodation

(1) A remand to youth detention accommodation is a remand to such accommodation of a kind listed in subsection (2) as the Secretary of State directs in the child's case.

(2) Those kinds of accommodation are—
  (a) a secure children's home,
  (b) a secure training centre,
  (c) a young offender institution, and
  (d) accommodation, or accommodation of a description, for the time being specified by order under section 107(1)(e) of the Powers of Criminal Courts (Sentencing) Act 2000 (youth detention accommodation for purposes of detention and training order provisions).

(3) A child's detention in one of those kinds of accommodation pursuant to a remand to youth detention accommodation is lawful.

(4) Where a court remands a child to youth detention accommodation, the court must—
  (a) state in open court that it is of the opinion mentioned in section 98(4), 99(7), 100(4) or 101(7) (as the case may be), and
  (b) explain to the child in open court and in ordinary language why it is of that opinion.

(5) A magistrates' court must ensure a reason that it gives under subsection (4)(b)—
  (a) is specified in the warrant of commitment, and
  (b) is entered in the register.

(6) Where a court remands a child to youth detention accommodation, the court must designate a local authority as the designated authority for the child for the purposes of—
  (a) subsection (8),
  (b) regulations under section 103 (arrangements for remands), and
  (c) section 104 (looked after child status).

(7) That authority must be—
  (a) in the case of a child who is being looked after by a local authority, otherwise than by virtue of section 104(1), that authority, and
  (b) in any other case, but subject to subsection (7B), a local authority in whose area it appears to the court that the child habitually resides or the offence or one of the offences was committed.

(7A) In a case to which subsection (7)(b) applies, the court is to designate a local authority in whose area it appears to the court that the child habitually resides (a 'home authority') except where the court—
  (a) considers as respects the home authority, or each home authority, that it is inappropriate to designate that authority, or
  (b) is unable to identify any place in England and Wales where the child habitually resides.

(7B) If in a case to which subsection (7)(b) applies—
  (a) the court is not required by subsection (7A) to designate a home authority, but
  (b) it appears to the court that the offence was not, or none of the offences was, committed in England and Wales, the court is to

designate a local authority which it considers appropriate in the circumstances of the case.

(7C) Where a child has been remanded to youth detention accommodation, the court—

(a) which remanded the child, or

(b) to which the child was remanded,

may designate a local authority ('B') as the designated authority for the child in substitution for the authority previously designated (whether that previous designation was made when the child was remanded or under this subsection).

(7D) Where a child has at any one time been subject to two or more remands to youth detention accommodation, a court which has jurisdiction to make a replacement designation under subsection (7C) in connection with one or some of the remands also has jurisdiction to make such a replacement designation in connection with each of the other remands.

(7E) Where a replacement designation is made under subsection (7C) after the end of the period of remand concerned, the substitution of B for the previously-designated authority has effect only for the purposes of regulations under section 103.

(7F) Where a replacement designation is made under subsection (7C) during the period of remand concerned, the substitution of B for the previously-designated authority—

(a) has effect, as respects the part of that period ending with the making of the replacement designation, only for the purposes of regulations under section 103, and

(b) has effect, as respects the remainder of that period, for all of the purposes listed in subsection (6).

(7G) A court may make a replacement designation under subsection (7C) only if it considers that, had everything it knows been known by the court which made the previous designation, that court would have designated B instead.

(7H) Where a replacement designation is made under subsection (7C) in relation to a remand, the previously-designated authority is to be repaid any sums it paid in respect of the remand pursuant to regulations under section 103.

(7J) A court which has jurisdiction to make a replacement direction under subsection (7C) may exercise that jurisdiction on an application by a local authority or of its own motion.

(8) Before giving a direction under subsection (1), the Secretary of State must consult the designated authority.

(9) A function of the Secretary of State under this section (other than the function of making regulations) is exercisable by the Youth Justice Board for England and Wales concurrently with the Secretary of State.

(10) The Secretary of State may by regulations provide that subsection (9) is not to apply, either generally or in relation to a particular description of case.

(11) In this Chapter 'secure children's home' means accommodation which is provided in a children's home, within the meaning of the Care Standards Act 2000—
    (a) which provides accommodation for the purposes of restricting liberty, and
    (b) in respect of which a person is registered under Part 2 of that Act.
(12) Before the coming into force in relation to England of section 107(2) of the Health and Social Care (Community Health and Standards) Act 2003, subsection (11) has effect as if it defined 'secure children's home' in relation to England as accommodation which—
    (a) is provided in a children's home, within the meaning of the Care Standards Act 2000, in respect of which a person is registered under Part 2 of that Act, and
    (b) is approved by the Secretary of State for the purpose of restricting the liberty of children.

B3 Breach of Orders, and New Offences Committed during an Order

See Powers of Criminal Courts (Sentencing) Act 2000, Schedule 1, Part 1, paragraphs 1–7.

B3.1 Referral orders

B3.1.1 *Which court will handle the case?*

> **Powers of Criminal Courts (Sentencing) Act 2000, Sch 1, Pt 1, para 1(2)**
>
> (2) the appropriate court is—
>   (a) in the case of an offender aged under 18 at the time when (in pursuance of the referral back) he first appears before the court, a youth court acting in the local justice area in which it appears to the youth offender panel that the offender resides or will reside; and
>   (b) otherwise, a magistrates' court (other than a youth court) acting in that area.

B3.1.2 *Powers of the court*

In dealing with the offender for such an offence, the appropriate court 'may deal with him in any way in which (assuming section 16 of this Act had not applied) he could have been dealt with for that offence by the court which made the order' (Sch 1, Pt 1, para 5(5)(a)). This provision disapplies the obligation to impose a referral order.

The court must be satisfied that the youth offender panel was entitled to make the finding of breach of the referral order, or that any discretion was exercised reasonably. Where a court is revoking and resentencing an offender, the court has the powers of the youth court, whatever the age of the defendant. As an alternative to revocation the court can impose a fine of up to £2,500 or the contract period may be increased up to a maximum of 12 months, and the court must have regard to the circumstances of the referral back and the extent of any compliance with it. The court may take no action.

B3.1.3 *Conviction whilst subject to a referral order*

See Powers of Criminal Courts (Sentencing) Act 2000, Schedule 1, Part 2, paragraphs 11–14.

The court sentencing for the new offence may extend the compliance period of the referral order. The total period may not exceed 12 months. If sentencing for the new offence in any other way (other than by an absolute or conditional discharge), the referral order may be revoked, but it may also be allowed to continue. The court may, if it is in the interests of justice, deal with the offender in any manner in which the offender could have been dealt with by the original court. The extent of any compliance must be taken into account.

B3.2 Youth rehabilitation order— breach proceedings

B3.2.1 *Which court will handle the case?*

> **Criminal Justice and Immigration Act 2008, Sch 2, para 5(3)**
>
> (3) 'appropriate court' means—
>   (a) if the offender is aged under 18, a youth court acting in the relevant local justice area, and
>   (b) if the offender is aged 18 or over, a magistrates' court (other than a youth court) acting in that local justice area.

In a youth rehabilitation order (YRO) case, a warning is required if the supervising officer finds there is a failure to comply without reasonable excuse. If, following a further, second warning within the 12-month 'warned period', there is then a third failure to comply without reasonable excuse, the officer must refer the case to court for breach proceedings, although Youth Offending Teams will have additional discretion in exceptional circumstances following a third failure to comply. The officer also has the discretion to refer the case to court at an earlier warning stage.

B3.2.2 *Powers of the court*

When dealing with the breach of a YRO, the court has the following options:

- no action;
- a fine of up to £2,500;
- amend the YRO, but not with Intensive Supervision and Surveillance Requirement (ISSR) or Intensive Fostering, unless that already applies;
- revoke the YRO and resentence, within the powers of the original (sentencing) court.

Custody is an option for breach of a YRO only if the original offence is imprisonable or, in the case of a non-imprisonable offence, if, following 'wilful and persistent' non-compliance (Criminal Justice and Immigration Act 2008, Sch 2), a YRO with an ISSR or Intensive Fostering provision is made and that further YRO is then also subject to non-compliance. The court, if passing a custodial sentence, must state that a YRO with an ISSR or Intensive Fostering provision is not appropriate and the reasons why. This is in addition to meeting the existing criteria, that is, the court forming the opinion that the offence(s) is so serious that a community sentence cannot be justified.

Paragraph 6 provides:

Criminal Justice and Immigration Act 2008, Sch 2, para 6

6 (1) This paragraph applies where—
  (a) an offender appears or is brought before a youth court or other magistrates' court under paragraph 5, and
  (b) it is proved to the satisfaction of the court that the offender has failed without reasonable excuse to comply with the youth rehabilitation order.

(2) The court may deal with the offender in respect of that failure in any one of the following ways—
  (a) by ordering the offender to pay a fine of an amount not exceeding £2,500;
  (b) by amending the terms of the youth rehabilitation order so as to impose any requirement which could have been included in the order when it was made—
    (i)   in addition to, or
    (ii) in substitution for
    any requirement or requirements already imposed by the order;
  (c) by dealing with the offender, for the offence in respect of which the order was made, in any way in which the court could have dealt with the offender for that offence (had the offender been before that court to be dealt with for it).

(3) Sub-paragraph (2)(b) is subject to sub-paragraphs (6) to (9).

(4) In dealing with the offender under sub-paragraph (2), the court must take into account the extent to which the offender has complied with the youth rehabilitation order.

(5) A fine imposed under sub-paragraph (2)(a) is to be treated, for the purposes of any enactment, as being a sum adjudged to be paid by a conviction.

(6) Any requirement imposed under sub-paragraph (2)(b) must be capable of being complied with before the date specified under paragraph 32(1) of Schedule 1.

---

(7) Where—
  (a) the court is dealing with the offender under sub-paragraph (2)(b), and
  (b) the youth rehabilitation order does not contain an unpaid work requirement,
  paragraph 10(2) of Schedule 1 applies in relation to the inclusion of such a requirement as if for '40' there were substituted '20'.
(8) The court may not under sub-paragraph (2)(b) impose—
  (a) an extended activity requirement, or
  (b) a fostering requirement,
  if the order does not already impose such a requirement.
(9) Where—
  (a) the order imposes a fostering requirement (the 'original requirement'), and
  (b) under sub-paragraph (2)(b) the court proposes to substitute a new fostering requirement ('the substitute requirement') for the original requirement,
  paragraph 18(2) of Schedule 1 applies in relation to the substitute requirement as if the reference to the period of 12 months beginning with the date on which the original requirement first had effect were a reference to the period of 18 months beginning with that date.
(10) Where—
  (a) the court deals with the offender under sub-paragraph (2)(b), and
  (b) it would not otherwise have the power to amend the youth rehabilitation order under paragraph 13 (amendment by reason of change of residence),
  that paragraph has effect as if references in it to the appropriate court were references to the court which is dealing with the offender.
(11) Where the court deals with the offender under sub-paragraph (2)(c), it must revoke the youth rehabilitation order if it is still in force.
(12) Sub-paragraphs (13) to (15) apply where—
  (a) the court is dealing with the offender under sub-paragraph (2)(c), and
  (b) the offender has wilfully and persistently failed to comply with a youth rehabilitation order.
(13) The court may impose a youth rehabilitation order with intensive supervision and surveillance notwithstanding anything in section 1(4) (a) or (b).
(14) If—
  (a) the order is a youth rehabilitation order with intensive supervision and surveillance, and
  (b) the offence mentioned in sub-paragraph (2)(c) was punishable with imprisonment,
  the court may impose a custodial sentence notwithstanding anything in section 152(2) of the Criminal Justice Act 2003 (c. 44) (general restrictions on imposing discretionary custodial sentences).

(15) If—
    (a) the order is a youth rehabilitation order with intensive supervision and surveillance which was imposed by virtue of sub-paragraph (13) or paragraph 8(12), and
    (b) the offence mentioned in sub-paragraph (2)(c) was not punishable with imprisonment,
    for the purposes of dealing with the offender under sub-paragraph (2)(c), the court is to be taken to have had power to deal with the offender for that offence by making a detention and training order for a term not exceeding 4 months.

(16) An offender may appeal to the Crown Court against a sentence imposed under sub-paragraph (2)(c).

B3.3 Youth rehabilitation orders made in the Crown Court

B3.3.1 *Powers of the court*

Criminal Justice and Immigration Act 2008, Sch 1, para 36

36 (1) Where the Crown Court makes a youth rehabilitation order, it may include in the order a direction that further proceedings relating to the order be in a youth court or other magistrates' court (subject to paragraph 7 of Schedule 2).

    (2) In sub-paragraph (1), 'further proceedings', in relation to a youth rehabilitation order, means proceedings—
        (a) for any failure to comply with the order within the meaning given by paragraph 1(2)(b) of Schedule 2, or
        (b) on any application for amendment or revocation of the order under Part 3 or 4 of that Schedule.

Criminal Justice and Immigration Act 2008, Sch 2, para 7

7 (1) Sub-paragraph (2) applies if—
    (a) the youth rehabilitation order was made by the Crown Court and contains a direction under paragraph 36 of Schedule 1, and
    (b) a youth court or other magistrates' court would (apart from that sub-paragraph) be required, or has the power, to deal with the offender in one of the ways mentioned in paragraph 6(2).

    (2) The court may instead—
        (a) commit the offender in custody, or
        (b) release the offender on bail,
    until the offender can be brought or appear before the Crown Court.

> (3) Where a court deals with the offender's case under sub-paragraph
> (2) it must send to the Crown Court—
>   (a) a certificate signed by a justice of the peace certifying that the
>   offender has failed to comply with the youth rehabilitation order
>   in the respect specified in the certificate, and
>   (b) such other particulars of the case as may be desirable;
>   and a certificate purporting to be so signed is admissible as evi-
>   dence of the failure before the Crown Court.

B3.3.2 *Conviction whilst subject to a youth rehabilitation order*

If the defendant is convicted of a new offence whilst subject to a YRO, the court has power to revoke the sentence and resentence. If the sentence was imposed in the Crown Court, it must commit to the Crown Court for sentence, unless the Crown Court made an order allowing the magistrates' court to deal with any breach under paragraph 36 of Schedule 1 to the Criminal Justice and Immigration Act 1998.

Paragraph 18 of Schedule 2 to the Criminal Justice and Immigration Act 2008 provides:

Criminal Justice and Immigration Act 2008, Sch 2, para 18

18 (1) This paragraph applies where—
    (a) a youth rehabilitation order is in force in respect of an offender, and
    (b) the offender is convicted of an offence (the 'further offence') by a youth court or other magistrates' court ('the convicting court').
  (2) Sub-paragraphs (3) and (4) apply where—
    (a) the youth rehabilitation order—
        (i) was made by a youth court or other magistrates' court, or
        (ii) was made by the Crown Court and contains a direction under paragraph 36 of Schedule 1, and
    (b) the convicting court is dealing with the offender for the further offence.
  (3) The convicting court may revoke the order.
  (4) Where the convicting court revokes the order under sub-paragraph (3), it may deal with the offender, for the offence in respect of which the order was made, in any way in which it could have dealt with the offender for that offence (had the offender been before that court to be dealt with for the offence).
  (5) The convicting court may not exercise its powers under sub-paragraph (3) or (4) unless it considers that it would be in the interests of justice to do so, having regard to circumstances which have arisen since the youth rehabilitation order was made.

(6) In dealing with an offender under sub-paragraph (4), the sentencing court must take into account the extent to which the offender has complied with the order.

(7) A person sentenced under sub-paragraph (4) for an offence may appeal to the Crown Court against the sentence.

(8) Sub-paragraph (9) applies where—
   (a) the youth rehabilitation order was made by the Crown Court and contains a direction under paragraph 36 of Schedule 1, and
   (b) the convicting court would, but for that sub-paragraph, deal with the offender for the further offence.

(9) The convicting court may, instead of proceeding under sub-paragraph (3)—
   (a) commit the offender in custody, or
   (b) release the offender on bail,
   until the offender can be brought before the Crown Court.

(10) Sub-paragraph (11) applies if the youth rehabilitation order was made by the Crown Court and does not contain a direction under paragraph 36 of Schedule 1.

(11) The convicting court may—
   (a) commit the offender in custody, or
   (b) release the offender on bail,
   until the offender can be brought or appear before the Crown Court.

B3.4 Detention and training order: breach of the supervision requirements

B3.4.1 *Which court handles the case?*

The Powers of Criminal Courts (Sentencing) Act 2000, section 104(1) provides that such matters must be dealt with by the youth court, even if the defendant has reached the age of 18 years.

B3.4.2 *Detention and training order—new offences*

Powers of Criminal Courts (Sentencing) Act 2000, s 105(1)–(4)

105 Offences during currency of order

(1) This section applies to a person subject to a detention and training order if—
   (a) after his release and before the date on which the term of the order ends, he commits an offence punishable with imprisonment in the case of a person aged 21 or over ('the new offence'); and
   (b) whether before or after that date, he is convicted of the new offence.

(2) Subject to section 8(6) above (duty of adult magistrates' court to remit young offenders to youth court for sentence), the court by or before which a person to whom this section applies is convicted of the new

offence may, whether or not it passes any other sentence on him, order him to be detained in such youth detention accommodation as the Secretary of State may determine for the whole or any part of the period which—

(a) begins with the date of the court's order; and

(b) is equal in length to the period between the date on which the new offence was committed and the date mentioned in subsection (1) above.

(3) The period for which a person to whom this section applies is ordered under subsection (2) above to be detained in youth detention accommodation—

(a) shall, as the court may direct, either be served before and be followed by, or be served concurrently with, any sentence imposed for the new offence; and

(b) in either case, shall be disregarded in determining the appropriate length of that sentence.

(4) Where the new offence is found to have been committed over a period of two or more days, or at some time during a period of two or more days, it shall be taken for the purposes of this section to have been committed on the last of those days.

...

 See *Blackstone's Criminal Practice 2017* **E7.15–E7.25**

B4 Jurisdiction of the Adult Magistrates' Court over Youths

B4.1 Youths in the adult court alone

A child or young person, who is not jointly charged with an adult and who is refused bail at the police station, may appear in an adult court when no youth court is sitting. The adult court may deal with the young person only for the purposes of making a decision with regard to a remand. It must then remit the young person to the next available youth court (Children and Young Persons Act 1933, s 46(2)) (see further **B7**).

B4.2 Jointly charged with an adult

A child or young person *must* appear before the adult court if jointly charged with an adult.

A child or young person *may* appear before the adult court if:

- charged with aiding or abetting an adult;
- an adult is charged with aiding or abetting the child or young person;
- charged with an offence arising out of the same circumstances as those giving rise to proceedings against an adult.

Children and Young Persons Act 1933, s 46

46 Assignment of certain matters to youth courts

(1) Subject as hereinafter provided, no charge against a child or young person, and no application whereof the hearing is by rules made under this section assigned to youth courts, shall be heard by a magistrates' court which is not a youth court:

Provided that—

  (a) a charge made jointly against a child or young person and a person who has attained the age of eighteen years shall be heard by a magistrates' court other than a youth court; and

  (b) where a child or young person is charged with an offence, the charge may be heard by a magistrates' court which is not a youth court if a person who has attained the age of eighteen years is charged at the same time with aiding, abetting, causing, procuring, allowing or permitting that offence; and

  (c) where, in the course of any proceedings before any magistrates' court other than a youth court, it appears that the person to whom the proceedings relate is a child or young person, nothing in this subsection shall be construed as preventing the court, if it thinks fit so to do, from proceeding with the hearing and determination of those proceedings.

Children and Young Persons Act 1963, s 18

18 Jurisdiction of magistrates' courts in certain cases involving children and young persons

Notwithstanding section 46(1) of the principal Act (which restricts the jurisdiction of magistrates' courts which are not youth courts in cases where a child or young person is charged with an offence) a magistrates' court which is not a youth court may hear an information against a child or young person if he is charged—

(a) with aiding, abetting, causing, procuring, allowing or permitting an offence with which a person who has attained the age of eighteen is charged at the same time; or

(b) with an offence arising out of circumstances which are the same as or connected with those giving rise to an offence with which a person who has attained the age of eighteen is charged at the same time.

B4.2.1 *What is a joint charge?*

It is not necessary for the charge to specify that the offence was committed 'jointly' or 'together with' the adult concerned (*R v Rowlands* [1972] 1 All ER 306).

Where there is a charge of taking a motor vehicle without consent or aggravated vehicle-taking, the driver and any passengers charged with allowing themselves to be carried are jointly charged (*R v Peterborough Justices, ex p Allgood* (1995) 159 JP 627, QBD).

B4.3 Severance of a youth from an adult

B4.3.1 *Sendings*

When the court sends the adult but is not obliged to send the youth, it shall, after following the plea before venue procedures (see **B5**), send the youth too if it considers it necessary in the interests of justice to do so (Crime and Disorder Act 1998, s 51(7)).

Relevant issues have been identified by the Sentencing Council in two Guidelines:

Allocation Guideline

Youths jointly charged with adults—interests of justice test

The proper venue for the trial of any youth is normally the youth court. Subject to statutory restrictions, that remains the case where a youth is charged jointly with an adult.

The following guidance must be applied in those cases where the interests of justice test falls to be considered:

1. If the adult is sent for trial to the Crown Court, the court should conclude that the youth must be tried separately in the youth court unless it is in the interests of justice for the youth and the adult to be tried jointly.

2. Examples of factors that should be considered when deciding whether it is in the interests of justice to send the youth to the Crown Court (rather than having a trial in the youth court) include:
   - whether separate trials will cause injustice to witnesses or to the case as a whole (consideration should be given to the provisions of sections 27 and 28 of the Youth Justice and Criminal Evidence Act 1999);
   - the age of the youth: the younger the youth, the greater the desirability that the youth be tried in the youth court;
   - the age gap between the youth and the adult: a substantial gap in age militates in favour of the youth being tried in the youth court;
   - the lack of maturity of the youth;
   - the relative culpability of the youth compared with the adult and whether the alleged role played by the youth was minor;
   - the lack of previous convictions on the part of the youth.

3. The court should bear in mind that the youth court now has a general power to commit for sentence following conviction pursuant to Section 3B of the Powers of Criminal Courts (Sentencing) Act 2000 (as amended). In appropriate cases this will permit the same court to sentence adults and youths who have been tried separately.

Guideline Overarching Principles—Youth Sentencing, paras 12.15–12.18

Jointly charged with an adult

12.15 A further exception to the presumption in favour of summary trial arises where a young person is charged jointly with a person aged 18 or over; if the court considers it necessary to commit them both for trial it will have the power to commit the young person to the Crown Court for trial.

12.16 Any presumption in favour of sending a youth to the Crown Court to be tried jointly with an adult must be balanced with the general presumption that young offenders should be dealt with in a youth court.

12.17 When deciding whether to separate the youth and adult defendants, a court must consider:
   - the young age of the offender, particularly where the age gap between the adult and youth is substantial,
   - the immaturity and intellect of the youth,
   - the relative culpability of the youth compared with the adult and whether or not the role played by the youth was minor, and
   - any lack of previous convictions on the part of the youth compared with the adult offender.

> **12.18** A very significant factor will be whether the trial of the adult and
> youth could be severed without inconvenience to witnesses or injus-
> tice to the case as a whole, including whether there are benefits in
> the same tribunal sentencing all offenders. In most circumstances,
> a single trial of all issues is likely to be most in the interests of justice.

In *Newham Justices, ex p Knight* [1976] Crim LR 323, it was stated:

> The advantage of committing the child or young person for trial is that
> he/she and the adult will be tried together in the Crown Court. Those
> charged with committing an offence jointly should generally be jointly
> tried. The disadvantage of such a committal/sending is that the Crown
> Court is now not generally thought to be the best place for the trial of
> young people, unless the offence is unusually serious. In deciding whether
> to commit the young person the magistrates should exercise their discre-
> tion judicially and should not automatically send him/her to the Crown
> Court just because he/she is jointly charged with an adult.

B4.4 Summary trials

If an adult and the youth plead not guilty to a joint charge, the trial
must take place in the adult court (Children and Young Persons
Act 1933, s 46(1)(a)). It may do so if the allegation is of aiding and
abetting, or arises out of the same circumstances (Children and
Young Persons Act 1933, s 46(1)(b); Children and Young Person
Act 1963, s 18(a) and (b)). (See **B4.2**.)

If the youth pleads guilty or is found guilty, the adult court may
sentence under its limited powers or remit to the youth court
(Powers of Criminal Courts (Sentencing) Act 2000, s 8(6)).

If the adult pleads guilty and the youth not guilty, it is to be
expected that the court will remit to the youth court for trial
(Magistrates' Courts Act 1980, s 29(2)) (see **B7**).

B4.5 Remittal

All cases not sent to the Crown Court, sentenced within the limited powers of the adult court (see **B9**) or listed for trial with an
adult, will be remitted to the youth court (see **B7**).

B5 **Managing the Case**

In order to handle the case appropriately, the steps shown in **Figure 3** must be followed where the youth is jointly charged with an adult. If the adult faces an indictable-only offence he

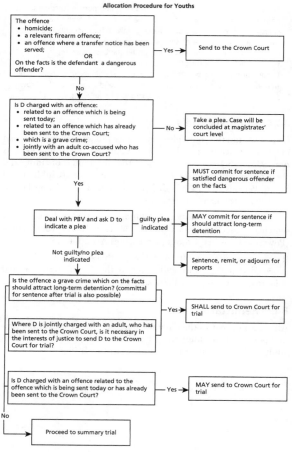

Allocation Procedure for Youths

The offence
- homicide;
- a relevant firearm offence;
- an offence where a transfer notice has been served;

OR

On the facts is the defendant a dangerous offender? —Yes→ Send to the Crown Court

↓ No

Is D charged with an offence:
- related to an offence which is being sent today;
- related to an offence which has already been sent to the Crown Court;
- which is a grave crime;
- jointly with an adult co-accused who has been sent to the Crown Court? —No→ Take a plea. Case will be concluded at magistrates' court level

↓ Yes

Deal with PBV and ask D to indicate a plea —guilty plea indicated→
- MUST commit for sentence if satisfied dangerous offender on the facts
- MAY commit for sentence if should attract long-term detention
- Sentence, remit, or adjourn for reports

↓ Not guilty/no plea indicated

Is the offence a grave crime which on the facts should attract long-term detention? (committal for sentence after trial is also possible) —Yes→ SHALL send to Crown Court for trial

Where D is jointly charged with an adult, who has been sent to the Crown Court, is it necessary in the interests of justice to send D to the Crown Court for trial?

Is D charged with an offence related to the offence which is being sent today or has already been sent to the Crown Court? —Yes→ MAY send to Crown Court for trial

↓ No

Proceed to summary trial

Figure 3 Allocation procedure for youths

must be sent to the Crown Court before dealing with this procedure. If the adult faces an either-way offence, this procedure should be followed but any plea should be taken first from the adult.

B5.1 Sendings to the Crown Court

The court *must* forthwith send the case to the Crown Court if the youth is charged with:

- homicide;
- an offence attracting a minimum sentence under section 51A of the Firearms Act 1968 or section 29(3) of the Violent Crime Reduction Act 2006, provided the youth was aged at least 16 at the date of the offence;
- a specified offence (see **Appendix 5**) and on the facts of the case an extended sentence may be required (so that for youths, a minimum sentence of four years would be required); *or*
- if notice has been given by the Crown under section 51B (serious fraud) or section 51C (children) of the Crime and Disorder Act 1998 (see **B5.5**).

When a child or young person is sent for trial, the court may also send for trial any either-way or summary offence for which he is charged if:

- it appears to the court to be related to the indictable-only offence; *and*
- in the case of a summary offence, it is punishable with imprisonment or involves obligatory or discretionary disqualification from driving (Crime and Disorder Act 1998, s 51(6) and (11)—see **B5.5**).

B5.1.1 Key points

- An offence of murder, attempted murder, manslaughter, causing or allowing the death of a child or vulnerable adult, or infanticide must be sent to the Crown Court for trial (Magistrates' Courts Act 1980, s 24(1)), along with any other offences with which the defendant is charged at the same time, if the charges for both offences could be joined in the same indictment (Magistrates' Courts Act 1980, s 24(1A)).
- The relevant offences under the Firearms Act 1968 are set out in section 51A of that Act:

Firearms Act 1968, s 51A

51A Minimum sentence for certain offences under s 5

(1) This section applies where—
  (a) an individual is convicted of—
    (i) an offence under section 5(1)(a), (ab), (aba), (ac), (ad), (ae), (af) or of this Act,
    (ii) an offence under section 5(1A)(a) of this Act, or
    (iii) an offence under any of the provisions of this Act listed in sub-section (1A) in respect of a firearm or ammunition specified in section 5(1)(a), (ab), (aba), (ac), (ad), (ae), (af) or (c) or section 5(1A)(a) of this Act, and
  (b) the offence was committed after the commencement of this section and at a time when he was aged 16 or over.

(1A) The provisions are—
  (a) section 16 (possession of firearm with intent to injure);
  (b) section 16A (possession of firearm with intent to cause fear of violence);
  (c) section 17 (use of firearm to resist arrest);
  (d) section 18 (carrying firearm with criminal intent);
  (e) section 19 (carrying a firearm in a public place);
  (f) section 20(1) (trespassing in a building with firearm).

(2) The court shall impose an appropriate custodial sentence (or order for detention) for a term of at least the required minimum term (with or without a fine) unless the court is of the opinion that there are exceptional circumstances relating to the offence or to the offender which justify its not doing so.

(3) Where an offence is found to have been committed over a period of two or more days, or at some time during a period of two or more days, it shall be taken for the purposes of this section to have been committed on the last of those days.

(4) In this section 'appropriate custodial sentence (or order for detention)' means—
  (a) in relation to England and Wales—
    (i) in the case of an offender who is aged 18 or over when convicted, a sentence of imprisonment, and
    (ii) in the case of an offender who is aged under 18 at that time, a sentence of detention under section 91 of the Powers of Criminal Courts (Sentencing) Act 2000;
  (b) ...

(5) In this section 'the required minimum term' means—
  (a) in relation to England and Wales—
    (i) in the case of an offender who was aged 18 or over when he committed the offence, five years, and
    (ii) in the case of an offender who was under 18 at that time, three years ...
  (b) ...

B5.2 Other indictable and all summary matters

The court must proceed to plea before venue if the case could be sent; or take a plea if it is a summary-only offence. This applies even when appearing jointly with an adult, though if both plead not guilty the court will have to consider whether it is appropriate to join the cases.

Tottenham Youth Court, ex p Fawzy [1999] 1 WLR 1350 confirms that the adult court must make the decision on venue under section 24. There is no power to remit the youth to the youth court for that court to make the mode of trial decision.

B5.3 Guilty plea indications

If a guilty plea is indicated, the court should proceed to sentence if the court's powers are sufficient (see **B9**) or remit to the youth court (see **B7**) *unless*:

- the offence is a specified offence (see **Appendix 5**) and on the developing facts an extended sentence may be required (so that for a youth a minimum sentence of at least four years may be required), in which case it *must* commit to the Crown Court for sentence;
- the offence is related to an offence which is being sent that day, or related to a matter which has already been sent, in which case it *may* commit to the Crown Court for sentence;
- the offence is capable of being a grave crime, in which case it *may* commit for sentence if on the facts the offence might attract a sentence of long-term detention.

If the youth pleads guilty and the adult is committed for sentence under section 4 of the Powers of Criminal Courts (Sentencing) Act 2000, he must be remitted for sentence to the youth court, unless either he is committed to the Crown Court for seriousness or dangerousness, or the court imposes a discharge, referral order, financial penalty, or bind over under section 8 of the 2000 Act.

B5.3.1 Key points

- Offences are *grave crimes* if they comprise:
  - an offence punishable in the case of a person aged 21 or over with imprisonment for 14 years or more, not being an offence the sentence for which is fixed by law; or
  - an offence under section 3 of the Sexual Offences Act 2003 ('the 2003 Act') (sexual assault); or
  - an offence under section 13 of the 2003 Act (child sex offences committed by children or young persons); or
  - an offence under section 25 of the 2003 Act (sexual activity with a child family member); or
  - an offence under section 26 of the 2003 Act (inciting a child family member to engage in sexual activity); or

- an offence under subsection (1)(a), (ab), (aba), (ac), (ad), (ae), (af), or (c) of section 5 of the Firearms Act 1968 (prohibited weapons), or under subsection (1A)(a) of that section; or
- an offence under section 51A(1A)(b), (e), or (f) of the Firearms Act 1968, which was committed in respect of a firearm or ammunition specified in section 5(1), (ab), (aba), (ac), (ad), (ae), (af), or (c), or section 5(1A)(a) of that Act; or
- an offence under section 28 of the Violent Crime Reduction Act 2006 (using someone to mind a weapon).
- An offence requiring a sentence of 'long-term detention' because it should exceed two years:
  - in determining whether a sentence of more than two years would be imposed, the court should ask itself what sentence was realistically possible, bearing in mind the sentencing range (*Crown Prosecution Service v Newcastle Upon Tyne Youth Court* [2010] EWHC 2773 (Admin));
  - the fact that a particular youth aged 12 to 14 years could not receive a detention and training order is not a ground for refusing jurisdiction when a sentence of more than two years' detention is not required; youths of this age should not be detained save in wholly exceptional circumstances (*R (B) v Norfolk Youth Court* and CPS [2013] EWHC 1459 (Admin));
  - in *BH v Llandudno Youth Court* [2014] EWHC 1833 (Admin) the court considered all the relevant authorities and applied the guideline, emphasizing that the correct question is, bearing in mind the age and the previous good character of the child concerned (there an 11-year-old facing an allegation of inducing a boy under 13 to engage in a sexual act against s 8 Sexual Offences Act 2003), and any other mitigation that is known and uncontentious, and bearing in mind aggravating factors, is there a real prospect that the Crown Court would exercise its powers under section 91 of the PCC(S) Act 2000 to impose custody? (It concluded that there was not.);
  - *R v H* [2014] EWCA Crim 2292 confirmed that while detention may have been appropriate for a 15-year-old in the same circumstances, a defendant who was 14 years old at the time of the offence had a youth rehabilitation order substituted. This was notwithstanding the seriousness of the burglary by 15 to 20 youths who entered a dwelling house and threatened violence, and his brandishing a carving knife to make his escape. He did not have 'a particularly bad record'—assaults on his mother; theft convictions; and various reprimands and warnings so as to be 'just' a persistent offender. The mitigation was a plea at the first opportunity; his being the only one arrested and being in the presence of much older boys who had serious criminal records and of whom he was in fear about attempting to separate himself;

- the overarching guideline on sentencing youths issued by the Sentencing Council states, in relation to the use of long-term detention:

Overarching Guideline—Youth Sentencing, paras 12.10 and 12.11

12.10 This general power should be used rarely since:
  (i) it is the general policy of Parliament that those under 18 should be tried in the youth court wherever possible;
  (ii) trial in the Crown Court under this provision should be reserved for the most serious cases, recognising the greater formality of the proceedings and the greatly increased number of people involved;
  (iii) offenders aged under 15 will rarely attract a period of detention under this provision and those under 12 even more rarely.

12.11 Accordingly,
  (i) a young person aged 10 or 11 (or aged 12–14 but not a persistent offender) should be committed to the Crown Court under this provision only where charged with an offence of such gravity that, despite the normal prohibition on a custodial sentence for a person of that age, a sentence exceeding two years is a realistic possibility; *R(D) v Manchester City Youth Court* [2001] EWHC Admin 860
  (ii) a young person aged 12–17 (for which a detention and training order could be imposed) should be committed to the Crown Court under this provision only where charged with an offence of such gravity that a sentence substantially beyond the 2 year maximum for a detention and training order is a realistic possibility[;] *C & D v Sheffield Youth Court* [2003] EWHC Admin 35 confirming the relevance of undisputed personal mitigation.

 See *Blackstone's Criminal Practice 2017* **D24.27**

B5.4 Not guilty and no plea indications

- If a youth is jointly charged with an adult who has been sent to the Crown Court, the court must first consider if the offence is a grave crime which on the facts should attract a sentence of long-term detention; and if it is, the court *must* send for trial. This provision is likely be seriously affected by the amendment of section 3B Powers of Criminal Courts (Sentencing) Act 2000 as the court may now commit a grave crime for sentence following a trial if long-term detention powers may be justified and fuller facts are (as is likely) available at the end of the trial (*DPP v South Tyneside Youth Court and B* [2015] EWHC 1455). As a result the court need not, at the allocation stage, take the prosecution case at its highest but may consider all relevant factors.

B5 Managing the Case

If the youth has not been sent for that reason but is jointly charged with an adult and it is necessary in the interests of justice (see **B4.3.1**) to send the youth to the Crown Court for trial, the court must then send the youth for that reason.

If the defendant is charged with an offence related to an offence which is sent that day, or has already been sent, the court *may* send to the Crown Court for trial.

In all other cases the court should proceed to summary trial or, if there is to be no effective trial of the adult, remit to the youth court (see **B7**).

B5.5 Statutory provisions

> **Magistrates' Courts Act 1980, ss 24A–24C**
>
> **24A Child or young person to indicate intention as to plea in certain cases**
>
> (1) This section applies where—
>
>   (a) a person under the age of 18 years appears or is brought before a magistrates' court on an information charging him with an offence other than one falling within section 51A(12) of the Crime and Disorder Act 1998 ('the 1998 Act'); and
>
>   (b) but for the application of the following provisions of this section, the court would be required at that stage, by virtue of section 51(7) or (8) or 51A(3)(b), (4) or (5) of the 1998 Act to determine, in relation to the offence, whether to send the person to the Crown Court for trial (or to determine any matter, the effect of which would be to determine whether he is sent to the Crown Court for trial).
>
> (2) Where this section applies, the court shall, before proceeding to make any such determination as is referred to in subsection (1)(b) above (the 'relevant determination'), follow the procedure set out in this section.
>
> (3) Everything that the court is required to do under the following provisions of this section must be done with the accused person in court.
>
> (4) The court shall cause the charge to be written down, if this has not already been done, and to be read to the accused.
>
> (5) The court shall then explain to the accused in ordinary language that he may indicate whether (if the offence were to proceed to trial) he would plead guilty or not guilty, and that if he indicates that he would plead guilty—
>
>   (a) the court must proceed as mentioned in subsection (7) below; and
>
>   (b) (in cases where the offence is one mentioned in section 91(1) of the Powers of Criminal Courts (Sentencing) Act 2000) he may be sent to the Crown Court for sentencing under section 3B or (if applicable) 3C of that Act if the court is of such opinion as is mentioned in subsection (2) of the applicable section.
>
> (6) The court shall then ask the accused whether (if the offence were to proceed to trial) he would plead guilty or not guilty.

(7) If the accused indicates that he would plead guilty, the court shall proceed as if—

  (a) the proceedings constituted from the beginning the summary trial of the information; and

  (b) section 9(1) above was complied with and he pleaded guilty under it, and, accordingly, the court shall not (and shall not be required to) proceed to make the relevant determination or to proceed further under section 51 or (as the case may be) section 51A of the 1998 Act in relation to the offence.

(8) If the accused indicates that he would plead not guilty, the court shall proceed to make the relevant determination and this section shall cease to apply.

(9) If the accused in fact fails to indicate how he would plead, for the purposes of this section he shall be taken to indicate that he would plead not guilty.

(10) Subject to subsection (7) above, the following shall not for any purpose be taken to constitute the taking of a plea—

  (a) asking the accused under this section whether (if the offence were to proceed to trial) he would plead guilty or not guilty;

  (b) an indication by the accused under this section of how he would plead.

24B Intention as to plea by child or young person: absence of accused

(1) This section shall have effect where—

  (a) a person under the age of 18 years appears or is brought before a magistrates' court on an information charging him with an offence other than one falling within section 51A(12) of the Crime and Disorder Act 1998;

  (b) but for the application of the following provisions of this section, the court would be required at that stage to make one of the determinations referred to in paragraph (b) of section 24A(1) above ('the relevant determination');

  (c) the accused is represented by a legal representative;

  (d) the court considers that by reason of the accused's disorderly conduct before the court it is not practicable for proceedings under section 24A above to be conducted in his presence; and

  (e) the court considers that it should proceed in the absence of the accused.

(2) In such a case—

  (a) the court shall cause the charge to be written down, if this has not already been done, and to be read to the representative;

  (b) the court shall ask the representative whether (if the offence were to proceed to trial) the accused would plead guilty or not guilty;

  (c) if the representative indicates that the accused would plead guilty the court shall proceed as if the proceedings constituted from the beginning the summary trial of the information, and as if section 9(1) above was complied with and the accused pleaded guilty under it;

(d) if the representative indicates that the accused would plead not guilty the court shall proceed to make the relevant determination and this section shall cease to apply.

(3) If the representative in fact fails to indicate how the accused would plead, for the purposes of this section he shall be taken to indicate that the accused would plead not guilty.

(4) Subject to subsection (2)(c) above, the following shall not for any purpose be taken to constitute the taking of a plea—

(a) asking the representative under this section whether (if the offence were to proceed to trial) the accused would plead guilty or not guilty;

(b) an indication by the representative under this section of how the accused would plead.

24C Intention as to plea by child or young person: adjournment

(1) A magistrates' court proceeding under section 24A or 24B above may adjourn the proceedings at any time, and on doing so on any occasion when the accused is present may remand the accused.

(2) Where the court remands the accused, the time fixed for the resumption of proceedings shall be that at which he is required to appear or be brought before the court in pursuance of the remand or would be required to be brought before the court but for section 128(3A) below.

Crime and Disorder Act 1998, ss 51–51C

51 Sending cases to the Crown Court: adults

(1) Where an adult appears or is brought before a magistrates' court ('the court') charged with an offence and any of the conditions mentioned in subsection (2) below is satisfied, the court shall send him forthwith to the Crown Court for trial for the offence.

...

(3) Where the court sends an adult for trial under subsection (1) above, it shall at the same time send him to the Crown Court for trial for any either-way or summary offence with which he is charged and which—

(a) (if it is an either-way offence) appears to the court to be related to the offence mentioned in subsection (1) above; or

(b) (if it is a summary offence) appears to the court to be related to the offence mentioned in subsection (1) above or to the either-way offence, and which fulfils the requisite condition (as defined in subsection (11) below).

...

(5) Where—

(a) the court sends an adult ('A') for trial under subsection (1) or (3) above;

(b) another adult appears or is brought before the court on the same or a subsequent occasion charged jointly with A with an either-way offence; and

(c) that offence appears to the court to be related to an offence for which A was sent for trial under subsection (1) or (3) above,

the court shall where it is the same occasion, and may where it is a subsequent occasion, send the other adult forthwith to the Crown Court for trial for the either-way offence.

...

(7) Where—

    (a) the court sends an adult ('A') for trial under subsection (1), (3) or (5) above; and

    (b) a child or young person appears or is brought before the court on the same or a subsequent occasion charged jointly with A with an indictable offence for which A is sent for trial under subsection (1), (3) or (5) above, or an indictable offence which appears to the court to be related to that offence,

the court shall, if it considers it necessary in the interests of justice to do so, send the child or young person forthwith to the Crown Court for trial for the indictable offence.

(8) Where the court sends a child or young person for trial under subsection (7) above, it may at the same time send him to the Crown Court for trial for any indictable or summary offence with which he is charged and which—

    (a) (if it is an indictable offence) appears to the court to be related to the offence for which he is sent for trial; and

    (b) (if it is a summary offence) appears to the court to be related to the offence for which he is sent for trial or to the indictable offence, and which fulfils the requisite condition.

(9) Subsections (7) and (8) above are subject to sections 24A and 24B of the Magistrates' Courts Act 1980 (which provide for certain cases involving children and young persons to be tried summarily).

(10) The trial of the information charging any summary offence for which a person is sent for trial under this section shall be treated as if the court had adjourned it under section 10 of the 1980 Act and had not fixed the time and place for its resumption.

(11) A summary offence fulfils the requisite condition if it is punishable with imprisonment or involves obligatory or discretionary disqualification from driving.

(13) The functions of a magistrates' court under this section, and its related functions under section 51D below, may be discharged by a single justice.

51A Sending cases to the Crown Court: children and young persons

(1) This section is subject to sections 24A and 24B of the Magistrates' Courts Act 1980 (which provide for certain offences involving children or young persons to be tried summarily).

(2) Where a child or young person appears or is brought before a magistrates' court ('the court') charged with an offence and any of the conditions mentioned in subsection (3) below is satisfied, the court shall send him forthwith to the Crown Court for trial for the offence.

(3) Those conditions are—
  (a) that the offence falls within subsection (12) below;
  (b) that the offence is such as is mentioned in subsection (1) of section 91 of the Powers of Criminal Courts (Sentencing) Act 2000 (other than one mentioned in paragraph (d) below in relation to which it appears to the court as mentioned there) and the court considers that if he is found guilty of the offence it ought to be possible to sentence him in pursuance of subsection (3) of that section;
  (c) that notice is given to the court under section 51B or 51C below in respect of the offence;
  (d) that the offence is a specified offence (within the meaning of section 224 of the Criminal Justice Act 2003) and it appears to the court that if he is found guilty of the offence the criteria for the imposition of a sentence under section 226B of that Act would be met.
(4) Where the court sends a child or young person for trial under subsection (2) above, it may at the same time send him to the Crown Court for trial for any indictable or summary offence with which he is charged and which—
  (a) (if it is an indictable offence) appears to the court to be related to the offence mentioned in subsection (2) above; or
  (b) (if it is a summary offence) appears to the court to be related to the offence mentioned in subsection (2) above or to the indictable offence, and which fulfils the requisite condition (as defined in subsection (9) below).
(5) Where a child or young person who has been sent for trial under subsection (2) above subsequently appears or is brought before a magistrates' court charged with an indictable or summary offence which—
  (a) appears to the court to be related to the offence mentioned in subsection (2) above; and
  (b) (in the case of a summary offence) fulfils the requisite condition,
  the court may send him forthwith to the Crown Court for trial for the indictable or summary offence.
(6) Where—
  (a) the court sends a child or young person ('C') for trial under subsection (2) or (4) above; and
  (b) an adult appears or is brought before the court on the same or a subsequent occasion charged jointly with C with an either-way offence for which C is sent for trial under subsection (2) or (4) above, or an either-way offence which appears to the court to be related to that offence,
  the court shall where it is the same occasion, and may where it is a subsequent occasion, send the adult forthwith to the Crown Court for trial for the either-way offence.
(7) Where the court sends an adult for trial under subsection (6) above, it shall at the same time send him to the Crown Court for trial for any either-way or summary offence with which he is charged and which—
  (a) (if it is an either-way offence) appears to the court to be related to the offence for which he was sent for trial; and
  (b) (if it is a summary offence) appears to the court to be related to the offence for which he was sent for trial or to the either-way offence, and which fulfils the requisite condition.

(8) The trial of the information charging any summary offence for which a person is sent for trial under this section shall be treated as if the court had adjourned it under section 10 of the 1980 Act and had not fixed the time and place for its resumption.

(9) A summary offence fulfils the requisite condition if it is punishable with imprisonment or involves obligatory or discretionary disqualification from driving.

(10) In the case of a child or young person charged with an offence—
   (a) if the offence satisfies any of the conditions in subsection (3) above, the offence shall be dealt with under subsection (2) above and not under any other provision of this section or section 51 above;
   (b) subject to paragraph (a) above, if the offence is one in respect of which the requirements of subsection (7) of section 51 above for sending the child or young person to the Crown Court are satisfied, the offence shall be dealt with under that subsection and not under any other provision of this section or section 51 above.

(11) The functions of a magistrates' court under this section, and its related functions under section 51D below, may be discharged by a single justice.

(12) An offence falls within this subsection if—
   (a) it is an offence of homicide;
   (b) each of the requirements of section 51A(1) of the Firearms Act 1968 would be satisfied with respect to—
      (i) the offence; and
      (ii) the person charged with it,
      if he were convicted of the offence; or
   (c) section 29(3) of the Violent Crime Reduction Act 2006 (minimum sentences in certain cases of using someone to mind a weapon) would apply if he were convicted of the offence.

51B Notices in serious or complex fraud cases

(1) A notice may be given by a designated authority under this section in respect of an indictable offence if the authority is of the opinion that the evidence of the offence charged—
   (a) is sufficient for the person charged to be put on trial for the offence; and
   (b) reveals a case of fraud of such seriousness or complexity that it is appropriate that the management of the case should without delay be taken over by the Crown Court …

(3) The notice must also specify the proposed place of trial, and in selecting that place the designated authority must have regard to the same matters as are specified in paragraphs (a) to (c) of section 51D(4) below.

51C Notices in certain cases involving children

(1) A notice may be given by the Director of Public Prosecutions under this section in respect of an offence falling within subsection (3) below if he is of the opinion—
   (a) that the evidence of the offence would be sufficient for the person charged to be put on trial for the offence;
   (b) that a child would be called as a witness at the trial; and

    (c) that, for the purpose of avoiding any prejudice to the welfare of the child, the case should be taken over and proceeded with without delay by the Crown Court...

(3) This subsection applies to an offence—

    (a) which involves an assault on, or injury or a threat of injury to, a person;

    (b) under section 1 of the Children and Young Persons Act 1933 (cruelty to persons under 16);

    (c) under the Sexual Offences Act 1956, the Protection of Children Act 1978 or the Sexual Offences Act 2003;

    (d) of kidnapping or false imprisonment, or an offence under section 1 or 2 of the Child Abduction Act 1984;

    (e) which consists of attempting or conspiring to commit, or of aiding, abetting, counselling, procuring or inciting the commission of, an offence falling within paragraph (a), (b), (c) or (d) above. ...

(7) In this section 'child' means—

    (a) a person who is under the age of 17; or

    (b) any person of whom a video recording (as defined in section 63(1) of the Youth Justice and Criminal Evidence Act 1999) was made when he was under the age of 17 with a view to its admission as his evidence in chief in the trial referred to in subsection (1) above.

B6 **Parents and Guardians**

B6.1 Definition of parent/guardian

B6.1.1 *Parent*

There is no definition of who is a 'parent', but it is likely to include a person with parental responsibility under the Children Act 1989.

B6.1.2 *Guardian*

> **Children and Young Persons Act 1933, s 107(1)**
>
> **107 Interpretation**
>
> 'Guardian', in relation to a child or young person, includes any person who, in the opinion of the court having cognisance of any case in relation to the child or young person or in which the child or young person is concerned, has for the time being the care of the child or young person ....

B6.2 Requiring attendance at court

> **Children and Young Persons Act 1933, s 34A**
>
> **34A Attendance at court of parent or guardian**
>
> (1) Where a child or young person is charged with an offence or is for any other reason brought before a court, the court—
>
>   (a) may in any case; and
>
>   (b) shall in the case of a child or a young person who is under the age of sixteen years,
>
> require a person who is a parent or guardian of his to attend at the court during all the stages of the proceedings, unless and to the extent that the court is satisfied that it would be unreasonable to require such attendance, having regard to the circumstances of the case.
>
> (2) In relation to a child or young person for whom a local authority have parental responsibility and who—
>
>   (a) is in their care; or
>
>   (b) is provided with accommodation by them in the exercise of any functions (in particular those under the Children Act 1989) which are social service functions within the meaning of the Local Authority Social Services Act 1970,
>
> the reference in subsection (1) above to a person who is a parent or guardian of his shall be construed as a reference to that authority or, where he is allowed to live with such a person, as including such a reference.
>
> In this subsection 'local authority' and 'parental responsibility' have the same meanings as in the Children Act 1989.

In the sentencing guideline, Overarching Principles—Sentencing Youths (to which the court must have regard), it is stated:

Overarching Principles—Sentencing Youths

The statutory framework clearly envisages the attendance of an adult with a degree of responsibility for the young person; this obligation reflects the principal aim of reducing offending, recognizing that that is unlikely to be achieved by the young person alone. A court must be aware of a risk that a young person will seek to avoid this requirement either by urging the court to proceed in the absence of an adult or in arranging for a person to come to court who purports to have (but in reality does not have) the necessary degree of responsibility. Insistence on attendance may produce a delay in the case before the court; however, it is important that this obligation is maintained and that it is widely recognized that a court will require such attendance, especially when imposing sentence.

The Criminal Procedure Rules, rule 7.4(9) provides:

Criminal Procedure Rules, r 7.4(9)

7.4 Summons, warrant, and requisition

(9) A summons or requisition issued to a defendant under 18 may require that defendant's parent or guardian to attend the court with the defendant, or a separate summons or requisition may be issued for that purpose.

B6.3 Responsibility for financial orders

Where the defendant is aged under 16 years, the court *must* order the parent or guardian to pay the fine, costs, surcharge, and compensation if ordered unless:

- he cannot be found; or
- it would be unreasonable to make an order for payment having regard to the circumstances of the case.

Where the defendant is aged 16 or 17 years, the court *may* order the parent or guardian to pay the fine, costs, surcharge, and compensation if ordered unless:

- he cannot be found; or
- it would be unreasonable to make an order for payment having regard to the circumstances of the case.

The court may make such an order in the absence of the parent or guardian where the court has required attendance but they have not attended.

Section 137 of the Powers of Criminal Courts (Sentencing) Act 2000 states that before making a financial order against a parent or guardian, the court may require details of their circumstances through a financial circumstances order. If there is no cooperation with this inquiry, the court may make such determination as it thinks fit.

Courts need not order parents to pay the victim surcharge if they are the victims of the crime. The liability may be delayed, possibly until the youth reaches 18 (see Ministry of Justice Circular 18/13).

B6.3.1 *When is it 'unreasonable' to make a financial order?*

In *R v Sheffield Crown Court, ex p Clarkson* [1986] Cr App R (S) 454, a compensation order payable by a mother who 'had done what she could to keep her son from criminal ways' was quashed. She was also of limited means, and the order meant that it would have taken her more than two years to pay.

In *TA v DPP* [1997] 1 Cr App R (S) 1, [1996] Crim LR 606, QBD, the parent of a child accommodated by the local authority under section 20 of the Children Act 1989 was not reasonably to be ordered to pay a financial penalty.

In *R (M) v Inner London Crown Court* [2003] EWHC 301 (Admin), the policy underlying the legislation meant that it was in the public interest that the financial order be recovered from the parent unless there were special circumstances which made that inappropriate.

In *R v JB* [2004] EWCA Crim 14, there seems to be an assumption that in the absence of parental fault it would be unreasonable to order the parent to pay.

B6.4 Local authorities

A local authority is responsible for payment of financial orders where the authority has parental responsibility for the defendant and the defendant is in the authority's care or is accommodated by it (Powers of Criminal Courts (Sentencing) Act 2000, s 137(8)).

An order remanding a young person to the care of the local authority does not confer parental responsibility on the local authority. Parental responsibility is acquired only with a full care order (*North Yorkshire County Council v Selby Youth Court* [1994] 1 All ER 991, QBD).

B6.4.1 *When is it 'unreasonable' to make a financial order?*

In *D and R v DPP* [1995] 16 Cr App R (S) 1040, [1995] Crim LR 748, a local authority that had done everything it reasonably and properly could to protect the public from the criminal behaviour of a young person in its care, could not be expected to assume responsibility for financial orders.

In *Bedfordshire County Council v DPP* [1996] 1 Cr App R (S) 322, [1995] Crim LR 962, the court stated that a causal link between the authority's lack of care and the offending needs to be established before the court should order payment of the financial penalty by the authority.

In *Marlowe Child and Family Services Ltd v DPP* [1998] Crim LR 594, a company contracted by the local authority to look after the young person could not be ordered to pay a financial order.

B6.5 Parental bind overs

Since the introduction of parenting orders, the imposition of parental bind overs has declined.

The making of a bind over requires consideration of its terms and the consent of the person being bound over.

Powers of the Criminal Courts (Sentencing) Act 2000, s 150

150 Binding over of parent or guardian

(1) Where a child or young person (that is to say, any person aged under 18) is convicted of an offence, the powers conferred by this section shall be exercisable by the court by which he is sentenced for that offence, and where the offender is aged under 16 when sentenced it shall be the duty of that court—

    (a) to exercise those powers if it is satisfied, having regard to the circumstances of the case, that their exercise would be desirable in the interests of preventing the commission by him of further offences; and

    (b) if it does not exercise them, to state in open court that it is not satisfied as mentioned in paragraph (a) above and why it is not so satisfied;

but this subsection has effect subject to section 19(5) above and paragraph 13(5) of Schedule 1 to this Act (cases where referral orders made or extended).

(2) The powers conferred by this section are as follows—

    (a) with the consent of the offender's parent or guardian, to order the parent or guardian to enter into a recognizance to take proper care of him and exercise proper control over him; and

---

(b) if the parent or guardian refuses consent and the court considers the refusal unreasonable, to order the parent or guardian to pay a fine not exceeding £1,000;

and where the court has passed on the offender a sentence which consists of or includes a youth rehabilitation order, it may include in the recognizance a provision that the offender's parent or guardian ensure that the offender complies with the requirements of that sentence.

(3) An order under this section shall not require the parent or guardian to enter into a recognizance for an amount exceeding £1,000.

(4) An order under this section shall not require the parent or guardian to enter into a recognizance—

(a) for a period exceeding three years; or

(b) where the offender will attain the age of 18 in a period shorter than three years, for a period exceeding that shorter period.

Article 7 Convention rights are engaged and the procedure set out in Part J19 of the Criminal Practice Direction 2013 EWCA Crim 1631 must be followed. This includes:

Criminal Practice Direction

J19 Where a court is considering binding over a parent or guardian under section 150 of the Powers of Criminal Courts (Sentencing) Act 2000 to enter into a recognizance to take proper care of and exercise proper control over a child or young person, the court should specify the actions which the parent or guardian is to take.

Where a bind over is not made, the court must explain its reasons in open court.

Where the court makes a referral order, it cannot impose a parental bind over (Powers of the Criminal Courts (Sentencing) Act 2000, s 19).

The parent who is made subject to a bind over has the right of appeal to the Crown Court from the youth court or adult magistrates' court, and to the Court of Appeal from the Crown Court.

B6.6 Parenting orders

A parenting order may be made by any criminal court—youth court, adult magistrates' court, or Crown Court. It may also be made by a Family Proceedings Court and an adult magistrates' court in the exercise of its civil jurisdiction.

Crime and Disorder Act 1998, s 8(1)–(4)

8 Parenting orders

(1) This section applies where, in any court proceedings—
  (a) a child safety order is made in respect of a child or the court deter-
      mines on an application under section 12(6) below that a child has
      failed to comply with any requirement included in such an order;
    (aa) a parental compensation order is made in relation to a child's
         behaviour;
  (b) an injunction is granted under s1 of the Anti-social Behaviour Crime
      and Policing Act 2104 , an order is made under s 22 of that Act or a
      sexual harm prevention order is made in respect of a child or young
      person;
  (c) a child or young person is convicted of an offence; or
  (d) a person is convicted of an offence under section 443 (failure to
      comply with school attendance order) or section 444 (failure to
      secure regular attendance at school of registered pupil) of the
      Education Act 1996.

(2) Subject to subsection (3) and section 9(1) below … if in the proceedings
    the court is satisfied that the relevant condition is fulfilled, it may make
    a parenting order in respect of a person who is a parent or guardian of
    the child or young person or, as the case may be, the person convicted
    of the offence under section 443 or 444 ('the parent').

(3) A court shall not make a parenting order unless it has been notified by
    the Secretary of State that arrangements for implementing such orders
    are available in the area in which it appears to the court that the parent
    resides or will reside and the notice has not been withdrawn.

(4) A parenting order is an order which requires the parent—
  (a) to comply, for a period not exceeding twelve months, with such
      requirements as are specified in the order, and
  (b) subject to subsection (5) below, to attend, for a concurrent period not
      exceeding three months, such counselling or guidance programme as
      may be specified in directions given by the responsible officer.

A parenting order is an order requiring a parent or guardian to
comply with requirements that the court considers desirable:

- in criminal proceedings, in the interests of preventing the commission of further offences;
- in civil proceedings, to prevent the behaviour which led to the
  making of a particular order.

Where an offender is aged under 16 years, the court must make a
parenting order if it considers it desirable as above. If the court is
not so satisfied, it must state this in open court and give reasons.

Where an offender is aged 16 or 17 years, the court has a discretionary power to make an order.

Before making an order, the court shall obtain and consider information about the family circumstances and the likely effect of the order on them. Where the court is considering making a referral order and a parenting order, this information shall be in a report by an appropriate officer.

B6.6.1 *Terms of the order*

The order will last for up to 12 months, and must include a requirement to attend a parenting programme for a period not exceeding three months and not more than once a week. The programme may be a residential course if it is likely to be more effective than a non-residential course and the likely interference with family life is proportionate.

The order must specify a responsible officer who may be:

- a probation officer;
- a social worker;
- a person nominated by the local education authority;
- a member of the Youth Offending Team.

B6.6.2 *Breach*

Breach of the order, without reasonable excuse, is punishable on conviction by a fine not exceeding level 3.

B6.6.3 *Variation, discharge, and appeal*

The responsible officer or parent may apply to the court which made the order to vary or discharge the order.

Appeal against an order made in the adult magistrates' court is to the Crown Court.

B7 Remittal to the Youth Court for Trial/Sentence

The magistrates' court may remit to:

- a youth court acting for the same place as the remitting court; or
- a youth court acting for the place where the young offender habitually resides.

It is generally good practice to remit for sentence to the young person's local court.

The powers to remit arise under section 46 of the Children and Young Persons Act 1933:

Children and Young Persons Act 1933, s 46

46 Assignment of certain matters to youth courts

(1) Subject as hereinafter provided, no charge against a child or young person, and no application whereof the hearing is by rules made under this section assigned to youth courts, shall be heard by a magistrates' court which is not a youth court:

Provided that—

(a) a charge made jointly against a child or young person and a person who has attained the age of eighteen years shall be heard by a magistrates' court other than a youth court; and

(b) where a child or young person is charged with an offence, the charge may be heard by a magistrates' court which is not a youth court if a person who has attained the age of eighteen years is charged at the same time with aiding, abetting, causing, procuring, allowing or permitting that offence; and

(c) where, in the course of any proceedings before any magistrates' court other than a youth court, it appears that the person to whom the proceedings relate is a child or young person, nothing in this subsection shall be construed as preventing the court, if it thinks fit so to do, from proceeding with the hearing and determination of those proceedings.

(1A) If a notification that the accused desires to plead guilty without appearing before the court is received by the designated officer for a court in pursuance of section 12 of the Magistrates' Courts Act 1980 and the court has no reason to believe that the accused is a child or young person, then, if he is a child or young person he shall be deemed to have attained the age of eighteen for the purposes of subsection (1) of this section in its application to the proceedings in question.

(2) No direction, whether contained in this or any other Act, that a charge shall be brought before a youth court shall be construed as restricting the powers of any justice or justices to entertain an application for bail or for a remand, and to hear such evidence as may be necessary for that purpose.

A power to remit is granted under section 29 of the Magistrates' Courts Act 1980 where there will be no effective trial of an adult in relation to a joint charge:

Magistrates' Courts Act 1980, s 29

29 Power of magistrates' court to remit a person under 17 for trial to a youth court in certain circumstances

(1) Where—
  (a) a person under the age of 18 years ('the juvenile') appears or is brought before a magistrates' court other than a youth court on an information jointly charging him and one or more other persons with an offence; and
  (b) that other person, or any of those other persons, has attained that age,
  subsection (2) below shall have effect notwithstanding proviso (a) in section 46(1) of the Children and Young Persons Act 1933 (which would otherwise require the charge against the juvenile to be heard by a magistrates' court other than a youth court).
  In the following provisions of this section 'the older accused' means such one or more of the accused as have attained the age of 18 years.

(2) If—
  (a) the court proceeds to the summary trial of the information in the case of both or all of the accused, and the older accused or each of the older accused pleads guilty; or
  (b) the court—
    (i) in the case of the older accused or each of the older accused, sends him to the Crown Court for trial under section 51 or 51A of the Crime and Disorder Act 1998; and
    (ii) in the case of the juvenile, proceeds to the summary trial of the information,
  then, if in either situation the juvenile pleads not guilty, the court may before any evidence is called in his case remit him for trial to a youth court acting for the same place as the remitting court or for the place where he habitually resides.

(3) A person remitted to a youth court under subsection (2) above shall be brought before and tried by a youth court accordingly.

(4) Where a person is so remitted to a youth court—
  (a) he shall have no right of appeal against the order of remission; and
  (b) the remitting court may, subject to section 25 of the Criminal Justice and Public Order Act 1994, give such directions as appear to be necessary with respect to his custody or for his release on bail until he can be brought before the youth court.

A duty to remit exists under section 8 of the Powers of Criminal Courts (Sentencing) Act 2000, for sentencing where the adult court powers are not regarded as sufficient:

Powers of Criminal Courts (Sentencing) Act 2000, s 8

8 Power and duty to remit young offenders to youth courts for sentence

(1) Subsection (2) below applies where a child or young person (that is to say, any person aged under 18) is convicted by or before any court of an offence other than homicide.

(2) The court may and, if it is not a youth court, shall unless satisfied that it would be undesirable to do so, remit the case—

    (a) if the offender was sent to the Crown Court for trial under section 51 or 51A of the Crime and Disorder Act 1998, to a youth court acting for the place where he was sent to the Crown Court for trial;

    (b) in any other case, to a youth court acting either for the same place as the remitting court or for the place where the offender habitually resides;

but in relation to a magistrates' court other than a youth court this subsection has effect subject to subsection (6) below.

(3) Where a case is remitted under subsection (2) above, the offender shall be brought before a youth court accordingly, and that court may deal with him in any way in which it might have dealt with him if he had been tried and convicted by that court.

(4) A court by which an order remitting a case to a youth court is made under subsection (2) above—

    (a) may, subject to section 25 of the Criminal Justice and Public Order Act 1994 (restrictions on granting bail), give such directions as appear to be necessary with respect to the custody of the offender or for his release on bail until he can be brought before the youth court; and

    (b) shall cause to be transmitted to the designated officer for the youth court a certificate setting out the nature of the offence and stating—

        (i) that the offender has been convicted of the offence; and

        (ii) that the case has been remitted for the purpose of being dealt with under the preceding provisions of this section.

(5) Where a case is remitted under subsection (2) above, the offender shall have no right of appeal against the order of remission, but shall have the same right of appeal against any order of the court to which the case is remitted as if he had been convicted by that court.

(6) Without prejudice to the power to remit any case to a youth court which is conferred on a magistrates' court other than a youth court by subsections (1) and (2) above, where such a magistrates' court convicts a child or young person of an offence it must exercise that power unless the case falls within subsection (7) or (8) below.

(7) The case falls within this subsection if the court would, were it not so to remit the case, be required by section 16(2) below to refer the offender to a youth offender panel (in which event the court may, but need not, so remit the case).

(8) The case falls within this subsection if it does not fall within subsection (7) above but the court is of the opinion that the case is one which can properly be dealt with by means of—

   (a) an order discharging the offender absolutely or conditionally, or
   (b) an order for the payment of a fine, or
   (c) an order (under section 150 below) requiring the offender's parent or guardian to enter into a recognizance to take proper care of him and exercise proper control over him,

   with or without any other order that the court has power to make when absolutely or conditionally discharging an offender.

(9) In subsection (8) above 'care' and 'control' shall be construed in accordance with section 150(11) below.

(10) A document purporting to be a copy of an order made by a court under this section shall, if it purports to be certified as a true copy by the justices' chief executive for the court, be evidence of the order.

B8 Reporting Restrictions

In the adult court, unlike the youth court, discretionary provisions apply. The court must specifically apply the restrictions which relate to the identification of victims, other witnesses, and defendants by stating in open court that it is doing so. The conflicting demands of Articles 8 and 10 of the European Convention on Human Rights must be balanced (see **A26.2.1**). Section 39 Children and Young Persons Act 1933 has been disapplied from criminal proceedings, and the relevant provisions are now sections 45 and 45A Youth Justice and Criminal Evidence Act 1999. The latter is considered at **A.26.1.1**.

Youth Justice and Criminal Evidence Act 1999, s 45

Power to restrict reporting of criminal proceedings involving persons under 18

(1) This section applies (subject to subsection (2)) in relation to—
  (a) any criminal proceedings in any court (other than a service court) in England and Wales

(2) This section does not apply in relation to any proceedings to which section 49 of the Children and Young Persons Act 1933 applies.

(3) The court may direct that no matter relating to any person concerned in the proceedings shall while he is under the age of 18 be included in any publication if it is likely to lead members of the public to identify him as a person concerned in the proceedings.

(4) The court or an appellate court may by direction ('an excepting direction') dispense, to any extent specified in the excepting direction, with the restrictions imposed by a direction under subsection (3) if it is satisfied that it is necessary in the interests of justice to do so.

(5) The court or an appellate court may also by direction ('an excepting direction') dispense, to any extent specified in the excepting direction, with the restrictions imposed by a direction under subsection (3) if it is satisfied—
  (a) that their effect is to impose a substantial and unreasonable restriction on the reporting of the proceedings, and
  (b) that it is in the public interest to remove or relax that restriction;
  but no excepting direction shall be given under this subsection by reason only of the fact that the proceedings have been determined in any way or have been abandoned.

(6) When deciding whether to make—
  (a) a direction under subsection (3) in relation to a person, or
  (b) an excepting direction under subsection (4) or (5) by virtue of which the restrictions imposed by a direction under subsection (3) would be dispensed with (to any extent) in relation to a person,
  the court or (as the case may be) the appellate court shall have regard to the welfare of that person.

---

(7) For the purposes of subsection (3) any reference to a person concerned in the proceedings is to a person—
  (a) against or in respect of whom the proceedings are taken, or
  (b) who is a witness in the proceedings.
(8) The matters relating to a person in relation to which the restrictions imposed by a direction under subsection (3) apply (if their inclusion in any publication is likely to have the result mentioned in that subsection) include in particular—
  (a) his name,
  (b) his address,
  (c) the identity of any school or other educational establishment attended by him,
  (d) the identity of any place of work, and
  (e) any still or moving picture of him.
(9) A direction under subsection (3) may be revoked by the court or an appellate court.
(10) An excepting direction—
  (a) may be given at the time the direction under subsection (3) is given or subsequently; and
  (b) may be varied or revoked by the court or an appellate court.

Considering earlier statutory provisions, the following principles were set out in *R (Y) v Aylesbury Crown Court* [2012] EWHC 1140 (Admin):

• The defendant had to satisfy the court that there was a good reason for restriction.
• The good reason for a young person would in most cases be his welfare. Publicity would have significant effects on the young person's prospects and opportunities.
• The court must have regard to Article 10 ECHR. A restriction order must be necessary and proportionate, and for a pressing social need. There was a public interest in knowing the outcome of proceedings.
• There is a balance to be struck. Prior to conviction it was unlikely that there should be publicity. After conviction, the age of the defendant and seriousness of the crime would be particularly relevant.
• Partial publicity was possible.
• If there was an even balance there should be no publicity.

B9 **Sentencing**

B9.1 Overview of section 8 of the Powers of Criminal Courts (Sentencing) Act 2000

Only the following sentencing options are available in relation to young offenders appearing in the adult court. Any case requiring a greater sentence must be remitted to the youth court (see **B7**).

Age (last birthday)	10–13	14	15	16–17
Absolute discharge	Yes	Yes	Yes	Yes
Conditional discharge (note that a conditional discharge cannot be imposed if the offender has received a final warning/youth caution in the previous 24 months unless exceptional circumstances are found). A conditional discharge in respect to a youth can be for a maximum period of 3 years.	Yes	Yes	Yes	Yes
Fine	Yes: maximum £250. Order must be made against parent/guardian unless unreasonable in the circumstances	Yes: maximum £1,000. Order must be made against parent/guardian unless unreasonable in the circumstances	Yes: maximum £1,000. Order must be made against parent/guardian unless unreasonable in the circumstances	Yes: maximum £1,000
Referral order	Yes	Yes	Yes	Yes

B9.2 Victim surcharge

The court must add the relevant victim surcharge which for youths is as follows:

Offenders under 18 years at the time the offence was committed	Victim surcharge for offences:	
	before 8 April 2016	on or after 8 April 2016
A conditional discharge	£10	£15
A fine	£15	£20
Youth rehabilitation order	£15	£20
Referral order	£15	£20

B9.3 Referral orders

The adult court may (but need not) make a referral order in circumstances where, in the youth court, such an order must be made. This obligation arises under section 17(1) of the Powers of Criminal Courts (Sentencing) Act 2000, where:

- the offence is punishable with imprisonment;
- the offender has pleaded guilty to the offence(s);
- the court is not imposing an absolute or conditional discharge, a hospital order, or a custodial sentence;
- the offender has never previously been convicted (in the United Kingdom) of an offence or bound over.

B9.4 Ancillary powers

In addition to exercising these powers, the court may make ancillary orders such as:

- an order (under section 150 of the Powers of Criminal Courts (Sentencing) Act 2000) binding over a parent or guardian to take proper care of the youth and exercise proper care over him (see **B6.5**), or a parenting order (see **B6.6**);
- ancillary orders such as disqualification from driving, endorsement of a driving licence, and to pay compensation and costs.

 See *Blackstone's Criminal Practice 2017* **D24.108** and **D24.109**

B10 **Summary Trials Involving Youths**

Before the trial of a youth in the adult court can begin, it is necessary to check the ability of the youth to understand the procedure.

B10.1 **Capacity of the youth to take part**

It is necessary to consider the youth's intellectual capacity to understand the proceedings.

There have been a number of cases where the defence have sought to raise a capacity issue, namely, that the defendant, whether due to immaturity or mental capacity, is unable to understand the proceedings, such that it would be an abuse of process to continue on the ground that he could not have a fair trial.

The elements of a fair trial (in this regard) are:

- the defendant had to understand what he is said to have done wrong;
- the court had to be satisfied that the defendant, when he had done wrong by act or omission, had the means of knowing that was wrong;
- he had to understand what, if any, defences were available to him;
- he had to have a reasonable opportunity to make relevant representations if he wished;
- he had to have the opportunity to consider what representation he wished to make once he understood the issues involved;
- he had, therefore, to be able to give proper instructions and to participate by way of providing answers to questions and suggesting questions to his lawyers in the circumstances of the trial as they arose.

The following guidance on how to approach the issue was issued by the court in *Crown Prosecution Service v P* [2007] EWHC 946 (Admin):

- the fitness to plead procedure (in so far as it applies in the magistrates' court—see **A21**) does not provide a complete answer to the defendant who lacks capacity, as there are fair trial issues to consider under Article 6 ECHR;
- in an exceptional case there may be grounds to stay a case as an abuse of process if the youth lacks capacity;
- medical evidence on the issue is not decisive;

- before considering a stay, the court should consider conducting a fact-finding exercise with a view to a medical disposal under the Mental Health Act 1983 in appropriate cases.

It can be seen, therefore, that only in cases where the capacity issue is not linked to mental health, or a mental health disposal is not appropriate, will a court consider a stay of proceedings.

B10.2 Assistance to the defendant

B10.2.1 *Live link direction for vulnerable young defendants*

The court has power to allow a vulnerable young defendant to give evidence via live link (Youth Justice and Criminal Evidence Act 1999, s 33A). An application is made under section 33A on the basis that the defendant's ability to participate effectively is compromised by his level of intellectual ability or social functioning. The fact that the defendant has a temper and does not like being challenged by authority is not a characteristic of social functioning. An expert report on communication with young people is not essential but can be of assistance (*R v Rahman* [2015] EWCA Crim 15).

Youth Justice and Criminal Evidence Act 1999, s 33A

33A Live link directions

(1) This section applies to any proceedings (whether in a magistrates' court or before the Crown Court) against a person for an offence.

(2) The court may, on the application of the accused, give a live link direction if it is satisfied—
   (a) that the conditions in subsection (4) or, as the case may be, subsection (5) are met in relation to the accused, and
   (b) that it is in the interests of justice for the accused to give evidence through a live link.

(3) A live link direction is a direction that any oral evidence to be given before the court by the accused is to be given through a live link.

(4) Where the accused is aged under 18 when the application is made, the conditions are that—
   (a) his ability to participate effectively in the proceedings as a witness giving oral evidence in court is compromised by his level of intellectual ability or social functioning, and
   (b) use of a live link would enable him to participate more effectively in the proceedings as a witness (whether by improving the quality of his evidence or otherwise).

---

(5) Where the accused has attained the age of 18 at that time, the conditions are that—

    (a) he suffers from a mental disorder (within the meaning of the Mental Health Act 1983) or otherwise has a significant impairment of intelligence and social function,

    (b) he is for that reason unable to participate effectively in the proceedings as a witness giving oral evidence in court, and

    (c) use of a live link would enable him to participate more effectively in the proceedings as a witness (whether by improving the quality of his evidence or otherwise).

(6) While a live link direction has effect the accused may not give oral evidence before the court in the proceedings otherwise than through a live link.

(7) The court may discharge a live link direction at any time before or during any hearing to which it applies if it appears to the court to be in the interests of justice to do so (but this does not affect the power to give a further live link direction in relation to the accused).

    The court may exercise this power of its own motion or on an application by a party.

(8) The court must state in open court its reasons for—

    (a) giving or discharging a live link direction, or

    (b) refusing an application for or for the discharge of a live link direction,

    and, if it is a magistrates' court, it must cause those reasons to be entered in the register of its proceedings.

B10.2.2 *Examination of accused through intermediary*

In *R (C) v Sevenoaks Youth Court* [2009] EWHC 3088 (Admin), the court held that an intermediary could be appointed under the court's common law power to ensure a fair trial process, until such time as statutory provisions are brought into force. In *R (AS) v Great Yarmouth Youth Court* [2011] EWHC 2059 (Admin), the court held that it was irrational to ignore the need for an intermediary of a youth suffering from attention deficit and hyperactive disorder (ADHD).

B10.3 Further assistance

The Criminal Practice Directions 2015 EWCA Crim 430 (as amended by 2016 EWCA Crim 97) give further assistance. The relevant provisions are in sections 3D, 3E, 3F, and 3G:

CPD General matters 3D: vulnerable people in the courts

3D.1 In respect of eligibility for special measures, 'vulnerable' and 'intimidated' witnesses are defined in sections 16 and 17 of the Youth Justice and Criminal Evidence Act 1999 (as amended by the Coroners and Justice Act 2009); 'vulnerable' includes those under 18 years of age and people with a mental disorder or learning disability; a physical disorder or disability; or who are likely to suffer fear or distress in giving evidence because of their own circumstances or those relating to the case.

3D.2 However, many other people giving evidence in a criminal case, whether as a witness or defendant, may require assistance: the court is required to take 'every reasonable step' to encourage and facilitate the attendance of witnesses and to facilitate the participation of any person, including the defendant (Rule 3.8(4)(a) and (b)). This includes enabling a witness or defendant to give their best evidence, and enabling a defendant to comprehend the proceedings and engage fully with his or her defence. The pre-trial and trial process should, so far as necessary, be adapted to meet those ends. Regard should be had to the welfare of a young defendant as required by section 44 of the Children and Young Persons Act 1933, and generally to Parts 1 and 3 of the Criminal Procedure Rules (the overriding objective and the court's powers of case management).

3D.3 Under Part 3 of the Rules, the court must identify the needs of witnesses at an early stage (Rule 3.2(2)(b)) and may require the parties to identify arrangements to facilitate the giving of evidence and participation in the trial (Rule 3.10(c)(iv) and (v)). There are various statutory special measures that the court may utilise to assist a witness in giving evidence. Part 29 of the Rules gives the procedures to be followed. Courts should note the 'primary rule' which requires the court to give a direction for a special measure to assist a child witness or qualifying witness and that in such cases an application to the court is not required (Rule 29.9).

CPD General matters 3E: ground rules hearings to plan the questioning of a vulnerable witness or defendant

3E.1 The judiciary is responsible for controlling questioning. Over-rigorous or repetitive cross-examination of a child or vulnerable witness should be stopped. Intervention by the judge, magistrates or intermediary (if any) is minimised if questioning, taking account of the individual's communication needs, is discussed in advance and ground rules are agreed and adhered to.

3E.2 Discussion of ground rules is required in all intermediary trials where they must be discussed between the judge or magistrates, advocates and intermediary before the witness gives evidence. The intermediary must be present but is not required to take the oath (the intermediary's declaration is made just before the witness gives evidence).

3E.3 Discussion of ground rules is good practice, even if no intermediary is used, in all young witness cases and in other cases where a witness or defendant has communication needs. Discussion before the day of trial is preferable to give advocates time to adapt their questions to the witness's needs. It may be helpful for a trial practice note of boundaries to be created at the end of the discussion. The judge may use such a document in ensuring that the agreed ground rules are complied with.

3E.4 All witnesses, including the defendant and defence witnesses, should be enabled to give the best evidence they can. In relation to young and/or vulnerable people, this may mean departing radically from traditional cross-examination. The form and extent of appropriate cross-examination will vary from case to case. For adult non vulnerable witnesses an advocate will usually put his case so that the witness will have the opportunity of commenting upon it and/or answering it. When the witness is young or otherwise vulnerable, the court may dispense with the normal practice and impose restrictions on the advocate 'putting his case' where there is a risk of a young or otherwise vulnerable witness failing to understand, becoming distressed or acquiescing to leading questions. Where limitations on questioning are necessary and appropriate, they must be clearly defined. The judge has a duty to ensure that they are complied with and should explain them to the jury and the reasons for them. If the advocate fails to comply with the limitations, the judge should give relevant directions to the jury when that occurs and prevent further questioning that does not comply with the ground rules settled upon in advance. Instead of commenting on inconsistencies during cross-examination, following discussion between the judge and the advocates, the advocate or judge may point out important inconsistencies after (instead of during) the witness's evidence. The judge should also remind the jury of these during summing up. The judge should be alert to alleged inconsistencies that are not in fact inconsistent, or are trivial.

CPD General matters 3F

[Sets out detailed provisions for the use of intermediaries.]

CPD General matters 3G [Sets put provisions for vulnerable defendants before the trial, sentencing, or appeal.]

Part C
Offences

C1 **Animal Offences**

C1.1 **Animal cruelty**

Sections 4, 5, 6, 7, 8, and 9 of the Animal Welfare Act 2006 provide for offences in relation to unnecessary suffering, mutilation, docking of dogs' tails, administration of poisons, and fighting.

Animal Welfare Act 2006, ss 4(1)–(2), 5(1)–(2), (6), 6(1)–(12), 7, 8, and 9

4 Unnecessary suffering

(1) A person commits an offence if—
  (a) an act of his, or a failure of his to act, causes an animal to suffer,
  (b) he knew, or ought reasonably to have known, that the act, or failure to act, would have that effect or be likely to do so,
  (c) the animal is a protected animal, and
  (d) the suffering is unnecessary.

(2) A person commits an offence if—
  (a) he is responsible for an animal,
  (b) an act, or failure to act, of another person causes the animal to suffer,
  (c) he permitted that to happen or failed to take such steps (whether by way of supervising the other person or otherwise) as were reasonable in all the circumstances to prevent that happening, and
  (d) the suffering is unnecessary ...

5 Mutilation

(1) A person commits an offence if—
  (a) he carries out a prohibited procedure on a protected animal;
  (b) he causes such a procedure to be carried out on such an animal.

(2) A person commits an offence if—
  (a) he is responsible for an animal,
  (b) another person carries out a prohibited procedure on the animal, and
  (c) he permitted that to happen or failed to take such steps (whether by way of supervising the other person or otherwise) as were reasonable in all the circumstances to prevent that happening.

...

(6) Nothing in this section applies to the removal of the whole or any part of a dog's tail.

6 Docking of dogs' tails

(1) A person commits an offence if—
  (a) he removes the whole or any part of a dog's tail, otherwise than for the purpose of its medical treatment;
  (b) he causes the whole or any part of a dog's tail to be removed by another person, otherwise than for the purpose of its medical treatment.

C1 Animal Offences

(2) A person commits an offence if—
   (a) he is responsible for a dog,
   (b) another person removes the whole or any part of the dog's tail, otherwise than for the purpose of its medical treatment, and
   (c) he permitted that to happen or failed to take such steps (whether by way of supervising the other person or otherwise) as were reasonable in all the circumstances to prevent that happening.

(3) Subsections (1) and (2) do not apply if the dog is a certified working dog that is not more than 5 days old.

(4) For the purposes of subsection (3), a dog is a certified working dog if a veterinary surgeon has certified, in accordance with regulations made by the appropriate national authority, that the first and second conditions mentioned below are met.

(5) The first condition referred to in subsection (4) is that there has been produced to the veterinary surgeon such evidence as the appropriate national authority may by regulations require for the purpose of showing that the dog is likely to be used for work in connection with—
   (a) law enforcement,
   (b) activities of Her Majesty's armed forces,
   (c) emergency rescue,
   (d) lawful pest control, or
   (e) the lawful shooting of animals.

(6) The second condition referred to in subsection (4) is that the dog is of a type specified for the purposes of this subsection by regulations made by the appropriate national authority.

(7) It is a defence for a person accused of an offence under subsection (1) or to show that he reasonably believed that the dog was one in relation to which subsection (3) applies.

(8) A person commits an offence if—
   (a) he owns a subsection (3) dog, and
   (b) fails to take reasonable steps to secure that, before the dog is 3 months old, it is identified as a subsection (3) dog in accordance with regulations made by the appropriate national authority.

(9) A person commits an offence if—
   (a) he shows a dog at an event to which members of the public are admitted on payment of a fee,
   (b) the dog's tail has been wholly or partly removed (in England and Wales or elsewhere), and
   (c) removal took place on or after the commencement day.

(10) Where a dog is shown only for the purpose of demonstrating its working ability, subsection (9) does not apply if the dog is a subsection (3) dog.

(11) It is a defence for a person accused of an offence under subsection (9) to show that he reasonably believed—
   (a) that the event was not one to which members of the public were admitted on payment of an entrance fee,
   (b) that the removal took place before the commencement day, or
   (c) that the dog was one in relation to which subsection (10) applies.

(12) A person commits an offence if he knowingly gives false information to a veterinary surgeon in connection with the giving of a certificate for the purposes of this section.

7 Administration of poisons etc

(1) A person commits an offence if, without lawful authority or reasonable excuse, he—

    (a) administers any poisonous or injurious drug or substance to a protected animal, knowing it to be poisonous or injurious, or

    (b) causes any poisonous or injurious drug or substance to be taken by a protected animal, knowing it to be poisonous or injurious.

(2) A person commits an offence if—

    (a) he is responsible for an animal,

    (b) without lawful authority or reasonable excuse, another person administers a poisonous or injurious drug or substance to the animal or causes the animal to take such a drug or substance, and

    (c) he permitted that to happen or, knowing the drug or substance to be poisonous or injurious, he failed to take such steps (whether by way of supervising the other person or otherwise) as were reasonable in all the circumstances to prevent that happening.

(3) In this section, references to a poisonous or injurious drug or substance include a drug or substance which, by virtue of the quantity or manner in which it is administered or taken, has the effect of a poisonous or injurious drug or substance.

8 Fighting etc

(1) A person commits an offence if he—

    (a) causes an animal fight to take place, or attempts to do so;

    (b) knowingly receives money for admission to an animal fight;

    (c) knowingly publicises a proposed animal fight;

    (d) provides information about an animal fight to another with the intention of enabling or encouraging attendance at the fight;

    (e) makes or accepts a bet on the outcome of an animal fight or on the likelihood of anything occurring or not occurring in the course of an animal fight;

    (f) takes part in an animal fight;

    (g) has in his possession anything designed or adapted for use in connection with an animal fight with the intention of its being so used;

    (h) keeps or trains an animal for use for in connection with an animal fight;

    (i) keeps any premises for use for an animal fight.

(2) A person commits an offence if, without lawful authority or reasonable excuse, he is present at an animal fight.

(3) A person commits an offence if, without lawful authority or reasonable excuse, he—

    (a) knowingly supplies a video recording of an animal fight,

    (b) knowingly publishes a video recording of an animal fight,

    (c) knowingly shows a video recording of an animal fight to another, or

    (d) possesses a video recording of an animal fight, knowing it to be such a recording, with the intention of supplying it.

(4) Subsection (3) does not apply if the video recording is of an animal fight that took place—

    (a) outside Great Britain, or

    (b) before the commencement date.
(5) Subsection (3) does not apply—
    (a) in the case of paragraph (a), to the supply of a video recording for
        inclusion in a programme service;
    (b) in the case of paragraph (b) or (c), to the publication or showing of
        a video recording by means of its inclusion in a programme service;
    (c) in the case of paragraph (d), by virtue of intention to supply for
        inclusion in a programme service.
...
(7) In this section—
    'animal fight' means an occasion on which a protected animal is placed
    with an animal, or with a human, for the purpose of fighting, wrestling
    or baiting;
    ...
    'programme service' has the same meaning as in the Communications
    Act 2003 (c. 21);
    'video recording' means a recording, in any form, from which a moving
    image may by any means be reproduced and includes data stored on a
    computer disc or by other electronic means which is capable of conver-
    sion into a moving image.
(8) In this section—
    (a) references to supplying or publishing a video recording are to sup-
        plying or publishing a video recording in any manner, including, in
        relation to a video recording in the form of data stored electroni-
        cally, by means of transmitting such data;
    (b) references to showing a video recording are to showing a moving
        image reproduced from a video recording by any means.

9 Duty of person responsible for animal to ensure welfare

(1) A person commits an offence if he does not take such steps as are
    reasonable in all the circumstances to ensure that the needs of an ani-
    mal for which he is responsible are met to the extent required by good
    practice.
(2) For the purposes of this Act, an animal's needs shall be taken to include—
    (a) its need for a suitable environment,
    (b) its need for a suitable diet,
    (c) its need to be able to exhibit normal behaviour patterns,
    (d) any need it has to be housed with, or apart from, other animals, and
    (e) its need to be protected from pain, suffering, injury and disease.
(3) The circumstances to which it is relevant to have regard when applying
    subsection (1) include, in particular—
    (a) any lawful purpose for which the animal is kept, and
    (b) any lawful activity undertaken in relation to the animal.
(4) Nothing in this section applies to the destruction of an animal in an
    appropriate and humane manner.

SO But note that a magistrates' court may try an Information
relating to an offence under this Act if the information is laid:

(a) before the end of the period of three years beginning with the date of the commission of the offence; and

(b) before the end of the period of six months beginning with the date on which evidence which the prosecutor thinks is sufficient to justify the proceedings comes to his knowledge.

 Fine and/or 6 months' imprisonment (ss 4, 5, 6(1) and (2), 7, 8, and 9)

C1.1.1 *Sentencing*

Note that this guideline is under review by the Sentencing Council (see **Appendix 7**).

Offence seriousness (culpability and harm) A. Identify the appropriate starting point Starting points based on first-time offender pleading not guilty		
Examples of nature of activity	**Starting point**	**Range**
One impulsive act causing little or no injury; short-term neglect	Band C fine	Band B fine to medium-level community order
Several incidents of deliberate ill-treatment/frightening animal(s); medium-term neglect	High-level community order	Medium-level community order to 12 weeks' custody
Attempt to kill/torture; animal baiting/conducting or permitting cock-fighting etc; prolonged neglect	18 weeks' custody	12 to 26 weeks' custody

Offence seriousness (culpability and harm) B. Consider the effect of aggravating and mitigating factors (other than those within examples above) The following may be particularly relevant but these lists are not exhaustive	
Factors indicating higher culpability 1. Offender in position of special responsibility 2. Adult involves children in offending 3. Animal(s) kept for livelihood 4. Use of weapon 5. Offender ignored advice/warnings 6. Offence committed for commercial gain **Factors indicating greater degree of harm** 1. Serious injury or death 2. Several animals affected	**Factors indicating lower culpability** 1. Offender induced by others 2. Ignorance of appropriate care 3. Offender with limited capacity

C1 Animal Offences

C1.1.2 *Deprivation order*

Section 33 of the Animal Welfare Act 2006 provides for a convicted person to be deprived of his animals:

Animal Welfare Act 2006, s 33

33 Deprivation

(1) If the person convicted of an offence under any of sections 4, 5, 6(1) and (2), 7, 8 and 9 is the owner of an animal in relation to which the offence was committed, the court by or before which he is convicted may, instead of or in addition to dealing with him in any other way, make an order depriving him of ownership of the animal and for its disposal.

(2) Where the owner of an animal is convicted of an offence under section 34(9) because ownership of the animal is in breach of a disqualification under section 34(2), the court by or before which he is convicted may, instead of or in addition to dealing with him in any other way, make an order depriving him of ownership of the animal and for its disposal.

(3) Where the animal in respect of which an order under subsection (1) or (2) is made has any dependent offspring, the order may include provision depriving the person to whom it relates of ownership of the offspring and for its disposal.

(4) Where a court makes an order under subsection (1) or (2), it may—
   (a) appoint a person to carry out, or arrange for the carrying out of, the order;
   (b) require any person who has possession of an animal to which the order applies to deliver it up to enable the order to be carried out;
   (c) give directions with respect to the carrying out of the order;
   (d) confer additional powers (including power to enter premises where an animal to which the order applies is being kept) for the purpose of, or in connection with, the carrying out of the order;
   (e) order the offender to reimburse the expenses of carrying out the order.

(5) Directions under subsection (4)(c) may—
   (a) specify the manner in which an animal is to be disposed of, or
   (b) delegate the decision about the manner in which an animal is to be disposed of to a person appointed under subsection (4)(a).

(6) Where a court decides not to make an order under subsection (1) or (2) in relation to an offender, it shall—
   (a) give its reasons for the decision in open court, and
   (b) if it is a magistrates' court, cause them to be entered in the register of its proceedings.

(7) Subsection (6) does not apply where the court makes an order under section 34(1) in relation to the offender.

(8) In subsection (1), the reference to an animal in relation to which an offence was committed includes, in the case of an offence under section 8, an animal which took part in an animal fight in relation to which the offence was committed.

(9) In this section, references to disposing of an animal include destroying it.

C1.1.3 *Disqualification order*

Section 34 of the Animal Welfare Act 2006 provides for disqualification orders to be made against convicted persons, thereby making it an offence for them to be involved with owning, keeping, or otherwise in the control of animals:

Animal Welfare Act 2006, s 34

34 Disqualification

(1) If a person is convicted of an offence to which this section applies, the court by or before which he is convicted may, instead of or in addition to dealing with him in any other way, make an order disqualifying him under any one or more of subsections (2) to (4) for such period as it thinks fit.

(2) Disqualification under this subsection disqualifies a person—
   (a) from owning animals,
   (b) from keeping animals,
   (c) from participating in the keeping of animals, and
   (d) from being party to an arrangement under which he is entitled to control or influence the way in which animals are kept.

(3) Disqualification under this subsection disqualifies a person from dealing in animals.

(4) Disqualification under this subsection disqualifies a person—
   (a) from transporting animals, and
   (b) from arranging for the transport of animals.

(5) Disqualification under subsection (2), (3) or (4) may be imposed in relation to animals generally, or in relation to animals of one or more kinds.

(6) The court by which an order under subsection (1) is made may specify a period during which the offender may not make an application under section 43(1) for termination of the order.
   ...

(9) A person who breaches a disqualification imposed by an order under subsection (1) commits an offence [carrying a ... fine and/or 6 months' imprisonment (s 32(2))].

(10) This section applies to an offence under any of sections 4, 5, 6(1) and (2), 7, 8, 9 and 13(6) and subsection (9).

C1.1.4 *Destruction orders*

Sections 37 and 38 of the Animal Welfare Act 2006 allow for destruction orders to be made in appropriate cases:

Animal Welfare Act 2006, ss 37 and 38

37 Destruction in the interests of the animal

(1) The court by or before which a person is convicted of an offence under any of sections 4, 5, 6(1) and (2), 7, 8(1) and (2) and 9 may order the destruction of an animal in relation to which the offence was committed

---

if it is satisfied, on the basis of evidence given by a veterinary surgeon, that it is appropriate to do so in the interests of the animal.

(2) A court may not make an order under subsection (1) unless—
  (a) it has given the owner of the animal an opportunity to be heard, or
  (b) it is satisfied that it is not reasonably practicable to communicate with the owner.

(3) Where a court makes an order under subsection (1), it may—
  (a) appoint a person to carry out, or arrange for the carrying out of, the order;
  (b) require a person who has possession of the animal to deliver it up to enable the order to be carried out;
  (c) give directions with respect to the carrying out of the order (including directions about how the animal is to be dealt with until it is destroyed);
  (d) confer additional powers (including power to enter premises where the animal is being kept) for the purpose of, or in connection with, the carrying out of the order;
  (e) order the offender or another person to reimburse the expenses of carrying out the order.

(4) Where a court makes an order under subsection (1), each of the offender and, if different, the owner of the animal may—
  (a) in the case of an order made by a magistrates' court, appeal against the order to the Crown Court;
  (b) in the case of an order made by the Crown Court, appeal against the order to the Court of Appeal.

(5) Subsection (4) does not apply if the court by which the order is made directs that it is appropriate in the interests of the animal that the carrying out of the order should not be delayed.

(6) In subsection (1), the reference to an animal in relation to which an offence was committed includes, in the case of an offence under section 8(1) or (2), an animal which took part in an animal fight in relation to which the offence was committed.

38 Destruction of animals involved in fighting offences

(1) The court by or before which a person is convicted of an offence under section 8(1) or (2) may order the destruction of an animal in relation to which the offence was committed on grounds other than the interests of the animal.

(2) A court may not make an order under subsection (1) unless—
  (a) it has given the owner of the animal an opportunity to be heard, or
  (b) it is satisfied that it is not reasonably practicable to communicate with the owner.

(3) Where a court makes an order under subsection (1), it may—
  (a) appoint a person to carry out, or arrange for the carrying out of, the order;
  (b) require a person who has possession of the animal to deliver it up to enable the order to be carried out;
  (c) give directions with respect to the carrying out of the order (including directions about how the animal is to be dealt with until it is destroyed);

    (d) confer additional powers (including power to enter premises where the animal is being kept) for the purpose of, or in connection with, the carrying out of the order;

    (e) order the offender or another person to reimburse the expenses of carrying out the order.

(4) Where a court makes an order under subsection (1) in relation to an animal which is owned by a person other than the offender, that person may—

    (a) in the case of an order made by a magistrates' court, appeal against the order to the Crown Court;

    (b) in the case of an order made by the Crown Court, appeal against the order to the Court of Appeal.

(5) In subsection (1), the reference to an animal in relation to which the offence was committed includes an animal which took part in an animal fight in relation to which the offence was committed.

C1.1.5 Key points

- The six-month limitation period for summary offences under this Act can be disapplied in certain circumstances (see s 31 of the 2006 Act and *RSPCA v Johnson* [2009] EWHC 2702 (Admin)).
- References to a person responsible for an animal are to a person responsible for an animal, whether on a permanent or a temporary basis.
- References to being responsible for an animal include being in charge of it.
- A person who owns an animal shall always be regarded as being a person who is responsible for it.
- A person shall be treated as responsible for any animal for which a person under the age of 16 years of whom he has actual care and control is responsible.
- Protected animal refers to an animal commonly domesticated in the British Isles, under the control of man, or not living in a wild state.

Section 4 is to be interpreted so as to require the Crown to prove that the defendant knew or ought to have known that the suffering was unnecessary. A conviction should not be recorded under section 9, where the standard is objective, when there is a conviction under section 4 and the offending behaviour is no wider (*R (Gray and Gray) v Aylesbury County Court* [2013] EWHC 500 (Admin)).

The considerations to which it is relevant to have regard when determining for the purposes of this section whether suffering is unnecessary include:

- whether the suffering could reasonably have been avoided or reduced;

- whether the conduct which caused the suffering was in compliance with any relevant enactment or any relevant provisions of a licence or code of practice issued under an enactment;
- whether the conduct which caused the suffering was for a legitimate purpose, such as:
  - benefiting the animal, or
  - protecting a person, property, or another animal;
- whether the suffering was proportionate to the purpose of the conduct concerned;
- whether the conduct concerned was in all the circumstances that of a reasonably competent and humane person.

Nothing in this section applies to the destruction of an animal in an appropriate and humane manner.

When considering making a disqualification order under section 4 of the Act, regard can be had to any previous convictions (*Ward v RSPCA*, 2010 EWHC 347). To be in breach of a disqualification order (s 34(2) of the Animal Welfare Act 2006) by participating in the keeping of animals or being party to an arrangement under which the defendant is entitled to control or influence the way in which animals are kept, there must be something more than contact with, or mere influence on the keeping of, the animals. There must be evidence of an entitlement to control the animals (*Patterson v RSPCA* [2013] EWHC 4531(Admin)).

In *RSPCA v McCormick* [2016] EWHC 928(Admin) 'animal fight' in section 8(7) was held to mean an occasion on which a protected animal (an animal under control) is placed with an animal, or a human, for the purpose of fighting, wrestling, or baiting. The effect is that the other animal must also be under some degree of control and not wild. The case confirmed that, whilst section 8(7) is aimed at animal fights that are organized or controlled, the payment of money does not have to be involved.

C1.1.6 *Animal welfare: section 9*

The welfare offence in this section extends to non-farmed animals; similar provisions are found in the Welfare of Farmed Animals (England) Regulations 2000 (SI 2000/1870) (made under Part 1 of the Agriculture (Miscellaneous Provisions) Act 1968), which ensure the welfare of livestock situated on agricultural land. A duty to ensure welfare will therefore apply to all animals for which someone is responsible, as defined in section 3. Where someone is responsible for an animal, he has a duty to take steps that are reasonable in all the circumstances to ensure its needs are met to the extent required by good practice (s 9(1)).

Section 9(3) specifies certain matters to which the courts should have regard when considering whether a person has committed an offence under this section. The provision recognizes that some otherwise lawful practices may prevent or hinder a person from ensuring that all of the welfare needs specified in section 9(2) can be met, and requires the courts to take this into account when considering what is reasonable in the circumstances of the case.

C1.2 Dangerous dogs

C1.2.1 *Dangerous Dogs Act 1991, section 1*

1 Dogs bred for fighting

(1) This section applies to—
    (a) any dog of the type known as the pit bull terrier;
    (b) any dog of the type known as the Japanese tosa;
    (c) any dog of any type designated for the purposes of this section by an order of the Secretary of State, being a type appearing to him to be bred for fighting or to have the characteristics of a type bred for that purpose.

(2) No person shall—
    (a) breed, or breed from, a dog to which this section applies;
    (b) sell or exchange such a dog or offer, advertise or expose such a dog for sale or exchange;
    (c) make or offer to make a gift of such a dog or advertise or expose such a dog as a gift;
    (d) allow such a dog of which he is the owner or of which he is for the time being in charge to be in a public place without being muzzled and kept on a lead; or
    (e) abandon such a dog of which he is the owner or, being the owner or for the time being in charge of such a dog, allow it to stray.

(3) After [30 November 1991] no person shall have any dog to which this section applies in his possession or custody except—
    (a) in pursuance of the power of seizure conferred by the subsequent provisions of this Act; or
    (b) in accordance with an order for its destruction made under those provisions;
but the Secretary of State shall by order make a scheme for the payment to the owners of such dogs who arrange for them to be destroyed before that day of sums specified in or determined under the scheme in respect of those dogs and the cost of their destruction.

(4) Subsection (2)(b) and (c) above shall not make unlawful anything done with a view to the dog in question being removed from the United Kingdom before the day appointed under subsection (3) above.

(5) The Secretary of State may by order provide that the prohibition in subsection (3) above shall not apply in such cases and subject to

> compliance with such conditions as are specified in the order and any
> such provision may take the form of a scheme of exemption containing
> such arrangements (including provision for the payment of charges or
> fees) as he thinks appropriate.
>
> (6) A scheme under subsection (3) or (5) above may provide for specified
> functions under the scheme to be discharged by such persons or bodies
> as the Secretary of State thinks.
>
> (6A) A scheme under subsection (3) or (5) may in particular include provi-
> sion requiring a court to consider whether a person is a fit and proper
> person to be in charge of a dog appropriate.
>
> (7) Any person who contravenes this section is guilty of an offence and
> liable on summary conviction to imprisonment for a term not exceed-
> ing six months or a fine or both except that a person who publishes an
> advertisement in contravention of subsection (2)(b) or (c)—
>
>   (a) shall not on being convicted be liable to imprisonment if he shows
> that he published the advertisement to the order of someone else
> and did not himself devise it; and
>
>   (b) shall not be convicted if, in addition, he shows that he did not know
> and had no reasonable cause to suspect that it related to a dog to
> which this section applies.

SO

6 months' imprisonment and/or a fine

In relation to an offence under section 1(2)(b) or (c), see section
1(7) which limits sentence in certain circumstances.

C1.2.2 *Sentencing guidelines*

**Offences under section 1(7): STEP ONE: determining the offence
category**

In order to determine the category the court should assess **culpability** and **harm**. The court should determine the offence category with reference only to the factors in the tables below. The
level of culpability is determined by weighing up all the factors
of the case. **Where there are characteristics present which fall
under different levels of culpability, the court should balance
these characteristics to reach a fair assessment of the offender's
culpability.**

CULPABILITY demonstrated by one or more of the following:	
A – Factors indicating higher culpability:	**B – Factors indicating lower culpability:**
Possessing a dog known to be prohibited Breeding from a dog known to be prohibited Selling, exchanging, or advertising a dog known to be prohibited Offence committed for gain Dog used to threaten or intimidate. Permitting fighting. Training and/or possession of paraphernalia for dog fighting.	All other cases.

HARM	
The level of harm is assessed by weighing up all the factors of the case.	
Greater harm	**Lesser harm**
High risk to the public and/or animals	Low risk to the public and/or animals

STEP TWO: starting point and category range

Having determined the category at step one, the court should use the corresponding starting point to reach a sentence within the category range below. The starting point applies to all offenders irrespective of plea or previous convictions.

	Culpability	
Harm	**A**	**B**
Greater harm	**Starting point** Medium-level community order	**Starting point** Band B fine
	Category range Band C fine – 6 months' custody	**Category range** Band A fine – low-level community order
Lesser harm	**Starting point** Band C fine	**Starting point** Band A fine
	Category range Band B fine – medium-level community order	**Category range** Discharge – Band B fine

The court should then consider any adjustment for any aggravating or mitigating factors. Below is a non-exhaustive list of additional factual elements providing the context of the offence and factors relating to the offender.

C1 Animal Offences

Identify whether any combination of these, or other relevant factors, should result in an upward or downward adjustment from the starting point.

Factors increasing seriousness	
Statutory aggravating factors:	*Other aggravating factors:*
Previous convictions, having regard to (a) the nature of the offence to which the conviction relates and its relevance to the current offence; and (b) the time that has elapsed since the conviction	Presence of children or others who are vulnerable because of personal circumstances
	Ill-treatment or failure to ensure welfare needs of the dog (where connected to the offence and where not charged separately)
Offence committed whilst on bail	Established evidence of community/ wider impact
	Failure to comply with current court orders
	Offence committed on licence
	Offences taken into consideration

Factors reducing seriousness or reflecting personal mitigation
No previous convictions or no relevant/recent convictions
Unaware that dog was prohibited type despite reasonable efforts to identify type
Evidence of safety or control measures having been taken by owner
Prosecution results from owner notification
Evidence of responsible ownership
Remorse
Good character and/or exemplary conduct
Serious medical condition requiring urgent, intensive or long-term treatment
Age and/or lack of maturity where it affects the responsibility of the offender
Mental disorder or learning disability
Sole or primary carer for dependent relatives
Determination and/or demonstration of steps having been taken to address offending behaviour
Lapse of time since the offence where this is not the fault of the offender ...

STEPS THREE to FIVE: (omitted: see D35)

Offences under section 1(7): STEP SIX

...

Other ancillary orders available include:

Disqualification from having a dog

The court **may** disqualify the offender from having custody of a dog for such period as it thinks fit. The test the court should consider is whether the offender is a fit and proper person to have custody of a dog.

Destruction order/contingent destruction order

In any case where the offender is not the owner of the dog, the owner must be given an opportunity to be present and make representations to the court. The court **shall** make a destruction order unless the court is satisfied that the dog would not constitute a danger to public safety.In reaching a decision, the court should consider the relevant circumstances, which must include:

• the temperament of the dog and its past behaviour;
• whether the owner of the dog, or the person for the time being in charge of it, is a fit and proper person to be in charge of the dog;

and **may** include:

• other relevant circumstances.

If the court is satisfied that the dog would not constitute a danger to public safety, it **shall** make a contingent destruction order requiring that the dog be exempted from the prohibition on possession or custody within the requisite period.

Where the court makes a destruction order, it **may** appoint a person to undertake destruction and order the offender to pay what it determines to be the reasonable expenses of destroying the dog and keeping it pending its destruction.

Fit and proper person

In determining whether a person is a fit and proper person to be in charge of a dog the following non-exhaustive factors may be relevant:

• any relevant previous convictions, cautions, or penalty notices;
• the nature and suitability of the premises that the dog is to be kept at by the person;
• where the police have released the dog pending the court's decision, whether the person has breached conditions imposed by the police; and
• any relevant previous breaches of court orders.

Note: the court must be satisfied that the person who is assessed by the court as a fit and proper person can demonstrate that they are the owner or the person ordinarily in charge of that dog at the time the court is considering whether the dog is a danger to public safety. Someone who has previously not been in charge of the dog should not be considered for this assessment, because it is an offence under the Dangerous Dogs Act 1991 to make a gift of a prohibited dog.

C1.2.3 *Dangerous Dogs Act 1991, section 3*

3 Keeping dogs under proper control

(1) If a dog is dangerously out of control in any place in England or Wales (whether or not a public place)—

    (a) the owner; and

    (b) if different, the person for the time being in charge of the dog, is guilty of an offence, or, if the dog while so out of control injures any person or assistance dog, an aggravated offence, under this subsection.

(1A) A person ('D') is not guilty of an offence under subsection (1) in a case which is a householder case.

(1B) For the purposes of subsection (1A) 'a householder case' is a case where—

    (a) the dog is dangerously out of control while in or partly in a building, or part of a building, that is a dwelling or is forces accommodation (or is both), and

    (b) at that time—

        (i) the person in relation to whom the dog is dangerously out of control ('V') is in, or is entering, the building or part as a trespasser, or

        (ii) D (if present at that time) believed V to be in, or entering, the building or part as a trespasser.

Section 76(8B) to (8F) of the Criminal Justice and Immigration Act 2008 (use of force at place of residence) apply for the purposes of this subsection as they apply for the purposes of subsection (8A) of that section (and for those purposes the reference in section 76(8D) to subsection (8A)(d) is to be read as if it were a reference to paragraph (b)(ii) of this subsection).

(2) In proceedings for an offence under subsection (1) above against a person who is the owner of a dog but was not at the material time in charge of it, it shall be a defence for the accused to prove that the dog was at the material time in the charge of a person whom he reasonably believed to be a fit and proper person to be in charge of it.

...

(4) A person guilty of an offence under subsection (1) above other than an aggravated offence is liable on summary conviction to imprisonment for a term not exceeding six months or a fine ... or both; and a person guilty of an aggravated offence under that subsection is liable—

    (a) on summary conviction, to imprisonment for a term not exceeding six months or a fine or both;

    (b) on conviction on indictment, to imprisonment for a term not exceeding the relevant maximum specified in subsection (4A) or a fine or both.

(4A) For the purposes of subsection (4)(b), the relevant maximum is—

    (a) 14 years if a person dies as a result of being injured;

    (b) 5 years in any other case where a person is injured;

    (c) 3 years in any case where an assistance dog is injured (whether or not it dies).

(5) It is hereby declared for the avoidance of doubt that an order under section 2 of the Dogs Act 1871 (order on complaint that dog is dangerous and not kept under proper control)—

    (a) may be made whether or not the dog is shown to have injured any person; and

(b) may specify the measures to be taken for keeping the dog under proper control, whether by muzzling, keeping on a lead, excluding it from specified places or otherwise.

(6) If it appears to a court on a complaint under section 2 of the said Act of 1871 that the dog to which the complaint relates is a male and would be less dangerous if neutered the court may under that section make an order requiring it to be neutered.

(7) The reference in section 1(3) of the Dangerous Dogs Act 1989 (penalties) to failing to comply with an order under section 2 of the said Act of 1871 to keep a dog under proper control shall include a reference to failing to comply with any other order made under that section; but no order shall be made under that section by virtue of subsection (6) above where the matters complained of arose before the coming into force of that subsection.

SO Non-aggravated offence

Fine and/or 6 months' imprisonment

EW Aggravated offence

Fine and/or on indictment terms of imprisonment, specified in section 4A

An offence is aggravated if the dog injures a person or assistance dog.

C1.2.4 *Sentencing guidelines*

The guidelines divide the offence under the Dangerous Dogs Act 1991, section 3(1) into four separate categories:

Category—Dangerous Dogs Act 1991 (section 3(1)):	Sentenced in:
Dog dangerously out of control in any place where death is caused	Normally, in the Crown Court
Dog dangerously out of control in any place where a person is injured	See **C1.2.4.1**
Dog dangerously out of control in any place where an assistance dog is injured or killed	See **C1.2.4.2**
Dog dangerously out of control in any place	See **C1.2.4.3**

C1.2.4.1 *Dog dangerously out of control, where a person is injured*

Owner or person in charge of a dog dangerously out of control in any place in England or Wales (whether or not a public place) where a person is injured: maximum five years' custody.

C1 Animal Offences

STEP ONE: determining the offence category

In order to determine the category the court should assess **culpability** and **harm**. The court should determine the offence category with reference only to the factors in the tables below. The level of culpability is determined by weighing up all the factors of the case. **Where there are characteristics present which fall under different levels of culpability, the court should balance these characteristics to reach a fair assessment of the offender's culpability**.

CULPABILITY demonstrated by one or more of the following:		
A – Factors indicating high culpability	**B – Factors indicating medium culpability**	**C – Factors indicating lesser culpability**
Dog used as a weapon or to intimidate people Dog known to be prohibited Dog trained to be aggressive Failure to respond to official warnings or to comply with orders concerning the dog Offender disqualified from owning a dog.	All other cases where characteristics for categories A or C are not present, and in particular: • failure to respond to warnings or concerns expressed by others about the dog's behaviour • failure to act on previous knowledge of the dog's aggressive behaviour • lack of safety or control measures taken in situations where an incident could reasonably have been foreseen • failure to intervene in the incident (where it would have been reasonable to do so) • ill-treatment or failure to ensure welfare needs of the dog (where connected to the offence and where not charged separately)	Attempts made to regain control of the dog and/or intervene Provocation of the dog without fault of the offender Evidence of safety or control measures having been taken Incident could not have reasonably been foreseen by the offender Momentary lapse of control/attention

HARM	
The level of harm is assessed by weighing up all the factors of the case	
Category 1	Serious injury (which includes disease transmission) Serious psychological harm
Category 2	Harm that falls between categories 1 and 3
Category 3	Minor injury and no significant psychological harm

STEP TWO: starting point and category range

Having determined the category at step one, the court should use the corresponding starting point to reach a sentence within the category range below. The starting point applies to all offenders irrespective of plea or previous convictions.

Harm	Culpability		
	A	**B**	**C**
Category 1	**Starting point** 3 years' custody	**Starting point** 1 year 6 months' custody	**Starting point** High-level community order
	Category range 2 years 6 months' – 4 years' custody	**Category range** 6 months' – 2 years 6 months' custody	**Category range** Medium-level community order – 6 months' custody
Category 2	**Starting point** 2 years 6 months' – 4 years' custody	**Starting point** 6 months' custody	**Starting point** Band C fine
	Category range 1 year – 3 years' custody	**Category range** Medium-level community order – 1 year's custody	**Category range** Band B fine – high-level community order
Category 3	**Starting point** 6 months' custody	**Starting point** Low-level community order	**Starting point** Band B fine
	Category range High-level community order – 1 year 6 months' custody	**Category range** Band C fine – 6 months' custody	**Category range** Discharge – Band C fine

The table is for single offences. Concurrent sentences reflecting the overall criminality of offending will ordinarily be appropriate where offences arise out of the same incident or facts: please refer to the Offences Taken into Consideration and Totality guidelines.

The court should then consider any adjustment for any aggravating or mitigating factors. There follows a **non-exhaustive** list of additional factual elements providing the context of the offence and factors relating to the offender.

Identify whether any combination of these, or other relevant factors, should result in an upward or downward adjustment from the starting point.

C1 Animal Offences

Factors increasing seriousness	
Statutory aggravating factors:	*Other aggravating factors:*
Previous convictions, having regard to (a) the **nature** of the offence to which the conviction relates and its **relevance** to the current offence; and (b) the **time** that has elapsed since the conviction Offence committed whilst on bail Offence motivated by, or demonstrating hostility based on any of the following characteristics or presumed characteristics of the victim: religion, race, disability, sexual orientation or transgender identity	Victim is a child or otherwise vulnerable because of personal circumstances Location of the offence Sustained or repeated attack Significant ongoing effect on witness(es) to the attack Serious injury caused to others (where not charged separately) Significant practical and financial effects of offence on relatives/carers Allowing person insufficiently experienced or trained, to be in charge of the dog Lack or loss of control of dog due to influence of alcohol or drugs Offence committed against those working in the public sector or providing a service to the public Injury to other animals Established evidence of community/wider impact Failure to comply with current court orders (except where taken into account in assessing culpability) Offence committed on licence Offences taken into consideration

Factors reducing seriousness or affecting personal mitigation
No previous convictions or no relevant/recent convictions
Isolated incident
No previous complaints against, or incidents involving, the dog
Evidence of responsible ownership
Remorse
Good character and/or exemplary conduct
Serious medical condition requiring urgent, intensive, or long-term treatment
Age and/or lack of maturity where it affects the responsibility of the offender
Mental disorder or learning disability
Sole or primary carer for dependent relatives
Determination and/or demonstration of steps having been taken to address offending behaviour

STEPS THREE to FIVE: (omitted: see **D35**)
STEP SIX

...

Other ancillary orders available include:

Disqualification from having a dog

The court **may** disqualify the offender from having custody of a dog. The test the court should consider is whether the offender is a fit and proper person to have custody of a dog.

Destruction order/contingent destruction order

In any case where the offender is not the owner of the dog, the owner must be given an opportunity to be present and make representations to the court.

If the dog is a **prohibited dog** refer to the guideline for possession of a prohibited dog in relation to destruction/contingent destruction orders.

The court **shall** make a destruction order unless the court is satisfied that the dog would not constitute a danger to public safety.

In reaching a decision, the court should consider the relevant circumstances which **must** include:

- the temperament of the dog and its past behaviour;
- whether the owner of the dog, or the person for the time being in charge of it is a fit and proper person to be in charge of the dog;

and **may** include:

- other relevant circumstances.

If the court is satisfied that the dog would not constitute a danger to public safety and the dog is not prohibited, it **may** make a contingent destruction order requiring the dog be kept under proper control. A contingent destruction order may specify the measures to be taken by the owner for keeping the dog under proper control, which include:

- muzzling;
- keeping on a lead;
- neutering in appropriate cases; and
- excluding it from a specified place.

Where the court makes a destruction order, it **may** appoint a person to undertake destruction and order the offender to pay what it determines to be the reasonable expenses of destroying the dog and keeping it pending its destruction.

Fit and proper person

In determining whether a person is a fit and proper person to be in charge of a dog the following non-exhaustive factors may be relevant:

- any relevant previous convictions, cautions or penalty notices;
- the nature and suitability of the premises that the dog is to be kept at by the person;

C1 Animal Offences

- where the police have released the dog pending the court's decision whether the person has breached conditions imposed by the police; and
- any relevant previous breaches of court orders.

C1.2.4.2 *Dog dangerously out of control, where an assistance dog is injured or killed*

Owner or person in charge of a dog dangerously out of control in any place in England or Wales (whether or not a public place) where an assistance dog is injured or killed: maximum three years' custody.

STEP ONE: determining the offence category

In order to determine the category the court should assess **culpability** and **harm**. The court should determine the offence category with reference only to the factors in the tables below.

The level of culpability is determined by weighing up all the factors of the case. **Where there are characteristics present which fall under different levels of culpability, the court should balance these characteristics to reach a fair assessment of the offender's culpability**.

CULPABILITY demonstrated by one or more of the following:		
A – Factors indicating high culpability	B – Factors indicating medium culpability	C – Factors indicating lesser culpability
Dog used as a weapon or to intimidate people or dogs Dog known to be prohibited Dog trained to be aggressive Offender disqualified from owning a dog, or failed to respond to official warnings, or to comply with orders concerning the dog Offence motivated by, or demonstrating hostility to the victim (assisted person) based on the victim's disability (or presumed disability)	All other cases where characteristics for categories A or C are not present, and in particular: • failure to respond to warnings or concerns expressed by others about the dog's behaviour • failure to act on previous knowledge of the dog's aggressive behaviour • lack of safety or control measures taken in situations where an incident could reasonably have been foreseen • failure to intervene in the incident (where it would have been reasonable to do so) • ill treatment or failure to ensure welfare needs of the dog (where connected to the offence and where not charged separately)	Attempts made to regain control of the dog and/or intervene Provocation of the dog without fault of the offender Evidence of safety or control measures having been taken Incident could not have reasonably been foreseen by the offender Momentary lapse of control/attention

HARM	
The level of harm is assessed by weighing up all the factors of the case.	
Category1	Fatality or serious injury to an assistance dog and/or Serious impact on the assisted person (whether psychological or other harm caused by the offence)
Category 2	Harm that falls between categories 1 and 3
Category 3	Minor injury to assistance dog and impact of the offence on the assisted person is limited

STEP TWO: starting point and category range

Having determined the category at step one, the court should use the corresponding starting point to reach a sentence within the category range below. The starting point applies to all offenders irrespective of plea or previous convictions.

Harm	Culpability		
	A	**B**	**C**
Category 1	**Starting point** 2 years' custody	**Starting point** 9 months' custody	**Starting point** Medium-level community order
	Category range 1 year – 2 years 6 months' custody	**Category range** Medium-level community order – 1 year's custody	**Category range** Low-level community order – high level community order
Category 2	**Starting point** **1** year's custody	**Starting point** High-level community order	**Starting point** Band B fine
	Category range 6 months' – 1 year 6 months' custody	**Category range** Low-level community order – 6 months' custody	**Category range** Band A fine – low– level community order
Category 3	**Starting point** High-level community order	**Starting point** Band C fine	**Starting point** Band A fine
	Category range Medium-level community order – 6 months' custody	**Category range** Band B fine – high-level community order	**Category range** Discharge – Band B fine

C1 Animal Offences

The court should then consider any adjustment for any aggravating or mitigating factors. Following is a **non-exhaustive** list of additional factual elements providing the context of the offence and factors relating to the offender.

Identify whether any combination of these, or other relevant factors, should result in an upward or downward adjustment from the starting point.

Factors increasing seriousness	
Statutory aggravating factors:	*Other aggravating factors:*
Previous convictions, having regard to (a) the **nature** of the offence to which the conviction relates and its **relevance** to the current offence; and (b) the **time** that has elapsed since the conviction Offence committed whilst on bail Offence motivated by, or demonstrating hostility based on any of the following characteristics or presumed characteristics of the victim: religion, race, disability, sexual orientation or transgender identity	Location of the offence Sustained or repeated attack Significant ongoing effect on witness(es) to the attack Allowing person insufficiently experienced or trained, to be in charge of the dog Lack or loss of control of dog owing to influence of alcohol or drugs Offence committed against those working in the public sector or providing a service to the public Injury to other animals Cost of retraining an assistance dog Established evidence of community/wider impact Failure to comply with current court orders (except where taken into account in assessing culpability) Offence committed on licence Offences taken into consideration

Factors reducing seriousness or reflecting personal mitigation
No previous convictions **or** no relevant/recent convictions
Isolated incident
No previous complaints against, or incidents involving the dog
Evidence of responsible ownership
Remorse
Good character and/or exemplary conduct
Serious medical condition requiring urgent, intensive or long-term treatment
Age and/or lack of maturity where it affects the responsibility of the offender
Mental disorder or learning disability
Sole or primary carer for dependent relatives
Determination and/or demonstration of steps having been taken to address offending behaviour

STEPS THREE to FIVE: (omitted: see **D35**)

STEP SIX:

…

Other ancillary orders available include

Disqualification from having a dog

The court **may** disqualify the offender from having custody of a dog. The test the court should consider is whether the offender is a fit and proper person to have custody of a dog.

Destruction order/contingent destruction order

In any case where the offender is not the owner of the dog, the owner must be given an opportunity to be present and make representations to the court.

If the dog is a **prohibited dog** refer to the guideline for possession of a prohibited dog in relation to destruction/contingent destruction orders.

The court **shall** make a destruction order unless the court is satisfied that the dog would not constitute a danger to public safety.

In reaching a decision, the court should consider the relevant circumstances which **must** include:

- the temperament of the dog and its past behaviour;
- whether the owner of the dog, or the person for the time being in charge of it is a fit and proper person to be in charge of the dog;

and **may** include:

- other relevant circumstances.

If the court is satisfied that the dog would not constitute a danger to public safety and the dog is not prohibited, it **may** make a contingent destruction order requiring the dog be kept under proper control. A contingent destruction order may specify the measures to be taken by the owner for keeping the dog under proper control, which include:

- muzzling;
- keeping on a lead;
- neutering in appropriate cases; and
- excluding it from a specified place.

Where the court makes a destruction order, it **may** appoint a person to undertake destruction and order the offender to pay what it determines to be the reasonable expenses of destroying the dog and keeping it pending its destruction.

Fit and proper person

In determining whether a person is a fit and proper person to be in charge of a dog the following non-exhaustive factors may be relevant:

- any relevant previous convictions, cautions or penalty notices;
- the nature and suitability of the premises that the dog is to be kept at by the person;
- where the police have released the dog pending the court's decision whether the person has breached conditions imposed by the police; and
- any relevant previous breaches of court orders.

C1.2.4.3 *Dog dangerously out of control in any place*

Owner or person in charge of a dog dangerously out of control in any place in England or Wales (whether or not a public place): maximum 6 months' custody.

STEP ONE: determining the offence category

In order to determine the category the court should assess **culpability** and **harm**. The court should determine the offence category with reference only to the factors in the tables below.

The level of culpability is determined by weighing up all the factors of the case. **Where there are characteristics present which fall under different levels of culpability, the court should balance these characteristics to reach a fair assessment of the offender's culpability**.

CULPABILITY demonstrated by one or more of the following:	
A – Factors indicating high culpability	B – Factors indicating lower culpability
Dog used as a weapon or to intimidate people Dog known to be prohibited Dog trained to be aggressive Offender disqualified from owning a dog, or failed to respond to official warnings, or to comply with orders concerning the dog	Attempts made to regain control of the dog and/or intervene Provocation of dog without fault of the offender Evidence of safety or control measures having been taken Incident could not have reasonably been foreseen by the offender Momentary lapse of control/attention

HARM	
The level of harm is assessed by weighing up all the factors of the case.	
Greater harm	Presence of children or others who are vulnerable because of personal circumstances. Injury to other animals.
Lesser harm	Low risk to the public.

STEP TWO: starting point and category range

Having determined the category at step one, the court should use the corresponding starting point to reach a sentence within the category range below. The starting point applies to all offenders irrespective of plea or previous convictions.

Harm	Culpability	
	A	**B**
Greater Harm	**Starting point** Medium-level community order	**Starting point** Band B fine
	Category range Band C fine – 6 months' custody	**Category range** Band A fine – Band C fine
Lesser harm	**Starting point** Band C fine	**Starting point** Band A fine
	Category range Band B fine – low-level community order	**Category range** Discharge – Band B fine

The court should then consider any adjustment for any aggravating or mitigating factors. Following is a **non-exhaustive** list of additional factual elements providing the context of the offence and factors relating to the offender.

Identify whether any combination of these, or other relevant factors, should result in an upward or downward adjustment from the starting point.

Factors increasing seriousness	
Statutory aggravating factors:	*Other aggravating factors:*
Previous convictions, having regard to (a) the **nature** of the offence to which the conviction relates and its **relevance** to the current offence; and (b) the **time** that has elapsed since the conviction Offence committed whilst on bail Offence motivated by, or demonstrating hostility based on any of the following characteristics or presumed characteristics of the victim: religion, race, disability, sexual orientation or transgender identity	Location of the offence Significant ongoing effect on the victim and/or others Failing to take adequate precautions to prevent the dog from escaping Allowing person insufficiently experienced or trained, to be in charge of the dog Ill treatment or failure to ensure welfare needs of the dog (where connected to the offence and where not charged separately) Lack or loss of control of dog owing to influence of alcohol or drugs Offence committed against those working in the public sector or providing a service to the public Established evidence of community/wider impact Failure to comply with current court orders (unless this has already been taken into account in assessing culpability) Offence committed on licence. Offences taken into consideration

Factors reducing seriousness or reflecting personal mitigation
No previous convictions **or** no relevant/recent convictions
Isolated incident
No previous complaints against, or incidents involving the dog
Evidence of responsible ownership
Remorse
Good character and/or exemplary conduct
Serious medical condition requiring urgent, intensive, or long-term treatment
Age and/or lack of maturity where it affects the responsibility of the offender Mental disorder or learning disability
Sole or primary carer for dependent relatives
Determination and/or demonstration of steps having been taken to address offending behaviour

STEPS THREE to FIVE: (omitted: see **D35**)

STEP SIX

...

Other ancillary orders available include:

Disqualification from having a dog

The court **may** disqualify the offender from having custody of a dog. The test the court should consider is whether the offender is a fit and proper person to have custody of a dog.

Destruction order/contingent destruction order

In any case where the offender is not the owner of the dog, the owner must be given an opportunity to be present and make representations to the court.

If the dog is a **prohibited dog** refer to the guideline for possession of a prohibited dog in relation to destruction/contingent destruction orders.

If the dog is not prohibited and the court is satisfied that the dog would constitute a danger to public safety the court **may** make a destruction order.

In reaching a decision, the court should consider the relevant circumstances which **must** include:

- the temperament of the dog and its past behaviour;
- whether the owner of the dog, or the person for the time being in charge of it is a fit and proper person to be in charge of the dog;

and **may** include:

• other relevant circumstances.

If the court is satisfied that the dog would not constitute a danger to public safety and the dog is not prohibited, it **may** make a contingent destruction order requiring the dog be kept under proper control. A contingent destruction order may specify the measures to be taken by the owner for keeping the dog under proper control, which include:

• muzzling;
• keeping on a lead;
• neutering in appropriate cases; and
• excluding it from a specified place.

Where the court makes a destruction order, it **may** appoint a person to undertake destruction and order the offender to pay what it determines to be the reasonable expenses of destroying the dog and keeping it pending its destruction.

Fit and proper person

In determining whether a person is a fit and proper person to be in charge of a dog the following non-exhaustive factors may be relevant:

• any relevant previous convictions, cautions, or penalty notices;
• the nature and suitability of the premises that the dog is to be kept at by the person;
• where the police have released the dog pending the court's decision whether the person has breached conditions imposed by the police; **and**
• any relevant previous breaches of court orders.

C1.2.5 *Dangerous Dogs Act 1991, sections 4(1)–(3) and 4A*

> **4 Destruction and disqualification orders**
>
> (1) Where a person is convicted of an offence under section 1 or 3(1) above or of an offence under an order made under section 2 above the court—
>
>   (a) may order the destruction of any dog in respect of which the offence was committed and, subject to subsection (1A) below, shall do so in the case of an offence under section 1 or an aggravated offence under section 3(1) above; and
>
>   (b) may order the offender to be disqualified, for such period as the court thinks fit, for having custody of a dog.

(1A) Nothing in subsection (1)(a) above shall require the court to order the destruction of a dog if the court is satisfied—
  (a) that the dog would not constitute a danger to public safety; and
  (b) where the dog was born before 30th November 1991 and is subject to the prohibition in section 1(3) above, that there is a good reason why the dog has not been exempted from that prohibition.

(1B) For the purposes of subsection (1A)(a), when deciding whether a dog would constitute a danger to public safety, the court—
  (a) must consider—
    (i) the temperament of the dog and its past behaviour, and
    (ii) whether the owner of the dog, or the person for the time being in charge of it, is a fit and proper person to be in charge of the dog, and
  (b) may consider any other relevant circumstances.

(2) Where a court makes an order under subsection (1)(a) above for the destruction of a dog owned by a person other than the offender, the owner may appeal to the Crown Court against the order.

(3) A dog shall not be destroyed pursuant to an order under subsection (1)(a) above—
  (a) until the end of the period for giving notice of appeal against the conviction or, against the order; and
  (b) if notice of appeal is given within that period, until the appeal is determined or withdrawn,
  unless the offender and, in a case to which subsection (2) above applies, the owner of the dog give notice to the court that made the order that there is to be no appeal

...

4A Contingent destruction orders

(1) Where—
  (a) a person is convicted of an offence under section 1 above or an aggravated offence under section 3(1) above;
  (b) the court does not order the destruction of the dog under section 4(1)(a) above; and
  (c) in the case of an offence under section 1 above, the dog is subject to the prohibition in section 1(3) above,
  the court shall order that, unless the dog is exempted from that prohibition within the requisite period, the dog shall be destroyed.

(2) Where an order is made under subsection (1) above in respect of a dog, and the dog is not exempted from the prohibition in section 1(3) above within the requisite period, the court may extend that period.

(3) Subject to subsection (2) above, the requisite period for the purposes of such an order is the period of two months beginning with the date of the order.

(4) Where a person is convicted of an offence under section 3(1) above, the court may order that, unless the owner of the dog keeps it under proper control, the dog shall be destroyed.

(5) An order under subsection (4) above—
  (a) may specify the measures to be taken for keeping the dog under proper control, whether by muzzling, keeping on a lead, excluding it from specified places or otherwise; and

(b) if it appears to the court that the dog is a male and would be less dangerous if neutered, may require it to be neutered.

(6) Subsections (2) to (4) of section 4 above shall apply in relation to an order under subsection (1) or (4) above as they apply in relation to an order under subsection (1)(a) of that section.

C1.2.6 Key points

- For 'type' see *Crown Court at Knightsbridge, ex p Dune* [1993] 4 All ER 491.
- 'Dangerously out of control' is defined under section 10(3) of the Act:

Dangerous Dogs Act 1991, s 10(3)

10 Short title, interpretation, commencement and extent

(3) For the purposes of this Act a dog shall be regarded as dangerously out of control on any occasion on which there are grounds for reasonable apprehension that it will injure any person or assistance dog, whether or not it actually does so, but references to a dog injuring a person or assistance dog or there being grounds for reasonable apprehension that it will do so do not include references to any case in which the dog is being used for a lawful purpose by a constable or a person in the service of the Crown.

- Regard must be had to the behaviour of the dog and the degree of control exercised by its handler. The fact that the dog has not displayed any previous bad traits was of relevance but not conclusive (*R v Gedminintaite* [2008] EWCA Crim 814).
- It is sufficient that the danger is only to other dogs (*Briscoe v Shattock* (1998) 163 JP 201), but hunting and killing rabbits and other small animals is part of a dog's nature and does not make it dangerous (*Sansom v Chief Constable of Kent* [1981] Crim LR 617).
- The owner of the dog has a defence under section 3(2) if another fit and proper person was in charge of the dog at the material time. Whether a person is a fit and proper person will depend on all of the circumstances. The dog must have been left with an identifiable person; it was not sufficient merely to say that different members of a family looked after the dog at different times (*R v Huddart* [1999] Crim LR 568).

Although section 3 creates an offence of strict liability, there must still be some causal connection between having charge of the dog and the occurrence of the serious injury (*R v Robinson-Pierre* [2013] EWCA Crim 2396).

- It is irrelevant that the owner did not anticipate the behaviour of the dog (*R v Bezzina* (1994) 158 JP 671).
- A person who relinquishes physical control of a dog by passing the lead to another may remain in joint control of the dog (*L v Crown Prosecution Service*, unreported, 10 February 2010). Plain evidence is required to demonstrate that control has been passed to another (*R v Huddart* [1999] Crim LR 568).
- 'Public place' includes the inside of a vehicle which is itself in a public place (*Bates v Director of Public Prosecutions* (1993) 157 JP 1004).
- There are no defences in relation to section 1 (see *Director of Public Prosecutions v Kellett* (1994) 158 JP 1138 (intoxication) and *Cichon v Director of Public Prosecutions* [1994] Crim LR (welfare of the animal—unmuzzling to allow the dog to be sick)).
- In relation to destruction orders, see the guidance issued by the Court of Appeal in *R v Flack* [2008] Cr App R (S) 395 and *R v Davies* [2010] 174 JP 514, CA, reviewed in *Kelleher v DPP* [2012] 176 JP 729, QBD.

Essentially the court must consider whether the dog constitutes a danger to the public. If it does not then no order is made. If it does, the court must consider whether a contingent destruction order would remove that danger. In the case of an aggravated offence, the burden of proof to show that the dog does not represent a danger is on the defence. The normal burden of proof applies in non-aggravated cases.

 See *Blackstone's Criminal Practice 2017* **B20**

C2 Breach Offences

C2.1 Criminal behaviour order and anti-social behaviour order

Upon implementation of the Anti-social Behaviour Crime and Policing Act (ASBPCA) 2014 earlier provisions were repealed and replaced by section 30 of that Act which provides that:

Anti-social Behaviour Crime and Policing Act 2014, s 30

30 Breach of order

(1) A person who without reasonable excuse—
  (a) does anything he or she is prohibited from doing by a criminal behaviour order, or
  (b) fails to do anything he or she is required to do by a criminal behaviour order,
  commits an offence.
(2) A person guilty of an offence under this section is liable—
  (a) on summary conviction, to imprisonment for a period not exceeding 6 months or to a fine, or to both;
  (b) on conviction on indictment, to imprisonment for a period not exceeding 5 years or to a fine, or to both.
(3) If a person is convicted of an offence under this section, it is not open to the court by or before which the person is convicted to make an order under subsection (1)(b) of section 12 of the Powers of Criminal Courts (Sentencing) Act 2000 (conditional discharge).

Crime and Disorder Act 1998, s 1(10)

1 Anti-social behaviour orders

If without reasonable excuse a person does anything which he is prohibited from doing by an anti-social behaviour order, he is guilty of an offence.

EW

 Fine and/or 6 months'/5 years' imprisonment.

C2 Breach Offences

C2.1.1 *Sentencing*

Nature of failure and harm	Starting point	Sentencing range
Serious harassment, alarm, or distress has been caused or where such harm was intended	26 weeks' custody	Custody threshold to 2 years' custody
Lesser degree of harassment, alarm, or distress, where such harm was intended, or where it would have been likely if the offender had not been apprehended	6 weeks' custody	Medium-level community order to 26 weeks' custody
No harassment, alarm, or distress was actually caused by the breach and none was intended by the offender	Low-level community order	Band B fine to medium-level community order

Aggravating factors	Mitigating factors
1. Offender has a history of disobedience to court orders 2. Breach was committed immediately or shortly after the order was made 3. Breach was committed subsequent to earlier breach proceedings arising from the same order 4. Targeting of a person the order was made to protect or a witness in the original proceedings	1. Breach occurred after a long period of compliance. 2. The prohibition(s) breached was not fully understood, especially where an interim order was made without notice.

C2.1.2 Key points

- The prosecution must be in a position to prove that the person before the court is the person in respect of whom the order was made (*Barber v Crown Prosecution Service* [2004] EWHC 2605 (Admin)).
- In *R v Nicholson* [2006] EWCA Crim 1518, the offender took part in a demonstration within a prohibited distance of a named property. She admitted, too, that she had not carefully checked the terms of the order, in particular the scheduled inclusion of premises named Halifax House. However, she maintained that she had a reasonable excuse for breaching the terms of the order within the statutory provision because she had no recollection of ever having heard before, or at the demonstration, of any reference to Halifax House as the address of the proposed laboratory, and she had mistakenly believed that she was entitled to

attend the demonstration as she did. Held: forgetfulness, misunderstanding, or ignorance could amount in law to a reasonable excuse.

- The fact that a person is appealing against the imposition of an order does not give rise to a reasonable excuse (*West Midlands Probation Board v Daly* [2008] EWHC 15 (Admin)).
- A belief that the order has come to an end is capable of amounting to a reasonable excuse (*Barber v Crown Prosecution Service* [2004] EWHC 2605 (Admin)).
- Where conduct forming the breach would also be a criminal offence in its own right, a court was not bound by the maximum sentence available for that offence, but should have regard to proportionality. It would be wrong for a prosecutor to proceed with a breach of an order simply because it was thought that the penalty for the substantive offence was too lenient (*R v Stevens* [2006] EWCA Crim 255).
- The burden of negativing reasonable excuse, once raised by evidence by the defence, falls on the prosecution (*R v Charles* [2009] EWCA Crim 1570).
- A defendant's state of mind is relevant to the issue of reasonable excuse, notwithstanding the fact that the offence is one of strict liability (*JB v Crown Prosecution Service* [2012] EWHC 72 (Admin)).

 See *Blackstone's Criminal Practice 2017* **D25**

C2.2 Breach of protective orders

- Protection from Harassment Act 1997, section 5(5).
- Family Law Act 1996, section 42A.

 EW

 Fine and/or 6 months'/5 years' imprisonment

 DO

C2 Breach Offences

C2.2.1 *Sentencing*

Offence seriousness (culpability and harm) A. Identify the appropriate starting point Starting points based on first-time offender pleading not guilty		
Examples of nature of activity	**Starting point**	**Range**
Single breach involving no/minimal direct contact	Low-level community order	Band C fine to medium-level community order
More than one breach involving no/ minimal contact or some direct contact	Medium-level community order	Low-level community order to high-level community order
Single breach involving some violence and/or significant physical or psychological harm to the victim	18 weeks' custody	13 to 26 weeks' custody
More than one breach involving some violence and/or significant physical or psychological harm to the victim	Crown Court	26 weeks' custody to Crown Court
Breach (whether one or more) involving significant physical violence and significant physical or psychological harm to the victim	Crown Court	Crown Court

Offence seriousness (culpability and harm) B. Consider the effect of aggravating and mitigating factors (other than those within examples above) The following may be particularly relevant but these lists are not exhaustive	
Factors indicating higher culpability 1. Proven history of violence or threats by the offender. 2. Using contact arrangements with a child to instigate offence. 3. Offence is a further breach, following earlier breach proceedings. 4. Offender has history of disobedience to court orders 5. Breach committed immediately or shortly after order made. **Factors indicating greater degree of harm** 1. Victim is particularly vulnerable. 2. Impact on children. 3. Victim is forced to leave home.	**Factors indicating lower culpability** 1. Breach occurred after long period of compliance. 2. Victim initiated contact.

C2.2.2 Key points

- A delusional schizophrenic's belief that his neighbour was committing crime could not be regarded as a reasonable excuse for such a breach, and the test of whether his conduct breached an order was objective. The belief was relevant to sentence, however (*R v Grazanfer* [2015] EWCA Crim 642).
- When considering a breach of a restraining order the word 'harass' in an order is to be read, as it would be under the Protection from Harassment Act 1997, so that a defendant would not be in breach of the order if he could make good the defence under section 1(3)(c) of that Act that, in the particular circumstances, the pursuit of the course of conduct had been reasonable (*R v O'Neill* [2016] EWCA Crim 92).
- Note that there is also an either-way offence carrying five years on indictment, under section 3 Protection from Harassment Act 1997, where there is a breach without reasonable excuse of a civil injunction obtained by an individual under ASBPCA.

 See *Blackstone's Criminal Practice 2017* **B14.134**

C2.3 Breach of sexual harm prevention order (SHPO)

> ### Sexual Offences Act 2003, s 103I
>
> #### Offence: breach of SHPO or interim SHPO, etc
>
> (1) A person who, without reasonable excuse, does anything that the person is prohibited from doing by—
>   (a) a sexual harm prevention order,
>   (b) an interim sexual harm prevention order,
>   (c) a sexual offences prevention order,
>   (d) an interim sexual offences prevention order, or
>   (e) a foreign travel order,
>   commits an offence.

EW

6 months' imprisonment and/or a fine/5 years' imprisonment

There is no sentencing guideline but a conditional discharge may not be imposed.

C2.4 Breach of a Modern Slavery Act protection order

Modern Slavery Act 2015, s 30

(1) A person who, without reasonable excuse, does anything that the person is prohibited from doing ... commits an offence.

EW

 6 months' imprisonment and/or a fine/5 years' imprisonment

C2.5 Breach of a female genital mutilation protection order

Female Genital Mutilation Act 2003, s 5A and Sch 2, para 4(1)

4 (1) A person who without reasonable excuse does anything that the person is prohibited from doing by an FGM protection order is guilty of an offence.

EW

 6 months' imprisonment and/or a fine/5 years' imprisonment

C2.6 Breach of a forced marriage protection order

Family Law Act 1996, s 63CA

(1) A person who without reasonable excuse does anything that the person is prohibited from doing by a forced marriage protection order is guilty of an offence.
(2) In the case of a forced marriage protection order made [ex parte] a person can be guilty of an offence under this section only in respect of conduct engaged in at a time when the person was aware of the existence of the order.

EW

 6 months' imprisonment and/or a fine/5 years' imprisonment

C2.7 Serious crime prevention order

Serious Crime Act 2007, s 25

(1) A person who, without reasonable excuse, fails to comply with a serious crime prevention order commits an offence.

6 months' imprisonment and/or a fine/5 years' imprisonment

C2.8 Breach of a football banning order

Football Spectators Act 1989, s 14J

(1) A person subject to a banning order who fails to comply with—
    (a) any requirement imposed by the order, or
    (b) any requirement imposed under section 19(2B) or (2C) below, is guilty of an offence.

SO

6 months and/or a fine

C2.9 Breach of bail

See **C3.1**.

C3 **Administration of Justice**

C3.1 Bail: failure to surrender

> ### Bail Act 1976, s 6(1) and (2)
>
> #### 6 Offence of absconding by person released on bail
> (1) If a person who has been released on bail in criminal proceedings fails without reasonable cause to surrender to custody he shall be guilty of an offence.
> (2) If a person who—
>   (a) has been released on bail in criminal proceedings, and
>   (b) having reasonable cause therefor, has failed to surrender to custody,
>   fails to surrender to custody at the appointed place as soon after the appointed time as is reasonably practicable he shall be guilty of an offence.

SO But with power to commit to the Crown Court

▦ Fine and/or 3 months'/12 months' imprisonment

C3.2 Sentencing

Offence seriousness (culpability and harm) A. Identify the appropriate starting point Starting points based on first-time offender pleading not guilty		
Example of nature of activity	**Starting point**	**Range**
Surrenders late on day but case proceeds as planned	Band A fine	Band A fine to Band B fine
Negligent or non-deliberate failure to attend causing delay and/or interference with the administration of justice	Band C fine	Band B fine to medium-level community order
Deliberate failure to attend causing delay and/or interference with the administration of justice. The type and degree of harm actually caused will affect where in the range the case falls	14 days' custody	Low-level community order to 10 weeks' custody

Offence seriousness (culpability and harm)	
B. Consider the effect of aggravating and mitigating factors	
(other than those within examples above)	
The following may be particularly relevant but these lists are not exhaustive	
Factors indicating higher culpability	**Factors indicating lower culpability**
1. Serious attempts to evade justice.	Where not amounting to a defence:
2. Determined attempt seriously to undermine the course of justice.	1. Misunderstanding;
	2. Failure to comprehend bail significance or requirements;
3. Previous relevant convictions and/or breach of court orders or police bail.	3. Caring responsibilities.
Factor indicating greater degree of harm	**Factor indicating lesser degree of harm**
1. Lengthy absence.	1. Prompt, voluntary surrender.

C3.3 Key points

- Guidance by Justices Clerks' Society in September 2014 advises that all courts should arrange for the surrender to bail to occur on appearance in the court room and not before on signing in with a court official. The effect is that those who arrive late, but whose cases are not called, will not be committing an offence. This reconciles *DPP v Richards* [1988] 3 All ER 406 (magistrates' courts) *with R v Scott Evans* [2011] 1WLR 1192 (Crown Courts) as appears below.

- In *R v Scott* [2007] EWCA Crim 2757, the court rejected an argument that surrendering to bail 30 minutes late was *de minimis* so as to make proceeding with a Bail Act charge *Wednesbury* unreasonable. The court held:

  We are prepared for the sake of argument to accept the possibility that there could be circumstances where a defendant's late arrival at court was so truly marginal that it would be Wednesbury unreasonable to pursue it but it would be a rare case. Even if a delay is small it can still cause inconvenience and waste of time. If a culture of lateness is tolerated the results can be cumulative and bad for the administration of justice.

- In *R v Gateshead Justices, ex p Usher* [1981] Crim LR 491, DC, a period of seven minutes was held to be *de minimis*; however, in *Scott* the court said that no gloss should be placed on the clear wording in the Bail Act and *Usher* established no clear principle of law.

- Proof of *bail* terms: section 6 of the Bail Act 1976 provides:

Bail Act 1976, s 6(8) and (9)

6 Offence of absconding by person released on bail

(8) In any proceedings for an offence under subsection (1) or (2) above a document purporting to be a copy of the part of the prescribed record which relates to the time and place appointed for the person specified in the record to surrender to custody and to be duly certified to be a true copy of that part of the record shall be evidence of the time and place appointed for that person to surrender to custody.

(9) For the purposes of subsection (8) above—
  (a) 'the prescribed record' means the record of the decision of the court, officer or constable made in pursuance of section 5(1) of this Act;
  (b) the copy of the prescribed record is duly certified if it is certified by the appropriate officer of the court or, as the case may be, by the constable who took the decision or a constable designated for the purpose by the officer in charge of the police station from which the person to whom the record relates was released.

- In *R v Liverpool Justices, ex p Santos*, The Times, 23 January 1997, the court held that reliance on mistaken information provided by a solicitor may be found a reasonable excuse for failing to surrender. The court went on to say that all relevant factors would need to be considered, and a mistake on the part of a solicitor in calculating the bail date did not automatically excuse the defendant's non-attendance.
- A failure to give the defendant a written bail notice does not amount to a reasonable excuse.
- A genuine, albeit mistaken, belief that bail was to another date would not amount to a reasonable excuse (*Laidlaw v Atkinson*, The Times, 2 August 1986).
- A reasonable excuse need be proved only to the civil standard (*R v Carr-Bryant* (1944) 29 Cr App R 76).
- A person who had overtly subjected himself to the court's direction (see *R v Central Criminal Court, ex p Guney* [1995] 2 All ER 577), or reported to court officials as directed, had surrendered to custody (see *Director of Public Prosecutions v Richards* [1988] QB 701 in relation to the magistrates' court). If the defendant later left court, no offence would be committed (although the court could issue a warrant for arrest). It is not essential that there be a formal surrender to an official (*R v Rumble* [2003] EWCA Crim 770), but simply arriving at the court at the proper time may not be enough (*R v Render* (1987) 84 Cr App R 294). In *Evans* [2011] EWCA Crim 2842, the court made clear that in the Crown Court a defendant who advises the usher and his own lawyer of

his presence but then leaves, does not surrender to bail. He must be identified before the judge, or surrender to the dock officer.

- If a person is acquitted of the offence for which he was on bail, that does not mitigate the penalty for failing to surrender (*R v Maguire* [1993] RTR 306).

 See *Blackstone's Criminal Practice 2017* **D7.97**

C3.4 Being unlawfully at large

Section 32ZA of the Crime (Sentences) Act 1997 and section 255ZA of the Criminal Justice Act 2003 apply in relation to a person recalled to prison before or after 13 April 2015.

Crime (Sentences) Act 1997, s 32ZA

Offence of remaining unlawfully at large after recall

(1) A person recalled to prison under section 32 commits an offence if the person—
   (a) has been notified of the recall orally or in writing, and
   (b) while unlawfully at large fails, without reasonable excuse, to take all necessary steps to return to prison as soon as possible.

(2) A person is to be treated for the purposes of subsection (1)(a) as having been notified of the recall if—
   (a) written notice of the recall has been delivered to an appropriate address, and
   (b) a period specified in the notice has elapsed.

(3) In subsection (2) 'an appropriate address' means—
   (a) an address at which, under the person's licence, the person is permitted to reside or stay, or
   (b) an address nominated, in accordance with the person's licence, for the purposes of this section.

(4) A person is also to be treated for the purposes of subsection (1)(a) as having been notified of the recall if—
   (a) the person's licence requires the person to keep in touch in accordance with any instructions given by an officer of a provider of probation services,
   (b) the person has failed to comply with such an instruction, and
   (c) the person has not complied with such an instruction for at least 6 months.

EW

6 months' and/or a fine/2 years' imprisonment

Criminal Justice Act 2003, s 255ZA

Offence of remaining unlawfully at large after recall

(1) A person recalled to prison under section 254 or 255 commits an offence if the person—
  (a) has been notified of the recall orally or in writing, and
  (b) while unlawfully at large fails, without reasonable excuse, to take all necessary steps to return to prison as soon as possible.
(2) A person is to be treated for the purposes of subsection (1)(a) as having been notified of the recall if—
  (a) written notice of the recall has been delivered to an appropriate address, and
  (b) a period specified in the notice has elapsed.
(3) In subsection (2) 'an appropriate address' means—
  (a) an address at which, under the person's licence, the person is permitted to reside or stay, or
  (b) an address nominated, in accordance with the person's licence, for the purposes of this section.
(4) A person is also to be treated for the purposes of subsection (1)(a) as having been notified of the recall if—
  (a) the person's licence requires the person to keep in touch in accordance with any instructions given by an officer of a provider of probation services,
  (b) the person has failed to comply with such an instruction, and
  (c) the person has not complied with such an instruction for at least 6 months.

EW

 6 months' and/or a fine/2 years' imprisonment

C3.5 Remaining at large after temporary release

Prisoners (Return to Custody) Act 1995, s 1

(1) Subject to subsection (2) below, a person who has been temporarily released in pursuance of rules made under section 47(5) of the Prison Act 1952 (rules for temporary release) is guilty of an offence if—
  (a) without reasonable excuse, he remains unlawfully at large at any time after becoming so at large by virtue of the expiry of the period for which he was temporarily released; or
  (b) knowing or believing an order recalling him to have been made and while unlawfully at large by virtue of such an order, he fails, without reasonable excuse, to take all necessary steps for complying as soon as reasonably practicable with that order.

(2) Subsection (1) above shall not apply in the case of a person temporarily released from a secure training centre.

...

(6) This section shall not apply where the period of temporary release expired, or the order of recall was made, before the commencement of this section.

EW

6 months' imprisonment and/or a fine/2 years' imprisonment

C4 **Communication Network Offenses**

C4.1 Improper use of public electronic communications network

> **Communications Act 2003, s 127(1) and (2)**
>
> **127 Improper use of public electronic communications network**
>
> (1) A person is guilty of an offence if he—
>   (a) sends by means of a public electronic communications network a message or other matter that is grossly offensive or of an indecent, obscene or menacing character; or
>   (b) causes any such message or matter to be so sent.
> (2) A person is guilty of an offence if, for the purpose of causing annoyance, inconvenience or needless anxiety to another, he—
>   (a) sends by means of a public electronic communications network, a message that he knows to be false,
>   (b) causes such a message to be sent; or
>   (c) persistently makes use of a public electronic communications network

SO

 Fine/6 months' imprisonment

Note that this guideline is under review by the Sentencing Council (see **Appendix 7**).

C4.1.1 *Sentencing*

Offence seriousness (culpability and harm) A. Identify the appropriate starting point Starting points based on first-time offender pleading not guilty		
Sending grossly offensive, indecent, obscene, or menacing messages (s 127(1))		
Example of nature of activity	**Starting point**	**Range**
Single offensive, indecent, obscene, or menacing call of short duration, having no significant impact on receiver	Band B fine	Band A fine to Band C fine
Single call where extreme language used, having only moderate impact on receiver	Medium-level community order	Low-level community order to high-level community order

Single call where extreme language used and substantial distress or fear caused to receiver; OR One of a series of similar calls as described in box above	6 weeks' custody	High-level community order to 12 weeks' custody

Sending false message/persistent use of communications network for purpose of causing annoyance, inconvenience, or needless anxiety (s 127(2))

Example of nature of activity	Starting point	Range
Persistent silent calls over short period to private individual, causing inconvenience or annoyance	Band B fine	Band A fine to Band C fine
Single hoax call to public or private organization resulting in moderate disruption or anxiety	Medium-level community order	Low-level community order to high-level community order
Single hoax call resulting in major disruption or substantial public fear or distress; OR One of a series of similar calls as described in box above	12 weeks' custody	High-level community order to 18 weeks' custody

C4.1.2 *Time limits*

Communications Act 2003, s 127

(5) An information or complaint relating to an offence under this section may be tried by a magistrates' court in England and Wales or Northern Ireland if it is laid or made—
   (a) before the end of the period of 3 years beginning with the day on which the offence was committed, and
   (b) before the end of the period of 6 months beginning with the day on which evidence comes to the knowledge of the prosecutor which the prosecutor considers sufficient to justify proceedings ...
(7) A certificate of a prosecutor as to the date on which evidence described in subsection (5)(b) or (6)(b) came to his or her knowledge is conclusive evidence of that fact.

C4.1.3 Key points

- In *Director of Public Prosecutions v Collins* [2006] UKHL 40, the court held that to be guilty of an offence under section 127:
  - the defendant must have intended his words to be offensive to those to whom they related; or

- must be aware that they might be taken to be so.
- It does not matter if the material sent was not received. The question of whether something is in fact offensive is to be determined by reference to whether or not reasonable persons would find the message grossly offensive, judged by the standards of an open and just multiracial society.
- Parliament cannot have intended to criminalize the conduct of a person using language which is, for reasons unknown to him, grossly offensive to those to whom it relates, or which may even be thought, however wrongly, to represent a polite or acceptable usage. On the other hand, a culpable state of mind will ordinarily be found where a message is couched in terms showing an intention to insult those to whom the message relates, or giving rise to the inference that a risk of doing so must have been recognized by the sender. The same will be true where facts known to the sender of a message about an intended recipient render the message peculiarly offensive to that recipient, or likely to be so, whether or not the message in fact reaches the recipient.
- While it is an offence to send by public electronic communication network a message of a menacing character (Communications Act 2003, s 127(1)(a)), the mental element requires the sender either to have intended that the message be of a menacing character, or to have been aware or to have recognized the risk that it might create fear or apprehension in any reasonable member of the public who reads or sees it.
- If the message was intended as a joke, however poor, the offence will rarely be made out (*Chambers v DPP* [2012] EWHC 2157 (QB)).
- For a call to be menacing within section 127(1)(a) Communications Act 2003 it must be more than offensive or nasty and anti-Semitic (*Karsten v Wood Green Crown Court* [2014] EWHC 2900 (Admin)).
- European Convention rights to freedom of expression will rarely provide a defence (see *Connolly v Director of Public Prosecutions* [2007] EWHC 237 (Admin), a case concerned with a different statute).

 See *Blackstone's Criminal Practice 2017* **B18.30**

C4.2 Sending indecent material through the post

Postal Services Act 2000, s 85

85 Prohibition on sending certain articles by post

(1) A person commits an offence if he sends by post a postal packet which encloses any creature, article or thing of any kind which is likely to injure other postal packets in course of their transmission by post or any person engaged in the business of a postal operator.

(2) Subsection (1) does not apply to postal packets which enclose anything permitted (whether generally or specifically) by the postal operator concerned.

(3) A person commits an offence if he sends by post a postal packet which encloses—

    (a) any indecent or obscene print, painting, photograph, lithograph, engraving, cinematograph film or other record of a picture or pictures, book, card or written communication, or

    (b) any other indecent or obscene article (whether or not of a similar kind to those mentioned in paragraph (a)).

(4) A person commits an offence if he sends by post a postal packet which has on the packet, or on the cover of the packet, any words, marks or designs which are of an indecent or obscene character.

(5) A person who commits an offence under this section shall be liable—

    (a) on summary conviction, to a fine not exceeding the statutory maximum,

    (b) on conviction on indictment, to a fine or to imprisonment for a term not exceeding twelve months or to both.

Summary trial—fine; on indictment—12 months' imprisonment and/or a fine

C4.2.1 Key points

Whether something is obscene is to be judged objectively.

In relation to Article 10 ECHR considerations, the court in *R v Kirk* [2006] EWCA Crim 725 held:

> We derive assistance, so far as the reference to the Convention is concerned, from the recent decision of the House of Lords in *K v London Borough of Lambeth* [2006] UKHL 10. We refer in particular to paragraph 110 of the opinion of Lord Hope. Article 10 protects the right of free speech; but the right is not absolute, and paragraph 2 of Article 10 permits restrictions on that right. It is not suggested, in the present case, that section 85 of the Postal Services Act 2000 is incompatible with the Convention. It follows that the restriction created by section 85 is accepted to be a restriction that is permitted by the Convention. That being so, the statute falls to be applied in the normal way: if a matter which is sent through the post is of an indecent or obscene character, there will be an offence under the Act.

See *Blackstone's Criminal Practice 2017* **B18.25**

C4.3 Indecent or offensive or threatening letters, etc

Malicious Communications Act 1988, s 1

1 Offence of sending letters etc with intent to cause distress or anxiety

(1) Any person who sends to another person—
   (a) a letter, electronic communication or article of any description which conveys—
      (i) a message which is indecent or grossly offensive;
      (ii) a threat; or
      (iii) information which is false and known or believed to be false by the sender; or
   (b) any article or electronic communication which is, in whole or part, of an indecent or grossly offensive nature,

is guilty of an offence if his purpose, or one of his purposes, in sending it is that it should, so far as falling within paragraph (a) or (b) above, cause distress or anxiety to the recipient or to any other person to whom he intends that it or its contents or nature should be communicated.

(2) A person is not guilty of an offence by virtue of subsection (1)(a)(ii) above if he shows—
   (a) that the threat was used to reinforce a demand made by him on reasonable grounds; and
   (b) that he believed, and had reasonable grounds for believing, that the use of the threat was a proper means of reinforcing the demand.

(2A) In this section 'electronic communication' includes—
   (a) any oral or other communication by means of an electronic communications network; and
   (b) any communication (however sent) that is in electronic form.

(3) In this section references to sending include references to delivering or transmitting and to causing to be sent, delivered or transmitted and 'sender' shall be construed accordingly.

 EW

 6 months' and/or fine/2 years' imprisonment

C4.3.1 Key points

See *Connolly v Director of Public Prosecutions* [2008] 1 WLR 276 for Articles 9 (religion) and 10 (free speech) considerations. Articles 9(2) and 10(2) allow for restrictions on the relevant rights.

 See *Blackstone's Criminal Practice 2017* **B18.30**

C4.4 Offences involving intent to cause distress, etc

Criminal Justice and Courts Act 2015, s 33

33 Disclosing private sexual photographs and films with intent to cause distress

(1) It is an offence for a person to disclose a private sexual photograph or film if the disclosure is made—
  (a) without the consent of an individual who appears in the photograph or film, and
  (b) with the intention of causing that individual distress.
(2) But it is not an offence under this section for the person to disclose the photograph or film to the individual mentioned in subsection (1)(a) and (b).
(3) It is a defence for a person charged with an offence under this section to prove that he or she reasonably believed that the disclosure was necessary for the purposes of preventing, detecting or investigating crime.
(4) It is a defence for a person charged with an offence under this section to show that—
  (a) the disclosure was made in the course of, or with a view to, the publication of journalistic material, and
  (b) he or she reasonably believed that, in the particular circumstances, the publication of the journalistic material was, or would be, in the public interest.
(5) It is a defence for a person charged with an offence under this section to show that—
  (a) he or she reasonably believed that the photograph or film had previously been disclosed for reward, whether by the individual mentioned in subsection (1)(a) and (b) or another person, and
  (b) he or she had no reason to believe that the previous disclosure for reward was made without the consent of the individual mentioned in subsection (1)(a) and (b).
(6) A person is taken to have shown the matters mentioned in subsection (4) or (5) if—
  (a) sufficient evidence of the matters is adduced to raise an issue with respect to it, and
  (b) the contrary is not proved beyond reasonable doubt.
(7) For the purposes of subsections (1) to (5)—
  (a) 'consent' to a disclosure includes general consent covering the disclosure, as well as consent to the particular disclosure, and
  (b) 'publication' of journalistic material means disclosure to the public at large or to a section of the public.
(8) A person charged with an offence under this section is not to be taken to have disclosed a photograph or film with the intention of causing distress merely because that was a natural and probable consequence of the disclosure.

EW

 6 months' imprisonment and/or fine/2 years' imprisonment

C4.4.1 *Interpretation*

Criminal Justice and Courts Act 2015, ss 34–35

34 Meaning of 'disclose' and 'photograph or film'

(1) The following apply for the purposes of section 33, this section and section 35.

(2) A person 'discloses' something to a person if, by any means, he or she gives or shows it to the person or makes it available to the person.

(3) Something that is given, shown or made available to a person is disclosed—
   (a) whether or not it is given, shown or made available for reward, and
   (b) whether or not it has previously been given, shown or made available to the person.

(4) 'Photograph or film' means a still or moving image in any form that—
   (a) appears to consist of or include one or more photographed or filmed images, and
   (b) in fact consists of or includes one or more photographed or filmed images.

(5) The reference in subsection (4)(b) to photographed or filmed images includes photographed or filmed images that have been altered in any way.

(6) 'Photographed or filmed image' means a still or moving image that—
   (a) was originally captured by photography or filming, or
   (b) is part of an image originally captured by photography or filming.

(7) 'Filming' means making a recording, on any medium, from which a moving image may be produced by any means.

(8) References to a photograph or film include—
   (a) a negative version of an image described in subsection (4), and
   (b) data stored by any means which is capable of conversion into an image described in subsection (4).

35 Meaning of 'private' and 'sexual'

(1) The following apply for the purposes of section 33.

(2) A photograph or film is 'private' if it shows something that is not of a kind ordinarily seen in public.

(3) A photograph or film is 'sexual' if—
   (a) it shows all or part of an individual's exposed genitals or pubic area,
   (b) it shows something that a reasonable person would consider to be sexual because of its nature, or
   (c) its content, taken as a whole, is such that a reasonable person would consider it to be sexual.

(4) Subsection (5) applies in the case of—
   (a) a photograph or film that consists of or includes a photographed or filmed image that has been altered in any way,
   (b) a photograph or film that combines two or more photographed or filmed images, and
   (c) a photograph or film that combines a photographed or filmed image with something else.

(5) The photograph or film is not private and sexual if—
    (a) it does not consist of or include a photographed or filmed image that is itself private and sexual,
    (b) it is only private or sexual by virtue of the alteration or combination mentioned in subsection (4), or
    (c) it is only by virtue of the alteration or combination mentioned in subsection (4) that the person mentioned in section 33(1)(a) and (b) is shown as part of, or with, whatever makes the photograph or film private and sexual.

C5 **Computer Misuse**

C5.1 **Unauthorised access to computer material**

Computer Misuse Act 1990, s 1

(1) A person is guilty of an offence if—
   (a) he causes a computer to perform any function with intent to secure access to any program or data held in any computer;
   (b) the access he intends to secure is unauthorised; and
   (c) he knows at the time when he causes the computer to perform the function that that is the case.
(2) The intent a person has to have to commit an offence under this section need not be directed at—
   (a) any particular program or data;
   (b) a program or data of any particular kind; or
   (c) a program or data held in any particular computer.

 6 months/2 years and/or a fine

C5.1.1 Key points

- For the offence to be made out there must be an interaction with the computer's programs but the interaction need not be sucesssful.
- In *DPP v Bignell* 1998 Crim LR 53 the court held that section 1 did not apply to the product of access by police officers who were authorised but acting outside their duties; however, the decision is limited by *Bow Street Stipendiary Magistrate ex p United States* 2000 1 Cr App R 61.
- Definitions are provided in section 17 Computer Misuse Act 1990.

C5.2 **Unauthorised access with intent to commit or facilitate commission of further offences**

Computer Misuse Act 1990, s 2

(1) A person is guilty of an offence under this section if he commits an offence under section 1 above ('the unauthorised access offence') with intent—
   (a) to commit an offence to which this section applies; or

(b) to facilitate the commission of such an offence (whether by himself or by any other person);

and the offence he intends to commit or facilitate is referred to below in this section as the further offence.

(2) This section applies to offences—

    (a) for which the sentence is fixed by law; or

    (b) for which a person who has attained the age of twenty-one years and has no previous convictions may be sentenced to imprisonment for a term of five years but for the restrictions imposed by section 33 of the Magistrates' Courts Act 1980).

(3) It is immaterial for the purposes of this section whether the further offence is to be committed on the same occasion as the unauthorised access offence or on any future occasion.

(4) A person may be guilty of an offence under this section even though the facts are such that the commission of the further offence is impossible.

EW

 6 months/5 years and/or a fine

C5.3 Unauthorised acts with intent to impair, or with recklessness as to impairing, operation of computer, etc

Computer Misuse Act 1990, s 3

3 (1) A person is guilty of an offence if—

    (a) he does any unauthorised act in relation to a computer;

    (b) at the time when he does the act he knows that it is unauthorised; and

    (c) either subsection (2) or subsection (3) below applies.

(2) This subsection applies if the person intends by doing the act—

    (a) to impair the operation of any computer;

    (b) to prevent or hinder access to any program or data held in any computer;

    (c) to impair the operation of any such program or the reliability of any such data.

(3) This subsection applies if the person is reckless as to whether the act will do any of the things mentioned in paragraphs (a) to (c) of subsection (2) above.

(4) The intention referred to in subsection (2) above, or the recklessness referred to in subsection (3) above, need not relate to—

    (a) any particular computer;

    (b) any particular program or data; or

    (c) a program or data of any particular kind.

> (5) In this section—
>   (a) a reference to doing an act includes a reference to causing an act to be done;
>   (b) 'act' includes a series of acts;
>   (c) a reference to impairing, preventing or hindering something includes a reference to doing so temporarily.

6 months/10 years and/or a fine

C5.3.1 Key point

The offence is made out if a bogus email is placed on another person's computer (*Zezev and Yarimaka v Governor of HMP Brixton* 202 EWHC 589(Admin)).

C5.4 Making, supplying, or obtaining articles for use in offence under section 1, 3, or 3ZA Computer Misuse Act 1990

Computer Misuse Act 1990, s 3A

(1) A person is guilty of an offence if he makes, adapts, supplies or offers to supply any article intending it to be used to commit, or to assist in the commission of, an offence under section 1, 3 or 3ZA.
(2) A person is guilty of an offence if he supplies or offers to supply any article believing that it is likely to be used to commit, or to assist in the commission of, an offence under section 1, 3 or 3ZA.
(3) A person is guilty of an offence if he obtains any article—
   (a) intending to use it to commit, or to assist in the commission of, an offence under section 1, 3 or 3ZA, or
   (b) with a view to its being supplied for use to commit, or to assist in the commission of, an offence under section 1, 3 or 3ZA.
(4) In this section 'article' includes any program or data held in electronic form.

6 months/2 years and/or a fine

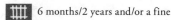

See *Blackstone's Criminal Practice 2017* **X.XX**

C6 **Criminal Damage**

C6.1 Destroying or damaging property

> ### Criminal Damage Act 1971, s 1
>
> **1 Destroying or damaging property**
>
> (1) A person who without lawful excuse destroys or damages any property belonging to another intending to destroy or damage any such property or being reckless as to whether any such property would be destroyed or damaged shall be guilty of an offence.
>
> (2) A person who without lawful excuse destroys or damages any property, whether belonging to himself or another—
>
> (a) intending to destroy or damage any property or being reckless as to whether any property would be destroyed or damaged; and
>
> (b) intending by the destruction or damage to endanger the life of another or being reckless as to whether the life of another would be thereby endangered;
>
> shall be guilty of an offence.
>
> (3) An offence committed under this section by destroying or damaging property by fire shall be charged as arson.

EW (If racially aggravated (see 6.1.6) but otherwise venue dictated by value and charge)

SO If value does not exceed £5,000 and offence is under section 1(1) and does not involve arson; the offence remains an indictable offence for all other purposes (*Fennell* [2000] EWCA Crim 3544) such as for time limits and costs. An offence under s1(2) is indictable only

IIII If SO: 3 months' imprisonment and/or fine level 4 (if value > £5,000, 6 months/10 years); but if on indictment section 1(2) or s1(3), Life

DO Section 1(2) offence

C6 Criminal Damage

C6.1.1 *Sentencing: criminal damage*

Offence seriousness (culpability and harm) A. Identify the appropriate starting point Starting points based on first-time offender pleading not guilty		
Examples of nature of activity	**Starting point**	**Range**
Minor damage, eg breaking small window; small amount of graffiti	Band B fine	Conditional discharge to Band C fine
Moderate damage, eg breaking large plate-glass or shop window; widespread graffiti	Low-level community order	Band C fine to medium-level community order
Significant damage up to £5,000, eg damage caused as part of a spree	High-level community order	Medium-level community order to 12 weeks' custody
Damage between £5,000 and £10,000	12 weeks' custody	6 to 26 weeks' custody
Damage over £10,000	Crown Court	Crown Court

Offence seriousness (culpability and harm) B. Consider the effect of aggravating and mitigating factors (other than those within examples above) The following may be particularly relevant but these lists are not exhaustive	
Factors indicating higher culpability	**Factors indicating lower culpability**
1. Revenge attack 2. Targeting vulnerable victim **Factors indicating greater degree of harm** 1. Damage to emergency equipment 2. Damage to public amenity 3. Significant public or private fear caused, eg in domestic context	1. Damage caused recklessly 2. Provocation

C6.1.2 *Sentencing: arson*

Offence seriousness (culpability and harm) A. Identify the appropriate starting point Starting points based on first-time offender pleading not guilty		
Examples of nature of activity	**Starting point**	**Range**
Minor damage by fire	High-level community order	Medium-level community order to 12 weeks' custody
Moderate damage by fire	12 weeks' custody	6 to 26 weeks' custody
Significant damage by fire	Crown Court	Crown Court

C6.1.3 *Criminal damage*

Offence seriousness (culpability and harm)	
B. Consider the effect of aggravating and mitigating factors	
(other than those within examples above)	
The following may be particularly relevant but these lists are not exhaustive	
Factors indicating higher culpability	**Factor indicating lower culpability**
1. Revenge attack	1. Damage caused recklessly
2. Targeting vulnerable victim	
Factors indicating greater degree of harm	
1. Damage to emergency equipment	
2. Damage to public amenity	
3. Significant public or private fear caused, eg in domestic context	

C6.1.4 Key points

- There is no bar on charging attempted criminal damage where, due to value, the matter can be tried summarily only (*R v Bristol Justices, ex p E* [1999] 1 WLR 390).
- Lawful excuse is defined in section 5:

Criminal Damage Act 1971, s 5(2)–(5)

5 'Without lawful excuse'

(2) A person charged with an offence to which this section applies, shall, whether or not he would be treated for the purposes of this Act as having a lawful excuse apart from this subsection, be treated for those purposes as having a lawful excuse—

    (a) if at the time of the act or acts alleged to constitute the offence he believed that the person or persons whom he believed to be entitled to consent to the destruction of or damage to the property in question had so consented, or would have so consented to it if he or they had known of the destruction or damage and its circumstances; or

    (b) if he destroyed or damaged or threatened to destroy or damage the property in question or, in the case of a charge of an offence under section 3 above, intended to use or cause or permit the use of something to destroy or damage it, in order to protect property belonging to himself or another or a right or interest in property which was or which he believed to be vested in himself or another, and at the time of the act or acts alleged to constitute the offence he believed—

        (i) that the property, right or interest was in immediate need of protection; and

        (ii) that the means of protection adopted or proposed to be adopted were or would be reasonable having regard to all the circumstances.

(3) For the purposes of this section it is immaterial whether a belief is justified or not if it is honestly held.

(4) For the purposes of subsection (2) above a right or interest in property includes any right or privilege in or over land, whether created by grant, licence or otherwise.

(5) This section shall not be construed as casting doubt on any defence recognised by law as a defence to criminal charges.

- A person can avail himself of the defence of lawful excuse, notwithstanding the fact that he was intoxicated (*Jaggard v Dickinson* (1981) 72 Cr App R 33). The test is subjective, that is, whether the belief is held honestly, not whether it is justified or reasonable. Conduct due to mental illness resulting from alcohol psychosis or hallucinosis may not be reckless if the defendant was thereby not aware of the risk (*R v Coley* [2013] EWCA Crim 223). However, whether a person is acting to protect property has an objective element (*R v Hunt* (1977) 66 Cr App R 105).

- It is clear that section 5(5) is intended to cover the situation whereby damage is caused to protect life or prevent injury (*R v Baker*, The Times, 26 November 1996).

- Damage does not need to be destruction and encompasses harm that is not permanent, such as graffiti. If expense or inconvenience is involved in putting right the matter then damage will have been caused (eg stamping on a policeman's helmet so that it had to be pushed back into shape). Damaging something that can be restored (eg deleting a computer program) constitutes damage (*Cox v Riley* (1986) 83 Cr App R 54). Spitting on a police officer's uniform is unlikely to cause damage (*A v R* [1978] Crim LR 689). The soaking of a blanket and the flooding of the floor of a police cell were held to amount to damage in *R v Fiak* [2005] EWCA Crim 2381, and the daubing of water-soluble paint on a pavement was equally found to amount to damage in *Hardman v Chief Constable of Avon and Somerset* [1986] Crim LR 330.

- Determining whether something has been damaged is a matter of fact and degree to be determined by the magistrates or the jury (*Roe v Kingerlee* [1986] Crim LR 735).

- It is an offence to damage jointly owned property. Section 10 provides:

Criminal Damage Act 1971, s 10

10 Interpretation

(1) In this Act 'property' means of a tangible nature, whether real or personal, including money and—

    (a) including wild creatures which have been tamed or are ordinarily kept in captivity, and any other wild creatures or their carcasses if, but only if, they have been reduced into possession which has not been lost or abandoned or are in the course of being reduced into possession; but

(b) not including mushrooms growing wild on any land or flowers, fruit or foliage of a plant growing wild on any land.

For the purposes of this subsection 'mushroom' includes any fungus and 'plant' includes any shrub or tree.

(2) Property shall be treated for the purposes of this Act as belonging to any person—

(a) having the custody or control of it;

(b) having in it any proprietary right or interest (not being an equitable interest arising only from an agreement to transfer or grant an interest); or

(c) having a charge on it.

(3) Where property is subject to a trust, the persons to whom it belongs shall be so treated as including any person having a right to enforce the trust.

(4) Property of a corporation sole shall be so treated as belonging to the corporation notwithstanding a vacancy in the corporation.

- The prosecution will have proved that the defendant was reckless if, having regard to all the available evidence, the court is sure:
  - that he was aware of a risk that property would be destroyed/damaged; and
  - that in the circumstances which were known to him it was unreasonable for him to take that risk.
- This test allows for some of the personal characteristics of a defendant to be taken into account (see *R v G* [2003] UKHL 50).

C6.1.5 *Criminal damage (by endangering life): Criminal Damage Act 1971, section 1(2)*

 An offence under section 1(2) is triable only on indictment: Life

See **C6.1**.

C6.1.6 *Racially or religiously aggravated criminal damage: Crime and Disorder Act 1998, section 30*

EW

 6 months' imprisonment and/or fine/14 years' imprisonment

C6.2 Threats to destroy or damage property

Criminal Damage Act 1971, s 2

2 Threats to destroy or damage property

A person who without lawful excuse makes to another a threat, intending that that other would fear it would be carried out—

(a) to destroy or damage any property belonging to that other or a third person; or

(b) to destroy or damage his own property in a way which he knows is likely to endanger the life of that other or third person;

shall be guilty of an offence.

 Fine and/or 6 months'/10 years' imprisonment

C6.2.1 *Sentencing*

There are no sentencing guidelines for this offence.

C6.2.2 Key points

- Whether a threat has been made under section 2(a) is to be assessed objectively with reference to the words and actions of the defendant (*R v Cakmak* [2002] EWCA Crim 500).
- The term 'without lawful excuse' is defined in section 5 of the Act:

Criminal Damage Act 1971, s 5

5 'Without lawful excuse'

(1) This section applies to any offence under section 1(1) above and any offence under section 2 or 3 above other than one involving a threat by the person charged to destroy or damage property in a way which he knows is likely to endanger the life of another or involving an intent by the person charged to use or cause or permit the use of something in his custody or under his control so to destroy or damage property.

C6.3 Possessing anything with intent to destroy or damage property

Criminal Damage Act 1971, s 3

3 Possessing anything with intent to destroy or damage property

A person who has anything in his custody or under his control intending without lawful excuse to use it or cause or permit another to use it—

(a) to destroy or damage any property belonging to some other person; or

(b) to destroy or damage his own or the user's property in a way which he knows is likely to endanger the life of some other person;

shall be guilty of an offence.

 Fine and/or 6 months'/10 years' imprisonment

C6.3.1 Key points

A conditional intent will suffice (*R v Buckingham* (1976) 63 Cr App R 159).

 See *Blackstone's Criminal Practice 2017* **B8**

C7 **Drugs**

C7.1 **Key points**

- A person must know that he is in possession of the drug; therefore a person holding drugs believing that they were something else would not be guilty (assuming the court believed the defendant). Note, however, that suspicion would be sufficient (see Misuse of Drugs Act 1971, s 28); and see later on containers.
- A person who 'forgot' that he had drugs would still be in possession of those drugs, but a person who had no knowledge at all would not (*R v Martindale* [1986] 3 All ER 25).
- A person need not be in physical possession of a drug, provided he is in control (sole or joint): see Misuse of Drugs Act 1971, section 37(3). It is not sufficient that the defendant might have knowledge of a confederate's possession of drugs; the test is whether the drugs were part of a common pool from which all could draw (*R v Searle* [1971] Crim LR 592).
- The fact that the quantity of drug was so miniscule as to be incapable of being used does not amount to a defence (*R v Boyesen* [1982] AC 768); it is merely an indication that the defendant may not have had knowledge of its presence.
- If a person is in possession of a container and he knows there is something inside, he will be in possession of the contents, even if he does not know their characteristics (*R v Lambert* [2002] 2 AC 545). If, however, the defendant had no right to open the container, he may not be in possession of its contents (*Warner v Metropolitan Police Commissioner* [1969] 2 AC 256), nor if he believed the contents to be different from what in fact they were (*R v McNamara* (1988) 87 Cr App R 246).
- Possession of drugs for religious purposes is not afforded any special protection under the European Convention (*R v Taylor* [2002] 1 Cr App R 519).
- Purchasing drugs on behalf of a third party, and passing those drugs to that party, even for no profit, amounts to supply.
- So-called social supply should be charged as simple possession. In *R v Denslow* [1998] Crim LR 566 the court observed:

> We wonder why it was thought necessary to charge supply in the circumstances of this case. How could it possibly serve the interests of the public that there should be either a trial or if not a trial as conventionally understood a hearing to determine this matter of law? It was inevitable that the appellant would be dealt with at worst as though he were in possession

of the drugs and, as turned out in this case, as though he were without any criminal responsibility for that particular part of the transaction. We are told that a plea had been offered to a charge of possession. It ought to have been accepted. We hope that those words will be borne in mind by prosecuting authorities in the future.

- A person who places drugs in the hands of a third party merely for safe keeping does not supply drugs (*R v Maginnis* [1987] AC 303).

- An offer to supply can be made by words or conduct, and once made cannot be withdrawn.

- It is the plant that must be cultivated, not the cannabis produced from the plant.

- The accused does not need to know that the plant was in fact cannabis (*R v Champ* (1981) 73 Cr App R 267).

- The defence of necessity (commonly pleaded by sufferers of certain illnesses) is not a defence available in law for this charge (*R v Quayle and others* [2006] 1 All ER 988).

- A statutory defence is provided by section 28 of the Misuse of Drugs Act 1971:

Misuse of Drugs Act 1971, s 28

28 Proof of lack of knowledge etc to be a defence in proceedings for certain offences

(1) This section applies to offences under any of the following provisions of this Act, that is to say section 4(2) and (3), section 5(2) and (3), section 6(2) and section 9.

(2) Subject to subsection (3) below, in any proceedings for an offence to which this section applies it shall be a defence for the accused to prove that he neither knew of nor suspected nor had reason to suspect the existence of some fact alleged by the prosecution which it is necessary for the prosecution to prove if he is to be convicted of the offence charged.

(3) Where in any proceedings for an offence to which this section applies it is necessary, if the accused is to be convicted of the offence charged, for the prosecution to prove that some substance or product involved in the alleged offence was the controlled drug which the prosecution alleges it to have been, and it is proved that the substance or product in question was that controlled drug, the accused—

    (a) shall not be acquitted of the offence charged by reason only of proving that he neither knew nor suspected nor had reason to suspect that the substance or product in question was the particular controlled drug alleged; but

    (b) shall be acquitted thereof—

        (i) if he proves that he neither believed nor suspected nor had reason to suspect that the substance or product in question was a controlled drug; or

---

> (ii) if he proves that he believed the substance or product in question
>   to be a controlled drug, or a controlled drug of a description, such
>   that, if it had in fact been that controlled drug or a controlled
>   drug of that description, he would not at the material time have
>   been committing any offence to which this section applies.
> (4) Nothing in this section shall prejudice any defence which it is open to
>   a person charged with an offence to which this section applies to raise
>   apart from this section.

- In considering a defence under section 28(3)(b), self-induced intoxication should not be considered (*R v Young* [1984] 2 All ER 164).

C7.2 Key points: Sentencing

- A minimum sentence of seven years must, unless not justified in all the circumstances, be imposed where an adult is convicted of a Class A drug trafficking offence (which excludes possession alone) if the offender has been convicted of two other drug trafficking offences in the circumstances set out in **D27**. Such offences may be tried on indictment only (Powers of Criminal Courts (Sentencing) Act 2000, s 110).
- Sentences are prescribed by Schedule 4 to the Misuse of Drugs Act 1971 in the table in the next section.

C7.3 Drugs—Class A: fail to attend/remain for initial or follow-up assessment (Sentencing Guideline at p 307)

Drugs Act 2005, s 12(1)–(3)

12 Attendance at initial assessment

(1) This section applies if a person is required to attend an initial assessment and remain for its duration by virtue of section 9(2).
(3) A person is guilty of an offence if without good cause—
    (a) he fails to attend an initial assessment at the specified time and place, or
    (b) he attends the assessment at the specified time and place but fails to remain for its duration.

...

SO

 6 months' imprisonment and/or level 4 fine

Misuse of Drugs Act 1971, Sch 4

Schedule 4

Prosecution and Punishment of Offences

Section Creation offence	General Nature of Offence	Mode of Prosecution	Punishment			
			Class A drug involved	Class B drug involved	Class C drug involved	General
Section 4(2)	Production, or being concerned in the production, of a controlled drug.	(a) Summary	6 months or fine, or both	6 months or fine, or both	3 months or £2,500 or both	
		(b) On indictment	Life	14 years	14 years	
Section 4(3)	Supplying or offering to supply a controlled drug or being concerned in the doing of either activity by another.		6 months or fine, or both	6 months or fine, or both	3 months or £2,500, or both	
		(b) On indictment	Life	14 years	14 years	
Section 5(2)	Having possession of a controlled drug.	(a) Summary	6 months or fine, or both	3 months or £2,500, or both	3 months or £1,000, or both	
		(b) On indictment	7 years	5 years	2 years	

(Continued)

C7 Drugs

Section Creation offence	General Nature of Offence	Mode of Prosecution	Punishment		
Section 5(3)	Having possession of a controlled drug with intent to supply it to another.	(a) Summary	6 months or fine, or both	6 months or fine, or both	3 months or £2,500, or both
		(b) On indictment	Life	14 years	14 years
Section 6(2)	Cultivation of cannabis plant.	(a) Summary			6 months or fine, or both
		(b) On indictment			14 years
Section 8	Being the occupier, or concerned in the management, of premises and permitting or suffering certain activities to take place there.	(a) Summary	6 months or fine, or both	6 months or fine, or both	3 months or £2,500, or both
		(b) On indictment	14 years	14 years	14 years
...					

> **Drugs Act 2005, s 14(1) and (3)**
>
> **14 Attendance at follow-up assessment**
> (1) This section applies if a person is required to attend a follow-up assessment and remain for its duration by virtue of section 10(2).
> …
> (3) A person is guilty of an offence if without good cause—
>   (a) he fails to attend a follow-up assessment at the specified time and place, or
>   (b) he attends the assessment at the specified time and place but fails to remain for its duration.
> …

 6 months and/or level 4 fine

C7.3.1 *Sentencing*

Note that this guideline refers to section 12 offences only *and that it is under review by the Sentencing Council* (see **Appendix 7**).

Offence seriousness (culpability and harm) A. Identify the appropriate starting point Starting points based on first-time offender pleading not guilty		
Examples of nature of activity	**Starting point**	**Range**
Failure to attend at the appointed place and time	Medium-level community order	Band C fine to high-level community order

Offence seriousness (culpability and harm) B. Consider the effect of aggravating and mitigating factors (other than those within examples above) The following may be particularly relevant but these lists are not exhaustive	
Factor indicating greater degree of harm	**Factors indicating lower culpability**
1. Threats or abuse to assessor or other staff	1. Offender turns up but at wrong place or time, or fails to remain for duration of appointment 2. Subsequent voluntary contact to rearrange appointment

C7.4 Drugs—Class A: fail/refuse to provide a sample

There are a considerable number of condition precedents that need to be satisfied before a lawful request for a sample can be made.

Police and Criminal Evidence Act 1984, s 63B

63B Testing for presence of Class A drugs

(1) A sample of urine or a non-intimate sample may be taken from a person in police detention for the purpose of ascertaining whether he has any specified Class A drug in his body if—
  (a) either the arrest condition or the charge condition is met;
  (b) both the age condition and the request condition are met; and
  (c) the notification condition is met in relation to the arrest condition, the charge condition or the age condition (as the case may be).

(1A) The arrest condition is that the person concerned has been arrested for an offence but has not been charged with that offence and either—
  (a) the offence is a trigger offence; or
  (b) a police officer of at least the rank of inspector has reasonable grounds for suspecting that the misuse by that person of a specified Class A drug caused or contributed to the offence and has authorised the sample to be taken.

(2) The charge condition is either—
  (a) that the person concerned has been charged with a trigger offence; or
  (b) that the person concerned has been charged with an offence and a police officer of at least the rank of inspector, who has reasonable grounds for suspecting that the misuse by that person of any specified Class A drug caused or contributed to the offence and has authorised the sample to be taken.

(3) The age condition is—
  (a) if the arrest condition is met, that the person concerned has attained the age of 18;
  (b) if the charge condition is met, that he has attained the age of 14.

(4) The request condition is that a police officer has requested the person concerned to give the sample.

(4A) ...

(4B) ...

(5) Before requesting the person concerned to give a sample, an officer must—
  (a) warn him that if, when so requested, he fails without good cause to do so he may be liable to prosecution, and
  (b) in a case within subsection (1A)(b) or (2)(b) above, inform him of the giving of the authorisation and of the grounds in question.

(5A) ...

(5B) ...

(5C) Despite subsection (1)(a) above, a sample may be taken from a person under this section if—
  (a) he was arrested for an offence (the first offence),
  (b) the arrest condition is met but the charge condition is not met,
  (c) before a sample is taken by virtue of subsection (1) above he would (but for his arrest as mentioned in paragraph (d) below) be required to be released from police detention,

> (d) he continues to be in police detention by virtue of his having
> been arrested for an offence not falling within subsection (1A)
> above, and
> (e) the sample is taken before the end of the period of 24 hours start-
> ing with the time when his detention by virtue of his arrest for the
> first offence began.
>
> (5D) A sample must not be taken from a person under this section if he
> is detained in a police station unless he has been brought before the
> custody officer.
> (6) A sample may be taken under this section only by a person prescribed
> by regulations made by the Secretary of State by statutory instrument.
> (6A) …
> (6B) …
> (7) …
> (8) A person who fails without good cause to give any sample which may
> be taken from him under this section shall be guilty of an offence.

 3 months and/or level 4 fine

Note that this guideline is under review by the Sentencing Council (see **Appendix 7**).

C7.4.1 *Sentencing*

Offence seriousness (culpability and harm) A. Identify the appropriate starting point Starting points based on first-time offender pleading not guilty		
Examples of nature of activity	**Starting point**	**Range**
Refusal to provide sample without good cause when required by police officer	Medium-level community order	Band C fine to high-level community order

Offence seriousness (culpability and harm) B. Consider the effect of aggravating and mitigating factors (other than those within examples above) The following may be particularly relevant but these lists are not exhaustive	
Factor indicating greater degree of harm	**Factors indicating lower culpability**
1. Threats or abuse to staff	1. Subsequent voluntary contact with drug workers 2. Subsequent compliance with testing on arrest/charge

C7.5 Drugs: fraudulent evasion of a prohibition by bringing into or taking out of the United Kingdom a controlled drug

Misuse of Drugs Act 1971, s 3

3 Restriction of importation and exportation of controlled drugs

(1) Subject to subsection (2) below—
   (a) the importation of a controlled drug; and
   (b) the exportation of a controlled drug, are hereby prohibited.
(2) Subsection (1) above does not apply—
   (a) to the importation or exportation of a controlled drug which is for the time being excepted from paragraph (a) or, as the case may be, paragraph (b) of subsection (1) above by regulations under section 7 of this Act or by provision made in a temporary class drug order by virtue of section 7A; or
   (b) to the importation or exportation of a controlled drug under and in accordance with the terms of a licence issued by the Secretary of State and in compliance with any conditions attached thereto.

Customs and Excise Management Act 1979, s 170(2)

170 Penalty for fraudulent evasion of duty, etc

(2) Without prejudice to any other provision of the Customs and Excise Acts 1979, if any person is, in relation to any goods, in any way knowingly concerned in any fraudulent evasion or attempt at evasion—
   (a) of any duty chargeable on the goods;
   (b) of any prohibition or restriction for the time being in force with respect to the goods under or by virtue of any enactment; or
   (c) of any provision of the Customs and Excise Acts 1979 applicable to the goods,
he shall be guilty of an offence under this section and may be detained.

6 months' imprisonment and/or £20,000/life (class A); 14 years' imprisonment (Classes B and C)

C7.5.1 *Sentencing*

STEP ONE: determining the offence category

Culpability demonstrated by offender's role. One or more of these characteristics may demonstrate the offender's role. The list is not exhaustive.	Category of harm. Indicative output or potential output (upon which the starting point is based):
LEADING role: • directing or organizing production on a commercial scale; • substantial links to, and influence on, others in a chain; • expectation of substantial financial gain; • uses business as cover; • abuses a position of trust or responsibility.	**Category 1** • heroin, cocaine—5kg; • ecstasy—10,000 tablets; • LSD—250,000 tablets; • amphetamine—20kg; • cannabis—200kg; • ketamine—5kg.
SIGNIFICANT role: • operational or management function within a chain; • involves others in the operation whether by pressure, influence, intimidation, or reward; • motivated by financial or other advantage, whether or not operating alone; • some awareness and understanding of scale of operation.	**Category 2** • heroin, cocaine—1kg; • ecstasy—2,000 tablets; • LSD—25,000 squares; • amphetamine—4kg; • cannabis—40kg; • ketamine—1kg. **Category 3** • heroin, cocaine—150g; • ecstasy—300 tablets; • LSD—2,500 squares; • amphetamine—750g; • cannabis—6kg; • ketamine—150g.
LESSER role: • performs a limited function under direction; • engaged by pressure, coercion, intimidation; • involvement through naivety/exploitation; • no influence on those above in a chain; • very little, if any, awareness or understanding of the scale of operation; • if own operation, solely for own use (considering reasonableness of account in all the circumstances).	**Category 4** • heroin, cocaine—5g; • ecstasy—20 tablets; • LSD—170 squares; • amphetamine—20g; • cannabis—100g; • ketamine—5g.

STEP TWO: Starting point and category range

CLASS A	Leading role	Significant role	Lesser role
Category 1	Crown Court	Crown Court	Crown Court
Category 2	Crown Court	Crown Court	Crown Court
Category 3	Crown Court	Crown Court	Crown Court
Category 4	Crown Court	Crown Court	Crown Court

C7 Drugs

CLASS B	Leading role	Significant role	Lesser role
Category 1	Crown Court	Crown Court	Crown Court
Category 2	Crown Court	Crown Court	1 year's custody Range: 26 weeks' to 3 years' custody
Category 3	Crown Court	Crown Court	Crown Court
Category 4	Crown Court	Crown Court	1 year's custody Range: 12 weeks' custody to 18 months' custody

CLASS C	Leading role	Significant role	Lesser role
Category 1	Crown Court	Crown Court	Crown Court
Category 2	Crown Court	Crown Court	26 weeks' custody Range: 12 weeks' to 18 months' custody
Category 3	Crown Court	26 weeks' custody Range: 12 weeks' to 18 months' custody	High level community order Range: low level community order to 26 weeks
Category 4	*	*	*

* Where the quantity falls below the indicative amount set out in the guideline for category 4, first identify the role for the importation offence, then refer to the starting point and ranges for possession or supply offences, depending on intent. Where the quantity is significantly larger than the indicative amounts for category 4 but below category 3 amounts, refer to the category 3 ranges.

Factors increasing seriousness	Factors reducing seriousness or reflecting personal mitigation
Statutory aggravating factors: Previous convictions, having regard to (a) nature of the offence to which conviction relates and relevance to current offence; and (b) time elapsed since offender used or permitted a person under 18 to deliver a controlled drug to a third person Offence committed on bail	Lack of sophistication as to nature of concealment. Involvement due to pressure, intimidation, or coercion falling short of duress, except where already taken into account at step 1 Mistaken belief of the offender regarding the type of drug, taking into account the reasonableness of such belief in all the circumstances

Other aggravating factors include:	Isolated incident
Sophisticated nature of concealment and/or attempts to avoid detection	Low purity
	No previous convictions or no relevant or recent convictions
Attempts to conceal or dispose of evidence, where not charged separately	Offender's vulnerability was exploited.
Exposure of others to more than usual danger, for example drugs cut with harmful substances	Remorse
	Good character and/or exemplary conduct
Presence of weapon, where not charged separately	Determination and/or demonstration of steps having been taken to address addiction or offending behaviour
High purity	Serious medical conditions requiring urgent, intensive, or long-term treatment
Failure to comply with current court orders.	Age and/or lack of maturity where it affects the responsibility of the offender
Offence committed on licence	Mental disorder or learning disability.
	Sole or primary carer for dependent relatives.

C7.5.1.1 *Additional steps*

Consider any factors which indicate a reduction, such as assistance to the prosecution; reduction for guilty plea; dangerousness; totality principle; compensation and ancillary orders; reasons; consideration for remand time.

C7.6 Drugs: supplying or offering to supply a controlled drug; possession of a controlled drug with intent to supply it to another

Misuse of Drugs Act 1971, ss 4(3) and 5(3)

4 Restriction of production and supply of controlled drugs

(3) Subject to section 28 of this Act, it is an offence for a person—
  (a) to supply or offer to supply a controlled drug to another in contravention of subsection (1) above; or
  (b) to be concerned in the supplying of such a drug to another in contravention of that subsection; or
  (c) to be concerned in the making to another in contravention of that subsection of an offer to supply such a drug.

  ...

5 Restriction of possession of controlled drugs

(3) Subject to section 28 of this Act, it is an offence for a person to have a controlled drug in his possession, whether lawfully or not, with intent to supply it to another in contravention of section 4(1) of this Act.

C7.6.1 *Sentencing*

STEP ONE: Determining the offence category

Culpability demonstrated by offender's role. One or more of these characteristics may demonstrate the offender's role. The list is not exhaustive.	Category of harm. Indicative output or potential output (upon which the starting point is based)
LEADING role: • directing or organizing production on a commercial scale; • substantial links to, and influence on, others in a chain; • expectation of substantial financial gain; • uses business as cover; • abuses a position of trust or responsibility. **SIGNIFICANT role:** • operational or management function within a chain; • involves others in the operation whether by pressure, influence, intimidation, or reward; • motivated by financial or other advantage, whether or not operating alone; • some awareness and understanding of scale of operation. **LESSER role:** • performs a limited function under direction; • engaged by pressure, coercion, intimidation; • involvement through naivety/exploitation; • no influence on those above in a chain; • very little, if any, awareness or understanding of the scale of operation; • if own operation, solely for own use (considering reasonableness of account in all the circumstances).	**Category 1** • heroin, cocaine—5kg; • ecstasy—10,000 tablets; • LSD—250,000 tablets; • amphetamine—20kg; • cannabis—200kg; • ketamine—5kg. **Category 2** • heroin, cocaine—1kg; • ecstasy—2,000 tablets; • LSD—25,000 squares; • amphetamine—4kg; • cannabis—40kg; • ketamine—1kg. **Category 3** Where the offence is selling directly to users* ('street dealing'), the starting point is not based on quantity, OR Where the offence is suppy of drugs in prison by a prison employee, the starting point is not based on quantity. • heroin, cocaine—150g; • ecstasy—300 tablets; • LSD—2,500 squares; • amphetamine—750g; • cannabis—6kg; • ketamine—150g. **Category 4** • heroin, cocaine—5g; • ecstasy—20 tablets; • LSD—170 squares; • amphetamine—20g; • cannabis—100g; • ketamine—5g. OR Where the offence is selling directly to users* ('street dealing') the starting point is not based on quantity—go to category 3.

* Including test purchase officers.

STEP TWO: Starting point and category range

CLASS A	Leading role	Significant role	Lesser role
Category 1	Crown Court	Crown Court	Crown Court
Category 2	Crown Court	Crown Court	Crown Court
Category 3	Crown Court	Crown Court	Crown Court
Category 4	Crown Court	Crown Court	18 months' custody Range: High-level community order to 3 years' custody

CLASS B	Leading role	Significant role	Lesser role
Category 1	Crown Court	Crown Court	Crown Court
Category 2	Crown Court	Crown Court	1 year's custody Range: 26 weeks' to 3 years' custody
Category 3	Crown Court	1 year's custody Range: 26 weeks' to 3 years' custody	High-level community order Range: Low-level community order to 26 weeks
Category 4	18 months' custody Range: 16 weeks' to 3 years custody	High-level community order Range: Medium-level community order to 26 weeks' custody	Low-level community order Range: Band B fine to medium-level community order

CLASS C	Leading role	Significant role	Lesser role
Category 1	Crown Court	Crown Court	Crown Court
Category 2	Crown Court	Crown Court	26 weeks' custody Range: 12 weeks' to 18 months' custody
Category 3	Crown Court	26 weeks' custody Range: 12 weeks' to 18 months' custody	High-level community order Range: Low-level community order to 12 weeks' custody
Category 4	26 weeks' custody Range: High-level community order to 18 months' custody	High-level community order Range: Low-level community order to 12 weeks' custody	Low-level community order Range: Band A fine to medium-level community order

Factors increasing seriousness	Factors reducing seriousness or reflecting personal mitigation
Statutory aggravating factors: Previous convictions, having regard to (a) nature of the offence to which conviction relates and relevance to current offence; and (b) time elapsed since conviction Offender used or permitted a person under 18 to deliver a controlled drug to a third person Offender 18 or over supplies or offers to supply a drug on, or in the vicinity of, school premises either when school in use as such or at a time between one hour before and one hour after they are to be used Offence committed on bail **Other aggravating factors include:** Targeting of any premises intended to locate vulnerable individuals or supply to such individuals and/or supply to those under 18 Exposure of others to more than usual danger, for example drugs cut with harmful substances Attempts to conceal or dispose of evidence, where not charged separately Presence of others, especially children and/or non-users Presence of weapon, where not charged separately Charged as importation of a very small amount. High purity Failure to comply with current court orders Offence committed on licence Established evidence of community impact	Involvement due to pressure, intimidation, or coercion falling short of duress, except where already taken into account at step 1 Supply only of drug to which offender addicted Mistaken belief of the offender regarding the type of drug, taking into account the reasonableness of such belief in all the circumstances Isolated incident Low purity No previous convictions or no relevant or recent convictions Offender's vulnerability was exploited Remorse Good character and/or exemplary conduct Determination and/or demonstration of steps having been taken to address addiction or offending behaviour Serious medical conditions requiring urgent, intensive, or long-term treatment Age and/or lack of maturity where it affects the responsibility of the offender Mental disorder or learning disability Sole or primary carer for dependent relatives

C7.6.1.1 *Additional steps*

Consider any factors which indicate a reduction, such as assistance to the prosecution; reduction for guilty plea; dangerousness; totality principle; compensation and ancillary orders; reasons; consideration for remand time.

C7.6.2 Key points

To be concerned in the supply of drugs under section 4(3)(b) Misuse of Drugs Act 1971 does not require proof of an actual supply but rather involvement in the process of supply. It is not limited to actual or past supply (*R v Martin (Dwain Ashley)* [2014] EWCA Crim 1940).

C7.7 Drugs: production of a controlled drug and cultivation of cannabis

C7.7.1 *Sentencing*

Misuse of Drugs Act 1971, ss 4(2)(a), (b) and 6

4 Restriction of production and supply of controlled drugs

(2) Subject to section 28 of this Act, it is an offence for a person—
   (a) to produce a controlled drug in contravention of subsection (1) above; or
   (b) to be concerned in the production of such a drug in contravention of that subsection by another.

6 Restriction of cultivation of cannabis plant

(1) Subject to any regulations under section 7 of this Act for the time being in force, it shall not be lawful for a person to cultivate any plant of the genus Cannabis.

(2) Subject to section 28 of this Act, it is an offence to cultivate any such plant in contravention of subsection (1) above.

STEP ONE: Determining the offence category

Culpability demonstrated by offender's role. One or more of these characteristics may demonstrate the offender's role. The list is not exhaustive.	Category of harm. Indicative output or potential output (upon which the starting point is based):
LEADING role: • directing or organizing production on a commercial scale; • substantial links to, and influence on, others in a chain; • expectation of substantial financial gain; • uses business as cover; • abuses a position of trust or responsibility.	**Category 1** • heroin, cocaine—5kg; • ecstasy—10,000 tablets; • LSD—250,000 tablets; • amphetamine—20kg; • cannabis—operation capable of producing industrial quantities for commercial use; • ketamine—5kg.

C7 Drugs

SIGNIFICANT role:
- operational or management function within a chain;
- involves others in the operation whether by pressure, influence, intimidation, or reward;
- motivated by financial or other advantage, whether or not operating alone;
- some awareness and understanding of scale of operation.

LESSER role:
- performs a limited function under direction;
- engaged by pressure, coercion, intimidation;
- involvement through naivety/exploitation;
- no influence on those above in a chain;
- very little, if any, awareness or understanding of the scale of operation;
- if own operation, solely for own use (considering reasonableness of account in all the circumstances).

Category 2
- heroin, cocaine—1kg;
- ecstasy—2,000 tablets;
- LSD—25,000 squares;
- amphetamine—4kg;
- cannabis—operation capable of producing significant quantities for commercial use;
- ketamine—1kg.

Category 3
- heroin, cocaine—150g;
- ecstasy—300 tablets;
- LSD—2,500 squares;
- amphetamine—750g;
- cannabis—28 plants;*
- ketamine—150g.

Category 4
- heroin, cocaine—5g;
- ecstasy—20 tablets;
- LSD—170 squares;
- amphetamine—20g;
- cannabis—9 plants (domestic operation);*
- ketamine—5g

*with an assumed yield of 40g per plant.

STEP TWO: Starting point and category range

CLASS A	Leading role	Significant role	Lesser role
Category 1	Crown Court	Crown Court	Crown Court
Category 2	Crown Court	Crown Court	Crown Court
Category 3	Crown Court	Crown Court	Crown Court
Category 4	Crown Court	Crown Court	Starting point 18 months' custody Range: High-level community order to 3 years' custody

CLASS B	Leading role	Significant role	Lesser role
Category 1	Crown Court	Crown Court	Crown Court
Category 2	Crown Court	Crown Court	1 year's custody Range: 26 weeks' to 3 years' custody
Category 3	Crown Court	1 year's custody Range: 26 weeks' to 3 years' custody	High-level community order Range: Low-level community order to 26 weeks' custody

CLASS B	Leading role	Significant role	Lesser role
Category 4	1 year's custody Range: High-level community order to 3 years' custody	High-level community order Range: Medium-level community order to 26 weeks' custody	Band C fine Range: Discharge to medium-level community penalty

CLASS C	Leading role	Significant role	Lesser role
Category 1	Crown Court	Crown Court	Crown Court
Category 2	Crown Court	Crown Court	26 weeks' custody Range: High-level community order to 18 months' custody
Category 3	Crown Court	26 weeks' custody Range: High-level community order to 18 months' custody	High-level community order Range: Low-level community order to 12 weeks' custody
Category 4	26 weeks' custody Range: High-level community order to 18 months' custody	High-level community order Range: Low-level community order to 12 weeks' custody	Band C fine Range: Discharge to medium-level community penalty

Factors increasing seriousness	Factors reducing seriousness or reflecting personal mitigation
Statutory aggravating factors: Previous convictions, having regard to (a) nature of the offence to which conviction relates and relevance to current offence; and (b) time elapsed since conviction Offence committed on bail **Other aggravating factors include:** Nature of any likely supply Level of any profit element Use of premises accompanied by unlawful access to electricity/other utility supply of others Ongoing/large-scale operation as evidenced by presence and nature of specialist equipment Exposure of others to more than usual danger, for example drugs cut with harmful substances	Involvement due to pressure, intimidation, or coercion falling short of duress, except where already taken into account at step 1 Isolated incident Low purity No previous convictions or no relevant or recent convictions Offender's vulnerability was exploited Remorse Good character and/or exemplary conduct Determination and/or demonstration of steps having been taken to address addiction or offending behaviour

Attempts to conceal or dispose of evidence, where not charged separately	Serious medical conditions requiring urgent, intensive, or long-term treatment
Presence of others, especially children and/ or non-users	Age and/or lack of maturity where it affects the responsibility of the offender
Presence of weapon, where not charged separately	Mental disorder or learning disability
High purity or high potential yield	Sole or primary carer for dependent relatives
Failure to comply with current court orders	
Offence committed on licence	
Established evidence of community impact	

C7.7.1.1 *Additional steps*

Consider any factors which indicate a reduction, such as assistance to the prosecution; reduction for guilty plea; dangerousness; totality principle; compensation and ancillary orders; reasons; consideration for remand time.

C7.7.2 Key points

In cases involving the cultivation of cannabis it is the capacity to produce that is central rather than the quantity (*R v Wiseman* [2013] EWCA Crim 2499).

In the case of M-Kat (mephedrone), which is not listed in the drugs guideline, reference should be made for comparative weights to amphetamine and not cannabis (*R v Pitts* [2014] EWCA Crim 1615).

C7.8 Drugs: permitting premises to be used

Misuse of Drugs Act 1971, s 8

8 Occupiers etc of premises to be punishable for permitting certain activities to take place there

A person commits an offence if, being the occupier or concerned in the management of any premises, he knowingly permits or suffers any of the following activities to take place on those premises, that is to say—

(a) producing or attempting to produce a controlled drug in contravention of section 4(1) of this Act;

(b) supplying or attempting to supply a controlled drug to another in contravention of section 4(1) of this Act, or offering to supply a controlled drug to another in contravention of section 4(1);

(c) preparing opium for smoking;

(d) smoking cannabis, cannabis resin or prepared opium.

C7.8.1 *Sentencing*

STEP ONE: Determining the offence category

Category 1	Higher culpability and greater harm
Category 2	Lower culpability and greater harm; or higher culpability and lesser harm
Category 3	Lower culpability and lesser harm

Factors indicating culpability (non-exhaustive)	**Factors indicating harm (non-exhaustive)**
Higher culpability: Permits premises to be used primarily for drug activity, for example crack house Permits use in expectation of substantial financial gain Uses legitimate business premises to aid and/or conceal illegal activity, for example public house or club **Lower culpability:** Permits use for limited or no financial gain No active role in any supply taking place Involvement through naivety	**Greater harm:** Regular drug-related activity Higher quantity of drugs, for example: heroin, cocaine—more than 5g; cannabis—more than 50g. **Lesser harm:** Infrequent drug-related activity Lower quantity of drugs, for example: heroin, cocaine—up to 5g; cannabis—up to 50g.

STEP TWO: Starting point and category range

Class A:

Offence category	Starting point	Category range
Category 1	Crown Court	Crown Court
Category 2	36 weeks' custody	High-level community order to 18 months' custody
Category 3	Medium-level community order	Low-level community order to high-level community order

Class B:

Offence category	Starting point	Category range
Category 1	1 year's custody	26 weeks' to 18 months' custody
Category 2	High-level community order	Low-level community order to 26 weeks' custody
Category 3	Band C fine	Band A fine to low-level community order

C7 **Drugs**

Class C:

Offence category	Starting point	Category range
Category 1	12 weeks' custody	High-level community order to 26 weeks' custody (max 12 weeks when tried summarily)
Category 2	Low-level community order	Band C fine to high-level community order
Category 3	Band A fine	Discharge to Band C fine

Factors increasing seriousness	Factors reducing seriousness or reflecting personal mitigation
Statutory aggravating factors: Previous convictions, having regard to (a) nature of the offence to which conviction relates and relevance to current offence; and (b) time elapsed since conviction Offence committed on bail **Other aggravating factors include:** Length of time over which premises used for drug activity Volume of drug activity permitted Premises adapted to facilitate drug activity Location of premises, for example proximity to school Attempts to conceal or dispose of evidence, where not charged separately Presence of others, especially children and/or non-users High purity Presence of weapons, where not charged separately Failure to comply with current court orders Offence committed on licence Established evidence of community impact	Involvement due to pressure, intimidation, or coercion falling short of duress Isolated incident Low purity No previous convictions or no relevant or recent convictions Offender's vulnerability was exploited Remorse Good character and/or exemplary conduct Determination and/or demonstration of steps having been taken to address addiction or offending behaviour Serious medical conditions requiring urgent, intensive or long-term treatment Age and/or lack of maturity where it affects the responsibility of the offender Mental disorder or learning disability Sole or primary carer for dependent relatives

C7.8.1.1 *Additional steps*

Consider any factors which indicate a reduction, such as assistance to the prosecution; reduction for guilty plea; dangerousness; totality principle; compensation and ancillary orders; reasons; consideration for remand time.

C7.8.2 Key points

Where the allegation is permitting premises to be used for the supply of drugs, in order to establish the offence the Crown must prove not only that the defendant knowingly permitted the supply of the drugs, but also that a supply of the drugs had actually taken place on the premises (*R v McGee* [2012] EWCA Crim 613 (Class A); *R v Auguiste* [2003] EWCA Crim 3329 (Class B)).

C7.9 Drugs: possession of a controlled drug

Misuse of Drugs Act 1971, s 5(2) and (4)

5 Restriction of possession of controlled drugs

(2) Subject to section 28 of this Act [see **C6.1**] and to subsection (4) below, it is an offence for a person to have a controlled drug in his possession in contravention of subsection (1) above.

...

(4) In any proceedings for an offence under subsection (2) above in which it is proved that the accused had a controlled drug in his possession, it shall be a defence for him to prove—

(a) that, knowing or suspecting it to be a controlled drug, he took possession of it for the purpose of preventing another from committing or continuing to commit an offence in connection with that drug and that as soon as possible after taking possession of it he took all such steps as were reasonably open to him to destroy the drug or to deliver it into the custody of a person lawfully entitled to take custody of it; or

(b) that, knowing or suspecting it to be a controlled drug, he took possession of it for the purpose of delivering it into the custody of a person lawfully entitled to take custody of it and that as soon as possible after taking possession of it he took all such steps as were reasonably open to him to deliver it into the custody of such a person.

C7.9.1 *Sentencing*

STEP ONE: Determine the offence category

Category 1	Class A drug
Category 2	Class B drug
Category 3	Class C drug

STEP TWO: Starting point and range

Offence category	Starting point	Category range
Category 1 (Class A)	Band C fine	Band A fine to 51 weeks' custody
Category 2 (Class B)	Band B fine	Discharge to26 weeks' custody
Category 3 (Class C)	Band A fine	Discharge to medium-level community order

Factors increasing seriousness	Factors reducing seriousness or reflecting personal mitigation
Statutory aggravating factors: Previous convictions, having regard to (a) nature of the offence to which conviction relates and relevance to current offence; and (b) time elapsed since conviction Offence committed on bail **Other aggravating factors include:** Possession of drug in prison Presence of others, especially children and/ or non-users Possession of drug in school or licensed premises Failure to comply with current court orders Offence committed on licence Attempts to conceal or dispose of evidence, where not charged separately Charged as importation of a very small amount Established evidence of community impact	No previous convictions or no relevant or recent convictions Remorse Good character and/or exemplary conduct Offender is using cannabis to help with a diagnosed medical condition Determination and/or demonstration of steps having been taken to address addiction or offending behaviour Serious medical conditions requiring urgent, intensive, or long-term treatment Isolated incident Age and/or lack of maturity where it affects the responsibility of the offender Mental disorder or learning disability Sole or primary carer for dependent relatives

C7.9.1.1 *Additional steps*

Consider any factors which indicate a reduction, such as assistance to the prosecution; reduction for guilty plea; dangerousness; totality principle; compensation and ancillary orders; reasons; consideration for remand time.

 See *Blackstone's Criminal Practice 2017* **B19**

C7.9.2 *Obstruction under the Misuse of Drugs Act 1971*

Section 23(4) of the Misuse of Drugs Act 1971 provides:

> ## Misuse of Drugs Act 1971, s 23(4)
>
> ### 23 Powers to search and obtain evidence
> (4) A person commits an offence if he—
>   (a) intentionally obstructs a person in the exercise of his powers under this section; or
>   (b) conceals from a person acting in the exercise of his powers under subsection (1) above any such books, documents, stocks or drugs as are mentioned in that subsection; or
>   (c) without reasonable excuse (proof of which shall lie on him) fails to produce any such books or documents as are so mentioned where their production is demanded by a person in the exercise of his power under that subsection.

6 months' imprisonment and/or fine/2 years' imprisonment

For there to be obstruction, the officer must be acting in the execution of his office. The officer must comply strictly with the requirements of the Police and Criminal Evidence Act 1984 in relation to a stop and search (*R v Bristol* [2007] EWHC 3214 (Admin); *B v DPP* [2008] EWHC 1655 (Admin); *R (Michaels) v Highbury Corner Magistrates' Court* [2009] EWHC 2928 (Admin)).

C7.10 Drugs: psychoactive substances

Psychoactive Substances Act 2016, ss 1, 4–9, and 26–271 Overview

(1) This Act contains provision about psychoactive substances.

(2) Section 2 defines what is meant by a 'psychoactive substance'.

(3) Sections 4 to 10 contain provision about offences relating to psychoactive substances.

(4) Section 11 provides for exceptions to those offences.

(5) Sections 12 to 35 contain powers for dealing with prohibited activities in respect of psychoactive substances, in particular powers to give prohibition notices and make prohibition orders.

(6) Sections 36 to 54 contain enforcement powers.

...

Offences

4 Producing a psychoactive substance

(1) A person commits an offence if—

  (a) the person intentionally produces a psychoactive substance,

  (b) the person knows or suspects that the substance is a psychoactive substance, and

  (c) the person—

    (i) intends to consume the psychoactive substance for itspsychoactive effects, or

    (ii) knows, or is reckless as to whether, the psychoactive substance is likely to be consumed by some other person for its psychoactive effects.

(2) This section is subject to section 11 (exceptions to offences).

5 Supplying, or offering to supply, a psychoactive substance

(1) A person commits an offence if—

  (a) the person intentionally supplies a substance to another person,

  (b) the substance is a psychoactive substance,

(c) the person knows or suspects, or ought to know or suspect, that the substance is a psychoactive substance, and

(d) the person knows, or is reckless as to whether, the psychoactive substance is likely to be consumed by the person to whom it is supplied, or by some other person, for its psychoactive effects.

(2) A person ('P') commits an offence if—

    (a) P offers to supply a psychoactive substance to another person ('R'), and

    (b) P knows or is reckless as to whether R, or some other person, would, if P supplied a substance to R in accordance with the offer, be likely to consume the substance for its psychoactive effects.

(3) For the purposes of subsection (2)(b), the reference to a substance's psychoactive effects includes a reference to the psychoactive effects which the substance would have if it were the substance which P had offered to supply to R.

(4) This section is subject to section 11 (exceptions to offences).

6 Aggravation of offence under section 5

(1) This section applies if—

    (a) a court is considering the seriousness of an offence under section 5, and

    (b) at the time the offence was committed the offender was aged 18 or over.

(2) If condition A, B or C is met the court—

    (a) must treat the fact that the condition is met as an aggravating factor (that is to say, a factor that increases the seriousness of the offence), and

    (b) must state in open court that the offence is so aggravated.

(3) Condition A is that the offence was committed on or in the vicinity of school premises at a relevant time.

(4) For the purposes of subsection (3) a 'relevant time' is—

    (a) any time when the school premises are in use by persons under the age of 18;

    (b) one hour before the start and one hour after the end of any such time.

(5) In this section—

'school premises' means land used for the purposes of a school, other than any land occupied solely as a dwelling by a person employed at the school;

'school' has the same meaning—

    (a) in England and Wales, as in section 4 of the Education Act 1996;

…

(6) Condition B is that in connection with the commission of the offence the offender used a courier who, at the time the offence was committed, was under the age of 18.

(7) For the purposes of subsection (6) a person ('P') uses a courier in connection with an offence under section 5 if P causes or permits another person (the courier)—

    (a) to deliver a substance to a third person, or

    (b) to deliver a drug-related consideration to P or a third person.

(8) A drug-related consideration is a consideration of any description which—
  (a) is obtained in connection with the supply of a psychoactive substance, or
  (b) is intended to be used in connection with obtaining a psychoactive substance.
(9) Condition C is that the offence was committed in a custodial institution.
(10) In this section—
  'custodial institution' means any of the following—
  (a) a prison;
  (b) a young offender institution, secure training centre, secure college, young offenders institution, young offenders centre, juvenile justice centre or remand centre;
  (c) a removal centre, a short-term holding facility or pre-departure accommodation;
  (d) service custody premises;
  'removal centre', 'short-term holding facility' and 'pre-departure accommodation' have the meaning given by section 147 of the Immigration and Asylum Act 1999;
  'service custody premises' has the meaning given by section 300(7) of the Armed Forces Act 2006.

7 Possession of psychoactive substance with intent to supply

(1) A person commits an offence if—
  (a) the person is in possession of a psychoactive substance,
  (b) the person knows or suspects that the substance is a psychoactive substance, and
  (c) the person intends to supply the psychoactive substance to another person for its consumption, whether by any person to whom it is supplied or by some other person, for its psychoactive effects.
(2) This section is subject to section 11 (exceptions to offences).

8 Importing or exporting a psychoactive substance

(1) A person commits an offence if—
  (a) the person intentionally imports a substance,
  (b) the substance is a psychoactive substance,
  (c) the person knows or suspects, or ought to know or suspect, that the substance is a psychoactive substance, and
  (d) the person—
    (i) intends to consume the psychoactive substance for its psychoactive effects, or
    (ii) knows, or is reckless as to whether, the psychoactive substance is likely to be consumed by some other person for its psychoactive effects.
(2) A person commits an offence if—
  (a) the person intentionally exports a substance,
  (b) the substance is a psychoactive substance,
  (c) the person knows or suspects, or ought to know or suspect, that the substance is a psychoactive substance, and

    (d) the person—
       (i) intends to consume the psychoactive substance for its psycho-
         active effects, or
       (ii) knows, or is reckless as to whether, the psychoactive substance
         is likely to be consumed by some other person for its psychoac-
         tive effects.
(3) In a case where a person imports or exports a controlled drug suspecting it to be a psychoactive substance, the person is to be treated for the
purposes of this section as if the person had imported or exported a
psychoactive substance suspecting it to be such a substance.
In this subsection 'controlled drug' has the same meaning as in the
Misuse of Drugs Act 1971.
(4) Section 5 of the Customs and Excise Management Act 1979 (time of
importation, exportation, etc) applies for the purposes of this section
as it applies for the purposes of that Act.
(5) This section is subject to section 11 (exceptions to offences).

9 Possession of a psychoactive substance in a custodial institution

(1) A person commits an offence if—
    (a) the person is in possession of a psychoactive substance in a custo-
       dial institution,
    (b) the person knows or suspects that the substance is a psychoactive
       substance, and
    (c) the person intends to consume the psychoactive substance for its
       psychoactive effects.
(2) In this section 'custodial institution' has the same meaning as in
section 6.
(3) This section is subject to section 11 (exceptions to offences).

...

26 Offence of failing to comply with a prohibition order or premises order

(1) A person against whom a prohibition order or a premises order is made
commits an offence by failing to comply with the order...
(3) A person does not commit an offence under this section if—
    (a) the person took all reasonable steps to comply with the order, or
    (b) there is some other reasonable excuse for the failure to comply.

27 Offence of failing to comply with an access prohibition, etc

(1) This section applies where a prohibition order or a premises order
imposes an access prohibition (see section 22(6)).
(2) A person, other than the person against whom the order was made,
who without reasonable excuse remains on or enters premises in contravention of the access prohibition commits an offence.
(3) A person who without reasonable excuse obstructs a person acting
under section 23(1) commits an offence.

EW ss 4–8

6 months and/or fine/7 years' imprisonment

EW ss 9 and 26

6 months and/or fine/2 years' imprisonment

SO s 27

6 months and/or fine

C7.10.1 Key points

Psychoactive Substances Act 2016, ss 2, 3, and 11

2 Meaning of 'psychoactive substance' etc

(1) In this Act 'psychoactive substance' means any substance which—
   (a) is capable of producing a psychoactive effect in a person who con-
       sumes it, and
   (b) is not an exempted substance (see section 3).
(2) For the purposes of this Act a substance produces a psychoactive effect in
    a person if, by stimulating or depressing the person's central nervous sys-
    tem, it affects the person's mental functioning or emotional state; and ref-
    erences to a substance's psychoactive effects are to be read accordingly.
(3) For the purposes of this Act a person consumes a substance if the
    person causes or allows the substance, or fumes given off by the sub-
    stance, to enter the person's body in any way.

3 Exempted substances

(1) In this Act 'exempted substance' means a substance listed in Schedule 1.

...

[SCHEDULE 1 Section 3—summary

EXEMPTED SUBSTANCES

Controlled drugs

Medicinal products

Alcohol

Nicotine and tobacco products

Caffeine

Food

Including drink;]

...

11 Exceptions to offences

(1) It is not an offence under this Act for a person to carry on any activity listed in subsection (3) if, in the circumstances in which it is carried on by that person, the activity is an exempted activity.

(2) In this section 'exempted activity' means an activity listed in Schedule 2.

(3) The activities referred to in subsection (1) are—
   (a) producing a psychoactive substance;
   (b) supplying such a substance;
   (c) offering to supply such a substance;
   (d) possessing such a substance with intent to supply it;
   (e) importing or exporting such a substance;
   (f) possessing such a substance in a custodial institution (within the meaning of section 9)…

[Schedule 2 EXEMPTED ACTIVITIES—summary

Healthcare-related activities

Research]

C8 Education Act

C8.1 School non-attendance

> **Education Act 1996, s 444(1), (1A), (1B), (2), (2A), and (3)**
>
> ### 444 Offence: failure to secure regular attendance at school of registered pupil
>
> (1) If a child of compulsory school age who is a registered pupil at a school fails to attend regularly at the school, his parent is guilty of an offence.
>
> (1A) If in the circumstances mentioned in subsection (1) the parent knows that his child is failing to attend regularly at the school and fails to cause him to do so, he is guilty of an offence.
>
> (1B) It is a defence for a person charged with an offence under subsection (1A) to prove that he had a reasonable justification for his failure to cause the child to attend regularly at the school.
>
> (2) Subsections (2A) to (6) below apply in proceedings for an offence under this section in respect of a child who is not a boarder at the school at which he is a registered pupil.
>
> (2A) The child shall not be taken to have failed to attend regularly at the school by reason of his absence from the school at any time if the parent proves that at that time the child was prevented from attending by reason of sickness or any unavoidable cause.
>
> (3) The child shall not be taken to have failed to attend regularly at the school by reason of his absence from the school—
>
> (a) with leave, or
>
> (b) [repealed]
>
> (c) on any day exclusively set apart for religious observance by the religious body to which his parent belongs.

SO

 Level 3 fine (s 444(1)); level 4 fine and/or 3 months' imprisonment (s 444(1A))

C8 Education Act

C8.1.1 *Sentencing*

Note that this guideline is under review by the Sentencing Council (see **Appendix 7**).

Offence seriousness (culpability and harm) A. Identify the appropriate starting point Starting points based on first-time offender pleading not guilty		
Example of nature of activity	**Starting point**	**Range**
Short period following previous good attendance (s 444(1))	Band A fine	Conditional discharge to Band A fine
Erratic attendance for long period (s 444(1))	Band B fine	Band B fine to Band C fine
Colluding in and condoning non-attendance or deliberately instigating non-attendance (s 444(1A))	Medium-level community order	Low-level community order to high-level community order

Offence seriousness (culpability and harm) B. Consider the effect of aggravating and mitigating factors (other than those within examples above) The following may be particularly relevant but these lists are not exhaustive	
Factors indicating higher culpability 1. Parental collusion (s 444(1) only) 2. Lack of parental effort to ensure attendance (s 444(1) only) 3. Threats to teachers and/or officials 4. Refusal to cooperate with school and/or officials **Factors indicating greater degree of harm** 1. More than one child 2. Harmful effect on other children in family	**Factors indicating lower culpability** 1. Parent unaware of child's whereabouts 2. Parent tried to ensure attendance 3. Parent concerned by child's allegations of bullying/unable to get school to address bullying

C8.1.2 Key points

- The offence under section 444(1) is strict, but the prosecution have the burden of proof. This is not contrary to the European Convention on Human Rights (*Barnfather v Islington Education Authority* [2003] EWHC 418 (Admin)). The term 'regularly' is not defined. The taking of an unauthorised holiday did not itself amount to an offence. Every case turned on its own facts. The Authority could not specify an unduly short period of time for consideration, such as the length of the holiday itself. The court must receive any explanation the parent wishes to give and, in *Isle of Wight Council v Platt* [2016] EWHC 1283 (Admin) the

court, finding an attendance rate in excess of 90 per cent, was
entitled to acquit.

- Difficulties in getting a child to school due to the child's behavioural and psychological difficulties did not equate to an unavoidable cause (s 444(1)), neither did it provide a defence under
  section 444(2A) (*Islington London Borough Council v TD*, [2011]
  EWHC 990 (Admin)). Unavoidable cause had to relate to the
  child, not the parent, and had to be something in the nature
  of an emergency. A child's chaotic lifestyle could not provide
  the defence of unavoidable cause for absence from school. The
  defence of reasonable justification to the aggravated version of
  the offence should only be considered if the general defence to
  both levels of the offence failed (*West Sussex County Council v C*
  [2013] EWHC 1757(Admin)).

- In relation to section 444(1A), the parent will have only an evidential burden to satisfy, the prosecution having then to prove
  to the criminal standard that the defence is not made out (*R
  (P) v Liverpool City Magistrates' Court* [2006] EWHC 2732
  (Admin)).

C8.2 Education Act: failure to comply with school attendance order

Education Act 1996, s 443(1) and (2)

443 Offence: failure to comply with school attendance order

(1) If a parent on whom a school attendance order is served fails to comply
with the requirements of the order, he is guilty of an offence, unless he
proves that he is causing the child to receive suitable education otherwise than at school.

(2) If, in proceedings for an offence under this section, the parent is acquitted, the court may direct that the school attendance order shall cease
to be in force.

 Level 3 fine

C8.2.1 Key points

Where a parent asserts the defence contained in section 443(1), the
burden of proving it remains with the parent (*Oxfordshire County
Council v L*, 3 March 2010).

C9 **Immigration Offences**

C9.1 **Offences**

C9.1.1 *Illegal entry and deception*

Immigration Act 1971, ss 24, 24A, and 24B

24 Illegal entry and similar offences

(1) [It is an offence—]
   (a) if contrary to this Act he knowingly enters the United Kingdom in breach of a deportation order or without leave;
   (b) if, having only a limited leave to enter or remain in the United Kingdom, he knowingly either—
       (i) remains beyond the time limited by the leave; or
       (ii) fails to observe a condition of the leave;
   (c) if, having lawfully entered the United Kingdom without leave by virtue of section 8(1) above, he remains without leave beyond the time allowed by section 8(1);
   (d) if, without reasonable excuse, he fails to comply with any requirement imposed on him under Schedule 2 to this Act to report to a medical officer of health, or to attend, or submit to a test or examination, as required by such an officer;
   (e) if, without reasonable excuse, he fails to observe any restriction imposed on him under Schedule 2 or 3 to this Act as to residence, as to his employment or occupation or as to reporting to the police, to an immigration officer or to the Secretary of State;
   (f) if he disembarks in the United Kingdom from a ship or aircraft after being placed on board under Schedule 2 or 3 to this Act with a view to his removal from the United Kingdom;
   (g) if he embarks in contravention of a restriction imposed by or under an Order in Council under section 3(7) of this Act.

(1A) A person commits an offence under subsection (1)(b)(i) above on the day when he first knows that the time limited by his leave has expired and continues to commit it throughout any period during which he is in the United Kingdom thereafter; but a person shall not be prosecuted under that provision more than once in respect of the same limited leave.

(3) The extended time limit for prosecutions which is provided for by section 28 below shall apply to offences under subsection (1)(a) and (c) above.

(4) In proceedings for an offence against subsection (1)(a) above of entering the United Kingdom without leave—
   (a) any stamp purporting to have been imprinted on a passport or other travel document by an immigration officer on a particular date for the purpose of giving leave shall be presumed to have been duly so imprinted, unless the contrary is proved;

    (b) proof that a person had leave to enter the United Kingdom shall lie on the defence if, but only if, he is shown to have entered within six months before the date when the proceedings were commenced.

24A Deception

(1) A person who is not a British citizen is guilty of an offence if, by means which include deception by him—

    (a) he obtains or seeks to obtain leave to enter or remain in the United Kingdom; or

    (b) he secures or seeks to secure the avoidance, postponement or revocation of enforcement action against him.

(2) 'Enforcement action', in relation to a person, means—

    (a) the giving of directions for his removal from the United Kingdom ('directions') under Schedule 2 to this Act or section 10 of the Immigration and Asylum Act 1999;

    (b) the making of a deportation order against him under section 5 of this Act; or

    (c) his removal from the United Kingdom in consequence of directions or a deportation order.

24B Illegal working

(1) A person ('P') who is subject to immigration control commits an offence if—

    (a) P works at a time when P is disqualified from working by reason of P's immigration status, and

    (b) at that time P knows or has reasonable cause to believe that P is disqualified from working by reason of P's immigration status.

(2) For the purposes of subsection (1) a person is disqualified from working by reason of the person's immigration status if—

    (a) the person has not been granted leave to enter or remain in the United Kingdom, or

    (b) the person's leave to enter or remain in the United Kingdom—

        (i) is invalid,

        (ii) has ceased to have effect (whether by reason of curtailment, revocation, cancellation, passage of time or otherwise), or

        (iii) is subject to a condition preventing the person from doing work of that kind...

(8) The reference in subsection (1) to a person who is subject to immigration control is to a person who under this Act requires leave to enter or remain in the United Kingdom.

(9) Where a person is on immigration bail within the meaning of Part 1 of Schedule 10 to the Immigration Act 2016—

    (a) the person is to be treated for the purposes of subsection (2) as if the person had been granted leave to enter the United Kingdom, but

    (b) any condition as to the person's work in the United Kingdom to which the person's immigration bail is subject is to be treated for those purposes as a condition of leave...

(10) The reference in subsection (1) to a person working is to that person working—

    (a) under a contract of employment,

    (b) under a contract of apprenticeship,

    (c) under a contract personally to do work,
    (d) under or for the purposes of a contract for services,
    (e) for a purpose related to a contract to sell goods,
    (f) as a constable,
    (g) in the course of Crown employment,
    (h) as a relevant member of the House of Commons staff, or
    (i) as a relevant member of the House of Lords staff...
(13) In this section 'contract' means a contract whether express or implied and, if express, whether oral or in writing.

SO Sections 24 and 25B

EW Section 24A

Fine/6 months' imprisonment (ss 24 and 25B)

6 months'/2 years' imprisonment (s 24A)

C9.1.2 *Assisting unlawful entry*

Immigration Act 1971, ss 25, 25A, and 25B

25 Assisting unlawful immigration to member state

(1) A person commits an offence if he—
    (a) does an act which facilitates the commission of a breach of immigration law by an individual who is not a citizen of the European Union,
    (b) knows or has reasonable cause for believing that the act facilitates the commission of a breach of immigration law by the individual, and
    (c) knows or has reasonable cause for believing that the individual is not a citizen of the European Union.

25A Helping asylum-seeker to enter United Kingdom

(1) A person commits an offence if—
    (a) he knowingly and for gain facilitates the arrival in, or the entry into, the United Kingdom of an individual, and
    (b) he knows or has reasonable cause to believe that the individual is an asylum-seeker.

25B Assisting entry to United Kingdom in breach of deportation or exclusion order

(1) A person commits an offence if he—
    (a) does an act which facilitates a breach of a deportation order in force against an individual who is a citizen of the European Union, and
    (b) knows or has reasonable cause for believing that the act facilitates a breach of the deportation order.

Fine/6 months' imprisonment/14 years' imprisonment

C9.1.2.1 Key points

Facilitation of a breach of immigration law under section 25 Immigration Act 1971 includes facilitating a breach by an asylum seeker (*R v Bina* [2014] EWCA Crim 1444). *R v Ali* [2013] EWCA Crim 43 confirms that, to prove an offence under section 25 Immigration Act 1971, it is not essential that breach actually occurs, and *R v Boateng* [2016] EWCA Crim 57 confirms that, for there to be an offence of facilitating the illegal entry of a person to the UK, it was not necessary that the person who enters be dishonest or aware of the position.

C9.1.3 *Possessing false passports, work permits, registration cards, etc*

> **Immigration Act 1971, ss 26 and 26A**
>
> **26 General offences in connection with administration of Act**
>
> (1) A person shall be guilty of an offence punishable on summary conviction with a fine or with imprisonment for not more than six months, or with both, in any of the following cases—
>
> (a) if, without reasonable excuse, he refuses or fails to submit to examination under Schedule 2 to this Act;
>
> (b) if, without reasonable excuse, he refuses to fails to furnish or produce any information in his possession, or any documents in his possession or control, which he is on an examination under that Schedule required to furnish or produce;
>
> (c) if on any such examination or otherwise he makes or causes to be made to an immigration officer or other person lawfully acting in the execution of a relevant enactment a return, statement or representation which he knows to be false or does not believe to be true;
>
> (d) if, without lawful authority, he alters any certificate of entitlement, entry clearance, work permit or other document issued or made under or for the purposes of this Act, or uses for the purposes of this Act, or has in his possession for such use, any passport, certificate of entitlement, entry clearance, work permit or other document which he knows or has reasonable cause to believe to be false;
>
> (e) if, without reasonable excuse, he fails to complete and produce a landing or embarkation card in accordance with any order under Schedule 2 to this Act;

    (f) if, without reasonable excuse, he fails to comply with any requirement of regulations under section 4(3) or of an order under section 4(4) above;

    (g) if, without reasonable excuse, he obstructs an immigration officer or other person lawfully acting in the execution of this Act.

(2) The extended time limit for prosecutions which is provided for by section 28 below shall apply to offences under subsection (1)(c) and (d) above.

26A Registration card

...

(3) A person commits an offence if he—

    (a) makes a false registration card,

    (b) alters a registration card with intent to deceive or to enable another to deceive,

    (c) has a false or altered registration card in his possession without reasonable excuse,

    (d) uses or attempts to use a false registration card for a purpose for which a registration card is issued,

    (e) uses or attempts to use an altered registration card with intent to deceive,

    (f) makes an article designed to be used in making a false registration card,

    (g) makes an article designed to be used in altering a registration card with intent to deceive or to enable another to deceive, or

    (h) has an article within paragraph (f) or (g) in his possession without reasonable excuse.

(4) In subsection (3) 'false registration card' means a document which is designed to appear to be a registration card.

EW

 Fine/6 months' imprisonment/10 years' imprisonment (subs (3)(a), (b), (d), (e), (f), or (g)), 2 years' imprisonment (subs (3)(c) or (h))

C9.2 Defences

Immigration and Asylum Act 1999, s 31

31 Defences based on Article 31(1) of the Refugee Convention

(1) It is a defence for a refugee charged with an offence to which this section applies to show that, having come to the United Kingdom directly from a country where his life or freedom was threatened (within the meaning of the Refugee Convention), he—

    (a) presented himself to the authorities in the United Kingdom without delay;

    (b) showed good cause for his illegal entry or presence; and

(c) made a claim for asylum as soon as was reasonably practicable after his arrival in the United Kingdom.

(2) If, in coming from the country where his life or freedom was threatened, the refugee stopped in another country outside the United Kingdom, subsection (1) applies only if he shows that he could not reasonably have expected to be given protection under the Refugee Convention in that other country.

(3) In England and Wales and Northern Ireland the offences to which this section applies are any offence, and any attempt to commit an offence, under—

   (a) Part I of the Forgery and Counterfeiting Act 1981 (forgery and connected offences);

   (b) section 24A of the 1971 Act (deception); or

   (c) section 26(1)(d) of the 1971 Act (falsification of documents).

…

(5) A refugee who has made a claim for asylum is not entitled to the defence provided by subsection (1) in relation to any offence committed by him after making that claim.

(6) 'Refugee' has the same meaning as it has for the purposes of the Refugee Convention.

(7) If the Secretary of State has refused to grant a claim for asylum made by a person who claims that he has a defence under subsection (1), that person is to be taken not to be a refugee unless he shows that he is.

C9.3 Key points

- Refugees are protected under Article 31 of the UN Convention relating to the status of refugees. This defence under section 31 above was fully considered in *R v Matete* [2013] EWCA Crim 1372. See **C15.11.2**; further case law is considered at **C15.11.3**.
- The six-month time limit does not apply to offences under section 26(1)(c) and (d), or section 28(1)(a) and (c).
- The burden of proving that entry was legal falls upon the defendant in relation to prosecutions commenced within six months of that entry (s 24(4)(b)).

 See *Blackstone's Criminal Practice 2017* **B22**

C10 **Prison Offences**

C10.1 Conveyance of articles into prison

The Prison Act 1952 lists the following prohibited articles (s 40A):

List A articles	List B articles
(a) a controlled drug (as defined for the purposes of the Misuse of Drugs Act 1971); (b) an explosive; (c) any firearm or ammunition (as defined in s 57 of the Firearms Act 1968); (d) any other offensive weapon (as defined in s 1(9) of the Police and Criminal Evidence Act 1984).	(a) alcohol (as defined for the purposes of the Licensing Act 2003); (b) a mobile telephone; (c) a camera; (d) a sound-recording device. 'Camera' includes any device by means of which a photograph (as defined in s 40E) can be produced; 'sound-recording device' includes any device by means of which a sound-recording (as defined in s 40E) can be made. The reference in paragraph (b), (c), or (d) of List B to a device of any description includes a reference to— (a) a component part of a device of that description; or (b) an article designed or adapted for use with a device of that description (including any disk, film, or other separate article on which images, sounds, or information may be recorded).

- A List C article is any article or substance proscribed for the purposes of section 40A by prison rules.
- Conveyance of an article in List A is triable only on indictment (Prison Act 1952, s 40B).

C10.1.1 *Conveyance of List B or C articles*

SO (For List C articles)

EW (For List B articles) (*Note*: List A items are indictable only)

|||| (For List B articles, fine and/or 6 months'/2 years' imprisonment; for List C articles, level 3 fine only)

> **Prison Act 1952, s 40C**
>
> **40C Conveyance etc of List B or C articles into or out of prison**
>
> (1) A person who, without authorisation—
>   (a) brings, throws or otherwise conveys a List B article into or out of a prison,

    (b) causes another person to bring, throw or otherwise convey a List B article into or out of a prison,

    (c) leaves a List B article in any place (whether inside or outside a prison) intending it to come into the possession of a prisoner, or

    (d) knowing a person to be a prisoner, gives a List B article to him, is guilty of an offence.

(2) A person who, without authorisation—

    (a) brings, throws or otherwise conveys a List C article into a prison intending it to come into the possession of a prisoner,

    (b) causes another person to bring, throw or otherwise convey a List C article into a prison intending it to come into the possession of a prisoner,

    (c) brings, throws or otherwise conveys a List C article out of a prison on behalf of a prisoner,

    (d) causes another person to bring, throw or otherwise convey a List C article out of a prison on behalf of a prisoner,

    (e) leaves a List C article in any place (whether inside or outside a prison) intending it to come into the possession of a prisoner, or

    (f) while inside a prison, gives a List C article to a prisoner, is guilty of an offence.

(3) A person who attempts to commit an offence under subsection (2) is guilty of that offence.

(4) In proceedings for an offence under this section it is a defence for the accused to show that—

    (a) he reasonably believed that he had authorisation to do the act in respect of which the proceedings are brought, or

    (b) in all the circumstances there was an overriding public interest which justified the doing of that act.

C10.2 Unauthorised possession of knives, etc in prison

Prison Act 1952, s 40CA

Unauthorised possession in prison of knife or offensive weapon

(1) A person who, without authorisation, is in possession of an article specified in subsection (2) inside a prison is guilty of an offence.

(2) The articles referred to in subsection (1) are—

    (a) any article that has a blade or is sharply pointed;

    (b) any other offensive weapon (as defined in section 1(9) of the Police and Criminal Evidence Act 1984).

(3) In proceedings for an offence under this section it is a defence for the accused to show that—

    (a) he reasonably believed that he had authorisation to be in possession of the article in question, or

    (b) in all the circumstances there was an overriding public interest which justified his being in possession of the article.

(5) In this section 'authorisation' means authorisation given for the purposes of this section; and subsections (1) to (3) of section 40E apply in relation to authorisations so given as they apply to authorisations given for the purposes of section 40D.

 Fine and/or 6 months'/4 years' imprisonment

C10.3 **Throwing articles into prison**

Prison Act 1952, s 40CB

40CB Throwing articles into prison

(1) A person who, without authorisation, throws any article or substance into a prison is guilty of an offence.
(2) For the purposes of subsection (1)—
  (a) the reference to an article or substance does not include a reference to a List A article, a List B article or a List C article (as defined by section 40A);
  (b) the reference to 'throwing' an article or substance into a prison includes a reference to doing anything from outside the prison that results in the article or substance being projected or conveyed over or through a boundary of the prison so as to land inside the prison.
(3) In proceedings for an offence under this section it is a defence for the accused to show that—
  (a) he reasonably believed that he had authorisation to do the act in respect of which the proceedings are brought, or
  (b) in all the circumstances there was an overriding public interest which justified the doing of that act.
(5) In this section 'authorisation' means authorisation given for the purposes of this section; and subsections (1) to (3) of section 40E apply in relation to authorisations so given as they apply to authorisations given for the purposes of section 40D.

Fine and/or 6 months'/2 years' imprisonment

C10.4 Other offences relating to prison security

Prison Act 1952, s 40D

40D Other offences relating to prison security

(1) A person who, without authorisation—

    (a) takes a photograph, or makes a sound-recording, inside a prison, or

    (b) transmits, or causes to be transmitted, any image, sound or information from inside a prison by electronic communications for simultaneous reception outside the prison,

  is guilty of an offence.

(2) It is immaterial for the purposes of subsection (1)(a) where the recording medium is located.

(3) A person who, without authorisation—

    (a) brings or otherwise conveys a restricted document out of a prison or causes such a document to be brought or conveyed out of a prison …

  is guilty of an offence.

(3A) A person who, without authorisation, is in possession of any of the items specified in subsection (3B) inside a prison is guilty of an offence.

(3B) The items referred to in subsection (3A) are—

    (a) a device capable of transmitting or receiving images, sounds or information by electronic communications (including a mobile telephone);

    (b) a component part of such a device;

    (c) an article designed or adapted for use with such a device (including any disk, film or other separate article on which images, sounds or information may be recorded).

(4) In proceedings for an offence under this section it is a defence for the accused to show that—

    (a) he reasonably believed that he had authorisation to do the act in respect of which the proceedings are brought, or

    (b) in all the circumstances there was an overriding public interest which justified the doing of that act.

EW

Fine and/or 6 months'/2 years' imprisonment

C11 **Public Order**

C11.1 Affray

> **Public Order Act 1986, ss 3(1)–(4), 6(2) and (5)**
>
> ### 3 Affray
>
> (1) A person is guilty of affray if he uses or threatens unlawful violence towards another and his conduct is such as would cause a person of reasonable firmness present at the scene to fear for his personal safety.
> (2) Where 2 or more persons use or threaten the unlawful violence, it is the conduct of them taken together that must be considered for the purposes of subsection (1).
> (3) For the purposes of this section a threat cannot be made by the use of words alone.
> (4) No person of reasonable firmness need actually be, or be likely to be, present at the scene
> ...
>
> ### 6 Mental element: miscellaneous
>
> (2) A person is guilty of violent disorder or affray only if he intends to use or threaten violence or is aware that his conduct may be violent or threaten violence.
> (5) For the purposes of this section a person whose awareness is impaired by intoxication shall be taken to be aware of that of which he would be aware if not intoxicated, unless he shows either that his intoxication was not self-induced or that it was caused solely by the taking or administration of a substance in the course of medical treatment.

EW

 6 months' imprisonment and/or fine/3 years' imprisonment

DO Dangerous offender

C11.1.1 *Sentencing*

Offence seriousness (culpability and harm) A. Identify the appropriate starting point Starting points based on first-time offender pleading not guilty		
Example of nature of activity	**Starting point**	**Range**
Brief offence involving low-level violence, no substantial fear created	Low-level community order	Band C fine to medium-level community order
Degree of fighting or violence that causes substantial fear	High-level community order	Medium-level community order to 12 weeks' custody
Fight involving a weapon/throwing objects, or conduct causing risk of serious injury	18 weeks' custody	12 weeks' custody to Crown Court

C11.1.2 Key points

- Section 6 provides that a threat cannot be made by the use of words alone.
- Affray may be committed in private as well as in public places. However, the fact that a third party could not be present may enable the court to hold that a hypothetical bystander would have viewed the threat as being restricted to the parties involved due to the turbulence of their relationship (*Leeson v Director of Public Prosecutions* [2010] EWHC 994 (Admin), where a conviction was quashed where L, who was drunk, had threatened a person with a knife in the bathroom of a private dwelling).
- In *R v Sanchez* (1996) 160 JP 321, the court approved the following academic commentary:

  The offence of affray envisages at least three persons: (i) the person using or threatening unlawful violence; (ii) a person towards whom the violence or threat is directed; and (iii) a person of reasonable firmness who need not actually be, or be likely to be, present at the scene. Thus the question in the present case was not whether a person of reasonable firmness in J's shoes would have feared for his personal safety but whether this hypothetical person, present in the room and seeing D's conduct towards J would have so feared.

- The definition of 'affray' is very wide, and in *Sanchez* (above) the court agreed with D's counsel that care has to be taken to avoid extending it so widely that it would cover every case of common assault:

  A common assault may be very trivial, so that it would not cause anyone to fear for his 'personal safety'. But where the assault threatens serious harm to the victim, there may be evidence of affray depending on the circumstances. The person of reasonable firmness present in a small room as in the present case might fear for his personal safety whereas the same person, observing the same conduct in an open space, would not.

The common law offence which it was intended to replace was, said the Law Commission, 'typically charged in cases of pitched street battles between rival gangs, spontaneous fights in public houses, clubs and at seaside resorts, and revenge attacks on individuals'.

- Reference should also be made to *R v Davison* [1992] Crim LR 31 and *R v Plavecz* [2002] Crim LR 837.
- The fact that a third party who is present does not feel afraid for their own safety is of evidential significance (*R v Blinkhorn* [2006] EWCA Crim 1416).

 See *Blackstone's Criminal Practice 2017* **B11.37–B11.46**

C11.2 Alcohol sale offences

Licensing Act 2003, s 141 (sale of alcohol to drunk person), s 146 (sale of alcohol to children), s 147 (allowing sale of alcohol to children), s 147A (persistently selling alcohol to children)

Section 147A of the Licensing Act 2003 makes it an offence if, on three or more different occasions within a period of three consecutive months, alcohol is sold unlawfully on the same premises to a person under 18.

 Level 3 fine (s 141), fine (ss 146, 147, and 147A)

C11.2.1 *Sentencing (for Licensing Act 2003 offences only)*

Note that this guideline is under review by the Sentencing Council (see **Appendix 7**).

Offence seriousness (culpability and harm) A. Identify the appropriate starting point Starting points based on first-time offender pleading not guilty		
Examples of nature of activity	**Starting point**	**Range**
Sale to a child (ie person under 18)/to a drunk person	Band B fine	Band A fine to Band C fine

Offence seriousness (culpability and harm)
B. Consider the effect of aggravating and mitigating factors (other than those within examples above)
The following may be particularly relevant but these lists are not exhaustive

Factors indicating higher culpability
1. No attempt made to establish age
2. Spirits/high-alcohol level of drink
3. Drunk person highly intoxicated
4. Large quantity of alcohol supplied
5. Sale intended for consumption by group of children/drunk people
6. Offender in senior or management position

Factors indicating greater degree of harm
1. Younger child/children
2. Drunk person causing distress to others
3. Drunk person aggressive

C11.2.2 Key points

• Provided a person has the authority to sell alcohol, it is irrelevant that he is unpaid (s 141).
• Section 146 provides:

Licensing Act 2003, s 146(4)–(6)

146 Sale of alcohol to children

(4) Where a person is charged with an offence under this section by reason of his own conduct it is a defence that—
 (a) he believed that the individual was aged 18 or over, and
 (b) either—
  (i) he had taken all reasonable steps to establish the individual's age, or
  (ii) nobody could reasonably have suspected from the individual's appearance that he was aged under 18.
(5) For the purposes of subsection (4), a person is treated as having taken all reasonable steps to establish an individual's age if—
 (a) he asked the individual for evidence of his age, and
 (b) the evidence would have convinced a reasonable person.
(6) Where a person ('the accused') is charged with an offence under this section by reason of the act or default of some other person, it is a defence that the accused exercised all due diligence to avoid committing it.

C11.3 **Alcohol on coaches and trains**

> ### Sporting Events (Control of Alcohol etc) Act 1985, s 1(1)–(5)
>
> **1 Offences in connection with alcohol on coaches and trains**
> (1) This section applies to a vehicle which—
>   (a) is a public service vehicle or railway passenger vehicle, and
>   (b) is being used for the principal purpose of carrying passengers for the whole or part of a journey to or from a designated sporting event.
> (2) A person who knowingly causes or permits alcohol to be carried on a vehicle to which this section applies is guilty of an offence—
>   (a) if the vehicle is a public service vehicle and he is the operator of the vehicle or the servant or agent of the operator, or
>   (b) if the vehicle is a hired vehicle and he is the person to whom it is hired or the servant or agent of that person.
> (3) A person who has alcohol in his possession while on a vehicle to which this section applies is guilty of an offence.
> (4) A person who is drunk on a vehicle to which this section applies is guilty of an offence.
> (5) In this section 'public service vehicle' and 'operator' have the same meaning as in the Public Passenger Vehicles Act 1981.

 Fine level 4 (s 1(2) offence), 3 months' imprisonment/fine level 3 (s 1(3) offence), fine level 2 (s 1(4) offence)

C11.4 **Begging**

Section 3 of the Vagrancy Act, as amended by section 70 of the Criminal Justice Act 1982, provides:

> ### Vagrancy Act, s 3
> Every person wandering abroad, or placing himself or herself in any public place, street, highway, court, or passage, to beg or gather alms, or causing or procuring or encouraging any child or children so to do; shall be deemed an idle and disorderly person within the true intent and meaning of this Act; and … it shall be lawful (to impose a fine).

Fine level 3

- Level 3 is for the situation where a weapon is used in danger-ous circumstances to threaten or cause fear; in those circum-stances, both the starting point and the range for a first-time adult offender who has pleaded not guilty are for sentencing in the Crown Court and, therefore, more than six months' custody.

'Dangerous circumstances' has not been judicially defined but was covered in the previous Court of Appeal guideline judgment in *Celaire and Poulton* [2002] EWCA Crim 2487. In relation to a knife, a circumstance is likely to be dangerous if there is a real pos-sibility that it could be used.

Offence seriousness (culpability and harm) A. Identify the appropriate starting point Starting points based on first-time offender pleading not guilty		
Examples of nature of activity	Starting point	Range
Weapon not used to threaten or cause fear	High-level community order	Band C fine to 12 weeks' custody
Weapon not used to threaten or cause fear but offence committed in dangerous circumstances	6 weeks' custody	High-level community order to Crown Court
Weapon used to threaten or cause fear and offence committed in dangerous circumstances	Crown Court	Crown Court

Offence seriousness (culpability and harm) B. Consider the effect of aggravating and mitigating factors (other than those within examples above) The following may be particularly relevant but these lists are not exhaustive	
Factors indicating higher culpability 1. Particularly dangerous weapon 2. Specifically planned use of weapon to commit violence, threaten violence, or intimidate 3. Offence motivated by hostility towards minority individual or group 4. Offender under influence of drink or drugs 5. Offender operating in group or gang **Factors indicating greater degree of harm** 1. Offence committed at school, hospital, or other place where vulnerable persons may be present 2. Offence committed on premises where people carrying out public services 3. Offence committed on or outside licensed premises 4. Offence committed on public transport 5. Offence committed at large public gathering, especially where there may be risk of disorder	1. Weapon carried only on temporary basis 2. Original possession legitimate, eg in course of trade or business

C11.5.2 Key points

- The Crown must prove that the person had the item with him and that it falls within the definition in the section. Only then must the defence establish a defence to the civil standard.
- 'Good reason' has been interpreted to mean the same as 'reasonable excuse' under the 1953 Act.
- A lock knife is not a folding knife, irrespective of the blade length (*Harris v Director of Public Prosecutions* [1993] 1 WLR 82).
- A screwdriver is not a bladed article (*R v Davis* [1998] Crim LR 564).
- A blade does not need to be sharp—a butter knife can be a bladed article (*Brooker v Director of Public Prosecutions* [2005] EWHC 1132 (Admin)).
- The fact that a defendant's employment was only casual was not a relevant consideration to prevent it being a good reason (*Chalal v Director of Public Prosecutions* [2010] EWHC 439 (Admin)).

C11.5.2.1 *Prevention of Crime Act 1953*

- The Crown must prove that the person had the weapon with him and that it falls within the definition in section 1(4), including proving any necessary intent. Only then must the defence establish the defence to the civil standard.
- It is necessary to show that the person knew that he was in possession of the offensive weapon (*R v Cugullere* [1961] 2 All ER 343).
- Weapons held by the appellate courts to be offensive per se include: a bayonet, a stiletto, a handgun, a butterfly knife, and a flickknife. Items that are inherently dangerous but manufactured for a lawful purpose are not offensive per se (eg razor blades, baseball bats, kitchen knives). It is likely that items prohibited for sale in England and Wales by virtue of the Criminal Justice Act 1988 (Offensive Weapons) (Amendment) Order 1988 (SI 1988/2019) are offensive per se. Whilst mere forgetfulness cannot amount to a reasonable excuse (or good reason) (*R v Glidewell* [1999] EWCA Crim 1221), the court must consider all the circumstances in which the forgetfulness arose (*R v Jolie* [2003] EWCA Crim 543).
- Fear of attack may amount to a reasonable excuse if the risk is imminent (*R v McAuley* [2009] EWCA Crim 2130).
- Whilst *Ohlson v Hylton* [1975] 1 WLR 724 confirms that an offence does not occur if a person lawfully in possession of an article, which is not offensive per se, suddenly uses it in the heat of an altercation, an offence does occur if a person leaves the scene to collect a weapon (*R v Tucker* [2016] EWCA Crim 13).
- A court should not approach the issue of 'good reason' (and thus 'reasonable excuse') wholly objectively, nor hold that an angry,

intoxicated, or traumatized state of mind could not contribute to good reason. A fear of attack can constitute good reason, the defendant's state of mind was relevant, and 'good reason' should be allowed a natural meaning. In *R v Clancy* [2012] EWCA Crim 8 (a decision under s 139 of the Criminal Justice Act 1988) the distorted thinking of the defendant following a sexual assault had to be considered. Only if the view was wholly unreasonable in all the circumstances as perceived by her should a court dismiss the defence.

C11.5.2.2 *Criminal Justice Act 1988*

Regarding the section 139A offence of having an article with a blade or point (or an offensive weapon) on school premises:

- school premises extend to surrounding land, playing fields, and yards;
- the offence can be committed when the school is closed;
- private schools' premises fall within the Act.

 See *Blackstone's Criminal Practice 2017* **B12.141–B12.191**

C11.6 Aggravated possession of bladed articles and offensive weapons

> ### Prevention of Crime Act 1953, s 1A
>
> #### 1A Offence of threatening with offensive weapon in public
>
> (1) A person is guilty of an offence if that person—
>   (a) has an offensive weapon with him or her in a public place,
>   (b) unlawfully and intentionally threatens another person with the weapon, and
>   (c) does so in such a way that there is an immediate risk of serious physical harm to that other person.
> (2) For the purposes of this section physical harm is serious if it amounts to grievous bodily harm for the purposes of the Offences against the Person Act 1861.
> (3) In this section 'public place' and 'offensive weapon' have the same meaning as in section 1.
>
> ...
>
> (5) Where a person aged 16 or over is convicted of an offence under this section, the court must impose an appropriate custodial sentence (with or without a fine) unless the court is of the opinion that there are particular circumstances which—
>   (a) relate to the offence or to the offender, and
>   (b) would make it unjust to do so in all the circumstances.

(6) In this section 'appropriate custodial sentence' means—

    (a) in the case of a person who is aged 18 or over when convicted, a sentence of imprisonment (or detention) for a term of at least 6 months;

    (b) in the case of a person who is aged at least 16 but under 18 when convicted, a detention and training order of at least 4 months.

(7) In considering whether it is of the opinion mentioned in subsection (5) in the case of a person aged under 18, the court must have regard to its duty under section 44 of the Children and Young Persons Act 1933.

...

(10) If on a person's trial for an offence under this section (whether on indictment or not) the person is found not guilty of that offence but it is proved that the person committed an offence under section 1, the person may be convicted of the offence under that section.

Criminal Justice Act 1988, s 139AA

139AA Offence of threatening with article with blade or point or offensive weapon

(1) A person is guilty of an offence if that person—

    (a) has an article to which this section applies with him or her in a public place or on school premises,

    (b) unlawfully and intentionally threatens another person with the article, and

    (c) does so in such a way that there is an immediate risk of serious physical harm to that other person.

(2) In relation to a public place this section applies to an article to which section 139 applies.

(3) In relation to school premises this section applies to each of these—

    (a) an article to which section 139 applies;

    (b) an offensive weapon within the meaning of section 1 of the Prevention of Crime Act 1953.

(4) For the purposes of this section physical harm is serious if it amounts to grievous bodily harm for the purposes of the Offences against the Person Act 1861.

(5) In this section—

    'public place' has the same meaning as in section 139;

    'school premises' has the same meaning as in section 139A.

(7) Where a person aged 16 or over is convicted of an offence under this section, the court must impose an appropriate custodial sentence (with or without a fine) unless the court is of the opinion that there are particular circumstances which—

    (a) relate to the offence or to the offender, and

    (b) would make it unjust to do so in all the circumstances.

(8) In this section 'appropriate custodial sentence' means—

    (a) in the case of a person who is aged 18 or over when convicted, a sentence of imprisonment (or detention) for a term of at least 6 months;

    (b) in the case of a person who is aged at least 16 but under 18 when convicted, a detention and training order of at least 4 months.

(9) In considering whether it is of the opinion mentioned in subsection (7) in the case of a person aged under 18, the court must have regard to its duty under section 44 of the Children and Young Persons Act 1933.

...

(12) If on a person's trial for an offence under this section (whether on indictment or not) the person is found not guilty of that offence but it is proved that the person committed an offence under section 139 or 139A, the person may be convicted of the offence under that section.

EW

 6 months' imprisonment and/or fine/4 years' imprisonment *but* with a minimum obligatory sentence unless it would be unjust in all the circumstances. In that situation community penalties may be imposed (s 305(4) Criminal Justice Act 2003). A 20 per cent reduction on that obligatory sentence is available for an early guilty plea, and there appears to be no statutory reason why a sentence on an adult should not be suspended.

C11.6.1 Key points

The defences available to the aggravated offences do not replicate those for the basic crimes.

C11.7 **Disorderly behaviour (harassment, alarm, or distress)**

Public Order Act 1986, s 5(1)

5 Harassment, alarm or distress

(1) A person is guilty of an offence if he—
   (a) uses threatening or abusive words or behaviour, or disorderly behaviour, or
   (b) displays any writing, sign or other visible representation which is threatening or abusive,

within the hearing or sight of a person likely to be caused harassment, alarm or distress thereby.

 Level 3 fine; level 4 fine if racially or religiously aggravated

C11.7.1 *Sentencing*

Offence seriousness (culpability and harm) A. Identify the appropriate starting point Starting points based on first-time offender pleading not guilty		
Examples of nature of activity	**Starting point**	**Range**
Shouting, causing disturbance for some minutes	Band A fine	Conditional discharge to Band B fine
Substantial disturbance caused	Band B fine	Band A fine to Band C fine

Offence seriousness (culpability and harm) B. Consider the effect of aggravating and mitigating factors (other than those within examples above) The following may be particularly relevant but these lists are not exhaustive	
Factors indicating higher culpability 1. Group action 2. Lengthy incident	**Factors indicating lower culpability** 1. Stopped as soon as police arrived 2. Brief/minor incident 3. Provocation
Factors indicating greater degree of harm 1. Vulnerable person(s) present 2. Offence committed at school, hospital, or other place where vulnerable persons may be present 3. Victim providing public service	

C11.7.2 Key points

• Section 5 provides:

Public Order Act 1986, s 5(3)

5 Harassment, alarm or distress

(3) It is a defence for the accused to prove—
  (a) that he had no reason to believe that there was any person within hearing or sight who was likely to be caused harassment, alarm or distress, or
  (b) that he was inside a dwelling and had no reason to believe that the words or behaviour used, or the writing, sign or other visible representation displayed, would be heard or seen by a person outside that or any other dwelling, or
  (c) that his conduct was reasonable.

• Section 6 provides:

Public Order Act 1986, s 6(4) and (5)

6 Mental element: miscellaneous

(4) A person is guilty of an offence under section 5 only if he intends his words or behaviour, or the writing, sign or other visible representation, to be threatening, abusive or insulting, or is aware that it may be threatening, abusive or insulting or (as the case may be) he intends his behaviour to be or is aware that it may be disorderly.

(5) For the purposes of this section a person whose awareness is impaired by intoxication shall be taken to be aware of that of which he would be aware if not intoxicated, unless he shows either that his intoxication was not self-induced or that it was caused solely by the taking or administration of a substance in the course of medical treatment.

• An offence under section 5 may be committed in a public or a private place, except that no offence is committed where the words or behaviour are used, or the writing, sign, or other visible representation is displayed, by a person inside a dwelling and the other person is also inside that or another dwelling.

• A person can be harassed without emotional upset (*Southard v Director of Public Prosecutions* [2006] EWHC 3449 (Admin)). In *Southard*, the defendant intervened in his brother's arrest, shouting 'fuck off' and 'fuck you' at the officer. The conviction was upheld. The harassment must not, however, be trivial (eg *R (R) v Director of Public Prosecutions* [2006] EWHC 1375 (Admin)— another case involving a police officer where the conviction was quashed).

- Concealing a video camera in a changing room can amount to disorderly behaviour (*Vigon v Director of Public Prosecutions* (1997) 162 JP 115).
- For considerations under the European Convention on Human Rights (and in particular Art 10 ECHR), see *Abdul and others v Crown Prosecution Service* [2011] EWHC 247 (Admin). The following principles emerge from Article 10 ECHR jurisprudence (para 49 of the judgment):

  (i) The starting point is the importance of the right to freedom of expression.

  (ii) In this regard, it must be recognized that legitimate protest can be offensive at least to some—and on occasions must be, if it is to have impact. Moreover, the right to freedom of expression would be unacceptably devalued if it did no more than protect those holding popular, mainstream views; it must plainly extend beyond that so that minority views can be freely expressed, even if distasteful. [The context of the remarks is a key factor.]

  (iii) The justification for interference with the right to freedom of expression must be convincingly established. Accordingly, while Article 10 does not confer an unqualified right to freedom of expression, the restrictions contained in Article 10.2 are to be narrowly construed.

  (iv) There is not and cannot be any universal test for resolving when speech goes beyond legitimate protest, so attracting the sanction of the criminal law. The justification for invoking the criminal law is the threat to public order. Inevitably, the context of the particular occasion will be of the first importance.

  (v) The relevance of the threat to public order should not be taken as meaning that the risk of violence by those reacting to the protest is, without more, determinative; sometimes it may be that protesters are to be protected. That said, in striking the right balance when determining whether speech is 'threatening, abusive or insulting', the focus on minority rights should not result in overlooking the rights of the majority.

  (vi) Plainly, if there is no prima facie case that speech was 'threatening, abusive or insulting' or that the other elements of the section 5 offence can be made good, then no question of prosecution will arise. However, even if there is otherwise a prima facie case for contending that an offence has been committed under section 5, it is still for the Crown to establish that prosecution is a proportionate response, necessary for the preservation of public order.

If the line between legitimate freedom of expression and a threat to public order has indeed been crossed, freedom of speech will not have been impaired by 'ruling ... out' threatening, abusive, or insulting speech.

• *Harvey v DPP* [2011] EWHC 3992 (Admin) confirms that it is not an offence under section 5 of the Public Order Act to use swear words in the presence of a police officer. The Crown must produce evidence of the likelihood of harassment, alarm, or distress. This cannot be implied for police officers or young people for whom they are a regular feature of life.

 See *Blackstone's Criminal Practice 2017* **B11.68–B11.82**

C11.8 Disorderly behaviour with intent to cause harassment, alarm, or distress

Public Order Act 1986, s 4A(1)

4A Intentional harassment, alarm or distress

(1) A person is guilty of an offence if, with intent to cause a person harassment, alarm or distress, he—

  (a) uses threatening, abusive or insulting words or behaviour, or disorderly behaviour, or

  (b) displays any writing, sign or other visible representation which is threatening, abusive or insulting,

thereby causing that or another person harassment, alarm or distress.

 6 months' imprisonment and/or fine

Note: racially or religiously aggravated offence is triable either way (2 years on indictment).

C11 Public Order

C11.8.1 *Sentencing*

Offence seriousness (culpability and harm) A. Identify the appropriate starting point Starting points based on first-time offender pleading not guilty		
Examples of nature of activity	**Starting point**	**Range**
Threats, abuse, or insults made more than once but on same occasion against the same person, eg while following down the street	Band C fine	Band B fine to low-level community order
Group action or deliberately planned action against targeted victim	Medium-level community order	Low-level community order to 12 weeks' custody
Weapon brandished or used or threats against vulnerable victim—course of conduct over longer period	12 weeks' custody	High-level community order to 26 weeks' custody

Offence seriousness (culpability and harm) B. Consider the effect of aggravating and mitigating factors (other than those within examples above) The following may be particularly relevant but these lists are not exhaustive	
Factors indicating higher culpability 1. High degree of planning 2. Offender deliberately isolates victim **Factors indicating greater degree of harm** 1. Offence committed in vicinity of victim's home 2. Large number of people in vicinity 3. Actual or potential escalation into violence 4. Particularly serious impact on victim	**Factors indicating lower culpability** 1. Very short period 2. Provocation

C11.8.2 Key points

• Section 4A(3) provides:

> **Public Order Act 1986, s 4A(3)**
>
> **4A Intentional harassment, alarm or distress**
>
> (3) It is a defence for the accused to prove—
>
> (a) that he was inside a dwelling and had no reason to believe that the words or behaviour used, or the writing, sign or other visible representation displayed, would be heard or seen by a person outside that or any other dwelling, or
>
> (b) that his conduct was reasonable.

• An offence under this section may be committed in a public or a private place, except that no offence is committed where the words or

behaviour are used, or the writing, sign, or other visible representation is displayed, by a person inside a dwelling and the person who is harassed, alarmed, or distressed is also inside that or another dwelling.
• For considerations under the European Convention on Human Rights (and in particular Art 10 ECHR), see *Abdul and others v Crown Prosecution Service* [2011] EWHC 247 (Admin).

 See *Blackstone's Criminal Practice 2017* **B11.60–11.68**

C11.9 Drunk and disorderly in a public place

> ### Criminal Justice Act 1967, s 91(1), (2), and (4)
>
> #### 91 Drunkenness in a public place
> (1) Any person who in any public place is guilty, while drunk, of disorderly behaviour … shall be liable on summary conviction to a fine not exceeding [level 3 on the standard scale].
> (2) The foregoing subsection shall have effect instead of any corresponding provision contained in section 12 of the Licensing Act 1872, section 58 of the Metropolitan Police Act 1839, section 37 of the City of London Police Act 1839, and section 29 of the Town Police Clauses Act 1847 (being enactments which authorise the imposition of a short term of imprisonment or of a fine not exceeding £10 or both for the corresponding offence) and instead of any corresponding provision contained in any local Act.
> (3) …
> (4) In this section 'public place' includes any highway and any other premises or place to which at the material time the public have or are permitted to have access, whether on payment or otherwise.

SO Level 3 fine

SO Summary only

C11.9.1 *Sentencing*

Note that this guideline is under review by the Sentencing Council (see **Appendix 7***).*

Offence seriousness (culpability and harm) A. Identify the appropriate starting point Starting points based on first-time offender pleading not guilty		
Examples of nature of activity	**Starting point**	**Range**
Shouting, causing disturbance for some minutes	Band A fine	Conditional discharge to band B fine
Substantial disturbance caused	Band B fine	Band A fine to band C fine

> Offence seriousness (culpability and harm)
> **B. Consider the effect of aggravating and mitigating factors (other than those within examples above)**
> The following may be particularly relevant but these lists are not exhaustive

Factors indicating higher culpability	Factors indicating lower culpability
1. Brandishing firearm	1. Firearm not in sight
2. Carrying firearm in a busy place	2. No intention to use firearm
3. Planned illegal use	3. Firearm to be used for lawful purpose
Factors indicating greater degree of harm	(not amounting to defence)
1. Person or people put in fear	
2. Offender participating in violent incident	

C11.9.2 Key points

• In *Carroll v Director of Public Prosecutions* [2009] EWHC 554 (Admin), the court stated that:

4. The offence requires proof of three elements, namely that (1) the defendant was drunk; (2) he was in a public place; and (3) he was guilty of disorderly behaviour. Only the first and third elements call for further comment:

...

9. As to the first element in *Neale v E (A Minor)* (1983) 80 Crim App R 20, this court (Robert Goff LJ and Mann J, as they each then were) decided that the word 'drunk' should be given its ordinary and natural meaning. In the end, therefore, whether a defendant was drunk is a simple question of fact in each case. On familiar principles it is the voluntary consumption of alcohol which is the requisite mens rea, such as it is, of this most basic offence. If that voluntary consumption results in the defendant becoming drunk then the first element of the offence is proved.

10. As to the third element, there is no requirement for mens rea at all. What is required is proof that objectively viewed the defendant was guilty of disorderly behaviour. Specific drunken intent and recklessness are nothing to the point. The words 'disorderly behaviour' are again to be given their ordinary and natural meaning. In the end, therefore, it is a simple question of fact in each case: whether the defendant is guilty of disorderly behaviour.

 See *Blackstone's Criminal Practice 2017* **B11.201–B11.205**

C11.10 **Firearms**

C11.10.1 *Possessing a prohibited weapon*

Firearms Act 1968 s 5(1)(b)

(1) A person commits an offence if, without the authority of the Defence Council he has in his possession, or purchases or acquires, or manufactures, sells or transfers—
  (b) any weapon of whatever description designed or adapted for the discharge of any noxious liquid, gas or other thing.

 6 months' imprisonment and/or fine/10 years' imprisonment

C11.10.1.2 Key points

This offence, usually used to prosecute those in possession of CS gas is a strict liability offence (*Deyemi* [2007] EWCA Crim, 2060). The fact of possession of the weapon must be proved but not necessarily knowledge of its contents (*Bradish* [1990] 1 All ER460).

Sentencing: There is no guideline for this offence. A fine is often imposed for possession of a CS gas container in the absence of any aggravating circumstances.

C11.10.2 *Carrying in public place*

Firearms Act 1968, s 19

19 Carrying a firearm in a public place
A person commits an offence if, without lawful authority or reasonable excuse (the proof whereof lies on him) he has with him in a public place—
(a) a loaded shot gun,
(b) an air weapon (whether loaded or not),
(c) any other firearm (whether loaded or not) together with ammunition suitable for use in that firearm, or
(d) an imitation firearm.

 (Summary only if an air weapon)

 6 months' imprisonment and/or fine/7 years' imprisonment (12 months if imitation weapon)

C11.10.2.1 *Sentencing*

Offence seriousness (culpability and harm) A. Identify the appropriate starting point Starting points based on first-time offender pleading not guilty		
Examples of nature of activity	**Starting point**	**Range**
Carrying an unloaded air weapon	Low-level community order	Band B fine to medium-level community order
Carrying loaded air weapon/ imitation firearm/ unloaded shot gun without ammunition	High-level community order	Medium-level community order to 26 weeks' custody (air weapon) Medium-level community order to Crown Court (imitation firearm, unloaded shot gun)
Carrying loaded shot gun/ carrying shot gun or any other firearm together with ammunition for it	Crown Court	Crown Court

Offence seriousness (culpability and harm) B. Consider the effect of aggravating and mitigating factors (other than those within examples above) The following may be particularly relevant but these lists are not exhaustive	
Factors indicating higher culpability 1. Brandishing firearm 2. Carrying firearm in a busy place 3. Planned illegal use **Factors indicating greater degree of harm** 1. Person or people put in fear 2. Offender participating in violent incident	**Factors indicating lower culpability** 1. Firearm not in sight 2. No intention to use firearm 3. Firearm to be used for lawful purpose (not amounting to defence)

C11.10.2.2 Key points

- It is not necessary to show that the defendant knew that a gun was loaded (*R v Harrison* [1996] Crim LR 200).
- An item is an imitation firearm if it 'looked like' a firearm at the time of its use (*R v Morris and King* (1984) 149 JP 60).
- A part of the body (eg fingers pointed under clothing) could not constitute an imitation firearm (*R v Bentham* [2005] UKHL 18).

 See *Blackstone's Criminal Practice 2017* **B12.108**

C11.11 Football-related offences

The Sporting Events (Control of Alcohol etc) Act 1985, section 2 concerns possession of alcohol whilst entering or trying to enter a designated sports ground (s 2(1)), and being drunk in, or whilst trying to enter, a sports ground (s 2(2)); the Football Offences Act 1991 covers throwing of missiles (s 2), indecent or racialist chanting (s 3), and going onto prohibited areas (s 4); and the Criminal Justice and Public Order Act 1994 deals with the unauthorised sale or attempted sale of tickets (s 166).

Sporting Events (Control of Alcohol etc) Act 1985, s 2(1), (1A), (2), and (3)

2 Offences in connection with alcohol, containers etc at sports grounds

(1) A person who has alcohol or an article to which this section applies in his possession—

    (a) at any time during the period of a designated sporting event when he is in any area of a designated sports ground from which the event may be directly viewed, or

    (b) while entering or trying to enter a designated sports ground at any time during the period of a designated sporting event at that ground,

is guilty of an offence.

(1A) Subsection (1)(a) above has effect subject to section 5A(1) of this Act.

(2) A person who is drunk in a designated sports ground at any time during the period of a designated sporting event at that ground or is drunk while entering or trying to enter such a ground at any time during the period of a designated sporting event at that ground is guilty of an offence.

(3) This section applies to any article capable of causing injury to a person struck by it, being—

    (a) a bottle, can or other portable container (including such an article when crushed or broken) which—

        (i) is for holding any drink, and

        (ii) is of a kind which, when empty, is normally discarded or returned to, or left to be recovered by, the supplier, or

    (b) part of an article falling within paragraph (a) above;

but does not apply to anything that is for holding any medicinal product (within the meaning of the Medicines Act 1968) or any veterinary medicinal product (within the meaning of the Veterinary Medicines Regulations 2006).

Football Offences Act 1991, ss 2, 3, and 4

2 Throwing of missiles

It is an offence for a person at a designated football match to throw anything at or towards—

(a) the playing area, or any area adjacent to the playing area to which spectators are not generally admitted, or

(b) any area in which spectators or other persons are or may be present, without lawful authority or lawful excuse (which shall be for him to prove).

3 Indecent or racialist chanting

(1) It is an offence to engage or take part in chanting of an indecent or racialist nature at a designated football match.

(2) For this purpose—

(a) 'chanting' means the repeated uttering of any words or sounds (whether alone or in concert with one or more others); and

(b) 'of a racialist nature' means consisting of or including matter which is threatening, abusive or insulting to a person by reason of his colour, race, nationality (including citizenship) or ethnic or national origins.

4 Going onto the playing area

It is an offence for a person at a designated football match to go onto the playing area, or any area adjacent to the playing area to which spectators are not generally admitted, without lawful authority or lawful excuse (which shall be for him to prove).

Criminal Justice and Public Order Act 1994, s 166

166 Sale of tickets by unauthorised persons

(1) It is an offence for an unauthorised person to—

(a) sell a ticket for a designated football match, or

(b) otherwise to dispose of such a ticket to another person.

(2) For this purpose—

(a) a person is 'unauthorised' unless he is authorised in writing to sell or otherwise dispose of tickets for the match by the organisers of the match;

(aa) a reference to selling a ticket includes a reference to—

(i) offering to sell a ticket;

(ii) exposing a ticket for sale;

(iii) making a ticket available for sale by another;

(iv) advertising that a ticket is available for purchase; and

(v) giving a ticket to a person who pays or agrees to pay for some other goods or services or offering to do so.

(b) a 'ticket' means anything which purports to be a ticket;

...

SO

3 months' imprisonment/level 3 fine (s 2(1) offence), level 2 fine (s 2(2) offence)

Level 3 fine (throwing missile; indecent or racialist chanting; going onto prohibited areas)

Fine (unauthorised sale of tickets)

Level 3 fine and/or 3 months' imprisonment (possession of alcohol)

C11.11.1 *Sentencing*

Note that this guideline is under review by the Sentencing Council (see **Appendix 7***).*

Offence seriousness (culpability and harm) A. Identify the appropriate starting point Starting points based on first-time offender pleading not guilty		
Examples of nature of activity	**Starting point**	**Range**
Being drunk in, or whilst trying to enter, ground	Band A fine	Conditional discharge to band B fine
Going onto playing or other prohibited area; unauthorised sale or attempted sale of tickets	Band B fine	Band A fine to band C fine
Throwing missile; indecent or racialist chanting	Band C fine	Band C fine
Possession of alcohol whilst entering or trying to enter ground	Band C fine	Band B fine to high-level community order

Offence seriousness (culpability and harm) B. Consider the effect of aggravating and mitigating factors (other than those within examples above) The following may be particularly relevant but these lists are not exhaustive
Factors indicating higher culpability 1. Commercial ticket operation; potential high cash value; counterfeit tickets 2. Inciting others to misbehave 3. Possession of large quantity of alcohol 4. Offensive language or behaviour (where not an element of the offence) **Factor indicating greater degree of harm** 1. Missile likely to cause serious injury, eg coin, glass, bottle, stone

See *Blackstone's Criminal Practice 2017* **B11.129–B11.132** and **B11.211–B11.215**

C11.12 Threatening behaviour, fear, or provocation of violence

Public Order Act 1986, ss 4(1), 6(3) and (5)

4 Fear or provocation of violence

(1) A person is guilty of an offence if he—
    (a) uses towards another person threatening, abusive or insulting words or behaviour, or
    (b) distributes or displays to another person any writing, sign or other visible representation which is threatening, abusive or insulting,
    with intent to cause that person to believe that immediate unlawful violence will be used against him or another by any person, or to provoke the immediate use of unlawful violence by that person or another, or whereby that person is likely to believe that such violence will be used or it is likely that such violence will be provoked.

...

6 Mental element: miscellaneous

(3) A person is guilty of an offence under section 4 only if he intends his words or behaviour, or the writing, sign or other visible representation, to be threatening, abusive or insulting, or is aware that it may be threatening, abusive or insulting.

...

(5) For the purposes of this section a person whose awareness is impaired by intoxication shall be taken to be aware of that of which he would be aware if not intoxicated, unless he shows either that his intoxication was not self-induced or that it was caused solely by the taking or administration of a substance in the course of medical treatment.

SO (Racially or religiously aggravated offence is triable either way)

▥ 6 months' imprisonment and/or fine. Racially or religiously aggravated offence carries a maximum 2 years' imprisonment on indictment

C11.12.1 *Sentencing*

Offence seriousness (culpability and harm) A. Identify the appropriate starting point Starting points based on first-time offender pleading not guilty		
Examples of nature of activity	**Starting point**	**Range**
Fear or threat of low-level immediate unlawful violence such as push, shove, or spit	Low-level community order	Band B fine to medium-level community order

Fear or threat of medium-level immediate unlawful violence such as punch	High-level community order	Low-level community order to 12 weeks' custody
Fear or threat of high-level immediate unlawful violence such as use of weapon; missile thrown; gang involvement	12 weeks' custody	6 to 26 weeks' custody

Offence seriousness (culpability and harm)
B. Consider the effect of aggravating and mitigating factors (other than those within examples above)
The following may be particularly relevant but these lists are not exhaustive

Factors indicating higher culpability	Factors indicating lower
1. Planning	culpability
2. Offender deliberately isolates victim	1. Impulsive action
3. Group action	2. Short duration
4. Threat directed at victim because of job	3. Provocation
5. History of antagonism towards victim	
Factors indicating greater degree of harm	
1. Offence committed at school, hospital, or other place where vulnerable persons may be present	
2. Offence committed on enclosed premises such as public transport	
3. Vulnerable victim(s)	
4. Victim needs medical help/counselling	

C11.12.2 Key points

- An offence under section 4 may be committed in a public or a private place, except that no offence is committed where the words or behaviour are used, or the writing, sign, or other visible representation is distributed or displayed, by a person inside a dwelling and the other person is also inside that or another dwelling.
- Subject to the Crown proving the use of threatening, etc words/behaviour and the mens rea, *Winn v DPP* (1992) 156 JP 881 confirmed that there are four ways in which the offence can be committed:
  - by intending to cause the person against whom the conduct is directed to believe that immediate unlawful violence will be used against him or another;
  - by intending to provoke the immediate use of unlawful violence by that person or another;
  - the person against whom the conduct is directed being likely to believe that immediate unlawful violence will be used; or
  - its being likely that immediate unlawful violence will be provoked.

C11 Public Order

- Actions taken in self-defence do not amount to unlawful violence.
- For the conduct to be used towards another, that other must be physically present (*Atkin v DPP* (1989) 89 Cr App R 199).
- The need for immediate unlawful violence means that it cannot be at some uncertain future time (*Horseferry Road Stipendiary Magistrate, ex p Siadatan* [1991] 1 QB 260), but it does not mean that it has to be instantaneous.
- For considerations under the European Convention on Human Rights (and in particular Art 10 ECHR), see *Abdul and others v Crown Prosecution Service* [2011] EWHC 247 (Admin).

 See *Blackstone's Criminal Practice 2017* **B11.47–B11.58**

C11.13 Taxi touting/soliciting for hire

Criminal Justice and Public Order Act 1994, s. 167

 Level 4 fine

 Sentence

C11.13.1 *Sentencing*

*Note that this guideline is under review by the Sentencing Council (see **Appendix 7**).*

Offence seriousness (culpability and harm) A. Identify the appropriate starting point Starting points based on first-time offender pleading not guilty		
Examples of nature of activity	**Starting point**	**Range**
Licensed taxi-driver touting for trade (ie making approach rather than waiting for a person to initiate hiring)	Band A fine	Conditional discharge to band A fine and consider disqualification 1–3 months
PHV licence held but touting for trade rather than being booked through an operator; an accomplice to touting	Band B fine	Band A fine to band C fine and consider disqualification 3–6 months
No PHV licence held	Band C fine	Band B fine to band C fine and disqualification 6–12 months

Offence seriousness (culpability and harm)
B. Consider the effect of aggravating and mitigating factors (other than those within examples above)
The following may be particularly relevant but these lists are not exhaustive

Factors indicating higher culpability	**Factor indicating lower culpability**
1. Commercial business/large-scale operation	1. Providing a service when no licensed taxi available
2. No insurance/invalid insurance	
3. No driving licence and/or no MOT	
4. Vehicle not roadworthy	
Factors indicating greater degree of harm	
1. Deliberately diverting trade from taxi rank	
2. PHV licence had been refused/offender ineligible for licence	

C11.13.2 Key points

Touting requires some form of invitation to a prospective hirer (*R (Oddy) v Bugbugs Ltd* [2003] EWHC 2865(Admin)).

C12 Road Traffic Offences—Definitions

C12.1 Accident

'Accident' is to be given its ordinary meaning (*Chief Constable of West Midlands v Billingham* [1979] 1 WLR 747). A deliberate act can amount to an accident (*Chief Constable of Staffordshire v Lees* [1981] RTR 506). A physical impact is not necessary (*R v Currie* [2007] EWCA Crim 927), but the *de minimis* principle applies (*R v Morris* [1972] 1 WLR 228).

C12.2 Causing

Causing requires a positive act (*Ross Hillman Ltd v Bond* [1974] QB 435) committed with prior knowledge.

C12.3 Driver

Section 192(1) of the Road Traffic Act 1988 provides:

> **Road Traffic Act 1988, s 192(1)**
>
> **192 General interpretation of Act**
>
> (1) ...
>
> 'driver', where a separate person acts as a steersman of a motor vehicle, includes (except for the purposes of section 1 of this Act) that person as well as any other person engaged in the driving of the vehicle, and 'drive' is to be interpreted accordingly,
>
> ...

A person supervising a driver will not be a driver unless he exercises some control over the vehicle (eg dual controls) (*Evans v Walkden* [1956] 1 WLR 1019).

C12.4 Driving

R v MacDonagh [1974] QB 448 defined 'driving' as use of the driver's controls for the purpose of directing the movement of the vehicle. The court gave the following guidance:

> There are an infinite number of ways in which a person may control the movement of a motor vehicle, apart from the orthodox one of sitting in the driving seat and using the engine for propulsion. He may be coasting down a hill with the gears in neutral and the engine switched off; he may be steering a vehicle which is being towed by another. As has already been

pointed out, he may be sitting in the driving seat whilst others push, or half sitting in the driving seat but keeping one foot on the road in order to induce the car to move. Finally, as in the present case, he may be standing in the road and himself pushing the car with or without using the steering wheel to direct it. Although the word 'drive' must be given a wide meaning, the Courts must be alert to see that the net is not thrown so widely that it includes activities which cannot be said to be driving a motor vehicle in any ordinary use of that word in the English language.

As a person may be driving a stationary vehicle, it is a matter of fact to be decided in each case, and factors such as the reason for the vehicle stopping and the duration of the stop will be relevant (*Planton v Director of Public Prosecutions* [2002] RTR 107).

Steering a vehicle being towed would amount to driving where there was an operational braking system (*McQuaid v Anderton* [1981] 1 WLR 154), as would freewheeling a vehicle down a hill while steering (*Saycell v Bool* [1948] 2 All ER 83). A person steering from the passenger seat is driving (*Tyler v Whatmore* [1976] RTR 83).

C12.5 In charge

In cases where the matter is not clear, the case of *Director of Public Prosecutions v Watkins* (1989) 89 Cr App R 112 should be considered in detail. The court laid down the following broad guidance:

Broadly there are two distinct classes of case. (1) If the defendant is the owner or lawful possessor of the vehicle or has recently driven it, he will have been in charge of it, and the question for the Court will be whether he is still in charge or whether he has relinquished his charge. Usually such a defendant will be prima facie in charge unless he has put the vehicle in someone else's charge. However, he would not be so if in all the circumstances he has ceased to be in actual control and there is no realistic possibility of his resuming actual control while unfit: eg if he is at home in bed for the night, if he is a great distance from the car, or if it is taken by another.

(2) If the defendant is not the owner, the lawful possessor, or recent driver but is sitting in the vehicle or is otherwise involved with it, the question for the Court is, as here, whether he has assumed being in charge of it. In this class of case the defendant will be in charge if, whilst unfit, he is voluntarily in de facto control of the vehicle or if, in the circumstances, including his position, his intentions and his actions, he may be expected imminently to assume control. Usually this will involve his having gained entry to the car and evinced an intention to take control of it. But gaining entry may not be necessary if he has manifested that intention some other way, eg by stealing the keys of a car in circumstances which show he means presently to drive it.

The circumstances to be taken into account will vary infinitely, but the following will be usually relevant:

(i)   Whether and where he is in the vehicle or how far he is from it.

(ii) What he is doing at the relevant time.

(iii) Whether he is in possession of a key that fits the ignition.

(iv) Whether there is evidence of an intention to take or assert control of the car by driving or otherwise

(v) Whether any other person is in, at or near the vehicle and if so, the like particulars in respect of that person.

It will be for the Court to consider all the above factors with any others which may be relevant and reach its decision as a question of fact and degree.

C12.6 Motor vehicle

There is no statutory definition of 'vehicle' and therefore its ordinary meaning of a carriage or conveyance should apply. Where the statute uses the phrase 'motor vehicle', the definition to be found in section 185 of the Road Traffic Act 1988 states that it is a 'mechanically propelled vehicle intended or adapted for use on roads'. The maximum speed of the vehicle is not a relevant factor (*Director of Public Prosecutions v King* [2008] EWHC 447 (Admin)). Section 20(1)(b) of the Chronically Sick and Disabled Persons Act 1970 means that a mechanically propelled invalid carriage, provided that it complies with the prescribed requirements and is being used in accordance with the prescribed conditions, is not a 'motor vehicle' for all the purposes of the Road Traffic Act 1988 save for the sole and specific exception of section 22A, and is thus excluded from the ambit of the nine sections of the 1988 Act that apply to mechanically propelled vehicles, including offences of driving with excess alcohol (*Croitoru v Crown Prosecution Service* [2016] EWHC 1645 (Admin)).

C12.7 Owner

This includes a person in possession of a vehicle under a hire or hire-purchase agreement.

C12.8 Permitting

A person permits use when he allows or authorizes use, or fails to take reasonable steps to prevent use. For permitting use with no insurance, the prosecution do not need to show that the person knew the driver to be uninsured. If, however, use is conditional (eg on the person having insurance), the outcome would be different (*Newbury v Davis* [1974] RTR 367).

C12.9 Public place

This is a place to which the public have access. However, the law draws a distinction between general public access and access for a defined group of persons. The law in this area is complex and voluminous, and advocates should always seek an adjournment where the answer is not clear.

C12.10 Road

This is defined as any highway or road to which the public have access. The following have been held to be a road:

- pedestrian pavement (*Randall v Motor Insurers' Bureau* [1968] 1 WLR 1900);
- grass verge at the side of a road (*Worth v Brooks* [1959] Crim LR 855);
- bridges over which a road passes.

It will be a matter of fact and degree as to whether something is a road, and whether or not the public have access. A car park will not generally be a road, even if there are roads running through it. In *Barrett v Director of Public Prosecutions*, 10 February 2009, the court held that a roadway running through a private caravan park, and facilitating entry to a beach, constituted a road.

A vehicle will be 'on' a road when part of the vehicle protrudes over a road (*Avery v Crown Prosecution Service* [2011] EWHC 2388 (Admin)).

C12.11 Highway

This is defined as land over which there is a right of way on foot, by riding, or with vehicles and cattle. A highway includes: bridleways, footpaths, footways, walkways, carriageways, and driftways.

 See generally *Blackstone's Criminal Practice 2017* **C1**

C13 **Road Traffic Offences**

C13.1 Careless driving (drive without due care and attention)

Road Traffic Act 1988, s 3

3 Careless, and inconsiderate, driving

If a person drives a mechanically propelled vehicle on a road or other public place without due care and attention, or without reasonable consideration for other persons using the road or place, he is guilty of an offence.

 Fine. Must endorse and may disqualify. If no disqualification, impose 3–9 points

C13.1.1 *Sentencing*

Note that this guideline is under review by the Sentencing Council (see **Appendix 7***).*

Offence seriousness (culpability and harm) A. Identify the appropriate starting point Starting points based on first-time offender pleading not guilty		
Example of nature of activity	**Starting point**	**Range**
Momentary lapse of concentration or misjudgement at low speed	Band A fine	Band A fine 3–4 points
Loss of control due to speed, mishandling, or insufficient attention to road conditions, or carelessly turning right across oncoming traffic	Band B fine	Band B fine 5–6 points
Overtaking manoeuvre at speed resulting in collision of vehicles, or driving bordering on the dangerous	Band C fine	Band C fine Consider disqualification OR 7–9 points

Careless driving (drive without due care and attention) C13.1

Offence seriousness (culpability and harm)
B. Consider the effect of aggravating and mitigating factors (other than those within examples above)
The following may be particularly relevant but these lists are not exhaustive

Factors indicating higher culpability	Factors indicating lower culpability
1. Excessive speed	1. Minor risk
2. Carrying out other tasks while driving	2. Inexperience of driver
3. Carrying passengers or heavy load	3. Sudden change in road or weather conditions
4. Tiredness	
Factors indicating greater degree of harm	
1. Injury to others	
2. Damage to other vehicles or property	
3. High level of traffic or pedestrians in vicinity	
4. Location, eg near school when children are likely to be present	

C13.1.2 Key points

- Careless driving is defined in the Act.
- Section 3ZA(2)–(4) of the Road Traffic Act 1988 provides:

Road Traffic Act 1988, s 3ZA(2)–(4)

3ZA Meaning of careless, or inconsiderate, driving

...

(2) A person is to be regarded as driving without due care and attention if (and only if) the way he drives falls below what would be expected of a competent and careful driver.

(3) In determining for the purposes of subsection (2) above what would be expected of a careful and competent driver in a particular case, regard shall be had not only to the circumstances of which he could be expected to be aware but also to any circumstances shown to have been within the knowledge of the accused.

(4) A person is to be regarded as driving without reasonable consideration for other persons only if those persons are inconvenienced by his driving.

- Examples of careless or inconsiderate driving:
  Careless driving
  - overtaking on the inside or driving inappropriately close to another vehicle;
  - inadvertent mistakes, such as driving through a red light or emerging from a side road into the path of another vehicle;
  - short distractions such as tuning a car radio.

Inconsiderate driving
- flashing of lights to force other drivers in front to give way;
- misuse of any lane to avoid queuing or to gain some other advantage over other drivers;
- driving that inconveniences other road users or causes unnecessary hazards, such as unnecessarily remaining in an overtaking lane, unnecessarily slow driving or braking without good cause, driving with undipped headlights which dazzle oncoming drivers, or driving through a puddle causing pedestrians to be splashed.

- If death has resulted from the driving, any trial should await the conclusion of any inquest (*Smith v Director of Public Prosecutions* [2000] RTR 36).
- Failure to drive in accordance with the Highway Code will generally amount to careless driving.
- An offence of careless driving can be tried alongside an offence of dangerous driving as an alternative. However, it is not clear as to why this is done in the magistrates' court, as the offence is a statutory alternative in any event.
- If the facts are such that in the absence of an explanation put forward by the defendant, or where that explanation is objectively inadequate, the only possible conclusion is that he was careless, he should be convicted (*Director of Public Prosecutions v Cox* (1993) 157 JP 1044).
- A court does not need to consider an alternative inference from facts, such as mechanical defect, without hearing evidence of the same (*Director of Public Prosecutions v Tipton* (1992) 156 JP 172).

 See *Blackstone's Criminal Practice 2017* **C6.1–C6.8**

C13.2 Causing death by disqualified, careless, unlicensed, or uninsured driving

Road Traffic Act 1988, ss 2B, 3ZB, and 3ZC

Causing death by:
- disqualified driving;
- careless or inconsiderate driving;
- unlicensed, or uninsured drivers.

Causing death by disqualified, careless driving C13.2

- Note: causing death by disqualified driving is triable only on indictment;
- Causing death by careless, etc driving: 6 months' imprisonment and/or a fine/5 years' imprisonment;
- Causing death by unlicensed or uninsured driving: 6 months' imprisonment and /or fine/2 years' imprisonment);
- Minimum disqualification of 12 months, discretionary retest, 3–11 penalty points.

C13.2.1 *Sentencing*

Death by careless or inconsiderate driving

Nature of offence	Starting point	Sentencing range
Careless or inconsiderate driving falling not far short of dangerous driving	15 months' custody	36 weeks to 3 years' custody
Other cases of careless or inconsiderate driving	36 weeks' custody	Community order (HIGH) to 2 years' custody
Careless or inconsiderate driving arising from momentary inattention with no aggravating factors	Community order (MEDIUM)	Community order (LOW) to community order (HIGH)

Additional aggravating factors	Additional mitigating factors
1. Other offences committed at the same time, such as driving other than in accordance with the terms of a valid licence; driving while disqualified; driving without insurance; taking a vehicle without consent; driving a stolen vehicle 2. Previous convictions for motoring offences, particularly offences that involve bad driving 3. More than one person was killed as a result of the offence 4. Serious injury to one or more persons in addition to the death(s) 5. Irresponsible behaviour, such as failing to stop or falsely claiming that one of the victims was responsible for the collision	1. Offender was seriously injured in the collision 2. The victim was a close friend or relative 3. The actions of the victim or a third party contributed to the commission of the offence 4. The offender's lack of driving experience contributed significantly to the likelihood of a collision 5. The driving was in response to a proven and genuine emergency falling short of a defence

Causing death by unlicensed, disqualified, or uninsured drivers

Nature of offence	Starting point	Sentencing range
The offender was disqualified from driving; OR The offender was unlicensed or uninsured plus two or more aggravating factors from the list below	12 months' custody	36 weeks to 2 years' custody

The offender was unlicensed or uninsured plus at least one aggravating factor from the list below	26 weeks' custody	Community order (HIGH) to 36 weeks' custody
The offender was unlicensed or uninsured—no aggravating factors	Community order (MEDIUM)	Community order (LOW) to community order (HIGH)

Additional aggravating factors	Additional mitigating factors
1. Previous convictions for motoring offences, whether involving bad driving or involving an offence of the same kind that forms part of the present conviction (ie unlicensed, disqualified, or uninsured driving)	1. The decision to drive was brought about by a proven and genuine emergency falling short of a defence
2. More than one person was killed as a result of the offence	2. The offender genuinely believed that he or she was insured or licensed to drive
3. Serious injury to one or more persons in addition to the death(s)	3. The offender was seriously injured as a result of the collision
4. Irresponsible behaviour such as failing to stop or falsely claiming that someone else was driving	4. The victim was a close friend or relative

C13.2.2 Key points

- Death must result from the act of driving but need not occur at the same time as the incident (*R v Jenkins* [2012] EWCA Crim 2909; dangerous parking).
- The driving must be more than a minimal cause of the death.
- Where the driver is faultless and the total responsibility for the death lies with the deceased, no offence is committed under section 3ZB (*R v Hughes* [2013] UKSC 56). *R v MH* [2011] EWCA Crim 1508 suggests it is open to the defence to argue that the defendant's contribution to the death was no more than minimal where, for example, in a stationary car or where the victim would have died anyway, say, because of a new act intervening.
- See *R v Coe* [2009] EWCA Crim 1452 in relation to the admission of samples taken in relation to alcohol.

 See *Blackstone's Criminal Practice 2017* **C3**

C13.3 Causing serious injury by dangerous driving or by disqualified driving

Road Traffic Act 1988, s 1A

1A Causing serious injury by dangerous driving

(1) A person who causes serious injury to another person by driving a mechanically propelled vehicle dangerously on a road or other public place is guilty of an offence.
(2) In this section 'serious injury' means—
   (a) in England and Wales, physical harm which amounts to grievous bodily harm for the purposes of the Offences against the Person Act 1861,
   (b) ...

C13.3.1 *Causing serious injury by disqualified driving*

Road Traffic Act 1988, s 3ZD

(1) A person is guilty of an offence under this section if he or she—
   (a) causes serious injury to another person by driving a motor vehicle on a road, and
   (b) at that time, is committing an offence under section 103(1)(b) of this Act (driving while disqualified).
(2) In this section 'serious injury' means—
   (a) in England and Wales, physical harm which amounts to grievous bodily harm for the purposes of the Offences against the Person Act 1861.

EW

- Dangerous driving: 6 months' imprisonment and/or fine/5 years' imprisonment
- Disqualified driving: 6 months' imprisonment and/or fine/ 4 years' imprisonment

Obligatory disqualification for 12 months (with obligatory retest if dangerous driving). If no disqualification then 3–11 penalty points

C13.3.2 Key points

- Dangerous driving is defined by section 2A of the Road Traffic Act 1988. See **C13.4.2**.
- This provision applies to driving only on or after 3 December 2012.
- There is no specific sentencing guideline, but there have been decisions where there have been convictions under section 20 of the Offences Against the Person Act 1861.

 See *Blackstone's Criminal Practice 2017* **C3.33**

C13.4 Dangerous driving

Road Traffic Act 1988, s 2

2 Dangerous driving

A person who drives a mechanically propelled vehicle dangerously on a road or other public place is guilty of an offence.

 EW

 6 months' imprisonment and/or fine/2 years' imprisonment. Must endorse and disqualify for a minimum period of 12 months; must order extended retest; must disqualify for at least 2 years if offender has had two or more disqualifications for periods of 56 days or more in preceding 3 years

C13.4.1 *Sentencing*

Offence seriousness (culpability and harm) A. Identify the appropriate starting point Starting points based on first-time offender pleading not guilty		
Example of nature of activity	**Starting point**	**Range**
Single incident where little or no damage or risk of personal injury	Medium-level community order	Low-level community order to high-level community order Disqualify 12–15 months
Incident(s) involving excessive speed or showing off, especially on busy roads or in built-up area; OR Single incident where little or no damage or risk of personal injury but offender was disqualified driver	12 weeks' custody	High-level community order to 26 weeks' custody Disqualify 15–24 months

Prolonged bad driving involving deliberate disregard for safety of others; OR Incident(s) involving excessive speed or showing off, especially on busy roads or in built-up area, by disqualified driver; OR Driving as described in box above while being pursued by police	Crown Court	Crown Court

Offence seriousness (culpability and harm) **B. Consider the effect of aggravating and mitigating factors (other than those within examples above)** **The following may be particularly relevant but these lists are not exhaustive**	
Factors indicating higher culpability 1. Disregarding warnings of others 2. Evidence of alcohol or drugs 3. Carrying out other tasks while driving 4. Carrying passengers or heavy load 5. Tiredness 6. Aggressive driving, such as driving much too close to vehicle in front, racing, inappropriate attempts to overtake, or cutting in after overtaking 7. Driving when knowingly suffering from a medical condition which significantly impairs the offender's driving skills 8. Driving a poorly maintained or dangerously loaded vehicle, especially where motivated by commercial concerns **Factors indicating greater degree of harm** 1. Injury to others 2. Damage to other vehicles or property	**Factors indicating lower culpability** 1. Genuine emergency 2. Speed not excessive 3. Offence due to inexperience rather than irresponsibility of driver

C13.4.2 Key points

- The Road Traffic Act 1988, section 2A provides:

Road Traffic Act 1988, s 2A

2A Meaning of dangerous driving

(1) For the purposes of sections 1 and 2 above a person is to be regarded as driving dangerously if (and, subject to subsection (2) below, only if)—
  (a) the way he drives falls far below what would be expected of a competent and careful driver, and
  (b) it would be obvious to a competent and careful driver that driving in that way would be dangerous.
(2) A person is also to be regarded as driving dangerously for the purposes of sections 1 and 2 above if it would be obvious to a competent and careful driver that driving the vehicle in its current state would be dangerous.

C13 Road Traffic Offences

> (3) In subsections (1) and (2) above 'dangerous' refers to danger either of injury to any person or of serious damage to property; and in determining for the purposes of those subsections what would be expected of, or obvious to, a competent and careful driver in a particular case, regard shall be had not only to the circumstances of which he could be expected to be aware but also to any circumstances shown to have been within the knowledge of the accused.
> (4) In determining for the purposes of subsection (2) above the state of a vehicle, regard may be had to anything attached to or carried on or in it and to the manner in which it is attached or carried.

- The special skill (or indeed lack of skill) of a driver is an irrelevant circumstance when considering whether the driving is dangerous (*R v Bannister* [2009] EWCA Crim 1571).
- The fact that the defendant had consumed alcohol is an admissible factor (*R v Webster* [2006] 2 Cr App R 103). Where drink is a major plank of the prosecution case, advocates should have regard to *R v McBride* [1962] 2 QB 167.
- Where a vehicle's dangerous state is due to its official design and not use, it will not usually be appropriate to prosecute (*R v Marchant* [2004] 1 All ER 1187).
- A vehicle is being driven in a dangerous state if the driver is aware that his ability to control the vehicle might be impaired such that the standard of his driving might fall below the requisite standard (*R v Marison* [1997] RTR 457).

 See *Blackstone's Criminal Practice 2017* **C3.39**

C13.5 Driving whilst disqualified

Road Traffic Act 1988, s 103(1)

103 Obtaining licence, or driving, while disqualified

(1) A person is guilty of an offence if, while disqualified for holding or obtaining a licence, he—
  (a) obtains a licence, or
  (b) drives a motor vehicle on a road.
...

SO

 6 months' imprisonment and/or fine. Must endorse and may disqualify. If no disqualification, impose 6 points

C13.5.1 *Sentencing*

*Note that this guideline is under review by the Sentencing Council (see **Appendix 7**).*

Offence seriousness (culpability and harm) A. Identify the appropriate starting point Starting points based on first-time offender pleading not guilty		
Example of nature of activity	**Starting point**	**Range**
Full period expired but retest not taken	Low-level community order	Band C fine to medium-level community order 6 points or disqualify for 3–6 months
Lengthy period of ban already served	High-level community order	Medium-level community order to 12 weeks custody Lengthen disqualification for 6–12 months beyond expiry of current ban
Recently imposed ban	12 weeks' custody	High-level community order to 26 weeks' custody Lengthen disqualification for 12–18 months beyond expiry of current ban

C13.5.2 Key points

- The prosecution do not need to prove that the defendant was aware of the prosecution that led to his being disqualified (*Taylor v Kenyon* [1952] 2 All ER 726); this is the case even where a driving licence has been returned to the defendant by mistake (*R v Bowsher* [1972] RTR 202). If the defendant was genuinely unaware of the disqualification and had no reason to anticipate one, prosecution is unlikely and an absolute discharge likely if one proceeds.
- Strict proof that the person disqualified by the court is the person now charged is required. This will normally arise from (a) admission, (b) fingerprints, (c) evidence of identity from someone in court when the disqualification was made (*R v Derwentside Justices, ex p Heaviside* [1996] RTR 384). Other evidence such as an unusual name will at least raise a prima facie case that the defendant will need to answer in order to avoid conviction (*Olakunori v Director of Public Prosecutions* [1998] COD 443).
- An admission made whilst giving evidence is sufficient to prove a disqualification, even in the absence of a certificate of conviction (*Moran v Crown Prosecution Service* (2000) 164 JP 562).
- A defendant's silence in interview (where he did not later rely on any fact) and his general attitude to the management of the case in accordance with the Criminal Procedure Rules, could not

provide sufficient proof (*Mills v Director of Public Prosecutions* [2008] EWHC 3304 (Admin)).

- Consistency of personal details will normally be sufficient to raise a prima facie case. If the defendant calls no evidence to contradict that prima facie case, it will be open to the court to be satisfied that identity is proved (*Pattison v Director of Public Prosecutions* [2006] RTR 13).
- A solicitor could be called as a witness to confirm identity, although the practice is discouraged (*R (Howe) v South Durham Magistrates' Court* [2005] RTR 4).
- A mistaken belief by the defendant that he was not driving on a road will not amount to a defence (*R v Miller* [1975] 1 WLR 1222).
- The fact that a disqualification was later quashed on appeal does not provide a defence (*R v Thames Magistrates' Court, ex p Levy*, The Times, 17 July 1997).
- A bad character application in relation to the disqualification is not necessary as it has to do with the facts of the alleged offence (Criminal Justice Act 2003, s 98) (*Director of Public Prosecutions v Agyemang* [2009] EWHC 1542 (Admin)).

 See *Blackstone's Criminal Practice 2017* **C6.40–C6.45**

C13.6 **Excess alcohol/Excess drugs**

Road Traffic Act 1988, s 5(1) and 5A

5 Driving or being in charge of a motor vehicle with alcohol concentration above prescribed limit

(1) If a person—
   (a) drives or attempts to drive a motor vehicle on a road or other public place, or
   (b) is in charge of a motor vehicle on a road or other public place, after consuming so much alcohol that the proportion of it in his breath, blood, or urine exceeds the prescribed limit he is guilty of an offence.

...

5A Driving or being in charge of a motor vehicle with concentration of specified controlled drug above specified limit.

(1) This section applies where a person ('D')—
   (a) drives or attempts to drive a motor vehicle on a road or other public place, or
   (b) is in charge of a motor vehicle on a road or other public place, and there is in D's body a specified controlled drug.
(2) D is guilty of an offence if the proportion of the drug in D's blood or urine exceeds the specified limit for that drug.

(3) It is a defence for a person ('D') charged with an offence under this section to show that—
  (a) the specified controlled drug had been prescribed or supplied to D for medical or dental purposes,
  (b) D took the drug in accordance with any directions given by the person by whom the drug was prescribed or supplied, and with any accompanying instructions (so far as consistent with any such directions) given by the manufacturer or distributor of the drug, and
  (c) D's possession of the drug immediately before taking it was not unlawful under section 5(1) of the Misuse of Drugs Act 1971 (restriction of possession of controlled drugs) because of an exemption in regulations made under section 7 of that Act (authorisation of activities otherwise unlawful under foregoing provisions).

(4) The defence in subsection (3) is not available if D's actions were—
  (a) contrary to any advice, given by the person by whom the drug was prescribed or supplied, about the amount of time that should elapse between taking the drug and driving a motor vehicle, or
  (b) contrary to any accompanying instructions about that matter (so far as consistent with any such advice) given by the manufacturer or distributor of the drug.

(5) If evidence is adduced that is sufficient to raise an issue with respect to the defence in subsection (3), the court must assume that the defence is satisfied unless the prosecution proves beyond reasonable doubt that it is not.

(6) It is a defence for a person ('D') charged with an offence by virtue of subsection (1)(b) to prove that at the time D is alleged to have committed the offence the circumstances were such that there was no likelihood of D driving the vehicle whilst the proportion of the specified controlled drug in D's blood or urine remained likely to exceed the specified limit for that drug.

(7) The court may, in determining whether there was such a likelihood, disregard any injury to D and any damage to the vehicle.

The specified drugs and limits are:

Illicit drugs	
Benzoylecgonine	50 µg per litre of blood
Cocaine	10 µg per litre of blood
Delta–9–tetrahydrocannabinol (cannabis and cannabinol)	2 µg per litre of blood
Ketamine	20 µg per litre of blood
Lysergic acid diethylamide (LSD)	1 µg per litre of blood
Methylamphetamine	10 µg per litre of blood
Methylenedioxymethaphetamine (MDMA–ecstasy)	10 µg per litre of blood
Monoacetylmorphine (6–MAM–heroin and diamorphine)	5 µg per litre of blood)
Amphetamine	250 µg per litre of blood

General prescription drugs	
Clonazepam	50 µg per litre of blood
Diazepam	550 µg per litre of blood
Flunitrazepam	300 µg per litre of blood
Lorazepam	100 µg per litre of blood
Methadone	500 µg per litre of blood
Morphine	80 µg per litre of blood
Oxazepam	300 µg per litre of blood
Temazepam	1000 µg per litre of blood

SO

- For driving: 6 months' imprisonment and/or fine. Must endorse and disqualify for at least 12 months. The offence carries between 3 and 11 points. Must disqualify for at least 2 years if offender has had two or more disqualifications for periods of 56 days or more in preceding 3 years. Must disqualify for at least 3 years if offender has been convicted of a relevant offence in preceding 10 years
- For being in charge: 3 months' imprisonment and/or level 4 fine. Discretionary disqualification, 10 points.

See **C13.14** for offence of being in charge.

C13.6.1 *Sentencing: driving with excess alcohol*

See the following table. *Note that this guideline is under review by the Sentencing Council* (see **Appendix 7**).

Offence seriousness(culpability and harm) A. Identify the appropriate starting point Starting points based on first-time offender pleading not guilty					
Level of alcohol			**Starting point**	**Range**	**Disqualification**	**Disqual. 2nd offence in 10 years—see note in 13.6**

Level of alcohol			Starting point	Range	Disqualification	Disqual. 2nd offence in 10 years—see note in 13.6
Breath (mg)	**Blood (ml)**	**Urine (ml)**				
36–59	81–137	108–183	Band C fine	Band C fine	12–16 months	36–40 months
60–89	138–206	184–274	Band C fine	Band C fine	17–22 months	36–46 months
90–119	207–275	275–366	Medium-level community order	Low-level community order to high-level community order	23–28 months	36–52 months
120–150 and above	276–345 and above	367–459 and above	12 weeks' custody	High-level community order to 26 weeks' custody	29–36 months	36–60 months

Offence seriousness (culpability and harm)
B. Consider the effect of aggravating and mitigating factors (other than those within examples above)
The following may be particularly relevant but these lists are not exhaustive

Factors indicating higher culpability	Factor indicating lower culpability
1. LGV, HGV, PSV, etc	1. Low likelihood of driving
2. Ability to drive seriously impaired	
3. High likelihood of driving	
4. Driving for hire or reward	

Driving with excess drugs: there is no guideline but it is suggested that reference may be made to the table at **C13.6.1**.

C13.6.2 Key points

- Section 5(2)–(3) provides:

> **Road Traffic Act 1988, s 5(2)–(3)**
>
> **5 Driving or being in charge of a motor vehicle with alcohol concentration above prescribed limit**
>
> (2) It is a defence for a person charged with an offence under subsection (1) (b) above to prove that at the time he is alleged to have committed the offence the circumstances were such that there was no likelihood of his driving the vehicle whilst the proportion of alcohol in his breath, blood or urine remained likely to exceed the prescribed limit.
>
> (3) The court may, in determining whether there was such a likelihood as is mentioned in subsection (2) above, disregard any injury to him and any damage to the vehicle.

- The burden of proof falls on the defendant (*Sheldrake v Director of Public Prosecutions* [2005] RTR 2).
- Duress is available as a defence. The defence will be available only for as long as the threat is active and a sober and reasonable person would have driven (*Crown Prosecution Service v Brown* [2007] EWHC 3274 (Admin)).
- Automatism is available as a defence.
- Where there has been no consumption of alcohol between the incidence of driving and the testing, the alcohol reading is conclusive (Road Traffic Offences Act 1988, s 15(2), and *Griffiths v Director of Public Prosecutions* [2002] EWHC 792 (Admin)). However, the presumption in section 15(2) applies only to trials and does not extend to a *Newton* hearing (*Goldsmith v Director of Public Prosecutions* [2009] EWHC 3010 (Admin)).
- Where there is post-driving consumption of alcohol, the defendant is able to 'back calculate' to obtain a reading at the time of

driving (Road Traffic Offences Act 1988, s 15(3)). The prosecution are also entitled to rely upon back calculations, but in practice rarely do so (*Gumbley v Cunningham* [1989] RTR 49).

- There will be no prosecution unless the alcohol level is at least 40 microgrammes (Home Office Circular 46/1982); it should be noted that this 'allowance' is already built into any blood or urine analysis.
- The equivalent defence for drug driving is at section 5A(6).

 See *Blackstone's Criminal Practice 2017* **C5.57**

C13.7 Fail to give information of driver's identity as required

Road Traffic Act 1988, s 172

Duty to give information as to identity of driver etc in certain circumstances

(1) This section applies—
  (a) to any offence under the preceding provisions of this Act except—
    (i) an offence under Part V, or
    (ii) an offence under section 13, 16, 51(2), 61(4), 67(9), 68(4), 96 or 120, and to an offence under section 178 of this Act,
  (b) to any offence under sections 25, 26 or 27 of the Road Traffic Offenders Act 1988,
  (c) to any offence against any other enactment relating to the use of vehicles on roads, and
  (d) to manslaughter.
(2) Where the driver of a vehicle is alleged to be guilty of an offence to which this section applies—
  (a) the person keeping the vehicle shall give such information as to the identity of the driver as he may be required to give by or on behalf of a chief officer of police, and
  (b) any other person shall if required as stated above give any information which it is in his power to give and may lead to identification of the driver.
(3) Subject to the following provisions, a person who fails to comply with a requirement under subsection (2) above shall be guilty of an offence.
(4) [see **C13.7.1** below]...
(5) Where a body corporate is guilty of an offence under this section and the offence is proved to have been committed with the consent or connivance of, or to be attributable to neglect on the part of, a director, manager, secretary or other similar officer of the body corporate, or a person who was purporting to act in any such capacity, he, as well as the body corporate, is guilty of that offence and liable to be proceeded against and punished accordingly.
(6) Where the alleged offender is a body corporate, or the proceedings are brought against him by virtue of subsection (5) above or subsection (11)

below, subsection (4) above shall not apply unless, in addition to the matters there mentioned, the alleged offender shows that no record was kept of the persons who drove the vehicle and that the failure to keep a record was reasonable.

(7) A requirement under subsection (2) may be made by written notice served by post; and where it is so made—

    (a) it shall have effect as a requirement to give the information within the period of 28 days beginning with the day on which the notice is served, and

    (b) the person on whom the notice is served shall not be guilty of an offence under this section if he shows either that he gave the information as soon as reasonably practicable after the end of that period or that it has not been reasonably practicable for him to give it.

(8) Where the person on whom a notice under subsection (7) above is to be served is a body corporate, the notice is duly served if it is served on the secretary or clerk of that body.

(9) For the purposes of section 7 of the Interpretation Act 1978 as it applies for the purposes of this section the proper address of any person in relation to the service on him of a notice under subsection (7) above is—

    (a) in the case of the secretary or clerk of a body corporate, that of the registered or principal office of that body or (if the body corporate is the registered keeper of the vehicle concerned) the registered address, and

    (b) in any other case, his last known address at the time of service.

(10) In this section—

'registered address', in relation to the registered keeper of a vehicle, means the address recorded in the record kept under the Vehicles Excise and Registration Act 1994 with respect to that vehicle as being that person's address, and

'registered keeper', in relation to a vehicle, means the person in whose name the vehicle is registered under that Act;

and references to the driver of a vehicle include references to the rider of a cycle.

SO 6 points (no endorsement for limited companies)

Ⅲ Level 3 fine

C13.7.1 Key points

• Section 172(4) provides:

Road Traffic Act 1988, s 172(4)

172 Duty to give information as to identity of driver etc in certain circumstances

(4) A person shall not be guilty of an offence by virtue of paragraph (a) of subsection (2) above if he shows that he did not know and could not with reasonable diligence have ascertained who the driver of the vehicle was.

- In *Krishevsky v DPP* [2014] EWHC 1755 (Admin) the court emphasized that the obligations under this provision arose on service and not on receipt.
- In *Duff v Director of Public Prosecutions* [2009] EWHC 675 (Admin), D's wife was served with a notice under section 172 of the Road Traffic Act 1988 requiring her to identify the name of the driver. D in fact replied to the notice, naming himself as the driver. As a result, a further section 172 notice was then served on D. Following legal advice, D did not respond to that notice and was subsequently convicted of failing to provide information. It was held that the conviction was sound, as the request to which he had in fact responded was a request of D's wife, not D himself.
- A driver is to be judged in relation to section 172(4) by the actions he did or did not take only from the time of the police request to ascertain the identity of the driver, not before (*Atkinson v Director of Public Prosecutions* [2011] EWHC 3363 (Admin)). In establishing the defence in section 172(4), in a case where either husband or wife was driving (as they indicated in their s 172 replies), the court will be sharp to seek real evidence of diligent attempts to identify which was the driver at the relevant time: *Marshall v CPS* [2015] EWHC 2333(Admin).
- For the defences available under section 172(7)(b), see *Purnell v Snaresbrook Crown Court* [2011] EWHC 934 (Admin) and *Whiteside v Director of Public Prosecutions* [2011] EWHC 3471 (Admin). *Whiteside* held that a lack of personal knowledge of the request was not itself a defence. But the defendant may be able to show that it was not reasonably practicable for him to have been aware of the notice and to provide the information sought.
- The notice is deemed served under section 1(3) of the Road Traffic Offenders Act 1974 unless the issue is raised by the defence by evidence (*Hall v DPP* [2013] EWHC 2544 (Admin)).

 See *Blackstone's Criminal Practice 2017* **C2.12**

C13.8 Fail to provide specimen for analysis

> **Road Traffic Act 1988, s 7(6) and (7)**
>
> **7 Provision of specimens for analysis**
>
> (6) A person who, without reasonable excuse, fails to provide a specimen when required to do so in pursuance of this section is guilty of an offence.
>
> (7) A constable must, on requiring any person to provide a specimen in pursuance of this section, warn him that a failure to provide it may render him liable to prosecution.

SO Driving/attempting to drive: 6 months' imprisonment and/ or fine. Must endorse and disqualify for at least 12 months. Must disqualify for at least 2 years if offender has had two or more disqualifications for periods of 56 days or more in preceding 3 years. Must disqualify for at least 3 years if offender has been convicted of a relevant offence in preceding 10 years

In-charge: 3 months' imprisonment and/or level 4 fine. Must endorse and may disqualify. If no disqualification, impose 10 points

C13.8.1 *Sentencing: driving or attempting to drive*

Note that this guideline is under review by the Sentencing Council (see **Appendix 7**).

Offence seriousness (culpability and harm) A. Identify the appropriate starting point Starting points based on first-time offender pleading not guilty				
Examples of nature of activity	**Starting point**	**Range**	**Disqual.**	**Disqual. 2nd offence in 10 years**
Defendant refused test when had honestly held but unreasonable excuse	Band C fine	Band C fine	12–16 months	36–40months
Deliberate refusal or deliberate failure	Low-level community order	Band C fine to high-level community order	17–28 months	36–52months
Deliberate refusal or deliberate failure where evidence of serious impairment	12 weeks' custody	High-level community order to 26 weeks' custody	29–36 months	36–60months

Offence seriousness (culpability and harm) B. Consider the effect of aggravating and mitigating factors (other than those within examples above) The following may be particularly relevant but these lists are not exhaustive	
Factors indicating higher culpability 1. Evidence of unacceptable standard of driving 2. LGV, HGV, PSV, etc 3. Obvious state of intoxication 4. Driving for hire or reward **Factor indicating greater degree of harm** 1. Involved in accident	**Factor indicating lower culpability** 1. Genuine but unsuccessful attempt to provide specimen

C13.8.2 *Sentencing: in-charge*

*Note that this guideline is under review by the Sentencing Council (see **Appendix 7**).*

Offence seriousness (culpability and harm) A. Identify appropriate starting point Starting points based on first-time offender pleading not guilty		
Examples of nature of activity	**Starting point**	**Range**
Defendant refused test when had honestly held but unreasonable excuse	Band B fine	Band B fine 10 points
Deliberate refusal or deliberate failure	Band C fine	Band C fine to medium-level community order Consider disqualification OR 10 points
Deliberate refusal or deliberate failure where evidence of serious impairment	Medium-level community order	Low-level community order to 6 weeks' custody Disqualify 6–12 months

Offence seriousness (culpability and harm) B. Consider the effect of aggravating and mitigating factors (other than those within examples above) The following may be particularly relevant but these lists are not exhaustive	
Factors indicating higher culpability 1. Obvious state of intoxication 2. LGV, HGV, PSV, etc 3. High likelihood of driving 4. Driving for hire of reward	**Factors indicating lower culpability** 1. Genuine but unsuccessful attempt to provide specimen 2. Low likelihood of driving

C13.8.3 Key points

- A reasonable excuse for failing to provide must relate to inability due to physical or mental issues (*R v Lennard* [1973] RTR 252).
- The suspect need not in fact be the driver if relevant investigation is being conducted by the police.
- Failure to mention a medical reason at the time of refusal does not preclude a court from finding that a reasonable excuse existed, although it was a factor to be taken into account (*Piggott v Director of Public Prosecutions* [2008] RTR 16).
- Once a reasonable excuse is raised, it is for the prosecution to disprove it (*McKeon v Director of Public Prosecutions* [2008] RTR 14).
- A failure to understand the statutory warning relating to prosecution may amount to a reasonable excuse if the accused's

understanding of English is poor (*Chief Constable of Avon and Somerset v Singh* [1988] RTR 107); but if an accredited interpreter is present there is an (rebuttable) inference that the warning was understood (*Bielecki v DPP* [2011] EWHC 2245 (Admin)). Failure to understand due to intoxication will not suffice.

- The taking of a specimen does not have to be delayed (over and above a couple of minutes) for the purpose of taking legal advice (*R v Gearing* [2008] EWHC 1695 (Admin)).
- To require the Crown to disprove a defence of reasonable excuse (in *R (Cuns) v Hammersmith Magistrates Court* [2016] EWHC 748 (Admin) in relation to needle phobia) the defence must lay an evidential basis, ie raise the issue by evidence. An assertion in the police station, during the statutory procedure, cannot meet that requirement by itself.

 See *Blackstone's Criminal Practice 2017* **C5.9**

C13.9 Fail to stop/report road accident

Road Traffic Act 1988, s 170

170 Duty of driver to stop, report accident and give information or documents

(1) This section applies in a case where, owing to the presence of a mechanically propelled vehicle on a road or other public place, an accident occurs by which—

  (a) personal injury is caused to a person other than the driver of that mechanically propelled vehicle, or

  (b) damage is caused—

    (i) to a vehicle other than that mechanically propelled vehicle or a trailer drawn by that mechanically propelled vehicle, or

    (ii) to an animal other than an animal in or on that mechanically propelled vehicle or a trailer drawn by that mechanically propelled vehicle, or

    (iii) to any other property constructed on, fixed to, growing in or otherwise forming part of the land on which the road or place in question is situated or land adjacent to such land.

(2) The driver of the mechanically propelled vehicle must stop and, if required to do so by any person having reasonable grounds for so requiring, give his name and address and also the name and address of the owner and the identification marks of the vehicle.

(3) If for any reason the driver of the mechanically propelled vehicle does not give his name and address under subsection (2) above, he must report the accident.

(4) A person who fails to comply with subsection (2) or (3) above is guilty of an offence.

(5) If, in a case where this section applies by virtue of subsection (1)(a) above, the driver of a motor vehicle does not at the time of the accident produce such a certificate of insurance or security, or other evidence, as is mentioned in section 165(2)(a) of this Act—

    (a) to a constable, or

    (b) to some person who, having reasonable grounds for so doing, has required him to produce it,

the driver must report the accident and produce such a certificate or other evidence.

This subsection does not apply to the driver of an invalid carriage.

(6) To comply with a duty under this section to report an accident or to produce such a certificate of insurance or security, or other evidence, as is mentioned in section 165(2)(a) of this Act, the driver—

    (a) must do so at a police station or to a constable, and

    (b) must do so as soon as is reasonably practicable and, in any case, within twenty-four hours of the occurrence of the accident.

(7) A person who fails to comply with a duty under subsection (5) above is guilty of an offence, but he shall not be convicted by reason only of a failure to produce a certificate or other evidence if, within seven days after the occurrence of the accident, the certificate or other evidence is produced at a police station that was specified by him at the time when the accident was reported.

(8) In this section 'animal' means horse, cattle, ass, mule, sheep, pig, goat or dog.

SO 6 months' imprisonment and/or fine. Must endorse and may disqualify. If no disqualification, impose 5–10 points.

C13.9.1 *Sentencing*

Note that this guideline is under review by the Sentencing Council (see **Appendix 7**).

Offence seriousness (culpability and harm) A. Identify the appropriate starting point Starting points based on first-time offender pleading not guilty		
Examples of nature of activity	**Starting point**	**Range**
Minor damage/injury or stopped at scene but failed to exchange particulars or report	Band B fine	Band B fine 5–6 points
Moderate damage/injury or failed to stop and failed to report	Band C fine	Band C fine 7–8 points Consider disqualification
Serious damage/injury and/or evidence of bad driving	High-level community order	Band C fine to 26 weeks custody Disqualify 6–12 months OR 9–10 points

Offence seriousness (culpability and harm)	
B. Consider the effect of aggravating and mitigating factors (other than those within examples above)	
The following may be particularly relevant but these lists are not exhaustive	
Factors indicating higher culpability	**Factors indicating lower culpability**
1. Evidence of drink or drugs/evasion of test	1. Believed identity known
2. Knowledge/suspicion that personal injury caused (where not an element of the offence)	2. Genuine fear of retribution
3. Leaving injured party at scene	3. Subsequently reported
4. Giving false details	

C13.9.2 Key points

A driver who is unaware of the accident cannot commit an offence under these provisons (*Harding v Price* [1948] 1 KB 695); but if he later becomes aware of the accident, he must report it personally if he becomes aware within 24 hours (*DPP v Drury* [1989] RTR 165).

If a driver was genuinely unaware that an accident had occurred, or remained of the view that none had occurred (even in circumstances where someone informed that person that there had been an accident), there is no duty to report.

However, if the appellant was unaware of the accident because of her drunken state, she could not rely upon that as a defence where she is voluntarily intoxicated. This is a crime of basic intent (*Magee v Crown Prosecution Service* [2014] EWHC 4089 (Admin)).

C13.9.3 *Power of police to stop vehicles*

> **Road Traffic Act 1988, s 163**
>
> (1) A person driving a mechanically propelled vehicle on a road must stop the vehicle on being required to do so by a constable in uniform or a traffic officer...
> (3) If a person fails to comply with this section he is guilty of an offence.

SO

 Level 3 fine with no endorsement

 See *Blackstone's Criminal Practice 2017* **C6.51–C6.55**

C13.10 No insurance, using, causing, or permitting

Road Traffic Act 1988, s. 143

SO Fine /discretionary disqualification/6–8 penalty points

C13.10.1 *Sentencing*

*Note that this guideline is under review by the Sentencing Council
(see **Appendix 7**).*

Offence seriousness (culpability and harm) A. Identify the appropriate starting point Starting points based on first-time offender pleading not guilty		
Examples of nature of activity	**Starting point**	**Range**
Using a motor vehicle on a road or other public place without insurance	Band C fine	Band C fine 6 points to 12 months' disqualification—see notes below

Offence seriousness (culpability and harm) B. Consider the effect of aggravating and mitigating factors (other than those within examples above) The following may be particularly relevant but these lists are not exhaustive	
Factors indicating higher culpability 1. Never passed test 2. Gave false details 3. Driving LGV, HGV, PSV, etc 4. Driving for hire or reward 5. Evidence of sustained uninsured use **Factors indicating greater degree of harm** 1. Involved in accident 2. Accident resulting in injury	**Factors indicating lower culpability** 1. Responsibility for providing insurance rests with another 2. Genuine misunderstanding 3. Recent failure to renew or failure to transfer vehicle details where insurance was in existence 4. Vehicle not being driven

Notes

Consider range from 7 points – 2 months' disqualification where vehicle was being driven and no evidence that the offender has held insurance.

Consider disqualification of 6–12 months if evidence of sustained uninsured use and/or involvement in accident.

C13.10.2 Key points

- See **C12** for definitions.
- Proceedings may be brought within six months of a prosecutor forming the opinion that there is sufficient evidence of an

offence having been committed (subject to an overall three-year time bar).

- It is for a defendant to show that he was insured, once it is established that a motor vehicle was used on a road or other public place. However, in *DPP v Whittaker* [2015] EWHC 1850 (Admin) it was held that once the defence have proved the existence of a valid insurance policy, it is for the Crown to prove to the normal criminal standard that it does not cover the driving at issue.
- It is not necessary that the vehicle be capable of being driven (*Pumbien v Vines* [1996] RTR 37).
- Employed drivers have the following defence available to them:

Road Traffic Act 1988, s 143(3)

143 Users of motor vehicles to be insured or secured against third-party risks

(3) A person charged with using a motor vehicle in contravention of this section shall not be convicted if he proves—
  (a) that the vehicle did not belong to him and was not in his possession under a contract of hiring or of loan,
  (b) that he was using the vehicle in the course of his employment, and
  (c) that he neither knew nor had reason to believe that there was not in force in relation to the vehicle such a policy of insurance or security as is mentioned in subsection (1) above.

 See *Blackstone's Criminal Practice 2017* **C6.46–C6.51**

C13.11 Offences concerning the driver

Offence	Maximum	Points	Starting point	Special considerations
Fail to cooperate with preliminary (roadside) breath test	L3	4	B	
Fail to give information of driver's identity as required	L3	6	C	For limited companies, endorsement is not available; a fine is the only available penalty
Fail to produce insurance certificate	L4	–	A	Fine per offence, not per document

Fail to produce test certificate	L3	–	A	
Drive otherwise than in accordance with licence (where could be covered)	L3	–	A	
Drive otherwise than in accordance with licence	L3	3–6	A	Aggravating factor if no licence ever held

 See *Blackstone's Criminal Practice 2017* **C6**

C13.12 Offences concerning the vehicle

The guidelines for some of the offences below differentiate between three types of offender when the offence is committed in the course of business: driver, owner-driver, and owner-company. For owner-drivers, the starting point is the same as for drivers; however, the court should consider an uplift of at least 25 per cent.

Offence	Maximum	Points	Starting point	Special considerations
No excise licence	L3 or 5 times annual duty, whichever is greater	–	A (1–3 months unpaid) B (4–6 months unpaid) C (7–12 months unpaid)	Add duty lost
Fail to notify change of ownership to DVLA	L3	–	A	If offence committed in course of business: A (driver) A* (owner-driver) B (owner-company)
No test certificate	L3	–	A	If offence committed in course of business: A (driver) A* (owner-driver) B (owner-company)

Brakes defective Key points: it is sufficient only to prove that any part of the braking system is defective (*Kennett v British Airports Authority* [1975] Crim LR 106). The fact that everything possible (eg servicing) has been done in order to ensure that the vehicle is in good condition does not amount to a defence (*Hawkins v Holmes* [1974] RTR 436), as maintenance of the braking system is an absolute obligation on the driver (*Green v Burnett* [1954] 3 All ER 273).	L4	3	B	If offence committed in course of business: B (driver) B* (owner-driver) C (owner-company) L5 if goods vehicle
Steering defective	L4	3	B	If offence committed in course of business: B (driver) B* (owner-driver) C (owner-company) L5 if goods vehicle
Tyres defective. It is a defence if the vehicle is not being used and there was no intention to use when the tyres were defective, regardless of the fact that the vehicle was on a road (*Eden v Mitchell* [1975] RTR 425). There is no requirement for the prosecution to have had the tyre examined by an authorised examiner as the issue was a simple question of fact (*Phillips v Thomas* [1974] RTR 28).	L4	3	B	If offence committed in course of business: B (driver) B* (owner-driver) C (owner-company) L5 if goods vehicle Penalty per tyre

Condition of vehicle/ accessories/ equipment involving danger of injury (Road Traffic Act 1988, s. 40A)	L4	3	B	Must disqualify for at least 6 months if offender has one or more previous convictions for same offence within 3 years If offence committed in course of business: B (driver) B* (owner-driver) C (owner-company) L5 if goods vehicle
Exhaust defective	L3	–	A	If offence committed in course of business: A (driver) A* (owner-driver) B (owner-company)
Lights defective	L3	–	A	If offence committed in course of business: A (driver) A* (owner-driver) B (owner-company)

 See *Blackstone's Criminal Practice 2017* **C6**

C13.13 Speeding

Road Traffic Regulation Act 1984, s. 89(1)

SO Level 3 fine (level 4 if motorway)

SO Summary only

C13.13.1 *Sentencing*

Note that this guideline is under review by the Sentencing Council (see **Appendix 7**).

Offence seriousness (culpability and harm) A. Identify the appropriate starting point Starting points based on first-time offender pleading not guilty			
Speed limit (mph)	Recorded speed (mph)		
20	21–30	31–40	41–50
30	31–40	41–50	51–60
40	41–55	56–65	66–75
50	51–65	66–75	76–85
60	61–80	81–90	91–100
70	71–90	91–100	101–110
Starting point	Band A fine	Band B fine	Band B fine
Range	Band A fine	Band B fine	Band B fine
Points/ disqualification	3 points	4–6 points OR Disqualify 7–28 days	Disqualify 7–56 days OR 6 points

Offence seriousness (culpability and harm) B. Consider the effect of aggravating and mitigating factors (other than those within examples above) The following may be particularly relevant but these lists are not exhaustive	
Factors indicating higher culpability 1. Poor road or weather conditions 2. LGV, HGV, PSV, etc 3. Towing caravan/trailer 4. Carrying passengers or heavy load 5. Driving for hire or reward 6. Evidence of unacceptable standard of driving over and above speed **Factors indicating greater degree of harm** 1. Location, eg near school 2. High level of traffic or pedestrians in the vicinity	**Factor indicating lower culpability** 1. Genuine emergency established

C13.13.2 Key points

- Necessity is available as a defence (*Moss v Howdle* [1997] SLT 782).
- Check that a notice of intended prosecution has been served in time.
- Save where the road is a restricted road, there needs to be signage in accordance with the regulations. A failure to provide adequate signage is fatal to any conviction. In *Jones v Director of Public*

Prosecutions [2011] EWHC 50 (Admin), the court held that the relevant question to be answered by the court was:

> Whether by the point on the road where the alleged offence took place (the point of enforcement) the driver by reference to the route taken thereto has been given (or drivers generally have been given) adequate guidance of the speed limit to be observed at that point on the road by the signs on the relevant part of parts of the road *in so far as (and thus to the extent that)* those traffic signs comply with the 2002 Regulations?

- In relation to restricted roads (where a 30 mph speed limit applies) there must be a system of street lighting not more than 200 yards apart. If this matter is put in issue (but not otherwise), the prosecution must establish this beyond reasonable doubt.
- The 200-yard rule relates to a 'system of street lighting', so some lights may be more than 200 yards apart, it being a question of fact whether the 'system of lighting' as a whole complies. In *Briere v Hailstone* (1968) 112 SJ 767, a conviction was upheld even though 50 per cent of the lamps were incorrectly distanced. Similarly, the fact that one lamp was in disrepair did not affect a conviction (*Spittle v Kent County Constabulary* [1985] Crim LR 744).

 See *Blackstone's Criminal Practice 2017* **C6.58–C6.62**

C13.14 Unfit through drink or drugs

Road Traffic Act 1988, s 4(1), (2), and (5)

4 Driving, or being in charge, when under influence of drink or drugs

(1) A person who, when driving or attempting to drive a mechanically pro-pelled vehicle on a road or other public place, is unfit to drive through drink or drugs is guilty of an offence.

(2) Without prejudice to subsection (1) above, a person who, when in charge of a mechanically propelled vehicle which is on a road or other public place, is unfit to drive through drink or drugs is guilty of an offence.

...

(5) For the purposes of this section, a person shall be taken to be unfit to drive if his ability to drive properly is for the time being impaired.

SO Drive/attempt to drive: 6 months' imprisonment and/or fine. Must endorse and disqualify for at least 12 months. Must dis-qualify for at least 2 years if offender has had two or more dis-qualifications for periods of 56 days or more in preceding years.

C13 Road Traffic Offences

Must disqualify for at least 3 years if offender has been convicted of a relevant offence in preceding 10 years.

In-charge: 3 months' imprisonment and/or level 4 fine. Must endorse and may disqualify. If no disqualification, impose 10 points.

C13.14.1 *Sentencing: driving or attempting to drive*

Note that this guideline is under review by the Sentencing Council (see **Appendix 7**).

Offence seriousness (culpability and harm) A. Identify the appropriate starting point Starting points based on first-time offender pleading not guilty				
Examples of nature of activity	**Starting point**	**Range**	**Disqual.**	**Disqual. 2nd offence in 10 years**
Evidence of moderate level of impairment and no aggravating factors	Band C fine	Band C fine	12–16 months	36–40 months
Evidence of moderate level of impairment and presence of one or more aggravating factors listed below	Band C fine	Band C fine	17–22 months	36–46 months
Evidence of high level of impairment and no aggravating factors	Medium-level community order	Low-level community order to high-level community order	23–28 months	36–52 months
Evidence of high level of impairment and presence of one or more aggravating factors listed below	12 weeks' custody	High-level community order to 26 weeks' custody	29–36 months	36–60 months

Offence seriousness (culpability and harm) B. Consider the effect of aggravating and mitigating factors (other than those within examples above) The following may be particularly relevant but these lists are not exhaustive	
Factors indicating higher culpability 1. LGV, HGV, PSV, etc 2. Poor road or weather conditions 3. Carrying passengers 4. Driving for hire or reward 5. Evidence of unacceptable standard of driving **Factors indicating greater degree of harm** 1. Involved in accident 2. Location, eg near school 3. High level of traffic or pedestrians in the vicinity	**Factors indicating lower culpability** 1. Genuine emergency established* 2. Spiked drinks* 3. Very short distance driven*

* even where not amounting to special reasons

C13.14.2 *Sentencing: in-charge*

Offence seriousness (culpability and harm) A. Identify the appropriate starting point Starting points based on first-time offender pleading not guilty		
Examples of nature of activity	**Starting point**	**Range**
Evidence of moderate level of impairment and no aggravating factors	Band B fine	Band B fine 10 points
Evidence of moderate level of impairment and presence of one or more aggravating factors listed below	Band B fine	Band B fine 10 points or consider disqualification
Evidence of high level of impairment and no aggravating factors	Band C fine	Band C fine to medium-level community order 10 points OR consider disqualification
Evidence of high level of impairment and presence of one or more aggravating factors listed below	High-level community order	Medium-level community order to 12 weeks' custody Consider disqualification OR 10 points

Offence seriousness (culpability and harm)
B. Consider the effect of aggravating and mitigating factors (other than those within examples above)
The following may be particularly relevant but these lists are not exhaustive

Factors indicating higher culpability	Factor indicating lower culpability
1. LGV, HGV, PSV, etc	1. Low likelihood of driving
2. High likelihood of driving	
3. Driving for hire or reward	

C13.14.3 Key points

- No likelihood of driving whilst unfit provides a defence in law to the in-charge offence. Section 4(3) and (4) of the Road Traffic Act 1988 provides:

Road Traffic Act 1988, s 4(3) and (4)

4 Driving, or being in charge, when under influence of drink or drugs

(3) For the purposes of subsection (2) above, a person shall be deemed not to have been in charge of a mechanically propelled vehicle if he proves that at the material time the circumstances were such that there was no likelihood of his driving it so long as he remained unfit to drive through drink or drugs.

(4) The court may, in determining whether there was such a likelihood as is mentioned in subsection (3) above, disregard any injury to him and any damage to the vehicle.

- Drugs include normal medicines.
- Evidence of impairment to drive may be provided by both expert and lay witnesses. Note, however, that a lay witness can give evidence as to a person's demeanour (and how much he drank, for example) but not on the ultimate question of whether the person was 'fit' to drive.
- The results of any evidential specimens are admissible (Road Traffic Offenders Act 1988, ss 15 and 16).

 See *Blackstone's Criminal Practice 2017* **C5.57**

C14 Sexual Offences

C14.1 Exposure

Sexual Offences Act 2003, s 66(1)

66 Exposure

(1) A person commits an offence if—
    (a) he intentionally exposes his genitals, and
    (b) he intends that someone will see them and be caused alarm or distress.

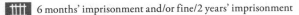 6 months' imprisonment and/or fine/2 years' imprisonment

EW Either way

C14.1.1 *Sentencing*

STEP ONE: determining the offence category

The court should determine the offence category using the table below.

Category 1	Raised harm **and** raised culpability
Category 2	Raised harm **or** raised culpability
Category 3	Exposure **without** raised harm or culpability factors present

The court should determine culpability and harm caused or intended, by reference **only** to the factors below, which comprise the principal factual elements of the offence. Where an offence does not fall squarely into a category, individual factors may require a degree of weighting before making an overall assessment and determining the appropriate offence category.

Factors indicating raised harm
• Victim followed/pursued
• Offender masturbated

Factors indicating raised culpability
• Specific or previous targeting of a particularly vulnerable victim
• Abuse of trust
• Use of threats (including blackmail)
• Offence racially or religiously aggravated
• Offence motivated by, or demonstrating, hostility to the victim based on his or her sexual orientation (or presumed sexual orientation) or transgender identity (or presumed transgender identity)
• Offence motivated by, or demonstrating, hostility to the victim based on his or her disability (or presumed disability)

STEP TWO: starting point and category range

Having determined the category, the court should use the corresponding starting points to reach a sentence within the category range [below]. The starting point applies to all offenders irrespective of plea or previous convictions. Having determined the starting point, step two allows further adjustment for aggravating or mitigating features, set out [below].

A case of particular gravity, reflected by multiple features of culpability or harm in step one, could merit upward adjustment from the starting point before further adjustment for aggravating or mitigating features, set out [below].

Where there is a sufficient prospect of rehabilitation, a community order with a sex offender treatment programme requirement under section 202 of the Criminal Justice Act 2003 can be a proper alternative to a short or moderate length custodial sentence.

Category 1	**Starting point** 26 weeks' custody **Category range** 12 weeks' to 1 year's custody
Category 2	**Starting point** High-level community order **Category range** Medium-level community order to 26 weeks' custody
Category 3	**Starting point** Medium-level community order **Category range** Band A fine to high-level community order

The table below contains a **non-exhaustive** list of additional factual elements providing the context of the offence and factors relating to the offender. Identify whether any combination of these, or other relevant factors, should result in an upward or downward adjustment from the starting point. **In particular, relevant recent convictions are likely to result in an upward adjustment**. In some cases, having considered these factors, it may be appropriate to move outside the identified category range.

When sentencing **category 2 offences**, the court should also consider the custody threshold as follows:

- has the custody threshold been passed?
- if so, is the nature of the offence be imposed?
- if so, can that sentence be suspended?

When sentencing **category 3 offences**, the court should also consider the community order threshold as follows:

- has the community order threshold been passed?

Aggravating factors	
Statutory aggravating factors	*Other aggravating factors*
• Previous convictions, having regard to (a) the nature of the offence to which the conviction relates and its relevance to the current offence; and (b) the time that has elapsed since the conviction • Offence committed whilst on bail	• Location of the offence • Timing of the offence • Any steps taken to prevent the victim reporting an incident, obtaining assistance, and/or from assisting or supporting the prosecution • Failure to comply with current court orders • Offence committed whilst on licence • Commission of offence whilst under the influence of alcohol or drugs • Presence of others, especially children
Mitigating factors	
• No previous convictions **or** no relevant/recent convictions • Remorse • Previous good character and/or exemplary conduct* • Age and/or lack of maturity where it affects the responsibility of the offender • Mental disorder or learning disability, particularly where linked to the commission of the offence • Demonstration of steps taken to address offending behaviour	

* Previous good character/exemplary conduct is different from having no previous convictions. The more serious the offence, the less the weight which should normally be attributed to this factor. Where previous good character/exemplary conduct has been used to facilitate the offence, this mitigation should not normally be allowed and such conduct may constitute an aggravating factor.

C14 Sexual Offences

C14.1.2 Key points

- This offence is committed where an offender intentionally exposes his or her genitals and intends that someone will see them and be caused alarm or distress. It is gender-neutral, covering exposure of male or female genitalia to a male or female witness.
- In accordance with section 80 of and Schedule 3 to the Sexual Offences Act 2003, automatic notification requirements apply upon conviction to an offender aged 18 or over where:
  - the victim was under 18; or
  - a term of imprisonment or a community sentence of at least 12 months is imposed.
- This guideline may be relevant by way of analogy to conduct charged as the common law offence of outraging public decency; the offence is triable either way and has a maximum penalty of a fine and/or 6 months' imprisonment when tried summarily.

 See *Blackstone's Criminal Practice 2017* **B3.286–B3.289**

C14.2 Indecent photographs of children

Protection of Children Act 1978, s 1(1)–(4)

1 Indecent photographs of children

(1) Subject to sections 1A and 1B, it is an offence for a person—
  (a) to take, or permit to be taken or to make, any indecent photograph or pseudo-photograph of a child; or
  (b) to distribute or show such indecent photographs or pseudo-photographs; or
  (c) to have in his possession such indecent photographs or pseudo-photographs, with a view to their being distributed or shown by himself or others; or
  (d) to publish or cause to be published any advertisement likely to be understood as conveying that the advertiser distributes or shows such indecent photographs or pseudo-photographs, or intends to do so.

(2) For purposes of this Act, a person is to be regarded as distributing an indecent photograph or pseudo-photograph if he parts with possession of it to, or exposes or offers it for acquisition by, another person.

(3) Proceedings for an offence under this Act shall not be instituted except by or with the consent of the Director of Public Prosecutions.

(4) Where a person is charged with an offence under subsection (1)(b) or (c), it shall be a defence for him to prove—
  (a) that he had a legitimate reason for distributing or showing the photographs or pseudo-photographs or (as the case may be) having them in his possession; or
  (b) that he had not himself seen the photographs or pseudo-photographs and did not know, nor had any cause to suspect, them to be indecent.
...

> **Criminal Justice Act 1988, s 160**
>
> **160 Possession of indecent photograph of child**
>
> (1) Subject to section 160A, it is an offence for a person to have any indecent photograph or pseudo-photograph of a child in his possession.
>
> (2) Where a person is charged with an offence under subsection (1) above, it shall be a defence for him to prove—
>
>   (a) that he had a legitimate reason for having the photograph or pseudophotograph in his possession; or
>
>   (b) that he had not himself seen the photograph or pseudo-photograph and did not know, nor had any cause to suspect, it to be indecent; or
>
>   (c) that the photograph or pseudo-photograph was sent to him without any prior request made by him or on his behalf and that he did not keep it for an unreasonable time.

 6 months' imprisonment and/or fine/10 years' imprisonment (5 years' if s 160)

C14.2.1 *Sentencing*

For section 1 offences committed on or after 3 December 2012, this is an offence listed in Part 1 of Schedule 15B for the purposes of section 224A (life sentence for second listed offence) of the Criminal Justice Act 2003.

For convictions on or after 3 December 2012 (irrespective of the date of commission of the offence), these are specified offences for the purposes of section 226A (extended sentence for certain violent or sexual offences) of the Criminal Justice Act 2003.

STEP ONE: determining the offence category

The court should determine the offence category using the table below.

	Possession	Distribution*	Production**
Category A	Possession of images involving penetrative sexual activity Possession of images involving sexual activity with an animal or sadism	Sharing images involving penetrative sexual activity Sharing images involving sexual activity with an animal or sadism	Creating images involving penetrative sexual activity Creating images involving sexual activity with an animal or sadism

Category B	Possession of images involving non-penetrative sexual activity	Sharing of images involving non-penetrative sexual activity	Creating images involving non-penetrative sexual activity
Category C	Possession of other indecent images not falling within categories A or B	Sharing of other indecent images not falling within categories A or B	Creating other indecent images not falling within categories A or B

* Distribution includes possession with a view to distributing or sharing images.

** Production includes the taking or making of any image at source, for instance the original image. Making an image by simple downloading should be treated as possession for the purposes of sentencing.

In most cases the intrinsic character of the most serious of the offending images will initially determine the appropriate category. If, however, the most serious images are unrepresentative of the offender's conduct a lower category may be appropriate. A lower category will not, however, be appropriate if the offender has produced or taken (for example photographed) images of a higher category.

STEP TWO: starting point and category range

Having determined the category, the court should use the corresponding starting points to reach a sentence within the category range below. The starting point applies to all offenders irrespective of plea or previous convictions. Having determined the starting point, step two allows further adjustment for aggravating or mitigating features, set out on the next page.

Where there is a sufficient prospect of rehabilitation, a community order with a sex offender treatment programme requirement under section 202 of the Criminal Justice Act 2003 can be a proper alternative to a short or moderate length custodial sentence.

	Possession	Distribution	Production
Category A	**Starting point** 1 year's custody **Category range** 26 weeks' to 3 years' custody	**Starting point** (Crown Court) **Category range** (Crown Court)	**Starting point** (Crown Court) **Category range** (Crown Court)
Category B	**Starting point** 26 weeks' custody **Category range** High-level community order to 18 months' custody	**Starting point** 1 year's custody **Category range** 26 weeks to 2 years' custody	**Starting point** (Crown Court) **Category range** (Crown Court)

| Category C | Starting point
High-level community order
Category range
Medium-level community
order to 26 weeks' custody | Starting point
13 weeks'
custody
Category range
High-level
community order to
26 weeks' custody | Starting point
(Crown Court)
Category range
(Crown Court) |

The table below contains a **non-exhaustive** list of additional factual elements providing the context of the offence and factors relating to the offender. Identify whether any combination of these, or other relevant factors, should result in an upward or downward adjustment from the starting point. **In particular, relevant recent convictions are likely to result in an upward adjustment.** In some cases, having considered these factors, it may be appropriate to move outside the identified category range.

When sentencing appropriate **category 2 or 3 offences**, the court should also consider the custody threshold as follows:

- has the custody threshold been passed?
- if so, is it unavoidable that a custodial sentence be imposed?
- if so, can that sentence be suspended?

Aggravating factors	
Statutory aggravating factors	*Other aggravating factors*
• Previous convictions, having regard to (a) the nature of the offence to which the conviction relates and its relevance to the current offence; and (b) the time that has elapsed since the conviction • Offence committed whilst on bail	• Failure to comply with current court orders • Offence committed whilst on licence • Age and/or vulnerability of the child depicted+ • Discernible pain or distress suffered by child depicted • Period over which images were possessed, distributed or produced • High volume of images possessed, distributed, or produced • Placing images where there is the potential for a high volume of viewers • Collection includes moving images • Attempts to dispose of or conceal evidence • Abuse of trust • Child depicted known to the offender • Active involvement in a network or process that facilitates or commissions the creation or sharing of indecent images of children • Commercial exploitation and/or motivation • Deliberate or systematic searching for images portraying young children, category A images, or the portrayal of familial sexual abuse • Large number of different victims • Child depicted intoxicated or drugged

	+Age and/or vulnerability of the child should be given significant weight. In cases where the actual age of the victim is difficult to determine sentencers should consider the development of the child (infant, pre-pubescent, post-pubescent)

Mitigating factors

- No previous convictions **or** no relevant/recent convictions
- Remorse
- Previous good character and/or exemplary conduct*
- Age and/or lack of maturity where it affects the responsibility of the offender
- Mental disorder or learning disability, particularly where linked to the commission of the offence
- Demonstration of steps taken to address offending behaviour

* Previous good character/exemplary conduct is different from having no previous convictions. The more serious the offence, the less the weight which should normally be attributed to this factor. Where previous good character/exemplary conduct has been used to facilitate the offence, this mitigation should not normally be allowed and such conduct may constitute an aggravating factor.

C14.2.2 Key points

- Photograph includes tracing or other image derived in whole or part from a photograph or pseudo-photograph.
- Whether a photograph is indecent depends on normally recognized standards of propriety.
- The age of the child may be relevant to the issue of indecency (*R v Owen* (1988) 88 Cr App R 291).
- The opening of an email or viewing of an image on the screen would amount to the making of an image if the defendant has the requisite knowledge of what he is doing.
- A person is not in possession of images if they have been deleted, if he is not able to recover those images (*R v Porter* [2006] EWCA Crim 560).
- A child is a person under 18 years of age (Sexual Offences Act 2003, s 45).

 See *Blackstone's Criminal Practice 2017* **B3.311–B3.322**

C14.3 Kerb crawling, paying for sexual services, loitering, and soliciting

Sexual Offences Act 2003, ss 51A and 53A

51A Soliciting

51A(1) It is an offence for a person in a street or public place to solicit another

(B) for the purpose of obtaining B's sexual services as a prostitute.

(2) The reference to a person in a street or public place includes a person in a vehicle in a street or public place.

...

(4) In this section 'street' has the meaning given by section 1(4) of the Street Offences Act 1959.

53A Paying for sexual services of a prostitute subjected to force etc

53A(1) A person (A) commits an offence if—

(a) A makes or promises payment for the sexual services of a prostitute (B),

(b) a third person (C) has engaged in exploitative conduct of a kind likely to induce or encourage B to provide the sexual services for which A has made or promised payment, and

(c) C engaged in that conduct for or in the expectation of gain for C or another person (apart from A or B).

(2) The following are irrelevant—

(a) where in the world the sexual services are to be provided and whether those services are provided,

(b) whether A is, or ought to be, aware that C has engaged in exploitative conduct.

(3) C engages in exploitative conduct if—

(a) C uses force, threats (whether or not relating to violence) or any other form of coercion, or

(b) C practises any form of deception.

Street Offences Act 1959, s 1(1)

1 Loitering or soliciting for purposes of prostitution

(1) It shall be an offence for a person aged 18 or over (whether male or female) persistently to loiter or solicit in a street or public place for the purpose of prostitution.

SO

Fine level 3 (for a first offence under Street Offences Act 1959, s 1, the fine is level 2)

See *Blackstone's Criminal Practice 2017* **B3.249–B3.312**

C14.4 Prohibited images of children

Coroners and Justice Act 2009, s 62

62 Possession of prohibited images of children

(1) It is an offence for a person to be in possession of a prohibited image of a child.

(2) A prohibited image is an image which—
   (a) is pornographic,
   (b) falls within subsection (6), and
   (c) is grossly offensive, disgusting or otherwise of an obscene character.

(3) An image is 'pornographic' if it is of such a nature that it must reasonably be assumed to have been produced solely or principally for the purpose of sexual arousal.

(4) Where (as found in the person's possession) an image forms part of a series of images, the question whether the image is of such a nature as is mentioned in subsection (3) is to be determined by reference to—
   (a) the image itself, and
   (b) (if the series of images is such as to be capable of providing a context for the image) the context in which it occurs in the series of images.

(5) So, for example, where—
   (a) an image forms an integral part of a narrative constituted by a series of images, and
   (b) having regard to those images as a whole, they are not of such a nature that they must reasonably be assumed to have been produced solely or principally for the purpose of sexual arousal,
   the image may, by virtue of being part of that narrative, be found not to be pornographic, even though it might have been found to be pornographic if taken by itself.

(6) An image falls within this subsection if it—
   (a) is an image which focuses solely or principally on a child's genitals or anal region, or
   (b) portrays any of the acts mentioned in subsection (7).

(7) Those acts are—
   (a) the performance by a person of an act of intercourse or oral sex with or in the presence of a child;
   (b) an act of masturbation by, of, involving or in the presence of a child;
   (c) an act which involves penetration of the vagina or anus of a child with a part of a person's body or with anything else;
   (d) an act of penetration, in the presence of a child, of the vagina or anus of a person with a part of a person's body or with anything else;
   (e) the performance by a child of an act of intercourse or oral sex with an animal (whether dead or alive or imaginary);
   (f) the performance by a person of an act of intercourse or oral sex with an animal (whether dead or alive or imaginary) in the presence of a child.

(8) For the purposes of subsection (7), penetration is a continuing act from entry to withdrawal.

(9) Proceedings for an offence under subsection (1) may not be instituted—
  (a) in England and Wales, except by or with the consent of the Director of Public Prosecutions;
...

 6 months' imprisonment and/or fine/3 years' imprisonment

C14.4.1 Key points

- Section 64 of the Act provides for the following defence:

Coroners and Justice Act 2009, s 64(1)

64 Defences

(1) Where a person is charged with an offence under section 62(1), it is a defence for the person to prove any of the following matters—
  (a) that the person had a legitimate reason for being in possession of the image concerned;
  (b) that the person had not seen the image concerned and did not know, nor had any cause to suspect, it to be a prohibited image of a child;
  (c) that the person—
    (i) was sent the image concerned without any prior request having been made by or on behalf of the person, and
    (ii) did not keep it for an unreasonable time.

- Section 63 of the Act defines the meaning of 'image' and 'child'.

 See *Blackstone's Criminal Practice 2017* **B3.323–B3.328**

C14.5 Extreme pornography

Criminal Justice and Immigration Act 2008, ss 63, 65–66

63 Possession of extreme pornographic images

(1) It is an offence for a person to be in possession of an extreme pornographic image.
(2) An 'extreme pornographic image' is an image which is both—
  (a) pornographic, and
  (b) an extreme image.
(3) An image is 'pornographic' if it is of such a nature that it must reasonably be assumed to have been produced solely or principally for the purpose of sexual arousal.

(4) Where (as found in the person's possession) an image forms part of a series of images, the question whether the image is of such a nature as is mentioned in subsection (3) is to be determined by reference to—
  (a) the image itself, and
  (b) (if the series of images is such as to be capable of providing a context for the image) the context in which it occurs in the series of images.

(5) So, for example, where—
  (a) an image forms an integral part of a narrative constituted by a series of images, and
  (b) having regard to those images as a whole, they are not of such a nature that they must reasonably be assumed to have been produced solely or principally for the purpose of sexual arousal,

  the image may, by virtue of being part of that narrative, be found not to be pornographic, even though it might have been found to be pornographic if taken by itself.

(5A) In relation to possession of an image in England and Wales, an 'extreme image' is an image which—
  (a) falls within subsection (7) or (7A), and
  (b) is grossly offensive, disgusting or otherwise of an obscene character.

(6) An 'extreme image' is an image which—
  (a) falls within subsection (7), and
  (b) is grossly offensive, disgusting or otherwise of an obscene character.

(7) An image falls within this subsection if it portrays, in an explicit and realistic way, any of the following—
  (a) an act which threatens a person's life,
  (b) an act which results, or is likely to result, in serious injury to a person's anus, breasts or genitals,
  (c) an act which involves sexual interference with a human corpse, or
  (d) a person performing an act of intercourse or oral sex with an animal (whether dead or alive), and a reasonable person looking at the image would think that any such person or animal was real.

(7A) An image falls within this subsection if it portrays, in an explicit and realistic way, either of the following—
  (a) an act which involves the non-consensual penetration of a person's vagina, anus or mouth by another with the other person's penis, or
  (b) an act which involves the non-consensual sexual penetration of a person's vagina or anus by another with a part of the other person's body or anything else,

  and a reasonable person looking at the image would think that the persons were real.

(7B) For the purposes of subsection (7A)—
  (a) penetration is a continuing act from entry to withdrawal;
  (b) 'vagina' includes vulva.

(8) In this section 'image' means—
  (a) a moving or still image (produced by any means); or

(b) data (stored by any means) which is capable of conversion into an image within paragraph (a).

(9) In this section references to a part of the body include references to a part surgically constructed (in particular through gender reassignment surgery).

(10) Proceedings for an offence under this section may not be instituted—

    (a) in England and Wales, except by or with the consent of the Director of Public Prosecutions;

...

65 Defences: general

(1) Where a person is charged with an offence under section 63, it is a defence for the person to prove any of the matters mentioned in subsection (2).

(2) The matters are—

    (a) that the person had a legitimate reason for being in possession of the image concerned;

    (b) that the person had not seen the image concerned and did not know, nor had any cause to suspect, it to be an extreme pornographic image;

    (c) that the person—

        (i) was sent the image concerned without any prior request having been made by or on behalf of the person, and

        (ii) did not keep it for an unreasonable time.

(3) In this section 'extreme pornographic image' and 'image' have the same meanings as in section 63.

66 Defence: participation in consensual acts

(A1) Subsection (A2) applies where in England and Wales—

    (a) a person ('D') is charged with an offence under section 63, and

    (b) the offence relates to an image that portrays an act or acts within subsection (7)(a) to (c) or (7A) of that section (but does not portray an act within subsection (7)(d) of that section).

(A2) It is a defence for D to prove—

    (a) that D directly participated in the act or any of the acts portrayed, and

    (b) that the act or acts did not involve the infliction of any non- consensual harm on any person, and

    (c) if the image portrays an act within section 63(7)(c), that what is portrayed as a human corpse was not in fact a corpse, and

    (d) if the image portrays an act within section 63(7A), that what is portrayed as non-consensual penetration was in fact consensual, and

(3) For the purposes of this section harm inflicted on a person is 'non-consensual' harm if—

    (a) the harm is of such a nature that the person cannot, in law, consent to it being inflicted on himself or herself; or

    (b) where the person can, in law, consent to it being so inflicted, the person does not in fact consent to it being so inflicted.

C14 Sexual Offences

C14.5.1 Key points

Section 63(3) means was the image produced for the purpose of sexually arousing anyone who comes to have it, be that the producer himself, a distributor, or an ultimate recipient. The section is designed to prevent the possession of such images by any person. The purpose of the subsection is to identify the types of image that are pornographic. The word 'pornographic' here deals with the assumed purpose of the image. The identity or purpose of the producer is immaterial; the circumstances in which the images are received are immaterial (*R v DB* [2016] EWCA Crim 474).

- 6 months' imprisonment and/or fine/3 years' imprisonment (2 years' if the offence relates to an image that does not portray any act within s 63(7)(a) or (b)).

See *Blackstone's Criminal Practice 2017* **B3.35–B3.340**

C14.6 Exploitation of prostitution

Sexual Offences Act 2003, ss 52 and 53

6 months' imprisonment and/or fine/7 years' imprisonment

C14.6.1 *Sentencing*

CAUSING OR INCITING PROSTITUTION FOR GAIN

Sexual Offences Act 2003 (section 52)

CONTROLLING PROSTITUTION FOR GAIN

Sexual Offences Act 2003 (section 53)

STEP ONE: determining the offence category

The court should determine which categories of harm and culpability the offence falls into by reference **only** to the tables below.

HARM	
Category 1	• Abduction/detention • Violence or threats of violence • Sustained and systematic psychological abuse • Individual(s) forced or coerced to participate in unsafe/degrading sexual activity • Individual(s) forced or coerced into seeing many 'customers' • Individual(s) forced/coerced/deceived into prostitution
Category 2	Factor(s) in category 1 not present

CULPABILITY		
A	B	C
• Causing, inciting or controlling prostitution on significant commercial basis • Expectation of significant financial or other gain • Abuse of trust • Exploitation of those known to be trafficked • Significant involvement in limiting the freedom of prostitute(s) • Grooming of individual(s) to enter prostitution including through cultivation of a dependency on drugs or alcohol	• Close involvement with prostitute(s) for example control of finances, choice of clients, working conditions, etc (where offender's involvement is not as a result of coercion)	• Performs limited function under direction • Close involvement but engaged by coercion/intimidation/exploitation

STEP TWO: starting point and category range

Having determined the category, the court should use the corresponding starting points to reach a sentence within the category range [below]. The starting point applies to all offenders irrespective of plea or previous convictions. Having determined the starting point, step two allows further adjustment for aggravating or mitigating features, set out [below].

A case of particular gravity, reflected by multiple features of culpability or harm in step one, could merit upward adjustment from the starting point before further adjustment for aggravating or mitigating features, set out [below].

Where there is a sufficient prospect of rehabilitation, a community order with a sex offender treatment programme requirement under section 202 of the Criminal Justice Act 2003 can be a proper alternative to a short or moderate length custodial sentence.

| Category 1 | **Starting point** (Crown Court) **Category range** (Crown Court) | **Starting point** (Crown Court) **Category range** (Crown Court) | **Starting point** 1 year's custody **Category range** 26 weeks' to 2 years' custody |
| Category 2 | **Starting point** (Crown Court) **Category range** (Crown Court) | **Starting point** 1 year's custody **Category range** High-level community order to 2 years' custody | **Starting point** Medium-level community order **Category range** Low-level community order to high-level community order |

The table below contains a **non-exhaustive** list of additional factual elements providing the context of the offence and factors relating to the offender. Identify whether any combination of these, or other relevant factors, should result in an upward or downward adjustment from the starting point. **In particular, relevant recent convictions are likely to result in an upward adjustment.** In some cases, having considered these factors, it may be appropriate to move outside the identified category range.

When sentencing appropriate **category 2 offences**, the court should also consider the custody threshold as follows:

- has the custody threshold been passed?
- if so, is it unavoidable that a custodial sentence be imposed?
- if so, can that sentence be suspended?

Aggravating factors	
Statutory aggravating factors	*Other aggravating factors*
• Previous convictions, having regard to (a) the nature of the offence to which the conviction relates and its relevance to the current offence; and (b) the time that has elapsed since the conviction • Offence committed whilst on bail	• Failure to comply with current court orders • Offence committed whilst on licence • Deliberate isolation of prostitute(s) • Threats made to expose prostitute(s) to the authorities (for example, immigration or police), family/friends or others • Harm threatened against the family/friends of prostitute(s) • Passport/identity documents removed • Prostitute(s) prevented from seeking medical treatment • Food withheld • Earnings withheld/kept by offender or evidence of excessive wage reduction or debt bondage, inflated travel or living expenses, or unreasonable interest rates • Any steps taken to prevent the reporting of an incident, obtaining assistance, and/or from assisting or supporting the prosecution • Attempts to dispose of or conceal evidence • Prostitute(s) forced or coerced into pornography • Timescale over which operation has been run

Mitigating factors
• No previous convictions **or** no relevant/recent convictions
• Remorse
• Previous good character and/or exemplary conduct*
• Age and/or lack of maturity where it affects the responsibility of the offender
• Mental disorder or learning disability, particularly where linked to the commission of the offence
• Demonstration of steps taken to address offending behaviour

* Previous good character/exemplary conduct is different from having no previous convictions. The more serious the offence, the less the weight which should normally be attributed to this factor. Where previous good character/exemplary conduct has been used to facilitate the offence, this mitigation should not normally be allowed and such conduct may constitute an aggravating factor.

 See *Blackstone's Criminal Practice 2017* **B3.243–B3.257**

C14.7 Keeping a brothel used for prostitution

Sexual Offences Act 1956, s 33

33 Keeping a brothel
It is an offence for a person to keep a brothel, or to manage, or act or assist in the management of, a brothel.

 SO

 3 months' imprisonment and/or level 3 fine. If previous conviction: 6 months' imprisonment and/or level 4 fine

Sexual Offences Act 1956, s 33A

33A Keeping a brothel used for prostitution
(1) It is an offence for a person to keep, or to manage, or act or assist in the management of, a brothel to which people resort for practices involving prostitution (whether or not also for other practices).

 EW

 6 months' imprisonment and/or fine/7 years' imprisonment

C14.7.1 *Sentencing*

STEP ONE: determining the offence category

The court should determine which categories of harm and culpability the offence falls into by reference **only** to the tables below.

Harm	
Category 1	• Under-18-year-olds working in brothel • Abduction/detention • Violence or threats of violence • Sustained and systematic psychological abuse • Those working in brothel forced or coerced to participate in unsafe/degrading sexual activity • Those working in brothel forced or coerced into seeing many 'customers' • Those working in brothel forced/coerced/deceived into prostitution • Established evidence of community impact
Category 2	Factor(s) in category 1 not present

Culpability		
A	B	C
• Keeping brothel on significant commercial basis • Involvement in keeping a number of brothels • Expectation of significant financial or other gain • Abuse of trust • Exploitation of those known to be trafficked • Significant involvement in limiting freedom of those working in brothel • Grooming of a person to work in the brothel including through cultivation of a dependency on drugs or alcohol	• Keeping/managing premises • Close involvement with those working in brothel eg control of finances, choice of clients, working conditions, etc (where offender's involvement is not as a result of coercion)	• Performs limited function under direction • Close involvement but engaged by coercion/intimidation/exploitation

STEP TWO: starting point and category range

Having determined the category, the court should use the corresponding starting points to reach a sentence within the category range [below]. The starting point applies to all offenders irrespective of plea or previous convictions. Having determined the starting point, step two allows further adjustment for aggravating or mitigating features, set out [below].

A case of particular gravity, reflected by multiple features of culpability or harm in step one, could merit upward adjustment from the starting point before further adjustment for aggravating or mitigating features, set out [below].

Where there is a sufficient prospect of rehabilitation, a community order with a sex offender treatment programme requirement under section 202 of the Criminal Justice Act 2003 can be a proper alternative to a short or moderate length custodial sentence.

	A	B	C
Category 1	**Starting point** (Crown Court) **Category range** (Crown Court)	**Starting point** (Crown Court) **Category range** (Crown Court)	**Starting point** 1 year's custody **Category range** High-level community order to 18 months' custody
Category 2	**Starting point** (Crown Court) **Category range** (Crown Court)	**Starting point** 12 months' custody **Category range** 26 weeks' to 2 years' custody	**Starting point** Medium-level community order **Category range** Low-level community order to high-level community order

The table below contains a **non-exhaustive** list of additional factual elements providing the context of the offence and factors relating to the offender. Identify whether any combination of these, or other relevant factors, should result in an upward or downward adjustment from the starting point. **In particular, relevant recent convictions are likely to result in an upward adjustment.** In some cases, having considered these factors, it may be appropriate to move outside the identified category range.

When sentencing appropriate **category 1 offences**, the court should also consider the custody threshold as follows:

• has the custody threshold been passed?
• if so, is it unavoidable that a custodial sentence be imposed?
• if so, can that sentence be suspended?

C14 Sexual Offences

Aggravating factors	
Statutory aggravating factors	*Other aggravating factors*
• Previous convictions, having regard to (a) the nature of the offence to which the conviction relates and its relevance to the current offence; and (b) the time that has elapsed since the conviction • Offence committed whilst on bail	• Failure to comply with current court orders • Offence committed whilst on licence • Deliberate isolation of those working in brothel • Threats made to expose those working in brothel to the authorities (for example, immigration or police), family/friends, or others • Harm threatened against the family/friends of those working in brothel • Passport/identity documents removed. • Those working in brothel prevented from seeking medical treatment • Food withheld • Those working in brothel passed around by offender and moved to other brothels • Earnings of those working in brothel withheld/kept by offender, or evidence of excessive wage reduction or debt bondage, inflated travel or living expenses, or unreasonable interest rates • Any steps taken to prevent those working in brothel reporting an incident, obtaining assistance, and/or from assisting or supporting the prosecution • Attempts to dispose of or conceal evidence • Those working in brothel forced or coerced into pornography • Timescale over which operation has been run

Mitigating factors

• No previous convictions **or** no relevant/recent convictions
• Remorse
• Previous good character and/or exemplary conduct*
• Age and/or lack of maturity where it affects the responsibility of the offender
• Mental disorder or learning disability, particularly where linked to the commission of the offence
• Demonstration of steps taken to address offending behaviour

* Previous good character/exemplary conduct is different from having no previous convictions. The more serious the offence, the less the weight which should normally be attributed to this factor. Where previous good character/exemplary conduct has been used to facilitate the offence, this mitigation should not normally be allowed and such conduct may constitute an aggravating factor.

 See *Blackstone's Criminal Practice 2017* **B3.347–B3.362**

C14.8 Possession of paedophile manual

Serious Crime Act 2015, s 69

Possession of paedophile manual

(1) It is an offence to be in possession of any item that contains advice or guidance about abusing children sexually.

(2) It is a defence for a person (D) charged with an offence under this section—
- (a) to prove that D had a legitimate reason for being in possession of the item;
- (b) to prove that—
    - (i) D had not read, viewed or (as appropriate) listened to the item, and
    - (ii) D did not know, and had no reason to suspect, that it contained advice or guidance about abusing children sexually; or
- (c) to prove that—
    - (i) the item was sent to D without any request made by D or on D's behalf, and
    - (ii) D did not keep it for an unreasonable time.

...

(4) Proceedings for an offence under this section may be brought—
- (a) in England and Wales, only by or with the consent of the Director of Public Prosecutions;

C14.8.1 Key points

Serious Crime Act 2015, s 69

(8) In this section—,
  'abusing children sexually' means doing anything that constitutes—
- (a) an offence under Part 1 of the Sexual Offences Act 2003, or under Part 2, 3, against a person under 16, or
- (b) an offence under section 1 of the Protection of Children Act 1978 involving indecent photographs (but not pseudo-photographs), or doing anything outside England and Wales that would constitute such an offence if done in England and Wales;
  'item' includes anything in which information of any description is recorded;
  'prohibited item' means an item within subsection (1).

EW

 6 months' imprisonment and/or a fine/2 years' imprisonment

C14.9 Sexual activity in a public lavatory

Sexual Offences Act 2003, s 71(1) and (2)

71 Sexual activity in a public lavatory

(1) A person commits an offence if—
   (a) he is in a lavatory to which the public or a section of the public has or is permitted to have access, whether on payment or otherwise,
   (b) he intentionally engages in an activity, and,
   (c) the activity is sexual.
(2) For the purposes of this section, an activity is sexual if a reasonable person would, in all the circumstances but regardless of any person's purpose, consider it to be sexual.

SO 6 months' imprisonment and/or fine

C14.9.1 *Sentencing*

Note that this guideline is under review by the Sentencing Council (see **Appendix 7***).*

Offence seriousness (culpability and harm) A. Identify the appropriate starting point Starting points based on first-time offender pleading not guilty		
Examples of nature of activity	**Starting point**	**Range**
Basic offence as defined in the Act, assuming no aggravating or mitigating factors	Band C fine	Band C fine
Offence with aggravating factors	Low-level community order	Band C fine to medium-level community order

Offence seriousness (culpability and harm) B. Consider the effect of aggravating and mitigating factors (other than those within examples above) The following may be particularly relevant but these lists are not exhaustive
Factors indicating higher culpability 1. Intimidating behaviour/threats of violence to member(s) of the public 2. Blatant behaviour

C14.9.2 Key points

- This offence is committed where an offender intentionally engages in sexual activity in a public lavatory. It was introduced to give adults and children the freedom to use public lavatories for the purpose for which they are designed, without the fear of being an unwilling witness to overtly sexual behaviour of a kind that most people would not expect to be conducted in public. It is primarily a public order offence rather than a sexual offence.

• When dealing with a repeat offender, the starting point should be a low-level community order, with a range of Band B and C fines to medium-level community order. The presence of aggravating factors may suggest that a sentence above the range is appropriate.

• This guideline may be relevant by way of analogy to conduct charged as the common law offence of outraging public decency; the offence is triable either way and has a maximum penalty of a fine and/or six months' imprisonment when tried summarily.

 See *Blackstone's Criminal Practice 2017* **B3.303–B3.305**

C14.10 Sexual assault

Sexual Offences Act 2003, ss 3(1)–(3), 4, 7(1), 8, and 9

3 Sexual assault

(1) A person (A) commits an offence if—
    (a) he intentionally touches another person (B),
    (b) the touching is sexual,
    (c) B does not consent to the touching, and
    (d) A does not reasonably believe that B consents.

(2) Whether a belief is reasonable is to be determined having regard to all the circumstances, including any steps A has taken to ascertain whether B consents.

(3) Sections 75 and 76 apply to an offence under this section....

4 Causing a person to engage in sexual activity without consent

(1) A person (A) commits an offence if—
    (a) he intentionally causes another person (B) to engage in an activity,
    (b) the activity is sexual,
    (c) B does not consent to engaging in the activity, and
    (d) A does not reasonably believe that B consents.

(2) Whether a belief is reasonable is to be determined having regard to all the circumstances, including any steps A has taken to ascertain whether B consents.

(3) Sections 75 and 76 apply to an offence under this section.

(4) A person guilty of an offence under this section, if the activity caused involved—
    (a) penetration of B's anus or vagina,
    (b) penetration of B's mouth with a person's penis,
    (c) penetration of a person's anus or vagina with a part of B's body or by B with anything else, or
    (d) penetration of a person's mouth with B's penis,
is liable, on conviction on indictment, to imprisonment for life.

---

7 Sexual assault of a child under 13

(1) A person commits an offence if—
   (a) he intentionally touches another person,
   (b) the touching is sexual, and
   (c) the other person is under 13....

8 Causing or inciting a child under 13 to engage in sexual activity

(1) A person commits an offence if—
   (a) he intentionally causes or incites another person (B) to engage in an activity,
   (b) the activity is sexual, and
   (c) B is under 13.
(2) A person guilty of an offence under this section, if the activity caused or incited involved—
   (a) penetration of B's anus or vagina,
   (b) penetration of B's mouth with a person's penis,
   (c) penetration of a person's anus or vagina with a part of B's body or by B with anything else, or
   (d) penetration of a person's mouth with B's penis,
   is liable, on conviction on indictment, to imprisonment for life.

9 Sexual activity with a child

(1) A person aged 18 or over (A) commits an offence if—
   (a) he intentionally touches another person (B),
   (b) the touching is sexual, and
   (c) either—
       (i) B is under 16 and A does not reasonably believe that B is 16 or over, or
       (ii) B is under 13.
(2) A person guilty of an offence under this section, if the touching involved—
   (a) penetration of B's anus or vagina with a part of A's body or anything else,
   (b) penetration of B's mouth with A's penis,
   (c) penetration of A's anus or vagina with a part of B's body, or
   (d) penetration of A's mouth with B's penis.

EW Save for sections 4, 8, and 9 where penetration is involved and the offences become triable only on indictment with maximum sentences of life for both sections 4 and 8 and 14 years' imprisonment for section 9

▥ 6 months' imprisonment and/or fine/10 years' (ss 3, 4), 14 years' (ss 7, 8), 14 years' imprisonment (s 9), save for sections 4 and 8 where penetration is involved and the offence is triable only on indictment with a maximum of life imprisonment

---

C14.10.1 *Sentencing*

[The guidelines set out below are applicable to adult offenders sentenced after 1 April 2014.]

Sexual Offences Act 2003, s 3

STEP ONE: determining the offence category
The court should determine which categories of harm and culpability the offence falls into by reference only to the tables below.

Harm		Culpability	
		A	**B**
Category 1	• Severe psychological or physical harm • Abduction • Violence or threats of violence • Forced/uninvited entry into victim's home	• Significant degree of planning • Offender acts together with others to commit the offence • Use of alcohol/drugs on victim to facilitate the offence • Abuse of trust • Previous violence against victim • Offence committed in course of burglary • Recording of offence	Factor(s) in category A not present
		• Commercial exploitation and/or motivation • Offence racially or religiously aggravated • Offence motivated by, or demonstrating, hostility to the victim based on his or her sexual orientation (or presumed sexual orientation) or transgender identity (or presumed transgender identity) • Offence motivated by, or demonstrating, hostility to the victim based on his or her disability (or presumed disability)	

Category 2	• Touching of naked genitalia or naked breasts • Prolonged detention/ sustained incident • Additional degradation/ humiliation • Victim is particularly vulnerable due to personal circumstances		
Category 3	• Factor(s) in categories 1 and 2 not present		

STEP TWO: starting point and category range

Having determined the category, the court should use the corresponding starting points to reach a sentence within the category range [below]. The starting point applies to all offenders irrespective of plea or previous convictions. Having determined the starting point, step two allows further adjustment for aggravating or mitigating features, set out on the next page.

A case of particular gravity, reflected by multiple features of culpability or harm in step one, could merit upward adjustment from the starting point before further adjustment for aggravating or mitigating features, set out [below].

Where there is a sufficient prospect of rehabilitation, a community order with a sex offender treatment programme requirement under section 202 of the Criminal Justice Act 2003 can be a proper alternative to a short or moderate length custodial sentence.

	A	B
Category 1	**Starting point** (Crown Court) **Category range** (Crown Court)	**Starting point** (Crown Court) **Category range** (Crown Court)
Category 2	**Starting point** (Crown Court) **Category range** (Crown Court)	**Starting point** 1 year's custody **Category range** High-level community order to 2 years' custody
Category 3	**Starting point** 26 weeks' custody **Category range** High-level community order to 1 year's custody	**Starting point** High-level community order **Category range** Medium-level community order to 26 weeks' custody

The table below contains a **non-exhaustive** list of additional factual elements providing the context of the offence and factors relating to the offender. Identify whether any combination of these, or other relevant factors, should result in an upward or downward adjustment from the starting point. **In particular, relevant recent convictions are likely to result in an upward adjustment.** In some cases, having considered these factors, it may be appropriate to move outside the identified category range.

When sentencing appropriate **category 2 or 3 offences**, the court should also consider the custody threshold as follows:

- has the custody threshold been passed?
- if so, is it unavoidable that a custodial sentence be imposed?
- if so, can that sentence be suspended?

Aggravating factors	
Statutory aggravating factors	*Other aggravating factors*
<ul><li>Previous convictions, having regard to (a) the nature of the offence to which the conviction relates and its relevance to the current offence; and (b) the time that has elapsed since the conviction</li><li>Offence committed whilst on bail</li></ul>	<ul><li>Specific targeting of a particularly vulnerable victim</li><li>Blackmail or other threats made (where not taken into account at step one)</li><li>Location of offence</li><li>Timing of offence</li><li>Use of weapon or other item to frighten or injure</li><li>Victim compelled to leave their home (including victims of domestic violence)</li><li>Failure to comply with current court orders</li><li>Offence committed whilst on licence</li><li>Exploiting contact arrangements with a child to commit an offence</li><li>Presence of others, especially children</li><li>Any steps taken to prevent the victim reporting an incident, obtaining assistance, and/or from assisting or supporting the prosecution</li><li>Attempts to dispose of or conceal evidence</li><li>Commission of offence whilst under the influence of alcohol or drugs</li></ul>
Mitigating factors	
<ul><li>No previous convictions **or** no relevant/recent convictions</li><li>Remorse</li><li>Previous good character and/or exemplary conduct*</li><li>Age and/or lack of maturity where it affects the responsibility of the offender</li><li>Mental disorder or learning disability, particularly where linked to the commission of the offence</li><li>Demonstration of steps taken to address offending behaviour</li></ul>	

* Previous good character/exemplary conduct is different from having no previous convictions. The more serious the offence, the less the weight which should normally be attributed to this factor. Where previous good character/exemplary conduct has been used to facilitate the offence, this mitigation should not normally be allowed and such conduct may constitute an aggravating factor.

C14 Sexual Offences

Sexual Offences Act 2003, s 7

STEP ONE: determining the offence category

The court should determine which categories of harm and culpability the offence falls into by reference **only** to the tables below.

Harm		Culpability	
		A	**B**
Category 1	• Severe psychological or physical harm • Abduction • Violence or threats of violence • Forced/uninvited entry into victim's home	• Significant degree of planning • Offender acts together with others to commit the offence • Use of alcohol/drugs on victim to facilitate the offence • Grooming behaviour used against victim • Abuse of trust • Previous violence against victim • Offence committed in course of burglary • Sexual images of victim recorded, retained, solicited, or shared • Deliberate isolation of victim • Commercial exploitation and/or motivation • Offence racially or religiously aggravated • Offence motivated by, or demonstrating, hostility to the victim based on his or her sexual orientation (or presumed sexual orientation) or transgender identity (or presumed transgender identity) • Offence motivated by, or demonstrating, hostility to the victim based on his or her disability (or presumed disability)	Factor(s) in category A not present
Category 2	• Touching of naked genitalia or naked breast area • Prolonged detention/sustained incident • Additional degradation/humiliation • Child is particularly vulnerable due to extreme youth and/or personal circumstances		
Category 3	Factor(s) in categories 1 and 2 not present		

STEP TWO: starting point and category range

Having determined the category, the court should use the corresponding starting points to reach a sentence within the category range [below]. The starting point applies to all offenders irrespective of plea or previous convictions. Having determined the starting point, step two allows further adjustment for aggravating or mitigating features, set out [below].

A case of particular gravity, reflected by multiple features of culpability or harm in step one, could merit upward adjustment from the starting point before further adjustment for aggravating or mitigating features, set out [below].

Where there is a sufficient prospect of rehabilitation, a community order with a sex offender treatment programme requirement under section 202 of the Criminal Justice Act 2003 can be a proper alternative to a short or moderate length custodial sentence.

	A	B
Category 1	**Starting point** (Crown Court) **Category range** (Crown Court)	**Starting point** (Crown Court) **Category range** (Crown Court)
Category 2	**Starting point** (Crown Court) **Category range** (Crown Court)	**Starting point** (Crown Court) **Category range** (Crown Court)
Category 3	**Starting point** 1 year's custody **Category range** 26 weeks' to 2 years' custody	**Starting point** 26 weeks' custody **Category range** High-level community order to 1 year's custody

The table below contains a **non-exhaustive** list of additional factual elements providing the context of the offence and factors relating to the offender. Identify whether any combination of these, or other relevant factors, should result in an upward or downward adjustment from the starting point. **In particular, relevant recent convictions are likely to result in an upward adjustment.** In some cases, having considered these factors, it may be appropriate to move outside the identified category range.

Aggravating factors	
Statutory aggravating factors	*Other aggravating factors*
• Previous convictions, having regard to (a) the nature of the offence to which the conviction relates and its relevance to the current offence; and (b) the time that has elapsed since the conviction • Offence committed whilst on bail	• Specific targeting of a particularly vulnerable child • Blackmail or other threats made (where not taken into account at step one) • Location of offence • Timing of offence • Use of weapon or other item to frighten or injure • Victim compelled to leave their home, school, etc • Failure to comply with current court orders • Offence committed whilst on licence • Exploiting contact arrangements with a child to commit an offence • Presence of others, especially other children • Any steps taken to prevent the victim reporting an incident, obtaining assistance, and/or from assisting or supporting the prosecution • Attempts to dispose of or conceal evidence • Commission of offence whilst under the influence of alcohol or drugs • Victim encouraged to recruit others

Mitigating factors
• No previous convictions **or** no relevant/recent convictions • Remorse • Previous good character and/or exemplary conduct* • Age and/or lack of maturity where it affects the responsibility of the offender • Mental disorder or learning disability, particularly where linked to the commission of the offence

* Previous good character/exemplary conduct is different from having no previous convictions. The more serious the offence, the less the weight which should normally be attributed to this factor. Where previous good character/exemplary conduct has been used to facilitate the offence, this mitigation should not normally be allowed and such conduct may constitute an aggravating factor.

In the context of this offence, previous good character/exemplary conduct should not normally be given any significant weight and will not normally justify a reduction in what would otherwise be the appropriate sentence.

C14.10.2 Key points

- A belief in consent arising from delusional psychotic illness must be objectively judged but the personality or disability of the defendant may be relevant to whether the belief was reasonably held where for instance it involved the reading of subtle social

signals. An irrational belief can never meet the reasonableness test (*R v B* [2013] EWCA Crim 3).
- A person under 16 years of age cannot in law consent.

 See *Blackstone's Criminal Practice 2014* **B3.53–B3.68** and **B3.78–B3.92**

C14.11 Sex offenders register—fail to comply with notification requirements

Sexual Offences Act 2003, s 91(1)

91 Offences relating to notification

(1) A person commits an offence if he—
    (a) fails, without reasonable excuse, to comply with section 83(1), 84(1), 4(4)(b), 85(1), 87(4) or 89(2)(b) or any requirement imposed by regulations made under section 86(1); or
    (b) notifies to the police, in purported compliance with section 83(1), 4(1) or 85(1) or any requirement imposed by regulations made under section 86(1), any information which he knows to be false.

EW

 Fine and/or 6 months'/5 years' imprisonment

C14.11.1 *Sentencing*

Offence seriousness (culpability and harm) A. Identify the appropriate starting point Starting points based on first-time offender (see note below) pleading not guilty		
Example of nature of activity	**Starting point**	**Range**
Negligent or inadvertent failure to comply with requirements	Medium-level community order	Band C fine to high-level community order
Deliberate failure to comply with requirements OR Supply of information known to be false	6 weeks' custody	High-level community order to 26 weeks' custody
Conduct as described in box above AND Long period of non-compliance OR Attempts to avoid detection	18 weeks' custody	6 weeks' custody to Crown Court

Offence seriousness (culpability and harm)	
B. Consider the effect of aggravating and mitigating factors (other than those within examples above)	
The following may be particularly relevant but these lists are not exhaustive	
Factor indicating higher culpability	**Factor indicating lower culpability**
1. Long period of non-compliance (where not in the examples above)	1. Genuine misunderstanding
Factors indicating greater degree of harm	
1. Alarm or distress caused to victim	
2. Particularly serious original offence	

C14.11.2 Key points

- A person who is subject to the notification requirements commits a criminal offence if he fails, without reasonable excuse, to:
  - make an initial notification, in accordance with section 83(1), of those matters set out in the Sexual Offences Act 2003 (Notification Requirements) (England and Wales) Regulations 2012;
  - notify a change of details in accordance with section 84(1);
  - make a renotification in accordance with section 85(1);
  - comply with any requirement imposed by regulations concerned with the notification of foreign travel (s 86(1));
  - notify the fact that a change did not happen as predicted when it had been notified in advance in accordance with section 84(4)(b);
  - allow a police officer to take his photograph or fingerprints (s 87(4));
  - ensure that a young offender on whose behalf he is required by a parental direction to comply with the notification requirements attends a police station when a notification is made (s 89(2)(b));
  - in the first four cases set out above, if he knowingly provides false information;
  - the prescribed information includes names, addresses, date of birth, National Insurance number, bank accounts, debit and credit card details, and details of passports or other identity documents.
- The offence occurs on the first day of breach and continues— only one breach can be prosecuted in such circumstances.
- A conditional discharge cannot be imposed on breach.

 See *Blackstone's Criminal Practice 2017* **E23**

C14.12 **Voyeurism**

Sexual Offences Act 2003, s 67(1)–(4)

67 Voyeurism

(1) A person commits an offence if—
   (a) for the purpose of obtaining sexual gratification, he observes another person doing a private act, and
   (b) he knows that the other person does not consent to being observed for his sexual gratification.

(2) A person commits an offence if—
   (a) he operates equipment with the intention of enabling another person to observe, for the purpose of obtaining sexual gratification, a third person (B) doing a private act, and
   (b) he knows that B does not consent to his operating equipment with that intention.

(3) A person commits an offence if—
   (a) he records another person (B) doing a private act,
   (b) he does so with the intention that he or a third person will, for the purpose of obtaining sexual gratification, look at an image of B doing the act, and
   (c) he knows that B does not consent to his recording the act with that intention.

(4) A person commits an offence if he installs equipment, or constructs or adapts a structure or part of a structure, with the intention of enabling himself or another person to commit an offence under subsection (1).

EW

6 months' imprisonment and/or fine/2 years' imprisonment

DO

C14.12.1 *Sentencing*

Sexual Offences Act 2003, s 67

STEP ONE: determining the offence category

The court should determine the offence category using the table below.

Category 1	Raised harm **and** raised culpability
Category 2	Raised harm **or** raised culpability
Category 3	Voyeurism **without** raised harm or culpability factors present

The court should determine culpability and harm caused or intended, by reference **only** to the factors below, which comprise the principal factual elements of the offence. Where an offence does not fall squarely into a category, individual factors may require a degree of weighting before making an overall assessment and determining the appropriate offence category.

Factors indicating raised harm
• Image(s) available to be viewed by others
• Victim observed or recorded in their own home or residence
Factors indicating raised culpability
• Significant degree of planning
• Image(s) recorded
• Abuse of trust
• Specific or previous targeting of a particularly vulnerable victim
• Commercial exploitation and/or motivation
• Offence racially or religiously aggravated
• Offence motivated by, or demonstrating, hostility to the victim based on his or her sexual orientation (or presumed sexual orientation) or transgender identity (or presumed transgender identity)
• Offence motivated by, or demonstrating, hostility to the victim based on his or her disability (or presumed disability)

STEP TWO: starting point and category range

Having determined the category, the court should use the corresponding starting points to reach a sentence within the category range [below]. The starting point applies to all offenders irrespective of plea or previous convictions. Having determined the starting point, step two allows further adjustment for aggravating or mitigating features, set out [below].

A case of particular gravity, reflected by multiple features of culpability or harm in step one, could merit upward adjustment from the starting point before further adjustment for aggravating or mitigating features, set out [below].

Where there is a sufficient prospect of rehabilitation, a community order with a sex offender treatment programme requirement under section 202 of the Criminal Justice Act 2003 can be a proper alternative to a short or moderate length custodial sentence.

Category 1	**Starting point**
	26 weeks' custody
	Category range
	12 weeks' to 18 months' custody

Category 2	**Starting point** High-level community order **Category range** Medium-level community order to 26 weeks' custody
Category 3	**Starting point** Medium-level community order **Category range** Band A fine to high-level community order

The table below contains a **non-exhaustive** list of additional factual elements providing the context of the offence and factors relating to the offender. Identify whether any combination of these, or other relevant factors, should result in an upward or downward adjustment from the starting point. **In particular, relevant recent convictions are likely to result in an upward adjustment.** In some cases, having considered these factors, it may be appropriate to move outside the identified category range.

When sentencing **category 2 offences**, the court should also consider the custody threshold as follows:

- has the custody threshold been passed?
- if so, is it unavoidable that a custodial sentence be imposed?
- if so, can that sentence be suspended?

When sentencing *category 3 offences*, the court should also consider the community order threshold as follows:

- has the community order threshold been passed?

Aggravating factors	
Statutory aggravating factors	*Other aggravating factors*
• Previous convictions, having regard to (a) the nature of the offence to which the conviction relates and its relevance to the current offence; and (b) the time that has elapsed since the conviction • Offence committed whilst on bail	• Location of offence • Timing of offence • Failure to comply with current court orders • Offence committed whilst on licence • Distribution of images, whether or not for gain • Placing images where there is the potential for a high volume of viewers • Period over which victim observed • Period over which images were made or distributed • Any steps taken to prevent victim reporting an incident, obtaining assistance, and/or from assisting or supporting the prosecution • Attempts to dispose of or conceal evidence

---

Mitigating factors

- No previous convictions **or** no relevant/recent convictions
- Remorse
- Previous good character and/or exemplary conduct*
- Age and/or lack of maturity where it affects the responsibility of the offender
- Mental disorder or learning disability, particularly where linked to the commission of the offence
- Demonstration of steps taken to address offending behaviour

---

* Previous good character/exemplary conduct is different from having no previous convictions. The more serious the offence, the less the weight which should normally be attributed to this factor. Where previous good character/exemplary conduct has been used to facilitate the offence, this mitigation should not normally be allowed and such conduct may constitute an aggravating factor.

C14.12.2 Key points

- Section 68 provides for the interpretation of key phrases:

Sexual Offences Act 2003, s 68

68 Voyeurism: interpretation

(1) For the purposes of section 67, a person is doing a private act if the person is in a place which, in the circumstances, would reasonably be expected to provide privacy, and—
   (a) the person's genitals, buttocks or breasts are exposed or covered only with underwear,
   (b) the person is using a lavatory, or
   (c) the person is doing a sexual act that is not of a kind ordinarily done in public.
(2) In section 67, 'structure' includes a tent, vehicle or vessel or other temporary or movable structure.

- Consent is defined under section 74 of the Act:

Sexual Offences Act 2003, s 74

74 'Consent'

For the purposes of this Part, a person consents if he agrees by choice, and has the freedom and capacity to make that choice.

- Sections 75 and 76 deal with evidential presumptions in relation to consent.

 See *Blackstone's Criminal Practice 2017* **B3.290–B3.294**

C15 **Dishonesty and Offences Against Property**

C15.1 Aggravated vehicle-taking

Theft Act 1968, s 12A(1)–(3)

12A Aggravated vehicle-taking

(1) Subject to subsection (3) below, a person is guilty of aggravated taking of a vehicle if—
  (a) he commits an offence under section 12(1) above (in this section referred to as a 'basic offence') in relation to a mechanically propelled vehicle; and
  (b) it is proved that, at any time after the vehicle was unlawfully taken (whether by him or another) and before it was recovered, the vehicle was driven, or injury or damage was caused, in one or more of the circumstances set out in paragraphs (a) to (d) of subsection (2) below.
(2) The circumstances referred to in subsection (1)(b) above are—
  (a) that the vehicle was driven dangerously on a road or other public place;
  (b) that, owing to the driving of the vehicle, an accident occurred by which injury was caused to any person;
  (c) that, owing to the driving of the vehicle, an accident occurred by which damage was caused to any property, other than the vehicle;
  (d) that damage was caused to the vehicle.
(3) A person is not guilty of an offence under this section if he proves that, as regards any such proven driving, injury or damage as is referred to in subsection (1)(b) above, either—
  (a) the driving, accident or damage referred to in subsection (2) above occurred before he committed the basic offence; or
  (b) he was neither in nor on nor in the immediate vicinity of the vehicle when that driving, accident or damage occurred.

EW Summary only if damage only and under £5,000

‖‖‖ Section 12A(2)(a) and (b): 6 months and/or fine/2 years' imprisonment (14 years' if accident caused death). Must endorse and disqualify for at least 12 months. Must disqualify for at least 2 years if offender has had two or more disqualifications for periods of 56 days or more in preceding 3 years.

‖‖‖ Section 12A(2)(c) and (d): 6 months' imprisonment and/or fine/ 2 years' imprisonment. Must endorse and disqualify for at least 12 months. Must disqualify for at least 2 years if offender has had two or more disqualifications for periods of 56 days or more in preceding 3 years.

C15.1.1 *Sentencing: dangerous driving or accident causing injury*

Offence seriousness (culpability and harm) A. Identify the appropriate starting point Starting points based on first-time offender pleading not guilty		
Example of nature of activity	**Starting point**	**Range**
Taken vehicle involved in single incident of bad driving where little or no damage or risk of personal injury	High-level community order	Medium-level community order to 12 weeks' custody
Taken vehicle involved in incident(s) involving excessive speed or showing off, especially on busy roads or in built-up area	18 weeks' custody	12 to 26 weeks' custody
Taken vehicle involved in prolonged bad driving involving deliberate disregard for safety of others	Crown Court	Crown Court

Offence seriousness (culpability and harm)
B. Consider the effect of aggravating and mitigating factors (other than those within examples above)
The following may be particularly relevant but these lists are not exhaustive

Factors indicating higher culpability
1. Disregarding warnings of others
2. Evidence of alcohol or drugs
3. Carrying out other tasks while driving
4. Tiredness
5. Trying to avoid arrest
6. Aggressive driving, such as driving much too close to vehicle in front, inappropriate attempts to overtake, or cutting in after overtaking

Factors indicating greater degree of harm
1. Injury to others
2. Damage to other vehicle or property

C15.1.2 *Sentencing: damage caused*

Offence seriousness (culpability and harm) A. Identify the appropriate starting point Starting points based on first-time offender pleading not guilty		
Examples of nature of activity	**Starting point**	**Range**
Exceeding authorised use of, eg employer's or relative's, vehicle; retention of hire car beyond return date; minor damage to taken vehicle	Medium-level community order	Low-level community order to high level community order

Greater damage to taken vehicle and/ or moderate damage to another vehicle and/or moderate damage to another vehicle and/or property	High-level community order	Medium-level community order to 12 weeks' custody
Vehicle taken as part of burglary or from private premises; severe damage	18 weeks' custody	12 to 26 weeks' custody (Crown Court if damage over £5,000)

Offence seriousness (culpability and harm)
B. Consider the effect of aggravating and mitigating factors (other than those within examples above)
The following may be particularly relevant but these lists are not exhaustive

Factors indicating higher culpability	Factors indicating lower culpability
1. Vehicle deliberately damaged/destroyed 2. Offender under influence of alcohol/drugs **Factors indicating greater degree of harm** 1. Passenger(s) carried 2. Vehicle belonging to elderly or disabled person 3. Emergency service vehicle 4. Medium to large goods vehicle 5. Damage caused in moving traffic accident	1. Misunderstanding with owner 2. Damage resulting from actions of another (where this does not provide a defence)

C15.1.3 Key points

- If aggravating factor is solely damage, then the offence is triable summarily only if the damage does not exceed £5,000.
- A magistrates' court can convict a defendant of the alternative offence of vehicle taking if it does not find the aggravating feature(s) (*H v Liverpool Youth Court* [2001] Crim LR 897).
- The allegation under section 12A Theft Act 1968 that there has been a taking and 'owing to the driving of the vehicle, an accident occurred by which injury was caused to any person' requires an element of fault in the driving. There must have been at least some act or omission in the control of the car which involved some element of fault and which contributed in some more than minimal way (*R v Taylor* [2016] UKSC 5). This will apply equally to an accident in which damage is caused.

 See *Blackstone's Criminal Practice 2017* **B4.127–B4.134**

C15.2 Alcohol/tobacco, fraudulently evade duty

Customs and Excise Management Act 1979, s. 170

6 months' imprisonment and/or £20,000/7 years' imprisonment

C15.2.1 *Sentencing*

See **Appendix 5**.

C15.2.2 Key points

- It is not sufficient for the prosecution to show that the defendant was merely reckless (*R v Panayi* [1989] 1 WLR 187).
- It is irrelevant that the defendant does not know the precise nature of the goods being imported (*R v Shivpuri* [1987] AC 1).
- The burden of proving that duty has been paid falls on the defendant (s 154).
- The prosecution have the right to appeal sentence (*Customs and Excise Commissioners v Brunt* (1998) 163 JP 161).

See *Blackstone's Criminal Practice 2017* **B16.40–B16.52**

C15.3 **Burglary**

> **Theft Act 1968, s 9(1) and (2)**
>
> **9 Burglary**
> (1) A person is guilty of burglary if—
>   (a) he enters any building or part of a building as a trespasser and with intent to commit any such offence as is mentioned in subsection (2) below; or
>   (b) having entered any building or part of a building as a trespasser he steals or attempts to steal anything in the building or that part of it or inflicts or attempts to inflict on any person therein any grievous bodily harm.
> (2) The offences referred to in subsection (1)(a) above are offences of stealing anything in the building or part of a building in question, of inflicting on any person therein any grievous bodily harm therein, and of doing unlawful damage to the building or anything therein.

 6 months' imprisonment and/or fine/10 years' imprisonment (14 years' if dwelling)

 Offence *is indictable only* and must be sent to the Crown Court if:

- the offender:
  - was 18 or over when he committed the offence,
  - committed the offence on or after 1 December 1999,
  - had previously been convicted of two other domestic burglary offences in England and Wales; one of those offences has been committed after conviction for the other and both of the previous domestic burglaries had been committed on or after 1 December 1999;
- any person was subjected to violence or the threat of violence: Magistrates' Courts Act 1980, Schedule 1.

C15.3.1 *Sentencing: non-dwelling*

STEP ONE: determine the offence category

Category 1	Greater harm and higher culpability
Category 2	Greater harm and lower culpability or lesser harm and higher culpability
Category 3	Lesser harm and lower culpability

Factors indicating greater harm	**Factors indicating higher culpability**
Theft of/damage to property causing a significant degree of loss to the victim (whether economic, commercial, or personal value) Soiling, ransacking, or vandalism of property Victim on the premises (or returns) while offender present Trauma to the victim, beyond the normal inevitable consequence of intrusion and theft Violence used or threatened against victim Context of general public disorder	Premises or victim deliberately targeted (to include pharmacy or doctor's surgery and targeting due to vulnerability of victim or hostility based on disability, race, sexual orientation, and so forth) A significant degree of planning or organization Knife or other weapon carried (where not charged separately) Equipped for burglary (eg implements carried and/or use of vehicle) Member of a group or gang
Factors indicating lesser harm	**Factors indicating lower culpability**
Nothing stolen or only property of very low value to the victim (whether economic, commercial, or personal) Limited damage or disturbance to property	Offence committed on impulse, with limited intrusion into property Offender exploited by others Mental disorder or learning disability, where linked to the commission of the offence

STEP TWO: **starting point and category range**

Offence category	Starting point	Category range
Category 1	Crown Court	Crown Court
Category 2	18 weeks' custody	Low-level community order to Crown Court (51 weeks' custody)
Category 3	Medium-level community order	Band B fine to 18 weeks' custody

Factors increasing seriousness	Factors reducing seriousness or reflecting personal mitigation
Statutory aggravating factors: Previous convictions, having regard to (a) the nature of the offence to which the conviction relates and its relevance to the current offence; and (b) the time that has elapsed since the conviction Offence committed whilst on bail **Other aggravating factors include:** Offence committed at night, particularly where staff present or likely to be present Abuse of a position of trust Gratuitous degradation of the victim Any steps taken to prevent the victim reporting the incident or obtaining assistance and/or from assisting or supporting the prosecution Established evidence of community impact Commission of offence whilst under the influence of alcohol or drugs Failure to comply with current court orders Offence committed whilst on licence Offences taken into consideration (TICs)	Offender has made voluntary reparation to the victim Subordinate role in a group or gang No previous convictions or no relevant/ recent convictions Remorse Good character and/or exemplary conduct Determination and/or demonstration of steps taken to address addiction or offending behaviour Serious medical conditions requiring urgent, intensive, or long-term treatment Age and/or lack of maturity where it affects the responsibility of the offender Lapse of time since the offence where this is not the fault of the offender Mental disorder or learning disability, where not linked to the commission of the offence Sole or primary carer for dependent relatives

C15.3.1.1 *Additional steps*

Consider any factors which indicate a reduction, such as: assistance to the prosecution; reduction for guilty plea; dangerousness; totality principle; compensation and ancillary orders; reasons; consideration for remand time.

C15.3.2 *Sentencing: dwelling*
STEP ONE: determine the offence category

Category 1	Greater harm and higher culpability
Category 2	Greater harm and lower culpability or lesser harm and higher culpability
Category 3	Lesser harm and lower culpability

Factors indicating greater harm	Factors indicating higher culpability
Theft of/damage to property causing a significant degree of loss to the victim (whether economic, sentimental, or personal value)	Victim or premises deliberately targeted (eg due to vulnerability or hostility based on disability, race, or sexual orientation)
Soiling, ransacking, or vandalism of property Occupier at home (or returns home) while offender present Trauma to the victim beyond the normal inevitable consequence of intrusion and theft Violence used or threatened against victim Context of general public disorder	A significant degree of planning or organization Knife or other weapon carried (where not charged separately) Equipped for burglary (eg implements carried and/or use of vehicle) Member of a group or gang
Factors indicating lesser harm	**Factors indicating lower culpability**
Nothing stolen or only property of very low value to the victim (whether economic, sentimental, or personal) Limited damage or disturbance to property	Offence committed on impulse, with limited intrusion into property Offender exploited by others Mental disorder or learning disability, where linked to the commission of the offence

STEP TWO: starting point and category range

Where the defendant is dependent on or has a propensity to misuse drugs and there is sufficient prospect of success, a community order with a drug rehabilitation requirement under section 209 of the Criminal Justice Act 2003 may be a proper alternative to a short or moderate length custodial sentence.

Offence category	Starting point	Category range
Category 1	Crown Court	Crown Court
Category 2	1 year's custody	High-level community order to Crown Court (2 years' custody)
Category 3	High-level community order	Low-level community order to 26 weeks' custody

Factors increasing seriousness	Factors reducing seriousness or reflecting personal mitigation
Statutory aggravating factors: Previous convictions, having regard to (a) the nature of the offence to which the conviction relates and its relevance to the current offence; and (b) the time that has elapsed since the conviction* Offence committed whilst on bail **Other aggravating factors include:** Child at home (or returns home) when offence committed Offence committed at night Gratuitous degradation of the victim Any steps taken to prevent the victim reporting the incident or obtaining assistance and/or from assisting or supporting the prosecution Victim compelled to leave their home (in particular victims of domestic violence) Established evidence of community impact Commission of offence whilst under the influence of alcohol or drugs Failure to comply with current court orders Offence committed whilst on licence Offences taken into consideration (TICs)	Offender has made voluntary reparation to the victim Subordinate role in a group or gang No previous convictions or no relevant/ recent convictions Remorse Good character and/or exemplary conduct Determination and/or demonstration of steps taken to address addiction or offending behaviour Serious medical conditions requiring urgent, intensive, or long-term treatment Age and/or lack of maturity where it affects the responsibility of the offender Lapse of time since the offence where this is not the fault of the offender Mental disorder or learning disability, where not linked to the commission of the offence Sole or primary carer for dependent relatives

* Where sentencing an offender for a qualifying third domestic burglary, the court must apply section 111 of the Powers of the Criminal Courts (Sentencing) Act 2000 and impose a custodial term of at least 3 years, unless it is satisfied that there are particular circumstances which relate to any of the offences or to the offender, which would make it unjust to do so.

C15.3.2.1 *Additional steps*

Consider any factors which indicate a reduction, such as: assistance to the prosecution; reduction for guilty plea; dangerousness; totality principle; compensation and ancillary orders; reasons; consideration for remand time.

C15.3.3 Key points

- Entry can be partial (*R v Brown* [1985] Crim LR 212), and may be effected without any part of the body entering the building (eg cane and hook burglaries).
- 'Building' is a factual not a legal issue, and will depend on all of the circumstances (*Caurti v Cozens* [1973] AC 854).
- Trespass can be committed knowingly or recklessly (*R v Collins* [1973] QB 100).

See *Blackstone's Criminal Practice 2017* **B4.75–B4.95**

C15.4 Trespass against property

C15.4.1 *Squatting*

> **Legal Aid, Sentencing and Punishment**
> **of Offenders Act 2012, s 144**
>
> **144 Offence of squatting in a residential building**
> (1) A person commits an offence if—
>   (a) the person is in a residential building as a trespasser having entered it as a trespasser,
>   (b) the person knows or ought to know that he or she is a trespasser, and
>   (c) the person is living in the building or intends to live there for any period.
> (2) The offence is not committed by a person holding over after the end of a lease or licence (even if the person leaves and re-enters the building).
> (3) For the purposes of this section—
>   (a) 'building' includes any structure or part of a structure (including a temporary or moveable structure), and
>   (b) a building is 'residential' if it is designed or adapted, before the time of entry, for use as a place to live.
> (4) For the purposes of this section the fact that a person derives title from a trespasser, or has the permission of a trespasser, does not prevent the person from being a trespasser.

 SO

 6 months' imprisonment and/or fine

C15.4.2 Key points

- The provision became effective on 1 September 2012 but applies to those who had entered before but remain after that date.
- It will be necessary to check that there was not even an informal licence; and whether a person intends to 'live' rather than stay temporarily will be a matter of fact in each case.

 See *Blackstone's Criminal Practice 2017* **B13.31**

C15.4.3 *Aggravated trespass*

> **Criminal Justice and Public Order Act 1994, s 68(1) and (2)**
>
> **68 Offence of aggravated trespass**
>
> (1) A person commits the offence of aggravated trespass if he trespasses on land and, in relation to any lawful activity which persons are engaging in or are about to engage in on that or adjoining land, does there anything which is intended by him to have the effect—
>   (a) of intimidating those persons or any of them so as to deter them or any of them from engaging in that activity,
>   (b) of obstructing that activity, or
>   (c) of disrupting that activity.
> (2) Activity on any occasion on the part of a person or persons on land is 'lawful' for the purposes of this section if he or they may engage in the activity on the land on that occasion without committing an offence or trespassing on the land.

 3 months' imprisonment and/or level 4 fine

C15.4.4 Key points

- There are four elements to the offence (*Richardson v DPP* [2014] UKSC 6; *Barnard v DPP* [2000] Crim LR 371):
  - trespass on land,
  - where a lawful activity is engaged,
  - the intention to have any one of the three effects specified (*Tilly v DPP* [2001] EWHC 821 (Admin)),
  - an act done towards that end. This must be distinct from the act of trespass (*Peppersharp v DPP* [2012] EWHC 474 (Admin)). However, a mass entry and demonstration would, on particular facts, meet this need if there was an intimidatory affect to prevent people from engaging in a lawful activity (*Bauer and others* [2013] EWHC 634 (Admin)).
- Actual disruption is not required if the necessary intention is proved (*Winder v DPP* (1996) 160 JP 713).
- Activity takes place only if there is someone on the land who is not allowed to go on with what he is entitled to do (*Tilly v DPP* [2001] EWHC 821 (Admin)). An activity will only be unlawful if it involves a criminal offence that is integral to the core activity carried on but not where the criminality is incidental, collateral, or remote.

The defence must by evidence raise the issue of such a specific criminal offence in English law, by the landowner. If that is done the burden passes to the Crown to disprove that proposition to the criminal standard (*Richardson v DPP* [2014] UKSC 8).

 See *Blackstone's Criminal Practice 2017* **B13.45**

C15.5 Electricity—abstract/use without authority

> **Theft Act 1968, s 13**
>
> **13 Abstracting of electricity**
> A person who dishonestly uses without due authority, or dishonestly causes to be wasted or diverted, any electricity shall be guilty of an offence.

 6 months' imprisonment and/or fine/5 years' imprisonment

C15.5.1 *Sentencing*

STEP ONE: determining the offence category

The court should determine the offence category with reference **only** to the factors identified in the following tables. In order to determine the category the court should assess **culpability** and **harm**.

The level of culpability is determined by weighing up all the factors of the case to determine the offender's role and the extent to which the offending was **planned** and the **sophistication** with which it was carried out.

CULPABILITY demonstrated by one or more of the following:
A – High culpability
A leading role where offending is part of a group activity
Involvement of others through coercion, intimidation, or exploitation
Sophisticated nature of offence/significant planning
Abuse of position of power or trust or responsibility
Commission of offence in association with or to further other criminal activity
B – Medium culpability
A significant role where offending is part of a group activity
All other cases where characteristics for categories A or C are not present
C – Lesser culpability
Performed limited function under direction
Involved through coercion, intimidation, or exploitation
Limited awareness or understanding of offence

Where there are characteristics present which fall under different levels of culpability, the court should balance these characteristics to reach a fair assessment of the offender's culpability.

The level of harm is assessed by weighing up all the factors of the case to determine the level of harm caused.

Greater harm

A significant risk of, or actual injury to persons or damage to property
Significant volume of electricity extracted as evidenced by length of time of offending and/or advanced type of illegal process used

Lesser harm

All other cases

STEP TWO; starting point and category range

Having determined the category at step one, the court should use the starting point to reach a sentence within the appropriate category range in the table below.

The starting point applies to all offenders irrespective of plea or previous convictions.

Harm		Culpability	
	A	B	C
Greater	**Starting point** 12 weeks' custody	**Starting point** Medium-level community order	**Starting point** Band C fine
	Category range High-level community order – 1 year's custody	**Category range** Low-level community order – 12 weeks' custody	**Category range** Band B fine – low-level community order
Lesser	**Starting point** High-level community order	**Starting point** Low-level community order	**Starting point** Band A fine
	Category range Medium-level community order – 12 weeks' custody	**Category range** Band C fine – medium-level community order	**Category range** Discharge – band C fine

The court should then consider further adjustment for any aggravating or mitigating factors. The table below contains a **non-exhaustive** list of additional factual elements providing the context of the offence and factors relating to the offender. Identify whether any combination of these, or other relevant factors, should result in an upward or downward adjustment from the starting point.

Factors increasing seriousness	
Statutory aggravating factors	*Other aggravating factors*
Previous convictions, having regard to (a) the **nature** of the offence to which the conviction relates and its **relevance** to the current offence; and (b) the **time** that has elapsed since the conviction Offence committed whilst on bail	Electricity abstracted from another person's property Attempts to conceal/dispose of evidence Failure to comply with current court orders
Factors reducing seriousness or reflecting personal mitigation	
No previous convictions **or** no relevant/recent convictions Good character and/or exemplary conduct Serious medical condition requiring urgent, intensive, or long-term treatment Age and/or lack of maturity where it affects the responsibility of the offender Mental disorder or learning disability Sole or primary carer for dependent relatives Determination and/or demonstration of steps having been taken to address addiction or offending behaviour	

 See *Blackstone's Criminal Practice 2017* **B4.140–B4.145**

C15.6 False accounting

Theft Act 1968, s 17(1)

17 False accounting

(1) Where a person dishonestly, with a view to gain for himself or another or with intent to cause loss to another,—
   (a) destroys, defaces, conceals or falsifies any account or any record or document made or required for any accounting purpose; or
   (b) in furnishing information for any purpose produces or makes use of any account, or any such record or document as aforesaid, which to his knowledge is or may be misleading, false or deceptive in a material particular,
   (c) he shall on conviction …

EW

 6 months' imprisonment and/or fine/7 years' imprisonment

C15.6.1 *Sentencing*

See **Appendix 5**.

 See *Blackstone's Criminal Practice 2017* **B6.3–B6.13**

C15.7 **Found on enclosed premises**

> **Vagrancy Act 1824, s 4**
>
> **4 Persons committing certain offences to be deemed rogues and vagabonds**
>
> [The following is an abbreviated version of the original] … [E]very person wandering abroad and lodging in any barn or outhouse, or in any deserted or unoccupied building, or in the open air, or under a tent, or in any cart or waggon, and not giving a good account of himself or herself; every person being found in or upon any dwelling house, warehouse, coach-house, stable, or outhouse, or in any inclosed yard, garden, or area, for any unlawful purpose; … is guilty of an offence.

C15.7.1 Key points

- An unlawful purpose is to commit an offence. Hiding from the police is therefore not enough (*L v CPS* [2007] EWHC 1843 (Admin)).

 SO

 Level 3 fine/3 months' imprisonment

 See *Blackstone's Criminal Practice 2017* **B4.95**

C15.8 **Fraud**

> **Fraud Act 2006, ss 1(1) and (2), 2, 3, 4, and 5**
>
> **1 Fraud**
>
> (1) A person is guilty of fraud if he is in breach of any of the sections listed in subsection (2) (which provide for different ways of committing the offence).
>
> (2) The sections are—
>
>   (a) section 2 (fraud by false representation),
>
>   (b) section 3 (fraud by failing to disclose information), and
>
>   (c) section 4 (fraud by abuse of position).

2 Fraud by false representation

(1) A person is in breach of this section if he—
  (a) dishonestly makes a false representation, and
  (b) intends, by making the representation—
    (i) to make a gain for himself or another, or
    (ii) to cause loss to another or to expose another to a risk of loss.
(2) A representation is false if—
  (a) it is untrue or misleading, and
  (b) the person making it knows that it is, or might be, untrue or misleading.
(3) 'Representation' means any representation as to fact or law, including a representation as to the state of mind of—
  (a) the person making the representation, or
  (b) any other person.
(4) A representation may be express or implied.
(5) For the purposes of this section a representation may be regarded as made if it (or anything implying it) is submitted in any form to any system or device designed to receive, convey or respond to communications (with or without human intervention).

3 Fraud by failing to disclose information

A person is in breach of this section if he—
  (a) dishonestly fails to disclose to another person information which he is under a legal duty to disclose, and
  (b) intends, by failing to disclose the information—
    (i) to make a gain for himself or another, or
    (ii) to cause loss to another or to expose another to a risk of loss.

4 Fraud by abuse of position

(1) A person is in breach of this section if he—
  (a) occupies a position in which he is expected to safeguard, or not to act against, the financial interests of another person,
  (b) dishonestly abuses that position, and
  (c) intends, by means of the abuse of that position—
    (i) to make a gain for himself or another, or
    (ii) to cause loss to another or to expose another to a risk of loss.
(2) A person may be regarded as having abused his position even though his conduct consisted of an omission rather than an act.

5 'Gain' and 'loss'

(1) The references to gain and loss in sections 2 to 4 are to be read in accordance with this section.
(2) 'Gain' and 'loss'—
  (a) extend only to gain or loss in money or other property;
  (b) include any such gain or loss whether temporary or permanent;
and 'property' means any property whether real or personal (including things in action and other intangible property).
(3) 'Gain' includes a gain by keeping what one has, as well as a gain by getting what one does not have.
(4) 'Loss' includes a loss by not getting what one might get, as well as a loss by parting with what one has.

6 months' imprisonment and/or fine/10 years' imprisonment

C15.8.1 *Sentencing*

See **Appendix 5**.

C15.8.2 Key points

The offence under section 2 requires that the defendant know that the representation was or might have been misleading. This is a subjective test. It is not a test of reasonableness or of what the defendant ought to have known. However, a defendant cannot close their eyes to obvious doubts about the genuineness of the representations (*R v Augunas* [2013] EWCA Crim 2046).

Whilst an offence under section 4 does not require a fiduciary relationship, there must be something akin to one. The test is objective and does not depend on the views of the defendant. In *R v Valujevs* [2014] EWCA Crim 2888 it was held that gang-masters might meet the test where there is an interference by them with the payment of wages due.

 See *Blackstone's Criminal Practice 2017* **B5.4–B5.20**

C15.9 Handling stolen goods

Theft Act 1968, s 22(1)

22 Handling stolen goods

(1) A person handles stolen goods if (otherwise than in the course of the stealing) knowing or believing them to be stolen goods he dishonestly receives the goods, or dishonestly undertakes or assists in their retention, removal, disposal or realisation by or for the benefit of another person, or if he arranges to do so.

 6 months' imprisonment and/or fine/14 years' imprisonment

C15.9.1 *Sentencing*

STEP ONE: determining the offence category

The court should determine the offence category with reference **only** to the factors identified in the following tables. In order to determine the category the court should assess **culpability** and **harm**.

The level of culpability is determined by weighing up all the factors of the case to determine the offender's role and the extent to which the offending was **planned** and the **sophistication** with which it was carried out.

CULPABILITY demonstrated by one or more of the following:
A – High culpability A leading role where offending is part of a group activity Involvement of others through coercion, intimidation, or exploitation Abuse of position of power, or trust, or responsibility Professional and sophisticated offence Advance knowledge of the primary offence Possession of very recently stolen goods from a domestic burglary or robbery
B – Medium culpability A significant role where offending is part of a group activity Offender acquires goods for resale All other cases where characteristics for categories A or C are not present
C – Lesser culpability Performed limited function under direction Involved through coercion, intimidation, or exploitation Little or no planning Limited awareness or understanding of offence Goods acquired for offender's personal use

Where there are characteristics present which fall under different levels of culpability, the court should balance these characteristics to reach a fair assessment of the offender's culpability.

HARM

Harm is assessed by reference to the **financial value** (to the loser) of the handled goods **and any significant additional harm** to the victim or others associated with the underlying offence—examples of additional harm may include **but are not limited to**:

Property stolen from a domestic burglary or a robbery (unless this has already been taken into account in assessing culpability) Items stolen were of substantial value to the loser, regardless of monetary worth Metal theft causing disruption to infrastructure Damage to heritage assets

Category 1	Very high value goods stolen (above £100,000) **or** high value with significant additional harm to the victim or others
Category 2	High-value goods stolen (£10,000 to £100,000) and no significant additional harm **or** medium-value with significant additional harm to the victim or others
Category 3	Medium-value goods stolen (£1,000 to £10,000) and no significant additional harm **or** low-value with significant additional harm to the victim or others
Category 4	Low-value goods stolen (up to £1,000) **and** little or no significant additional harm to the victim or others

STEP TWO: starting point and category range

Having determined the category at step one, the court should use the starting point to reach a sentence within the appropriate category range in the table below.

The starting point applies to all offenders irrespective of plea or previous convictions.

Harm	Culpability		
	A	B	C
Category 1 Where the value greatly exceeds £100,000, it may be appropriate to move outside the identified range. Adjustment should be made for any significant additional harm where very high value stolen goods are handled.	**Starting point** 5 years' custody	**Starting point** 3 years' custody	**Starting point** 1 year's custody
	Category range 3–8 years' custody	**Category range** 1 year 6 months' – 4 years' custody	**Category range** 26 weeks' – 1 year 6 months' custody
Category 2	**Starting point** 3 years' custody	**Starting point** 1 year's custody	**Starting point** High-level community order
	Category range 1 year 6 months' – 4 years' custody	**Category range** 26 weeks' – 1 year 6 months' custody	**Category range** Low-level community order – 26 weeks' custody

Category 3	Starting point 1 year's custody	Starting point High-level community order	Starting point Band C fine
	Category range 26 weeks' – 2 years' custody	Category range Low-level community order – 26 weeks' custody	Category range Band B fine – low-level community order
Category 4	Starting point High-level community order	Starting point Low-level community order	Starting point Band B fine
	Category range Medium-level community order – 26 weeks' custody	Category range Band C fine – high-level community order	Category range Discharge – band C fine

Consecutive sentences for multiple offences may be appropriate—
please refer to the *Offences Taken into Consideration* and *Totality*
guidelines.

The court should then consider further adjustment for any aggravating or mitigating factors. The following is a **non-exhaustive**
list of additional factual elements providing the context of the
offence and factors relating to the offender. Identify whether any
combination of these, or other relevant factors, should result in
an upward or downward adjustment from the starting point.

Factors increasing seriousness	
Statutory aggravating factors	*Other aggravating factors*
Previous convictions, having regard to (a) the nature of the offence to which the conviction relates and its relevance to the current offence; and (b) the time that has elapsed since the conviction Offence committed whilst on bail	Seriousness of the underlying offence, for example, armed robbery Deliberate destruction, disposal, or defacing of stolen property Damage to a third party Failure to comply with current court orders Offence committed on licence Offences taken into consideration Established evidence of community/wider impact

Factors reducing seriousness or reflecting personal mitigation
No previous convictions **or** no relevant/recent convictions Good character and/or exemplary conduct Serious medical condition requiring urgent, intensive, or long-term treatment Age and/or lack of maturity where it affects the responsibility of the offender Mental disorder or learning disability Sole or primary carer for dependent relatives Determination and/or demonstration of steps having been taken to address addiction or offending behaviour

C15.9.2 Key points

- Mere suspicion that goods are stolen will not suffice.
- In *R v Hall* (1985) 81 Cr App R 260, belief was said to be present when someone thought: 'I cannot say for certain that those goods are stolen, but there can be no other reasonable conclusion in the light of all the circumstances of all I have heard and seen.' Similarly if the person admits that 'my brain is telling me [they are stolen] despite what I have heard'.
- If the defendant argues that he has paid an adequate consideration for the goods, it falls upon the prosecution to disprove (*Hogan v Director of Public Prosecutions* [2007] EWHC 978 (Admin)).

 See *Blackstone's Criminal Practice 2017* **B4.159–B4.185**

C15.10 Money laundering

Proceeds of Crime Act 2002, ss 327–329

327 Concealing etc

(1) A person commits an offence if he—
  (a) conceals criminal property;
  (b) disguises criminal property;
  (c) converts criminal property;
  (d) transfers criminal property;
  (e) removes criminal property from England and Wales or from Scotland or from Northern Ireland.

(2) But a person does not commit such an offence if—
  (a) he makes an authorised disclosure under section 338 and (if the disclosure is made before he does the act mentioned in subsection (1)) he has the appropriate consent;
  (b) he intended to make such a disclosure but had a reasonable excuse for not doing so;
  (c) the act he does is done in carrying out a function he has relating to the enforcement of any provision of this Act or of any other enactment relating to criminal conduct or benefit from criminal conduct.

(2A) Nor does a person commit an offence under subsection (1) if—
  (a) he knows, or believes on reasonable grounds, that the relevant criminal conduct occurred in a particular country or territory outside the United Kingdom, and
  (b) the relevant criminal conduct—
    (i) was not, at the time it occurred, unlawful under the criminal law then applying in that country or territory, and
    (ii) is not of a description prescribed by an order made by the Secretary of State.

(2B) In subsection (2A) 'the relevant criminal conduct' is the criminal conduct by reference to which the property concerned is criminal property.

(2C) A deposit-taking body that does an act mentioned in paragraph (c) or (d) of subsection (1) does not commit an offence under that subsection if—

    (a) it does the act in operating an account maintained with it, and

    (b) the value of the criminal property concerned is less than the threshold amount determined under section 339A for the act.

(3) Concealing or disguising criminal property includes concealing or disguising its nature, source, location, disposition, movement or ownership or any rights with respect to it.

328 Arrangements

(1) A person commits an offence if he enters into or becomes concerned in an arrangement which he knows or suspects facilitates (by whatever means) the acquisition, retention, use or control of criminal property by or on behalf of another person.

(2) But a person does not commit such an offence if—

    (a) he makes an authorised disclosure under section 338 and (if the disclosure is made before he does the act mentioned in subsection (1)) he has the appropriate consent;

    (b) he intended to make such a disclosure but had a reasonable excuse for not doing so;

    (c) the act he does is done in carrying out a function he has relating to the enforcement of any provision of this Act or of any other enactment relating to criminal conduct or benefit from criminal conduct.

329 Acquisition, use and possession

(1) A person commits an offence if he—

    (a) acquires criminal property;

    (b) uses criminal property;

    (c) has possession of criminal property.

(2) But a person does not commit such an offence if—

    (a) he makes an authorised disclosure under section 338 and (if the disclosure is made before he does the act mentioned in subsection (1)) he has the appropriate consent;

    (b) he intended to make such a disclosure but had a reasonable excuse for not doing so;

    (c) he acquired or used or had possession of the property for adequate consideration;

    (d) the act he does is done in carrying out a function he has relating to the enforcement of any provision of this Act or of any other enactment relating to criminal conduct or benefit from criminal conduct.

(3) For the purposes of this section—

    (a) a person acquires property for inadequate consideration if the value of the consideration is significantly less than the value of the property;

    (b) a person uses or has possession of property for inadequate consideration if the value of the consideration is significantly less than the value of the use or possession;

    (c) the provision by a person of goods or services which he knows or suspects may help another to carry out criminal conduct.

C15 Dishonesty and Offences Against Property

The critical definitions for these offences are contained in section 340 of the Proceeds of Crime Act 2002:

> ### Proceeds of Crime Act 2002, s 340(2)–(4)(b)
>
> #### 340 Interpretation
> (2) Criminal conduct is conduct which—
>   (a) constitutes an offence in any part of the United Kingdom, or
>   (b) would constitute an offence in any part of the United Kingdom if it occurred there.
> (3) Property is criminal property if—
>   (a) it constitutes a person's benefit from criminal conduct or it represents such a benefit (in whole or part and whether directly or indirectly), and
>   (b) the alleged offender knows or suspects that it constitutes or represents such a benefit.
> (4) It is immaterial—
>   (a) who carried out the conduct;
>   (b) who benefited from it;
> ...

EW

 6 months' imprisonment and/or fine/14 years' imprisonment

C15.10.1 *Sentencing*

STEP ONE: determining the offence category

The court should determine the offence category with reference to the tables below. In order to determine the category the court should assess **culpability** and **harm**.

The level of **culpability** is determined by weighing up all the factors of the case to determine the offender's role and the extent to which the offending was planned and the sophistication with which it was carried out.	**Harm A** Harm is initially assessed by the value of the money laundered.
Culpability demonstrated by one or more of the following:	
A – High culpability	**Category 1** £10 million or more Starting point based on £30 million
A leading role where offending is part of a group activity	**Category 2** £2 million–£10 million Starting point based on £5 million

Involvement of others through pressure, influence	**Category 3** £500,000–£2 million Starting point based on £1 million
Abuse of position of power, or trust, or responsibility	**Category 4** £100,000–£500,000 Starting point based on £300,000
Sophisticated nature of offence/significant planning	**Category 5** £10,000–£100,000 Starting point based on £50,000
Criminal activity conducted over sustained period of time	**Category 6** Less than £10,000 Starting point based on £5,000
B – Medium culpability	**Harm B**
Other cases where characteristics for categories A or C are not present A significant role where offending is part of a group activity	Money laundering is an integral component of much serious criminality. **To complete the assessment of harm, the court should take into account the level of harm associated with the underlying offence to determine whether it warrants upward adjustment of the starting point within the range, or in appropriate cases, outside the range.**
C – Lesser culpability	
Performed limited function under direction Involved through coercion, intimidation or exploitation Not motivated by personal gain Opportunistic 'one-off' offence; very little or no planning Limited awareness or understanding of extent of criminal activity	Where it is possible to identify the underlying offence, regard should be given to the relevant sentencing levels for that offence.

STEP TWO: starting point and category range

Having determined the category at step one, the court should use the appropriate starting point (as adjusted in accordance with step one above) to reach a sentence within the category range in the table below. The starting point applies to all offenders irrespective of plea or previous convictions.

Where the value is larger or smaller than the amount on which the starting point is based, this should lead to upward or downward adjustment as appropriate.

Where the value greatly exceeds the amount of the starting point in category 1, it may be appropriate to move outside the identified range.

Section 327 of the Proceeds of Crime Act 2002: Concealing/disguising/converting/transferring/removing criminal property from England & Wales

Section 328 of the Proceeds of Crime Act 2002: Entering into arrangements concerning criminal property

Section 329 of the Proceeds of Crime Act 2002: Acquisition, use and possession of criminal property

Maximum: 14 years' custody

Categories 1 to 3 refer to sums in excess of £500,000 and guideline sentencing levels are beyond the jurisdiction of the magistrates' court.

Harm	Culpability		
	A	**B**	**C**
Category 4 £100,000–£500,000 Starting point based on £300,000	**Starting point** 5 years' custody	**Starting point** 3 years' custody	**Starting point** 18 months' custody
	Category range 3 to 6 years' custody	**Category range** 18 months' to 4 years' custody	**Category range** 26 weeks' to 3 years' custody
Category 5 £10,000–£100,000 Starting point based on £50,000	**Starting point** 3 years' custody	**Starting point** 18 months' custody	**Starting point** 26 weeks' custody
	Category range 18 months' to 4 years' custody	**Category range** 26 weeks' to 3 years' custody	**Category range** Medium-level community order to 1 year's custody
Category 6 Less than £10,000 Starting point based on £5,000	**Starting point** 1 year's custody	**Starting point** High-level community order	**Starting point** Low-level community order
	Category range 26 weeks' to 2 years' custody	**Category range** Low-level community order to 1 year's custody	**Category range** Band B fine to medium-level community order

The table below contains a non-exhaustive list of additional factual elements providing the context of the offence and factors relating to the offender.

Identify whether any combination of these or other relevant factors should result in an upward or downward adjustment of the sentence arrived at thus far.

Consecutive sentences for multiple offences may be appropriate where large sums are involved.

Factors increasing seriousness	
Statutory aggravating factors:	*Other aggravating factors:*
Previous convictions, having regard to (a) the nature of the offence to which the conviction relates and its relevance to the current offence; and (b) the time that has elapsed since the conviction Offence committed whilst on bail	Attempts to conceal/dispose of evidence Established evidence of community/wider impact Failure to comply with current court orders Offence committed on licence Offences taken into consideration Failure to respond to warnings about behaviour Offences committed across borders Blame wrongly placed on others Damage to third party, for example loss of employment by legitimate employees

Factors reducing seriousness or reflecting personal mitigation
No previous convictions **or** no relevant/recent convictions
Remorse
Little or no prospect of success
Good character and/or exemplary conduct
Serious medical conditions requiring urgent, intensive, or long-term treatment
Age and/or lack of maturity where it affects the responsibility of the offender
Lapse of time since apprehension where this does not arise from the conduct of the offender
Mental disorder or learning disability
Sole or primary carer for dependent relatives
Offender cooperated with investigation, made early admissions, and/or voluntarily reported offending
Determination and/or demonstration of steps having been taken to address addiction or offending behaviour
Activity originally legitimate

C15.10.2 Key points

- For there to be criminal property, there must be an intent or a suspicion that there is a benefit from criminal conduct.
- Knowledge of a potential breach of trust was not of itself the same as knowledge or suspicion of crime. That the defendant ought to have known is not enough (*Holt v Attorney General* [2014] UKPC 4).
- In *Wilkinson v DPP* [2006] EWHC 3012 (Admin), the court discouraged the use of this offence (with its requirement only for suspicion rather than belief) when a handling charge would adequately have reflected the seriousness of the offence.
- For there to be an offence there must be actual criminal conduct and the proceeds must already be the product of that crime (*R v Gabriel* [2006] EWCA Crim 229). However, a court might decide that 'clean' money had changed its nature and become 'criminal property' because it was obtained by fraud (*R v GH*

[2015] UKSC 24). This case also confirmed that the money need not be 'criminal property' at the moment the parties come to a prohibited arrangement, but it must amount to 'criminal property' at the time the arrangement begins to operate upon it.

- *R v Ogden* [2016] EWCA Crim 6 confirms that an offence of conspiracy to convert criminal property (s 327 of Proceeds of Crime Act 2000) is committed when A, who is in possession of controlled drugs, agrees to supply B with what B is aware is a controlled drug. The drugs are criminal property.
- There are two ways in which the Crown can prove that the property derives from crime. Either:
  - by showing that it derives from criminal conduct of a specific kind; or
  - by proving that the circumstances in which it was handled create an irresistible inference that it can only have derived from crime (*Kuchhadia v R* [2015] EWCA Crim 1252).
- *R v Rogers (Bradley)* [2014] EWCA Crim 1680 confirms that payments into a Spanish bank account by reason of frauds committed in England are amenable to the jurisdiction of the English courts, as sections 327–329 POCA 2002 have extra-territorial effect.

 See *Blackstone's Criminal Practice 2017* **B21**

C15.11 Possession of false identity documents, etc without reasonable excuse

Identity Documents Act 2010, ss 6 and 7

6 Possession of false identity documents, etc without reasonable excuse

(1) It is an offence for a person ('P'), without reasonable excuse, to have in P's possession or under P's control—
   (a) an identity document that is false,
   (b) an identity document that was improperly obtained,
   (c) an identity document that relates to someone else,
   (d) any apparatus which, to P's knowledge, is or has been specially designed or adapted for the making of false identity documents, or
   (e) any article or material which, to P's knowledge, is or has been specially designed or adapted to be used in the making of such documents.

...

7 Meaning of 'identity document'

(1) For the purposes of sections 4 to 6 'identity document' means any document that is or purports to be—
   (a) an immigration document,

(b) a United Kingdom passport (within the meaning of the Immigration Act 1971),
(c) a passport issued by or on behalf of the authorities of a country or territory outside the United Kingdom or by or on behalf of an international organisation,
(d) a document that can be used (in some or all circumstances) instead of a passport,
(e) a licence to drive a motor vehicle granted under Part 3 of the Road Traffic Act 1988 or under Part 2 of the Road Traffic (Northern Ireland) Order 1981, or
(f) a driving licence issued by or on behalf of the authorities of a country or territory outside the United Kingdom.
(2) In subsection (1)(a) 'immigration document' means—
   (a) a document used for confirming the right of a person under the EU Treaties in respect of entry or residence in the United Kingdom,
   (b) a document that is given in exercise of immigration functions and records information about leave granted to a person to enter or to remain in the United Kingdom, or
   (c) a registration card (within the meaning of section 26A of the Immigration Act 1971).
(3) In subsection (2)(b) 'immigration functions' means functions under the Immigration Acts (within the meaning of the Asylum and Immigration (Treatment of Claimants, etc.) Act 2004).
(4) References in subsection (1) to the issue of a document include its renewal, replacement or re-issue (with or without modifications).
(5) In this section 'document' includes a stamp or label.
(6) The Secretary of State may by order amend the definition of 'identity document'.

 6 months' imprisonment and/or fine/2 years' imprisonment

C15.11.1 *Sentencing*

Offence seriousness (culpability and harm) A. Identify the appropriate starting point Starting points based on first-time offender pleading not guilty		
Examples of nature of activity	**Starting point**	**Range**
Single document possessed	Medium-level community order	Band C fine to high-level community order
Small number of documents, no evidence of dealing	12 weeks' custody	6 weeks' custody to Crown Court
Considerable number of documents possessed, evidence of involvement in larger operation	Crown Court	Crown Court

C15 Dishonesty and Offences Against Property

Offence seriousness (culpability and harm) B. Consider the effect of aggravating and mitigating factors (other than those within examples above) The following may be particularly relevant but these lists are not exhaustive	
Factors indicating higher culpability 1. Clear knowledge that documents false 2. Number of documents possessed (where not in offence descriptions above) **Factor indicating greater degree of harm** 1. Genuine mistake or ignorance	**Factors indicating lower culpability** 1. Group activity 2. Potential impact of use (where not in offence descriptions above)

C15.11.2 *Defences*

Immigration and Asylum Act 1999, s 31

31 Defences based on Article 31(1) of the Refugee Convention

(1) It is a defence for a refugee charged with an offence to which this section applies to show that, having come to the United Kingdom directly from a country where his life or freedom was threatened (within the meaning of the Refugee Convention), he—

   (a) presented himself to the authorities in the United Kingdom without delay;

   (b) showed good cause for his illegal entry or presence; and

   (c) made a claim for asylum as soon as was reasonably practicable after his arrival in the United Kingdom.

(2) If, in coming from the country where his life or freedom was threatened, the refugee stopped in another country outside the United Kingdom, subsection (1) applies only if he shows that he could not reasonably have expected to be given protection under the Refugee Convention in that other country.

(3) In England and Wales and Northern Ireland the offences to which this section applies are any offence, and any attempt to commit an offence, under—

   (a) Part I of the Forgery and Counterfeiting Act 1981 (forgery and connected offences);

   (b) section 24A of the 1971 Act (deception); or

   (c) section 26(1)(d) of the 1971 Act (falsification of documents).

...

(5) A refugee who has made a claim for asylum is not entitled to the defence provided by subsection (1) in relation to any offence committed by him after making that claim.

(6) 'Refugee' has the same meaning as it has for the purposes of the Refugee Convention.

(7) If the Secretary of State has refused to grant a claim for asylum made by a person who claims that he has a defence under subsection (1), that person is to be taken not to be a refugee unless he shows that he is.

C15.11.3 Key points

- Refugees are protected under Article 31 of the UN Convention relating to the status of refugees. The defence, set out in section 31 Immigration and Asylum Act 1999, was considered in *R v Matete* [2013] EWCA Crim 1372.

The requirement that the claim for asylum must be made as soon as was reasonably practicable does not necessarily mean at the earliest possible moment (*Asfaw* [2008] UKHL 31).

It follows that the fact a refugee stopped in a third country in transit is not necessarily fatal and may be explicable: the refugee has some choice as to where he might properly claim asylum. The main touchstones by which exclusion from protection should be judged are the length of the stay in the intermediate country, the reasons for delaying there, and whether or not the refugee sought or found protection de jure or de facto from the persecution from which he or she was seeking to escape (*Asfaw*). The Court of Appeal has found that stays as long as three months in countries where a refugee could not reasonably be expected to seek asylum do not necessarily exclude reliance on the defence. Even where the third country is a signatory to the Refugee Convention, this is not necessarily fatal to the statutory defence. Short stopovers in 'safe' countries have been accepted by the Court of Appeal as falling within the description of 'in transit' for the purposes of the 'come directly' provision in section 31. Examples include:

- stays in Turkey of up to one month (see *Jaddi* [2012] EWCA Crim 2565)
- stays in Greece of up to two weeks (see *Mohamed v R* [2010] EWCA Crim 2400)
- stays in Spain of up to 20 days (see *Mateta v R* [2013] EWCA Crim 1372), and
- stays in France of up to 10 days (*R v Nguidjol (Richard Sohe)* 18 June 2015 unreported).

A short stopover within the UK has also been found to be in transit for the purposes of section 31 where the defendant was in the hands of an agent organising their journey, and/or had been advised to seek asylum elsewhere, and always intended to do so (*Sadeghi* [2014] EWCA Crim 2933).

The courts will consider the individual circumstances of the case, such as the length of the stay and the reason for delay in coming to the UK. The fact that the defendant has not made an application for asylum immediately on entry to the UK will not necessarily mean a section 31 defence is not available to them. A stay of 13 days in the UK has been found by the Court of Appeal to satisfy the requirements of section 31 for the purposes of making a clam for asylum as soon as reasonably practicable (*Mulugeta v R* [2015] EWCA Crim 6).

The requirement that the refugee demonstrates 'good cause' for his illegal entry or presence in the United Kingdom will be satisfied by showing that he was reasonably travelling on false papers (*R v Uxbridge MC ex p Adimi* [2001] QB 667).

- If the document itself is false then it is no defence in a case where the document was being used for establishing a registrable fact, that it bore the correct details of the defendant (*R v Jamalov*, The Times, 17 March 2010), but the defendant's ignorance of a document's falsity could amount to a reasonable cause for possessing it (*R v Unah* [2011] EWCA Crim 1837).

In *L; HVN; THN; T v R* [2013] EWCA Crim 991 the court considered that the abuse of process jurisdiction should be used to stay cases where the defendant was the subject of human trafficking and there was a connection with their criminality.

The review by the court was wider than a *Wednesbury* review. The court discharged its responsibilities under the European Parliament and Council Directive 2011/36/EU by:

(i) reviewing decisions to prosecute;
(ii) staying inappropriate prosecutions; and
(iii) discharging defendants when prosecution was appropriate but punishment was not.

It was essential that a court made full enquiries as to the defendant's true age and their involvement in human trafficking—when it may still provide arguments in favour of an abuse of process or at least mitigation (see **A1.1**).

 See *Blackstone's Criminal Practice 2017* **B6.59–B6.63**

C15.12 Making off without payment

> **Theft Act 1978, s 3**
>
> **3 Making off without payment**
>
> (1) Subject to subsection (3) below, a person who, knowing that payment on the spot for any goods supplied or service done is required or expected from him, dishonestly makes off without having paid as required or expected and with intent to avoid payment of the amount due shall be guilty of an offence.
>
> (2) For purposes of this section 'payment on the spot' includes payment at the time of collecting goods on which work has been done or in respect of which service has been provided.

(3) Subsection (1) above shall not apply where the supply of the goods or the doing of the service is contrary to law, or where the service done is such that payment is not legally enforceable.

 6 months' imprisonment and/or fine/2 years' imprisonment

C15.12.1 *Sentencing*

STEP ONE: determining the offence category

The court should determine the offence category with reference **only** to the factors identified in the following tables. In order to determine the category the court should assess **culpability** and **harm**.

The level of culpability is determined by weighing up all the factors of the case to determine the offender's role and the extent to which the offending was **planned** and the **sophistication** with which it was carried out.

CULPABILITY demonstrated by one or more of the following:
A – High culpability
A leading role where offending is part of a group activity Involvement of others through coercion, intimidation, or exploitation Sophisticated nature of offence/significant planning Offence involving intimidation or the use or threat of force Deliberately targeting victim on basis of vulnerability
B – Medium culpability
A significant role where offending is part of a group activity Some degree of planning involved All other cases where characteristics for categories A or C are not present
C – Lesser culpability
Performed limited function under direction Involved through coercion, intimidation or exploitation Little or no planning Limited awareness or understanding of offence

Where there are characteristics present which fall under different levels of culpability, the court should balance these characteristics to reach a fair assessment of the offender's culpability.

HARM

Harm is assessed by reference to the **actual loss** that results from the offence **and any significant additional harm** suffered by the victim—examples of additional harm may include **but are not limited to**:

A high level of inconvenience caused to the victim Emotional distress Fear/loss of confidence caused by the crime A greater impact on the victim due to the size or type of their business	
Category 1	Goods or services obtained above £200 **or** goods/services up to £200 with significant additional harm to the victim
Category 2	Goods or services obtained up to £200 **and** little or no significant additional harm to the victim

STEP TWO: starting point and category range

Having determined the category at step one, the court should use the starting point to reach a sentence within the appropriate category range in the table below.

The starting point applies to all offenders irrespective of plea or previous convictions.

Harm		Culpability	
	A	**B**	**C**
Category 1 Where the value greatly exceeds £200, it may be appropriate to move outside the identified range. Adjustment should be made for any significant additional harm for offences above £200.	**Starting point** 12 weeks' custody	**Starting point** Low-level community order	**Starting point** Band B fine
	Category range High-level community order – 36 weeks' custody	**Category range** Band C fine – high-level community order	**Category range** Band A fine – low-level community order
Category 2	**Starting point** Medium-level community order	**Starting point** Band C fine	**Starting point** Band A fine
	Category range Low-level community order – 12 weeks' custody	**Category range** Band B fine – low-level community order	**Category range** Discharge – band B fine

Consecutive sentences for multiple offences may be appropriate – please refer to the *Offences Taken into Consideration* and *Totality* guidelines.

The court should then consider further adjustment for any aggravating or mitigating factors. The following list is a non-exhaustive list of additional factual elements providing the context of the offence and factors relating to the offender. Identify whether any combination of these, or other relevant factors, should result in an upward or downward adjustment from the starting point.

Factors increasing seriousness	
Statutory aggravating factors	Other aggravating factors
Previous convictions, having regard to (a) the **nature** of the offence to which the conviction relates and its relevance to the current offence; and (b) the **time** that has elapsed since the conviction Offence committed whilst on bail Offence motivated by, or demonstrating hostility based on, any of the following characteristics or presumed characteristics of the victim: religion, race, disability, sexual orientation, or transgender identity	Steps taken to prevent the victim reporting or obtaining assistance and/or from assisting or supporting the prosecution Attempts to conceal/dispose of evidence Failure to comply with current court orders Offence committed on licence Offences taken into consideration Established evidence of community/ wider impact
Factors reducing seriousness or reflecting personal mitigation	
No previous convictions **or** no relevant/recent convictions Remorse, particularly where evidenced by voluntary reparation to the victim Good character and/or exemplary conduct Serious medical condition requiring urgent, intensive, or long-term treatment Age and/or lack of maturity where it affects the responsibility of the offender Mental disorder or learning disability Sole or primary carer for dependent relatives Determination and/or demonstration of steps having been taken to address addiction or offending behaviour	

C15.12.2 Key points

The intention to avoid making payment means a permanent intention not to pay, so a person who genuinely disputes a bill and challenges someone to bring legal action cannot be said to have committed an offence.

 See *Blackstone's Criminal Practice 2017* **B5.38–B5.45**

C15.13 Obtaining services dishonestly

Fraud Act 2006, s 11(1) and (2)

11 Obtaining services dishonestly

(1) A person is guilty of an offence under this section if he obtains services for himself or another—
   (a) by a dishonest act, and
   (b) in breach of subsection (2).

(2) A person obtains services in breach of this subsection if—
  (a) they are made available on the basis that payment has been, is being or will be made for or in respect of them,
  (b) he obtains them without any payment having been made for or in respect of them or without payment having been made in full, and
  (c) when he obtains them, he knows—
    (i) that they are being made available on the basis described in paragraph (a), or
    (ii) that they might be,
  but intends that payment will not be made, or will not be made in full.

 6 months' imprisonment and/or fine/5 years' imprisonment

C15.13.1 *Sentencing*

The offence of *obtaining services dishonestly* may be committed in circumstances that otherwise could be charged as an offence contrary to section 1 of the Fraud Act 2006, or may be more akin to *making off without payment*, contrary to section 3 of the Theft Act 1978. For this reason, it has not been included specifically within any of the guidelines for fraud, and one of the following approaches should be used:

- where it involves conduct which can be characterized as a fraud offence (such as obtaining credit through fraud or payment card fraud), the court should apply the guideline for the relevant type of fraud (see **Appendix 5**); or
- where the conduct could be characterized as *making off without payment* (ie where an offender, knowing that payment on the spot for any goods supplied or service done is required or expected, dishonestly makes off without having paid and with intent to avoid payment), the guideline for that offence should be used (see **C15.12.1**).

 See *Blackstone's Criminal Practice 2017* **B5.31–B5.37**

C15.14 Possession of articles for fraud

Fraud Act 2006, s 6

6 Possession etc of articles for use in frauds

(1) A person is guilty of an offence if he has in his possession or under his control any article for use in the course of or in connection with any fraud.

Fine/6 months'/5 years' imprisonment

C15.14.1 *Sentencing*
See **Appendix 5**.

C15.14.2 Key points

Section 8 provides:

> **Fraud Act 2006, s 8**
>
> **8 'Article'**
> (1) For the purposes of—
>   (a) sections 6 and 7, and
>   (b) the provisions listed in subsection (2), so far as they relate to articles
>   for use in the course of or in connection with fraud,
>   'article' includes any program or data held in electronic form.

R v Sakalauskas [2013] EWCA Crim 2278 confirms that an 'article'
in section 6 of the Fraud Act 2006 (as was the case under s 25 Theft
Act 1968) meant any article that the defendant had with him for
the purposes of fraud but not articles which he had possessed for
that purpose in the past.

 See *Blackstone's Criminal Practice 2017* **B5.21** and **B5.22**

C15.15 Making, adapting, supplying, or offering to supply articles for fraud

> **Fraud Act 2006, s 7**
>
> **7 Making or supplying articles for use in frauds**
> (1) A person is guilty of an offence if he makes, adapts, supplies or offers
>   to supply any article—
>   (a) knowing that it is designed or adapted for use in the course of or in
>   connection with fraud, or
>   (b) intending it to be used to commit, or assist in the commission of, fraud.

 Fine/6 months'/10 years' imprisonment

C15 Dishonesty and Offences Against Property

C15.15.1 *Sentencing*

See **Appendix 5**.

C15.15.2 Key points

For definition of an 'article', see **C15.14.2**.

 See *Blackstone's Criminal Practice 2017* **B5.24** and **B5.25**

C15.16 Railway fare evasion

> **Regulation of Railways Act 1889, s 5(1) and (3)**

 SO

 Level 3 fine or 3 months' imprisonment (s 5(3)); level 2 fine (s 5(1))

C15.16.1 *Sentencing*

*Note that this guideline is under review by the Sentencing Council (see **Appendix 7**).*

Offence seriousness (culpability and harm) A. Identify the appropriate starting point Starting points based on first-time offender pleading not guilty		
Examples of nature of activity	**Starting point**	**Range**
Failing to produce ticket or pay fare on request	Band A fine	Conditional discharge to band B fine
Travelling on railway without having paid the fare or knowingly and wilfully travelling beyond the distance paid for, with intent to avoid payment	Band B fine	Band A fine to band C fine

Offence seriousness (culpability and harm) B. Consider the effect of aggravating and mitigating factors (other than those within examples above) The following may be particularly relevant but these lists are not exhaustive
Factor indicating higher culpability 1. Offensive or intimidating language or behaviour towards railway staff **Factor indicating greater degree of harm** 1. High level of loss caused or intended to be caused

C15.17 False statement/representation to obtain social security benefit

Social Security Administration Act 1992, ss 111A and 112

111A Dishonest representations for obtaining benefit etc

(1) If a person dishonestly—

    (a) makes a false statement or representation; or

    (b) produces or furnishes, or causes or allows to be produced or furnished, any document or information which is false in a material particular;

with a view to obtaining any benefit or other payment or advantage under the relevant social security legislation (whether for himself or for some other person), he shall be guilty of an offence.

(1A) A person shall be guilty of an offence if—

    (a) there has been a change of circumstances affecting any entitlement of his to any benefit or other payment or advantage under any provision of the relevant social security legislation;

    (b) the change is not a change that is excluded by regulations from the changes that are required to be notified;

    (c) he knows that the change affects an entitlement of his to such a benefit or other payment or advantage; and

    (d) he dishonestly fails to give a prompt notification of that change in the prescribed manner to the prescribed person.

(1B) A person shall be guilty of an offence if—

    (a) there has been a change of circumstances affecting any entitlement of another person to any benefit or other payment or advantage under any provision of the relevant social security legislation;

    (b) the change is not a change that is excluded by regulations from the changes that are required to be notified;

    (c) he knows that the change affects an entitlement of that other person to such a benefit or other payment or advantage; and

    (d) he dishonestly causes or allows that other person to fail to give a prompt notification of that change in the prescribed manner to the prescribed person.

(1C) This subsection applies where—

    (a) there has been a change of circumstances affecting any entitlement of a person ('the claimant') to any benefit or other payment or advantage under any provision of the relevant social security legislation;

    (b) the benefit, payment or advantage is one in respect of which there is another person ('the recipient') who for the time being has a right to receive payments to which the claimant has, or (but for the arrangements under which they are payable to the recipient) would have, an entitlement; and

    (c) the change is not a change that is excluded by regulations from the changes that are required to be notified.

(1D) In a case where subsection (1C) above applies, the recipient is guilty of an offence if—
  (a) he knows that the change affects an entitlement of the claimant to a benefit or other payment or advantage under a provision of the relevant social security legislation;
  (b) the entitlement is one in respect of which he has a right to receive payments to which the claimant has, or (but for the arrangements under which they are payable to the recipient) would have, an entitlement; and
  (c) he dishonestly fails to give a prompt notification of that change in the prescribed manner to the prescribed person.

(1E) In a case where that subsection applies, a person other than the recipient is guilty of an offence if—
  (a) he knows that the change affects an entitlement of the claimant to a benefit or other payment or advantage under a provision of the relevant social security legislation;
  (b) the entitlement is one in respect of which the recipient has a right to receive payments to which the claimant has, or (but for the arrangements under which they are payable to the recipient) would have, an entitlement; and
  (c) he dishonestly causes or allows the recipient to fail to give a prompt notification of that change in the prescribed manner to the prescribed person.

(1F) In any case where subsection (1C) above applies but the right of the recipient is confined to a right, by reason of his being a person to whom the claimant is required to make payments in respect of a dwelling, to receive payments of housing benefit—
  (a) a person shall not be guilty of an offence under subsection (1D) or (1E) above unless the change is one relating to one or both of the following—
    (i) the claimant's occupation of that dwelling;
    (ii) the claimant's liability to make payments in respect of that dwelling; but
  (b) subsections (1D)(a) and (1E)(a) above shall each have effect as if after 'knows' there were inserted 'or could reasonably be expected to know'.

(1G) For the purposes of subsections (1A) to (1E) above a notification of a change is prompt if, and only if, it is given as soon as reasonably practicable after the change occurs.

112 False representations for obtaining benefit etc

(1) If a person for the purpose of obtaining any benefit or other payment under the relevant social security legislation whether for himself or some other person, or for any other purpose connected with that legislation—
  (a) makes a statement or representation which he knows to be false; or
  (b) produces or furnishes, or knowingly causes or knowingly allows to be produced or furnished, any document or information which he knows to be false in a material particular, he shall be guilty of an offence.

(1A) A person shall be guilty of an offence if—
  (a) there has been a change of circumstances affecting any entitle-
    ment of his to any benefit or other payment or advantage under
    any provision of the relevant social security legislation;
  (b) the change is not a change that is excluded by regulations from the
    changes that are required to be notified;
  (c) he knows that the change affects an entitlement of his to such a
    benefit or other payment or advantage; and
  (d) he fails to give a prompt notification of that change in the pre-
    scribed manner to the prescribed person.
(1B) A person is guilty of an offence under this section if—
  (a) there has been a change of circumstances affecting any entitle-
    ment of another person to any benefit or other payment or advan-
    tage under any provision of the relevant social security legislation;
  (b) the change is not a change that is excluded by regulations from the
    changes that are required to be notified;
  (c) he knows that the change affects an entitlement of that other
    person to such a benefit or other payment or advantage; and
  (d) he causes or allows that other person to fail to give a prompt noti-
    fication of that change in the prescribed manner to the prescribed
    person.
(1C) In a case where subsection (1C) of section 111A above applies, the
  recipient is guilty of an offence if—
  (a) he knows that the change affects an entitlement of the claimant to
    a benefit or other payment or advantage under a provision of the
    relevant social security legislation;
  (b) the entitlement is one in respect of which he has a right to receive
    payments to which the claimant has, or (but for the arrangements
    under which they are payable to the recipient) would have, an
    entitlement; and
  (c) he fails to give a prompt notification of that change in the pre-
    scribed manner to the prescribed person.
(1D) In a case where that subsection applies, a person other than the recipient is guilty of an offence if—
  (a) he knows that the change affects an entitlement of the claimant to
    a benefit or other payment or advantage under a provision of the
    relevant social security legislation;
  (b) the entitlement is one in respect of which the recipient has a
    right to receive payments to which the claimant has, or (but for
    the arrangements under which they are payable to the recipient)
    would have, an entitlement; and
  (c) he causes or allows the recipient to fail to give a prompt notification
    of that change in the prescribed manner to the prescribed person.
(1E) Subsection (1F) of section 111A above applies in relation to subsections (1C) and (1D) above as it applies in relation to subsections (1D)
  and (1E) of that section.
(1F) For the purposes of subsections (1A) to (1D) above a notification of
  a change is prompt if, and only if, it is given as soon as reasonably
  practicable after the change occurs.

C15 Dishonesty and Offences Against Property

Section 111A:

EW

⚏ 6 months' imprisonment and/or fine/7 years' imprisonment

Section 112:

SO

⚏ 3 months' imprisonment and/or level 3 fine

C15.17.1 *Sentencing*

For offences under section 111A, refer to the 'Fraud Guideline' at **Appendix 5**. For section 112:

Offence seriousness (culpability and harm) A. Identify the appropriate starting point Starting points based on first-time offender pleading not guilty		
Examples of nature of activity	**Starting point**	**Range**
Claim fraudulent from the start, up to £5,000 obtained (s 111A or s 112)	Medium-level community order	Band B fine to high-level community order
Claim fraudulent from the start, more than £5,000 but less than £20,000 obtained	12 weeks' custody	Medium-level community order to Crown Court
Claim fraudulent from the start, large-scale, professional offending	Crown Court	Crown Court

Offence seriousness (culpability and harm)

B. Consider the effect of aggravating and mitigating factors

(other than those within examples above)

The following may be particularly relevant but these lists are not exhaustive

Factors indicating higher culpability	**Factors indicating lower culpability**
1. Offending carried out over a long period	1. Pressurized by others
2. Offender acting in unison with one or more others	2. Claim initially legitimate
3. Planning	**Factor indicating lesser degree of harm**
4. Offender motivated by greed or desire to live beyond his/her means	1. Voluntary repayment of amounts overpaid
5. False identities or other personal details used	
6. False or forged documents used	
7. Official documents altered or falsified	

R v Noel [2012] EWCA Crim 956 confirmed that a custodial sentence was not appropriate for an offence under section 112(1A)(2) (failing to notify change of circumstances) of the Social Security Amendment Act 1982 by a woman of good character, involving £12,500 over nearly 5 years. The committal to the Crown Court had been only for the purposes of confiscation. *R v Vitorio Condomiti* [2015] EWCA Crim 806 held that a legitimate entitlement to benefits not claimed is also a mitigating factor and is a form of set-off based against what the applicant would have received, had a claim been made.

C15.17.2 Key points

Allocation:

In guidance published by the CPS, including guidance on diversion from prosecution, it is suggested that administrative penalties may be suitable (subject to an absence of aggravating factors) for offences to a value of £2,000, and that summary jurisdiction may be accepted (subject to mitigating and aggravating factors) to the sum of £35,000. By the Social Security (Penalty as Alternative to Prosecution)(Maximum Amount) Order 2015 the maximum amount of the penalty that may be offered as an alternative to prosecution is set at £5,000 for matters occurring wholly on or after 1 April 2015.

- In *R v Laku* [2008] EWCA Crim 1748, L made false representations in order to claim benefits and was prosecuted under sections 111A and 111A(1A) of the Social Security Administration Act 1992. On subsequent claims he did not correct the falsehoods. Held: convictions under section 111A(1A) quashed; he had not failed to notify a change in circumstances as the same false circumstances that founded the convictions under section 111A continued.
- An offence under section 111A(1B) requires a positive act on the part of the defendant. Sitting back and doing nothing does not amount to (allowing) an offence (*R v Tilley* [2009] EWCA Crim 1426).
- The offence under section 112(1A) of the Social Security Administration Act 1992 was interpreted in *Coventry City Council v Vassell* [2011] EWHC 1542 (Admin), and is committed if:
  - there is a change of circumstances affecting entitlement to benefit;
  - that change is not excluded from reporting by regulations; and
  - the defendant knows that change affects his entitlement to benefit; the court held this meant 'would' affect (not 'could' affect) that entitlement;

- in relation to the requirement that the defendant fails to give prompt notification in the prescribed manner to the prescribed person the court held that whether there was prompt notice is a matter of fact. In considering who is the prescribed person, the court confirmed that the DWP will not suffice if the regulations specify the local authority. However, the defendant must *know* who is the correct person for the offence to be committed. In considering that aspect, relevant issues include the information provided by the local authority and the unexpected continuation of benefit.

C15.17.3 *Time limits for prosecution*

The normal six-month time limit for summary-only offences is extended in relation to section 112 by section 116(2):

Social Security Administration Act 1992, s 116(2)–(3)

116 Legal proceedings

(2) Notwithstanding anything in any Act—
  (a) proceedings for an offence under this Act (other than proceedings to which paragraph (b) applies), or for an offence under the Jobseekers Act 1995, may be begun at any time within the period of 3 months from the date on which evidence, sufficient in the opinion of the Secretary of State to justify a prosecution for the offence, comes to his knowledge or within a period of 12 months from the commission of the offence, whichever period last expires; and
  (b) proceedings brought by the appropriate authority for an offence under this Act relating to housing benefit or council tax benefit may be begun at any time within the period of 3 months from the date on which evidence, sufficient in the opinion of the appropriate authority to justify a prosecution for the offence, comes to the authority's knowledge or within a period of 12 months from the commission of the offence, whichever period last expires.

(2A) Subsection (2) above shall not be taken to impose any restriction on the time when proceedings may be begun for an offence under section 111A above.

(3) For the purposes of subsection (2) above—
  (a) a certificate purporting to be signed by or on behalf of the Secretary of State as to the date on which such evidence as is mentioned in paragraph (a) of that subsection came to his knowledge shall be conclusive evidence of that date; and.
  (b) a certificate of the appropriate authority as to the date on which such evidence as is mentioned in paragraph (b) of that subsection came to the authority's knowledge shall be conclusive evidence of that date.

See *Blackstone's Criminal Practice 2017* **B5.8** and **B16.55–B16.63**

C15.18 Tax credit fraud

Tax Credits Act 2002, s 35

35 Offence of fraud

A person commits an offence if he is knowingly concerned in any fraudulent activity undertaken with a view to obtaining payments of a tax credit by him or any other person.

EW

 6 months' imprisonment and/or fine/7 years' imprisonment

C15.18.1 *Sentencing*

See **Appendix 5**.

C15.18.2 Key points

- Disposing of the proceeds of fraud amounts to a fraudulent activity (*R v Kolapo* [2009] EWCA Crim 545).
- *R v Nolan and Howard* [2012] EWCA Crim 671 confirmed that the passive receipt of moneys and failure to report did not amount to 'fraudulent activity', which requires a positive act of misrepresentation with a view to gain. The statute requires behaviour calculated to achieve, rather than to capitalize on what had already been achieved.

 See *Blackstone's Criminal Practice 2017* **B16.7**

C15.19 Theft

Theft Act 1968, s 1(1) and (2)

1 Basic definition of theft

(1) A person is guilty of theft if he dishonestly appropriates property belonging to another with the intention of permanently depriving the other of it; and 'thief' and 'steal' shall be construed accordingly.

(2) It is immaterial whether the appropriation is made with a view to gain, or is made for the thief's own benefit.

C15 Dishonesty and Offences Against Property

 6 months' imprisonment and/or fine/7 years' imprisonment

C15.19.1 *Sentencing*

General theft : Theft Act 1968 (section 1)

Including:

> Theft from the person
> Theft in a dwelling
> Theft in breach of trust
> Theft from a motor vehicle
> Theft of a motor vehicle
> Theft of a pedal bicycle
> and all other section 1 Theft Act 1968 offences, but
> excluding theft from a shop or stall.

STEP ONE: determining the offence category

The court should determine the offence category with reference **only** to the factors identified in the following tables. In order to determine the category the court should assess **culpability** and **harm**.

The level of culpability is determined by weighing up all the factors of the case to determine the offender's role and the extent to which the offending was **planned** and the **sophistication** with which it was carried out.

CULPABILITY demonstrated by one or more of the following:
A – High culpability
A leading role where offending is part of a group activity Involvement of others through coercion, intimidation, or exploitation Breach of a high degree of trust or responsibility Sophisticated nature of offence/significant planning Theft involving intimidation or the use or threat of force Deliberately targeting victim on basis of vulnerability
B – Medium culpability
A significant role where offending is part of a group activity Some degree of planning involved Breach of some degree of trust or responsibility All other cases where characteristics for categories A or C are not present

C – Lesser culpability
Performed limited function under direction
Involved through coercion, intimidation, or exploitation
Little or no planning
Limited awareness or understanding of offence

Where there are characteristics present which fall under different levels of culpability, the court should balance these characteristics to reach a fair assessment of the offender's culpability.

HARM

Harm is assessed by reference to the **financial loss** that results from the theft and **any significant additional harm** suffered by the victim or others—examples of significant additional harm may include **but are not limited to**:

Items stolen were of substantial value to the loser—regardless of monetary worth
High level of inconvenience caused to the victim or others
Consequential financial harm to victim or others
Emotional distress
Fear/loss of confidence caused by the crime
Risk of or actual injury to persons or damage to property
Impact of theft on a business
Damage to heritage assets
Disruption caused to infrastructure

Intended loss should be used where actual loss has been prevented.

Category 1	Very-high-value goods stolen (above £100,000) **or** high-value with significant additional harm to the victim or others
Category 2	High-value goods stolen (£10,000 to £100,000) **and** no significant additional harm **or** medium-value with significant additional harm to the victim or others
Category 3	Medium-value goods stolen (£500 to £10,000) **and** no significant additional harm **or** low-value with significant additional harm to the victim or others
Category 4	Low-value goods stolen (up to £500) **and** little or no significant additional harm to the victim or others

STEP TWO: Starting point and category range

Having determined the category at step one, the court should use the starting point to reach a sentence within the appropriate category range in the table below.

The starting point applies to all offenders irrespective of plea or previous convictions.

Harm	Culpability		
	A	**B**	**C**
Category 1 Adjustment should be made for any significant additional harm factors where very high value goods are stolen	**Starting point** 3 years 6 months' custody	**Starting point** 2 years' custody	**Starting point** 1 year's custody
	Category range 2 years 6 months' – 6 years' custody	**Category range** 1–3 years 6 months' custody	**Category range** 26 weeks' – 2 years' custody
Category 2	**Starting point** 2 years' custody	**Starting point** 1 year's custody	**Starting point** High-level community order
	Category range 1 year – 3 years 6 months' custody	**Category range** 26 weeks' – 2 years' custody	**Category range** Low-level community order – 36 weeks' custody
Category 3	**Starting point** 1 year's custody	**Starting point** High-level community order	**Starting point** Band C fine
	Category range 26 weeks' – 2 years' custody	**Category range** Low-level community order – 36 weeks' custody	**Category range** Band B fine – low-level community order
Category 4	**Starting point** High-level community order	**Starting point** Low-level community order	**Starting point** Band B fine
	Category range Medium-level community order – 36 weeks' custody	**Category range** Band C fine – medium-level community order	**Category range** Discharge – band C fine

The table above refers to single offences. Where there are multiple offences, consecutive sentences may be appropriate: please refer to the *Offences Taken into Consideration* and *Totality* guidelines.

Where multiple offences are committed in circumstances which justify consecutive sentences, and the total amount stolen is in excess of £1 million, then an aggregate sentence in excess of 7 years may be appropriate.

Where the offender is dependent on or has a propensity to misuse drugs or alcohol and there is sufficient prospect of success, a community order with a drug rehabilitation requirement under section 209, or an alcohol treatment requirement under section 212 of the Criminal Justice Act 2003, may be a proper alternative to a short or moderate custodial sentence.

Where the offender suffers from a medical condition that is susceptible to treatment but does not warrant detention under a hospital order, a community order with a mental health treatment requirement under section 207 of the Criminal Justice Act 2003 may be a proper alternative to a short or moderate custodial sentence.

The court should then consider further adjustment for any aggravating or mitigating factors. The following is a non-exhaustive list of additional factual elements providing the context of the offence and factors relating to the offender. Identify whether any combination of these, or other relevant factors, should result in an upward or downward adjustment from the sentence arrived at so far.

Factors increasing seriousness	
Statutory aggravating factors	*Other aggravating factors*
Previous convictions, having regard to (a) the **nature** of the offence to which the conviction relates and its relevance to the current offence; and (b) the **time** that has elapsed since the conviction	Stealing goods to order
	Steps taken to prevent the victim reporting or obtaining assistance and/or from assisting or supporting the prosecution
Offence committed whilst on bail	Offender motivated by intention to cause harm or revenge
Offence motivated by, or demonstrating hostility based on, any of the following characteristics or presumed characteristics of the victim: religion, race, disability, sexual orientation, or transgender identity	Offence committed over sustained period of time
	Attempts to conceal/dispose of evidence
	Failure to comply with current court orders
	Offence committed on licence
	Offences taken into consideration
	Established evidence of community/wider impact (for issues other than prevalence)
	Prevalence—see below

Factors reducing seriousness or reflecting personal mitigation
No previous convictions **or** no relevant/recent convictions
Remorse, particularly where evidenced by voluntary reparation to the victim
Good character and/or exemplary conduct
Serious medical condition requiring urgent, intensive, or long-term treatment
Age and/or lack of maturity where it affects the responsibility of the offender
Mental disorder or learning disability
Sole or primary carer for dependent relatives
Determination and/or demonstration of steps having been taken to address addiction or offending behaviour
Inappropriate degree of trust or responsibility

C15.19.1.1 *Prevalence*

There may be exceptional local circumstances that arise which may lead a court to decide that prevalence should influence sentencing levels. The pivotal issue in such cases will be the harm caused to the community. It is essential that the court, before taking account of prevalence:

- has supporting evidence from an external source, for example, community impact statements, to justify claims that a particular crime is prevalent in their area, and is causing particular harm in that community, and
- is satisfied that there is a compelling need to treat the offence more seriously than elsewhere.

C15.19.1.2 *Theft from a shop or stall*

STEP ONE: determining the offence category

The court should determine the offence category with reference **only** to the factors identified in the following tables. In order to determine the category the court should assess **culpability** and **harm**.

The level of culpability is determined by weighing up all the factors of the case to determine the offender's role and the extent to which the offending was **planned** and the **sophistication** with which it was carried out.

A – High culpability
A leading role where offending is part of a group activity
Involvement of others through coercion, intimidation, or exploitation
Sophisticated nature of offence/significant planning
Significant use or threat of force
Offender subject to a banning order from the relevant shop or stall
Child accompanying offender is actively used to facilitate the offence (not merely present when offence is committed)
B – Medium culpability
A significant role where offending is part of a group activity
Some degree of planning involved
Limited use or threat of force
All other cases where characteristics for categories A or C are not present
C – Lesser culpability
Performed limited function under direction
Involved through coercion, intimidation, or exploitation
Little or no planning
Mental disorder/learning disability where linked to commission of the offence

Where there are characteristics present which fall under different levels of culpability, the court should balance these characteristics to reach a fair assessment of the offender's culpability.

HARM

Harm is assessed by reference to the **financial loss** that results from the theft and **any significant additional harm** suffered by the victim—examples of significant additional harm may include **but are not limited to**:

Emotional distress
Damage to property
Effect on business
A greater impact on the victim due to the size or type of their business
A particularly vulnerable victim

Intended loss should be used where actual loss has been prevented.

Category 1	High-value goods stolen (above £1,000) **or** medium-value with significant additional harm to the victim
Category 2	Medium-value goods stolen (£200 to £1,000) **and** no significant additional harm **or** low-value with significant additional harm to the victim
Category 3	Low-value goods stolen (up to £200) **and** little or no significant additional harm to the victim

STEP TWO: starting point and category range

Having determined the category at step one, the court should use the starting point to reach a sentence within the appropriate category range in the table below.

The starting point applies to all offenders irrespective of plea or previous convictions.

Harm	Culpability		
	A	B	C
Category 1 Where the value greatly exceeds £1,000 it may be appropriate to move outside the identified range. Adjustment should be made for any significant additional harm where high value goods are stolen.	**Starting point** 26 weeks' custody	**Starting point** Medium-level community order	**Starting point** Band C fine
	Category range 12 weeks' – 3 years' custody	**Category range** Low-level community order – 26 weeks' custody	**Category range** Band B fine – low-level community order

Category 2	**Starting point** 12 weeks' custody	**Starting point** Low-level community order	**Starting point** Band B fine
	Category range High-level community order – 26 weeks' custody	**Category range** Band C fine – medium-level community order	**Category range** Band A fine – band C fine
Category 3	**Starting point** High-level community order	**Starting point** Band C fine	**Starting point** Band A fine
	Category range Low-level community order – 12 weeks' custody	**Category range** Band B fine – low-level community order	**Category range** Discharge – band B fine

Consecutive sentences for multiple offences may be appropriate—please refer to the *Offences Taken into Consideration* and *Totality* guidelines. Previous diversionary work with an offender does not preclude the court from considering this type of sentencing option again if appropriate.

Where the offender is dependent on or has a propensity to misuse drugs or alcohol and there is sufficient prospect of success, a community order with a drug rehabilitation requirement under section 209, or an alcohol treatment requirement under section 212 of the Criminal Justice Act 2003, may be a proper alternative to a short or moderate length custodial sentence.

Where the offender suffers from a medical condition that is susceptible to treatment but does not warrant detention under a hospital order, a community order with a mental health treatment requirement under section 207 of the Criminal Justice Act 2003 may be a proper alternative to a short or moderate length custodial sentence.

The court should then consider further adjustment for any aggravating or mitigating factors. The following is a non-exhaustive list of additional factual elements providing the context of the offence and factors relating to the offender. Identify whether any combination of these, or other relevant factors, should result in an upward or downward adjustment from the sentence arrived at so far.

Factors increasing seriousness	
Statutory aggravating factors	*Other aggravating factors*
Previous convictions, having regard to (a) the **nature** of the offence to which the conviction relates and its relevance to the current offence; and (b) the **time** that has elapsed since the conviction. Relevant recent convictions may justify an upward adjustment, including outside the category range. In cases involving significant persistent offending, the community and custodial thresholds may be crossed even though the offence otherwise warrants a lesser sentence. Any custodial sentence must be kept to the necessary minimum Offence committed whilst on bail Offence motivated by, or demonstrating hostility based on, any of the following characteristics or presumed characteristics of the victim: religion, race, disability, sexual orientation, or transgender identity	Stealing goods to order Steps taken to prevent the victim reporting or obtaining assistance and/ or from assisting or supporting the prosecution Attempts to conceal/dispose of evidence Offender motivated by intention to cause harm or revenge Failure to comply with current court orders Offence committed on licence Offences taken into consideration Established evidence of community/ wider impact (for issues other than prevalence) Prevalence—see below

Factors reducing seriousness or reflecting personal mitigation
No previous convictions **or** no relevant/recent convictions Remorse, particularly where evidenced by voluntary reparation to the victim Good character and/or exemplary conduct Serious medical condition requiring urgent, intensive, or long-term treatment Age and/or lack of maturity where it affects the responsibility of the offender Mental disorder or learning disability (where not linked to the commission of the offence) Sole or primary carer for dependent relatives. Determination and/or demonstration of steps having been taken to address addiction or offending behaviour. Offender experiencing exceptional financial hardship.

C15.19.1.3 *Prevalence*

There may be exceptional local circumstances that arise which may lead a court to decide that prevalence should influence sentencing levels. The pivotal issue in such cases will be the harm caused to the community. It is essential that the court, before taking account of prevalence:

- has supporting evidence from an external source, for example, community impact statements, to justify claims that a particular crime is prevalent in their area, and is causing particular harm in that community, and
- is satisfied that there is a compelling need to treat the offence more seriously than elsewhere.

C15.19.2 Key points

- Dishonesty is a two-part test:
  (i) Were the accused's actions dishonest according to the ordinary standards of reasonable and honest people?
  (ii) If so, did the accused know that those actions were dishonest according to those standards? (*R v Ghosh* [1982] QB 1058)

The first, objective limb of *Ghosh* is tested by the ordinary standards of the honest and reasonable person generally, not by the standards of a particular market. Those may be relevant to the second, subjective limb, which considers the defendant's beliefs as to what an honest and reasonable person would think (*Hayes* [2015] EWCA 1944).

- 'Dishonestly' is considered in section 2 of the Theft Act 1968:

> **Theft Act 1968, s 2**
>
> **2 'Dishonestly'**
>
> (1) A person's appropriation of property belonging to another is not to be regarded as dishonest—
>   (a) if he appropriates the property in the belief that he has in law the right to deprive the other of it, on behalf of himself or of a third person; or
>   (b) if he appropriates the property in the belief that he would have the other's consent if the other knew of the appropriation and the circumstances of it; or
>   (c) (except where the property came to him as trustee or personal representative) if he appropriates the property in the belief that the person to whom the property belongs cannot be discovered by taking reasonable steps.
> (2) A person's appropriation of property belonging to another may be dishonest notwithstanding that he is willing to pay for the property.

'Appropriation' means the assumption of any of the rights of an owner (*R v Gomez* [1993] AC 442).

The intention permanently to deprive is also considered in section 6 of the Theft Act 1968:

> **Theft Act 1968, s 6**
>
> **6 'With the intention of permanently depriving the other of it'**
>
> (1) A person appropriating property belonging to another without meaning the other permanently to lose the thing itself is nevertheless to be regarded as having the intention of permanently depriving the other of it if his intention is to treat the thing as his own to dispose of regardless of the other's rights; and a borrowing or lending of it may

amount to so treating it if, but only if, the borrowing or lending is for a period and in circumstances making it equivalent to an outright taking or disposal.

(2) Without prejudice to the generality of subsection (1) above, where a person, having possession or control (lawfully or not) of property belonging to another, parts with the property under a condition as to its return which he may not be able to perform, this (if done for purposes of his own and without the other's authority) amounts to treating the property as his own to dispose of regardless of the other's rights.

C15.19.3 *Low-value theft from a shop*

Magistrates' Courts Act 1980, s 22A

(1) Low-value shoplifting is triable only summarily.

(2) But where a person accused of low-value shoplifting is aged 18 or over, and appears or is brought before the court before the summary trial of the offence begins, the court must give the person the opportunity of electing to be tried by the Crown Court for the offence and, if the person elects to be so tried—

    (a) subsection (1) does not apply, and

    (b) the court must send the person to the Crown Court for trial for the offence.

(3) 'Low-value shoplifting' means an offence under section 1 of the Theft Act 1968 in circumstances where—

    (a) the value of the stolen goods does not exceed £200,

    (b) the goods were being offered for sale in a shop or any other premises, stall, vehicle or place from which there is carried on a trade or business, and

    (c) at the time of the offence, the person accused of low-value shoplifting was, or was purporting to be, a customer or potential customer of the person offering the goods for sale.

(4) For the purposes of subsection (3)(a)—

    (a) the value of the stolen goods is the price at which they were being offered for sale at the time of the offence, and

    (b) where the accused is charged on the same occasion with two or more offences of low-value shoplifting, the reference to the value involved has effect as if it were a reference to the aggregate of the values involved....

(6) A person convicted of low-value shoplifting by a magistrates' court may not appeal to the Crown Court against the conviction on the ground that the convicting court was mistaken as to whether the offence was one of low-value shoplifting.

(7) For the purposes of this section, any reference to low-value shoplifting includes aiding, abetting, counselling or procuring the commission of low-value shoplifting.

> **Criminal Attempts Act 1981, s 1(5)**
>
> This section also applies to low-value shoplifting (which is defined in, and is triable only summarily by virtue of, section 22A of the Magistrates' Courts Act 1980).

SO 6 months' imprisonment and/or a fine

C15.20 Going equipped for theft

> **Theft Act 1968, s 25(1)–(3), (5)**
>
> **25 Going equipped for stealing etc**
> (1) A person shall be guilty of an offence if, when not at his place of abode, he has with him any article for use in the course of or in connection with any burglary or theft.
> (2) A person guilty of an offence under this section shall on conviction on indictment be liable to imprisonment for a term not exceeding three years.
> (3) Where a person is charged with an offence under this section, proof that he had with him any article made or adapted for use in committing a burglary or theft shall be evidence that he had it with him for such use.
> (4) ...
> (5) For purposes of this section an offence under section 12(1) of this Act of taking a conveyance shall be treated as theft.

EW

▥ 6 months' imprisonment and/or fine/3 years' imprisonment

C15.20.1 *Sentencing*

STEP ONE: determining the offence category

The court should determine the offence category with reference **only** to the factors identified in the following tables. In order to determine the category the court should assess **culpability** and **harm**.

The level of culpability is determined by weighing up all the factors of the case to determine the offender's role and the extent to which the offending was **planned** and the **sophistication** with which it was carried out.

CULPABILITY demonstrated by one or more of the following:
A – High culpability
A leading role where offending is part of a group activity Involvement of others through coercion, intimidation, or exploitation Significant steps taken to conceal identity and/or avoid detection Sophisticated nature of offence/significant planning Offender equipped for robbery or domestic burglary
B – Medium culpability
A significant role where offending is part of a group activity All other cases where characteristics for categories A or C are not present
C – Lesser culpability
Involved through coercion, intimidation, or exploitation Limited awareness or understanding of offence Little or no planning

Where there are characteristics present which fall under different levels of culpability, the court should balance these characteristics to reach a fair assessment of the offender's culpability.

HARM

This guideline refers to preparatory offences where no theft has been committed. The level of harm is determined by weighing up all the factors of the case to determine the harm that would be caused if the item(s) were used to commit a substantive offence.

Greater harm

Possession of item(s) which have the potential to facilitate an offence affecting a large number of victims Possession of item(s) which have the potential to facilitate an offence involving high-value items

Lesser harm

All other cases

STEP TWO: starting point and category range

Having determined the category at step one, the court should use the starting point to reach a sentence within the appropriate category range in the table below.

The starting point applies to all offenders irrespective of plea or previous convictions.

C15 Dishonesty and Offences Against Property

Harm	Culpability		
	A	B	C
Greater	**Starting point** 1 year's custody	**Starting point** 18 weeks' custody	**Starting point** Medium-level community order
	Category range 26 weeks' – 1 year 6 months' custody	**Category range** High-level community order – 36 weeks' custody	**Category range** Low-level community order – high-level community order
Lesser	**Starting point** 26 weeks' custody	**Starting point** High-level community order	**Starting point** Band C fine
	Category range 12 weeks' – 36 weeks' custody	**Category range** Medium-level community order – 12 weeks' custody	**Category range** Discharge – medium-level community order

Consecutive sentences for multiple offences may be appropriate – please refer to the *Offences Taken into Consideration* and *Totality* guidelines.

The court should then consider further adjustment for any aggravating or mitigating factors. The following is a **non-exhaustive** list of additional factual elements providing the context of the offence and factors relating to the offender. Identify whether any combination of these, or other relevant factors, should result in an upward or downward adjustment from the starting point.

Factors increasing seriousness	
Statutory aggravating factors	*Other aggravating factors*
Previous convictions, having regard to (a) the **nature** of the offence to which the conviction relates and its **relevance** to the current offence; and (b) the **time** that has elapsed since the conviction Offence committed whilst on bail	Attempts to conceal/dispose of evidence Established evidence of community/ wider impact Failure to comply with current court orders Offence committed on licence Offences taken into consideration

Factors reducing seriousness or reflecting personal mitigation
No previous convictions **or** no relevant/recent convictions Good character and/or exemplary conduct Serious medical condition requiring urgent, intensive, or long-term treatment Age and/or lack of maturity where it affects the responsibility of the offender Mental disorder or learning disability Sole or primary carer for dependent relatives Determination and/or demonstration of steps having been taken to address addiction or offending behaviour

C15.20.2 Key points

The article need not be intended for immediate use but it must be intended for future use (see *R v Ellames* [1974] 1 WLR 1391). Proof of intent is required and not mere contemplation of an offence (see *R v Hargreaves* [1985] Crim LR 243).

 See *Blackstone's Criminal Practice 2017* **B4.150–4.158**

C15.21 Unauthorised use of trade mark, etc

Trade Marks Act 1994, s 92(1)–(4)

92 Unauthorised use of trade mark, etc in relation to goods

(1) A person commits an offence who with a view to gain for himself or another, or with intent to cause loss to another, and without the consent of the proprietor—
  (a) applies to goods or their packaging a sign identical to, or likely to be mistaken for, a registered trade mark, or
  (b) sells or lets for hire, offers or exposes for sale or hire or distributes goods which bear, or the packaging of which bears, such a sign, or
  (c) has in his possession, custody or control in the course of a business any such goods with a view to the doing of anything, by himself or another, which would be an offence under paragraph (b).

(2) A person commits an offence who with a view to gain for himself or another, or with intent to cause loss to another, and without the consent of the proprietor—
  (a) applies a sign identical to, or likely to be mistaken for, a registered trade mark to material intended to be used—
    (i) for labelling or packaging goods,
    (ii) as a business paper in relation to goods, or
    (iii) for advertising goods, or
  (b) uses in the course of a business material bearing such a sign for labelling or packaging goods, as a business paper in relation to goods, or for advertising goods, or
  (c) has in his possession, custody or control in the course of a business any such material with a view to the doing of anything, by himself or another, which would be an offence under paragraph (b).

(3) A person commits an offence who with a view to gain for himself or another, or with intent to cause loss to another, and without the consent of the proprietor—
  (a) makes an article specifically designed or adapted for making copies of a sign identical to, or likely to be mistaken for, a registered trade mark, or
  (b) has such an article in his possession, custody or control in the course of a business,

---

knowing or having reason to believe that it has been, or is to be, used to produce goods, or material for labelling or packaging goods, as a business paper in relation to goods, or for advertising goods.

(4) A person does not commit an offence under this section unless—
   (a) the goods are goods in respect of which the trade mark is registered, or
   (b) the trade mark has a reputation in the United Kingdom and the use of the sign takes or would take unfair advantage of, or is or would be detrimental to, the distinctive character or the repute of the trade mark.

EW

 6 months' imprisonment and/or fine/10 years' imprisonment

C15.21.1 *Sentencing*

Offence seriousness (culpability and harm) A. Identify the appropriate starting point Starting points based on first-time offender pleading not guilty		
Examples of nature of activity	**Starting point**	**Range**
Small number of counterfeit items	Band C fine	Band B fine to low-level community order
Larger number of counterfeit items but no involvement in wider operation	Medium-level community order, plus fine*	Low-level community order to 12 weeks' custody, plus fine*
High number of counterfeit items or involvement in wider operation, eg manufacture or distribution	12 weeks' custody	6 weeks' custody to Crown Court
Central role in large-scale operation	Crown Court	Crown Court

* This may be an offence where it is appropriate to combine a fine with a community order.

Offence seriousness (culpability and harm) B. Consider the effect of aggravating and mitigating factors (other than those within examples above) The following may be particularly relevant but these lists are not exhaustive	
Factors indicating higher culpability 1. High degree of professionalism 2. High level of profit **Factor indicating greater degree of harm** 1. Purchasers at risk of harm, eg from counterfeit drugs	**Factor indicating lower culpability** 1. Mistake or ignorance about provenance of goods

C15.21.2 Key points

It is a defence for a person charged with an offence under section 92 to show that he believed on reasonable grounds that the use of the sign in the manner in which it was used, or was to be used, was not an infringement of the registered trade mark. In order to be able to satisfy the statutory defence under section 95(2) of the Trade Marks Act 1994, the defendant must show not only that he had an honest belief that the trade marks did not infringe registered trade marks, but also that he had reasonable grounds for so believing. Section 97 makes provision for the forfeiture of counterfeit goods and packaging.

See *Blackstone's Criminal Practice 2017* **B6.102**

C15.22 TV licence payment evasion

> **Communications Act 2003, s 363**
> 363 Licence required for use of TV receiver

 Level 3 fine

C15.22.1 *Sentencing*

Note that this guideline is under review by the Sentencing Council (see **Appendix 7**).

Offence seriousness (culpability and harm) A. Identify the appropriate starting point Starting points based on first-time offender pleading not guilty		
Examples of nature of activity	**Starting point**	**Range**
Up to 6 months' unlicensed use	Band A fine	Band A fine
Over 6 months' unlicensed use	Band B fine	Band A fine to band B fine

> **Offence seriousness (culpability and harm)**
> **B. Consider the effect of aggravating and mitigating factors**
> **(other than those within examples above)**
> **The following may be particularly relevant but these lists are not exhaustive**
>
> **Factors indicating lower culpability**
> 1. Accidental oversight or belief licence held
> 2. Confusion of responsibility
> 3. Licence immediately obtained

C15.23 TWOC (vehicle-taking without consent)

> ### Theft Act 1968, s 12(1), (5), (6), and (7)
>
> #### 12 Taking motor vehicle or other conveyance without authority
>
> (1) Subject to subsections (5) and (6) below, a person shall be guilty of an offence if, without having the consent of the owner or other lawful authority, he takes any conveyance for his own or another's use or knowing that any conveyance has been taken without such authority, drives it or allows himself to be carried in or on it.
> (5) Subsection (1) above shall not apply in relation to pedal cycles; but, subject to subsection (6) below, a person who, without having the consent of the owner or other lawful authority, takes a pedal cycle for his own or another's use, or rides a pedal cycle knowing it to have been taken without such authority, shall on summary conviction be liable to a fine not exceeding level 3 on the standard scale.
> (6) A person does not commit an offence under this section by anything done in the belief that he has lawful authority to do it or that he would have the owner's consent if the owner knew of his doing it and the circumstances of it.
> (7) For purposes of this section—
>   (a) 'conveyance' means any conveyance constructed or adapted for the carriage of a person or persons whether by land, water or air, except that it does not include a conveyance constructed or adapted for use only under the control of a person not carried in or on it, and 'drive' shall be construed accordingly; and
>   (b) 'owner', in relation to a conveyance which is the subject of a hiring agreement or hire-purchase agreement, means the person in possession of the conveyance under that agreement.

SO

 6 months' imprisonment and/or fine

C15.23.1 *Sentencing*

*Note that this guideline is under review by the Sentencing Council (see **Appendix 7**).*

Offence seriousness (culpability and harm) A. Identify the appropriate starting point Starting points based on first-time offender pleading not guilty		
Examples of nature of activity	Starting point	Range
Exceeding authorised use of, eg employer's or relative's, vehicle; retention of hire car beyond return date	Low-level community order	Band B fine to medium-level community order
As above with damage caused to lock/ignition; OR stranger's vehicle involved but no damage caused	Medium-level community order	Low-level community order to high-level community order
Taking vehicle from private premises; OR causing damage to, eg lock/ignition of stranger's vehicle	High-level community order	Medium-level community order to 26 weeks' custody

Offence seriousness (culpability and harm) B. Consider the effect of aggravating and mitigating factors (other than those within examples above) The following may be particularly relevant but these lists are not exhaustive	
Factors indicating greater degree of harm 1. Vehicle later burnt 2. Vehicle belonging to elderly/disabled person 3. Emergency services vehicle 4. Medium to large goods vehicle 5. Passengers carried	**Factor indicating lower culpability** 1. Misunderstanding with owner
	Factor indicating lesser degree of harm 1. Offender voluntarily returned vehicle to owner

C15.23.2 Key points

- This offence is summary only, but subject to the following exception in relation to limitation period. Section 12(4A)–(4C) of the Act provides:

Theft Act 1968, s 12(4A)–(4C)

(4A) Proceedings for an offence under subsection (1) above (but not proceedings of a kind falling within subsection (4) above) in relation to a mechanically propelled vehicle—

(a) shall not be commenced after the end of the period of three years beginning with the day on which the offence was committed; but

    (b) subject to that, may be commenced at any time within the period of six months beginning with the relevant day.

(4B) In subsection (4A)(b) above 'the relevant day' means—

    (a) in the case of a prosecution for an offence under subsection (1) above by a public prosecutor, the day on which sufficient evidence to justify the proceedings came to the knowledge of any person responsible for deciding whether to commence any such prosecution;

    (b) in the case of a prosecution for an offence under subsection (1) above which is commenced by a person other than a public prosecutor after the discontinuance of a prosecution falling within paragraph (a) above which relates to the same facts, the day on which sufficient evidence to justify the proceedings came to the knowledge of the person who has decided to commence the prosecution or (if later) the discontinuance of the other prosecution;

    (c) in the case of any other prosecution for an offence under subsection (1) above, the day on which sufficient evidence to justify the proceedings came to the knowledge of the person who has decided to commence the prosecution.

(4C) For the purposes of subsection (4A)(b) above a certificate of a person responsible for deciding whether to commence a prosecution of a kind mentioned in subsection (4B)(a) above as to the date on which such evidence as is mentioned in the certificate came to the knowledge of any person responsible for deciding whether to commence any such prosecution shall be conclusive evidence of that fact.

- There must be movement for a vehicle to be taken (*R v Bogacki* [1973] QB 832). The vehicle must be taken as a conveyance (*R v Stokes* [1983] RTR 59). The burden of proving that the defendant did not have a belief that he had the authority of the owner lies on the Crown once the defendant has raised the issue by evidence (*R v Gannon* (1987) 87 Cr App R 254). The belief must exist at the time of the taking (*R v Ambler* [1979] RTR 217).

 See *Blackstone's Criminal Practice 2017* **B4.116–B4.126**

C15.24 Vehicle interference

Criminal Attempts Act 1981, s 9(1) and (2)

9 Interference with vehicles

(1) A person is guilty of the offence of vehicle interference if he interferes with a motor vehicle or trailer or with anything carried in or on a motor vehicle or trailer with the intention that an offence specified

in subsection (2) below shall be committed by himself or some other person.

(2) The offences mentioned in subsection (1) above are—

   (a) theft of the motor vehicle or trailer or part of it;

   (b) theft of anything carried in or on the motor vehicle or trailer; and

   (c) an offence under section 12(1) of the Theft Act 1968 (taking and driving away without consent);

and, if it is shown that a person accused of an offence under this section intended that one of those offences should be committed, it is immaterial that it cannot be shown which it was.

 3 months' imprisonment and/or level 4 fine

C15.24.1 *Sentencing*

Note that this guideline is under review by the Sentencing Council (see **Appendix 7**).

Offence seriousness (culpability and harm) A. Identify the appropriate starting point Starting points based on first-time offender pleading not guilty		
Examples of nature of activity	**Starting point**	**Range**
Trying door handles; no entry gained to vehicle; no damage caused	Band C fine	Band A fine to low-level community order
Entering vehicle, little or no damage caused	Medium-level community order	Band C fine to high-level community order
Entering vehicle, with damage caused	High-level community order	Medium-level community order to 12 weeks' custody

Offence seriousness (culpability and harm) B. Consider the effect of aggravating and mitigating factors (other than those within examples above) The following may be particularly relevant but these lists are not exhaustive
Factor indicating higher culpability   1. Targeting vehicle in dark/isolated location   **Factors indicating greater degree of harm**   1. Emergency services vehicle   2. Disabled driver's vehicle   3. Part of series

 See *Blackstone's Criminal Practice 2017* **B4.136–B4.139**

C15.25 Vehicle licence/registration fraud

Vehicle Excise and Registration Act 1994, s 44(1) and (2)

44 Forgery and fraud

(1) A person is guilty of an offence if he forges, fraudulently alters, fraudulently uses, fraudulently lends or fraudulently allows to be used by another person anything to which subsection (2) applies

(2) This subsection applies to—

    (a) a vehicle licence,

    (b) a trade licence,

    (c) a nil licence,

    (d) a registration mark,

    (e) a registration document, and

    (f) a trade plate (including a replacement trade plate).

 Fine/2 years' imprisonment

C15.25.1 *Sentencing*

Offence seriousness (culpability and harm) A. Identify the appropriate starting point Starting points based on first-time offender pleading not guilty		
Examples of nature of activity	**Starting point**	**Range**
Use of unaltered licence from another vehicle	Band B fine	Band B fine
Forged licence bought for own use, or forged/altered for own use	Band C fine	Band C fine
Use of number plates from another vehicle; OR licence/number plates forged or altered for sale to another	High-level community order (in Crown Court)	Medium-level community order to Crown Court (Note: community order and custody available only in Crown Court)

Offence seriousness (culpability and harm)
B. Consider the effect of aggravating and mitigating factors (other than those within examples above)
The following may be particularly relevant but these lists are not exhaustive

Factors indicating higher culpability	Factors indicating lower culpability
1. LGV, PSV, taxi, etc	1. Licence/registration mark from another vehicle owned by defendant
2. Long-term fraudulent use	2. Short-term use
Factors indicating greater degree of harm	
1. High financial gain	
2. Innocent victim deceived	
3. Legitimate owner inconvenienced	

 See *Blackstone's Criminal Practice 2017* **C4.10**

C15.26 Use of threat or violence for the purpose of securing entry to premises

Criminal Law Act 1977, s 6

6 Violence for securing entry

(1) Subject to the following provisions of this section, any person who, without lawful authority, uses or threatens violence for the purpose of securing entry into any premises for himself or for any other person is guilty of an offence, provided that—

    (a) there is someone present on those premises at the time who is opposed to the entry which the violence is intended to secure; and

    (b) the person using or threatening the violence knows that that is the case.

(1A) Subsection (1) above does not apply to a person who is a displaced residential occupier or a protected intending occupier of the premises in question or who is acting on behalf of such an occupier; and if the accused adduces sufficient evidence that he was, or was acting on behalf of, such an occupier he shall be presumed to be, or to be acting on behalf of, such an occupier unless the contrary is proved by the prosecution.

(2) Subject to subsection (1A) above, the fact that a person has any interest in or right to possession or occupation of any premises shall not for the purposes of subsection (1) above constitute lawful authority for the use or threat of violence by him or anyone else for the purpose of securing his entry into those premises.

(3) (repealed).

(4) It is immaterial for the purposes of this section—

    (a) whether the violence in question is directed against the person or against property; and

    (b) whether the entry which the violence is intended to secure is for the purpose of acquiring possession of the premises in question or for any other purpose.

SO

6 months' imprisonment and/or fine

C15.26.1 Key points

The terms premises, displaced residential occupier, and protected intending occupier are defined by sections 12 and 12A of the Criminal Law Act 1977.

C16 **Offences Against the Person**

C16.1 Assault occasioning actual bodily harm

Offences Against the Person Act 1861, s 47

47 Assault occasioning bodily harm
Whosoever shall be convicted ... of any assault occasioning actual bodily harm shall be liable ...

 Fine and/or 6 months'/5 years' imprisonment (7 years' if racially aggravated)

C16.1.1 *Sentencing*

STEP ONE: determining the offence category

Category 1	Greater harm (serious injury must normally be present) and higher culpability
Category 2	Greater harm (serious injury must normally be present) and lower culpability or lesser harm and higher culpability
Category 3	Lesser harm and lower culpability

Factors indicating greater harm	Factors indicating higher culpability
Injury (which includes disease transmission and/or psychological harm) which is serious in the context of the offence (must normally be present) Victim is particularly vulnerable because of personal circumstances Sustained or repeated assault on the same victim	**Statutory aggravating factors:** Offence motivated by, or demonstrating, hostility to, the victim based on his or her sexual orientation (or presumed sexual orientation) Offence motivated by, or demonstrating, hostility to, the victim based on the victim's disability (or presumed disability) **Other aggravating factors:** A significant degree of premeditation Use of weapon or weapon equivalent (eg shod foot, head-butting, use of acid, use of animal) Intention to commit more serious harm than actually resulted from the offence

	Deliberately causes more harm than is necessary for commission of offence Deliberate targeting of vulnerable victim Leading role in group or gang Offence motivated by, or demonstrating, hostility based on the victim's age, sex, gender identity (or presumed gender identity)
Factors indicating lesser harm	**Factors indicating lower culpability**
Injury which is less serious in the context of the offence	Subordinate role in group or gang A greater degree of provocation than normally expected Lack of premeditation Mental disorder or learning disability, where linked to commission of the offence Excessive self-defence

A person could be seen as particularly vulnerable because he was intoxicated even where he struck the first blow, if there is an excessive response (*R v Halane* [2014] EWCA Crim 477). Not every victim of domestic violence is to be treated as particularly vulnerable for the purpose of the guideline. Serious injury must be interpreted in the context of the particular offence. It means not on the margins and more substantial injury (*R v Thomas* [2014] EWCA Crim 1715). In *R v Maloney (James)* [2015] EWCA Crim 798 the Crown alleged the deliberate targeting of a vulnerable victim, acknowledging that this may involve an element of double counting, thus increasing both harm and culpability. The court found that there was not enough evidence that the defendant targeted the victim *because* she was vulnerable; rather, he was angry with her and she happened to be vulnerable.

STEP TWO: starting point and category range

Offence category	Starting point	Category range
Category 1	Crown Court	Crown Court
Category 2	26 weeks' custody	Low-level community order to Crown Court (51 weeks' custody)
Category 3	Medium-level community order	Band A fine to high-level community order

Factors increasing seriousness	
Statutory aggravating factors	*Other aggravating factors*
Previous convictions, having regard to (a) the **nature** of the offence to which the conviction relates and its relevance to the current offence; and (b) the **time** that has elapsed since the conviction	Location of the offence
	Timing of the offence
	Ongoing effect upon the victim
	Offence committed against those working in the public sector or providing a service to the public
	Presence of others including relatives, especially children or partner of the victim
	Gratuitous degradation of victim
Offence committed whilst on bail	In domestic violence cases, victim forced to leave their home
	Failure to comply with current court orders
	Offence committed whilst on licence
	Attempt to conceal or dispose of evidence
	Failure to respond to warnings or concerns expressed by others about the offender's behaviour
	Commission of offence whilst under the influence of alcohol or drugs
	Abuse of power and/or position of trust
	Exploiting contact arrangements with a child to commit an offence
	Established evidence of community impact
	Any steps taken to prevent the victim reporting an incident, obtaining assistance, and/or from assisting or supporting the prosecution
	Offences taken into consideration (TICs)

Factors reducing seriousness or reflecting personal mitigation
No previous convictions or no relevant/recent convictions
Single blow
Remorse
Good character and/or exemplary conduct
Determination and/or demonstration of steps taken to address addiction or offending behaviour
Serious medical conditions requiring urgent, intensive, or long-term treatment
Isolated incident
Age and/or lack of maturity where it affects the responsibility of the offender
Lapse of time since the offence where this is not the fault of the offender
Mental disorder or learning disability, where not linked to the commission of the offence
Sole or primary carer for dependent relatives

C16.1.1.1 *Additional steps*

Consider any factors which indicate a reduction, such as: assistance to the prosecution; reduction for guilty plea; dangerousness; totality principle; compensation and ancillary orders; reasons; consideration for remand time.

C16.1.2 Key points

- Action or words causing the person to apprehend imminent unlawful force. A conditional threat amounts to an assault, as does a threat to do something in the future (how far into the future is a matter of debate: see *R v Constanza* [1997] 2 Cr App R 492). Words in themselves could suffice, as could a gesture (eg using fingers to imitate a gun being fired, or a slashing action across the throat). An extreme example can be found in *R v Ireland* [1998] AC 147, a case where the appellant made silent phone calls to the victim. Conditional actions—for example, 'get out of my house or I will hurt you'—will amount to an assault. The words may also indicate that no assault is going to happen, as in the famous case of *Tuberville v Savage* (1669) 1 Mod Rep 3 ('if it were not assize time, I would not take such language from you'). Creating a danger can amount to an assault; for example if a prisoner knows that he has a needle secreted on him and dishonestly does not inform a police officer carrying out a search, he may be liable if the officer injures himself on that needle, such a risk being reasonably foreseeable (*Director of Public Prosecutions v Santana-Bermudez* [2003] EWHC 2908 (Admin)).
- A battery involves the use of actual force being applied to the victim.
- Harm, which must be more than merely transient or trifling, encompasses not only injury but also hurt and damage. The concept of bodily harm is wide-ranging, and includes the cutting off of someone's hair (*DPP v Smith* [2006] 2 Cr App R 1). Psychiatric injury, in a medically diagnosed form, can amount to bodily harm, but anything short of this, for example upset or distress, will not.
- Mens rea is intention or recklessness. Note that the mens rea relates to the act of assault or battery; there is no requirement to prove that harm was intended, or that the defendant was reckless as to whether or not harm would be caused.

C16.1.3 *Defences*

The following defences should be considered:

- Consent, although *R v Brown* [1994] 1 AC 212 limits the application of this defence in sado-masochistic situations. It remains available, for instance, in sport or medical treatment, or where a wife agrees to be 'branded' (*R v Wilson* [1996] 2 Cr App R 241).
- Lawful correction or chastisement, but subject to section 58 of the Children Act 2004:

Children Act 2004, s 58(1)–(2)

58 Reasonable punishment

(1) In relation to any offence specified in subsection (2), battery of a child cannot be justified on the ground that it constituted reasonable punishment.

(2) The offences referred to in subsection (1) are—

  (a) an offence under section 18 or 20 of the Offences against the Person Act 1861 (c. 100) (wounding and causing grievous bodily harm);

  (b) an offence under section 47 of that Act (assault occasioning actual bodily harm);

  (c) an offence under section 1 of the Children and Young Persons Act 1933 (c. 12) (cruelty to persons under 16).

- Self-defence. Because there must be an unlawful act, a person acting in self-defence cannot be guilty of an assault; and once the issue has been raised by the defence in evidence, the Crown must prove that the defendant was not acting in self-defence. Householders enjoy a wider definition of self-defence under the amended section 76 of the Criminal Justice and Immigration Act 2008.

The 'householder' version of self-defence (was the act grossly disproportionate) applies to all lawful occupiers of a property and not just to the owner. In *R v Day* [2015] EWCA Crim 1646 a student pushing an unwelcome caller from her room was entitled to take advantage of it.

- Defence of property.
- Prevention of crime.
- Horseplay. Consent to rough and undisciplined play where there is no intention to harm is a defence to a charge of assault including where, consent being absent, there is a genuine (however unreasonable) belief by a defendant that consent was present (*R v Jones and others* (1986) 83 Cr App R 375).

 See *Blackstone's Criminal Practice 2017* **B2.27–B2.36**

C16.2 Assault with intent to resist arrest

Offences Against the Person Act 1861, s 38

38 Assault with intent to resist apprehension, etc

Whosoever shall assault any person with intent to resist or prevent the lawful apprehension or detainer of himself or of any other person for any offence, shall be guilty of an offence.

6 months' imprisonment and/or fine/2 years' imprisonment

C16.2.1 *Sentencing*

STEP ONE: determining the offence category

Category 1	Greater harm and higher culpability
Category 2	Greater harm and lower culpability; or lesser harm and higher culpability
Category 3	Lesser harm and lower culpability

Factors indicating greater harm	Factors indicating higher culpability
Sustained or repeated assault on the same victim	**Statutory aggravating factors:** Offence racially or religiously aggravated Offence motivated by, or demonstrating, hostility to the victim based on his or her sexual orientation (or presumed sexual orientation) Offence motivated by, or demonstrating, hostility to the victim based on the victim's disability (or presumed disability) **Other aggravating factors:** A significant degree of premeditation Use of weapon or weapon equivalent (eg shod foot, head-butting, use of acid, use of animal)
	Intention to commit more serious harm than actually resulted from the offence Deliberately causes more harm than is necessary for commission of offence Leading role in group or gang Offence motivated by, or demonstrating, hostility based on the victim's age, sex, gender identity (or presumed gender identity)
Factors indicating lesser harm	Factors indicating lower culpability
Injury that is less serious in the context of the offence	Subordinate role in group or gang Lack of premeditation Mental disorder or learning disability, where linked to commission of the offence

STEP TWO: starting point and category range

Offence category	Starting point	Category range
Category 1	26 weeks' custody	12 weeks' custody to Crown Court (51 weeks' custody)
Category 2	Medium-level community order	Low-level community order to high-level community order
Category 3	Band B fine	Band A fine to band C fine

Factors increasing seriousness

Statutory aggravating factors
Previous convictions, having regard to (a) the **nature** of the offence to which the conviction relates and its relevance to the current offence; and (b) the **time** that has elapsed since the conviction
Offence committed whilst on bail

Other aggravating factors
Location of the offence
Timing of the offence
Ongoing effect upon the victim
Gratuitous degradation of victim
Failure to comply with current court orders
Offence committed whilst on licence
Attempt to conceal or dispose of evidence
Failure to respond to warnings or concerns expressed by others about the offender's behaviour
Commission of offence whilst under the influence of alcohol or drugs
Established evidence of community impact
Any steps taken to prevent the victim reporting an incident, obtaining assistance, and/or assisting or supporting the prosecution
Offences taken into consideration (TICs)

Factors reducing seriousness or reflecting personal mitigation

No previous convictions or no relevant/recent convictions
Single blow
Remorse
Good character and/or exemplary conduct
Determination and/or demonstration of steps taken to address addiction or offending behaviour
Serious medical conditions requiring urgent, intensive, or long-term treatment
Isolated incident
Age and/or lack of maturity where it affects the responsibility of the defendant
Lapse of time since the offence where this is not the fault of the offender
Mental disorder or learning disability, where not linked to the commission of the offence
Sole or primary carer for dependent relatives

C16.2.1.1 *Additional step*

Consider any factors which indicate a reduction, such as: assistance to the prosecution; reduction for guilty plea; dangerousness;

totality principle; compensation and ancillary orders; reasons; consideration for remand time.

C16.2.2 Key points

- The arrest must be a lawful one, and the defendant's honest but mistaken belief in that regard does not afford a defence (*R v Lee* (2001) 165 JP 344).
- The prosecution do not need to prove that the defendant knew that the person was a police officer (*R v Brightling* [1991] Crim LR 364).

 See *Blackstone's Criminal Practice 2017* **B2.22–B2.26**

C16.3 Assaulting a police constable or resisting or obstructing a police constable

---

Police Act 1996, s 89(1)–(2)

89 Assaults on constables

(1) Any person who assaults a constable in the execution of his duty, or a person assisting a constable in the execution of his duty, shall be guilty of an offence …

(2) Any person who resists or wilfully obstructs a constable in the execution of his duty, or a person assisting a constable in the execution of his duty, shall be guilty of an offence ….

SO

 6 months' imprisonment and/or fine (assaults), and/or 1 month imprisonment/level 3 fine/(resist/obstruct)

C16.3.1 *Sentencing, section 89(1) Assault*

STEP ONE: determining the offence category

Category 1	Greater harm and higher culpability
Category 2	Greater harm and lower culpability; or lesser harm and higher culpability
Category 3	Lesser harm and lower culpability

Factors indicating greater harm	Factors indicating higher culpability
Sustained or repeated assault on the same victim	**Statutory aggravating factors:** Offence racially or religiously aggravated Offence motivated by, or demonstrating, hostility to the victim based on his or her sexual orientation (or presumed sexual orientation) Offence motivated by, or demonstrating, hostility to the victim based on the victim's disability (or presumed disability) **Other aggravating factors:** A significant degree of premeditation Use of weapon or weapon equivalent (eg shod foot, headbutting, use of acid, use of animal) Intention to commit more serious harm than actually resulted from the offence Deliberately causes more harm than is necessary for commission of offence Leading role in group or gang Offence motivated by, or demonstrating, hostility based on the victim's age, sex, gender identity (or presumed gender identity)
Factors indicating lesser harm	**Factors indicating lower culpability**
Injury which is less serious in the context of the offence	Subordinate role in group or gang Lack of premeditation Mental disorder or learning disability, where linked to commission of the offence

STEP TWO: starting point and category range

Offence category	Starting point	Category range
Category 1	12 weeks' custody	Low-level community order to 26 weeks' custody
Category 2	Medium-level community order	Low-level community order to high-level community order
Category 3	Band B fine	Band A fine to band C fine

Factors increasing seriousness	
Statutory aggravating factors Previous convictions, having regard to (a) the nature of the offence to which the conviction relates and its relevance to the current offence; and (b) the time that has elapsed since the conviction Offence committed whilst on bail	*Other aggravating factors* Location of the offence Timing of the offence Ongoing effect upon the victim Gratuitous degradation of victim Failure to comply with current court orders Offence committed whilst on licence Attempt to conceal or dispose of evidence Failure to respond to warnings or concerns expressed by others about the offender's behaviour Commission of offence whilst under the influence of alcohol or drugs Established evidence of community impact Any steps taken to prevent the victim reporting an incident, obtaining assistance, and/or assisting or supporting the prosecution Offences taken into consideration (TICs)
Factors reducing seriousness or reflecting personal mitigation	

No previous convictions or no relevant/recent convictions
Single blow
Remorse
Good character and/or exemplary conduct
Determination and/or demonstration of steps taken to address addiction or offending behaviour
Serious medical conditions requiring urgent, intensive, or long-term treatment
Isolated incident
Age and/or lack of maturity where it affects the responsibility of the offender
Lapse of time since the offence where this is not the fault of the offender
Mental disorder or learning disability, where not linked to the commission of the offence
Sole or primary carer for dependent relatives

C16.3.1.1 *Sentencing (s 89(2)) Wilful Obstruction*

Note that this guideline is under review by the Sentencing Council (see **Appendix 7**).

Offence seriousness (culpability and harm) A. Identify the appropriate starting point Starting points based on first-time offender pleading not guilty.		
Examples of nature of activity	**Starting point**	**Range**
Failure to move when required to do so	Band A fine	Conditional discharge to band B fine
Attempt to prevent arrest or other lawful police action; or giving false details	Band B fine	Band A fine to band C fine
Several people attempting to prevent arrest or other lawful police action	Low-level community order	Band C fine to medium-level community order

Offence seriousness (culpability and harm) B. Consider the effect of aggravating and mitigating factors (other than those within examples above)	
Factors indicating higher culpability	**Factors indicating lower culpability**
1. Premeditated action 2. Aggressive words/threats 3. Aggressive group action	1. Genuine mistake or misjudgement 2. Brief incident

C16.3.1.2 *Additional steps*

Consider any factors which indicate a reduction, such as: assistance to the prosecution; reduction for guilty plea; dangerousness; totality principle; compensation and ancillary orders; reasons; consideration for remand time.

C16.3.2 Key points

- The constable must be acting lawfully (ie in execution of his duty).
- The prosecution do not need to prove that the defendant knew that the person was a police officer (*R v Brightling* [1991] Crim LR 364).
- If officer A is not acting lawfully in arresting a suspect, officer B who in good faith seeks to assist officer A will not be acting lawfully (*Cumberbatch v Crown Prosecution Service* [2009] EWHC 3353 (Admin)).
- If a suspect is accused of trying to impede the arrest of a third party, it must be shown that the arrest of that third party was lawful (*Riley v Director of Public Prosecutions* (1990) 91 Cr App R 14).
- Where the defendant interfered with the lawful detention by a police officer of another, an officer pushing the defendant away cannot
  (i) legitimize an earlier obstruction by the defendant of an officer in execution of his duty; or
  (ii) provide an indemnity against all further actions of the defendant including a continuing obstruction.
  This is a different scenario to that when the only issue is whether the officer was touching the person without any intention to arrest. In any event the officer's push was a lawful act in accordance with section 3 Criminal Law Act 1967 (*Metcalfe v CPS* [2015] EWHC 1091 (Admin)).
- For the lawfulness of a police officer entering premises to save life or limb, see *Baker v Crown Prosecution Service* [2009] EWHC 299 (Admin). An officer may enter premises to prevent a potential breach of the peace (*Laporte v MPC* [2014] EWHC 3574 (QB)).
- For the situation where a police officer has had a licence to remain on property revoked, see *R (Fullard) v Woking Magistrates' Court* [2005] EWHC 2922 (Admin).

- An officer who had not yet established grounds for arrest was acting unlawfully in restraining a suspect (*Wood v Director of Public Prosecutions* [2008] EWHC 1056 (Admin)). It was unlawful to take hold of a woman to question her (*Collins v Wilcock* [1984] 1 WLR 1172), but not every interference with a citizen's liberty will be sufficient to take the officer outside the course of his duty. A police officer may take hold of a person's arm to attract his attention and calm him down (*Mepstead v DPP* (1996) 160 JP 175).
  Whilst a police officer may touch someone to gain their attention, if they are told to desist, a further touching will take the officer outside the execution of their duty (*R (Shah) v Central Criminal Court* [2013] EWHC 1747 (Admin)). A police officer may not detain a person, beyond acceptable conduct by any member of the public, even for one second, without intending to exercise a power of arrest. This included the use of an implied threat of force if the person did not remain (*Walker v Commissioner of the Metropolitan Police* [2014] EWCA Civ 897). However where an officer seeks to have the defendant stop but does not use or threaten violence the action is lawful notwithstanding that he may have had an unlawful intent to detain without an arrest. It is what is said and done and not what is intended that is critical (*Tester v DPP* 2015 EWHC 1353 (Admin)).
- The powers of the police to stop and search, and of entry under the Police and Criminal Evidence Act 1984, are interpreted strictly (see *R v Bristol* [2007] EWCA Crim 3214 and *B v Director of Public Prosecutions* [2008] EWHC 1655 (Admin)).
- A police officer who had a mere belief in the existence of a search warrant was not acting in the execution of their duty. But the existence of a warrant could be inferred by the court from other facts proved such as evidence that it was a planned raid by a specialist unit (*Sykes v CPS* [2013] EWHC 3600 (Admin)).
- An arrest is lawful if the factual grounds are explained. It is not necessary to identify the statute creating the offence (*McCann v CPS* [2015] EWHC 2461 (Admin)).

 See *Blackstone's Criminal Practice 2017* **B2.37–B2.47**

C16.4 Common assault

Criminal Justice Act 1988, s 39

SO (Racially or religiously aggravated: either way)

6 months' imprisonment and/or fine (racially or religiously aggravated: 2 years' imprisonment)

 (Racially or religiously aggravated: common assault)

C16.4.1 *Sentencing*

STEP ONE: determining the offence category

Category 1	Greater harm (injury or fear of injury must normally be present) and higher culpability
Category 2	Greater harm (injury or fear of injury must normally be present) and lower culpability; or lesser harm and higher culpability
Category 3	Lesser harm and lower culpability

Factors indicating greater harm	Factors indicating higher culpability
Injury or fear of injury which is serious in the context of the offence (must normally be present) Victim is particularly vulnerable because of personal circumstances Sustained or repeated assault on the same victim	**Statutory aggravating factors:** Offence motivated by, or demonstrating, hostility to the victim based on his or her sexual orientation (or presumed sexual orientation) Offence motivated by, or demonstrating, hostility to the victim based on the victim's disability (or presumed disability) **Other aggravating factors:** A significant degree of premeditation Threatened or actual use of weapon or weapon equivalent (eg shod foot, head-butting, use of acid, use of animal) Intention to commit more serious harm than actually resulted from the offence Deliberately causes more harm than is necessary for commission of offence Deliberate targeting of vulnerable victim Leading role in group or gang Offence motivated by, or demonstrating, hostility based on the victim's age, sex, gender identity (or presumed gender identity)
Factors indicating lesser harm	Factors indicating lower culpability
Injury which is less serious in the context of the offence	Subordinate role in group or gang A greater degree of provocation than normally expected Lack of premeditation Mental disorder or learning disability, where linked to commission of the offence Excessive self-defence

STEP TWO: starting point and category range

Offence category	Starting point	Category range
Category 1	High-level community order	Low-level community order to 23 weeks' custody
Category 2	Medium-level community order	Band A fine to high-level community order
Category 3	Band A fine	Discharge to band C fine

Factors increasing seriousness	
Statutory aggravating factors	*Other aggravating factors*
Previous convictions, having regard to (a) the **nature** of the offence to which the conviction relates and its relevance to the current offence; and (b) the **time** that has elapsed since the conviction Offence committed whilst on bail	Location of the offence Timing of the offence Ongoing effect upon the victim Offence committed against those working in the public sector or providing a service to the public Presence of others including relatives, especially children or partner of the victim Gratuitous degradation of victim In domestic violence cases, victim forced to leave their home Failure to comply with current court orders Offence committed whilst on licence Attempt to conceal or dispose of evidence Failure to respond to warnings or concerns expressed by others about the offender's behaviour Commission of offence whilst under the influence of alcohol or drugs Abuse of power and/or position of trust. Exploiting contact arrangements with a child to commit an offence Established evidence of community impact. Any steps taken to prevent the victim reporting an incident, obtaining assistance, and/or assisting or supporting the prosecution Offences taken into consideration (TICs)

Factors reducing seriousness or reflecting personal mitigation

No previous convictions or no relevant/recent convictions
Single blow
Remorse
Good character and/or exemplary conduct
Determination and/or demonstration of steps taken to address addiction or offending behaviour
Serious medical conditions requiring urgent, intensive, or long-term treatment
Isolated incident
Age and/or lack of maturity where it affects the responsibility of the offender
Lapse of time since the offence where this is not the fault of the offender
Mental disorder or learning disability, where not linked to the commission of the offence
Sole or primary carer for dependent relative

Racially aggravated offences: the court should determine the appropriate sentence for the offence without taking account of the element of aggravation and then make an addition to the sentence, considering the level of aggravation involved. It may be appropriate to move outside the identified category range, taking into account the increased statutory maximum.

C16.4.1.1 *Additional steps*

Consider any factors which indicate a reduction, such as: assistance to the prosecution; reduction for guilty plea; dangerousness; totality principle; compensation and ancillary orders; reasons; consideration for remand time.

C16.4.2 Key points

- Common assault comprises both assault (where 'assault' means the intentional or reckless causing of another to apprehend immediate unlawful violence) and assault by beating (battery—the intentional or reckless inflicting of unlawful force).

  The element of assault described as 'hostility' conveys that some non-hostile contact is an ordinary incident of life to which there is implied consent. A genuine belief that an assault is necessary to save a life or prevent a third party attack is a defence but a wish to do good is not. Forced feeding is an offence. (*R v B* [2013] EWCA Crim 3).
- Defences (see **C16.1.3**):
  - Consent: evidence of a lack of consent can be inferred from evidence in the case and need not come from the complainant (see *Director of Public Prosecutions v Shabbir* [2009] EWHC 2754 (Admin)).
  - Lawful correction or chastisement: this defence survives the implementation of section 58 of the Children Act 2004.
  - Self-defence.
  - Defence of property.
  - Prevention of crime.

 See *Blackstone's Criminal Practice 2017* **B2.1–B2.21**

C16.5 Child neglect, etc

Children and Young Persons Act 1933, s 1(1)

1 Cruelty to persons under 16

(1) If any person who has attained the age of sixteen years and has responsibility for any child or young person under that age, wilfully assaults, ill-treats, (whether physically or mentally), neglects, abandons, or exposes

> him, or causes or procures him to be assaulted, ill-treated (whether physically or mentally), neglected, abandoned, or exposed, in a manner likely to cause him unnecessary suffering or injury to health (whether the suffering or injury is of a physical or a psychological nature), that person shall be guilty of an offence.

EW

6 months' imprisonment and/or fine/10 years' imprisonment

DO

C16.5.1 *Sentencing*

- The same starting point and sentencing range are proposed for offences that might fall into the four categories (assault, ill-treatment or neglect, abandonment, and failure to protect). These are designed to take into account the fact that the victim is particularly vulnerable, assuming an abuse of trust or power and the likelihood of psychological harm, and are designed to reflect the seriousness with which society as a whole regards these offences.
- As noted above, the starting points have been calculated to reflect the likelihood of psychological harm, and this cannot be treated as an aggravating factor. Where there is an especially serious physical or psychological effect on the victim, even if unintended, this should increase sentence.
- The normal sentencing starting point for an offence of child cruelty should be a custodial sentence. The length of that sentence will be influenced by the circumstances in which the offence took place.
- However, in considering whether a custodial sentence is the most appropriate disposal, the court should take into account any available information concerning the future care of the child.
- Where the offender is the sole or primary carer of the victim or other dependants, this potentially should be taken into account for sentencing purposes, regardless of whether the offender is male or female. In such cases, an immediate custodial sentence may not be appropriate.
- The most relevant areas of personal mitigation are likely to be:
  - mental illness/depression;
  - inability to cope with pressures of parenthood;
  - lack of support;

- sleep deprivation;
- offender dominated by an abusive or a stronger partner;
- extreme behavioural difficulties in the child, often coupled with a lack of support;
- inability to secure assistance or support services in spite of every effort having been made by the offender.
- Some of the factors identified above, in particular sleep deprivation, lack of support, and an inability to cope, could be regarded as an inherent part of caring for children, especially when a child is very young, and could be put forward as mitigation by most carers charged with an offence of child cruelty. It follows that, before being accepted as mitigation, there must be evidence that these factors were present to a high degree, and had an identifiable and significant impact on the offender's behaviour.

Offence seriousness (culpability and harm) A. Identify the appropriate starting point Starting points based on first-time offender pleading not guilty		
Example of nature of activity	**Starting point**	**Range**
(i) Short-term neglect or ill-treatment (ii) Single incident of short-term abandonment (iii) Failure to protect a child from any of the above	12 weeks' custody	Low-level community order to 26 weeks' custody
(i) Assault(s) resulting in injuries consistent with ABH (ii) More than one incident of neglect or ill-treatment (but not amounting to long-term behaviour) (iii) Single incident of long-term abandonment OR regular incidents of short-term abandonment (the longer the period of long-term abandonment or the greater the number of incidents of short-term abandonment, the more serious the offence) (iv) Failure to protect a child from any of the above	Crown Court	26 weeks' custody to Crown Court
(i) Series of assaults (ii) Protracted neglect or ill-treatment (iii) Serious cruelty over a period of time (iv) Failure to protect a child from any of the above	Crown Court	Crown Court

Offence seriousness (culpability and harm)	
B. Consider the effect of aggravating and mitigating factors	
(other than those within examples above)	
The following may be particularly relevant but these lists are not exhaustive	
Factors indicating higher culpability	**Factor indicating lower culpability**
1. Targeting one particular child from the family	1. Seeking medical help or bringing the situation to the notice of the authorities
2. Sadistic behaviour	
3. Threats to prevent the victim from reporting the offence	
4. Deliberate concealment of the victim from the authorities	
5. Failure to seek medical help	

C16.5.2 Key points

- Section 1(2) of the Children and Young Persons Act 1933 provides that:
  - a parent or other person legally liable to maintain a child or young person, or the legal guardian of a child or young person, shall be deemed to have neglected him in a manner likely to cause injury to his health if he has failed to provide adequate food, clothing, medical aid, or lodging for him, or if, having been unable otherwise to provide such food, clothing, medical aid, or lodging, he has failed to take steps to procure it to be provided under the enactments applicable in that behalf;
  - where it is proved that the death of an infant under three years of age was caused by suffocation (not being suffocation caused by disease or the presence of any foreign body in the throat or air passages of the infant) while the infant was in bed, or lying next to an adult in or on any kind of furniture or surface being used by the adult for the purpose of sleeping, with some other person who has attained the age of 16 years, that other person shall, if he was, when he went to bed, under the influence of drink or drugs, be deemed to have neglected the infant in a manner likely to cause injury to its health.
- Section 1(3) provides that a person may be convicted of an offence under this section:
  - notwithstanding that actual suffering or injury to health, or the likelihood of actual suffering or injury to health, was obviated by the action of another person;
  - notwithstanding the death of the child or young person in question.

R v Turbill and Broadway [2012] EWCA Crim 1422 confirms that offences requiring wilful neglect require more than carelessness (even gross carelessness) or negligence. The neglect must be wilful.

The definition in *Shepherd* (1981) AC 394 applies to child neglect and to neglect under the Mental Capacity Act 2005.

 See *Blackstone's Criminal Practice 2017* **B2.137–B2.148**

C16.6 Domestic abuse

Serious Crime Act 2015, s 76

Controlling or coercive behaviour in an intimate or family relationship

(1) A person (A) commits an offence if—
   (a) A repeatedly or continuously engages in behaviour towards another person (B) that is controlling or coercive,
   (b) at the time of the behaviour, A and B are personally connected,
   (c) the behaviour has a serious effect on B, and
   (d) A knows or ought to know that the behaviour will have a serious effect on B.

(2) A and B are 'personally connected' if—
   (a) A is in an intimate personal relationship with B, or
   (b) A and B live together and—
      (i) they are members of the same family, or
      (ii) they have previously been in an intimate personal relationship with each other.

(3) But A does not commit an offence under this section if at the time of the behaviour in question—
   (a) A has responsibility for B, for the purposes of Part 1 of the Children and Young Persons Act 1933 (see section 17 of that Act), and
   (b) B is under 16.

(4) A's behaviour has a 'serious effect' on B if—
   (a) it causes B to fear, on at least two occasions, that violence will be used against B, or
   (b) it causes B serious alarm or distress which has a substantial adverse effect on B's usual day-to-day activities.

(5) For the purposes of subsection (1)(d) A 'ought to know' that which a reasonable person in possession of the same information would know.

(6) For the purposes of subsection (2)(b)(i) A and B are members of the same family if—
   (a) they are, or have been, married to each other;
   (b) they are, or have been, civil partners of each other;
   (c) they are relatives;
   (d) they have agreed to marry one another (whether or not the agreement has been terminated);
   (e) they have entered into a civil partnership agreement (whether or not the agreement has been terminated);
   (f) they are both parents of the same child;
   (g) they have, or have had, parental responsibility for the same child.

(7) In subsection (6)—

'civil partnership agreement' has the meaning given by section 73 of the Civil Partnership Act 2004;

'child' means a person under the age of 18 years;

'parental responsibility' has the same meaning as in the Children Act 1989;

'relative' has the meaning given by section 63(1) of the Family Law Act 1996.

(8) In proceedings for an offence under this section it is a defence for A to show that—

    (a) in engaging in the behaviour in question, A believed that he or she was acting in B's best interests, and

    (b) the behaviour was in all the circumstances reasonable.

(9) A is to be taken to have shown the facts mentioned in subsection (8) if—

    (a) sufficient evidence of the facts is adduced to raise an issue with respect to them, and

    (b) the contrary is not proved beyond reasonable doubt.

(10) The defence in subsection (8) is not available to A in relation to behaviour that causes B to fear that violence will be used against B.

EW

 6 months' imprisonment and/or a fine/5 years' imprisonment

C16.7 Forced labour and human trafficking

The Modern Slavery Act 2015 creates two major offences and a new general defence to all crime.

C16.7.1 *Slavery, etc*

Modern Slavery Act 2015, s 1

1 Slavery, servitude and forced or compulsory labour

(1) A person commits an offence if—.

    (a) the person holds another person in slavery or servitude and the circumstances are such that the person knows or ought to know that the other person is held in slavery or servitude, or.

    (b) the person requires another person to perform forced or compulsory labour and the circumstances are such that the person knows or ought to know that the other person is being required to perform forced or compulsory labour...

(2) In subsection (1) the references to holding a person in slavery or servitude or requiring a person to perform forced or compulsory labour are to be construed in accordance with Article 4 of the Human Rights Convention.

(3) In determining whether a person is being held in slavery or servitude or required to perform forced or compulsory labour, regard may be had to all the circumstances.

(4) For example, regard may be had—

    (a) to any of the person's personal circumstances (such as the person being a child, the person's family relationships, and any mental or physical illness) which may make the person more vulnerable than other persons;.

    (b) to any work or services provided by the person, including work or services provided in circumstances which constitute exploitation within section 3(3) to (6)…

(5) The consent of a person (whether an adult or a child) to any of the acts alleged to constitute holding the person in slavery or servitude, or requiring the person to perform forced or compulsory labour, does not preclude a determination that the person is being held in slavery or servitude, or required to perform forced or compulsory labour.

A16.7.2 *Trafficking*

Modern Slavery Act 2015, ss 2 and 3

2 Human trafficking

(1) A person commits an offence if the person arranges or facilitates the travel of another person ('V') with a view to V being exploited…

(2) It is irrelevant whether V consents to the travel (whether V is an adult or a child)…

(3) A person may in particular arrange or facilitate V's travel by recruiting V, transporting or transferring V, harbouring or receiving V, or transferring or exchanging control over V.

(4) A person arranges or facilitates V's travel with a view to V being exploited only if—

    (a) the person intends to exploit V (in any part of the world) during or after the travel, or

    (b) the person knows or ought to know that another person is likely to exploit V (in any part of the world) during or after the travel.

(5) 'Travel' means—

    (a) arriving in, or entering, any country,

    (b) departing from any country,

    (c) travelling within any country.

(6) A person who is a UK national commits an offence under this section regardless of—
  (a) where the arranging or facilitating takes place, or
  (b) where the travel takes place.

(7) A person who is not a UK national commits an offence under this section if—
  (a) any part of the arranging or facilitating takes place in the United Kingdom, or
  (b) the travel consists of arrival in or entry into, departure from, or travel within, the United Kingdom.

3 Meaning of exploitation

(1) For the purposes of section 2 a person is exploited only if one or more of the following subsections apply in relation to the person.

Slavery, servitude and forced or compulsory labour

(2) The person is the victim of behaviour—.
  (a) which involves the commission of an offence under section 1, or.
  (b) which would involve the commission of an offence under that section if it took place in England and Wales.

Sexual exploitation

(3) Something is done to or in respect of the person—.
  (a) which involves the commission of an offence under—.
    (i) section 1(1)(a) of the Protection of Children Act 1978 (indecent photographs of children), or.
    (ii) Part 1 of the Sexual Offences Act 2003 (sexual offences), as it has effect in England and Wales, or
  (b) which would involve the commission of such an offence if it were done in England and Wales.

Removal of organs, etc

(4) The person is encouraged, required or expected to do anything—.
  (a) which involves the commission, by him or her or another person, of an offence under section 32 or 33 of the Human Tissue Act 2004 (prohibition of commercial dealings in organs and restrictions on use of live donors) as it has effect in England and Wales, or
  (b) which would involve the commission of such an offence, by him or her or another person, if it were done in England and Wales.

Securing services, etc by force, threats or deception

(5) The person is subjected to force, threats or deception designed to induce him or her—
  (a) to provide services of any kind,
  (b) to provide another person with benefits of any kind, or
  (c) to enable another person to acquire benefits of any kind.

Securing services, etc from children and vulnerable persons

(6) Another person uses or attempts to use the person for a purpose within paragraph (a), (b) or (c) of subsection (5), having chosen him or her for that purpose on the grounds that—

(a) he or she is a child, is mentally or physically ill or disabled, or has a family relationship with a particular person, and
(b) an adult, or a person without the illness, disability, or family relationship, would be likely to refuse to be used for that purpose.

C16.7.3

 6 months' imprisonment and/or fine/life

C16.7.4 *General defence*

Modern Slavery Act 2015, s 45

45 Defence for slavery or trafficking victims who commit an offence

(1) A person is not guilty of an offence if—
   (a) the person is aged 18 or over when the person does the act which constitutes the offence,
   (b) the person does that act because the person is compelled to do it,
   (c) the compulsion is attributable to slavery or to relevant exploitation, and
   (d) a reasonable person in the same situation as the person and having the person's relevant characteristics would have no realistic alternative to doing that act.
(2) A person may be compelled to do something by another person or by the person's circumstances.
(3) Compulsion is attributable to slavery or to relevant exploitation only if—
   (a) it is, or is part of, conduct which constitutes an offence under section 1 or conduct which constitutes relevant exploitation, or
   (b) it is a direct consequence of a person being, or having been, a victim of slavery or a victim of relevant exploitation.
(4) A person is not guilty of an offence if—
   (a) the person is under the age of 18 when the person does the act which constitutes the offence,
   (b) the person does that act as a direct consequence of the person being, or having been, a victim of slavery or a victim of relevant exploitation, and
   (c) a reasonable person in the same situation as the person and having the person's relevant characteristics would do that act.
(5) For the purposes of this section—
   'relevant characteristics' means age, sex and any physical or mental illness or disability;
   'relevant exploitation' is exploitation (within the meaning of section 3) that is attributable to the exploited person being, or having been, a victim of human trafficking.
(6) In this section references to an act include an omission.
(7) Subsections (1) and (4) do not apply to an offence listed in Schedule 4 (most sexual and violent offences).

C16.8 Forced marriages

C16.8.1 *Breach of a forced marriage protection order*

Family Law Act 1996, s 63CA

63CA Offence of breaching order

(1) A person who without reasonable excuse does anything that the person is prohibited from doing by a forced marriage protection order is guilty of an offence.

(2) In the case of a forced marriage protection order made by virtue of section 63D(1), a person can be guilty of an offence under this section only in respect of conduct engaged in at a time when the person was aware of the existence of the order.

(3) Where a person is convicted of an offence under this section in respect of any conduct, that conduct is not punishable as a contempt of court.

(4) A person cannot be convicted of an offence under this section in respect of any conduct which has been punished as a contempt of court.

 6 months' imprisonment and/or fine/5 years' imprisonment

C16.8.2 *Offence of forced marriage*

Anti-social Behaviour Crime and Policing Act 2014, s 121

121 (1) A person commits an offence under the law of England and Wales if he or she—
    (a) uses violence, threats or any other form of coercion for the purpose of causing another person to enter into a marriage, and
    (b) believes, or ought reasonably to believe, that the conduct may cause the other person to enter into the marriage without free and full consent.

(2) In relation to a victim who lacks capacity to consent to marriage, the offence under subsection (1) is capable of being committed by any conduct carried out for the purpose of causing the victim to enter into a marriage (whether or not the conduct amounts to violence, threats or any other form of coercion).

(3) A person commits an offence under the law of England and Wales if he or she—
    (a) practises any form of deception with the intention of causing another person to leave the United Kingdom, and
    (b) intends the other person to be subjected to conduct outside the United Kingdom that is an offence under subsection (1) or would be an offence under that subsection if the victim were in England or Wales.

(4) 'Marriage' means any religious or civil ceremony of marriage (whether or not legally binding).

(5) 'Lacks capacity' means lacks capacity within the meaning of the Mental Capacity Act 2005.

(6) It is irrelevant whether the conduct mentioned in paragraph (a) of subsection (1) is directed at the victim of the offence under that subsection or another person.

(7) A person commits an offence under subsection (1) or (3) only if, at the time of the conduct or deception—

(a) the person or the victim or both of them are in England or Wales,

(b) neither the person nor the victim is in England or Wales but at least one of them is habitually resident in England and Wales, or

(c) neither the person nor the victim is in the United Kingdom but at least one of them is a UK national.

(8) 'UK national' means an individual who is—

(a) a British citizen, a British overseas territories citizen, a British National (Overseas) or a British Overseas citizen;

(b) a person who under the British Nationality Act 1981 is a British subject; or

(c) a British protected person within the meaning of that Act.

 6 months' imprisonment and/or fine/7 years' imprisonment

C16.9 Grievous bodily harm/unlawful wounding

Offences Against the Person Act 1861, s 20

20 Inflicting bodily injury, with or without weapon

Whosoever shall unlawfully and maliciously wound or inflict any grievous bodily harm upon any other person, either with or without any weapon or instrument, shall be guilty of an offence.

 6 months' imprisonment and/or fine/5 years' imprisonment (7 years' if racially or religiously aggravated)

C16.9.1 *Sentencing*

STEP ONE: determining the offence category

Category 1	Greater harm (serious injury must normally be present) and higher culpability
Category 2	Greater harm (serious injury must normally be present) and lower culpability; or lesser harm and higher culpability
Category 3	Lesser harm and lower culpability

Factors indicating greater harm	Factors indicating higher culpability
Injury (which includes disease transmission and/or psychological harm) which is serious in the context of the offence (must normally be present) Victim is particularly vulnerable because of personal circumstances Sustained or repeated assault on the same victim	**Statutory aggravating factors:** Offence motivated by, or demonstrating, hostility to the victim based on his or her sexual orientation (or presumed sexual orientation) Offence motivated by, or demonstrating, hostility to the victim based on the victim's disability (or presumed disability) **Other aggravating factors:** A significant degree of premeditation Use of weapon or weapon equivalent (eg shod foot, head-butting, use of acid, use of animal) Intention to commit more serious harm than actually resulted from the offence Deliberately causes more harm than is necessary for commission of offence Deliberate targeting of vulnerable victim Leading role in group or gang Offence motivated by, or demonstrating, hostility based on the victim's age, sex, gender identity (or presumed gender identity
Factors indicating lesser harm	
Injury which is less serious in the context of the offence	

STEP TWO: starting point and category range

Offence category	Starting point	Category range
Category 1	Crown Court	Crown Court
Category 2	Crown Court	Crown Court
Category 3	High-level community order	Low-level community order to Crown Court (51 weeks' custody)

Factors increasing seriousness	
Statutory aggravating factors	*Other aggravating factors*
Previous convictions, having regard to (a) the **nature** of the offence to which the conviction relates and its relevance to the current offence; and (b) the **time** that has elapsed since the conviction Offence committed whilst on bail	Location of the offence Timing of the offence Ongoing effect upon the victim Offence committed against those working in the public sector or providing a service to the public Presence of others including relatives, especially children or partner of the victim Gratuitous degradation of victim In domestic violence cases, victim forced to leave their home Failure to comply with current court orders Offence committed whilst on licence. Attempt to conceal or dispose of evidence Failure to respond to warnings or concerns expressed by others about the offender's behaviour Commission of offence whilst under the influence of alcohol or drugs Abuse of power and/or position of trust Exploiting contact arrangements with a child to commit an offence Established evidence of community impact Any steps taken to prevent the victim reporting an incident, obtaining assistance, and/or assisting or supporting the prosecution Offences taken into consideration (TICs)

Factors reducing seriousness or reflecting personal mitigation
No previous convictions or no relevant/recent convictions Single blow Remorse Good character and/or exemplary conduct Determination and/or demonstration of steps taken to address addiction or offending behaviour Serious medical conditions requiring urgent, intensive, or long-term treatment Isolated incident Age and/or lack of maturity where it affects the responsibility of the offender Lapse of time since the offence where this is not the fault of the offender Mental disorder or learning disability, where not linked to the commission of the offence Sole or primary carer for dependent relatives

C16.9.1.1 *Additional steps*

Consider any factors which indicate a reduction, such as: assistance to the prosecution; reduction for guilty plea; dangerousness;

totality principle; compensation and ancillary orders; reasons; consideration for remand time.

C16.9.2 Key points

Wounding requires the breaking of the continuity of the whole of the skin. Although this may include relatively minor injuries, charging standards indicate that this offence should not be used in such cases. Harm can be inflicted without the need for an assault (*R v Ireland* [1998] AC 147). To be malicious there must be intention or subjective recklessness, but the harm foreseen need not be serious. This is a crime of basic intent.

C16.9.3 *Defences*

For defences see **C16.1.3**.

 See *Blackstone's Criminal Practice 2017* **B2.48–B2.63**

C16.10 Harassment—putting people in fear of violence

Protection from Harassment Act 1997, s 4

4 Putting people in fear of violence

(1) A person whose course of conduct causes another to fear, on at least two occasions, that violence will be used against him is guilty of an offence if he knows or ought to know that his course of conduct will cause the other so to fear on each of those occasions…

(2) For the purposes of this section, the person whose course of conduct is in question ought to know that it will cause another to fear that violence will be used against him on any occasion if a reasonable person in possession of the same information would think the course of conduct would cause the other so to fear on that occasion.

(3) It is a defence for a person charged with an offence under this section to show that—

   (a) his course of conduct was pursued for the purpose of preventing or detecting crime,

   (b) his course of conduct was pursued under any enactment or rule of law or to comply with any condition or requirement imposed by any person under any enactment, or

   (c) the pursuit of his course of conduct was reasonable for the protection of himself or another or for the protection of his or another's property.

---

6 months' imprisonment and/or fine/5 years' imprisonment
(7 years' if racially or religiously aggravated)

C16.10.1 *Sentencing*

Offence seriousness (culpability and harm) A. Identify the appropriate starting point Starting points based on first-time offender pleading not guilty		
Examples of nature of activity	**Starting point**	**Range**
A pattern of two or more incidents of unwanted contact	6 weeks' custody	High-level community order to 18 weeks' custody
Deliberate threats, persistent action over a longer period; or intention to cause fear of violence	18 weeks' custody	12 weeks' custody to Crown Court
Sexual threats, vulnerable person targeted	Crown Court	Crown Court

Offence seriousness (culpability and harm) B. Consider the effect of aggravating and mitigating factors (other than those within examples above) The following may be particularly relevant but these lists are not exhaustive	
Factors indicating higher culpability 1. Planning 2. Offender ignores obvious distress 3. Visits in person to victim's home or workplace 4. Offender involves others 5. Using contact arrangements with a child to instigate offence **Factors indicating greater degree of harm** 1. Victim needs medical help/counselling 2. Physical violence used 3. Victim aware that offender has history of using violence 4. Grossly violent or offensive material sent 5. Children frightened 6. Evidence that victim changed lifestyle to avoid contact	**Factors indicating lower culpability** 1. Limited understanding of effect on victim 2. Initial provocation

C16.10.2 Key points

- The question of what constitutes a course of conduct has been considered in a number of cases, and the answer will always be fact-sensitive. In *R v Curtis* [2010] EWCA Crim 123, the court allowed a defence appeal where the defendant, in the context of there being a volatile relationship, had been responsible for six incidents over a period of nine months. The court held that the conduct must be unacceptable to a degree which would sustain criminal liability and also must be oppressive, and went on to say:

Courts are well able to separate the wheat from the chaff at an early stage of the proceedings. They should be astute to do so. In most cases courts should have little difficulty in applying the 'close connection' test. Where the claim meets that requirement, and the quality of the conduct said to constitute harassment is being examined, courts will have in mind that irritations, annoyances, even a measure of upset, arise at times in everybody's day-to-day dealings with other people. Courts are well able to recognise the boundary between conduct which is unattractive, even unreasonable, and conduct which is oppressive and unacceptable. To cross the boundary from the regrettable to the unacceptable the gravity of the misconduct must be of an order which would sustained *[sic]* criminal liability under section 2.

- References to harassing a person include alarming the person or causing the person distress (s 7). The person whose course of conduct is in question ought to know that it will cause another to fear that violence will be used against him on any occasion, if a reasonable person in possession of the same information would think the course of conduct would cause the other so to fear on that occasion.
- *R v O'Neill* [2016] EWCA Crim 92 confirmed that the definition in section 7 is inclusive and not exhaustive. 'Harassment' is generally understood to involve improper, oppressive, and unreasonable conduct that is targeted at an individual and calculated to produce the consequences described in section 7. Harassment cannot simply be equated with 'causing alarm or distress'. The danger of doing this is that not all conduct, even if unattractive, unreasonable, and causing alarm or distress, will be of an order justifying the sanction of the criminal law. By section 1(3) of the Act '… reasonable and/or lawful courses of conduct may be excluded'. But the Crown does not need to prove that a defendant's conduct is unreasonable.
- In *R v Haque* [2011] EWCA Crim 1871, the following requirements were identified for there to be proof of harassment:
  - the conduct must be targeted at an individual;
  - conduct must be calculated to produce the consequences in section 7 (alarm or distress);

- conduct must have been oppressive and unreasonable;
- provocation may possibly be relevant to causation and reasonableness;
- there must also be proof that the defendant knew or ought to have known that conduct would cause the complainant to fear violence.

- In *R v Widdows* [2011] EWCA Crim 1500, the court held that, in bringing a charge under section 4, the prosecutor (and the judge when summing up) should have in mind the concept of harassment which is at the core of the 1997 Act—though the word is not used in section 4—and the explanation of 'harassment' in *Majrowski v Guy's and St Thomas' NHS Trust* [2007] 1 AC 224 ('stalkers, racial abusers, disruptive neighbours, bullying at work and so forth') and in *Thomas v News Group Newspapers Ltd* [2001] EWCA Civ 1233 (where the practice of stalking was said to be a prime example). The section is not normally appropriate for use as a means of criminalizing conduct, not charged as violence, during incidents in a long and predominantly affectionate relationship in which both parties persisted and wanted to continue.

- It is a defence for a person charged with an offence under section 4 to show that:
  - his course of conduct was pursued for the purpose of preventing or detecting crime. There is a test of rationality to this defence which applies a minimum objective standard to the relevant person's mental processes. It imposes a requirement for good faith and an absence of arbitrariness. Detection or prevention need not be the sole purpose but it must be a dominant purpose of the defendant (*Hayes v Willoughby* [2012] UKSC 17);
  - his course of conduct was pursued under any enactment or rule of law, or to comply with any condition or requirement imposed by any person under any enactment; or
  - the pursuit of his course of conduct was reasonable for the protection of himself or another, or for the protection of his or another's property.

- The naming of two complainants in one charge is not duplicitous, but at least one of the complainants must have feared violence on at least two occasions (*Caurti v Director of Public Prosecutions* [2002] EWHC 867 (Admin)).

  See *Blackstone's Criminal Practice 2017* **B2.189–B2.196**

C16.11 Harassment (without violence)

Protection from Harassment Act 1997, ss 1 and 2(1)

1 Prohibition of harassment

(1) A person must not pursue a course of conduct—
   (a) which amounts to harassment of another, and
   (b) which he knows or ought to know amounts to harassment of the other.
(2) For the purposes of this section, the person whose course of conduct is in question ought to know that it amounts to harassment of another if a reasonable person in possession of the same information would think the course of conduct amounted to harassment of the other.
(3) Subsection (1) does not apply to a course of conduct if the person who pursued it shows—
   (a) that it was pursued for the purpose of preventing or detecting crime,
   (b) that it was pursued under any enactment or rule of law or to comply with any condition or requirement imposed by any person under any enactment, or
   (c) that in the particular circumstances the pursuit of the course of conduct was reasonable.

2 Offence of harassment

(1) A person who pursues a course of conduct in breach of section 1 is guilty of an offence.

SO (Either way if racially or religiously aggravated)

‖‖‖ 6 months' imprisonment and/or fine (2 years' if racially or religiously aggravated)

C16.11.1 *Sentencing*

Offence seriousness (culpability and harm) A. Identify the appropriate starting point Starting points based on first-time offender pleading not guilty		
Examples of nature of activity	**Starting point**	**Range**
Small number of incidents	Medium-level community order	Band C fine to high-level community order
Constant contact at night, trying to come into workplace or home, involving others	6 weeks' custody	Medium-level community order to 12 weeks' custody
Threatening violence, taking personal photographs, sending offensive material	18 weeks' custody	12 to 26 weeks' custody

Offence seriousness (culpability and harm)
B. Consider the effect of aggravating and mitigating factors
(other than those within examples above)
The following may be particularly relevant but these lists are not exhaustive

Factors indicating higher culpability	Factors indicating lower culpability
1. Planning	1. Limited understanding of effect on victim
2. Offender ignores obvious distress	2. Initial provocation
3. Offender involves others	
4. Using contact arrangements with a child to instigate offence	
Factors indicating greater degree of harm	
1. Victim needs medical help/counselling	
2. Action over long period	
3. Children frightened	
4. Use or distribution of photographs	

C16.11.2 Key points

- See key points at **C16.10.2**.
- The naming of two complainants in one charge is not duplicitous, but unlike the charge under section 4, there need only be conduct against at least two people on at least one occasion each (*Director of Public Prosecutions v Dunn* (2008) 165 JP 130).

 See *Blackstone's Criminal Practice 2017* **B2.173–B2.185**

C16.12 Ill-treatment or wilful neglect: care workers

Criminal Justice and Courts Act 2015, s 20

Ill-treatment or wilful neglect: care worker offence

(1) It is an offence for an individual who has the care of another individual by virtue of being a care worker to ill-treat or wilfully to neglect that individual.

...

(3) 'Care worker' means an individual who, as paid work, provides—
   (a) health care for an adult or child, other than excluded health care, or
   (b) social care for an adult,
   including an individual who, as paid work, supervises or manages individuals providing such care or is a director or similar officer of an organisation which provides such care.

(4) An individual does something as 'paid work' if he or she receives or is entitled to payment for doing it other than—
  (a) payment in respect of the individual's reasonable expenses,
  (b) payment to which the individual is entitled as a foster parent,
  (c) a benefit under social security legislation, or
  (d) a payment made under arrangements under section 2 of the Employment and Training Act 1973 (arrangements to assist people to select, train for, obtain and retain employment).
(5) 'Health care' includes—
  (a) all forms of health care provided for individuals, including health care relating to physical health or mental health and health care provided for or in connection with the protection or improvement of public health, and
  (b) procedures that are similar to forms of medical or surgical care but are not provided in connection with a medical condition,
  and 'excluded health care' has the meaning given in Schedule 4.
(6) 'Social care' includes all forms of personal care and other practical assistance provided for individuals who are in need of such care or assistance by reason of age, illness, disability, pregnancy, childbirth, dependence on alcohol or drugs or any other similar circumstances.
(7) References in this section to a person providing health care or social care do not include a person whose provision of such care is merely incidental to the carrying out of other activities by the person.
(8) In this section—
  'adult' means an individual aged 18 or over;
  'child' means an individual aged under 18;
  'foster parent' means—
    (a) a local authority foster parent within the meaning of the Children Act 1989,
    (b) a person with whom a child has been placed by a voluntary organisation under section 59(1)(a) of that Act, or
    (c) a private foster parent within the meaning of section 53 of the Safeguarding Vulnerable Groups Act 2006.

 6 months' imprisonment and/or a fine/5 years' imprisonment.

C16.13 Stalking

The offences of stalking mirror the approach of the basic and aggravated forms of the harassment offences set out at **C16.10** and **C16.11**.

The defences in section 1(3) of the Protection from Harassment Act 1997 are available (see **C16.11**).

C16.13.1 *The basic offence*

Protection from Harassment Act 1997, s 2A

2A Offence of stalking

(1) A person is guilty of an offence if—
   (a) the person pursues a course of conduct in breach of section 1(1), and
   (b) the course of conduct amounts to stalking.

(2) For the purposes of subsection (1)(b) (and section 4A(1)(a)) a person's course of conduct amounts to stalking of another person if—
   (a) it amounts to harassment of that person,
   (b) the acts or omissions involved are ones associated with stalking, and
   (c) the person whose course of conduct it is knows or ought to know that the course of conduct amounts to harassment of the other person.

(3) The following are examples of acts or omissions which, in particular circumstances, are ones associated with stalking—
   (a) following a person,
   (b) contacting, or attempting to contact, a person by any means,
   (c) publishing any statement or other material—
      (i) relating or purporting to relate to a person, or
      (ii) purporting to originate from a person,
   (d) monitoring the use by a person of the internet, email or any other form of electronic communication,
   (e) loitering in any place (whether public or private),
   (f) interfering with any property in the possession of a person,
   (g) watching or spying on a person.
   …
(6) This section is without prejudice to the generality of section 2.

SO (Either way if racially or religiously aggravated)

6 months' imprisonment and/or fine (2 years' if racially or religiously aggravated)

It is suggested that, until a specific guideline is published, regard should be had to the guideline at **C16.11.1**, as both offences carry the same maximum penalty.

C16.13.2 *Aggravated stalking*

Protection from Harassment Act 1997, s 4A

4A Stalking involving fear of violence or serious alarm or distress

(1) A person ('A') whose course of conduct—
  (a) amounts to stalking, and
  (b) either—
    (i) causes another ('B') to fear, on at least two occasions, that violence will be used against B, or
    (ii) causes B serious alarm or distress which has a substantial adverse effect on B's usual day-to-day activities,
  is guilty of an offence if A knows or ought to know that A's course of conduct will cause B so to fear on each of those occasions or (as the case may be) will cause such alarm or distress.

(2) For the purposes of this section A ought to know that A's course of conduct will cause B to fear that violence will be used against B on any occasion if a reasonable person in possession of the same information would think the course of conduct would cause B so to fear on that occasion.

(3) For the purposes of this section A ought to know that A's course of conduct will cause B serious alarm or distress which has a substantial adverse effect on B's usual day-to-day activities if a reasonable person in possession of the same information would think the course of conduct would cause B such alarm or distress.

(4) It is a defence for A to show that—
  (a) A's course of conduct was pursued for the purpose of preventing or detecting crime,
  (b) A's course of conduct was pursued under any enactment or rule of law or to comply with any condition or requirement imposed by any person under any enactment, or
  (c) the pursuit of A's course of conduct was reasonable for the protection of A or another or for the protection of A's or another's property.

...

(9) This section is without prejudice to the generality of section 4.

EW

 6 months' imprisonment and/or fine/5 years' imprisonment (7 years' if racially or religiously aggravated)

It is suggested that, until a specific guideline is published, regard should be had to the guideline at **C16.10.1**, as both offences carry the same maximum penalty.

C16.14 Threats to kill

Offences Against the Person Act 1861, s 16

16 Threats to kill
A person who without lawful excuse makes to another a threat, intending that that other would fear it would be carried out, to kill that other or a third person shall be guilty of an offence.

 6 months' imprisonment and/or fine/10 years' imprisonment

C16.14.1 *Sentencing*

Offence seriousness (culpability and harm) A. Identify the appropriate starting point Starting points based on first-time offender pleading not guilty		
Examples of nature of activity	**Starting point**	**Range**
One threat uttered in the heat of the moment, no more than fleeting impact on victim	Medium-level community order	Low-level community order to high-level community order
Single, calculated threat or victim fears that threat will be carried out	12 weeks' custody	6 to 26 weeks' custody
Repeated threats or visible weapon	Crown Court	Crown Court

Offence seriousness (culpability and harm) B. Consider the effect of aggravating and mitigating factors (other than those within examples above) The following may be particularly relevant but these lists are not exhaustive	
Factors indicating higher culpability 1. Planning 2. Offender deliberately isolates victim 3. Group action 4. Threat directed at victim because of job 5. History of antagonism towards victim **Factors indicating greater degree of harm** 1. Vulnerable victim 2. Victim needs medical help/counselling	**Factor indicating lower culpability** 1. Provocation

 See *Blackstone's Criminal Practice 2017* **B1.140–B1.144**

C16.15 **Witness intimidation**

Criminal Justice and Public Order Act 1994, s 51(1)–(5)

51 Intimidation, etc of witnesses, jurors and others

(1) A person commits an offence if—
  (a) he does an act which intimidates, and is intended to intimidate, another person ('the victim'),
  (b) he does the act knowing or believing that the victim is assisting in the investigation of an offence or is a witness or potential witness or a juror or potential juror in proceedings for an offence, and
  (c) he does it intending thereby to cause the investigation or the course of justice to be obstructed, perverted or interfered with.

(2) A person commits an offence if—
  (a) he does an act which harms, and is intended to harm, another person or, intending to cause another person to fear harm, he threatens to do an act which would harm that other person,
  (b) he does or threatens to do the act knowing or believing that the person harmed or threatened to be harmed ('the victim'), or some other person, has assisted in an investigation into an offence or has given evidence or particular evidence in proceedings for an offence, or has acted as a juror or concurred in a particular verdict in proceedings for an offence, and
  (c) he does or threatens to do it because of that knowledge or belief.

(3) For the purposes of subsections (1) and (2) it is immaterial that the act is or would be done, or that the threat is made—
  (a) otherwise than in the presence of the victim, or
  (b) to a person other than the victim.

(4) The harm that may be done or threatened may be financial as well as physical (whether to the person or a person's property) and similarly as respects an intimidatory act which consists of threats.

(5) The intention required by subsection (1)(c) and the motive required by subsection (2)(c) above need not be the only or the predominating intention or motive with which the act is done or, in the case of subsection (2), threatened.

EW

 6 months and/or fine/5 years

C16.15.1 *Sentencing*

Offence seriousness (culpability and harm) A. Identify the appropriate starting point Starting points based on first-time offender pleading not guilty		
Examples of nature of activity	**Starting point**	**Range**
Sudden outburst in chance encounter	6 weeks' custody	Medium-level community order to 18 weeks' custody
Conduct amounting to a threat; staring at, approaching, or following witnesses; talking about the case; trying to alter or stop evidence	18 weeks' custody	12 weeks' custody to Crown Court
Threats of violence to witnesses and/ or their families; deliberately seeking out witnesses	Crown Court	Crown Court

Offence seriousness (culpability and harm) B. Consider the effect of aggravating and mitigating factors (other than those within examples above) The following may be particularly relevant but these lists are not exhaustive
Factors indicating higher culpability 1. Breach of bail conditions 2. Offender involves others **Factors indicating greater degree of harm** 1. Detrimental impact on administration of justice 2. Contact made at or in vicinity of victim's home

C16.15.2 Key points

For there to be an offence under section 51(1) of the Criminal Justice and Public Order Act 1994 the witness, etc must be proved to have been intimidated. Intent alone is not enough. It might, however, be possible to establish an attempt (*R v ZN* [2013] EWCA Crim 989).

 See *Blackstone's Criminal Practice 2017* **B14.46**

Part D
Sentencing

D1 **Age of Offender**

D1.1 General principles

The age of the offender is important in relation to the court's power to impose different types of sentence. If age is in doubt, the court should consider all available evidence and make a determination before proceeding to sentence.

Generally speaking, the relevant age is the age of the offender on the date of conviction, not the date of offence. As a matter of public policy, however, the courts have been willing to sentence in relation to offence date, as opposed to conviction date. In *R v Ghafoor* [2002] EWCA Crim 1857, the court said:

> The approach to be adopted where a defendant crosses a relevant age threshold between the date of the commission of the offence and date of conviction should now be clear. The starting point is the sentence that the defendant would have been likely to receive if he had been sentenced at the date of the commission of the offence. It has been described as a 'powerful factor'. That is for the obvious reason that as Mr Emmerson points out, the philosophy of restricting sentencing powers in relation to young persons reflects both (a) society's acceptance that young offenders are less responsible for their actions and therefore less culpable than adults, and (b) the recognition that, in consequence, sentencing them should place greater emphasis on rehabilitation and less on retribution and deterrence than in the case of adults. It should be noted that the 'starting point' is not the maximum sentence that could lawfully have been imposed, but the sentence that the offender would have been likely to receive.

However, in *R v Bowker* [2007] EWCA Crim 1608, the court said that *Ghafoor* was a powerful starting point but other factors (such as the need for deterrent sentencing) may justify departing from it.

 See *Blackstone's Criminal Practice 2017* **E7.3**

D1.2 Exceptions to general rule

Where a court activates a conditional discharge, the relevant age for the purpose of resentencing is determined by the date on which the offender appears for resentence (s 136, Powers of Criminal Courts (Sentencing) Act 2000).

D2 **Alteration of Sentence**

D2.1 **Section 142 of the Magistrates' Courts Act 1980**

Section 142 of the Magistrates' Courts Act 1980 gives the court power to reopen sentence. There are no time restrictions, but a court must have regard to the principle of finality of sentence, meaning that in many cases it will not be proper to interfere (*R (Trigger) v Northampton Magistrates' Court* [2011] EWHC 149 (Admin)). For case law see **A6.2**. Section 142(1) provides:

> ### Magistrates' Courts Act 1980, s 142(1)
>
> #### 142 Power of magistrates' court to re-open cases to rectify mistakes etc
>
> (1) A magistrates' court may vary or rescind a sentence or other order imposed or made by it when dealing with an offender if it appears to the court to be in the interests of justice to do so, and it is hereby declared that this power extends to replacing a sentence or order which for any reason appears to be invalid by another which the court has power to impose or make.

 See *Blackstone's Criminal Practice 2017* **D23.23–D23.28**

D3 **Banning Orders (Football)**

Banning orders are imposed under section 14A of the Football Spectators Act 1989.

D3.1 **Criteria and effect**

Banning orders must be imposed when an offender is convicted of a relevant offence, and if the court is satisfied that there are reasonable grounds to believe that making a banning order would help to prevent violence or disorder at or in connection with any regulated football matches.

The core requirements of such an order are to prohibit the offender from attending regulated football matches in England and Wales. When matches are being played abroad, the order will require the offender to report to a police station and surrender his passport (unless there are exceptional circumstances certified by the court as to why this should not be done). Other requirements can be imposed, for example not to go within a certain distance of a football ground.

The order must be for a period of between three and five years, or six and 10 years if a custodial sentence (including a sentence of detention) is imposed for the original offence. A banning order cannot be limited to matches between particular teams (*Commissioner of Police of the Metropolis v Thorpe* [2015] EWHC 3339 (Admin)).

In *Newman v Commissioner of Police of the Metropolis* [2009] EWHC 1642 (Admin), the court held that the police were entitled to rely upon compilation witness statements and compilation video footage, and had no duty to disclose the underlying material from which they were drawn. There is no statutory disclosure regime applicable to the making of banning orders and a court should apply normal principles of 'fairness'. Advocates seeking disclosure should be careful to specify the material that they wish to view and the reasons why. An application that amounts to nothing more than a 'fishing expedition' ought to be refused.

D3.2 **Relevant offences**

Relevant offences are listed in Schedule 1 to the 1989 Act. For some offences, the court will need to make a declaration of relevance (see **D3.3**).

Football Spectators Act 1989, Sch 1

1. This Schedule applies to the following offences:
    (a) any offence under section 14J(1) or 21C(2) of this Act,
    (b) any offence under section 2 or 2A of the Sporting Events (Control of Alcohol etc) Act 1985 (alcohol, containers, and fireworks) committed by the accused at any football match to which this Schedule applies or while entering or trying to enter the ground,
    (c) any offence under section 4A or 5 of the Public Order Act 1986 (harassment, alarm, or distress) or any provision of Part III of that Act (racial hatred) committed during a period relevant to a football match to which this Schedule applies at any premises while the accused was at, or was entering or leaving or trying to enter or leave, the premises,
    (d) any offence involving the use or threat of violence by the accused towards another person committed during a period relevant to a football match to which this Schedule applies at any premises while the accused was at, or was entering or leaving or trying to enter or leave, the premises,
    (e) any offence involving the use or threat of violence towards property committed during a period relevant to a football match to which this Schedule applies at any premises while the accused was at, or was entering or leaving or trying to enter or leave, the premises,
    (f) any offence involving the use, carrying or possession of an offensive weapon or a firearm committed during a period relevant to a football match to which this Schedule applies at any premises while the accused was at, or was entering or leaving or trying to enter or leave, the premises,
    (g) any offence under section 12 of the Licensing Act 1872 (persons found drunk in public places, etc) of being found drunk in a highway or other public place committed while the accused was on a journey to or from a football match to which this Schedule applies being an offence as respects which the court makes a declaration that the offence related to football matches,
    (h) any offence under section 91(1) of the Criminal Justice Act 1967 (disorderly behaviour while drunk in a public place) committed in a highway or other public place while the accused was on a journey to or from a football match to which this Schedule applies being an offence as respects which the court makes a declaration that the offence related to football matches, ...
    (j) any offence under section 1 of the Sporting Events (Control of Alcohol etc) Act 1985 (alcohol on coaches or trains to or from sporting events) committed while the accused was on a journey to or from a football match to which this Schedule applies being an offence as respects which the court makes a declaration that the offence related to football matches,
    (k) any offence under section 4A or 5 of the Public Order Act 1986 (harassment, alarm, or distress) or any provision of Part III of that Act (racial hatred) committed while the accused was on a journey

to or from a football match to which this Schedule applies being an offence as respects which the court makes a declaration that the offence related to football matches,

(l) any offence under section 4 or 5 of the Road Traffic Act 1988 (driving etc when under the influence of drink or drugs or with an alcohol concentration above the prescribed limit) committed while the accused was on a journey to or from a football match to which this Schedule applies being an offence as respects which the court makes a declaration that the offence related to football matches,

(m) any offence involving the use or threat of violence by the accused towards another person committed while one or each of them was on a journey to or from a football match to which this Schedule applies being an offence as respects which the court makes a declaration that the offence related to football matches,

(n) any offence involving the use or threat of violence towards property committed while the accused was on a journey to or from a football match to which this Schedule applies being an offence as respects which the court makes a declaration that the offence related to football matches,

(o) any offence involving the use, carrying or possession of an offensive weapon or a firearm committed while the accused was on a journey to or from a football match to which this Schedule applies being an offence as respects which the court makes a declaration that the offence related to football matches,

(p) any offence under the Football (Offences) Act 1991,

(q) any offence under section 4A or 5 of the Public Order Act 1986 (harassment, alarm, or distress) or any provision of Part 3 or 3A of that Act (hatred by reference to race etc)—
   (i) which does not fall within paragraph (c) or (k) above,
   (ii) which was committed during a period relevant to a football match to which this Schedule applies, and
   (iii) as respects which the court makes a declaration that the offence related to that match or to that match and any other football match which took place during that period,

(r) any offence involving the use or threat of violence by the accused towards another person—
   (i) which does not fall within paragraph (d) or (m) above,
   (ii) which was committed during a period relevant to a football match to which this Schedule applies, and
   (iii) as respects which the court makes a declaration that the offence related to that match or to that match and any other football match which took place during that period,

(s) any offence involving the use or threat of violence towards property—
   (i) which does not fall within paragraph (e) or (n) above,
   (ii) which was committed during a period relevant to a football match to which this Schedule applies, and
   (iii) as respects which the court makes a declaration that the offence related to that match or to that match and any other football match which took place during that period,

(t) any offence involving the use, carrying or possession of an offensive weapon or a firearm—
   (i) which does not fall within paragraph (f) or (o) above,
   (ii) which was committed during a period relevant to a football match to which this Schedule applies, and
   (iii) as respects which the court makes a declaration that the offence related to that match or to that match and any other football match which took place during that period.
(u) any offence under section 166 of the Criminal Justice and Public Order Act 1994 (sale of tickets by unauthorised persons) which relates to tickets for a football match.

D3.3 Declaration of relevance

The prosecution must give five days' notice that they intend to invite a court to make a declaration of relevance. That notice period may be waived by the defence; it can also be dispensed with by the court if the interests of justice do not require a longer notice period to be given. Note that the court can grant an adjournment to facilitate the five-day notice period.

The declaration is that the offence related to that match, or to that match and any other football match which took place during that period.

Each of the following periods is 'relevant to' a football match to which Schedule 1 applies:

- in the case of a match which takes place on the day on which it is advertised to take place, the period:
  - beginning 24 hours before whichever is the earlier of the start of the match and the time at which it was advertised to start, and
  - ending 24 hours after it ends;
- in the case of a match which does not take place on the day on which it was advertised to take place, the period:
  - beginning 24 hours before the time at which it was advertised to start on that day, and
  - ending 24 hours after that time.

In *R v Arbery* [2008] EWCA Crim 702, the offenders were drinking in a public house following a football match, waiting for their train home, when violence broke out with rival supporters. A football banning order was quashed on appeal, as the court held that the offence arose out of a disagreement in the pub, completely unrelated to football.

In *R v Eliot* [2007] EWCA Crim 1002, the court gave a helpful insight into how the issue of 'relevance' might be approached:

> Did the offences committed in the present case relate to the match? Clearly, the presence of the applicants in London and indeed at Leicester Square related to the match. But it is not their presence, nor their allegiance, which is the touchstone of the declaration; it is the relationship between the offence and the match. Here, the offences were sparked by the presence of a group of football supporters in London. The spark, however, had nothing to do with the match itself on the facts as found by the judge. The violence took place, not because of anything that had happened at the football match, or between supporters but because of disparaging remarks made to a lady who had nothing to do with the football match and remarks which had nothing to do with the football match. In those circumstances, we do not consider that, in this case, the statutory requirement was satisfied.

In *Director of Public Prosecutions v Beaumont* [2008] EWHC 523 (Admin), the court rejected an argument that there was a temporal limit to the making of a banning order. In that case the violence erupted more than one hour after the end of the match.

A travel restriction, imposed as part of a banning order, does not infringe EU law, or the European Convention on Human Rights (*Gough v Chief Constable of Derbyshire* [2002] EWCA Civ 351).

Reviewing the law in *R v Doyle* [2012] EWCA Crim 1869, the court said that two requirements must be met in order to require the mandatory imposition of an order:

- Conviction of a relevant offence (Sch 1—see **D3.2**). These offences must 'relate' to football matches, which is an issue of fact—one match will suffice. Merely being on a journey to a match is not enough. Groups of fans will more easily meet the test. It is not enough that the violence would not have occurred 'but for' the journey to the football match.
- There are reasonable grounds to believe that the making of an order would help to prevent violence or disorder at or in connection with a regulated football match. One match can raise an inquiry, but there must be a risk of repetition.
- In *R v Irving* [2013] EWCA Crim 1932, the court confirmed:
  - Where the particular offence in Schedule 1 Football Spectators Act 1989 requires a declaration that the offence related to a particular football match, the failure to make such a declaration meant that no order could be made.
  - An offence could relate to a football match even though the defendant supported neither team and did not go to the game, as where there is an ambush of supporters.

D3 Banning Orders (Football)

- The court must also find that there are reasonable grounds for believing that such an order would help to prevent violence or disorder. This required specific reasoning.
- Requirements attached to the order must be considered individually and be proportionate.

D3.4 Appeals

An appeal lies to the Crown Court in respect to the making of a banning order or dismissal of prosecution application (Football Spectators Act 1989, s 14D).

 See *Blackstone's Criminal Practice 2017* **E21.3–E21.7**

D4 **Bind Over**

D4.1 Criteria

Any person before the court, as defendant or witness (provided that he has given evidence), may be bound over.

A bind over can be made only by consent, and the court should, as a matter of good practice, hear representations (but see *R v Woking Justices, ex p Gossage* [1973] QB 448, where the court held that there was no duty to hear representations if the court was binding over a person in his own recognizance for a 'just and suitable' sum); refusal can result in committal to prison. The order is to keep the peace and be of good behaviour; further conditions are not permitted.

The court will set a recognizance to be forfeit on breach. If the sum set is more than trivial, inquiry should be made in relation to means; a failure to do so may give rise to a successful challenge (*R v Lincoln Crown Court, ex p Jude*, The Times, 30 April 1997).

Generally, a binding over to keep the peace is typically warranted only where there is evidence of likely personal danger to others, involving violence or the threat of violence (see, eg, *Percy v Director of Public Prosecutions* [1995] 3 All ER 124).

In *R v Middlesex Crown Court, ex p Khan* (1997) 161 JP 240, the court held that:

> if a judge is going to require a man to be bound over in circumstances where he has been acquitted, it is particularly important that he should be satisfied beyond a reasonable doubt that the man poses a potential threat to other persons and that he is a man of violence.

D4.2 Criminal Practice Direction sentencing

All aspects relating to the imposition of an order binding over to keep the peace are dealt with in the Criminal Practice Direction 2015 EWCA Crim 1567 Part VII sentencing J.

D5 **Breach of Prison Licence Supervision**

Under section 256AA Criminal Justice Act 2003, if a person is sentenced to under two years in custody, they will be subject to supervision for a year from the date of their actual release 'for the purposes of rehabilitation'.

Similar arrangements are made for 'youths' who are 18 on the date of their release from post-January 2015 sentences of detention and training, or detention, under section 91 Powers of Criminal Courts (Sentencing) Act 2000, extending their period of supervision in these cases.

D5.1 **Breach of supervision requirements imposed under section 256AA**

A new application for legal aid may be made under section 14(b) of the Legal Aid Sentencing and Punishment of Offenders Act 2012.

Criminal Justice Act 2003, s 256AC

(1) Where it appears on information to a justice of the peace that a person has failed to comply with a supervision requirement imposed under section 256AA, the justice may—

    (a) issue a summons requiring the offender to appear at the place and time specified in the summons, or

    (b) if the information is in writing and on oath, issue a warrant for the offender's arrest.

...

(3) Where the person does not appear in answer to a summons issued under subsection (1)(a), the court may issue a warrant for the person's arrest.

(4) If it is proved to the satisfaction of the court that the person has failed without reasonable excuse to comply with a supervision requirement imposed under section 256AA, the court may—

    (a) order the person to be committed to prison for a period not exceeding 14 days (subject to subsection (7)),

    (b) order the person to pay a fine not exceeding level 3 on the standard scale, or

    (c) make an order (a 'supervision default order') imposing on the person—

        (i) an unpaid work requirement (as defined by section 199), or

        (ii) a curfew requirement (as defined by section 204).

(5) Section 177(3) (obligation to impose electronic monitoring requirement) applies in relation to a supervision default order that imposes a curfew requirement as it applies in relation to a community order that imposes such a requirement.

---

(6) If the court deals with the person under subsection (4), it must revoke any supervision default order which is in force at that time in respect of that person.

(7) Where the person is under the age of 21—

    (a) an order under subsection (4)(a) in respect of the person must be for committal to a young offender institution instead of to prison,

(8) A person committed to prison or a young offender institution by an order under subsection (4)(a) is to be regarded as being in legal custody.

(9) A fine imposed under subsection (4)(b) is to be treated, for the purposes of any enactment, as being a sum adjudged to be paid by a conviction.

(10) In Schedule 19A (supervision default orders)—

    (a) Part 1 makes provision about requirements of supervision default orders, and

    (b) Part 2 makes provision about the breach, revocation and amendment of supervision default orders.

(11) A person dealt with under this section may appeal to the Crown Court against the order made by the court.

D5.2 Breach of a supervision default order

Breach of a supervision default order, without reasonable excuse, can be dealt with by using either:

- up to 14 days' custody;
- up to level 3 fine, or
- amended supervision default orders, taking account of what has already been done.

Supervision default orders are to be revoked if custody is later imposed (Sch 19A CJA 2003).

D6 Committal for Sentence

D6.1 Criteria

A magistrates' court may commit an offender for sentence following a guilty plea (Powers of Criminal Courts (Sentencing) Act 2000 (PCC(S)A 2000), s 3). When a magistrates' court has retained jurisdiction for an offence and the offender is convicted, it will require new circumstances to do so. See **A4**.

A magistrates' court will commit for sentence if the court is of the opinion:

- that the offence or the combination of the offence and one or more offences associated with it was so serious that greater punishment should be inflicted for the offence than the court has power to impose; or
- in the case of a violent or sexual offence, that a custodial sentence for a term longer than the court has power to impose is necessary to protect the public from serious harm from the offender.

Additional committal powers are provided for under sections 4 and 6 of the PCC(S)A 2000. The powers of the Crown Court depend on the use of the correct section.

Powers of Criminal Courts (Sentencing) Act 2000, ss 3–6

3 Committal for sentence on summary trial of offence triable either way

(1) Subject to subsection (4) below, this section applies where on the summary trial of an offence triable either way a person aged 18 or over is convicted of the offence.

(2) If the court is of the opinion—
   (a) that the offence or the combination of the offence and one or more offences associated with it was so serious that greater punishment should be inflicted for the offence than the court has power to impose, or
   (b) in the case of a violent or sexual offence, that a custodial sentence for a term longer than the court has power to impose is necessary to protect the public from serious harm from him,
   the court may commit the offender in custody or on bail to the Crown Court for sentence in accordance with section 5(1) below.

(3) Where the court commits a person under subsection (2) above, section 6 below (which enables a magistrates' court, where it commits a person under this section in respect of an offence, also to commit him to the Crown Court to be dealt with in respect of certain other offences) shall apply accordingly.

---

(4) This section does not apply in relation to an offence as regards which this section is excluded by section 33 of the Magistrates' Courts Act 1980 (certain offences where value involved is small).

(5) The preceding provisions of this section shall apply in relation to a corporation as if—

    (a) the corporation were an individual aged 18 or over; and

    (b) in subsection (2) above, paragraph (b) and the words 'in custody or on bail' were omitted.

4 Committal for sentence on indication of guilty plea to offence triable either way

(1) This section applies where—

    (a) a person aged 18 or over appears or is brought before a magistrates' court ('the court') on an information charging him with an offence triable either way ('the offence');

    (b) he or his representative indicates that he would plead guilty if the offence were to proceed to trial; and

    (c) proceeding as if section 9(1) of the Magistrates' Courts Act 1980 were complied with and he pleaded guilty under it, the court convicts him of the offence.

(2) If the court has committed the offender to the Crown Court for trial for one or more related offences, that is to say, one or more offences which, in its opinion, are related to the offence, it may commit him in custody or on bail to the Crown Court to be dealt with in respect of the offence in accordance with section 5(1) below.

(3) If the power conferred by subsection (2) above is not exercisable but the court is still to inquire, as examining justices, into one or more related offences—

    (a) it shall adjourn the proceedings relating to the offence until after the conclusion of its inquiries; and

    (b) if it commits the offender to the Crown Court for trial for one or more related offences, it may then exercise that power.

(4) Where the court—

    (a) under subsection (2) above commits the offender to the Crown Court to be dealt with in respect of the offence, and

    (b) does not state that, in its opinion, it also has power so to commit him under section 3(2) above,

section 5(1) below shall not apply unless he is convicted before the Crown Court of one or more of the related offences.

(5) Where section 5(1) below does not apply, the Crown Court may deal with the offender in respect of the offence in any way in which the magistrates' court could deal with him if it had just convicted him of the offence.

(6) Where the court commits a person under subsection (2) above, section 6 below (which enables a magistrates' court, where it commits a person under this section in respect of an offence, also to commit him to the Crown Court to be dealt with in respect of certain other offences) shall apply accordingly.

(7) For the purposes of this section one offence is related to another if, were they both to be prosecuted on indictment, the charges for them could be joined in the same indictment.

5 Power of Crown Court on committal for sentence under sections 3 and 4

(1) Where an offender is committed by a magistrates' court for sentence under section 3 or 4 above, the Crown Court shall inquire into the circumstances of the case and may deal with the offender in any way in which it could deal with him if he had just been convicted of the offence on indictment before the court.

(2) In relation to committals under section 4 above, subsection (1) above has effect subject to section 4(4) and (5) above.

6 Committal for sentence in certain cases where offender committed in respect of another offence

(1) This section applies where a magistrates' court ('the committing court') commits a person in custody or on bail to the Crown Court under any enactment mentioned in subsection (4) below to be sentenced or otherwise dealt with in respect of an offence ('the relevant offence').

(2) Where this section applies and the relevant offence is an indictable offence, the committing court may also commit the offender, in custody or on bail as the case may require, to the Crown Court to be dealt with in respect of any other offence whatsoever in respect of which the committing court has power to deal with him (being an offence of which he has been convicted by that or any other court).

(3) Where this section applies and the relevant offence is a summary offence, the committing court may commit the offender, in custody or on bail as the case may require, to the Crown Court to be dealt with in respect of—

   (a) any other offence of which the committing court has convicted him, being either—

      (i) an offence punishable with imprisonment; or

      (ii) an offence in respect of which the committing court has a power or duty to order him to be disqualified under section 34, 35 or 36 of the Road Traffic Offenders Act 1988 (disqualification for certain motoring offences); or

   (b) any suspended sentence in respect of which the committing court has under paragraph 11(1) of Schedule 12 to the Criminal Justice Act 2003 power to deal with him.

(4) The enactments referred to in subsection (1) above are—

   (a) the Vagrancy Act 1824 (incorrigible rogues);

   (b) sections 3 to 4A above (committal for sentence for offences triable either way);

   (c) section 13(5) below (conditionally discharged person convicted of further offence);

   (d) paragraph 11(2) of Schedule 12 to the Criminal Justice Act 2003 (committal to Crown Court where offender convicted during operational period of suspended sentence).

Where a summary-only offence has been committed in breach of a Crown Court suspended sentence the new offence may (Sch 12 para 11 CJA 2003) be committed, under section 6 above, to the Crown Court (*R v Jepson* [2013] EWCA Crim 1362). However, where a summary-only offence is committed in breach of a Crown Court community order, there is no such power to commit the new offence when the breach is committed under Schedule 8 paragraph 22 Criminal Justice Act 2003 (*R v De Bitto* [2013] EWCA Crim 1134).

 See *Blackstone's Criminal Practice 2017* **D23.29**

D7 Community Orders

D7.1 Criteria

Section 148 of the Criminal Justice Act 2003 (as amended) provides:

> ### Criminal Justice Act 2003, s 148
>
> #### 148 Restrictions on imposing community sentences
>
> (1) A court must not pass a community sentence on an offender unless it is of the opinio3n that the offence, or the combination of the offence and one or more offences associated with it, was serious enough to warrant such a sentence.
> (2) Where a court passes a community sentence which consists of or includes a community order—
>   (a) the particular requirement or requirements forming part of the community order must be such as, in the opinion of the court, is, or taken together are, the most suitable for the offender, and
>   (b) the restrictions on liberty imposed by the order must be such as in the opinion of the court are commensurate with the seriousness of the offence, or the combination of the offence and one or more offences associated with it.
> (3) Subsections (1) and (2) (b) have effect subject to section 151(2).
> (4) The fact that by virtue of any provision of this section—
>   (a) a community sentence may be passed in relation to an offence; or
>   (b) particular restrictions on liberty may be imposed by a community order or youth rehabilitation order,
>   does not require a court to pass such a sentence or to impose those restrictions.

Because a court is not required to impose a community sentence in cases where the offence is serious enough to justify such a sentence, there is a wider discretion to impose financial penalties. Section 150A of the Criminal Justice Act 2003 restricts community orders for those aged 18 or above to offences that are punishable with imprisonment:

> ### Criminal Justice Act 2003, s 150A
>
> #### 150A Community order available only for offences punishable with imprisonment or for persistent offenders previously fined
>
> (1) The power to make a community order is only exercisable in respect of an offence if—
>   (a) the offence is punishable with imprisonment; or
>   (b) in any other case, section 151(2) confers power to make such an order.

> (2) For the purposes of this section and section 151 an offence triable either way that was tried summarily is to be regarded as punishable with imprisonment only if it is so punishable by the sentencing court (and for this purpose section 148(1) is to be disregarded).

D7.2 Reports

The court must obtain a report unless the court is of the view that one is unnecessary. (See **D28**.)

No custodial sentence or community sentence is invalidated by the failure of a court to obtain and consider a pre-sentence report (CJA 2003, s 156(6)).

D7.3 Sentencing guidelines

The Sentencing Council's guideline provides that the seriousness of the offence should be the initial factor in determining which requirements to include in a community order. It establishes three sentencing ranges within the community order band based on offence seriousness (low, medium, and high), and identifies non-exhaustive examples of requirements that might be appropriate in each. These are set out below. The examples focus on punishment in the community; other requirements of a rehabilitative nature may be more appropriate in some cases.

The particular requirements imposed within the range must be suitable for the individual offender and will be influenced by a wide range of factors, including the stated purpose(s) of the sentence, the risk of reoffending, the ability of the offender to comply, and the availability of the requirements in the local area. Sentencers must ensure that the sentence strikes the right balance between proportionality and suitability. The resulting restriction on liberty must be a proportionate response to the offence that was committed.

Low	Medium	High
Offences only just cross community order threshold, where the seriousness of the offence or the nature of the offender's record means that a discharge or fine is inappropriate.	Offences that obviously fall within the community order band.	Offences only just fall below the custody threshold or the custody threshold is crossed but a community order is more appropriate in the circumstances.
In general, only one requirement will be appropriate and the length may be curtailed if additional requirements are necessary.		More intensive sentences which combine two or more requirements may be appropriate.

Low	Medium	High
Suitable requirements might include: • 40–80 hours' unpaid work • curfew requirement within the lowest range (eg up to 12 hours per day for a few weeks) • exclusion requirement, without electronic monitoring, for a few months • prohibited activity requirement • attendance centre requirement (where available).	Suitable requirements might include: • greater number of hours of unpaid work (eg 80–150 hours) • curfew requirement within the middle range (eg up to 12 hours per day for 2–3 months) • exclusion requirement lasting in the region of 6 months • prohibited activity requirement.	Suitable requirements might include: • 150–300 hours' unpaid work • activity requirement up to the maximum of 60 days • curfew requirement up to 12 hours per day for 4–6 months • exclusion order lasting in the region of 12 months.

D7.4 Requirements

Criminal Justice Act 2003, s 177(2A)–(2B)

Obligations when imposing a community order)

177 (2A) Where the court makes a community order, the court must—

   (a) include in the order at least one requirement imposed for the purpose of punishment, or

   (b) impose a fine for the offence in respect of which the community order is made, or

   (c) comply with both of paragraphs (a) and (b).

(2B) Subsection (2A) does not apply where there are exceptional circumstances which—

   (a) relate to the offence or to the offender,

   (b) would make it unjust in all the circumstances for the court to comply with subsection (2A)(a) in the particular case, and

   (c) would make it unjust in all the circumstances for the court to impose a fine for the offence concerned.

When imposing requirements on the offender as part of the community order, a court should balance the requirements, or combination of requirements, with the offender's personal circumstances, and avoid conflict with work, schooling, or religious beliefs.

The available requirements are:

• unpaid work of between 40 and 300 hours;
• rehabilitation activity requirement;
• programme; the court must specify the initial length (*R v Price* [2013] EWCA Crim 1283);

- prohibited activity;
- curfew for up to 16 hours a day for up to 12 months;
- exclusion, normally with electronic monitoring; such a requirement to exclude the offender from the UK is unlawful (*R (Dragoman) v Camberwell Green Magistrates' Court* [2012] EWHC 4105 (Admin));
- residence;
- mental health treatment;
- drug treatment;
- alcohol treatment;
- (if under 25) attendance centre;
- foreign travel restriction for up to 12 months;
- alcohol abstinence and monitoring (not fully in force), if alcohol an element of the offence or a factor contributing to it and the offender is not dependent on alcohol.

 See *Blackstone's Criminal Practice 2017* **E8**

D7.5 Community order made after long remand in custody

It is not uncommon in a magistrates' court for the offender to have served time on remand equivalent to the maximum custodial sentence available. Some courts, instead of imposing a custodial sentence that allows for immediate release, go on to sentence the offender to a community penalty, effectively visiting upon the offender a greater punishment than is deserved for the crime. In *R v Hemmings* [2008] 1 Cr App R (S) 106, the court held:

> A sentence of a community order, and all the more so one coupled with requirements which have a real impact on the offender's liberty, is a form of punishment. It does not seem to us to be right that the appellant should receive a substantial further punishment in circumstances where he has already received what was in practice the maximum punishment by way of imprisonment which the law could have imposed. That reasoning seems to us to be in line with the reasoning in [earlier cases where] ... the court took the course of imposing a conditional discharge.

The court went on to impose a conditional discharge that expired immediately upon sentence to ensure that the appellant could not fall foul of the consequences of any breach of the order. In *R v Rakib* [2011] EWCA Crim 870, the court, considering *Hemmings*, held that time spent in custody was not a determinative factor, and the rehabilitative aims of sentencing (s 142(1) of the Criminal Justice Act 2003) may in some cases justify a community penalty even if the offender had served on remand the equivalent of the maximum custodial sentence.

D7.6 Breach of and offences while on a community order

D7.6.1 *Criteria*

Breach of community orders imposed under the Criminal Justice Act 2003 is dealt with in accordance with Schedule 8 to that Act (as amended). A general defence of reasonable excuse is open to the defendant. The fact that a person is appealing against a community order does not give him a reasonable excuse not to comply (*West Midlands Probation Board v Sutton Coldfield Magistrates' Court* [2008] EWHC 15 (Admin)).

On breach of a community order due to the offender having failed to comply with the terms of the order, the court must act in one of the following ways:

- impose a fine of up to £2,500;
- impose more onerous requirements than the original order (having taken into account the offender's level of cooperation with the order) and let the order continue (including, on one occasion, lengthening the order by up to six months beyond its original date);
- if the order was made by the Crown Court, commit the offender for sentence;
- revoke the order and deal with the offender in any manner in which it could deal with him if he had just been convicted by the court of the offence (having taken into account the offender's level of cooperation with the order).

It should be noted that, with respect to an offender aged 18 years or older, imprisonment for a term of up to six months can be imposed following a wilful and persistent failure to comply, even if the original offence is not in itself imprisonable.

A court must be 'satisfied' that a breach has occurred to the criminal standard of proof (*West Yorkshire Probation Board v Boulter* (2005) 169 JP 601).

If the breach has occurred due to the offender's ill-health, a court should not resentence (*R v Bishop* [2004] EWCA Crim 2956).

If a person breaches an order that does not already include an unpaid work requirement, and the court is minded to impose such a requirement, the minimum hours to be worked shall be 20 (CJA 2003, Sch 8, para 9(3A)).

There is no power to commence breach proceedings once the operational period has expired (*West Yorkshire Probation Board v Cruickshanks* [2010] EWHC 615 (Admin)).

D7.6.2 *Further offences whilst subject to a community order (Sch 8, para 21)*

If the offender has committed a further offence during the life of the community order and is convicted whilst that order is in force, the court has three options open to it in respect to the original order:

- do nothing, and sentence for the new offence; or
- if the order was made by the Crown Court, commit the offender for sentence; or
- revoke the order and deal with the offender in any manner in which it could deal with him if he had just been convicted by the court of the offence (having taken into account the offender's level of cooperation with the order).

D7.6.3 *Approach to be taken by the court*

The Sentencing Council provides guidance (*Guideline: New Sentences: Criminal Justice Act 2003*, paras 1.1.44–1.1.47):

- When increasing the onerousness of requirements, the court must consider the impact on the offender's ability to comply and the possibility of precipitating a custodial sentence for further breach. For that reason, and particularly where the breach occurs towards the end of the sentence, the court should take account of compliance to date and may consider that extending the supervision or operational periods will be more sensible; in other cases it might choose to add punitive or rehabilitative requirements instead. In making these changes the court must be mindful of the legislative restrictions on the overall length of community sentences and on the supervision and operational periods allowed for each type of requirement.
- The court dealing with breach of a community sentence should have as its primary objective ensuring that the requirements of the sentence are finished, and this is important if the court is to have regard to the statutory purposes of sentencing. A court that imposes a custodial sentence for breach without giving adequate consideration to alternatives is in danger of imposing a sentence that is not commensurate with the seriousness of the original offence and is solely a punishment for breach. This risks undermining the purposes it has identified as being important. Nonetheless, courts will need to be vigilant to ensure that there is a realistic prospect of the purposes of the order being achieved.
- A court sentencing for breach must take account of the extent to which the offender has complied with the requirements of the community order, the reasons for breach, and the point at which the breach has occurred. Where a breach takes place towards the

end of the operational period and the court is satisfied that the offender's appearance before the court is likely to be sufficient in itself to ensure future compliance, then given that it is not open to the court to make no order, an approach that the court might wish to adopt could be to resentence in a way that enables the original order to be completed properly—for example, a differently constructed community sentence that aims to secure compliance with the purposes of the original sentence. (Note the restriction on making no order has now been removed.)

- If the court decides to make the order more onerous, it must give careful consideration, with advice from the Probation Service, to the offender's ability to comply. A custodial sentence should be the last resort, where all reasonable efforts to ensure that an offender completes a community sentence have failed.

 See *Blackstone's Criminal Practice 2017* **E8.30**

D8 **Compensation Order**

D8.1 **Criteria**

> **Powers of Criminal Courts (Sentencing) Act 2000, s 130(1)–(10)**
>
> ### 130 Compensation orders against convicted persons
>
> (1) A court by or before which a person is convicted of an offence, instead of or in addition to dealing with him in any other way, may, on application or otherwise, make an order (in this Act referred to as a 'compensation order') requiring him—
>   - (a) to pay compensation for any personal injury, loss or damage resulting from that offence or any other offence which is taken into consideration by the court in determining sentence; or
>   - (b) to make payments for funeral expenses or bereavement in respect of a death resulting from any such offence, other than a death due to an accident arising out of the presence of a motor vehicle on a road; but this is subject to the following provisions of this section and to section 131 below.
>
> (2) Where the person is convicted of an offence the sentence for which is fixed by law or falls to be imposed under 110(2) or 111(2) above, section 51A(2) of the Firearms Act 1968, section 225, 226, 227 or 228 of the Criminal Justice Act 2003 or section 29(4) or (6) of the Violent Crime Reduction Act 2006, subsection (1) above shall have effect as if the words 'instead of or' were omitted.
>
> (2A) A court must consider making a compensation order in any case where this section empowers it to do so.
>
> (3) A court shall give reasons, on passing sentence, if it does not make a compensation order in a case where this section empowers it to do so.
>
> (4) Compensation under subsection (1) above shall be of such amount as the court considers appropriate, having regard to any evidence and to any representations that are made by or on behalf of the accused or the prosecutor.
>
> (5) In the case of an offence under the Theft Act 1968 or Fraud Act 2006, where the property in question is recovered, any damage to the property occurring while it was out of the owner's possession shall be treated for the purposes of subsection (1) above as having resulted from the offence, however and by whomever the damage was caused.
>
> (6) A compensation order may only be made in respect of injury, loss or damage (other than loss suffered by a person's dependants in consequence of his death) which was due to an accident arising out of the presence of a motor vehicle on a road, if—
>   - (a) it is in respect of damage which is treated by subsection (5) above as resulting from an offence under the Theft Act 1968 or Fraud Act 2006; or

> (b) it is in respect of injury, loss or damage as respects which—
>> (i) the offender is uninsured in relation to the use of the vehicle; and
>> (ii) compensation is not payable under any arrangements to which the Secretary of State is a party.
>
> (7) Where a compensation order is made in respect of injury, loss or damage due to an accident arising out of the presence of a motor vehicle on a road, the amount to be paid may include an amount representing the whole or part of any loss of or reduction in preferential rates of insurance attributable to the accident.
>
> (8) A vehicle the use of which is exempted from insurance by section 144 of the Road Traffic Act 1988 is not uninsured for the purposes of subsection (6) above.
>
> (9) A compensation order in respect of funeral expenses may be made for the benefit of any one who incurred the expenses.
>
> (10) A compensation order in respect of bereavement may be made only for the benefit of a person for whose benefit a claim for damages for bereavement could be made under section 1A of the Fatal Accidents Act 1976; and the amount of compensation in respect of bereavement shall not exceed the amount for the time being specified in section 1A (3) of that Act.

D8.2 **Principles**

A magistrates' court can order compensation for each offence without limit of amount, and may also award compensation in relation to offences taken into consideration.

In relation to motor vehicle damage, the maximum payable will generally be the excess not paid by the Motor Insurers Bureau (MIB) (£300 in untraced driver cases with significant personal injury; otherwise nil), save where it is in respect of a vehicle stolen or taken without consent and there is damage to that vehicle, or the claim is not covered by the MIB.

If the amount of compensation is not agreed, the prosecution must be in a position to call evidence. In cases where the loss is unclear or subject to complex argument, the best course of action is to leave the matter to the civil courts to resolve (*R v Horsham Justices, ex p Richards* [1985] 2 All ER 1114); the Court of Appeal did, however, uphold a compensation order made in respect of injuries occasioned as a result of health and safety-related failures, in the sum of £90,000 (*R v Pola* [2009] EWCA Crim 655). In *R v Bewick* [2007] EWCA Crim 3297, the court observed that it would generally not be appropriate to resolve compensation applications where it was necessary to hear from a third party in evidence. A court can, however, make a common-sense determination (eg £50 for a small broken window).

D8.3 Assessment of means

In determining whether to make a compensation order against any person, and in determining the amount to be paid by any person under such an order, the court shall have regard to his means so far as they appear or are known to the court. An order made in the absence of a means inquiry is at risk of being ruled unlawful (*R v Gray* [2011] EWCA Crim 225).

Where the court considers:

- that it would be appropriate both to impose a fine and to make a compensation order, but
- that the offender has insufficient means to pay both an appropriate fine and appropriate compensation,

the court shall give preference to compensation (though it may impose a fine as well).

Save where a sentence of custody impacts on the offender's ability to pay, there is nothing wrong in principle with imposing compensation in addition to a custodial penalty.

D8.4 Time for payment

Whilst payment within a year is often required, and the defendant's means are relevant to the amount of an order, the time for payment must be proportionate. A one-year period was inappropriate and was increased on the facts in *R v Campbell (Natalie)* [2015] EWCA Crim 1876.

D8.5 Suggested levels of compensation

The Magistrates' Court Sentencing Guidelines set out the following scales for the award of compensation:

Physical injury		
Type of injury	**Description**	**Starting point**
Graze	Depending on size	Up to £75
Bruise	Depending on size	Up to £100
Cut: no permanent scar	Depending on size and whether stitched	£100–500
Black eye		£125
Eye	Blurred or double vision lasting up to 6 weeks	Up to £1,000
	Blurred or double vision lasting for 6–13 weeks	£1,000

D8 Compensation Order

Physical injury		
Type of injury	**Description**	**Starting point**
	Blurred or double vision lasting for more than 13 weeks (recovery expected)	£1,750
Brain	Concussion lasting 1 week	£1,500
Nose	Undisplaced fracture of nasal bone	£1,000
	Displaced fracture requiring manipulation	£2,000
	Deviated nasal septum requiring septoplasty	£2,000
Loss of non-front tooth	Depending on cosmetic effect	£1,250
Loss of front tooth		£1,750
Facial scar	Minor disfigurement (permanent)	£1,500
Arm	Fractured humerus, radius, ulna (substantial recovery)	£3,300
Shoulder	Dislocated (substantial recovery)	£1,750
Wrist	Dislocated/fractured—including scaphoid fracture (substantial recovery)	£3,300
	Fractured—colles type (substantial recovery)	£4,400
Sprained wrist, ankle	Disabling for up to 6 weeks	Up to £1,000
	Disabling for 6–13 weeks	£1,000
	Disabling for more than 13 weeks	£2,500
Finger	Fractured finger other than index finger (substantial recovery)	£1,000
	Fractured index finger (substantial recovery)	£1,750
	Fractured thumb (substantial recovery)	£2,000
Leg	Fractured fibula (substantial recovery)	£2,500
	Fractured femur, tibia (substantial recovery)	£3,800
Abdomen	Injury requiring laparotomy	£3,800

Mental injury	
Description	**Starting point**
Temporary mental anxiety (including terror, shock, distress), not medically verified	Up to £1,000
Disabling mental anxiety, lasting more than 6 weeks, medically verified	£1,000
Disability mental illness, lasting up to 28 weeks, confirmed by psychiatric diagnosis	£2,500

Physical and sexual abuse		
Type of abuse	**Description**	**Starting point**
Physical abuse of adult	Intermittent physical assaults resulting in accumulation of healed wounds, burns, or scalds, but with no appreciable disfigurement	£2,000
Physical abuse of child	Isolated or intermittent assault(s) resulting in weals, hair pulled from scalp, etc	£1,000
	Intermittent physical assaults resulting in accumulation of healed wounds, burns, or scalds, but with no appreciable disfigurement	£2,000
Sexual abuse of adult	Non-penetrative indecent physical acts over clothing	£1,000
	Non-penetrative indecent act(s) under clothing	£2,000
Sexual abuse of child (under 18)	Non-penetrative indecent physical act(s) over clothing	£1,000
	Non-penetrative frequent assaults over clothing or non-penetrative indecent act under clothing	£2,000
	Repetitive indecent acts under clothing	£3,300

 See *Blackstone's Criminal Practice 2017* **E16**

D9 Confiscation: Proceeds of Crime Act 2002

D9.1 Criteria

A magistrates' court has no power to make a confiscation order. However, in some cases it will be appropriate to accept jurisdiction for an offence but find that the prosecution or court later consider that confiscation proceedings are appropriate (a common example is in relation to counterfeit goods). A magistrates' court may commit an offender to the Crown Court for the purposes of activating the confiscation regime under the Proceeds of Crime Act 2002, even where a discharge is considered the proper sentence (see *R v Varma* [2012] UKSC 42 and **D16**) or the offence is summary only (*R v Sumal & Sons (Properties) Limited* 2012 EWCA Crim 1840).

In the event that the prosecution wish to proceed with confiscation proceedings, the court *must* commit the offender to the Crown Court for sentence.

Proceeds of Crime Act 2002, s 70

70 Committal by magistrates' court

(1) This section applies if—
   (a) defendant is convicted of an offence by a magistrates' court, and
   (b) the prosecutor asks the court to commit the defendant to the Crown Court with a view to a confiscation order being considered under section 6.
(2) In such a case the magistrates' court—
   (a) must commit the defendant to the Crown Court in respect of the offence, and
   (b) may commit him to the Crown Court in respect of any other offence falling within subsection (3).
(3) An offence falls within this subsection if—
   (a) the defendant has been convicted of it by the magistrates' court or any other court, and
   (b) the magistrates' court has power to deal with him in respect of it.
(4) If a committal is made under this section in respect of an offence or offences—
   (a) section 6 applies accordingly, and
   (b) the committal operates as a committal of the defendant to be dealt with by the Crown Court in accordance with section 71.

---

(5) If a committal is made under this section in respect of an offence for which (apart from this section) the magistrates' court could have committed the defendant for sentence under section 3(2) of the Sentencing Act (offences triable either way) the court must state whether it would have done so.

(6) A committal under this section may be in custody or on bail.

Particular note should be made of section 70(5), with the court being invited to confirm that it would not otherwise have committed for sentence. Later clarification cannot be relied upon and it is therefore essential that a full contemporaneous note is taken (*R v Blakeburn* [2007] EWCA Crim 1803).

 See *Blackstone's Criminal Practice 2017* **E19**

D10 **Criminal Behaviour Orders**

D10.1 **Notice**

Criminal Procedure Rule 31.3 requires the prosecutor to give notice, on a prescribed form, of his intention to apply for a criminal behaviour order (CBO). There are therefore no circumstances in which a defence lawyer should feel pressurized into dealing with what can be a complex area of law without adequate notice.

D10.2 **Criteria**

Criminal behaviour orders are made following conviction.

Anti-social Behaviour Crime and Policing Act 2014, Pt 2, ss 22 and 25

22 Power to make orders

(1) This section applies where a person ('the offender') is convicted of an offence.
(2) The court may make a criminal behaviour order against the offender if two conditions are met.
(3) The first condition is that the court is satisfied, beyond reasonable doubt, that the offender has engaged in behaviour that caused or was likely to cause harassment, alarm or distress to any person.
(4) The second condition is that the court considers that making the order will help in preventing the offender from engaging in such behaviour.
(5) A criminal behaviour order is an order which, for the purpose of preventing the offender from engaging in such behaviour—
   (a) prohibits the offender from doing anything described in the order;
   (b) requires the offender to do anything described in the order.
(6) The court may make a criminal behaviour order against the offender only if it is made in addition to—
   (a) a sentence imposed in respect of the offence, or
   (b) an order discharging the offender conditionally.
(7) The court may make a criminal behaviour order against the offender only on the application of the prosecution.
(8) The prosecution must find out the views of the local youth offending team before applying for a criminal behaviour order to be made if the offender will be under the age of 18 when the application is made.
(9) Prohibitions and requirements in a criminal behaviour order must, so far as practicable, be such as to avoid—
   (a) any interference with the times, if any, at which the offender normally works or attends school or any other educational establishment;
   (b) any conflict with the requirements of any other court order or injunction to which the offender may be subject.

...

---

25 Duration of order etc

(1) A criminal behaviour order takes effect on the day it is made, subject to subsection (2).

(2) If on the day a criminal behaviour order ('the new order') is made the offender is subject to another criminal behaviour order ('the previous order'), the new order may be made so as to take effect on the day on which the previous order ceases to have effect.

(3) A criminal behaviour order must specify the period ('the order period') for which it has effect.

(4) In the case of a criminal behaviour order made before the offender has reached the age of 18, the order period must be a fixed period of—
  (a) not less than 1 year, and
  (b) not more than 3 years.

(5) In the case of a criminal behaviour order made after the offender has reached the age of 18, the order period must be—
  (a) a fixed period of not less than 2 years, or
  (b) an indefinite period (so that the order has effect until further order).

(6) A criminal behaviour order may specify periods for which particular prohibitions or requirements have effect.

D10.3 Relevant case law

CBOs were considered in *DPP v Bulmer* 2015 EWHC 2323 (Admin). The second requirement, under section 22(4), that the order should help to prevent further harassment, alarm, or distress is an easier test than that of necessity. There is no burden of proof as such. It is an evaluative exercise. However such orders are not to be lightly imposed. The issue is not one of pure discretion. Whilst the availability of positive requirements is important their absence does not mean that an order cannot be made. A failure to comply with past orders is a relevant consideration but not of itself a reason for refusing an order—variation of the existing order or imposition of a new one may assist. Any requirement must be proportionate and tailored to the specific circumstances. The ordinary power to arrest may not be sufficient, without an order, for the police to prevent anti-social behaviour in advance.

The earlier case law is that relating to anti-social behaviour orders (ASBOs). This will only be applicable to the first condition but will not assist in relation to the second, which sets a lower threshold than applied to ASBOs, which required an order to be necessary. CBOs can impose positive as well as negative obligations and can apply to members of the same household.

Evidence of post-complaint behaviour is admissible to show whether a person has acted in an anti-social manner (and whether an order is necessary) (*Birmingham City Council v Dixon* [2009] EWHC 761 (Admin)).

That conduct was likely to cause harassment, alarm, or distress does not require evidence that the conduct was actually witnessed as long as there were people in the vicinity (street drug dealing) who were likely to see it, and thereby be caused harassment, etc (*R v Hashi* [2014] EWCA Crim 2119).

Many of the principles established in the leading case, *R v Boness* [2005] EWCA Crim 2395, and other cases (notably *R v P (Shane Tony)* [2004] EWCA Crim 287, *R v McGrath* [2005] EWCA Crim 353, and *W v Director of Public Prosecutions* [2005] EWCA Civ 1333), will continue to apply to CBOs.

- The requirement that a prohibition was necessary (helpful) to protect persons from further anti-social acts by the defendant means that the use of an ASBO to punish a defendant is unlawful.
- Each separate prohibition must be targeted at the individual and the specific form of anti-social behaviour it is intended to prevent. The order must be tailored to the defendant and not designed on a word processor for generic use. Therefore the court must ask itself when considering a specific order, 'Is this order necessary (helpful) to protect persons in any place in England and Wales from further anti-social acts by the defendant?'
- Each prohibition must be precise and capable of being understood by the defendant. Therefore the court should ask itself before making an order: 'Are the terms of this order clear so that the defendant will know precisely what it is that he is prohibited from doing?' (So unfamiliar words like 'curtilage' and 'environs' should be avoided, as should vague ones like 'implement' or 'paraphernalia'.) For example, a prohibition should clearly delineate any exclusion zone by reference to a map and clearly identify those whom the defendant must not contact or associate with.
- The terms of the order must be proportionate in the sense that they must be commensurate with the risk to be guarded against. This is particularly important where an order may interfere with a Convention right protected by the Human Rights Act 1998, for example Articles 8, 10, and 11 ECHR.
- There is no requirement that the prohibited acts should by themselves give rise to harassment, alarm, or distress.
- An ASBO should not be used merely to increase the sentence of imprisonment which an offender is liable to receive.
- Different considerations may apply if the maximum sentence is only a fine, but the court must still go through all the steps to make sure that an ASBO is necessary (helpful).

The fact that an order prohibits a defendant from committing a specified criminal offence does not automatically invalidate it. However, the court should not make such an order if the sentence which could be passed following conviction for the offence would be a sufficient deterrent. In addition, the Court of Appeal has indicated that prohibiting behaviour that is in any event a crime does not necessarily address the aim of an ASBO, which is to prevent anti-social behaviour. The better course is to make an anticipatory form of order, namely an order which prevents a defendant from doing an act preparatory to the commission of the offence, thereby helping to prevent the criminal offence from being committed in the first place. For example, an order might prevent a defendant from entering a shopping centre rather than stealing from shops.

In *Boness*, Hooper LJ gave other examples, drawing an analogy with bail conditions designed to prevent a defendant from committing further offences. He said:

> If, for example, a court is faced by an offender who causes criminal damage by spraying graffiti then the order should be aimed at facilitating action to be taken to prevent graffiti spraying by him and/or his associates before it takes place. An order in clear and simple terms preventing the offender from being in possession of a can of spray paint in a public place gives the police or others responsible for protecting the property an opportunity to take action in advance of the actual spraying and makes it clear to the offender that he has lost the right to carry such a can for the duration of the order.

If a court wishes to make an order prohibiting a group of youngsters from racing cars or motorbikes on an estate or driving at excessive speed (anti-social behaviour for those living on the estate), then the order should not (normally) prohibit driving whilst disqualified. It should prohibit, for example, the offender whilst on the estate from taking part in, or encouraging, racing or driving at an excessive speed. It might also prevent the group from congregating with named others in a particular area of the estate. Such an order gives those responsible for enforcing order on the estate the opportunity to take action to prevent the anti-social conduct, it is to be hoped, before it takes place.

In *R (Cooke) v Director of Public Prosecutions* [2008] EWHC 2703 (Admin), the court held that an order was not appropriate in relation to an offender who due to mental incapacity was not able to understand its terms, as such an order would fail to protect the public and could therefore not be said to be necessary to protect others. It is suggested that this will apply all the more forcefully under the CBO regime as an order cannot help to prevent anti-social behaviour where the defendant does not understand its terms or his obligations.

D10 Criminal Behaviour Orders

A condition not to cause harassment, alarm, or distress was too imprecise; conditions had to be clear as to what behaviour the order was seeking to discourage (*Heron v Plymouth City Council* [2009] EWHC 3562 (Admin)).

 See *Blackstone's Criminal Practice 2017* **D25.1–D25.47**

D11 Custodial Sentences

D11.1 Criteria

The court must not pass a custodial sentence unless it is of the opinion that the offence, or the combination of the offence and one or more offences associated with it, was so serious that neither a fine alone nor a community sentence can be justified for the offence.

Nothing prevents the court from passing a custodial sentence on the offender if:

- he fails to express his willingness to comply with a requirement which is proposed by the court to be included in a community order and which requires an expression of such willingness; or
- he fails to comply with an order under section 161(2) of the Criminal Justice Act 2003 (pre-sentence drug testing *when in force*).

The custodial sentence must be for the shortest term (not exceeding the permitted maximum) that in the opinion of the court is commensurate with the seriousness of the offence, or the combination of the offence and one or more offences associated with it.

Type of sentence	Age requirement	Notes
Detention in young offender institution	18–20 years	Minimum sentence of 21 days. Maximum 6 months for any one offence. Maximum 12 months for two or more either-way offences. Subject always to the statutory maximum for the offences in question. See **D15**.
Imprisonment	21 years+	Minimum 5 days save for detention imposed under Magistrates' Courts Act 1980, ss 135 and 136. Maximum 6 months for any one offence. Maximum 12 months for two or more either-way offences. Subject always to the statutory maximum for the offences in question.

 See *Blackstone's Criminal Practice 2017* **E2**

D12 **Dangerous Offenders**

D12.1 **Criteria**

Generally speaking, the dangerous offender provisions are of concern to the magistrates' court only when determining venue. The only sentence now available is an extended sentence, and this is available for those who commit a specified violent or sexual offence, as listed in **Appendix 4**, where the court is of the opinion that 'there is a significant risk to members of the public of serious harm occasioned by the commission by him of further specified offences' (CJA 2003, s 227). If new information becomes available during a summary trial, there is a residuary power to commit for sentence under these dangerous offender provisions (PCC(S) A 2000, s 3A).

D12.2 **Specified offences**

Specified offences are those listed in Schedule 15 to the Criminal Justice Act 2003 and appear in **Appendix 4**.

 See *Blackstone's Criminal Practice 2017* **D24.38–D24.41**

D13 **Deferment of Sentence**

D13.1 **Criteria**

The magistrates' court can defer sentence, on one occasion, for a maximum period of six months, to enable the court to assess the offender's capacity to change or carry out reparation to the victim. Such cases are simply adjourned (not on bail), and a warrant can be issued (PCC(S)A 2000, s 1(7)(b)) if the offender fails to attend for sentence (the court also has the option of issuing a summons, and the court should always be invited to try this option first). If the offender reoffends before the period of deferment has expired, he may be dealt with for the deferred matter.

The power to defer shall be exercisable only if:

- the offender consents;
- the offender undertakes to comply with any requirements as to his conduct during the period of the deferment that the court considers it appropriate to impose; and
- the court is satisfied, having regard to the nature of the offence and the character and circumstances of the offender, that it would be in the interests of justice to exercise the power.

See **D13.3** for the legislative framework.

D13.2 **Sentencing Council: deferred sentences: definitive guideline on new sentences (CJA 2003), paragraphs 1.2.6–1.2.9**

Under the new framework, there is a wider range of sentencing options open to the courts, including the increased availability of suspended sentences, and deferred sentences are likely to be used in very limited circumstances. A deferred sentence enables the court to review the conduct of the defendant before passing sentence, having first prescribed certain requirements. It also provides several opportunities for an offender to have some influence as to the sentence passed—

(a) it tests the commitment of the offender not to re-offend;
(b) it gives the offender an opportunity to do something where progress can be shown within a short period;
(c) it provides the offender with an opportunity to behave or refrain from behaving in a particular way that will be relevant to sentence.

Given the new power to require undertakings and the ability to enforce those undertakings before the end of the period of deferral, the decision to defer sentence should be predominantly for a small group of cases at either the custody threshold or the community sentence threshold, where the sentencer feels that there would be particular value in giving the offender the opportunities listed because, if the offender complies with the requirements, a different sentence will be justified at the end of the deferment period.

This could be a community sentence instead of a custodial sentence, or a fine or discharge instead of a community sentence. It may, rarely, enable a custodial sentence to be suspended rather than imposed immediately.

> The use of deferred sentences should be predominantly for a small group of cases close to a significant threshold where, should the defendant be prepared to adapt his behaviour in a way clearly specified by the sentencer, the court may be prepared to impose a lesser sentence.

A court may impose any conditions during the period of deferment that it considers appropriate. These could be specific requirements as set out in the provisions for community sentences, or requirements that are drawn more widely. The requirements may include restorative justice requirements. These should be specific, measurable conditions so that the offender knows exactly what is required and the court can assess compliance; the restriction on liberty should be limited to ensure that the offender has a reasonable expectation of being able to comply whilst maintaining his or her social responsibilities.

Given the need for clarity in the mind of the offender and the possibility of sentence by another court, the court should give a clear indication (and make a written record) of the type of sentence it would be minded to impose if it had not decided to defer and ensure that the offender understands the consequences of failure to comply with the court's wishes during the deferral period.

> When deferring sentence, the sentencer must make clear the consequence of not complying with any requirements and should indicate the type of sentence it would be minded to impose. Sentencers should impose specific, measurable conditions that do not involve a serious restriction on liberty.

D13.3 Legislation

Sections 1–1D of the PCC(S)A 2000 provide:

> ### Powers of Criminal Courts (Sentencing) Act 2000, ss 1, 1A, 1B, 1C, 1D, and 1ZA
>
> #### 1 Deferment of sentence
>
> (1) The Crown Court or a magistrates' court may defer passing sentence on an offender for the purpose of enabling the court, or any other court to which it falls to deal with him, to have regard in dealing with him to—
>
> > (a) his conduct after conviction (including, where appropriate, the making by him of reparation for his offence); or
> >
> > (b) any change in his circumstances;
>
> but this is subject to subsections (3) and (4) below.
>
> (2) Without prejudice to the generality of subsection (1) above, the matters to which the court to which it falls to deal with the offender may have regard by virtue of paragraph (a) of that subsection include the extent to which the offender has complied with any requirements imposed under subsection (3)(b) below.
>
> (3) The power conferred by subsection (1) above shall be exercisable only if—
>
> > (a) the offender consents;
> >
> > (b) the offender undertakes to comply with any requirements as to his conduct during the period of the deferment that the court considers it appropriate to impose; and
> >
> > (c) the court is satisfied, having regard to the nature of the offence and the character and circumstances of the offender, that it would be in the interests of justice to exercise the power.
>
> (4) Any deferment under this section shall be until such date as may be specified by the court, not being more than six months after the date on which the deferment is announced by the court; and, subject to section 1D(3) below, where the passing of sentence has been deferred under this section it shall not be further so deferred …
>
> (6) Notwithstanding any enactment, a court which under this section defers passing sentence on an offender shall not on the same occasion remand him.
>
> (7) Where—
>
> > (a) a court which under this section has deferred passing sentence on an offender proposes to deal with him on the date originally specified by the court, or
> >
> > (b) the offender does not appear on the day so specified,
>
> the court may issue a summons requiring him to appear before the court at a time and place specified in the summons, or may issue a warrant to arrest him and bring him before the court at a time and place specified in the warrant.
>
> (8) Nothing in this section or sections 1ZA to 1D below shall affect—
>
> > (a) the power of the Crown Court to bind over an offender to come up for judgment when called upon; or

(b) the power of any court to defer passing sentence for any purpose for which it may lawfully do so apart from this section.

1ZA Undertakings to participate in restorative justice activities

(1) Without prejudice to the generality of paragraph (b) of section 1(3), the requirements that may be imposed under that paragraph include restorative justice requirements.

(2) Any reference in this section to a restorative justice requirement is to a requirement to participate in an activity—
   (a) where the participants consist of, or include, the offender and one or more of the victims,
   (b) which aims to maximise the offender's awareness of the impact of the offending concerned on the victims, and
   (c) which gives an opportunity to a victim or victims to talk about, or by other means express experience of, the offending and its impact.

(3) Imposition under section 1(3)(b) of a restorative justice requirement requires, in addition to the offender's consent and undertaking under section 1(3), the consent of every other person who would be a participant in the activity concerned.

(4) For the purposes of subsection (3), a supervisor appointed under section 1A(2) does not count as a proposed participant …

(7) In this section 'victim' means a victim of, or other person affected by, the offending concerned.

1A Further provision about undertakings

(1) Without prejudice to the generality of paragraph (b) of section 1(3) above, the requirements that may be imposed by virtue of that paragraph include requirements as to the residence of the offender during the whole or any part of the period of deferment.

(2) Where an offender has undertaken to comply with any requirements imposed under section 1(3)(b) above the court may appoint—
   (a) an officer of a local probation board or an officer of a provider of probation services, or
   (b) any other person whom the court thinks appropriate, to act as a supervisor in relation to him.

1B Breach of undertakings

(1) A court which under section 1 above has deferred passing sentence on an offender may deal with him before the end of the period of deferment if—
   (a) he appears or is brought before the court under subsection (3) below; and
   (b) the court is satisfied that he has failed to comply with one or more requirements imposed under section 1(3)(b) above in connection with the deferment.

(2) Subsection (3) below applies where—
   (a) a court has under section 1 above deferred passing sentence on an offender;
   (b) the offender undertook to comply with one or more requirements imposed under section 1(3)(b) above in connection with the deferment; and

    (c) a person appointed under section 1A(2) above to act as a supervisor in relation to the offender has reported to the court that the offender has failed to comply with one or more of those requirements.

(3) Where this subsection applies, the court may issue—
    (a) a summons requiring the offender to appear before the court at a time and place specified in the summons; or
    (b) a warrant to arrest him and bring him before the court at a time and place specified in the warrant.

1C Conviction of offence during period of deferment

(1) A court which under section 1 above has deferred passing sentence on an offender may deal with him before the end of the period of deferment if during that period he is convicted in Great Britain of any offence.

(2) Subsection (3) below applies where a court has under section 1 above deferred passing sentence on an offender in respect of one or more offences and during the period of deferment the offender is convicted in England and Wales of any offence ('the later offence').

(3) Where this subsection applies, then (without prejudice to subsection (1) above and whether or not the offender is sentenced for the later offence during the period of deferment), the court which passes sentence on him for the later offence may also, if this has not already been done, deal with him for the offence or offences for which passing of sentence has been deferred, except that—
    (a) the power conferred by this subsection shall not be exercised by a magistrates' court if the court which deferred passing sentence was the Crown Court; and
    (b) the Crown Court, in exercising that power in a case in which the court which deferred passing sentence was a magistrates' court, shall not pass any sentence which could not have been passed by a magistrates' court in exercising that power.

(4) Where a court which under section 1 above has deferred passing sentence on an offender proposes to deal with him by virtue of subsection (1) above before the end of the period of deferment, the court may issue—
    (a) a summons requiring him to appear before the court at a time and place specified in the summons; or
    (b) a warrant to arrest him and bring him before the court at a time and place specified in the warrant.

1D Deferment of sentence: supplementary

(1) In deferring the passing of sentence under section 1 above a magistrates' court shall be regarded as exercising the power of adjourning the trial conferred by section 10(1) of the Magistrates' Courts Act 1980, and accordingly sections 11(1) and 13(1) to (3A) and (5) of that Act (non-appearance of the accused) apply (without prejudice to section 1(7) above) if the offender does not appear on the date specified under section 1(4) above.

(2) Where the passing of sentence on an offender has been deferred by a court ('the original court') under section 1 above, the power of that court

under that section to deal with the offender at the end of the period of deferment and any power of that court under section 1B(1) or 1C(1) above, or of any court under section 1C(3) above, to deal with the offender—

  (a) is power to deal with him, in respect of the offence for which passing of sentence has been deferred, in any way in which the original court could have dealt with him if it had not deferred passing sentence; and

  (b) without prejudice to the generality of paragraph (a) above, in the case of a magistrates' court, includes the power conferred by section 3 below to commit him to the Crown Court for sentence.

(3) Where—

  (a) the passing of sentence on an offender in respect of one or more offences has been deferred under section 1 above, and

  (b) a magistrates' court deals with him in respect of the offence or any of the offences by committing him to the Crown Court under section 3 below,

the power of the Crown Court to deal with him includes the same power to defer passing sentence on him as if he had just been convicted of the offence or offences on indictment before the court.

 See *Blackstone's Criminal Practice 2017* **D20.103–D20.109**

D14 **Deprivation Order**

D14.1 Criteria

Orders of this kind should not be made without warning the defendant in advance and inviting representations, otherwise they are liable to be quashed on appeal (*R v Ball* [2002] EWCA Crim 2777). The court should not proceed without first ascertaining the value of the property, and should also ensure that an order made against just one offender does not result in an overly disproportionate sentence (*Ball*). Such an order will be invalid if the financial consequences and the value of the property have not been considered (*Trans Berckx BVBA v North Avon and Swindon Magistrates' Court* [2011] EWHC 2605 (Admin)).

The power can be used to deprive the defendant of their interest in property intended to be used for any offence, not just the particular offence before the court (*R v O'Farrell* [1988] Crim LR 387). Deprivation orders are intended only for straightforward cases involving unencumbered property (*R v Troth* [1980] Crim LR 249). In connection with child pornography the order should be proportionate in the particular circumstances (*R v Connelly* [2012] EWCA Crim 2049).

Powers of Criminal Courts (Sentencing) Act 2000, s 143

143 Powers to deprive offenders of property used etc for purposes of crime

(1) Where a person is convicted of an offence and the court by or before which he is convicted is satisfied that any property which has been lawfully seized from him, or which was in his possession or under his control at the time when he was apprehended for the offence or when a summons in respect of it was issued—

    (a) has been used for the purpose of committing, or facilitating the commission of, any offence, or

    (b) was intended by him to be used for that purpose,

    the court may (subject to subsection (5) below) make an order under this section in respect of that property.

(2) Where a person is convicted of an offence and the offence, or an offence which the court has taken into consideration in determining his sentence, consists of unlawful possession of property which—

    (a) has been lawfully seized from him, or

    (b) was in his possession or under his control at the time when he was apprehended for the offence of which he has been convicted or when a summons in respect of that offence was issued,

---

the court may (subject to subsection (5) below) make an order under this section in respect of that property.

(3) An order under this section shall operate to deprive the offender of his rights, if any, in the property to which it relates, and the property shall (if not already in their possession) be taken into the possession of the police.

(4) Any power conferred on a court by subsection (1) or (2) above may be exercised—

    (a) whether or not the court also deals with the offender in any other way in respect of the offence of which he has been convicted; and

    (b) without regard to any restrictions on forfeiture in any enactment contained in an Act passed before 29th July 1988.

(5) In considering whether to make an order under this section in respect of any property, a court shall have regard—

    (a) to the value of the property; and

    (b) to the likely financial and other effects on the offender of the making of the order (taken together with any other order that the court contemplates making).

(6) Where a person commits an offence to which this subsection applies by—

    (a) driving, attempting to drive, or being in charge of a vehicle, or

    (b) failing to comply with a requirement made under section 7 or 7A of the Road Traffic Act 1988 (failure to provide specimen for analysis or laboratory test or to give permission for such a test) in the course of an investigation into whether the offender had committed an offence while driving, attempting to drive or being in charge of a vehicle, or

    (c) failing, as the driver of a vehicle, to comply with subsection (2) or (3) of section 170 of the Road Traffic Act 1988 (duty to stop and give information or report accident),

the vehicle shall be regarded for the purposes of subsection (1) above (and section 144(1)(b) below) as used for the purpose of committing the offence (and for the purpose of committing any offence of aiding, abetting, counselling or procuring the commission of the offence).

(7) Subsection (6) above applies to—

    (a) an offence under the Road Traffic Act 1988 which is punishable with imprisonment;

    (b) an offence of manslaughter; and

    (c) an offence under section 35 of the Offences Against the Person Act 1861 (wanton and furious driving).

(8) Facilitating the commission of an offence shall be taken for the purposes of subsection (1) above to include the taking of any steps after it has been committed for the purpose of disposing of any property to which it relates or of avoiding apprehension or detection.

 See *Blackstone's Criminal Practice 2017* **E18**

D15 **Detention in Young Offender Institution**

D15.1 **Criteria**

The general requirements for the imposition of a custodial sentence (see **D11**) must be met. A minimum sentence of 21 days must be imposed.

A suspended sentence order (see **D41**) may be imposed.

D15.2 **Breach of YOI licence**

A new application for legal aid may be made under section 14(b) Legal Aid Sentencing and Punishment of Offenders Act 2012.

Section 256C of the Criminal Justice Act 2003 provides:

> ### Criminal Justice Act 2003, s 256C
>
> #### 256C(4) Breach of supervision requirements
>
> (4) If it is proved to the satisfaction of the court that the offender has failed to comply with requirements under section 256B(6) (the supervision requirements), the court may—
>   (a) order the offender to be detained, in prison or such youth detention accommodation as the Secretary of State may determine, for such period, not exceeding 30 days, as the court may specify, or
>   (b) impose on the offender a fine not exceeding level 3 on the standard scale.
>
> If returned to custody the offender serves the whole of the period involved and the supervision period is reduced by the time served.

 See *Blackstone's Criminal Practice 2017* **E7.4**

D16 Discharges: Conditional and Absolute

D16.1 Criteria

An order can be imposed where it is inexpedient to inflict any punishment. A conditional discharge can be for up to three years. Only the orders mentioned in section 12(7) of the PCC(S)A 2000 can be made alongside a discharge, but a magistrates' court may commit an offender to the Crown Court for the purposes of activating the confiscation regime under the Proceeds of Crime Act 2002 even where a discharge is considered the proper sentence (*R v Varma* [2012] UKSC 42).

Powers of Criminal Courts (Sentencing) Act 2000, s 12(7)

12 Absolute and conditional discharge

(7) Nothing in this section shall be construed as preventing a court, on discharging an offender absolutely or conditionally in respect of any offence, from making an order for costs against the offender or imposing any disqualification on him or from making in respect of the offence an order under section 130, 143 or 148 below (compensation orders, deprivation orders and restitution orders).

Where a person who has received a youth caution is convicted of an offence committed within two years of the caution, the court by or before which he is so convicted:

- shall not impose a conditional discharge in respect of the offence unless it is of the opinion that there are exceptional circumstances relating to the offence or the offender which justify its doing so; and
- where it does so, shall state in open court that it is of that opinion and why it is.

A person convicted of breaching a CBO may not receive a conditional discharge (Anti-social Behaviour Crime and Policing Act 2014, s 30(3)).

If a person commits an offence during the life of a conditional discharge, he may be resentenced for that original offence even if the period of discharge has expired at the date of sentence. The offender will be sentenced with reference to his age at the date of resentence, not the date of the previous offence, and can be sentenced in any way as if he had just been convicted of the offence.

If the conditional discharge was imposed by the Crown Court, the offender may be committed to that court for resentence.

There is no requirement to resentence, and a court could sentence for a new offence and leave the conditional discharge in place if it saw fit to do so.

See also section 12 of the PCC(S)A 2000.

 See *Blackstone's Criminal Practice 2017* **E12**

D17 **Discounts for Early Plea**

The Sentencing Council has completed a consultation on discounts for guilty plea and a new guideline is likely to be introduced during the life of this edition. Once an implementation date is known the details will appear at www.oup.com/blackstones/criminal.

D17.1 **Criteria**

A court must discount a sentence in return for a guilty plea. A magistrates' court may impose a maximum sentence as an alternative to committing the case for sentence to the Crown Court. A reduced discount must be given even if the prosecution case is overwhelming. The amount of discount will depend upon the timing of the plea. The Magistrates' Sentencing Guidelines state:

> The reduction has no impact on sentencing decisions in relation to ancillary orders, including disqualification. The level of the reduction should reflect the stage at which the offender indicated a willingness to admit guilt and will be gauged on a sliding scale, ranging from a recommended one third (where the guilty plea was entered at the first reasonable opportunity), reducing to a recommended one quarter (where a trial date has been set) and to a recommended one tenth (for a guilty plea entered at the 'door of the court' or after the trial has begun). There is a presumption that the recommended reduction will be given unless there are good reasons for a lower amount. The application of the reduction may affect the type, as well as the severity, of the sentence. It may also take the sentence below the range in some cases. The court must state that it has reduced a sentence to reflect a guilty plea. It should usually indicate what the sentence would have been if there had been no reduction as a result of the plea.

In each category, there is a presumption that the recommended reduction will be given unless there are good reasons for a lower amount		
First reasonable opportunity	After a trial date is set	Door of the court/after trial has begun
recommended 1/3	**recommended** 1/4	**recommended** 1/10

The issue has been comprehensively reviewed in *R v Caley* [2012] EWCA Crim 2821. The court held that the following points should apply:

- The Sentencing Council's Guideline on discount for guilty plea remains the starting point for the consideration of the relevant issues.

- The discount is given for the indication of the guilty plea. This is based on the need to alleviate the anxieties of victims and witnesses, and to contribute to an effective criminal justice system.
- It is separate to the issue of remorse.

D17.1.1 *First reasonable opportunity*

When the first reasonable opportunity arises is a matter for the judge.

For the police interview to be the first reasonable opportunity would require a significant adjustment to general practice. It may affect the caution and rules of practice on how interviews are conducted. The charge will not have been formulated. An admission in interview is, however, very relevant as mitigation prior to the application of the discount.

It is necessary to distinguish cases where the defendant will know of his guilt and where he needs advice. The discount is not for knowing that the case can be proved. Relevant facts can be admitted if not specific charges. Case management forms seek an indication of plea at a sending. Early guilty plea schemes have this in mind. An indication at the magistrates' court or immediately on arrival at the Crown Court, and certainly by the plea and case management hearing (PTPH), is desirable. However, the PTPH is not usually the first reasonable opportunity. It will usually allow a discount of 25 per cent. The other two opportunities will ordinarily attract the maximum one-third discount. An indication may be to indicate a plea to a lesser charge where that is reasonable.

D17.1.2 *Overwhelming evidence*

Discount should be given in accordance with the guideline and *R v Wilson* [2012] EWCA Crim 386. In any event, a case may not be as overwhelming as part of the evidence only suggests. Twenty per cent is the minimum appropriate discount. *R v Blaydes* [2014] EWCA Crim 798 held that where there is a plea at the first opportunity, the presumption is of a full discount even if the evidence is overwhelming.

D17.1.3 *Available penalties*

A low maximum sentence is not relevant.

D17.1.4 *Unsuccessful Newton hearings*

A normal reduction is not appropriate. The actual discount will depend on the circumstances and number of issues in dispute.

D17.1.5 *Residual flexibility*

There is a residual discretion to deal with the facts of individual cases such as the following:

- Where expert evidence is involved in a serious case, if the significance of the act is in dispute but not the occurrence of the act itself (*R v Peters* [2005] EWCA Crim 605).
- To blame poor advice on plea to an inexperienced defendant rather than an experienced one, but there may have to be a full waiver of privilege.
- The avoidance of an exceptionally long or complex trial may also lead to an exceptional discount. Care is needed to ensure those who plead early see a benefit. There is not to be a detailed investigation of the savings in individual cases.

D17.1.6 *Case law decisions*

Because all relevant documents had not been served, a full discount was given when they were (*R v Thompson* [2012] EWCA Crim 1431). In *R v Carlisle* [2012] EWCA Crim 2501, a 20 per cent discount was appropriate when the defence prevaricated after the Crown had refused to accept a plea to a lesser charge. An acceptance of guilt to a lesser offence whilst denying a greater, of which he is then acquitted, should result in a lower starting point for sentence. This is not so if an indication of willingness to plead is refused by the Crown and then withdrawn entirely (*R v Wilson (Lee)* [2103] EWCA Crim 830). Discount for guilty plea can be lost by an earlier failure to surrender to police bail delaying the court process by a year in this case (*R v Ward* [2013] EWCA Crim 2667).

Where a defendant suffered serious injury leading to amnesia he should not suffer a loss of discount whilst his lawyers obtained sufficient information to advise him on plea, here to causing death by careless driving. Courts should be slow to gainsay a solicitor's opinion as to what further evidence was required so as to advise (*R v Creathorne* [2014] EWCA Crim 502).

R v Joy [2014] EWCA Crim 2321 confirmed that the fact that on charge the defendant had said not guilty was not a relevant factor.

To secure a maximum discount at the Crown Court, an indication of plea should be given at or immediately after a sending if a guilty plea has not been entered in the magistrates' court.

D18 **Disqualification from Driving**

D18.1 Criteria

Disqualification (or in the fifth example, more accurately a revocation) may arise in one of five ways:

(1) Offence carrying obligatory disqualification (see **D18.4**).
(2) Offence carrying discretionary disqualification (see **D18.6**).
(3) As a result of accumulating 12 or more penalty points (see **D18.7**).
(4) As a result of conviction for any offence, or an offence where a vehicle was used for crime (PCC(S)A 2000, ss 146 and 147) (see **D18.9**).
(5) As a result of a 'new driver' accumulating six penalty points (see **D18.10**)

If a mandatory disqualification is imposed then the licence should be endorsed but not with any number of penalty points. Section 44(1) of the Road Traffic Offenders Act (RTOA) 1988 continues the previous position (*R v Usaceva* [2015] EWCA Crim 166).

D18.2 Interim disqualification

An interim disqualification can be imposed when the court commits an offender for sentence to the Crown Court, remits the case to another court, or defers or adjourns sentence (RTOA 1988, s 26). More than one interim disqualification may be imposed, but the total term must not exceed six months.

 See *Blackstone's Criminal Practice 2017* **C7.11**

D18.3 Disqualification with an immediate custodial sentence

A period of disqualification has to be extended by the time actually served in custody in accordance with sections 35A and 35B of the Road Traffic Offenders Act 1988.

Road Traffic Offenders Act 1988, ss 35A and 35B

35A Extension of disqualification where custodial sentence also imposed

(1) This section applies where a person is convicted in England and Wales of an offence for which the court—
   (a) imposes a custodial sentence, and

(b) orders the person to be disqualified under section 34 or 35.
(2) The order under section 34 or 35 must provide for the person to be disqualified for the appropriate extension period, in addition to the discretionary disqualification period.
(3) The discretionary disqualification period is the period for which, in the absence of this section, the court would have disqualified the person under section 34 or 35.
(4) The appropriate extension period is—
    ...
    (h) a period equal to half the custodial sentence imposed ...
(5) If a period determined under subsection (4) includes a fraction of a day, that period is to be rounded up to the nearest number of whole days.
(7) This section does not apply where—
    (a) the custodial sentence was a suspended sentence.

35B Effect of custodial sentence in other cases

(1) This section applies where a person is convicted in England and Wales of an offence for which a court proposes to order the person to be disqualified under section 34 or 35 and—
    (a) the court proposes to impose on the person a custodial sentence (other than a suspended sentence) for another offence, or
    (b) at the time of sentencing for the offence, a custodial sentence imposed on the person on an earlier occasion has not expired.
(2) In determining the period for which the person is to be disqualified under section 34 or 35, the court must have regard to the consideration in subsection (3) if and to the extent that it is appropriate to do so.
(3) The consideration is the diminished effect of disqualification as a distinct punishment if the person who is disqualified is also detained in pursuance of a custodial sentence.
(4) If the court proposes to order the person to be disqualified under section 34 or 35 and to impose a custodial sentence for the same offence, the court may not in relation to that disqualification take that custodial sentence into account for the purposes of subsection (2).

Similar provisions apply where the sentence is imposed under section 146 or 147 Powers of Criminal Courts (Sentencing) Act 2000.

These provisions were given detailed consideration in *R v Needham and others* [2016] EWCA Crim 455 which offered the following staged guidance:

Step 1—Does the court intend to impose a 'discretionary' disqualification under section 34 or section 35 for any offence?

YES—go to step 2

Step 2—Does the court intend to impose a custodial term for that same offence?

YES—section 35A applies and the court must impose an extension period (see section 35A(4)(h) for that same offence and consider step 3.

NO—section 35A does not apply at all—go on to consider section 35B and step 4

Step 3—Does the court intend to impose a custodial term for another offence (which is longer or consecutive) or is the defendant already serving a custodial sentence?

YES—then consider what increase ('uplift') in the period of 'discretionary disqualification' is required to comply with section 35B(2) and (3). In accordance with section 35B(4) ignore any custodial term imposed for an offence involving disqualification under section 35A.

Discretionary period + extension period + uplift = total period of disqualification

NO—no need to consider section 35B at all

Discretionary period + extension period = total period of disqualification

Step 4—Does the court intend to impose a custodial term for another offence or is the defendant already serving a custodial sentence?

YES—then consider what increase ('uplift') in the period of 'discretionary disqualification' is required to comply with section 35B(2) and (3).

Discretionary period + uplift = total period of disqualification

D18.4 Obligatory disqualification

Where a person is convicted of an offence involving obligatory disqualification, the court must order him to be disqualified for such period not less than 12 months as the court thinks fit, unless the court for special reasons (see **D18.5**) thinks fit to order him to be disqualified for a shorter period or not to order him to be disqualified at all (RTOA 1988, s 34).

A person disqualified for dangerous driving must also be ordered to undertake an extended driving test.

A mandatory disqualification does not have the effect of removing any penalty points existing on the licence.

There are certain exceptions to the minimum 12-month period that are applicable to those sentenced in the magistrates' court, as set out in **D18.4.1–D18.4.3**.

D18.4.1 *Minimum three-year disqualification*

A minimum three-year disqualification follows where, within the 10 years immediately preceding the commission of the offence, a person has been convicted of any such offence, and is again convicted of an offence under any of the following provisions of the Road Traffic Act 1988, that is:

• section 3A (causing death by careless driving when under the influence of drink or drugs);

- section 4(1) (driving or attempting to drive while unfit);
- section 5(1)(a) (driving or attempting to drive with excess alcohol);
- section 7(6) (failing to provide a specimen) where that is an offence involving obligatory disqualification;
- section 7A(6) (failing to allow a specimen to be subjected to laboratory test) where that is an offence involving obligatory disqualification.

D18.4.2 *Minimum two-year disqualification*

A minimum two-year disqualification follows in relation to a person on whom more than one disqualification for a fixed period of 56 days or more has been imposed within the three years immediately preceding the commission of the offence.

D18.4.3 *Minimum six-months' disqualification*

A minimum six-months' disqualification follows where a person convicted of an offence under section 40A of the Road Traffic Act 1988 (using vehicle in dangerous condition, etc) has, within the three years immediately preceding the commission of the offence, been convicted of any such offence.

D18.5 Special reasons

There is no statutory definition of 'special reasons', but it must not amount to a defence in law, must be directly connected with the offence in question (not the offender), and must be a mitigating or extenuating circumstance. The burden (civil standard) falls on the defendant. Good character, personal service to the community (eg being a doctor), financial hardship as a result of a disqualification, and the fact the offence was not particularly serious have all been held not to amount to special reasons.

An ignorance of the terms of motor insurance cannot generally amount to special reasons (*Rennison v Knowler* [1947] 1 All ER 302), unless the person was misled or there is a particularly good reason for the ignorance (eg illness, confusion brought about by others).

If special reasons are found, the court has a discretion not to endorse points, and to reduce or not impose a mandatory period of disqualification. Note, however, that for an offence involving mandatory disqualification, where special reasons are found and the court does not disqualify, it must impose points, unless it finds special reasons also for not doing so.

Common special reasons are:

- spiked drinks or mistake as to item drunk;
- shortness of distance driven;
- medical or other emergencies.

In *R v Mander*, unreported, 13 May 2008, CA, the court found special reasons where a taxi driver, upon three of five passengers alighting without paying, drove dangerously for approximately nine-tenths of a mile. The court declined, however, to exercise its discretion to reduce the period of disqualification on the grounds that the defendant had overreacted to the circumstances.

In *Warring-Davies v Director of Public Prosecutions* [2009] EWHC 1172 (Admin), the court emphasized the need to find a causal link between any alleged medical condition and the driving in question.

In *Director of Public Prosecutions v Harrison* [2007] EWHC 556 (Admin), the court held it wrong to find special reasons where a drunken person drove 446 yards in order to find youths who had harassed him earlier.

In *Director of Public Prosecutions v Oram* [2005] EWHC 964 (Admin), the court held that special reasons would not be arguable to a drunk driver who relied upon shortness of distance driven alone.

Taylor v Rajan [1974] RTR 304 deals with the principles involved in 'emergency' cases:

> This is not the first case in which the court has had to consider whether driving in an emergency could justify a conclusion that there are special reasons for not disqualifying the driver. If a man, in the well-founded belief that he will not drive again, puts his car in the garage, goes into his house and has a certain amount to drink in the belief that he is not going to drive again, and if thereafter is an emergency which requires him in order to deal with it to take his car out despite his intention to leave it in the garage, then that is a situation which can in law amount to a special reason for not disqualifying a driver. On the other hand, Justices who are primarily concerned with dealing with this legislation should approach the exercise of the resulting discretion with great care. The mere fact that the facts disclose a special reason does not mean that the driver is to escape disqualification as a matter of course. There is a very serious burden upon the Justices, even when a special reason has been disclosed, to decide whether in their discretion they should decline to disqualify a particular case. The Justices should have very much in mind that if a man deliberately drives when he knows he has consumed a considerable quantity of drink, he presents a potential source of danger to the public which no private crisis can likely excuse. One of the most important matters which Justices have to consider in the exercise of this discretion is whether the emergency (and I call it such for want of a more convenient word) was sufficiently acute to justify the driver taking his car out. The

> Justices should only exercise a discretion in favour of the driver in clear and compelling circumstances … The Justices therefore must consider the whole of the circumstances. They must consider the nature and degree of the crisis or emergency which has caused the defendant to take the car out. They must consider with particular care whether there were alternative means of transport or methods of dealing with the crisis other than and alternative to the use by the defendant of his own car. They should have regard to the manner in which the defendant drove … and they should generally have regard to whether the defendant acted responsibly or otherwise … The matter must be considered objectively and the quality and gravity of the crisis must be assessed in that way. Last, but by no means least, if the alcohol content in the defendant's blood and body is very high, that is a powerful reason for saying that the discretion should not be exercised in his favour. Indeed, if the alcohol content exceeds 100 milligrammes per hundred millilitres of blood, the Justices should rarely, if ever, exercise this discretion in favour of the defendant driver. …

In *DPP v Heathcote* [2011] EWHC 2536 (Admin), it was held that in deciding whether an 'emergency' justified driving, the court should ask whether a sober, reasonable, and responsible friend would have advised the defendant to drive. Relevant factors included:

- amount drunk;
- threat to others;
- state of the roads;
- distance to be driven;
- nature of the emergency;
- what alternatives were available.

The court confirmed that the use of an emergency as a special reason was not limited to life and limb cases; but, on the facts, to chase the thieves of a relative's car was not acceptable.

Chatters v Burke [1986] 3 All ER 168 details the seven factors relevant to a 'shortness of distance driven' argument:

- distance;
- manner of driving;
- state of the vehicle;
- whether there was an intention to drive further;
- road and traffic conditions;
- possibility of danger to road users and pedestrians;
- reason for the driving.

In order to establish a spiked drinks defence, it will be necessary to prove that the drink was laced, that the defendant did not know it was laced, and that but for the lacing of the drink his alcohol level would not have exceeded the legal limit. It will normally be necessary to call expert evidence in relation to the last point. The higher the reading, the less likely it is that a defendant will be able to prove he had no knowledge. If a court is of the view that the defendant ought to have realized his drink was spiked, it will not find special reasons (*Pridige v Grant* [1985] RTR 196).

McCormick and Hitchins [1988] RTR 182 held that special reasons could be available not to endorse points, where the allegation was of failing to provide a specimen when in charge, if the court was satisfied there was no intention to drive and that the defendant could not have been a danger on the road.

 See *Blackstone's Criminal Practice 2017* **C7.8** and **C7.55**

D18.6 Discretionary disqualification

Where an offence carries discretionary disqualification, the court must consider disqualification before it considers the imposition of penalty points. This is the case even if the offender would be liable to disqualification under the 'totting-up' provisions.

Practitioners will consider the tactical considerations of inviting a court to impose a discretionary disqualification as opposed to points that could trigger a totting-up disqualification. The benefit of a discretionary disqualification is that it can be for as short a period as the court directs; the negative side is that any previous points remain on the licence. If a totting-up disqualification were imposed, all the points would be removed but the defendant would face a minimum six-month period of disqualification. This applies only if the court is minded to impose a shorter period, as a defendant may prefer to tot up and clear his licence after a six-month disqualification, rather than have, say, four months disqualified and still have the existing points hanging over him. If a court disqualifies then no additional penalty points are imposed. The period of disqualification can be for any period the court thinks proper.

D18.7 As a result of accumulating 12 or more penalty points

Under section 35 of the Road Traffic Offenders Act 1988 (see **D18.8**), if a driver has accumulated 12 or more points on his licence, the court must order him to be disqualified for not less than the minimum period, unless it is satisfied, having regard to all the circumstances, that there are grounds for disqualifying him for a shorter period or not to disqualify him. In calculating the points on the licence ('totting up'), the court will have regard to:

• the points to be imposed for the new offence, and

- any points on the licence for offences committed no longer than three years from the date of commission of the new offence (therefore, points run from the date of the old offence to the date of new offence) (RTOA 1988, s 29).

If there has been in the three-year period a disqualification under the totting-up provisions, then points imposed prior to that disqualification would be disregarded.

The minimum period of disqualification is:

- six months if no previous disqualification;
- 12 months if one previous disqualification (for 56 days or more);
- two years if two or more previous disqualifications (for 56 days or more).

The previous disqualifications must have been imposed within three years of the date of the new offence to count.

D18.8 Mitigating circumstances

'Mitigating circumstances' may be argued in order to escape disqualification as a result of totting-up (see **D18.7**).

Section 35 of the Road Traffic Offenders Act 1988 provides:

Road Traffic Offenders Act 1988, s 35

35 Disqualification for repeated offences

(1) Where—
   (a) a person is convicted of an offence to which this subsection applies, and
   (b) the penalty points to be taken into account on that occasion number twelve or more,

   the court must order him to be disqualified for not less than the minimum period unless the court is satisfied, having regard to all the circumstances, that there are grounds for mitigating the normal consequences of the conviction and thinks fit to order him to be disqualified for a shorter period or not to order him to be disqualified.

(1A) Subsection (1) above applies to—
   (a) an offence involving discretionary disqualification and obligatory endorsement, and
   (b) an offence involving obligatory disqualification in respect of which no order is made under section 34 of this Act.

(2) The minimum period referred to in subsection (1) above is—
   (a) six months if no previous disqualification imposed on the offender is to be taken into account, and
   (b) one year if one, and two years if more than one, such disqualification is to be taken into account;

---

and a previous disqualification imposed on an offender is to be taken into account if it was for a fixed period of 56 days or more and was imposed within the three years immediately preceding the commission of the latest offence in respect of which penalty points are taken into account under section 29 of this Act.

(3) Where an offender is convicted on the same occasion of more than one offence to which subsection (1) above applies—

  (a) not more than one disqualification shall be imposed on him under subsection (1) above,

  (b) in determining the period of the disqualification the court must take into account all the offences, and

  (c) for the purposes of any appeal any disqualification imposed under subsection (1) above shall be treated as an order made on the conviction of each of the offences.

(4) No account is to be taken under subsection (1) above of any of the following circumstances—

  (a) any circumstances that are alleged to make the offence or any of the offences not a serious one,

  (b) hardship, other than exceptional hardship, or

  (c) any circumstances which, within the three years immediately preceding the conviction, have been taken into account under that subsection in ordering the offender to be disqualified for a shorter period or not ordering him to be disqualified.

(5) References in this section to disqualification do not include a disqualification imposed under section 26 of this Act or section 147 of the Powers of Criminal Courts (Sentencing) Act 2000 or section 223A or 436A of the Criminal Procedure (Scotland) Act 1975 (offences committed by using vehicles) or a disqualification imposed in respect of an offence of stealing a motor vehicle, an offence under section 12 or 25 of the Theft Act 1968, an offence under section 178 of the Road Traffic Act 1988, or an attempt to commit such an offence.

(5A) The preceding provisions of this section shall apply in relation to a conviction of an offence committed by aiding, abetting, counselling, procuring, or inciting to the commission of, an offence involving obligatory disqualification as if the offence were an offence involving discretionary disqualification.

It should be noted that the burden of establishing mitigating circumstances is on the defendant; and those circumstances will generally need to be proved by way of evidence as opposed to submission. If hardship is argued as a mitigating circumstance it must be exceptional but hardship is not a prerequisite for finding mitigating circumstances in all the circumstances of a particular case (*R v Preston* [1986] RTR 136).

 See *Blackstone's Criminal Practice 2017* **C7.28**

D18.9 As a result of conviction for any offence, or an offence where a vehicle was used for crime

Section 146 of the PCC(S)A 2000 gives a court the power to disqualify an offender from holding a driving licence following a conviction for any offence. There need be no nexus between driving and the offence in question, and nothing additional should be written into the statute over and above what is already present; this allows a court to use the provision whenever it feels it to be appropriate in all of the circumstances (*R v Sofekun* [2008] EWCA Crim 2035).

Section 147 of the PCC(S)A 2000 gives courts a narrower power to disqualify where a motor vehicle was involved in the commission of the offence. In the magistrates' court the power is limited solely to the offences of assault:

> **Powers of Criminal Courts (Sentencing) Act 2000, s 147(1) and (3)**
>
> **147 Driving disqualification when vehicle used for purposes of crime**
>
> (1) This section ... applies where a person is convicted by or before any court of common assault or of any other offence involving an assault (including an offence of aiding, abetting, counselling or procuring, or inciting to the commission of, an offence).
>
> (2) ...
>
> (3) If, in a case to which this section applies by virtue of subsection (2) above, the court is satisfied that the assault was committed by driving a motor vehicle, the court may order the person convicted to be disqualified, for such period as the court thinks fit, for holding or obtaining a driving licence.

 See *Blackstone's Criminal Practice 2017* **E21.11** and **E21.12**

D18.10 Road Traffic (New Drivers) Act 1995

Newly qualified drivers are subject to a two-year probationary period. If at any time during that period the points to be endorsed on a driving licence amount to six or more, the licence will be automatically revoked. The relevant date is the date of offence not conviction, so revocation cannot be avoided by delaying court proceedings.

In appropriate cases, advocates may seek to invite courts to disqualify instead of endorse points, in order to try to avoid the draconian consequences of accumulating six or more penalty points.

 See *Blackstone's Criminal Practice 2017* **C7.44**

D18.11 Disqualification in the offender's absence

The Magistrates' Court Sentencing Guidelines provide that when considering disqualification in absence the starting point should be that disqualification in absence should be imposed if there is no reason to believe the defendant is not aware of the proceedings, and after the statutory notice has been served pursuant to section 11(4) of MCA 1980 where appropriate. Section 11(4) provides that there can be no disqualification in absence except on the resumption of a hearing after adjournment. Disqualification should not be imposed in absence where there is evidence that the defendant has an acceptable reason for not attending or where there are reasons to believe it would be contrary to the interests of justice to do so.

D18.12 Return of driving licence

D18.12.1 *Overview*

Section 42 of the Road Traffic Offenders Act 1988 provides for a disqualified driver to apply to the court for the return of his driving licence, prior to the expiry of the disqualification period. These proceedings may be funded at the magistrates' court by way of a means-tested representation order.

Period of disqualification	Minimum period of disqualification that must have elapsed before court can consider an application
Less than 4 years	2 years
4 years, but less than 10 years	One half of the disqualification period
10 years or more	5 years

If a disqualification is imposed by virtue of section 36(1) of the Act (disqualification until test is passed), there is no power to return a licence under section 43.

D18.12.2 *Criteria to be applied*

On any such application the court may, as it thinks proper having regard to:

- the character of the person disqualified and his conduct subsequent to the order;
- the nature of the offence; and
- any other circumstances of the case,

either by order remove the disqualification as from such date as may be specified in the order, or refuse the application.

D18.12.3 *Further application following refusal*

Where an application is refused, a further application shall not be entertained if made within three months after the date of the refusal.

 See *Blackstone's Criminal Practice 2017* **C7.42**

D19 Exclusion from Licensed Premises

D19.1 Criteria

The term of the order must be between three months and two years. Section 1 of the Licensed Premises (Exclusion of Certain Persons) Act 1980 provides:

> ### Licensed Premises (Exclusion of Certain Persons) Act 1980, s 1(1) and (2)
>
> **1 Exclusion orders**
>
> (1) Where a court by or before which a person is convicted of an offence committed on licensed premises is satisfied that in committing that offence he resorted to violence or offered or threatened to resort to violence, the court may, subject to subsection (2) below, make an order (in this Act referred to as an 'exclusion order') prohibiting him from entering those premises or any other specified premises, without the express consent of the licensee of the premises or his servant or agent.
>
> (2) An exclusion order may be made either—
>
>   (a) in addition to any sentence which is imposed in respect of the offence of which the person is convicted; or
>
>   (b) where the offence was committed in England and Wales, notwithstanding the provisions of sections 12 and 14 of the Powers of Criminal Courts (Sentencing) Act 2000 (cases in which absolute and conditional discharges may be made, and their effect), in addition to an order discharging him absolutely or conditionally.

 See *Blackstone's Criminal Practice 2017* **E21.1**

D20 **Financial Orders: Priority for Payment**

In the magistrates' court the order of priority between financial orders, when a defendant does not have sufficient funds, is as follows:

(1) compensation (**D8**),
(2) victim surcharge (**D40**),
(3) fine (**D21**),
(4) prosecution costs (**D30**).

D21 **Fines**

D21.1 **Criteria**

The Magistrates' Court Sentencing Guidelines set out the following approach to fines: these guidelines are up to date as of 11 September 2015. For offences committed on or after 12 March 2015 there is no upper limit to the level of fine that may be imposed in a magistrates' court. The Legal Aid Sentencing and Punishment of Offenders Act 2012 (Fines on summary conviction) Regulations 2015 contain detailed exceptions to this rule. The Criminal Practice Direction X111 Annex 3 contains provisions requiring certain serious offences to be identified by the Crown so that an authorised district judge may be appointed to deal with the case.

Fine band starting points and ranges

In these guidelines, where the starting point or range for an offence is or includes a fine, it is expressed as one of three fine bands (A, B, or C). Each fine band has both a starting point and a range. In some cases bands D–F may be used even where the community or custody threshold have been passed.

On some offence guidelines, both the starting point and the range are expressed as a single fine band; see, for example, careless driving, where the starting point and range for the first level of offence activity are 'fine band A'. This means that the starting point will be the starting point for fine band A (50 per cent of the offender's relevant weekly income) and the range will be the range for fine band A (25–75 per cent of relevant weekly income). On other guidelines, the range encompasses more than one fine band; see, for example, drunk and disorderly in a public place on page 55 of the Sentencing Guidelines, where the starting point for the second level of offence activity is 'fine band B' and the range is 'fine band A to fine band C'. This means that the starting point will be the starting point for fine band B (100 per cent of relevant weekly income) and the range will be the lowest point of the range for fine band A to the highest point of the range for fine band C (25–175 per cent of relevant weekly income).

1. The amount of a fine must reflect the seriousness of the offence.
2. The court must also take into account the financial circumstances of the offender; this applies whether it has the effect of increasing or reducing the fine. Normally a fine should be of an amount that is capable of being paid within 12 months.
3. The aim is for the fine to have an equal impact on offenders with different financial circumstances; it should be a hardship but should not force the offender below a reasonable 'subsistence' level.

---

4. The guidance below aims to establish a clear, consistent, and principled approach to the assessment of fines that will apply fairly in the majority of cases. However, it is impossible to anticipate every situation that may be encountered and in each case the court will need to exercise its judgement to ensure that the fine properly reflects the seriousness of the offence and takes into account the financial circumstances of the offender.

5. For the purpose of the offence guidelines, a fine is based on one of six bands (A–F). The selection of the relevant fine band, and the position of the individual offence within that band, is determined by the seriousness of the offence.

	Starting point	**Range**
Fine band A	50% of relevant weekly income	25–75% of relevant weekly income
Fine band B	100% of relevant weekly income	75–125% of relevant weekly income
Fine band C	150% of relevant weekly income	125–175% of relevant weekly income
Fine band D	250% of relevant weekly income	200–300% of relevant weekly income
Fine band E	400% of relevant weekly income	300–500% of relevant weekly income
Fine band F	600% of relevant weekly income	500–700% of relevant weekly income

...Definition of relevant weekly income

7. The seriousness of an offence determines the choice of fine band and the position of the offence within the range for that band. The offender's financial circumstances are taken into account by expressing that position as a proportion of the offender's relevant weekly income.

8. Where an offender is in receipt of income from employment or is self-employed and that income is more than £110 per week after deduction of tax and National Insurance (or equivalent where the offender is self-employed), the actual income is the relevant weekly income.

9. Where an offender's only source of income is state benefit (including where there is relatively low additional income as permitted by the benefit regulations) or the offender is in receipt of income from employment or is self-employed but the amount of income after deduction of tax and national insurance is £110 or less, the relevant weekly income is deemed to be £110.

10. In calculating relevant weekly income, no account should be taken of tax credits, housing benefit, child benefit, or similar.

No reliable information

11. Where an offender has failed to provide information, or the court is not satisfied that it has been given sufficient reliable information, it

is entitled to make such determination as it thinks fit regarding the financial circumstances of the offender. Any determination should be clearly stated on the court records for use in any subsequent variation or enforcement proceedings. In such cases, a record should also be made of the applicable fine band and the court's assessment of the position of the offence within that band based on the seriousness of the offence.

12. Where there is no information on which a determination can be made, the court should proceed on the basis of an assumed relevant weekly income of £400. This is derived from national median pre-tax earnings; a gross figure is used as, in the absence of financial information from the offender, it is not possible to calculate appropriate deductions.

13. Where there is some information that tends to suggest a significantly lower or higher income than the recommended £400 default sum, the court should make a determination based on that information.

14. A court is empowered to remit a fine in whole or part if the offender subsequently provides information as to means. The assessment of offence seriousness and, therefore, the appropriate fine band and the position of the offence within that band is not affected by the provision of this information.

Assessment of financial circumstances

15. While the initial consideration for the assessment of a fine is the offender's relevant weekly income, the court is required to take account of the offender's financial circumstances more broadly. Guidance on important parts of this assessment is set out below.

16. An offender's financial circumstances may have the effect of increasing or reducing the amount of the fine; however, they are not relevant to the assessment of offence seriousness. They should be considered separately from the selection of the appropriate fine band and the court's assessment of the position of the offence within the range for that band.

Out-of-the-ordinary expenses

17. In deciding the proportions of relevant weekly income that are the starting points and ranges for each fine band, account has been taken of reasonable living expenses. Accordingly, no further allowance should normally be made for these. In addition, no allowance should normally be made where the offender has dependants.

18. Outgoings will be relevant to the amount of the fine only where the expenditure is out of the ordinary and substantially reduces the ability to pay a financial penalty so that the requirement to pay a fine based on the standard approach would lead to undue hardship.

Unusually low outgoings

19. Where the offender's living expenses are substantially lower than would normally be expected, it may be appropriate to adjust the amount of the fine to reflect this. This may apply, for example, where an offender does not make any financial contribution towards his or her living costs.

Savings

20. Where an offender has savings these will not normally be relevant to the assessment of the amount of a fine although they may influence the decision on time to pay.

21. However, where an offender has little or no income but has substantial savings, the court may consider it appropriate to adjust the amount of the fine to reflect this.

Household has more than one source of income

22. Where the household of which the offender is a part has more than one source of income, the fine should normally be based on the income of the offender alone.

23. However, where the offender's part of the income is very small (or the offender is wholly dependent on the income of another), the court may have regard to the extent of the household's income and assets which will be available to meet any fine imposed on the offender.

Potential earning capacity

24. Where there is reason to believe that an offender's potential earning capacity is greater than his or her current income, the court may wish to adjust the amount of the fine to reflect this. This may apply, for example, where an unemployed offender states an expectation to gain paid employment within a short time. The basis for the calculation of fine should be recorded in order to ensure that there is a clear record for use in variation or enforcement proceedings.

High income offenders

25. Where the offender is in receipt of very high income, a fine based on a proportion of relevant weekly income may be disproportionately high when compared with the seriousness of the offence. In such cases, the court should adjust the fine to an appropriate level; as a general indication, in most cases the fine for a first time offender pleading not guilty should not exceed 75 per cent of the maximum fine.

Approach to offenders on low income

26. An offender whose primary source of income is state benefit will generally receive a base level of benefit (e.g. jobseeker's allowance, a relevant disability benefit, or income support) and may also be eligible for supplementary benefits depending on his or her individual circumstances (such as child tax credits, housing benefit, council tax benefit, and similar). In some cases these benefits may have been replaced by Universal Credit.

27. If relevant weekly income were defined as the amount of benefit received, this would usually result in higher fines being imposed on offenders with a higher level of need; in most circumstances that would not properly balance the seriousness of the offence with the financial circumstances of the offender. While it might be possible to exclude from the calculation any allowance above the basic entitlement of a single person, that could be complicated and time-consuming.

28. Similar issues can arise where an offender is in receipt of a low earned income since this may trigger eligibility for means-related benefits such as working tax credits and housing benefit depending on the particular

circumstances. It will not always be possible to determine with any confidence whether such a person's financial circumstances are significantly different from those of a person whose primary source of income is state benefit.

29. For these reasons, a simpler and fairer approach to cases involving offenders in receipt of low income (whether primarily earned or as a result of benefit) is to identify an amount that is deemed to represent the offender's relevant weekly income.

30. While a precise calculation is neither possible nor desirable, it is considered that an amount that is approximately half-way between the base rate for jobseeker's allowance and the net weekly income of an adult earning the minimum wage for 30 hours per week represents a starting point that is both realistic and appropriate; this is currently £120.

   The calculation is based on a 30-hour working week in recognition of the fact that many of those on minimum wage do not work a full 37-hour week and that lower minimum wage rates apply to younger people.

31. The figures will be updated in due course in accordance with any changes to benefit and minimum wage levels.

Offence committed for 'commercial' purposes

32. Some offences are committed with the intention of gaining a significant commercial benefit. These often occur where, in order to carry out an activity lawfully, a person has to comply with certain processes which may be expensive. They include, for example, 'taxi touting' (where unauthorised persons seek to operate as taxi drivers) and 'fly-tipping' (where the cost of lawful disposal is considerable).

33. In some of these cases, a fine based on the standard approach set out above may not reflect the level of financial gain achieved or sought through the offending.

   Accordingly:

   (a) where the offender has generated income or avoided expenditure to a level that can be calculated or estimated, the court may wish to consider that amount when determining the financial penalty;

   (b) where it is not possible to calculate or estimate that amount, the court may wish to draw on information from the enforcing authorities about the general costs of operating within the law...

Reduction for a guilty plea

36. Where a guilty plea has been entered, the amount of the fine should be reduced by the appropriate proportion.

Maximum fines

37. A fine must not exceed the statutory limit. Where this is expressed in terms of a 'level', the maxima are:

Level 1	£200
Level 2	£500
Level 3	£1,000

Level 4	£2,500
Level 5	Unlimited

Multiple offences

38. Where an offender is to be fined for two or more offences that arose out of the same incident, it will often be appropriate to impose on the most serious offence a fine which reflects the totality of the offending where this can be achieved within the maximum penalty for that offence. 'No separate penalty' should be imposed for the other offences.

39. Where compensation is being ordered, that will need to be attributed to the relevant offence as will any necessary ancillary orders.

Imposition of fines with custodial sentences

40. A fine and a custodial sentence may be imposed for the same offence, although there will be few circumstances in which this is appropriate, particularly where the custodial sentence is to be served immediately. One example might be where an offender has profited financially from an offence but there is no obvious victim to whom compensation can be awarded. Combining these sentences is most likely to be appropriate only where the custodial sentence is short and/or the offender clearly has, or will have, the means to pay.

41. Care must be taken to ensure that the overall sentence is proportionate to the seriousness of the offence and that better-off offenders are not able to 'buy themselves out of custody'...

Payment

43. A fine is payable in full on the day on which it is imposed. The offender should always be asked for immediate payment when present in court and some payment on the day should be required wherever possible.

44. Where that is not possible, the court may, in certain circumstances, require the offender to be detained. More commonly, a court will allow payments to be made over a period set by the court:

    (a) if periodic payments are allowed, the fine should normally be payable within a maximum of 12 months. However, it may be unrealistic to expect those on very low incomes to maintain payments for as long as a year;

    (b) compensation should normally be payable within 12 months. However, in exceptional circumstances it may be appropriate to allow it to be paid over a period of up to three years.

45. Where fine bands D, E and F apply, it may be appropriate for the fine to be of an amount that is larger than can be repaid within 12 months. In such cases, the fine should normally be payable within a maximum of 18 months (band D) or two years (bands E and F).

46. It is generally recognized that the maximum weekly payment by a person in receipt of state benefit should rarely exceed £5.

47. When allowing payment by instalments by an offender in receipt of earned income, the following approach may be useful. If the offender

has dependants or larger than usual commitments, the weekly payment is likely to be decreased.

Net weekly income	Starting point for weekly payment
£60	£5
£120	£10
£200	£25
£250	£30
£300	£50
£400	£80

The rate of payment for fines in bands D and E was approved in *R (Purnell) v South Western Magistrates' Court* [2013] EWHC 64 (Admin), which confirmed also that the responsibility to advise the court of other fines outstanding falls upon the offender. *R v Rance* [2012] EWCA Crim 2023 confirmed that it was for the defendant to provide the court with all relevant financial information, but that fines must have regard only to the means of the offender—there is no concept of a 'tainted gift'.

If the defendant fails to put all relevant information before the court, he cannot later complain that the court has failed to take account of financial circumstances as required by section 164 of the Criminal Justice Act 2003.

R v Rance also held that whilst the court should have regard to any financial benefit from the crime, this is merely one consideration and does not mean that an equivalent or large proportion of the amount should be included in the fine.

D21.2 The detention alternative

Section 135 of the Magistrates' Courts Act 1980 provides:

Magistrates' Courts Act 1980, s 135

135 Detention of offender for one day in court-house or police station

(1) A magistrates' court that has power to commit to prison a person convicted of an offence, or would have that power but for section 82 or 88 above, may order him to be detained within the precincts of the court-house or at any police station until such hour, not later than 8 o'clock in the evening of the day on which the order is made, as the court may

direct, and, if it does so, shall not, where it has power to commit him to prison [or detention if aged 18–20 years], exercise that power.

(2) A court shall not make such an order under this section as will deprive the offender of a reasonable opportunity of returning to his abode on the day of the order.

 See *Blackstone's Criminal Practice 2017* **E15**

D22 **Forfeiture Order**

D22.1 **Criteria**

Section 27 of the Misuse of Drugs Act 1971 provides:

Misuse of Drugs Act 1971, s 27

27 Forfeiture

(1) Subject to subsection (2) below, the court by or before which a person is convicted of an offence under this Act or an offence falling within subsection (3) below or an offence to which section 1 of the Criminal Justice (Scotland) Act 1987 relates may order anything shown to the satisfaction of the court to relate to the offence, to be forfeited and either destroyed or dealt with in such other manner as the court may order.

(2) The court shall not order anything to be forfeited under this section, where a person claiming to be the owner of or otherwise interested in it applies to be heard by the court, unless an opportunity has been given to him to show cause why the order should not be made.

(3) An offence falls within this subsection if it is an offence which is specified in—

    (a) paragraph 1 of Schedule 2 to the Proceeds of Crime Act 2002 (drug trafficking offences), or

    (b) so far as it relates to that paragraph, paragraph 10 of that Schedule.

There are also powers of forfeiture in other statutes, such as the Knives Act 1997 and the Obscene Publications Act 1959.

Section 1 of the Prevention of Crime Act 1953 provides that, where any person is convicted of an offence under that section, the court may make an order for the forfeiture or disposal of any weapon in respect of which the offence was committed. See also **D14** on deprivation orders.

 See *Blackstone's Criminal Practice 2017* **E18.7** and, in relation to deprivation orders, **D21**

D23 Guardianship and Hospital Orders

D23.1 Criteria

Section 37 of the Mental Health Act 1983 provides:

Mental Health Act 1983, s 37

37 Powers of court to order hospital admission or guardianship

(1) Where a person is convicted … by a magistrates' court of an offence punishable on summary conviction with imprisonment, and the conditions mentioned in subsection (2) below are satisfied, the court may by order authorise his admission to and detention in such hospital as may be specified in the order or, as the case may be, place him under the guardianship of a local social services authority or of such other person approved by a local social services authority as may be so specified.

(1A) …

(1B) …

(2) The conditions referred to in subsection (1) above are that—

    (a) the court is satisfied, on the written or oral evidence of two registered medical practitioners, that the offender is suffering from mental illness, psychopathic disorder, severe mental impairment or mental impairment and that either—

        (i) the mental disorder from which the offender is suffering is of a nature or degree which makes it appropriate for him to be detained in a hospital for medical treatment and, in the case of psychopathic disorder or mental impairment, that such treatment is likely to alleviate or prevent a deterioration of his condition; or

        (ii) in the case of an offender who has attained the age of 16 years, the mental disorder is of a nature or degree which warrants his reception into guardianship under this Act; and

    (b) the court is of the opinion, having regard to all the circumstances including the nature of the offence and the character and antecedents of the offender, and to the other available methods of dealing with him, that the most suitable method of disposing of the case is by means of an order under this section.

(3) Where a person is charged before a magistrates' court with any act or omission as an offence and the court would have power, on convicting him of that offence, to make an order under subsection (1) above in his case as being a person suffering from mental illness or severe mental impairment, then, if the court is satisfied that the accused did the act or made the omission charged, the court may, if it thinks fit, make such an order without convicting him.

(4) An order for the admission of an offender to a hospital (in this Act referred to as 'a hospital order') shall not be made under this section unless the court is satisfied on the written or oral evidence of the registered medical practitioner who would be in charge of his treatment or of some other person representing the managers of the hospital that arrangements have been made for his admission to that hospital, and for his admission to it within the period of 28 days beginning with the date of the making of such an order; and the court may, pending his admission within that period, give such directions as it thinks fit for his conveyance to and detention in a place of safety …

(8) Where an order is made under this section, the court shall not—

(a) pass sentence of imprisonment or impose a fine or make a community order (within the meaning of Part 12 of the Criminal Justice Act 2003) in respect of the offence,

(b) if the order under this section is a hospital order, make a referral order (within the meaning of the Powers of Criminal Courts (Sentencing) Act 2000) in respect of the offence, or

(c) make in respect of the offender an order under section 150 of that Act (binding over of parent or guardian),

but the court may make any other order which it has power to make apart from this section; and for the purposes of this subsection 'sentence of imprisonment' includes any sentence or order for detention.

 See *Blackstone's Criminal Practice 2017* **E22**

D24 *Newton* Hearings

D24.1 The rule in *Newton*

The rule in *R v Newton* (1982) 77 Cr App R 13 indicates that an offender will be sentenced on the prosecution's version of the facts unless the defence make clear that they are pleading on an alternative basis. In that situation, the Crown must prove its version of the facts by admissible evidence to the criminal standard of proof.

The purpose of a *Newton* hearing is to establish the factual basis for sentence in a case where there is a factual dispute and that dispute is material to sentence. Once a *Newton* hearing takes place the defendant is at risk of findings conflicting with an earlier basis of plea (*Nicholls v DPP* [2013] EWHC 4365 (Admin)).

D24.2 Criteria

R v Cairns [2013] EWCA Crim 467 confirmed that there is no obligation to hold a *Newton* hearing

(a) if the difference between the two versions of fact is immaterial to sentence (in which event the defendant's version must be adopted): *R v Hall* (1984) 6 Cr App R (S) 321;

(b) where the defence version can be described as 'manifestly false' or 'wholly implausible': *R v Hawkins* (1985) Cr App R (S) 351; or

(c) where the matters put forward by the defendant do not contradict the prosecution case but constitute extraneous mitigation where the court is not bound to accept the truth of the matters put forward whether or not they are challenged by the prosecution: *R v Broderick* (1994) 15 Cr App R (S) 476.

Guidance in relation to the holding of *Newton* hearings was set down in *R v Underwood* [2004] EWCA Crim 2256:

(1) The starting point has to be the defendant's instructions. His advocate will appreciate whether any significant facts about the prosecution evidence are disputed and the factual basis on which the defendant intends to plead guilty. Responsibility for taking initiative and alerting the prosecutor to the disputed areas rests with the defence.

(2) Where the Crown accepts the defendant's account of the disputed facts, the agreement should be written down and signed by both advocates. It should then be made available to the judge. If pleas have already been accepted and approved then it should be available before the sentencing hearing begins. If the agreed basis of plea is not signed by both advocates, the judge is entitled to ignore it. The Crown might reject the defendant's version. If so, the areas of

dispute should be identified in writing, focusing the court's attention on the precise facts in dispute.

(3) The prosecution's position might be that they have no evidence to contradict the defence's assertions. In those circumstances, particularly if the facts relied on by the defendant arise from his personal knowledge and depend on his own account of the facts, the Crown should not normally agree the defendant's account unless supported by other material. The court should be notified at the outset in writing of the points in issue and the Crown's responses.

(4) After submissions, the judge will decide how to proceed. If not already decided, he would address the question of whether he should approve the Crown's acceptance of pleas. Then he would address the proposed basis of plea. It should be emphasized that whether or not the basis of plea is agreed, the judge is not bound by any such agreement and is entitled of his own motion to insist that any evidence relevant to the facts in dispute should be called before him, paying appropriate regard to any agreement reached by the advocates and any reasons which the Crown, in particular, might advance to justify him proceeding immediately to sentence. The judge is responsible for the sentencing decision and may order a *Newton* hearing to ascertain the truth about disputed facts.

(5) Relevant evidence should be called by prosecution and defence, particularly where the issue arises from facts which are within the exclusive knowledge of the defendant. If the defendant is willing to give evidence he should be called and, if not, subject to any explanation offered, the judge may draw such inference as he sees fit. The judge can reject the evidence called by the prosecution or by the defendant or his witnesses even if the Crown has not called contradictory evidence. The judge's conclusions should be explained in the judgment …

(7) Normally, matters of mitigation are not dealt with by way of a *Newton* hearing but it is always open to the court to allow a defendant to give evidence on matters of mitigation which are within his own knowledge. The judge is entitled to decline to hear evidence about disputed facts if the case advanced is, for good reason, to be regarded as absurd or obviously untenable.

(8) If the issues at the *Newton* hearing are wholly resolved in the defendant's favour, mitigation for guilty pleas should not be reduced. If the defendant is disbelieved or obliges the prosecution to call evidence from the victim, who is then subjected to cross-examination which, because it is entirely unfounded, causes unnecessary and inappropriate distress, or if the defendant conveys that he has no insight into the consequences of his offence, and no genuine remorse, the judge might reduce the discount for the guilty pleas. There may be a few exceptional cases in which the normal entitlement to credit for a plea of guilty is wholly dissipated by the *Newton* hearing, and, in such cases, the judge should explain his reasons.

 See *Blackstone's Criminal Practice 2017* **D20.8–D20.29**

D25 **Offences Taken into Consideration (TICs) and the Totality Principle**

D25.1 **Criteria for TICs**

In *R v Miles* [2006] EWCA Crim 256, the court made the following observations:

[T]he sentence is intended to reflect a defendant's overall criminality. Offences cannot be taken into consideration without the express agreement of the offender. That is an essential prerequisite. The offender is pleading guilty to the offences. If they are to be taken into account (and the court is not obliged to take them into account) they have relevance to the overall criminality. When assessing the significance of TICs, as they are often called, of course the court is likely to attach weight to the demonstrable fact that the offender has assisted the police, particularly if they are enabled to clear up offences which might not otherwise be brought to justice. It is also true that cooperative behaviour of that kind will often provide its own very early indication of guilt, and usually means that no further proceedings at all need be started. They may also serve to demonstrate a genuine determination by the offender (and we deliberately use the colloquialism) to wipe the slate clean, so that when he emerges from whatever sentence is imposed on him, he can put his past completely behind him, without having worry or concern that offences may be revealed and that he is then returned to court. As in so many aspects of sentencing, of course, the way in which the court deals with offences to be taken into consideration depends on context. In some cases the offences taken into consideration will end up by adding nothing or nothing very much to the sentence which the court would otherwise impose. On the other hand, offences taken into consideration may aggravate the sentence and lead to a substantial increase in it. For example, the offences may show a pattern of criminal activity which suggests careful planning or deliberate rather than casual involvement in a crime. They may show an offence or offences committed on bail, after an earlier arrest. They may show a return to crime immediately after the offender has been before the court and given a chance that, by committing the crime, he has immediately rejected. There are many situations where similar issues may arise. One advantage to the defendant, of course, is that if once an offence is taken into consideration, there is no likely risk of any further prosecution for it. If, on the other hand, it is not, that risk remains. In short, offences taken into consideration are indeed taken into consideration. They are not ignored or expunged or disregarded.

The Sentencing Council has issued a definitive guideline in relation to offences taken into consideration (TICs), which was intended to reflect the existing law. It confirms that, when sentencing an offender who requests offences to be taken into consideration, courts should pass a total sentence which reflects all the offending behaviour. The sentence must be just and proportionate, and must not exceed the statutory maximum for the conviction offence.

The court is likely to consider that the fact that the offender has assisted the police (particularly if the offences would not otherwise have been detected) and avoided the need for further proceedings demonstrates a genuine determination by the offender to wipe the slate clean.

The sentence imposed on the offender should, in most circumstances, be increased to reflect the fact that other offences have been taken into consideration. The court should:

- determine the sentencing starting point for the conviction offence;
- consider aggravating and mitigating circumstances. The presence of TICs should generally be treated as an aggravating feature that justifies an upward adjustment from the starting point. Where there is a large number of TICs, it may be appropriate to move outside the category range, although this must be considered in the context of the case and subject to the principle of totality. The court is limited to the statutory maximum for the conviction offence;
- consider whether the frank admission of a number of offences is an indication of a defendant's remorse or determination and/or demonstration of steps taken to address addiction or offending behaviour.

Any reduction for guilty plea should be applied to the total sentence, as should the totality principle.

Ancillary orders may take account of TICs to the limit allowed by the offences for which there is a conviction.

D25.2 Totality principle

The principle of totality comprises two elements:

(1) all courts, when sentencing for more than a single offence, should pass a total sentence which reflects all the offending behaviour before it and is just and proportionate. This is so whether the sentences are structured as concurrent or consecutive. Therefore, concurrent sentences will ordinarily be longer than a single sentence for a single offence.

(2) it is usually impossible to arrive at a just and proportionate sentence for multiple offending simply by adding together notional single sentences. It is necessary to address the offending behaviour, together with the factors personal to the offender as a whole.

D25.2.1 *Concurrent/consecutive sentences*

There is no inflexible rule governing whether sentences should be structured as concurrent or consecutive components. The overriding principle is that the overall sentence must be just and proportionate.

D25.3 Specific applications—custodial sentences

For an existing determinate sentence, where determinate sentence is still to be passed:

Circumstance	Approach
Offender serving a determinate sentence (offence(s) committed before original sentence imposed)	Consider what the sentence length would have been if the court had dealt with the offences at the same time and ensure that the totality of the sentence is just and proportionate in all the circumstances. If it is not, an adjustment should be made to the sentence imposed for the latest offence.
Offender serving a determinate sentence (offence(s) committed after original sentence imposed)	Generally the sentence will be consecutive as it will have arisen out of an unrelated incident. The court must have regard to the totality of the offender's criminality when passing the second sentence, to ensure that the total sentence to be served is just and proportionate. Where a prisoner commits acts of violence in prison, any reduction for totality is likely to be minimal.
Offender serving a determinate sentence but released from custody	The new sentence should start on the day it is imposed: s. 265 Criminal Justice Act 2003 prohibits a sentence of imprisonment running consecutively to a sentence from which a prisoner has been released. The sentence for the new offence will take into account the aggravating feature that it was committed on licence. However, it must be commensurate with the new offence and cannot be artificially inflated with a view to ensuring that the offender serves a period in custody additional to the recall period (which will be an unknown quantity in most cases) this is so even if the new sentence will, in consequence, add nothing to the period actually served.
Offender sentenced to a determinate term and subject to an existing suspended sentence order	Where an offender commits an additional offence during the operational period of a suspended sentence and the court orders the suspended sentence to be activated, the additional sentence will generally be consecutive to the activated suspended sentence, as it will arise out of unrelated facts.

 See *Blackstone's Criminal Practice 2017* **D20**

D26 Penalty Points for Driving Offences

(See RTOA 1988, ss 28 *et seq.*)

D26.1 Criteria

Penalty points must be imposed for all offences that are subject to obligatory endorsement, unless the court finds special reasons for not imposing points (see RTOA 1988, s 44(2) and **D18.5**).

A person who acts as a secondary party to an offence carrying obligatory disqualification is liable to ten penalty points.

If a person is found guilty, on one or more occasions, of more than one offence committed on the same occasion, the range of penalty points is taken as being whichever is the highest available for any one offence (eg a person convicted of speeding (3–6 points) and no insurance (6–8 points) is liable to receive up to 8 points). A court does, however, have discretion to disapply this rule if reasons are given (Road Traffic Act 1988, s 28).

Where a court orders obligatory disqualification and there are further offences to be sentenced, it should not order points for the further offences.

 See *Blackstone's Criminal Practice 2017* **C7.10–C7.23**

D27 Prescribed Minimum Sentences

D27.1 Criteria

Burglary	<ul><li>Latest offence committed on or after 1 December 1999.</li><li>Offender aged 18 or over at date of this offence.</li><li>Convicted of two previous domestic burglaries, both of which occurred after 1 December 1999, and had been convicted of the first burglary before he committed the second. Must have been sentenced to a penalty greater than a discharge.</li><li>Minimum 3-year sentence (discount of 20% permissible for guilty plea).</li><li>The case must be sent to the Crown Court.</li></ul>
Drug trafficking	<ul><li>Latest offence committed on or after 1 October 1997.</li><li>Offender aged 18 or over at date of this offence.</li><li>Convicted of two previous drug trafficking offences and had been convicted of the first offence before he committed the second but the dates of conviction are not relevant. Must have been sentenced to a penalty greater than a discharge.</li><li>7-year sentence (discount of 20% permissible for guilty plea).</li><li>The case must be sent to the Crown Court.</li></ul>

Firearms	Minimum 5 years, or 3 years (depending on whether offender aged under or over 18 years at time of commission of offence): **Firearms Act 1968, s 51A**
	(1) This section applies where—
	  (a) an individual is convicted of—
	    (i) an offence under section 5(1)(a), (ab), (aba), (ac), (ad), (ae), (af) or (c) of this Act,
	    (ii) an offence under section 5(1A)(a) of this Act, or
	    (iii) an offence under any of the provisions of this Act listed in subsection (1A) in respect of a firearm or ammunition specified in section 5(1)(a), (ab), (aba), (ac), (ad), (ae), (af) or (c) or section 5(1A)(a) of this Act, and
	  (b) the offence was committed after the commencement of this section and at a time when he was aged 16 or over.
	(1A) The provisions are—
	  (za) section 5(1A) (manufacture, sale, or transfer of firearm or possession etc for sale or transfer);
	  (a) section 16 (possession of firearm with intent to injure);
	  (b) section 16A (possession of firearm with intent to cause fear of violence);
	  (c) section 17 (use of firearm to resist arrest);

	(d) section 18 (carrying firearm with criminal intent);
	(e) section 19 (carrying a firearm in a public place);
	(f) section 20(1) (trespassing in a building with firearm).
	(2) The court shall impose an appropriate custodial sentence (or order for detention) for a term of at least the required minimum term (with or without a fine) unless the court is of the opinion that there are exceptional circumstances relating to the offence or to the offender which justify its not doing so.
	The relevant date for the section 51(1A) offences is 6 April 2007. For all other offences, it is 22 January 2004.
Aggravated possession of weapons (Prevention of Crime Act 1953, s 1A; Criminal Justice Act 1988, s 139AA)	• Offence committed on or after 3 December 2012. • Minimum 6-month sentence unless unjust in all the circumstances of the offence or of the offender, with a 20% discount available for a guilty plea. • A suspended sentence appears to be available.
Second offence under any of s 1 Prevention of Crime Act 1953, s 139 and s 139A Criminal Justice Act 1988	• Offence committed on or after implementation of s 28 Criminal Justice and Courts Act 2015 • Already convicted when over 16 of any of these offences. • Minimum 6-month sentence unless unjust in all the circumstances of the offence or of the offender, with a 20% discount available for a guilty plea. • A suspended sentence appears to be available.

 See *Blackstone's Criminal Practice 2017* **E5** and **B12.171**

D28 **Pre-Sentence Reports**

D28.1 **Criteria**

Section 156 of the Criminal Justice Act 2003 provides:

Criminal Justice Act 2003, s 156

156 Pre-sentence reports and other requirements

(1) In forming any such opinion as is mentioned in section 148(1) or (2) (b), section 152(2) or section 153(2), or in section 1 (4)(b) or (c) of the Criminal Justice and Immigration Act 2008 (youth rehabilitation orders with intensive supervision and surveillance or fostering), a court must take into account all such information as is available to it about the circumstances of the offence or (as the case may be) of the offence and the offence or offences associated with it, including any aggravating or mitigating factors.

(2) In forming any such opinion as is mentioned in section 148(2)(a), the court may take into account any information about the offender which is before it.

(3) Subject to subsection (4), a court must obtain and consider a pre-sentence report before—

   (a) in the case of a custodial sentence, forming any such opinion as is mentioned in section 152(2), section 153(2), section 225(1)(b), section 226(1)(b), section 227(1)(b) or section 228(1)(b)(i), or

   (b) in the case of a community sentence, forming any such opinion as is mentioned in section 148(1) or (2)(b), or in section 1(4)(b) or (c) of the Criminal Justice and Immigration Act 2008, or any opinion as to the suitability for the offender of the particular requirement or requirements to be imposed by the community order or youth rehabilitation order.

(4) Subsection (3) does not apply if, in the circumstances of the case, the court is of the opinion that it is unnecessary to obtain a pre-sentence report.

(5) In a case where the offender is aged under 18, the court must not form the opinion mentioned in subsection (4) unless—

   (a) there exists a previous pre-sentence report obtained in respect of the offender, and

   (b) the court has had regard to the information contained in that report, or, if there is more than one such report, the most recent report.

(6) No custodial sentence or community sentence is invalidated by the failure of a court to obtain and consider a pre-sentence report before forming an opinion referred to in subsection (3), but any court on an appeal against such a sentence—

   (a) must, subject to subsection (7), obtain a pre-sentence report if none was obtained by the court below, and

   (b) must consider any such report obtained by it or by that court.

---

(7) Subsection (6)(a) does not apply if the court is of the opinion—
  (a) that the court below was justified in forming an opinion that it was unnecessary to obtain a pre-sentence report, or
  (b) that, although the court below was not justified in forming that opinion, in the circumstances of the case at the time it is before the court, it is unnecessary to obtain a pre-sentence report.
(8) In a case where the offender is aged under 18, the court must not form the opinion mentioned in subsection (7) unless—
  (a) there exists a previous pre-sentence report obtained in respect of the offender, and
  (b) the court has had regard to the information contained in that report, or, if there is more than one such report, the most recent report.

D28.2 Reports in anticipated guilty plea cases when sending cases to the Crown Court

D28.2.1 *Criminal Procedure Rule 3A9*

Where a magistrates' court is considering committal for sentence or the defendant has indicated an intention to plead guilty in a matter which is to be sent to the Crown Court, the magistrates' court should request the preparation of a pre-sentence report for the Crown Court's use if the magistrates' court considers that:

(a) there is a realistic alternative to a custodial sentence; or
(b) the defendant may satisfy the criteria for classification as a dangerous offender; or
(c) there is some other appropriate reason for doing so.

D28.2.2 *Judicial guidance*

To assist in identifying such cases the following factors may in addition be relevant.

  It will usually be appropriate to order a report where (in some of these cases a recent report may be sufficient):
    The defendant is 17 and under.
    The defendant is under 21 and is a first-time offender/has not served a prison sentence.
  It will *not* usually be appropriate to order a report (or have a recent report available) in the cases where:
    The defendant has a previous prison sentence(s).
    Supply of Class A offences.
    False passport/ID docs.
    3rd strike burglary.

Cultivation of cannabis at or above level 2, significant role.

Offences in breach of a suspended sentence order save as to progress on requirements.

High-level frauds (in excess of £100,000).

'Custody inevitable' cases where dangerousness is not a consideration and the defendant is not under 18 (cf 'length of sentence' cases).

When magistrates' courts consider the need for reports, they should record their decision as 'PSR' (Pre-Sentence Report), or 'No Report'. This will ensure, at later hearings, that it is clear that the court did indeed consider the need for a report and what its decision was. In like manner, the CPS and defence should assume a duty to assist the magistrates by ensuring that the decision is addressed and should note their files. Where a report has been ordered, defence solicitors should be alert to check with and ensure that Probation has indeed been made aware of the need for the report and that they have the defendant's details.

Solicitors will also be aware of the ability to make representations to the Crown Court in any particular case where a decision has been made that no report is required, or where the court has not been asked to make such a decision.

 See *Blackstone's Criminal Practice 2017* **E1.26** and **E1.27**

D29 **Previous Convictions**

D29.1 **Criteria**

Section 143 of the Criminal Justice Act 2003 provides:

Criminal Justice Act 2003, s 143

143 Determining the seriousness of an offence

(1) In considering the seriousness of any offence, the court must consider the offender's culpability in committing the offence and any harm which the offence caused, was intended to cause or might foreseeably have caused.

(2) In considering the seriousness of an offence ('the current offence') committed by an offender who has one or more previous convictions, the court must treat each previous conviction as an aggravating factor if (in the case of that conviction) the court considers that it can reasonably be so treated having regard, in particular, to—
  (a) the nature of the offence to which the conviction relates and its relevance to the current offence, and
  (b) the time that has elapsed since the conviction.

(3) In considering the seriousness of any offence committed while the offender was on bail, the court must treat the fact that it was committed in those circumstances as an aggravating factor.

(4) Any reference in subsection (2) to a previous conviction is to be read as a reference to—
  (a) previous conviction by a court in the United Kingdom,
  (aa) previous conviction by a court in another member State of a relevant offence under the law of that State,
  (b) previous conviction of a service offence within the meaning of the Armed Forces Act 2006 ('conviction' here including anything that under section 376(1) and (2) of that Act is to be treated as a conviction), or
  (c) finding of guilt in respect of a member State service offence.

(5) Subsections (2) and (4) do not prevent the court from treating—
  (a) previous conviction by a court outside both the United Kingdom and any other member State, or
  (b) previous conviction by a court in any member State (other than the United Kingdom) of an offence which is not a relevant offence,
  as an aggravating factor in any case where the court considers it appropriate to do so.

(6) For the purposes of this section—
  (a) an offence is 'relevant' if the offence would constitute an offence under the law of any part of the United Kingdom if it were done in that part at the time of the conviction of the defendant for the current offence,
  (b) 'member State service offence' means an offence which—

>   (i) was the subject of proceedings under the service law of a member State other than the United Kingdom, and
>
>   (ii) would constitute an offence under the law of any part of the United Kingdom, or a service offence (within the meaning of the Armed Forces Act 2006), if it were done in any part of the United Kingdom, by a member of Her Majesty's forces, at the time of the conviction of the defendant for the current offence,
>
>   (c) 'Her Majesty's forces' has the same meaning as in the Armed Forces Act 2006, and
>
>   (d) 'service law', in relation to a member State other than the United Kingdom, means the law governing all or any of the naval, military or air forces of that State.

 See *Blackstone's Criminal Practice 2017* **D20.45** and **D20.51**

D30 **Prosecution Costs**

D30.1 **Criteria**

The following principles may be derived from the Criminal Practice Direction and *R v Northallerton Magistrates' Court, ex p Dove* [2000] 1 Cr App R (S) 136:

(1) An order to pay costs to the prosecutor should never exceed the sum which, having regard to the defendant's means and any other financial order imposed upon him, the defendant was able to pay and which it was reasonable to order the defendant to pay.

(2) Such an order should never exceed the sum that the prosecutor had actually and reasonably incurred (or was liable to a third party to pay, for example when that third party commissions a report on behalf of the prosecution).

(3) The purpose of such an order was to compensate the prosecutor and not punish the defendant. Where the defendant had by his conduct put the prosecutor to avoidable expense he might, subject to his means, be ordered to pay some or all of that sum to the prosecutor. However, he was not to be punished for exercising his constitutional right to defend himself.

(4) Whilst there was no requirement that any sum ordered by justices to be paid to a prosecutor by way of costs should stand in any arithmetical relationship to any fine imposed, the costs ordered to be paid should not in any ordinary way be grossly disproportionate to the fine. Justices should ordinarily begin by deciding on the appropriate fine to reflect the criminality of the defendant's offence, always bearing in mind his means and ability to pay, and then consider what, if any, costs he should be ordered to pay to the prosecutor. If, when the costs sought by the prosecutor were added to the proposed fine, the total exceeded the sum which in the light of the defendant's means and all other relevant circumstances the defendant could reasonably be ordered to pay, it was preferable to achieve an acceptable total by reducing the sum of costs which the defendant was ordered to pay rather than by reducing the fine.

(5) If the offender fails to disclose properly his means to the court, reasonable inferences can be drawn as to his means from evidence they had heard and all the circumstances of the case.

D30 Prosecution Costs

In determining the amount of costs to be paid by an offender, consideration should be given to any time that the offender has spent in custody on remand, if the court is to go on to impose any further punishment (eg a community order) (*R v Rakib* [2011] EWCA Crim 870).

 See Blackstone's Criminal Practice 2017 **D33.20**

D31 Racially and Religiously Aggravated Crimes

D31.1 Meaning of 'racially aggravated'

Crime and Disorder Act 1998, s 28

28 Meaning of racially or religiously aggravated

(1) An offence is racially or religiously aggravated for the purposes of sections 29 to 32 below if—
   (a) at the time of committing the offence, or immediately before or after doing so, the offender demonstrates towards the victim of the offence hostility based on the victim's membership (or presumed membership) of a racial or religious group; or
   (b) the offence is motivated (wholly or partly) by hostility towards members of a racial or religious group based on their membership of that group.

(2) In subsection (1)(a) above—
   'membership', in relation to a racial or religious group, includes association with members of that group;
   'presumed' means presumed by the offender.

(3) It is immaterial for the purposes of paragraph (a) or (b) of subsection (1) above whether or not the offender's hostility is also based, to any extent, on any other factor not mentioned in that paragraph.

(4) In this section 'racial group' means a group of persons defined by reference to race, colour, nationality (including citizenship) or ethnic or national origins.

(5) In this section 'religious group' means a group of persons defined by reference to religious belief or lack of religious belief.

D31.2 Specific racially aggravated offences

The Crime and Disorder Act 1988 provides for increased sentences for specific offences that are racially or religiously aggravated.

Section 29 of the Crime and Disorder Act 1998 provides for increased penalties for the following specific offences:

- sections 20 **(C16.9)**, 39 **(C16.4)**, and 47 **(C16.1)** Offences Against the Person Act 1861;
- section 30 criminal damage **(C6.1.6)** Crime and Disorder Act 1998;
- section 31, sections 4 **(C11.12)**, 4A **(C11.8.2)**, and 5 **(C11.7)** Public Order Act 1986; and
- section 32 for harassment offences under the Protection from Harassment Act 1997 **(C16.10** and **C16.11)**.

D31.3 **Criteria for other offences**

Section 145 of the Criminal Justice Act 2003 provides:

Criminal Justice Act 2003, s 145

145 Increase in sentences for racial or religious aggravation

(1) This section applies where a court is considering the seriousness of an offence other than one under sections 29 to 32 of the Crime and Disorder Act 1998 (c 37) (racially or religiously aggravated assaults, criminal damage, public order offences and harassment etc).

(2) If the offence was racially or religiously aggravated, the court—
   (a) must treat that fact as an aggravating factor, and
   (b) must state in open court that the offence was so aggravated.

(3) Section 28 of the Crime and Disorder Act 1998 (meaning of 'racially or religiously aggravated') applies for the purposes of this section as it applies for the purposes of sections 29 to 32 of that Act. An offence is racially or religiously aggravated if—
   (a) at the time of committing the offence, or immediately before or after doing so, the offender demonstrates towards the victim of the offence hostility based on the victim's membership (or presumed membership) of a racial or religious group; or
   (b) the offence is motivated (wholly or partly) by hostility towards members of a racial or religious group based on their membership of that group.

Following the guidance given by the court in *R v Kelly and Donnelly* [2001] 2 Cr App R (S) 73, the court should follow a two-stage process, identifying first the sentence it would have passed if the offence had not been racially aggravated and then adding an appropriate uplift to reflect the racial element, so that the sentencing process is transparent and the public can see to what extent the racial element has been reflected. There is no fixed uplift, but in *Kelly and Donnelly*, an uplift of 50 per cent was applied.

When sentencing a judge may take account of matters relating to racial, etc aggravation where there had been no acquittal of the aggravated offence, such an allegation had not been deleted, and the issue had been addressed in evidence: *R v O'Leary* [2015] EWCA Crim 1306.

For other aggravating factors, see **D39**.

 See *Blackstone's Criminal Practice 2017* **B11.148–B11.154** and **E1.16**

D32 Remand to Hospital for Reports

D32.1 Criteria

Section 35 of the Mental Health Act 1983 provides:

> **Mental Health Act 1983, s 35**
>
> **35 Remand to hospital for report on accused's mental condition**
>
> (1) Subject to the provisions of this section, the Crown Court or a magistrates' court may remand an accused person to a hospital specified by the court for a report on his mental condition.
>
> (2) For the purposes of this section an accused person is—
>
> (a) ...
>
> (b) in relation to a magistrates' court, any person who has been convicted by the court of an offence punishable on summary conviction with imprisonment and any person charged with such an offence if the court is satisfied that he did the act or made the omission charged or he has consented to the exercise by the court of the powers conferred by this section.
>
> (3) Subject to subsection (4) below, the powers conferred by this section may be exercised if—
>
> (a) the court is satisfied, on the written or oral evidence of a registered medical practitioner, that there is reason to suspect that the accused person is suffering from mental disorder; and
>
> (b) the court is of the opinion that it would be impracticable for a report on his mental condition to be made if he were remanded on bail; but those powers shall not be exercised by the Crown Court in respect of a person who has been convicted before the court if the sentence for the offence of which he has been convicted is fixed by law.
>
> (4) The court shall not remand an accused person to a hospital under this section unless satisfied, on the written or oral evidence of the registered medical practitioner who would be responsible for making the report or of some other person representing the managers of the hospital, that arrangements have been made for his admission to that hospital and for his admission to it within the period of seven days beginning with the date of the remand; and if the court is so satisfied it may, pending his admission, give directions for his conveyance to and detention in a place of safety.
>
> (5) Where a court has remanded an accused person under this section it may further remand him if it appears to the court, on the written or oral evidence of the approved clinician responsible for making the report, that a further remand is necessary for completing the assessment of the accused person's mental condition.

(6) The power of further remanding an accused person under this section may be exercised by the court without his being brought before the court if he is represented by an authorised person who is given an opportunity of being heard.

(7) An accused person shall not be remanded or further remanded under this section for more than 28 days at a time or for more than 12 weeks in all; and the court may at any time terminate the remand if it appears to the court that it is appropriate to do so.

(8) An accused person remanded to hospital under this section shall be entitled to obtain at his own expense an independent report on his mental condition from a registered medical practitioner or approved clinician chosen by him and to apply to the court on the basis of it for his remand to be terminated under subsection (7) above.

(9) Where an accused person is remanded under this section—

   (a) constable or any other person directed to do so by the court shall convey the accused person to the hospital specified by the court within the period mentioned in subsection (4) above; and

   (b) the managers of the hospital shall admit him within that period and thereafter detain him in accordance with the provisions of this section.

(10) If an accused person absconds from a hospital to which he has been remanded under this section, or while being conveyed to or from that hospital, he may be arrested without warrant by any constable and shall, after being arrested, be brought as soon as practicable before the court that remanded him; and the court may thereupon terminate the remand and deal with him in any way in which it could have dealt with him if he had not been remanded under this section.

 See *Blackstone's Criminal Practice 2017* **D20.74**

D33 **Restitution Order**

D33.1 **Criteria**

A court passing sentence in handling cases should always have in mind the power to make restitution orders (*R v Webbe and others* [2002] 1 Cr App R (S) 22), but section 148 of the PCC(S)A 2000 provides:

> ### Powers of Criminal Courts (Sentencing) Act 2000, s 148(1)–(5)
>
> #### 148 Restitution orders
> (1) This section applies where goods have been stolen, and either—
>   (a) a person is convicted of any offence with reference to the theft (whether or not the stealing is the gist of his offence); or
>   (b) a person is convicted of any other offence, but such an offence as is mentioned in paragraph (a) above is taken into consideration in determining his sentence.
> (2) Where this section applies, the court by or before which the offender is convicted may on the conviction (whether or not the passing of sentence is in other respects deferred) exercise any of the following powers—
>   (a) the court may order anyone having possession or control of the stolen goods to restore them to any person entitled to recover them from him; or
>   (b) on the application of a person entitled to recover from the person convicted any other goods directly or indirectly representing the stolen goods (as being the proceeds of any disposal or realisation of the whole or part of them or of goods so representing them), the court may order those other goods to be delivered or transferred to the applicant; or
>   (c) the court may order that a sum not exceeding the value of the stolen goods shall be paid, out of any money of the person convicted which was taken out of his possession on his apprehension, to any person who, if those goods were in the possession of the person convicted, would be entitled to recover them from him;
>   and in this subsection 'the stolen goods' means the goods referred to in subsection (1) above.
> (3) Where the court has power on a person's conviction to make an order against him both under paragraph (b) and under paragraph (c) of subsection (2) above with reference to the stealing of the same goods, the court may make orders under both paragraphs provided that the person in whose favour the orders are made does not thereby recover more than the value of those goods.

D33 Restitution Order

(4) Where the court on a person's conviction makes an order under subsection (2)(a) above for the restoration of any goods, and it appears to the court that the person convicted—

    (a) has sold the goods to a person acting in good faith, or

    (b) has borrowed money on the security of them from a person so acting, the court may order that there shall be paid to the purchaser or lender, out of any money of the person convicted which was taken out of his possession on his apprehension, a sum not exceeding the amount paid for the purchase by the purchaser or, as the case may be, the amount owed to the lender in respect of the loan.

(5) The court shall not exercise the powers conferred by this section unless in the opinion of the court the relevant facts sufficiently appear from evidence given at the trial or the available documents, together with admissions made by or on behalf of any person in connection with any proposed exercise of the powers.

 See *Blackstone's Criminal Practice 2017* **E17**

D34 **Restraining Order**

D34.1 **Criteria**

Under the Protection from Harassment Act 1997, a court may impose a restraining order following conviction or acquittal (acquittal includes where the prosecution offer no evidence on a charge). Section 5 provides:

Protection from Harassment Act 1997, s 5(2)–(6)

5 Restraining orders

(1) …
(2) The order may, for the purpose of protecting the victim or victims of the offence, or any other person mentioned in the order, from further conduct which—
   (a) amounts to harassment, or
   (b) will cause a fear of violence,
   prohibit the defendant from doing anything described in the order.
(3) The order may have effect for a specified period or until further order.
(4) The prosecutor, the defendant or any other person mentioned in the order may apply to the court which made the order for it to be varied or discharged by a further order.
(5) If without reasonable excuse the defendant does anything which he is prohibited from doing by an order under this section, he is guilty of an offence.
(6) A person guilty of an offence under this section is liable—
   (a) on conviction on indictment, to imprisonment for a term not exceeding five years, or a fine, or both, or
   (b) on summary conviction, to imprisonment for a term not exceeding six months, or a fine not exceeding the statutory maximum, or both.

The terms of the order must be proportionate and not violate the offender's human rights. However, a person can harass someone by publishing truthful things (eg that someone is gay), and an order may be made preventing publication of information that is the truth; such an order will not violate a person's right to freedom of expression under the European Convention (*R v Debnath* [2006] 2 Cr App R (S) 25).

An order must name the person it is seeking to protect (*R v Mann*, The Times, 11 April 2000), but there is no reason in principle why an order cannot be made to protect a group of individuals or a company (*R v Buxton* [2010] EWCA Crim 2023).

In relation to restraining orders after acquittal, a new legal aid order may be sought from the court and the matter billed separately (as a

CRM 7 non-standard claim). The following points emerge from *R v Major* [2010] EWCA Crim 3016:

- it was not Parliament's intention that orders be made only when the facts are uncontested, nor that orders should be made only rarely;
- the civil standard of proof applies;
- there is no contradiction in making an order post-acquittal, as the standard of proof required for a conviction is higher than that for making a restraining order;
- the evidence did not have to establish on the balance of probabilities that there had been harassment; it was enough if the evidence established conduct which fell short of harassment but which might well, if repeated in the future, amount to harassment and so make an order necessary;
- the court should set out the factual basis for making an order.

Section 5A of the Protection from Harassment Act 1997 provides:

> ## Protection from Harassment Act 1997, s 5A(1), (2), and (5)
>
> ### 5A Restraining orders on acquittal
> (1) A court before which a person ('the defendant') is acquitted of an offence may, if it considers it necessary to do so to protect a person from harassment by the defendant, make an order prohibiting the defendant from doing anything described in the order.
> (2) Subsections (3) to (7) of section 5 apply to an order under this section as they apply to an order under that one.
> (3) ...
> (4) ...
> (5) A person made subject to an order under this section has the same right of appeal against the order as if—
>   (a) he had been convicted of the offence in question before the court which made the order, and
>   (b) the order had been made under section 5.

In making an order on acquittal, the court must ensure that the defendant is not denied the opportunity to make submissions on the propriety and the terms of an order. See *R v Trott* [2011] EWCA Crim 2395, following *R v Kapotra* [2011] EWCA Crim 1843 (see also Criminal Procedure Rules Part 31). In *R v M J Smith* [2012] EWCA Crim 2566, the court quashed an order on acquittal following a finding that the defendant was not guilty by reason of insanity, as that meant there was no sufficient intent and it unnecessarily criminalized acts that were otherwise lawful; and held that the order was not for the benefit of a sufficiently identifiable group of persons.

R v Brown [2012] EWCA Crim 1152 confirms that a court should not make an order preventing contact with a complainant who had capacity to decide and who genuinely (and not in fear) wished the relationship to continue, notwithstanding a course of violence against her.

Even though the defendant had been convicted of an offence against a neighbour under section 3 of the Sexual Offences Act 2003, an order excluding him from his home, where he cared for elderly parents, for five years could not be justified. The order already prevented him from contacting the neighbour directly or indirectly. Neither the fact of knowing he was living next door nor anxiety from knowing there might be a sighting of him, made this part of the order necessary for the protection of the victim from conduct of the defendant which would cause fear of violence (see *R v M* [2012] EWCA Crim 1144).

 See *Blackstone's Criminal Practice 2017* **E21.34** and **E21.38**

D35 **Return to Custody**

This power has ceased to exist and it should be noted that section 265 CJA 2003 means a new sentence cannot be made consecutive to a sentence following recall (following *R v Kerrigan* [2014] EWCA Crim 2348) and a sentence cannot be artificially increased to allow for this (see *Costello* [2010] EWCA Crim 371).

D36 **Sentencing guidelines**

Coroners and Justice Act 2009, s 125

125 Sentencing guidelines: duty of court

(1) Every court—
- (a) must, in sentencing an offender, follow any sentencing guidelines which are relevant to the offender's case, and
- (b) must, in exercising any other function relating to the sentencing of offenders, follow any sentencing guidelines which are relevant to the exercise of the function,

unless the court is satisfied that it would be contrary to the interests of justice to do so.

(2) Subsections (3) and (4) apply where—
- (a) a court is deciding what sentence to impose on a person ('P') who is guilty of an offence, and
- (b) sentencing guidelines have been issued in relation to that offence which are structured in the way described in section 121(2) to (5) ('the offence-specific guidelines').

(3) The duty imposed on a court by subsection (1)(a) to follow any sentencing guidelines which are relevant to the offender's case includes—
- (a) in all cases, a duty to impose on P, in accordance with the offence-specific guidelines, a sentence which is within the offence range, and
- (b) where the offence-specific guidelines describe categories of case in accordance with section 121(2), a duty to decide which of the categories most resembles P's case in order to identify the sentencing starting point in the offence range;

but nothing in this section imposes on the court a separate duty, in a case within paragraph (b), to impose a sentence which is within the category range.

(4) Subsection (3)(b) does not apply if the court is of the opinion that, for the purpose of identifying the sentence within the offence range which is the appropriate starting point, none of the categories sufficiently resembles P's case.

(5) Subsection (3)(a) is subject to—
- (a) section 144 of the Criminal Justice Act 2003 (c 44) (reduction in sentences for guilty pleas),
- (b) sections 73 and 74 of the Serious Organised Crime and Police Act 2005 (c 15) (assistance by defendants: reduction or review of sentence) and any other rule of law by virtue of which an offender may receive a discounted sentence in consequence of assistance given (or offered to be given) by the offender to the prosecutor or investigator of an offence, and
- (c) any rule of law as to the totality of sentences.

(6) The duty imposed by subsection (1) is subject to the following provisions—

    (a) section 148(1) and (2) of the Criminal Justice Act 2003 (restrictions on imposing community sentences);

    (b) section 152 of that Act (restrictions on imposing discretionary custodial sentences);

    (c) section 153 of that Act (custodial sentence must be for shortest term commensurate with seriousness of offence);

    (d) section 164(2) of that Act (fine must reflect seriousness of offence);

    (e) section 269 of and Schedule 21 to that Act (determination of minimum term in relation to mandatory life sentence);

    (f) section 51A of the Firearms Act 1968 (c 27) (minimum sentence for certain offences under section 5 etc);

    (g) sections 110(2) and 111(2) of the Powers of Criminal Courts (Sentencing) Act 2000 (c 6) (minimum sentences for certain drug trafficking and burglary offences);

    (h) section 29(4) and (6) of the Violent Crime Reduction Act 2006 (c 38) (minimum sentences for certain offences involving firearms).

(7) Nothing in this section or section 126 is to be taken as restricting any power (whether under the Mental Health Act 1983 (c 20) or otherwise) which enables a court to deal with a mentally disordered offender in the manner it considers to be most appropriate in all the circumstances.

(8) In this section—

'mentally disordered', in relation to a person, means suffering from a mental disorder within the meaning of the Mental Health Act 1983;

'sentencing guidelines' means definitive sentencing guidelines.

D36.1 Process

Guidelines are normally structured in a series of steps:

STEP ONE: determining the offence category

The court should determine the offence category with reference **only** to the factors identified in the published tables. In order to determine the category the court should assess **culpability** and **harm**.

STEP TWO: starting point and category range

Having determined the category at step one, the court should use the starting point to reach a sentence within the appropriate category range in the published table.

STEP THREE: consider any factors which indicate a reduction, such as assistance to the prosecution

The court should take into account sections 73 and 74 of the Serious Organised Crime and Police Act 2005.

STEP FOUR: reduction for guilty pleas (see D17)

The court should take account of any potential reduction for a guilty plea in accordance with section 144 of the Criminal Justice Act 2003 and the *Guilty Plea* guideline.

STEP FIVE: totality principle (see D25.2)

If sentencing an offender for more than one offence, or where the offender is already serving a sentence, consider whether the total sentence is just and proportionate to the overall offending behaviour in accordance with the *Offences Taken into Consideration* and *Totality* guidelines.

STEP SIX: confiscation, compensation (see D9), and ancillary orders

D36.2 Key points

R v Balogh [2015] EWCA Crim 44 considered section 125(7) and held that a relevant guideline applies to mentally disordered offenders unless in the interests of justice it should be disapplied, and in those circumstances a mental health disposal might be used.

D37 Sexual Offences Notification Requirements

D37.1 Criteria

It is not a requirement that a court 'orders' a notification requirement, as this will follow automatically as a result of a qualifying conviction (ie those offences specified in Sch 3 to the Sexual Offences Act 2003).

An offender will be given a notice to sign and be provided with his own copy that sets down the requirements to be satisfied. For some offences a specific sentence is required before the liability arises. In *R v Davison* [2008] EWCA Crim 2795, D was ordered to complete 220 hours of unpaid work within a 12-month period. An issue arose as to whether the defendant was, therefore, subject to notification requirements (Sexual Offences Act 2003). D submitted that a community order which contains solely an unpaid work requirement to be completed within 12 months is not a community sentence of at least 12 months' duration, as it is open to the offender to complete the work within the 12-month period and on completion of the work the community order ceases. He relied on *Odam* [2008] EWCA Crim 1087. The court held:

> We have had the benefit of helpful written and oral argument on behalf of both the applicant and the respondent which were not available to the court in *Odam*. These have led us to the conclusion that the length of a community order must be capable of being determined on the date it is made. In our judgement the period specified under section 177(5) of the Criminal Justice Act 2003 by a court when imposing a community order is the relevant period for the purpose of determining the duration of the order under paragraph 18(b)(ii)(c) of Schedule 3 to the Sexual Offences Act 2003 however long it in fact takes the offender to carry out the requirements under the order. It follows that in our judgement the opinion expressed in *Odam* was wrong.

Penalty	Notification period for an adult (Sexual Offences Act 2003, s 82)
Conditional discharge	Period of discharge
A person sentenced otherwise than as mentioned elsewhere	5 years
Imprisonment for a term of 6 months or less	7 years

Imprisonment for a minimum term of 6 months but less than 30 months	10 years
A person sentenced to imprisonment for life or for 30 months or more	Indeterminate
Note: Where the registration is indeterminate there is a power to apply for removal once 15 years has been served and then every 8 years.	

 See *Blackstone's Criminal Practice 2017* **E23**

D38 **Sexual Harm Prevention Order**

D38.1 **Criteria**

Following conviction for an offence specified in Schedule 3 (in some cases dependent on the sentence imposed) or 5 to the Sexual Offences Act 2003, the court may go on to consider whether or not to make a sexual harm prevention order. Schedule 5 contains a wide range of non-sexual offences.

D38.2 **Grounds for application**

Sexual Offences Act 2003, ss 103A–D

103A Sexual harm prevention orders: applications and grounds

(1) A court may make an order under this section (a 'sexual harm prevention order') in respect of a person ('the defendant') where subsection (2) or (3) applies to the defendant.

(2) This subsection applies to the defendant where—
   (a) the court deals with the defendant in respect of—
      (i) an offence listed in Schedule 3 or 5, or
      (ii) a finding that the defendant is not guilty of an offence listed in Schedule 3 or 5 by reason of insanity, or
      (iii) a finding that the defendant is under a disability and has done the act charged against the defendant in respect of an offence listed in Schedule 3 or 5,

   and

   (b) the court is satisfied that it is necessary to make a sexual harm prevention order, for the purpose of—
      (i) protecting the public or any particular members of the public from sexual harm from the defendant, or
      (ii) protecting children or vulnerable adults generally, or any particular children or vulnerable adults, from sexual harm from the defendant outside the United Kingdom.

103B Section 103A: supplemental

(1) In section 103A—
   'child' means a person under 18;
   'the public' means the public in the United Kingdom;
   'sexual harm' from a person means physical or psychological harm caused—
   (a) by the person committing one or more offences listed in Schedule 3, or
   (b) (in the context of harm outside the United Kingdom) by the person doing, outside the United Kingdom, anything which would constitute an offence listed in Schedule 3 if done in any part of the United Kingdom;
   'vulnerable adult' means a person aged 18 or over whose ability to protect himself or herself from physical or psychological harm is significantly impaired through physical or mental disability or illness, through old age or otherwise.

103C SHPOs: effect

(1) A sexual harm prevention order prohibits the defendant from doing anything described in the order.

(2) Subject to section 103D(1), a prohibition contained in a sexual harm prevention order has effect—

    (a) for a fixed period, specified in the order, of at least 5 years, or

    (b) until further order.

(3) A sexual harm prevention order—

    (a) may specify that some of its prohibitions have effect until further order and some for a fixed period;

    (b) may specify different periods for different prohibitions.

(4) The only prohibitions that may be included in a sexual harm prevention order are those necessary for the purpose of—

    (a) protecting the public or any particular members of the public from sexual harm from the defendant, or

    (b) protecting children or vulnerable adults generally, or any particular children or vulnerable adults, from sexual harm from the defendant outside the United Kingdom.

(5) In subsection (4) 'the public', 'sexual harm', 'child' and 'vulnerable adult' each has the meaning given in section 103B(1).

(6) Where a court makes a sexual harm prevention order in relation to a person who is already subject to such an order (whether made by that court or another), the earlier order ceases to have effect.

103D SHPOs: prohibitions on foreign travel

(1) A prohibition on foreign travel contained in a sexual harm prevention order must be for a fixed period of not more than 5 years.

(2) A 'prohibition on foreign travel' means—

    (a) a prohibition on travelling to any country outside the United Kingdom named or described in the order,

    (b) a prohibition on travelling to any country outside the United Kingdom other than a country named or described in the order, or

    (c) a prohibition on travelling to any country outside the United Kingdom.

(3) Subsection (1) does not prevent a prohibition on foreign travel from being extended for a further period (of no more than 5 years each time) under section 103E.

(4) A sexual harm prevention order that contains a prohibition within subsection (2)(c) must require the defendant to surrender all of the defendant's passports at a police station specified in the order—

    (a) on or before the date when the prohibition takes effect, or

    (b) within a period specified in the order.

(5) Any passports surrendered must be returned as soon as reasonably practicable after the person ceases to be subject to a sexual harm prevention order containing a prohibition within subsection (2)(c) (unless the person is subject to an equivalent prohibition under another order).

(6) Subsection (5) does not apply in relation to—

    (a) a passport issued by or on behalf of the authorities of a country outside the United Kingdom if the passport has been returned to those authorities;

    (b) a passport issued by or on behalf of an international organisation if the passport has been returned to that organisation.

(7) In this section 'passport' means—
   (a) a United Kingdom passport within the meaning of the Immigration Act 1971;
   (b) a passport issued by or on behalf of the authorities of a country outside the United Kingdom, or by or on behalf of an international organisation;
   (c) a document that can be used (in some or all circumstances) instead of a passport.

D38.3 Key points

- There is nothing in these provisions to indicate that a court must believe a defendant to be 'dangerous' (within the meaning of the sentencing regime) before it can make such an order (*R v Richards* [2006] EWCA Crim 2519).
- Notice of at least two working days of an application for a sexual harm prevention order should always be given under Part 31 of the Criminal Procedure Rules.
- Cases on the predecessor order would appear to remain valid.

The burden of proof for obtaining such an order is the criminal standard (*MPC v Ebanks* [2012] EWHC 2368 (Admin)).

The order must be capable of being complied with without unreasonable difficulty, and free of the risk of unintended breach (*R v Hemsley* [2012] EWCA Crim 225). It must be clear and necessary, and avoid a total ban on the use of the internet, though it can require a history of use of the internet to be kept (*R v Smith* [2012] EWCA Crim 1772; *Mortimer* [2010] EWCA Crim 1303).

R v Smith [2011] EWCA Crim 3142 confirms that if it is intended to allow access to children under 16 only with the consent of their parent/guardian, provision should be made for accidental or inadvertent contact: see also *R v Jackson* [2012] EWCA Crim 2602, confirming that to order that the police have access at all times to any computer is too great an invasion of privacy.

In *R v Christopher James* [2012] EWCA Crim 81, where a defendant was convicted of offences of making indecent photographs, it was not on the facts necessary, whilst controlling the use of the internet, to insert non-contact provisions with children as there was no identified risk, and a 10-year order substituted for lifetime control.

 See *Blackstone's Criminal Practice 2017* **E21.24–E21.33**

D39 **Sexual Orientation, Disability, or Transgender Identity**

Section 146 of the Criminal Justice Act 2003 provides:

Criminal Justice Act 2003, s 146

146 Increase in sentences for aggravation related to disability or sexual orientation

(1) This section applies where the court is considering the seriousness of an offence committed in any of the circumstances mentioned in subsection (2).

(2) Those circumstances are—

   (a) that, at the time of committing the offence, or immediately before or after doing so, the offender demonstrated towards the victim of the offence hostility based on—

      (i) the sexual orientation (or presumed sexual orientation) of the victim, or

      (ii) a disability (or presumed disability) of the victim,

      (iii) the victim being or being presumed to be transgender; or

   (b) that the offence is motivated (wholly or partly)—

      (i) by hostility towards persons who are of a particular sexual orientation, or

      (ii) by hostility towards persons who have a disability or a particular disability,

      (iii) by hostility to persons who are transgender.

(3) The court—

   (a) must treat the fact that the offence was committed in any of those circumstances as an aggravating factor, and

   (b) must state in open court that the offence was committed in such circumstances.

(4) It is immaterial for the purposes of paragraph (a) or (b) of subsection (2) whether or not the offender's hostility is also based, to any extent, on any other factor not mentioned in that paragraph.

(5) In this section 'disability' means any physical or mental impairment.

(6) In this section references to being transgender include references to being transsexual, or undergoing, proposing to undergo or having undergone a process or part of a process of gender reassignment.

 See *Blackstone's Criminal Practice 2017* **E1.17**

D40 **Victim Surcharge Order**

D40.1 **Criteria**

In any case relating to an offence committed on or after 1 October 2012, the court must impose a surcharge order in accordance with the following table (Criminal Justice Act 2003, s 161A and the Criminal Justice Act 2003 (Surcharge) Order 2012 (SI 2012/1696)). For offences wholly committed on or after 8 April 2016 the figures are increased as shown in the final column (Criminal Justice Act 2003 (Surcharge)(Amendment) Order 2016 (SI 2016/389)).

The charge may be reduced if the offender would not be able to pay both the surcharge and compensation. If the offender would not be able to pay both a surcharge and a fine, the surcharge takes precedence and the fine should be reduced.

D40.2 **The charges**

Sentence	Adult		Youths		Company	
	to 08.04.16	after 08.04.16	to 08.04.16	after 08.04.16	to 08.04.16	after 08.04.16
Conditional discharge	£15	£20	£10	£15	£15	£20
Fine	10% in range £20 to £120	10% in range £30 to £170	£15	£20	10% in range £20 to £120	10% in range £30 to £170
YRO/Referral order			£15	£20		
Community order	£60	£85				
Suspended or immediate custodial sentence	£80 if 6 months or less	£115 if 6 months or less				

D40 Victim Surcharge Order

One surcharge (at the highest rate) is payable if more than one sentence (including more than one fine) is imposed.

If any one offence was committed as a youth then the youth court figures apply.

TICs are not relevant to the calculation of the surcharge (*R v Bailey; R v Kirk; R v Tote* [2013] EWCA Crim 1551).

R v George (Michael) [2015] EWCA Crim 1096 confirms that a second surcharge is not payable on sentence for breach of an order. Liability stems from conviction and the 'notional' existence of a 'victim'.

 See *Blackstone's Criminal Practice 2017* **E15.24**

D41 **Suspended Sentences**

See section 189 of the Criminal Justice Act 2003.

D41.1 Length of suspended sentences

A magistrates' court may suspend a sentence of not less than 14 days and not more than six months (CJA 2003, s 189). Where a person has served such time on remand that a custodial sentence would result in immediate release, it is not appropriate to impose a suspended sentence order (*R v Waters and Young* [2008] EWCA Crim 2538).

The court may suspend the sentence for between six months and two years, and may add appropriate requirement(s) to be completed as part of the order.

D41.2 Breach of suspended sentence order

See Schedule 12 to the Criminal Justice Act 2003.

An order will be breached if the offender does not comply with any community requirement during the period of suspension, or commits a further offence during the operational period. Following conviction for a new offence, a magistrates' court has no jurisdiction to deal with breach of a suspended sentence order imposed by the Crown Court; it must either commit the offender for sentence upon conviction for the new offence, or notify the Crown Court of the breach so that that court can take action if it so wishes. A Crown Court order will specify whether or not any breach of its requirements should result in a return to the Crown Court or be left to the magistrates' court (it is the norm for a Crown Court to order any breach be reserved to itself).

Upon a breach being proved the court has the following options open to it:

- order the sentence to take effect (ie send the offender to prison); or
- order the sentence to take effect but with a reduced term of imprisonment; or with an extended operational period; or
- impose more onerous community requirements; or
- impose a fine of up to £2,500.

Note: the court must order one of the first two options unless it would be unjust to do so in all the circumstances. A court must give reasons for so ordering.

 See Blackstone's Criminal Practice 2017 **E6**

D42 Time on Remand or Qualifying Curfew

D42.1 Criteria

Section 240ZA of the Criminal Justice Act 2003 provides that any immediate custodial sentence shall be reduced automatically by any time spent on remand in custody.

Section 240A of the Criminal Justice Act 2003 requires the sentencing court to direct that time spent on bail under an electronically monitored curfew should be credited against an immediate custodial sentence in a similar way. A person will receive credit at the rate of a half a day for every day spent subject to a qualifying electronically monitored curfew (ie a curfew of nine hours a day or more). There is no general discretion to disallow this time and deductions may only be made in accordance with section 240A(3A and 3B) (eg if already serving another sentence) (*R v Lord* [2015] EWCA Crim 1545). Section 240ZA means that time spent on remand in relation to a new offence cannot count if it coincides with a recall. There would have to be an excessive delay to reduce an otherwise appropriate sentence (*R v Phillips (Nathan)* [2015] EWCA Crim 427).

The section sets out the procedure as follows:

Criminal Justice Act 2003, s 240A

240A Crediting periods of remand on bail: terms of imprisonment and detention

(3) The credit period is calculated by taking the following steps.

Step 1

Add—

    (a) the day on which the offender's bail was first subject to the relevant conditions (and for this purpose a condition is not prevented from being a relevant condition by the fact that it does not apply for the whole of the day in question), and

    (b) the number of other days on which the offender's bail was subject to those conditions (but exclude the last of those days if the offender spends the last part of it in custody).

Step 2

Deduct the number of days on which the offender, whilst on bail subject to the relevant conditions, was also—

    (a) subject to any requirement imposed for the purpose of securing the electronic monitoring of the offender's compliance with a curfew requirement, or

    (b) on temporary release under rules made under section 47 of the Prison Act 1952.

Step 3

From the remainder, deduct the number of days during that remainder on which the offender has broken either or both of the relevant conditions.

Step 4

Divide the result by 2.

Step 5

If necessary, round up to the nearest whole number.

(3A) A day of the credit period counts as time served—

    (a) in relation to only one sentence, and

    (b) only once in relation to that sentence.

(3B) A day of the credit period is not to count as time served as part of any period of 28 days served by the offender before automatic release (see section 255B(1)).

If there is a dispute as to the time to be allowed, the burden to the criminal standard is on the Crown but the strict rules of evidence do not apply (*R v Hoggard* (2013) EWCA Crim 1024). The matter was further examined in *R v Marshall and others* [2015] EWCA Crim 1999, which emphasized that approved wording should be used so that any error could be corrected administratively under section 142 Magistrates' Courts Act 1980 **(A6.2.1)**:

> The defendant will receive full credit for half the time spent under curfew if the curfew qualified under the provisions of section 240A. On the information before me the total period is … days (subject to the deduct of … days that I have directed under the Step(s) 2 and/or 3 making a total of … days), but if this period is mistaken, this court will order an amendment of the record for the correct period to be recorded.

Appendices

Appendix 1

Preparation for Effective Trial

These notes are prepared by reference to questions for the defence raised by the current Preparation for effective trial form.

6 Advice on plea and absence/7 Partial or different guilty plea

The current law on discount for guilty plea is summarized at **D17**.

The law on trials in the absence of a defendant is at **A2.2.2**.
The law on disclosure of the initial details of the prosecution case is set out in Rule 8 of the Criminal Procedure Rules.

> **8.3.** Initial details of the prosecution case must include—
>   (a) where, immediately before the first hearing in the magistrates' court, the defendant was in police custody for the offence charged—
>   (i) a summary of the circumstances of the offence, and
>   (ii) the defendant's criminal record, if any;
>   (b) where paragraph (a) does not apply—
>   (i) a summary of the circumstances of the offence,
>   (ii) any account given by the defendant in interview, whether contained in that summary or in another document,
>   (iii) any written witness statement or exhibit that the prosecutor then has available and considers material to plea, or to the allocation of the case for trial, or to sentence,
>   (iv) the defendant's criminal record, if any, and
>   (v) any available statement of the effect of the offence on a victim, a victim's family or others.

The Law Society has given guidance on entering a plea when there is insufficient disclosure fully to advise:

> #### 4 Meeting your professional obligation
> If your client is unsure about how to plead to the charge/s but you require further information in order to meet your professional obligations in providing adequate advice, you should make both the court and your client aware of any problems this may present.
>
> #### 4.1 Providing advice
> You should advise your client about the sentencing discount they will be entitled to if they plead guilty at the first opportunity.
>
> If you advise the client to enter a not guilty plea, or to enter no plea, to protect his or her position due to the lack of information, you should ask the court to make a note of the circumstances and the reasons for pleading so.

Appendix 1

To help your client retain the maximum credit for any subsequent guilty plea, you should both:

advise your client about the situation

inform the court of the predicament you face due to the lack of disclosure.

There is a risk that any admission of a lesser offence may be used in evidence to prove ingredients of the greater. However, consideration should be given to *R v Newell* [2012] EWCA Crim 650:

Whilst an answer by a lawyer on a case management form may be admissible as hearsay under the agency rule, a discretion should be exercised to exclude the answer from evidence under section 78 of the Police and Criminal Evidence Act 1984, provided that the case is conducted in accordance with the letter and spirit of the Criminal Procedure Rules. It would be otherwise if there was an ambush.

The *Newton* principles in relation to a basis of plea appear at **D24**.

8 Case management information

8.1 Agreed facts

Facts agreed in section 9 may be used in evidence by the Crown. There was again a risk that other responses in this section 8 might also be used by the Crown in evidence, but that risk has been largely removed by the decision in *R v Newell* (above). However, care should be taken before admissions are made, and specific authority obtained from the client.

The tape summary cannot be agreed unless the solicitor was present or the tape has been played. Obtaining a copy of the tape or disc of interview is often problematic. The court has a jurisdiction to order production to the defence under PACE Code E paragraph 14.9.

4.19 The suspect shall be handed a notice which explains:
- how the audio recording will be used;
- the arrangements for access to it;
- that if they are charged or informed they will be prosecuted, a copy of the audio recording will be supplied as soon as practicable or as otherwise agreed between the suspect and the police or on the order of a court.

Information about the defendant's previous convictions held by a solicitor is confidential and must not be disclosed to the client's detriment, but great care must be taken not to mislead the court. It is for the Crown to prove to the criminal standard the existence of previous convictions if they are not agreed.

8.2 Disputed issues

Generally the areas in dispute should be identified. However, a defendant is entitled to put the Crown to proof. In that situation the form should indicate that the defence put the Crown to proof and do not raise any positive defence. Care should be taken, as the absence of a defence may be used in cross-examination should the defendant later raise a specific issue. The law is set out in *R v Rochford* [2010] EWCA Crim 1928. The words in square brackets are so marked because defence statements are not obligatory in the magistrates' court:

> What is the duty of the lawyer if the defendant has no positive case to advance at trial but declines to plead guilty? That is a realistic (if rare) practical possibility. It may occur in at least two situations. It might happen that a defendant within the cloak of privilege confides in his lawyer that he is in fact guilty of the offence charged but refuses to plead guilty. He cannot be prevented from taking that course and his instructions to his lawyer are covered by privilege. He is entitled in those circumstances to sit through the trial and to see whether the Crown can prove the case or not. What he is not entitled to do is to conduct the trial by the putting in issue of specific matters and advancing evidence or argument towards them without giving notice [in his defence statement] that he is going to do it. A less extreme but equally possible example is the defendant who refuses to give instructions either at all or on specific points. That too can occur. In neither of those situations can it possibly be the obligation of the defendant to put in [to his defence statement] an admission of guilt or a refusal to give instructions. What are the lawyers to do? It seems to us that we can give an answer only in general terms because it would be unhelpful for us to attempt the impossible task of foreseeing every factual scenario that might occur in future. They will have to be dealt with as they arise, case by case. But in general terms our answer is this. The defence [statement] must say that the defendant does not admit the offence or the relevant part of it as the case may be, and calls for the Crown to prove it. But it must also say that he advances no positive case because if he is going to advance a positive case [that must appear in the defence statement and] notice of it must be given.

In its guidance on the Criminal Procedure Rules, the Law Society states:

> Your client is entitled to put the prosecution to proof and you are not required by the CPR to cease acting simply because you are unable to assist the court further. However, you will note the consequent limitation on your client's ability to raise any positive case at his trial.

Thus whilst entitled to put the prosecution to proof, care should be taken in the preparation of the effective trial form because Direction 24B.4 of the Criminal Practice Directions confirms that:

The identification of issues at the case management stage will have been made without the risk that they would be used at trial as statement of the defendant admissible in evidence against the defendant, provided the advocate follows the letter and the spirit of the Criminal Procedure Rules. The court may take the view that a party is not acting in the spirit of the Criminal Procedure Rules in seeking to ambush the other party or raising late and technical legal arguments that were not previously raised as issues. No party that seeks to ambush the other at trial should derive an advantage from such a course of action. The court may also take the view that a defendant is not acting in the spirit of the Criminal Procedure Rules if he or she refuses to identify the issues and puts the prosecutor to proof at the case management stage. In both such circumstances the court may limit the proceedings on the day of trial in accordance with CrimPR 3.11(d). In addition any significant divergence from the issues identified at case management at this late stage may well result in the exercise of the court's powers under CrimPR 3.5(6), the powers to impose sanctions.

8.3 Defence statements

These are not obligatory in the magistrates' court but will be required if there are disclosure issues, and such issues cannot be raised without one. A defence statement cannot be filed without the defendant's consent. *R v Rochford* (above) has made clear that compliance with the requirement for a defence statement cannot require a breach of privilege.

9 Admissions

These are formal admissions that will be admitted at trial and on which a defendant can be cross-examined.

10 Application for directions

Check that you will be able to comply with the standard time limits, or apply to vary them. Consider particularly issues around disclosure, expert evidence, CCTV, and tapes. Under 2010/64/EU a defendant who does not speak English is entitled to an interpreter and translation of 'essential documents'.

Consideration should also be given to special measures required for the defendant or defence witnesses. See **B10.3** and **A28**.

11 Prosecution witnesses

Appropriate assistance should be given in identifying the relevant witnesses and witnesses whose evidence can be read, but this should always be checked with the client. Nothing that is said, including by the court, can make hearsay evidence admissible upon the completion of the form (*T v R* [2012] EWCA Crim 2358). Either there must be agreement under section 10 of the Criminal Justice Act

1967, or there must be compliance with section 9 of the Criminal Justice Act 1967 or section 114(1)(d) of the Criminal Justice Act 2003. The latter is likely to be used unless the defence identifies the grounds on which the witness is required to attend. (See **A10.10** and **A18.3**.)

The form seeks to identify the time needed to examine and cross-examine each witness. Generous estimates should be given particularly if time is needed to establish a picture to enable effective cross-examination. However, whilst courts will seek to set (*Drinkwater v Solihull MC* [2012] EWHC 765 (Admin)) and enforce a timetable, the resulting trial must be fair. In *R v Jisl* [2004] EWCA Crim 296 the court said:

> The starting point is simple. Justice must be done. The judge should consider whether to direct a timetable to cover pre-trial steps, and eventually the conduct of the trial itself, not rigid, nor immutable, and fully recognising that during the trial at any rate the unexpected must be treated as normal, and making due allowance for it in the interests of justice. To enable the trial judge to manage the case in a way which is fair to every participant, pre-trial, the potential problems as well as the possible areas for time saving, should be canvassed. In short, a sensible informed discussion about the future management of the case and the most convenient way to present the evidence, whether disputed or not, and where appropriate, with admissions by one or other or both *sides*, should enable the judge to make a fully informed analysis of the future timetable, and the proper conduct of the trial. The objective is not haste and rush, but greater efficiency and better use of limited resources by closer identification of and focus on critical rather than peripheral issues.

In principle, the trial judge should exercise firm control over the timetable, where necessary, making clear in advance and throughout the trial that the timetable will be subject to appropriate constraints, with such necessary even-handedness and flexibility as the interests of the justice require as the case unfolds (*R v Chabban* [2003] EWCA Crim 1012).

12 Expected defence witnesses

An estimate of the number of defence witnesses and details of known witnesses can be given, though there is no obligation to do so and it is unlikely that they have been proofed at this stage. The defence comply with their obligations to notify the details of witnesses if they do so once there is an intention to call them (see **A10.7**).

Appendix 2

Extracts from the Criminal Procedure Rules

Extracts from the following rules are reproduced in this appendix:

- Rule 1 (the overriding objective); and
- Rule 3 (case management).

Part 1 The Overriding Objective

The overriding objective

1.1—(1) The overriding objective of this new code is that criminal cases be dealt with justly.

(2) Dealing with a criminal case justly includes—

(a) acquitting the innocent and convicting the guilty;

(b) dealing with the prosecution and the defence fairly;

(c) recognising the rights of a defendant, particularly those under Article 6 of the European Convention on Human Rights;

(d) respecting the interests of witnesses, victims and jurors and keeping them informed of the progress of the case;

(e) dealing with the case efficiently and expeditiously;

(f) ensuring that appropriate information is available to the court when bail and sentence are considered; and

(g) dealing with the case in ways that take into account—

(i) the gravity of the offence alleged,

(ii) the complexity of what is in issue,

(iii) the severity of the consequences for the defendant and others affected, and

(iv) the needs of other cases.

The duty of the participants in a criminal case

1.2—(1) Each participant, in the conduct of each case, must—

(a) prepare and conduct the case in accordance with the overriding objective;

(b) comply with these Rules, practice directions and directions made by the court; and

(c) at once inform the court and all parties of any significant failure (whether or not that participant is responsible for that failure) to take any procedural step required by these Rules, any practice direction or any direction of the court. A failure is significant if it might hinder the court in furthering the overriding objective.

(2) Anyone involved in any way with a criminal case is a participant in its conduct for the purposes of this rule.

Extracts from the Criminal Procedure Rules

The application by the court of the overriding objective

1.3 The court must further the overriding objective in particular when—
  (a) exercising any power given to it by legislation (including these Rules);
  (b) applying any practice direction; or
  (c) interpreting any rule or practice direction.

Part 3 Case Management

The duty of the court

3.2—(1) The court must further the overriding objective by actively managing the case.
  (2) Active case management includes—
    (a) the early identification of the real issues;
    (b) the early identification of the needs of witnesses;
    (c) achieving certainty as to what must be done, by whom, and when, in particular by the early setting of a timetable for the progress of the case;
    (d) monitoring the progress of the case and compliance with directions;
    (e) ensuring that evidence, whether disputed or not, is presented in the shortest and clearest way;
    (f) discouraging delay, dealing with as many aspects of the case as possible on the same occasion, and avoiding unnecessary hearings;
    (g) encouraging the participants to co-operate in the progression of the case; and
    (h) making use of technology.
  (3) The court must actively manage the case by giving any direction appropriate to the needs of that case as early as possible.

The duty of the parties

3.3—...
  (2) Active assistance for the purposes of this rule includes—
    (a) at the beginning of the case, communication between the prosecutor and the defendant at the first available opportunity and in any event no later than the beginning of the day of the first hearing;
    (b) after that, communication between the parties and with the court officer until the conclusion of the case;
    (c) by such communication establishing, among other things—
      (i) whether the defendant is likely to plead guilty or not guilty,
      (ii) what is agreed and what is likely to be disputed,
      (iii) what information, or other material, is required by one party of another, and why, and
      (iv) what is to be done, by whom, and when (without or if necessary with a direction); and
    (d) reporting on that communication to the court—
      (i) at the first hearing, and
      (ii) after that, as directed by the court...

Appendix 2

Case preparation and progression

3.9—(1) At every hearing, if a case cannot be concluded there and then the court must give directions so that it can be concluded at the next hearing or as soon as possible after that.

(2) At every hearing the court must, where relevant—

(a) if the defendant is absent, decide whether to proceed nonetheless;

(b) take the defendant's plea (unless already done) or if no plea can be taken then find out whether the defendant is likely to plead guilty or not guilty;

(c) set, follow or revise a timetable for the progress of the case, which may include a timetable for any hearing including the trial or (in the Crown Court) the appeal;

(d) in giving directions, ensure continuity in relation to the court and to the parties' representatives where that is appropriate and practicable; and

(e) where a direction has not been complied with, find out why, identify who was responsible, and take appropriate action…

(3) In order to prepare for the trial, the court must take every reasonable step—

(a) to encourage and to facilitate the attendance of witnesses when they are needed; and

(b) to facilitate the participation of any person, including the defendant.

(4) Facilitating the participation of the defendant includes finding out whether the defendant needs interpretation because—

(a) the defendant does not speak or understand English; or

(b) the defendant has a hearing or speech impediment.

(5) Where the defendant needs interpretation—

(a) the court officer must arrange for interpretation to be provided at every hearing which the defendant is due to attend;

(b) interpretation may be by an intermediary where the defendant has a speech impediment, without the need for a defendant's evidence direction;

(c) on application or on its own initiative, the court may require a written translation to be provided for the defendant of any document or part of a document, unless—

(i) translation of that document, or part, is not needed to explain the case against the defendant, or

(ii) the defendant agrees to do without and the court is satisfied that the agreement is clear and voluntary and that the defendant has had legal advice or otherwise understands the consequences;

(d) on application by the defendant, the court must give any direction which the court thinks appropriate, including a direction for interpretation by a different interpreter, where—

(i) no interpretation is provided,

(ii) no translation is ordered or provided in response to a previous application by the defendant, or

(iii) the defendant complains about the quality of interpretation or of any translation.

Extracts from the Criminal Procedure Rules

(6) Facilitating the participation of any person includes giving directions for the appropriate treatment and questioning of a witness or the defendant, especially where the court directs such questioning is to be conducted through an intermediary.

(7) Where directions for appropriate treatment and questioning are required, the court must—

    (a) invite representations by the parties and by any intermediary; and

    (b) set ground rules for the conduct of the questioning, which rules may include—

        (i) a direction relieving a party of any duty to put that party's case to a witness or a defendant in its entirety,

        (ii) directions about the manner of questioning,

        (iii) directions about the duration of questioning,

        (iv) if necessary, directions about the questions that may or may not be asked,

        (v) where there is more than one defendant, the allocation among them of the topics about which a witness may be asked, and

        (vi) directions about the use of models, plans, body maps or similar aids to help communicate a question or an answer.

Indictable-Only Offences and Offences Carrying Life Imprisonment

Act	Offence	Max sentence
Common Law	Kidnapping	Life
Common Law	False imprisonment	Life
Common Law	Attempting to pervert the course of public justice	Life
Common Law	Absconding from lawful custody	Life
Common Law	Conspiracy to outrage public decency	Life
Common Law	Conspiracy to corrupt public morals	Life
Common Law	Obstructing coroner in the execution of his duty	Life
Common Law	Duty to aid constables	Life
Common Law	Rescuing a prisoner in custody	Life
Common Law	Showing an indecent exhibition	Life
Common Law	Removing corpse from grave	Life
Common Law	Murder of persons aged 1 yr or over	Life
Common Law	Murder of persons under 1 yr of age	Life
Common Law	Common Law offences not listed separately	Life
Common Law Criminal Attempts Act 1981	Attempted murder	Life
Common Law Criminal Justice Act 1987, s 12	Conspiracy to defraud	10 years
Common Law Offences against the Person Act 1861, s 5	Manslaughter	Life
Anti-Terrorism, Crime and Security Act 2001, s 47	Use etc of nuclear weapons	Life
Anti-Terrorism, Crime and Security Act 2001, s 50	Weapons-related acts overseas	Life

Act	Offence	Max sentence
Aviation and Maritime Security Act 1990, s 1	Endangering safety at aerodromes	Life
Aviation and Maritime Security Act 1990, s 11	Destroying ships or fixed platforms, endangering their safety	Life
Aviation and Maritime Security Act 1990, s 12	Other acts endangering or likely to endanger safe navigation	Life
Aviation and Maritime Security Act 1990, s 13	Compelling by threatening to destroy or damage ship or sea platform or property used in navigation	Life
Aviation and Maritime Security Act 1990, s 14(4)	Inducing commission of offence relating to safety of ship, cargo, or sea platform outside UK	Life
Aviation and Maritime Security Act 1990, s 14(4)	Assisting commission of offence relating to safety of ship, cargo, or sea platform outside UK	Life
Aviation Security Act 1982, ss 1, 6	Hijacking	Life
Aviation Security Act 1982, ss 2, 6	Destroying, damaging, or endangering safety of aircraft	Life
Aviation Security Act 1982, ss 3, 6	Other acts endangering safety of aircraft	Life
Aviation and Maritime Security Act 1990, s 1	Endangering safety at aerodromes	Life
Census Act 1920, s 8(2)	Census official contravening provisions	2 years
Channel Tunnel Act 1987, s 1(7)	Destroying, damaging etc a Channel Tunnel train or the Tunnel system or committing acts of violence likely to endanger safety of operation	Life
Channel Tunnel (Security) Order 1994, art 6		
Channel Tunnel Act 1987, s 1(7)	Hijacking, destroying, or damaging Channel Tunnel train or system	Life
Channel Tunnel (Security) Order 1994, arts 4, 5, 7, 8		
Chemical Weapons Act 1996, s 2	Use of chemical weapons	Life
Chemical Weapons Act 1996, s 11	Premises or equipment for producing chemical weapons	Life
Computer Misuse Act 1990 s 3ZA	Unauthorised acts causing serious damage	14 years/Life

Appendix 3

Act	Offence	Max sentence
Coroners and Justice Act 2009, Sch 6, para 5A(1) and (8) as amended by Criminal Justice and Courts Act 2015, s 75	Member of a jury at an inquest researching the case during the inquest period	2 years
Coroners and Justice Act 2009, Sch 6, para 5A(1) and (8) as amended by Criminal Justice and Courts Act 2015, s 75	Member of a jury at inquest sharing research with another member of the jury during the inquest period	2 years
Coroners and Justice Act 2009, Sch 6, para 5A(1) and (8) as amended by Criminal Justice and Courts Act 2015, s 75	Member of a jury at an inquest engaging in prohibited conduct	2 years
Coroners and Justice Act 2009, Sch 6, para 5D(1) and (2) as amended by Criminal Justice and Courts Act 2015, s 75	Intentionally disclosing jury's deliberations at an inquest	2 years
Corporate Homicide Act 2007, s 1(1)	Corporate manslaughter	Unlimited fine
Corporate Manslaughter and Corporate Homicide Act 2007, s 9	Organization convicted of corporate manslaughter/homicide fails to comply with remedial order	Fine
Corporate Manslaughter and Corporate Homicide Act 2007, s 10	Organization convicted of corporate manslaughter/homicide fails to comply with order to publish particulars of offences	Fine
Counter-Terrorism Act 2008, Sch 7, para 31	Knowingly or recklessly providing false information or a document to obtain grant of an exemption licence	2 years
Criminal Damage Act 1971, s 1(2)	Criminal damage with intent to endanger life	Life
Criminal Justice Act 1988, s 134	Torture	Life
Criminal Justice and Courts Act 2015, s 26	Corrupt etc exercise of police powers	14 years
Criminal Law Act 1967, s 4(1) in part	Assist offender (offences triable on indictment only)	7 years
Criminal Law Act 1967, s 4(1)	Assisting offender by impeding his apprehension or prosecution in a case of murder	10 years

Act	Offence	Max sentence
Criminal Law Act 1977, s 1	Conspiracy to commit murder	Life
Customs and Excise Management Act 1979, s 50(1), (2), (3), (4), and (5A)	Offence in relation to the unlawful importation of any weapon or ammunition of a kind mentioned in s5(1)(a), (ab), (aba), (ac), (ad), (ae), (af), or (c) of Firearms Act 1968	Life
Customs and Excise Management Act 1979, s 50(1), (2), (3), (4), and (5A)	Unship/unload prohibited weapon/ammunition with intent to evade prohibition/restriction	Life
Customs and Excise Management Act 1979, s 50(1), (2), (3), (4), and (5A)	Remove prohibited weapons/ammunition from their place of importation with intent to evade prohibition/restriction	Life
Customs and Excise Management Act 1979, s 50(3), (4), and 5A(a)	Import prohibited weapons/ammunition with intent to evade a prohibition/restriction	Life
Customs and Excise Management Act 1979, s 68(2), (3), and (4A)	Offence in relation to the unlawful exportation of any weapon or ammunition of a kind mentioned in s 5(1)(a), (ab), (aba), (ac), (ad), (ae), (af), or (c) of Firearms Act 1968	Life
Customs and Excise Management Act 1979, s 68(2), (3), and (4A)	Export prohibited weapon/ammunition with intent to evade prohibition/restriction	Life
Customs & Excise Management Act 1979, s 85(2)	Shooting at naval or revenue vessels	5 years
Customs and Excise Management Act 1979, s 170(1)(b) and (3)	Carry/remove/deposit etc prohibited weapons/ammunition with intent to evade a prohibition/restriction	Life
Customs and Excise Management Act 1979, s 170(2), (3), and (4A)(a)	Knowingly concerned in fraudulent evasion of prohibition/restriction on prohibited weapon/ammunition	Life
Customs & Excise Management Act 1979, s 170	Fraudulent evasion of duty, an offence in connection with a prohibition or restriction on the importation or exportation of any weapon or ammunition, etc	10 years
Domestic Violence, Crime and Victims Act 2004, s 5	Causing or allowing death of child or vulnerable person	14 years

Appendix 3

Act	Offence	Max sentence
Domestic Violence, Crime and Victims Act 2004, as added by the Domestic Violence, Crime and Victims (Amendment) Act 2012	Cause or allow a child or vulnerable adult to suffer serious physical harm	10 years
Explosive Substances Act 1883, ss 2, 3	Criminal damage to a dwelling endangering life	Life
Explosive Substances Act 1883, ss 2, 3	Criminal damage to a building other than a dwelling endangering life	Life
Explosive Substances Act 1883, ss 2, 3	Criminal damage to a vehicle endangering life	Life
Explosive Substances Act 1883, ss 2, 3	Criminal damage endangering life, other	Life
Explosive Substances Act 1883, s 3(1)(b)	Possession of explosives with intent to endanger life	Life
Explosive Substances Act 1883, s 4	Possession of explosive substance	14 years/Life
Fair Trading Act 1973, s 62	Enforcement provisions relating to newspaper mergers	2 years
Firearms Act 1968, s 5(1)	Possessing or distributing prohibited weapons or ammunition	10 years
Firearms Act 1968, s 5(1A)(a), as amended by the Criminal Justice Act 2003, s 288	Possessing or distributing firearm designed as other object	10 years
Firearms Act 1968, s 5(2A)	Manufacturing or distributing, or possessing for distribution, prohibited weapons, or ammunition	Life
Firearms Act 1968, s 16	Possession of firearm with intent to injure (Group I)	Life
Firearms Act 1968, s 16	Possession of firearm with intent to injure (Group II)	Life
Firearms Act 1968, s 16	Possession of firearm with intent to injure (Group III)	Life
Firearms Act 1968, s 16A	Possessing firearm or imitation firearm with intent to cause fear of violence	10 years
Firearms Act 1968, s 17(1)	Use of firearm to resist arrest	Life

Indictable-Only Offences

Act	Offence	Max sentence
Firearms Act 1968, s 17(2)	Possessing firearm or imitation firearm while committing or being arrested for offence specified below	Life
Firearms Act 1968, s 18(1)	Possessing firearm or imitation firearm with intent to commit indictable offence or resist arrest	Life
Forgery Act 1861, s 34	Acknowledging bail in false name	7 years
Forgery Act 1861, s 36	Destroying, forging, or falsifying registers of births, marriages, deaths, burials etc	Life
Forgery Act 1861, s 37	Forgery of copy of registrar's record	Life
Genocide Act 1969, s 1(1)	Prevention and punishment of the crime of genocide	Life
Human Reproductive Cloning Act 2001, s 1	Placing in a woman a human embryo which has been created otherwise than by fertilization	10 years
Identity Documents Act 2010, s 4	Possess/control identity documents with intent	10 years
Identity Documents Act 2010, s 5	Make/possess/control apparatus/article/material designed/adapted for making false identity documents	10 years
Infant Life (Preservation) Act 1929, s 1	Child destruction	Life
Infanticide Act 1938, s 1(1)	Infanticide	Life
International Criminal Court Act 2001, ss 51, 53	Genocide or crime against humanity	Life
International Criminal Court Act 2001, ss 52, 53, and 55	Conspiring, aiding, abetting, counselling, procuring, or inciting commission of genocide or crime against humanity	Life
International Criminal Court Act 2001, ss 52, 53, 55	Attempted genocide or crime against humanity	Life
International Criminal Court Act 2001, ss 52, 53, 55	Concealing commission of genocide or crime against humanity	Life
Juries Act 1974, ss 20A, 20B, 20C, and 20D	Research/disclosure of research/prohibited practices/disclosure of deliberations	2 years
Law of Property Act 1925, s 183	Frauds in connection with sale of land etc	2 years

Act	Offence	Max sentence
Magistrates' Court Act 1980, s 106	False written statements tendered in evidence	2 years
Criminal Justice Act 1967, s 89		
Merchant Shipping Act 1995, s 245	Selling abroad wreck found in British waters	5 years
Modern Slavery Act 2015, s 1	Slavery etc	Life (but either-way offence)
Modern Slavery Act 2015, s 2	Human trafficking	Life (but either-way offence)
National Health Service Act 2006, s 259 and Sch 21	Prohibition of sale of medical practices	Indefinite
Offences Against the Person Act 1861, s 64	Making or possessing explosives etc with intent	Life
Explosive Substances Act 1883, s 3		
Offences Against the Person Act 1861, s 4	Soliciting to commit murder	Life
Criminal Law Act 1977, s 1		
Offences Against the Person Act 1861, s 17	Impeding the saving of life from shipwreck	Life
Offences Against the Person Act 1861, s 18	Wounding with intent to do grievous bodily harm	Life
Offences Against the Person Act 1861, s 21	Attempting to choke etc in order to commit indictable offence	Life
Offences Against the Person Act 1861, s 22	Using chloroform etc to commit indictable offence	Life
Offences Against the Person Act 1861, s 23	Administering poison so as to endanger life	10 years
Offences Against the Person Act 1861, s 24	Administering poison with intent to injure or annoy	5 years
Offences Against the Person Act 1861, s 28	Causing bodily injury by explosion	Life
Offences Against the Person Act 1861, s 29	Causing explosions, sending explosive substance or throwing corrosive fluids with intent to do grievous bodily harm	Life
Offences Against the Person Act 1861, s 30	Placing explosives in or near buildings with intent to do bodily harm	14 years

Act	Offence	Max sentence
Offences Against the Person Act 1861, s 31	Setting spring guns, etc to injure trespassers	5 years
Offences Against the Person Act 1861, s 32	Endangering railway passengers by placing anything on railway, taking up rails, changing points and signals etc	Life
Offences Against the Person Act 1861, s 33	Endangering railway passengers by throwing anything at railway carriages etc	Life
Offences Against the Person Act 1861, s 35	Drivers injuring persons by furious driving	2 years
Offences Against the Person Act 1861, s 37	Assault on person preserving wreck	7 years
Offences Against the Person Act 1861, s 58	Administering drugs or using instruments to procure abortion	Life
Offences Against the Person Act 1861, s 59	Procuring drugs etc to cause abortion	5 years
Perjury Act 1911, s 1	Perjury—judicial proceedings	7 years
Pharmacy Act 1954, s 18	Falsification by the registrar	1 year
Piracy Act 1837, s 2	Piracy with violence	Life
Piracy Acts 1698–1721 and Piracy Act 1837, s 3	Piracy	Life
Prison Act 1952, s 39	Assisting a prisoner to escape	10 years
Prison Act 1952, s 40	Conveyance etc of List A articles into or out of prison	10 years
Prison Security Act 1992, s 1	Prison mutiny	10 years
Prison Security Act 1992, s 1(1) and (4)	Participating in prison mutiny with or without failing to submit to lawful authority	10 years
Public Order Act 1986, s 1	Riot	10 years
Road Traffic Act 1988, s 1	Causing death by dangerous driving	14 years
Road Traffic Act 1988, s 3A	Causing death by careless driving when under the influence of drink or drugs	14 years
Road Traffic Act 1988, s 3ZA	Causing death by disqualified driving	10 years
Serious Crime Act 2007, s 44 (pt)	Intentionally encouraging or assisting commission of murder	Life

Appendix 3

Act	Offence	Max sentence
Serious Crime Act 2007, s 45 (pt)	Encouraging or assisting in the commission of murder believing it will be committed	Life
Serious Crime Act 2007, s 46 (pt)	Encouraging or assisting in the commission of one or more offences of murder, believing one or more will be committed	Life
Serious Crime Act 2015, s 45	Participating in organised crime group	5 years
Sexual Offences (Conspiracy and Incitement) Act 1996, s 2	Conspiracy to commit a listed sexual offence	Life
Sexual Offences Act 2003, s 1	Rape of a female aged under 16	Life
Sexual Offences Act 2003, s 1	Rape of a female aged 16 or over	Life
Sexual Offences Act 2003, s 1	Rape of a male aged under 16	Life
Sexual Offences Act 2003, s 1	Rape of a male aged 16 or over	Life
Sexual Offences Act 2003, s 1	Attempted rape of a female aged under 16	Life
Sexual Offences Act 2003, s 1	Attempted rape of a female aged 16 or over	Life
Sexual Offences Act 2003, s 1	Attempted rape of a male aged under 16	Life
Sexual Offences Act 2003, s 1	Attempted rape of a male aged 16 or over	Life
Sexual Offences Act 2003, s 2	Assault on a male by penetration	Life
Sexual Offences Act 2003, s 2	Assault on a female by penetration	Life
Sexual Offences Act 2003, s 4	Causing a person to engage in sexual activity without consent—female person	Life
Sexual Offences Act 2003, s 4	Causing a person to engage in sexual activity without consent—male person	Life
Sexual Offences Act 2003, s 5	Rape of a female child under 13 by a male	Life

Indictable-Only Offences

Act	Offence	Max sentence
Sexual Offences Act 2003, s 5	Rape of a male child under 13 by a male	Life
Sexual Offences Act 2003, s 5	Attempted rape of a female child under 13 by a male	Life
Sexual Offences Act 2003, s 5	Attempted rape of a male child under 13 by a male	Life
Sexual Offences Act 2003, s 6	Assault on a male child under 13 by penetration	Life
Sexual Offences Act 2003, s 6	Assault on a female child under 13 by penetration	Life
Sexual Offences Act 2003, s 8	Causing or inciting a child under 13 to engage in sexual activity—female child	Life
Sexual Offences Act 2003, s 8	Causing or inciting a child under 13 to engage in sexual activity—male child	Life
Sexual Offences Act 2003, s 9	Sexual activity with a child under 16—female child	14 years
Sexual Offences Act 2003, s 9	Sexual activity with a child under 16—male child	14 years
Sexual Offences Act 2003, s 10	Causing or inciting a child under 16 to engage in sexual activity—female child	14 years
Sexual Offences Act 2003, s 10	Causing or inciting a child under 16 to engage in sexual activity—male child	14 years
Sexual Offences Act 2003, s 25	Sexual activity with a child family member—penetration—offender 18 or over—victim female 13 to 17	14 years
Sexual Offences Act 2003, s 25	Sexual activity with a child family member—penetration—offender 18 or over—victim male 13 to 17	14 years
Sexual Offences Act 2003, s 25	Sexual activity with a child family member—penetration—offender 18 or over—victim female under 13	14 years
Sexual Offences Act 2003, s 25	Sexual activity with a child family member—penetration—offender 18 or over—victim male under 13	14 years
Sexual Offences Act 2003, s 26	Inciting a child family member to engage in sexual activity—penetration—offender 18 or over—victim female 13 to 17	14 years

Appendix 3

Act	Offence	Max sentence
Sexual Offences Act 2003, s 26	Inciting a child family member to engage in sexual activity—penetration—offender 18 or over—victim male 13 to 17	14 years
Sexual Offences Act 2003, s 26	Inciting a child family member to engage in sexual activity—penetration—offender 18 or over—victim female under 13	14 years
Sexual Offences Act 2003, s 26	Inciting a child family member to engage in sexual activity—penetration—offender 18 or over—victim male under 13	14 years
Sexual Offences Act 2003, s 30	Sexual activity with a person with a mental disorder impeding choice—male person	Life
Sexual Offences Act 2003, s 30	Sexual activity with a person with a mental disorder impeding choice—female person	Life
Sexual Offences Act 2003, s 31	Causing or inciting a person with a mental disorder impeding choice to engage in sexual activity—male person	Life
Sexual Offences Act 2003, s 31	Causing or inciting a person with a mental disorder impeding choice to engage in sexual activity—female person	Life
Sexual Offences Act 2003, s 34	Inducement, threat, or deception to procure sexual activity with a person with a mental disorder—penetration	Life
Sexual Offences Act 2003, s 35	Causing a person with a mental disorder to engage in sexual activity by inducement, threat, or deception—penetration	Life
Sexual Offences Act 2003, s 38	Care workers: sexual activity with a person with a mental disorder—male person	14 years
Sexual Offences Act 2003, s 38	Care workers: sexual activity with a person with a mental disorder—female person	14 years
Sexual Offences Act 2003, s 39	Care workers: causing or inciting sexual activity (person with mental disorder)—penetration	14 years

Act	Offence	Max sentence
Sexual Offences Act 2003, s 47	Paying for the sexual services of a child—female child under 13	Life
Sexual Offences Act 2003, s 47	Paying for the sexual services of a child—male child under 13	Life
Sexual Offences Act 2003, s 47	Paying for the sexual services of a child—female child under 16	14 years
Sexual Offences Act 2003, s 47	Paying for the sexual services of a child—male child under 16	14 years
Specialist Printing Equipment and Materials (Offences) Act 2015, s 1	Supplying printing equipment for criminal purposes	10 years
Solicitors Act 1974, s 20	Unqualified person acting as a solicitor	2 years
Suicide Act 1961, s 2(1)	Intentionally doing an act capable of encouraging or assisting the suicide or attempted suicide of another	14 years
Taking of Hostages Act 1982, s 1	Detaining and threatening to kill or injure a hostage	Life
Terrorism Act 2000, s 54(6)(a)	Weapon training for terrorism	Life
Terrorism Act 2006, s 5	With intent that self/to assist another to commit an act of terrorism/engage in preparation	Life
Terrorism Act 2006, s 6(5)(a)	Training for terrorism	Life
Terrorism Act 2006, s 9	Possess radioactive material with intent to use it in commission/preparation for terrorism	Life
Terrorism Act 2006, s 9(1)(a)	Make/possess radioactive device with intent to use it in commission/preparation for terrorism	Life
Terrorism Act 2006, s 10	Use radioactive device/material in the course of/in connection with commission/purposes of terrorism	Life
Terrorism Act 2006, s 10	In course of/in connection with commission/purposes of terrorism use/damage nuclear facility to cause release/ask of release of radioactive material	Life
Terrorism Act 2006, s 11	Terrorist makes demands relating to devices/materials/facilities	Life

Appendix 3

Act	Offence	Max sentence
Terrorism Act 2006, s 11	Terrorist makes threats to use radioactive device/material	Life
Theft Act 1968, s 8	Robbery—personal	Life
Theft Act 1968, s 8	Robbery—business	Life
Theft Act 1968, s 8	Assault with intent to rob—personal	Life
Theft Act 1968, s 8	Assault with intent to rob—business	Life
Theft Act 1968, s 9	Burglary Triable either way unless there is the commission or intent to commit an indictable-only offence or burglary in a dwelling if a person was subjected to violence or the threat of violence	14 years
Theft Act 1968, s 10	Aggravated burglary in a dwelling	Life
Theft Act 1968, s 10	Aggravated burglary in building other than a dwelling	Life
Theft Act 1968, s 21	Blackmail	14 years
Treason Acts 1351–1814	Treason	Life
Treason Act 1842, s 2	Attempting to injure or alarm the sovereign	Life
Treason Felony Act 1848, s 3	Treason—felony	Life
United Nations Personnel Act 1997, ss 2, 3	Threats of attack on United Nations' workers	10 years
Unlawful Drilling Act 1819, s 1	Meeting for training or drilling to the use of arms or for practising military exercise movement or evolution without lawful authority	7 years
Violent Crime Reduction Act 2006, s 28	Using someone to look after a dangerous weapon—offensive/weapon/knife/bladed weapon	4 years
Violent Crime Reduction Act 2006, s 28	Using someone to look after a dangerous weapon—firearm	10 years

Specified Offences under the Criminal Justice Act 2003, Schedule 15 (Dangerous Offender Provisions)

Schedule 15 Specified offences for purposes of Chapter 5 of Part 12

Part 1 Specified violent offences

1. Manslaughter.
2. Kidnapping.
3. False imprisonment.
4. An offence under section 4 of the Offences Against the Person Act 1861 (c 100) (soliciting murder).
5. An offence under section 16 of that Act (threats to kill).
6. An offence under section 18 of that Act (wounding with intent to cause grievous bodily harm).
7. An offence under section 20 of that Act (malicious wounding).
8. An offence under section 21 of that Act (attempting to choke, suffocate, or strangle in order to commit or assist in committing an indictable offence).
9. An offence under section 22 of that Act (using chloroform etc to commit or assist in the committing of any indictable offence).
10. An offence under section 23 of that Act (maliciously administering poison etc so as to endanger life or inflict grievous bodily harm).
11. An offence under section 27 of that Act (abandoning children).
12. An offence under section 28 of that Act (causing bodily injury by explosives).
13. An offence under section 29 of that Act (using explosives etc with intent to do grievous bodily harm).
14. An offence under section 30 of that Act (placing explosives with intent to do bodily injury).
15. An offence under section 31 of that Act (setting spring guns etc with intent to do grievous bodily harm).
16. An offence under section 32 of that Act (endangering the safety of railway passengers).

17. An offence under section 35 of that Act (injuring persons by furious driving).
18. An offence under section 37 of that Act (assaulting officer preserving wreck).
19. An offence under section 38 of that Act (assault with intent to resist arrest).
20. An offence under section 47 of that Act (assault occasioning actual bodily harm).
21. An offence under section 2 of the Explosive Substances Act 1883 (c 3) (causing explosion likely to endanger life or property).
22. An offence under section 3 of that Act (attempt to cause explosion, or making or keeping explosive with intent to endanger life or property).
22A. An offence under section 4 of that Act (making or possession of explosive under suspicious circumstances).
23. An offence under section 1 of the Infant Life (Preservation) Act 1929 (c 34) (child destruction).
24. An offence under section 1 of the Children and Young Persons Act 1933 (c 12) (cruelty to children).
25. An offence under section 1 of the Infanticide Act 1938 (c 36) (infanticide).
26. An offence under section 16 of the Firearms Act 1968 (c 27) (possession of firearm with intent to endanger life).
27. An offence under section 16A of that Act (possession of firearm with intent to cause fear of violence).
28. An offence under section 17(1) of that Act (use of firearm to resist arrest).
29. An offence under section 17(2) of that Act (possession of firearm at time of committing or being arrested for offence specified in Schedule 1 to that Act).
30. An offence under section 18 of that Act (carrying a firearm with criminal intent).
31. An offence under section 8 of the Theft Act 1968 (c 60) (robbery or assault with intent to rob).
32. An offence under section 9 of that Act of burglary with intent to—inflict grievous bodily harm on a person, or do unlawful damage to a building or anything in it.
33. An offence under section 10 of that Act (aggravated burglary).
34. An offence under section 12A of that Act (aggravated vehicle-taking) involving an accident which caused the death of any person.
35. An offence of arson under section 1 of the Criminal Damage Act 1971 (c 48).

36. An offence under section 1(2) of that Act (destroying or damaging property) other than an offence of arson.
37. An offence under section 1 of the Taking of Hostages Act 1982 (c 28) (hostage-taking).
38. An offence under section 1 of the Aviation Security Act 1982 (c 36) (hijacking).
39. An offence under section 2 of that Act (destroying, damaging or endangering safety of aircraft).
40. An offence under section 3 of that Act (other acts endangering or likely to endanger safety of aircraft).
41. An offence under section 4 of that Act (offences in relation to certain dangerous articles).
42. An offence under section 127 of the Mental Health Act 1983 (c 20) (ill-treatment of patients).
43. An offence under section 1 of the Prohibition of Female Circumcision Act 1985 (c 38) (prohibition of female circumcision).
44. An offence under section 1 of the Public Order Act 1986 (c 64) (riot).
45. An offence under section 2 of that Act (violent disorder).
46. An offence under section 3 of that Act (affray).
47. An offence under section 134 of the Criminal Justice Act 1988 (c 33) (torture).
48. An offence under section 1 of the Road Traffic Act 1988 (c 52) (causing death by dangerous driving).
49. An offence under section 3A of that Act (causing death by careless driving when under influence of drink or drugs).
50. An offence under section 1 of the Aviation and Maritime Security Act 1990 (c 31) (endangering safety at aerodromes).
51. An offence under section 9 of that Act (hijacking of ships).
52. An offence under section 10 of that Act (seizing or exercising control of fixed platforms).
53. An offence under section 11 of that Act (destroying fixed platforms or endangering their safety).
54. An offence under section 12 of that Act (other acts endangering or likely to endanger safe navigation).
55. An offence under section 13 of that Act (offences involving threats).
56. An offence under Part II of the Channel Tunnel (Security) Order 1994 (SI 1994/570) (offences relating to Channel Tunnel trains and the tunnel system).
57. An offence under section 4 of the Protection from Harassment Act 1997 (c 40) (putting people in fear of violence).
58. An offence under section 29 of the Crime and Disorder Act 1998 (c 37) (racially or religiously aggravated assaults).

59. An offence falling within section 31(1) (a) or (b) of that Act (racially or religiously aggravated offences under section 4 or 4A of the Public Order Act 1986 (c 64)).

59A. An offence under section 54 of the Terrorism Act 2000 (c 11) (weapons training).

59B. An offence under section 56 of that Act (directing terrorist organisation).

59C. An offence under section 57 of that Act (possession of article for terrorist purposes).

59D. An offence under section 59 of that Act (inciting terrorism overseas).

60. An offence under section 51 or 52 of the International Criminal Court Act 2001 (c 17) (genocide, crimes against humanity, war crimes and related offences), other than one involving murder.

60A. An offence under section 47 of the Anti-terrorism, Crime and Security Act 2001 (c 24) (use etc of nuclear weapons).

60B. An offence under section 50 of that Act (assisting or inducing certain weapons-related acts overseas).

60C. An offence under section 113 of that Act (use of noxious substance or thing to cause harm or intimidate).

61. An offence under section 1 of the Female Genital Mutilation Act 2003 (c 31) (female genital mutilation).

62. An offence under section 2 of that Act (assisting a girl to mutilate her own genitalia).

63. An offence under section 3 of that Act (assisting a non-UK person to mutilate overseas a girl's genitalia).

63A. An offence under section 5 of the Domestic Violence, Crime and Victims Act 2004 (c 28) (causing or allowing the death of a child or vulnerable adult).

63B. An offence under section 5 of the Terrorism Act 2006 (c 11) (preparation of terrorist acts).

63C. An offence under section 6 of that Act (training for terrorism).

63D. An offence under section 9 of that Act (making or possession of radioactive device or material).

63E. An offence under section 10 of that Act (use of radioactive device or material for terrorist purposes etc).

63F. An offence under section 11 of that Act (terrorist threats relating to radioactive devices etc).

63G. An offence under section 1 of the Modern Slavery Act 2015 (c 30) (slavery, servitude and forced or compulsory labour).

63H. An offence under section 2 of that Act (human trafficking) which is not within Part 2 of this Schedule.

64 (1) Aiding, abetting, counselling or procuring the commission of an offence specified in the preceding paragraphs of this Part of this Schedule.

   (2) An attempt to commit such an offence.

   (3) Conspiracy to commit such an offence.

   (4) Incitement to commit such an offence.

   (5) An offence under Part 2 of the Serious Crime Act 2007 (c 9) in relation to which an offence specified in the preceding paragraphs of this Part of this Schedule is the offence (or one of the offences) which the person intended or believed would be committed.

65 (1) An attempt to commit murder.

   (2) Conspiracy to commit murder.

   (3) Incitement to commit murder.

   (4) An offence under Part 2 of the Serious Crime Act 2007 in relation to which murder is the offence (or one of the offences) which the person intended or believed would be committed.

Part 2 Specified sexual offences

66. An offence under section 1 of the Sexual Offences Act 1956 (c 69) (rape).

67. An offence under section 2 of that Act (procurement of woman by threats).

68. An offence under section 3 of that Act (procurement of woman by false pretences).

69. An offence under section 4 of that Act (administering drugs to obtain or facilitate intercourse).

70. An offence under section 5 of that Act (intercourse with girl under 13).

71. An offence under section 6 of that Act (intercourse with girl under 16).

72. An offence under section 7 of that Act (intercourse with a defective).

73. An offence under section 9 of that Act (procurement of a defective).

74. An offence under section 10 of that Act (incest by a man).

75. An offence under section 11 of that Act (incest by a woman).

76. An offence under section 14 of that Act (indecent assault on a woman).

77. An offence under section 15 of that Act (indecent assault on a man).

78. An offence under section 16 of that Act (assault with intent to commit buggery).
79. An offence under section 17 of that Act (abduction of woman by force or for the sake of her property).
80. An offence under section 19 of that Act (abduction of unmarried girl under 18 from parent or guardian).
81. An offence under section 20 of that Act (abduction of unmarried girl under 16 from parent or guardian).
82. An offence under section 21 of that Act (abduction of defective from parent or guardian).
83. An offence under section 22 of that Act (causing prostitution of women).
84. An offence under section 23 of that Act (procuration of girl under 21).
85. An offence under section 24 of that Act (detention of woman in brothel).
86. An offence under section 25 of that Act (permitting girl under 13 to use premises for intercourse).
87. An offence under section 26 of that Act (permitting girl under 16 to use premises for intercourse).
88. An offence under section 27 of that Act (permitting defective to use premises for intercourse).
89. An offence under section 28 of that Act (causing or encouraging the prostitution of, intercourse with or indecent assault on girl under 16).
90. An offence under section 29 of that Act (causing or encouraging prostitution of defective).
91. An offence under section 32 of that Act (soliciting by men).
92A. An offence under section 33A of that Act (keeping a brothel used for prostitution).
93. An offence under section 128 of the Mental Health Act 1959 (c 72) (sexual intercourse with patients).
94. An offence under section 1 of the Indecency with Children Act 1960 (c 33) (indecent conduct towards young child).
95. An offence under section 4 of the Sexual Offences Act 1967 (c 60) (procuring others to commit homosexual acts).
96. An offence under section 5 of that Act (living on earnings of male prostitution).
97. An offence under section 9 of the Theft Act 1968 (c 60) of burglary with intent to commit rape.
98. An offence under section 54 of the Criminal Law Act 1977 (c 45) (inciting girl under 16 to have incestuous sexual intercourse).
99. An offence under section 1 of the Protection of Children Act 1978 (c 37) (indecent photographs of children).

Specified Offences under the Criminal Justice Act 2003

100. An offence under section 170 of the Customs and Excise Management Act 1979 (c 2) (penalty for fraudulent evasion of duty etc) in relation to goods prohibited to be imported under section 42 of the Customs Consolidation Act 1876 (c 36) (indecent or obscene articles).
101. An offence under section 160 of the Criminal Justice Act 1988 (c 33) (possession of indecent photograph of a child).
102. An offence under section 1 of the Sexual Offences Act 2003 (c 42) (rape).
103. An offence under section 2 of that Act (assault by penetration).
104. An offence under section 3 of that Act (sexual assault).
105. An offence under section 4 of that Act (causing a person to engage in sexual activity without consent).
106. An offence under section 5 of that Act (rape of a child under 13).
107. An offence under section 6 of that Act (assault of a child under 13 by penetration).
108. An offence under section 7 of that Act (sexual assault of a child under 13).
109. An offence under section 8 of that Act (causing or inciting a child under to engage in sexual activity).
110. An offence under section 9 of that Act (sexual activity with a child).
111. An offence under section 10 of that Act (causing or inciting a child to engage in sexual activity).
112. An offence under section 11 of that Act (engaging in sexual activity in the presence of a child).
113. An offence under section 12 of that Act (causing a child to watch a sexual act).
114. An offence under section 13 of that Act (child sex offences committed by children or young persons).
115. An offence under section 14 of that Act (arranging or facilitating commission of a child sex offence).
116. An offence under section 15 of that Act (meeting a child following sexual grooming etc).
117. An offence under section 16 of that Act (abuse of position of trust: sexual activity with a child).
118. An offence under section 17 of that Act (abuse of position of trust: causing or inciting a child to engage in sexual activity).
119. An offence under section 18 of that Act (abuse of position of trust: sexual activity in the presence of a child).
120. An offence under section 19 of that Act (abuse of position of trust: causing a child to watch a sexual act).
121. An offence under section 25 of that Act (sexual activity with a child family member).

122. An offence under section 26 of that Act (inciting a child family member to engage in sexual activity).
123. An offence under section 30 of that Act (sexual activity with a person with a mental disorder impeding choice).
124. An offence under section 31 of that Act (causing or inciting a person with a mental disorder impeding choice to engage in sexual activity).
125. An offence under section 32 of that Act (engaging in sexual activity in the presence of a person with a mental disorder impeding choice).
126. An offence under section 33 of that Act (causing a person with a mental disorder impeding choice to watch a sexual act).
127. An offence under section 34 of that Act (inducement, threat or deception to procure sexual activity with a person with a mental disorder).
128. An offence under section 35 of that Act (causing a person with a mental disorder to engage in or agree to engage in sexual activity by inducement, threat or deception).
129. An offence under section 36 of that Act (engaging in sexual activity in the presence, procured by inducement, threat or deception, of a person with a mental disorder).
130. An offence under section 37 of that Act (causing a person with a mental disorder to watch a sexual act by inducement, threat or deception).
131. An offence under section 38 of that Act (care workers: sexual activity with a person with a mental disorder).
132. An offence under section 39 of that Act (care workers: causing or inciting sexual activity).
133. An offence under section 40 of that Act (care workers: sexual activity in the presence of a person with a mental disorder).
134. An offence under section 41 of that Act (care workers: causing a person with a mental disorder to watch a sexual act).
135. An offence under section 47 of that Act (paying for sexual services of a child).
136. An offence under section 48 of that Act (causing or inciting child prostitution or pornography).
137. An offence under section 49 of that Act (controlling a child prostitute or a child involved in pornography).
138. An offence under section 50 of that Act (arranging or facilitating child prostitution or pornography).
139. An offence under section 52 of that Act (causing or inciting prostitution for gain).
140. An offence under section 53 of that Act (controlling prostitution for gain).

141. An offence under section 57 of that Act (trafficking into the UK for sexual exploitation).
142. An offence under section 58 of that Act (trafficking within the UK for sexual exploitation).
143. An offence under section 59 of that Act (trafficking out of the UK for sexual exploitation).
144. An offence under section 61 of that Act (administering a substance with intent).
145. An offence under section 62 of that Act (committing an offence with intent to commit a sexual offence).
146. An offence under section 63 of that Act (trespass with intent to commit a sexual offence).
147. An offence under section 64 of that Act (sex with an adult relative: penetration).
148. An offence under section 65 of that Act (sex with an adult relative: consenting to penetration).
149. An offence under section 66 of that Act (exposure).
150. An offence under section 67 of that Act (voyeurism).
151. An offence under section 69 of that Act (intercourse with an animal).
152. An offence under section 70 of that Act (sexual penetration of a corpse).
152A. An offence under section 2 of the Modern Slavery Act 2015 (human trafficking) committed with a view to exploitation that consists of or includes behaviour within section 3(3) of that Act (sexual exploitation).
153 (1) Aiding, abetting, counselling or procuring the commission of an offence specified in this Part of this Schedule.
   (2) An attempt to commit such an offence.
   (3) Conspiracy to commit such an offence.
   (4) Incitement to commit such an offence.
   (5) An offence under Part 2 of the Serious Crime Act 2007 in relation to which an offence specified in this Part of this Schedule is the offence (or one of the offences) which the person intended or believed would be committed.

Appendix 5

Fraud Guideline (Note: The Sentencing Council has also published a guideline for corporate defendants accused of fraud, bribery, and money laundering offences, which will usually be handled at the Crown Court.)

GROUP A: General fraud offences

Fraud by false representation, fraud by failing to disclose information, fraud by abuse of position
Fraud Act 2006 (section 1)
Triable either way
Maximum: 10 years' custody
Offence range: Discharge –8 years' custody

False accounting
Theft Act 1968 (section 17)
Triable either way
Maximum: 7 years' custody
Offence range: Discharge – 6 years and 6 months' custody

STEP ONE Determining the offence category

The court should determine the offence category with reference to the tables below. In order to determine the category the court should assess **culpability** and **harm**.

> The level of **culpability** is determined by weighing up all the factors of the case to determine the offender's role and the extent to which the offending was planned and the sophistication with which it was carried out.

Culpability demonstrated by one or more of the following:
A—High culpability
A leading role where offending is part of a group activity
Involvement of others through pressure, influence
Abuse of position of power or trust or responsibility
Sophisticated nature of offence/significant planning
Fraudulent activity conducted over sustained period of time

Culpability demonstrated by one or more of the following:
Large number of victims
Deliberately targeting victim on basis of vulnerability
B—Medium culpability
Other cases where characteristics for categories A or C are not present
A significant role where offending is part of a group activity
C—Lesser culpability
Involved through coercion, intimidation or exploitation
Not motivated by personal gain
Peripheral role in organised fraud
Opportunistic 'one-off' offence; very little or no planning
Limited awareness or understanding of the extent of fraudulent activity

Where there are characteristics present which fall under different levels of culpability, the court should balance these characteristics to reach a fair assessment of the offender's culpability.

Harm is initially assessed by the actual, intended, or risked loss as may arise from the offence.

The values in the table below are to be used for **actual** or **intended** loss only.

Intended loss relates to offences where circumstances prevent the actual loss that is intended to be caused by the fraudulent activity.

> **Risk of loss** (for instance in mortgage frauds) involves consideration of both the likelihood of harm occurring and the extent of it if it does. Risk of loss is less serious than actual or intended loss. Where the offence has caused risk of loss but no (or much less) actual loss the normal approach is to move down to the corresponding point in the next category. This may not be appropriate if either the likelihood or extent of risked loss is particularly high.

Harm A—Loss caused or intended		
Category 1	£500,000 or more	Starting point based on £1 million
Category 2	£100,000–£500,000 **or** Risk of category 1 harm	Starting point based on £300,000
Category 3	£20,000–£100,000 **or** Risk of category 2 harm	Starting point based on £50,000

Appendix 5

Harm A—Loss caused or intended		
Category 4	£5,000–£20,000 **or** Risk of category 3 harm	Starting point based on £12,500
Category 5	Less than £5,000 **or** Risk of category 4 harm	Starting point based on £2,500
Risk of category 5 harm, move down the range within the category		

Harm B—Victim impact demonstrated by one or more of the following:
The court should then take into account the level of harm caused to the victim(s) or others to determine whether it warrants the sentence being moved up to the corresponding point in the next category or further up the range of the initial category.
High impact—move up a category; if in category 1 move up the range
Serious detrimental effect on the victim whether financial or otherwise, for example substantial damage to credit rating
Victim particularly vulnerable (due to factors including but not limited to their age, financial circumstances, mental capacity)
Medium impact—move upwards within the category range
Considerable detrimental effect on the victim whether financial or otherwise
Lesser impact—no adjustment
Some detrimental impact on victim, whether financial or otherwise

STEP TWO Starting point and category range

Having determined the category at step one, the court should use the appropriate starting point (as adjusted in accordance with step one above) to reach a sentence within the category range in the table below. The starting point applies to all offenders irrespective of plea or previous convictions.

Where the value is larger or smaller than the amount on which the starting point is based, this should lead to upward or downward adjustment as appropriate.

Where the value greatly exceeds the amount of the starting point in category 1, it may be appropriate to move outside the identified range.

TABLE 1

Section 1 Fraud Act 2006: Conspiracy to defraud

Maximum: 10 years' custody

Culpability			
Harm	**A**	**B**	**C**
Category 1 £500,000 or more Starting point based on £1 million	**Starting point** 7 years' custody **Category range** 5–8 years' custody	**Starting point** 5 years' custody **Category range** 3–6 years' custody	**Starting point** 3 years' custody **Category range** 18 months' – 4 years' custody
Category 2 £100,000–£500,000 Starting point based on £300,000	**Starting point** 5 years' custody **Category range** 3–6 years' custody	**Starting point** 3 years' custody **Category range** 18 months' – 4 years' custody	**Starting point** 18 months' custody **Category range** 26 weeks' – 3 years' custody
Category 3 £20,000–£100,000 Starting point based on £50,000	**Starting point** 3 years' custody **Category range** 18 months' – 4 years' custody	**Starting point** 18 months' custody **Category range** 26 weeks' – 3 years' custody	**Starting point** 26 weeks' custody **Category range** Medium-level community order – 1 year's custody
Category 4 £5,000–£20,000 Starting point based on £12,500	**Starting point** 18 months' custody **Category range** 26 weeks' – 3 years' custody	**Starting point** 26 weeks' custody **Category range** Medium-level community order – 1 year's custody	**Starting point** Medium-level community order **Category range** Band B fine – high-level community order
Category 5 Less than £5,000 Starting point based on £2,500	**Starting point** 36 weeks' custody **Category range** High-level community order – 1 year's custody	**Starting point** Medium-level community order **Category range** Band B fine – 26 weeks' custody	**Starting point** Band B fine **Category range** Discharge – medium-level community order

TABLE 2

Section 17 Theft Act 1968: False accounting

Maximum: 7 years' custody

Culpability			
Harm	**A**	**B**	**C**
Category 1 £500,000 or more Starting point based on £1 million	**Starting point** 5 years 6 months' custody **Category range** 4 years' – 6 years 6 months' custody	**Starting point** 4 years' custody **Category range** 2 years 6 months' – 5 years' custody	**Starting point** 2 years 6 months' custody **Category range** 15 months' – 3 years 6 months' custody
Category 2 £100,000–£500,000 Starting point based on £300,000	**Starting point** 4 years' custody **Category range** 2 years 6 months' – 5 years' custody	**Starting point** 2 years 6 months' custody **Category range** 15 months' – 3 years 6 months' custody	**Starting point** 15 months' custody **Category range** 26 weeks' – 2 years 6 months' custody
Category 3 £20,000–£100,000 Starting point based on £50,000	**Starting point** 2 years 6 months' custody **Category range** 15 months' – 3 years 6 months' custody	**Starting point** 15 months' custody **Category range** High-level community order – 2 years 6 months' custody	**Starting point** High-level community order **Category range** Low-level community order – 36 weeks' custody
Category 4 £5,000–£20,000 Starting point based on £12,500	**Starting point** 15 months' custody **Category range** High-level community order – 2 years 6 months' custody	**Starting point** High-level community order **Category range** Low-level community order – 36 weeks' custody	**Starting point** Low-level community order **Category range** Band B fine – medium-level community order
Category 5 Less than £5,000 Starting point based on £2,500	**Starting point** 26 weeks' custody **Category range** Medium-level community order – 36 weeks' custody	**Starting point** Low-level community order **Category range** Band B fine – medium-level community order	**Starting point** Band B fine **Category range** Discharge – low-level community order

The table below contains a non-exhaustive list of additional factual elements providing the context of the offence and factors relating to the offender.

Identify whether any combination of these or other relevant factors should result in an upward or downward adjustment from the sentence arrived at so far.

> Consecutive sentences for multiple offences may be appropriate where large sums are involved.

Factors increasing seriousness	Factors reducing seriousness or reflecting personal mitigation
Statutory aggravating factors:	No previous convictions **or** no relevant/recent convictions
Previous convictions, having regard to (a) the nature of the offence to which the conviction relates and its relevance to the current offence; and (b) the time that has elapsed since the conviction	Remorse
Offence committed whilst on bail	Good character and/or exemplary conduct
Other aggravating factors:	Little or no prospect of success
Steps taken to prevent the victim reporting or obtaining assistance and/or from assisting or supporting the prosecution	Serious medical conditions requiring urgent, intensive or long-term treatment
Attempts to conceal/dispose of evidence	Age and/or lack of maturity where it affects the responsibility of the offender
Established evidence of community/wider impact	Lapse of time since apprehension where this does not arise from the conduct of the offender
Failure to comply with current court orders	Mental disorder or learning disability
Offence committed on licence	Sole or primary carer for dependent relatives
Offences taken into consideration	Offender co-operated with investigation, made early admissions and/or voluntarily reported offending
Failure to respond to warnings about behaviour	Determination and/or demonstration of steps having been taken to address addiction or offending behaviour
Offences committed across borders	Activity originally legitimate
Blame wrongly placed on others	

Appendix 5

GROUP B: Articles for fraud

Possessing, making or supplying articles for use in fraud
Possession of articles for use in frauds
Fraud Act 2006 (section 6)
Triable either way
Maximum: 5 years' custody
Offence range: Band A fine – 3 years' custody

Making or supplying articles for use in frauds
Fraud Act 2006 (section 7)
Triable either way
Maximum: 10 years' custody
Offence range: Band C fine – 7 years' custody

STEP ONE Determining the offence category

The court should determine the offence category with reference to the tables below. In order to determine the category the court should assess **culpability** and **harm**.

> The level of **culpability** is determined by weighing up all the factors of the case to determine the offender's role and the extent to which the offending was planned and the sophistication with which it was carried out.

Culpability demonstrated by one or more of the following:
A—High culpability
A leading role where offending is part of a group activity
Involvement of others through pressure, influence
Abuse of position of power or trust or responsibility
Sophisticated nature of offence/significant planning
Fraudulent activity conducted over sustained period of time
Articles deliberately designed to target victims on basis of vulnerability
B—Medium culpability
Other cases where characteristics for categories A or C are not present
A significant role where offending is part of a group activity
C—Lesser culpability
Performed limited function under direction
Involved through coercion, intimidation or exploitation
Not motivated by personal gain
Opportunistic 'one-off' offence; very little or no planning
Limited awareness or understanding of extent of fraudulent activity

Where there are characteristics present which fall under different levels of culpability, the court should balance these characteristics to reach a fair assessment of the offender's culpability.

Harm
This guideline refers to preparatory offences where no substantive fraud has been committed. The level of **harm** is determined by weighing up all the factors of the case to determine the harm that would be caused if the article(s) were used to commit a substantive offence.
Greater harm
Large number of articles created/supplied/in possession
Article(s) have potential to facilitate fraudulent acts affecting large number of victims
Article(s) have potential to facilitate fraudulent acts involving significant sums
Use of third party identities
Offender making considerable gain as result of the offence
Lesser harm
All other offences

STEP TWO Starting point and category range

Having determined the category at step one, the court should use the appropriate starting point to reach a sentence within the category range in the table below. The starting point applies to all offenders irrespective of plea or previous convictions.

Section 6 Fraud Act 2006: Possessing articles for use in fraud
Maximum: 5 years' custody

Culpability			
Harm	A	B	C
Greater	**Starting point** 18 months' custody	**Starting point** 36 weeks' custody	**Starting point** High-level community order
	Category range 36 weeks' custody – 3 years' custody	**Category range** High-level community order – 2 years' custody	**Category range** Medium-level community order – 26 weeks' custody

Culpability			
Harm	A	B	C
Lesser	**Starting point** 26 weeks' custody	**Starting point** Medium-level community order	**Starting point** Band B fine
	Category range High-level community order – 18 months' custody	**Category range** Low-level community order – 26 weeks' custody	**Category range** Band A fine – medium-level community order

Section 7 Fraud Act 2006: Making or adapting or supplying articles for use in fraud

Maximum: 10 years' custody

Culpability			
Harm	A	B	C
Greater	**Starting point** 4 years 6 months' custody	**Starting point** 2 years 6 months' custody	**Starting point** 1 year's custody
	Category range 3–7 years' custody	**Category range** 18 months' – 5 years' custody	**Category range** High-level community order – 3 years' custody
Lesser	**Starting point** 2 years' custody	**Starting point** 36 weeks' custody	**Starting point** Medium-level community order
	Category range 26 weeks' – 4 years' custody	**Category range** Low-level community order – 2 years' custody	**Category range** Band C fine – 26 weeks' custody

The table below contains a non-exhaustive list of additional factual elements providing the context of the offence and factors relating to the offender.

Identify whether any combination of these or other relevant factors should result in an upward or downward adjustment from the starting point.

Consecutive sentences for multiple offences may be appropriate where large sums are involved.

Factors increasing seriousness	Factors reducing seriousness or reflecting personal mitigation
Statutory aggravating factors:	No previous convictions **or** no relevant/recent convictions
Previous convictions, having regard to (a) the nature of the offence to which the conviction relates and its relevance to the current offence; and (b) the time that has elapsed since the conviction	Remorse Good character and/or exemplary conduct
Offence committed whilst on bail	Little or no prospect of success
Other aggravating factors:	Serious medical conditions requiring urgent, intensive or long-term treatment
Steps taken to prevent the victim reporting or obtaining assistance and/or from assisting or supporting the prosecution	Age and/or lack of maturity where it affects the responsibility of the offender
Attempts to conceal/dispose of evidence	Lapse of time since apprehension where this does not arise from the conduct of the offender
Established evidence of community/wider impact	Mental disorder or learning disability
Failure to comply with current court orders	Sole or primary carer for dependent relatives
Offence committed on licence	Offender co-operated with investigation, made early admissions and/or voluntarily reported offending
Offences taken into consideration	Determination and/or demonstration of steps having been taken to address addiction or offending behaviour
Failure to respond to warnings about behaviour	Activity originally legitimate
Offences committed across borders	
Blame wrongly placed on others	

Appendix 5

GROUP C: Revenue fraud

Fraud
Conspiracy to defraud (common law)
Triable on indictment only

Fraud Act 2006 (section 1)
Triable either way
Maximum: 10 years' custody
Offence range: Low-level community order – 8 years' custody
False accounting
Theft Act 1968 (section 17)
**Fraudulent evasion of VAT; False statement for VAT purposes;
Conduct amounting to an offence**
Value Added Tax Act 1994 (section 72)
Fraudulent evasion of income tax
Taxes Management Act 1970 (section 106A)
**Fraudulent evasion of excise duty; Improper importation
of goods**
**Customs and Excise Management Act 1979 (sections 50, 170
and 170B)**
Triable either way
Maximum: 7 years' custody
Offence range: Band C fine – 6 years and 6 months' custody

Fraud
Cheat the public revenue (common law)
Triable on indictment only
Maximum: Life imprisonment
Offence range: 3–17 years' custody

STEP ONE Determining the offence category

The court should determine the offence category with reference
to the tables below. In order to determine the category the court
should assess **culpability** and **harm**.

> The level of **culpability** is determined by weighing up all the factors
> of the case to determine the offender's role and the extent to which
> the offending was planned and the sophistication with which it was
> carried out.
>
> **Harm**—Gain/intended gain to offender or loss/intended loss to HMRC.

Culpability demonstrated by one or more of the following:	Category 1 £50 million or more Starting point based on £80 million
A—High culpability	**Category 2** £10 million–£50 million Starting point based on £30 million
A leading role where offending is part of a group activity	**Category 3** £2 million–£10 million Starting point based on £5 million
Involvement of others through pressure/influence	**Category 4** £500,000–£2 million Starting point based on £1 million
Abuse of position of power or trust or responsibility	**Category 5** £100,000–£500,000 Starting point based on £300,000
Sophisticated nature of offence/significant planning	**Category 6** £20,000–£100,000 Starting point based on £50,000
Fraudulent activity conducted over sustained period of time	**Category 7** Less than £20,000 Starting point based on £12,500
B—Medium culpability	
Other cases where characteristics for categories A or C are not present	
A significant role where offending is part of a group activity	
C—Lesser culpability	
Involved through coercion, intimidation or exploitation	
Not motivated by personal gain	
Opportunistic 'one-off' offence; very little or no planning	
Performed limited function under direction	
Limited awareness or understanding of extent of fraudulent activity	

Where there are characteristics present which fall under different levels of culpability, the court should balance these characteristics to reach a fair assessment of the offender's culpability.

Appendix 5

STEP TWO Starting point and category range

Having determined the category at step one, the court should use the appropriate starting point to reach a sentence within the category range in the table below. The starting point applies to all offenders irrespective of plea or previous convictions.

Where the value is larger or smaller than the amount on which the starting point is based, this should lead to upward or downward adjustment as appropriate.

Where the value greatly exceeds the amount of the starting point in category 1, it may be appropriate to move outside the identified range.

TABLE 1

Section 1 Fraud Act 2006: Conspiracy to defraud (common law)

Maximum: 10 years' custody

For offences where the value of the fraud is over £2 million refer to the corresponding category in Table 3 subject to the maximum sentence of 10 years for this offence.

Culpability			
Harm	**A**	**B**	**C**
Category 4 £500,000–£2million	**Starting point** 7 years' custody	**Starting point** 5 years' custody	**Starting point** 3 years' custody
Starting point based on £1 million	**Category range** 5–8 years' custody	**Category range** 3–6 years' custody	**Category range** 18 months' – 4 years' custody
Category 5 £100,000–£500,000	**Starting point** 5 years' custody	**Starting point** 3 years' custody	**Starting point** 18 months' custody
Starting point based on £300,000	**Category range** 3–6 years' custody	**Category range** 18 months' – 4 years' custody	**Category range** 26 weeks' – 3 years' custody
Category 6 £20,000–£100,000	**Starting point** 3 years' custody	**Starting point** 18 months' custody	**Starting point** 26 weeks' custody
Starting point based on £50,000	**Category range** 18 months' – 4 years' custody	**Category range** 26 weeks' – 3 years' custody	**Category range** Medium-level community order – 1 year's custody
Category 7 Less than £20,000	**Starting point** 18 months' custody	**Starting point** 36 weeks' custody	**Starting point** Medium-level community order

Culpability			
Harm	**A**	**B**	**C**
Starting point based on £12,500	**Category range** 36 weeks' – 3 years' custody	**Category range** Medium-level community order – 18 months' custody	**Category range** Low-level community order – high-level community order

TABLE 2

Section 17 Theft Act 1968: False Accounting

Section 72(1) Value Added Tax Act 1994: Fraudulent evasion of VAT

Section 72(3) Valued Added Tax Act 1994: False statement for VAT purposes

Section 72(8) Value Added Tax Act 1994: Conduct amounting to an offence

Section 106(a) Taxes Management Act 1970: Fraudulent evasion of income tax

Section 170(1)(a)(i), (ii), (b), 170(2)(a), 170B Customs and Excise Management Act 1979: Fraudulent evasion of excise duty

Section 50(1)(a), (2) Customs and Excise Management Act 1979: Improper importation of goods

Maximum: 7 years' custody

Culpability			
Harm	**A**	**B**	**C**
Category 4 £500,000–£2 million	**Starting point** 5 years 6 months' custody	**Starting point** 4 years' custody	**Starting point** 2 years 6 months' custody
Starting point based on £1 million	**Category range** 4 years' – 6 years 6 months' custody	**Category range** 2 years 6 months' – 5 years' custody	**Category range** 15 months' – 3 years 6 months' custody
Category 5 £100,000–£500,000	**Starting point** 4 years' custody	**Starting point** 2 years 6 months' custody	**Starting point** 15 months' custody
Starting point based on £300,000	**Category range** 2 years 6 months' – 5 years' custody	**Category range** 15 months' – 3 years 6 months' custody	**Category range** 26 weeks' – 2 years 6 months' custody

Culpability			
Harm	**A**	**B**	**C**
Category 6 £20,000–£100,000	**Starting point** 2 years 6 months' custody	**Starting point** 15 months' custody	**Starting point** High-level community order
Starting point based on £50,000	**Category range** 15 months' – 3 years 6 months' custody	**Category range** High-level community order – 2 years 6 months' custody	**Category range** Low-level community order – 36 weeks' custody
Category 7 Less than £20,000	**Starting point** 15 months' custody	**Starting point** 26 weeks' custody	**Starting point** Medium-level community order
Starting point based on £12,500	**Category range** 26 weeks' – 2 years 6 months' custody	**Category range** Medium-level community order – 15 months' custody	**Category range** Band C fine – high-level community order

TABLE 3

Cheat the Revenue (common law)

Maximum: Life imprisonment

Where the offending is on the most serious scale, involving sums significantly higher than the starting point in category 1, sentences of 15 years and above may be appropriate depending on the role of the offender. In cases involving sums below £2 million the court should refer to Table 1.

Culpability			
Harm	**A**	**B**	**C**
Category 1 £50 million or more	**Starting point** 12 years' custody	**Starting point** 8 years' custody	**Starting point** 6 years' custody
Starting point based on £80 million	**Category range** 10–17 years' custody	**Category range** 7–12 years' custody	**Category range** 4–8 years' custody
Category 2 £10 million–£50 million	**Starting point** 10 years' custody	**Starting point** 7 years' custody	**Starting point** 5 years' custody
Starting point based on £30 million	**Category range** 8–13 years' custody	**Category range** 5–9 years' custody	**Category range** 3–6 years' custody
Category 3 £2 million–£10 million	**Starting point** 8 years' custody	**Starting point** 6 years' custody	**Starting point** 4 years' custody
Starting point based on £5 million	**Category range** 6–10 years' custody	**Category range** 4–7 years' custody	**Category range** 3–5 years' custody

The table below contains a non-exhaustive list of additional factual elements providing the context of the offence and factors relating to the offender.

Identify whether any combination of these or other relevant factors should result in any further upward or downward adjustment from the starting point.

> Consecutive sentences for multiple offences may be appropriate where large sums are involved.

Factors increasing seriousness	Factors reducing seriousness or reflecting personal mitigation
Statutory aggravating factors:	No previous convictions **or** no relevant/recent convictions
Previous convictions, having regard to (a) the nature of the offence to which the conviction relates and its relevance to the current offence; and (b) the time that has elapsed since the conviction	Remorse
Offence committed whilst on bail	Good character and/or exemplary conduct
Other aggravating factors:	Little or no prospect of success
Involves multiple frauds	Serious medical condition requiring urgent, intensive or long-term treatment
Number of false declarations	Age and/or lack of maturity where it affects the responsibility of the offender
Attempts to conceal/dispose of evidence	Lapse of time since apprehension where this does not arise from the conduct of the offender
Failure to comply with current court orders	Mental disorder or learning disability
Offence committed on licence	Sole or primary carer for dependent relatives
Offences taken into consideration	Offender co-operated with investigation, made early admissions and/or voluntarily reported offending
Failure to respond to warnings about behaviour	Determination and/or demonstration of steps having been taken to address addiction or offending behaviour
Blame wrongly placed on others	Activity originally legitimate
Damage to third party (for example as a result of identity theft)	
Dealing with goods with an additional health risk	
Disposing of goods to under age purchasers	

Appendix 5

GROUP D: Benefit fraud

Dishonest representations for obtaining benefit etc
Social Security Administration Act 1992 (section 111A)
Tax Credit fraud
Tax Credits Act 2002 (section 35)
False accounting
Theft Act 1968 (section 17)
Triable either way
Maximum: 7 years' custody
Offence range: Discharge – 6 years 6 months' custody

False representations for obtaining benefit etc
Social Security Administration Act 1992 (section 112)
Triable summarily only
Maximum: Level 5 fine and/or 3 months' custody
Offence range: Discharge – 12 weeks' custody

Fraud by false representation, fraud by failing to disclose information, fraud by abuse of position
Fraud Act 2006 (section 1)
Triable either way

Conspiracy to defraud
Common law
Triable on indictment only
Maximum: 10 years' custody
Offence range: Discharge – 8 years' custody

STEP ONE Determining the offence category

The court should determine the offence category with reference to the tables below. In order to determine the category the court should assess **culpability** and **harm**.

> The level of **culpability** is determined by weighing up all the factors of the case to determine the offender's role and the extent to which the offending was planned and the sophistication with which it was carried out.
>
> **Harm**—Amount obtained or intended to be obtained

Culpability demonstrated by one or more of the following:	Category 1 £500,000–£2 million Starting point based on £1 million
A—High culpability	Category 2 £100,000–£500,000 Starting point based on £300,000
A leading role where offending is part of a group activity	**Category 3** £50,000–£100,000 Starting point based on £75,000
Involvement of others through pressure/influence	**Category 4** £10,000–£50,000 Starting point based on £30,000
Abuse of position of power, or trust, or responsibility	**Category 5** £2,500–£10,000 Starting point based on £5,000
Sophisticated nature of offence/significant planning	**Category 6** Less than £2,500 Starting point based on £1,000
B—Medium culpability	
Other cases where characteristics for categories A or C are not present	
Claim not fraudulent from the outset	
A significant role where offending is part of a group activity	
C—Lesser culpability	
Involved through coercion, intimidation, or exploitation	
Performed limited function under direction	

Where there are characteristics present which fall under different levels of culpability, the court should balance these characteristics to reach a fair assessment of the offender's culpability.

STEP TWO Starting point and category range

Having determined the category at step one, the court should use the appropriate starting point to reach a sentence within the category range in the table below. The starting point applies to all offenders irrespective of plea or previous convictions.

Where the value is larger or smaller than the amount on which the starting point is based, this should lead to upward or downward adjustment as appropriate.

Appendix 5

Where the value greatly exceeds the amount of the starting point in category 1, it may be appropriate to move outside the identified range.

TABLE 1

Section 111A Social Security Administration Act 1992: Dishonest representations to obtain benefit etc

Section 35 Tax Credits Act 2002: Tax Credit fraud
Section 17 Theft Act 1968: False accounting

Maximum: 7 years' custody

Culpability			
Harm	**A**	**B**	**C**
Category 1 £500,000 or more	**Starting point** 5 years 6 months' custody	**Starting point** 4 years' custody	**Starting point** 2 years 6 months' custody
Starting point based on £1 million	**Category range** 4 years' – 6 years 6 months' custody	**Category range** 2 years 6 months' – 5 years' custody	**Category range** 15 months' – 3 years 6 months' custody
Category 2 £100,000–£500,000	**Starting point** 4 years' custody	**Starting point** 2 years 6 months' custody	**Starting point** 1 year's custody
Starting point based on £300,000	**Category range** 2 years 6 months' – 5 years' custody	**Category range** 15 months' – 3 years 6 months' custody	**Category range** 26 weeks' – 2 years 6 months' custody
Category 3 £50,000–£100,000	**Starting point** 2 years 6 months' custody	**Starting point** 1 year's custody	**Starting point** 26 weeks' custody
Starting point based on £75,000	**Category range** 2 years' – 3 years 6 months' custody	**Category range** 26 weeks' – 2 years 6 months' custody	**Category range** High-level community order – 36 weeks' custody
Category 4 £10,000–£50,000	**Starting point** 18 months' custody	**Starting point** 36 weeks' custody	**Starting point** Medium-level community order
Starting point based on £30,000	**Category range** 36 weeks' – 2 years 6 months' custody	**Category range** Medium-level community order – 21 months' custody	**Category range** Low-level community order – 26 weeks' custody

Harm	Culpability		
	A	B	C
Category 5 £2,500–£10,000 Starting point based on £5,000	**Starting point** 36 weeks' custody **Category range** Medium-level community order – 18 months' custody	**Starting point** Medium-level community order **Category range** Low-level community order – 26 weeks' custody	**Starting point** Low-level community order **Category range** Band B fine – medium-level community order
Category 6 Less than £2,500 Starting point based on £1,000	**Starting point** Medium-level community order **Category range** Low-level community order – 26 weeks' custody	**Starting point** Low-level community order **Category range** Band A fine – medium-level community order	**Starting point** Band A fine **Category range** Discharge – Band B fine

TABLE 2

Section 112

Social Security Administration Act 1992: False representations for obtaining benefit etc

Maximum: Level 5 fine and/or 3 months' custody

Harm	Culpability		
	A	B	C
Category 5 Above £2,500 Starting point based on £5,000	**Starting point** High-level community order **Category range** Medium-level community order – 12 weeks' custody	**Starting point** Medium-level community order **Category range** Band B fine – high-level community order	**Starting point** Low-level community order **Category range** Band A fine – medium-level community order
Category 6 Less than £2,500 Starting point based on £1,000	**Starting point** Medium-level community order **Category range** Low-level community order – high-level community order	**Starting point** Band B fine **Category range** Band A fine – Band C fine	**Starting point** Band A fine **Category range** Discharge – Band B fine

TABLE 3

Section 1 Fraud Act 2006

Conspiracy to defraud (common law)

Maximum: 10 years' custody

Harm	Culpability		
	A	B	C
Category 1 £500,000 or more Starting point based on £1 million	**Starting point** 7 years' custody **Category range** 5–8 years' custody	**Starting point** 5 years' custody **Category range** 3–6 years' custody	**Starting point** 3 years' custody **Category range** 18 months' – 4 years' custody
Category 2 £100,000–£500,000 Starting point based on £300,000	**Starting point** 5 years' custody **Category range** 3–6 years' custody	**Starting point** 3 years' custody **Category range** 18 months' – 4 years' custody	**Starting point** 15 months' custody **Category range** 26 weeks' – 3 years' custody
Category 3 £50,000–£100,000 Starting point based on £75,000	**Starting point** 3 years' custody **Category range** 2 years 6 months' – 4 years' custody	**Starting point** 15 months' custody **Category range** 36 weeks' – 3 years' custody	**Starting point** 36 weeks' custody **Category range** 26 weeks' – 1 year's custody
Category 4 £10,000–£50,000 Starting point based on £30,000	**Starting point** 21 months' custody **Category range** 1 year's – 3 years' custody	**Starting point** 1 year's custody **Category range** High-level community order – 2 years' custody	**Starting point** High-level community order **Category range** Low-level community order – 26 weeks' custody
Category 5 £2,500–£10,000 Starting point based on £5,000	**Starting point** 1 year's custody **Category range** High-level community order – 2 years' custody	**Starting point** High-level community order **Category range** Low-level community order – 26 weeks' custody	**Starting point** Medium-level community order **Category range** Band C fine – high- level community order
Category 6 Less than £2,500 Starting point based on £1,000	**Starting point** High-level community order **Category range** Low-level community order – 26 weeks' custody	**Starting point** Low-level community order **Category range** Band B fine – medium-level community order	**Starting point** Band B fine **Category range** Discharge – Band C fine

The table below contains a non-exhaustive list of additional factual elements providing the context of the offence and factors relating to the offender.

Identify whether any combination of these or other relevant factors should result in any further upward or downward adjustment from the starting point.

> Consecutive sentences for multiple offences may be appropriate where large sums are involved.

Factors increasing seriousness	Factors reducing seriousness or reflecting personal mitigation
Statutory aggravating factors:	No previous convictions **or** no relevant/recent convictions
Previous convictions, having regard to (a) the nature of the offence to which the conviction relates and its relevance to the current offence; and (b) the time that has elapsed since the conviction	Remorse
Offence committed whilst on bail	Good character and/or exemplary conduct
Other aggravating factors:	Serious medical condition requiring urgent, intensive, or long-term treatment
Claim fraudulent from the outset	Legitimate entitlement to benefits not claimed
Proceeds of fraud funded lavish lifestyle	Little or no prospect of success
Length of time over which the offending was committed	Age and/or lack of maturity where it affects the responsibility of the offender
Number of false declarations	Age and/or lack of maturity where it affects the responsibility of the offender
Attempts to conceal/dispose of evidence Failure to comply with current court orders	Lapse of time since apprehension where this does not arise from the conduct of the offender
Offence committed on licence	Mental disorder or learning disability
Offences taken into consideration	Sole or primary carer for dependent relatives
Failure to respond to warnings about behaviour	Offender co-operated with investigation, made early admissions and/or voluntarily reported offending
Blame wrongly placed on others	Determination and/or demonstration of steps having been taken to address addiction or offending behaviour
Damage to third party (for example as a result of identity theft)	Offender experiencing significant financial hardship or pressure at time fraud was committed due to **exceptional** circumstances

Rehabilitation Periods

A Basic Criminal Record Certificates

Rehabilitation of Offenders Act 1974 as amended

The rehabilitation 'period' for a sentence is the period listed in the following table

Sentence	End of rehabilitation period for adult offenders	End of rehabilitation period for offenders under 18 at date of conviction
A custodial sentence of more than 30 months and up to, or consisting of, 48 months	The end of the period of 7 years beginning with the day on which the sentence (including any licence period) is completed	The end of the period of 42 months beginning with the day on which the sentence (including any licence period) is completed
A custodial sentence of more than 6 months and up to, or consisting of, 30 months	The end of the period of 48 months beginning with the day on which the sentence (including any licence period) is completed	The end of the period of 24 months beginning with the day on which the sentence (including any licence period) is completed
A custodial sentence of 6 months or less	The end of the period of 24 months beginning with the day on which the sentence (including any licence period) is completed	The end of the period of 18 months beginning with the day on which the sentence (including any licence period) is completed
Removal from Her Majesty's service	The end of the period of 12 months beginning with the date of the conviction in respect of which the sentence is imposed	The end of the period of 6 months beginning with the date of the conviction in respect of which the sentence is imposed
A sentence of service detention	The end of the period of 12 months beginning with the day on which the sentence is completed	The end of the period of 6 months beginning with the day on which the sentence is completed
A fine	The end of the period of 12 months beginning with the date of the conviction in respect of which the sentence is imposed	The end of the period of 6 months beginning with the date of the conviction in respect of which the sentence is imposed

Sentence	End of rehabilitation period for adult offenders	End of rehabilitation period for offenders under 18 at date of conviction
A compensation order	The date on which the payment is made in full	The date on which the payment is made in full
A community or youth rehabilitation order	The end of the period of 12 months beginning with the day provided for by or under the order as the last day on which the order is to have effect	The end of the period of 6 months beginning with the day provided for by or under the order as the last day on which the order is to have effect
A relevant order e.g. conditional discharge	The day provided for by or under the order as the last day on which the order is to have effect	The day provided for by or under the order as the last day on which the order is to have effect
Conditional caution	The day 3 months from the date of imposition	The day 3 months from the date of imposition
Absolute discharges and other alternatives to prosecution including cautions	Immediately rehabilitated	Immediately rehabilitated

Note 1. Where no provision is made by or under a community or youth rehabilitation order or a relevant order for the last day on which the order is to have effect, the rehabilitation period for the order is to be the period of 24 months beginning with the date of conviction

Note 2. Endorsements on driving licences are excluded from rehabilitation.

B Basic and Standard Criminal Record Certificates

'Protected convictions' and 'protected cautions' are provided for by the Police Act 1997 (Criminal Record Certificates: Relevant Matters) (Amendment) (England and Wales) Order 2013 (SI 2013/1200) and Police Act 1997 (Criminal Records) (Amendment) Regulations 2013 (SI 2013/1194); The Rehabilitation of Offenders Act 1974 (Exceptions) Order 1975 (Amendment) (England and Wales) Order 2013 (SI 2013/1198) makes further amendments.

The effect of these amendments in relation to convictions is that:

(1) convictions that resulted in a custodial sentence, convictions for serious sexual or violent offences, and convictions for certain other specified offences will always be disclosed;

(2) in relation to all other convictions for persons aged 18 or over, convictions that fall within an 11-year period ending with the day on which the certificate is issued will be disclosed;

(3) in relation to all other convictions for persons aged under 18, convictions that fall within a five-and-a-half-year period

ending with the day on which the certificate is issued will be disclosed; but

(4) persons with more than one conviction will have all their convictions disclosed.

The effect of the amendments in relation to cautions is that—

(1) cautions for serious sexual and violent offences and certain other offences will always be disclosed;

(2) in relation to all other cautions for persons aged 18 or over, cautions that fall within a six-year period ending with the day on which the certificate is issued will be disclosed; and

(3) in relation to all other cautions for person aged under 18, cautions that fall within a two-year period ending with the day on which the certificate is issued will be disclosed.

The 1974 Act is no longer disapplied (and so no disclosure need be made), save in defined circumstances, in respect of a 'protected caution' or a 'protected conviction' (as defined in Rehabilitation of Offenders Act 1974 (Exceptions) Order 1975 (SI 1975/1023), art 2A) when a question is asked to assess a person's suitability for certain purposes, or when a decision is made for certain purposes.

C Enhanced Criminal Record Certificates (s 115 Police Act 1997)

In defined circumstances, an enhanced certificate may be sought which enables the police to disclose additional information held by them as being relevant and proportionate to the particular application. This may include spent and protected data and background information in relation to acquittals, harassment warnings, and other intelligence held by the police (s 113B Police Act 1997).

Appendix 7

Sentencing Guidelines for Summary-Only Offences under Consultation by the Sentencing Council

If these become effective during the life of this edition they will appear at www.oup.com/blackstones/criminal.

- Alcohol sale offences—*Licensing Act 2003, ss 141, 146, and 147*
- Animal cruelty—*Animal Welfare Act 2006, ss 4, 8, and 9*
- Careless driving—*Road Traffic Act 1988, s 3*
- Communication network offences—*Communications Act 2003, s 127(1)*
- Communication network offences—*Communications Act 2003, s 127(2)*
- Drive whilst disqualified—*Road Traffic Act 1988, s 103*
- Drugs – fail to attend/remain for initial assessment—*Drugs Act 2005, s 12*
- Drugs – fail/refuse to provide a sample—*Police and Criminal Evidence Act 1984, s 63B*
- Drunk and disorderly in a public place—*Criminal Justice Act 1967, s 91*
- Excess alcohol (drive/attempt)—*Road Traffic Act 1988, s 5(1)(a)*
- Excess alcohol (in charge) —*Road Traffic Act 1988, s 5(1)(b)*
- Fail to provide specimen for analysis (drive/attempt)—*Road Traffic Act 1988, s 7(6)*
- Fail to provide specimen for analysis (in charge)—*Road Traffic Act 1988, s 7(6)*
- Fail to stop/report road accident—*Road Traffic Act 1988, s 170(4)*
- Football-related offences—*Sporting Events (Control of Alcohol etc.) Act 1985, ss 2(1) and 2(2); Football Offences Act 1991, ss 2, 3, and 4; and Criminal Justice and Public Order Act 1994, s 166*
- No insurance—*Road Traffic Act 1988, s 143*
- Obstruct/resist a police constable in execution of duty—*Police Act 1996, s 89(2)*
- Railway fare evasion—*Regulation of Railways Act 1889, ss 5(1) and 5(3)*
- School non-attendance—*Education Act 1996, ss 444(1) and 444(1A)*
- Sexual activity in a public lavatory—*Sexual Offences Act 2003, s 71*

- Speeding—*Road Traffic Regulation Act 1984, s 89(10)*
- Taxi Touting/soliciting for hire—*Criminal Justice and Public Order Act 1994, s 167*
- TV licence payment evasion—*Communications Act 2003, s 363*
- Unfit through drink or drugs (drive/attempt)—*Road Traffic Act 1988, s 4(1)*
- Unfit through drink or drugs (in charge)—*Road Traffic Act 1988, s 4(2)*
- Vehicle interference—*Criminal Attempts Act 1981, s 9*
- Vehicle taking, without consent—*Theft Act 1968, s 12*

Index

Index

Index

Index

Index

Index

Index

Index

Index

Index

Index

Index

Index

Index

Index

Index

Index

Index

Index

Index

Index

Index

Index

Index

Index

Index

Index